BENEATH A RAINBOW

BENEATH A RAINBOW

The National Library of Poetry

Chris Tyler, Editor

Beneath a Rainbow

Library of Congress
Cataloging in Publication Data

ISBN 1-57553-575-0

Manufactured in The United States of America by
Watermark Press
One Poetry Plaza
Owings Mills, MD 21117

Foreword

Throughout life, we store information collected from experiences and try in some way to make sense of it. When we are not able to fully understand the things which occur in our lives, we often externalize the information. By doing this, we are afforded a different perspective, thus allowing us to think more clearly about difficult or perplexing events and emotions. Art is one of the ways in which people choose to externalize their thoughts.

Within the arts, modes of expression differ, but poetry is a very powerful tool by which people can share sometimes confusing, sometimes perfectly clear concepts and feelings with others. Intentions can run the gamut as well: the artists may simply want to share something that has touched their lives in some way, or they may want to get help to allay anxiety or uncertainty. The poetry within *Beneath a Rainbow* is from every point on the spectrum: every topic, every intention, every event or emotion imaginable. Some poems will speak to certain readers more than others, but it is always important to keep in mind that each verse is the voice of a poet, of a mind which needs to make sense of this world, of a heart which feels the effects of every moment in this life, and perhaps of a memory which is striving to surface. Nonetheless, recalling our yesterdays gives birth to our many forms of expression.

Melisa S. Mitchell
Editor

EDITOR'S NOTE

F. Scott Fitzgerald closes his masterpiece *The Great Gatsby* with the following poignant words: "So we beat on, boats against the current, borne back ceaselessly into the past." While this passage aptly describes the fate of the larger-than-life characters in that tragic tale, it can apply to everyday people. Many of us have struggled with issues and situations that reappear just when we think we have conquered them; sometimes it seems that we will never truly forge ahead.

For some people, one of the best ways to deal with this helpless feeling is to express the sentiments within. Sharing such private matters is risky and requires courage, but the payoff is added control over the situation: One may not be able to change what's happening, but one can manage it in one's own way. Various forms of art serve as such outlets, yet, as the poetry in this volume demonstrates, writing is arguably the most used medium.

One poem that adeptly employs this method is "Welfare" (p. 12) by Liberty Boor. This piece illustrates the dynamic of a relationship between two women who are seeking independence. The first woman, seemingly the older of the two, originally serves as a guide for the woman narrating the poem: "'A hot water bottle is better than a man,' you say, / and I believe you, because you are the prophetess." These two characters appear to come from different generations, and the narrator's dubbing the older woman "the prophetess" suggests that the first woman was something of a leader in the women's movement.

As the poem continues, it becomes obvious that the younger persona's respect for her mentor has diminished. The power of this "bright and fierce and indignant" pioneer becomes muted when it turns out that her words are spoken more strongly than they are believed. The narrator comments on the hot water bottle statement in the following passage:

> *[You are] tattooing fairy tales of peace*
> *to the roof of your mouth*
> *with the dark sharpness of your tongue*
> *as you lie curled around your red rubber life raft.*

This description implies that the older woman has made the same needle-sharp statements often enough that speaking them has left a "tattoo" in her mouth. However, these utterances are useless if the only mark they make is a hidden one. A tattoo often makes a brazen statement to the world, yet this woman's tattoo is on "the roof of [her] mouth." In addition, the older woman seems weak, even pathetic, saying these words while she is "curled around [the] red rubber life raft" that is her hot water bottle.

Later images in the poem also reveal the diminished strength of the elder's remarks:

> . . . *the black rivulets*
> *of your frustrated prophesy*
> *drip slowly down the curves of your mouth*
> . . . .
> *and when you speak the ink is*
> *flicked from your lips, spattering my cheek. . . .*

These assertions carry little weight, as they "drip slowly" out of her mouth and are merely "flicked from [her] lips." The action of these words being sprinkled onto the narrator's cheek suggests the feeble attempts of "the prophetess" to pass on her experience. The poet further illustrates this idea when the older lady tells the narrator, "'You can be the new voice.'" However, when the younger woman says, "I need a hotter water bottle / and a more permanent ink / if I'm going to get my soul off welfare," it is clear that she is left wondering how much progress her mentor has really made.

"Recognition (For E.H.)" (p. 10), by Jeaneen McAmis, is another work expressing a seemingly futile situation. The speaker has tried unsuccessfully to bring her partner out of depression:

> *Longtime I tried in vain to draw your attention*
> *to my humble offerings of dawns and daylilies;*
> *your eyes fixed on the gingery shores*
> *of the echoing country of remorse. . . .*

The persona's mention of "dawns and daylilies"—both bright, uplifting references—shows her desire to bring light into her companion's world. Her partner, on the other hand, cannot see this light because he does not want to be happy. His drinking "the rich, poisoned honey of regret" illustrates how he has allowed gloominess to keep him in its bittersweet grasp.

Although the reason for the man's depression is not disclosed, it is immaterial because it is the melancholia itself that holds him. Perhaps this emotional state has such a grip on this character because it serves as a sort of penance for something that occurred in his past. In fact, being sad has become a type of religion for the man, as seen by the poem's numerous mythological images. For example, the speaker always tried to reach her companion but she could not: "You were ever at the bergamot-scented shrine of Melancholy, / attentive to your Cimmerian oracle. . . ." Of course the word "shrine" carries religious connotations, but the capitalization of "melancholy" gives the word a god-like status. This technique evokes ancient Greek mythology, which personified war, love, and wisdom, for example, in the form of gods and goddesses. This concept is further upheld by the mention of a "Cimmerian oracle." Homer said that the Cimmerians, a tribe from ancient mythology, lived in a dark place barely separated from the Greek underworld; therefore, the gloomy Cimmerians were practically dead themselves.

The man's persistent sadness eventually leads the speaker to abandon her attempts to uplift him. In addition, she now sees that she also must find fulfillment in her own isolation. Separation is symbolized once again with mythological imagery, in the form of an ancient temple: ". . . in resignation, I turn from you / into the cool, white pillared place within me / and kneel at the priestess-pool of my solitude. . . ."

An intriguing aspect of this piece is that resolution occurs when the persona accepts the hopelessness of her situation. For so long the man's gaze was "fixed on the gingery shores / of the echoing country of remorse" but now his "sloe-eyed, elusive gaze finally" connects with hers. At this point, the title "Recognition" comes into play because it is then that the couple sees the same thing. Perhaps they are similar in now being alone, or maybe it is only when the woman turns away that the man recognizes that he needs her more than he needs his regret; what really matters is that at last they share the same vision.

The aforementioned sentiment that concludes F. Scott Fitzgerald's *The Great Gatsby* is well-expressed by Patricia Claire Eggleston in her poem "F. Scott Fitzgerald" (p. 1). While *The Great Gatsby* illustrates the wealth and decadence that abounded in America in the 1920's, it also expounds on the futility of trying to use money to satisfy dreams. Fitzgerald himself was caught between these worlds, aware that money could not be fulfilling but always wanting more of it. While Fitzgerald's characters espoused some of his qualities, the author himself was something of a character: During the Twenties, his exploits led him to be as well-known a personality as he was a writer. Eggleston deftly mirrors Fitzgerald's style of mixing fictional and autobiographical events, shown by lines like "You wrote about yellow cocktail music and the green light on Daisy's dock" and "You said . . . That the rich are different from you and me. . . ." Like his character Jay Gatsby, who tried to win upper class Daisy Buchanan with self-made wealth, Fitzgerald could not wed his wife Zelda until he amassed a sufficient amount of money. The author and his wife knew all about "yellow cocktail music," too, as they lived the highlife. However, this situation resulted in Fitzgerald's never being able to sell enough of his work to satisfy their extravagant lifestyle.

Fitzgerald's situation worsened soon after *The Great Gatsby* was released in 1925. His works enjoyed less critical acclaim and public popularity, a decline Eggleston addresses with the question, ". . .when did you begin to see your leaf was in the sere? / That you were lost. . . ." A sere is a level in an ecological plant community, so being a mere "leaf" in this ecosystem represents having no outstanding qualities. The cleverness of Eggleston's comparison is seen by her including the idea of Fitzgerald's being "lost" in this system because he belonged to the Lost Generation, a group of disillusioned American authors who wrote after World War I. Therefore, she notes how Fitzgerald became less remarkable for his talent as a writer than for being a part of a larger group.

Fitzgerald was a spokesman of his era; therefore, as the Roaring Twenties died, so did his popularity as a writer. When the Great Depression hit in the 1930's, the public had neither the money nor the desire to indulge in the ritzy world of Fitzgerald's books: "The 30's subsumed you; the country forgot / That you were a wordsmith while millions were not." Furthermore, Eggleston draws attention to the mounting problems in Fitzgerald's personal life as the decade turned: "Gatsby was great; Zelda was not / And Hemingway said how dry was your rot." "Gatsby was great" refers to Fitzgerald's success in the 1920's, defined by *The Great Gatsby*; "Zelda was not" alludes to Zelda's mental illness, made manifest by her first nervous breakdown in 1930. Eggleston's allusion to Hemingway touches on the friendship between the two authors. Hemingway's success rose as Fitzgerald's fell, and the friendship deteriorated around this same time. "Hemingway said how dry was your rot" most likely refers to the culmination of this disintegration—a published Hemingway story that decried Fitzgerald's writing ability.

Despite Fitzgerald's perceived failure during his own lifetime, his talent was recognized soon after his death. Fitzgerald was not representative of his time merely because he reported facts about the 1920's; the author expertly described the opulence of that era through his work. Eggleston states, "Your vision was Keatsian sensual, / Your dialogue visible to the ear." The result of this superb style is that Fitzgerald was able to capture his world in writing: ". . . the words that you wrote were a movement in time / To exist in the ether of brazen sublime." One way in which Fitzgerald creates a sumptuous atmosphere in *The Great Gatsby* is through his extensive, symbolic use of color. In her poem, Eggleston judiciously establishes the more prominent *Gatsby* colors. The "yellow cocktail music" points to Fitzgerald's use of that color, similar to gold, to represent affluence; "the green light on Daisy's dock" refers to his employing green to represent promise; and a "waltz in blue gardens" echoes Fitzgerald's descriptions of Gatsby's nighttime parties, which spilled out to the lawns and gardens under the dark blue night sky.

Certain aspects of Eggleston's technique also capture Fitzgerald's sensuous sound. She consistently uses rhythm and rhyme, so the reader gets caught up in and carried away by her poem. In addition, the poet uses words and images that suggest an ethereal nature behind Fitzgerald's talent. For instance, she says his written words transcend that of the norm with the line "Your dialogue visible to the ear" and winds down the poem by stating "the angels that brought you will not come again. . . ." Due to her ability to weave a skillful representation of Fitzgerald's life into her own unique style, Patricia Claire Eggleston was awarded the Grand Prize for the contest held in association with this anthology.

Other poems in this anthology that merit special recognition include "Point Pleasant in November" (p. 9) by Barrett Brokaw, "Sonnet #8" (p. 12) by Suzanne Cerreta, "Motel on Atlantic Avenue" by Kendra Griffin (p. 12), Margaret Kist's "Melancholia" (p. 9), "Carwash" (p. 8) by Alan Parks, "While You Were Asleep (Ariel's Requiem)"

(p. 9) by Frank James Ryan Jr., "Watercoloured Stranger" (p. 13) by Kirsten Volnes, and "Deathwatch" (p. 11) by D. M. Weiss. Please be sure to experience the many other notable poems in this anthology as well.

The production of this book was made possible by the contributions of many individuals. Thank you to the editors, assistant editors, and office personnel, who all helped create this anthology.

Chris Tyler
Editor

Cover Art: Chaya Schapiro

Winners of the North American Open Poetry Contest

Grand Prize Winner

Patricia Claire Eggleston / Saginaw, MI

Second Prize Winners

Liberty Boor / Radford, VA
Barrett Brokaw / Oceanport, NJ
Suzanne Cerreta / Spring, TX
Kendra Griffin / Bridgeville, PA
Margaret Kist / Woodhaven, MI

Jeaneen McAmis / Silver Spring, MD
Alan Parks / Lake Mary, FL
Frank James Ryan Jr. / Yonkers, NY
Kirsten Volnes / Dennison, MN
D. M. Weiss / Hampton, VA

Third Prize Winners

Diane Abbinanti / Palatine, IL
Brandon Avery / San Francisco, CA
Michael Baker / North Potomac, MD
L. L. Ball / Edmond, OK
Terena Elizabeth Bell / Hopkinsville, KY
Elizabeth Bourland / Mon Mouth, OR
Michael F. Brady / Westfield, NJ
Donald L. Brase / Portland, OR
John W. Buckley / Tewksbury, MA
Jia Chen / Carmichael, CA
Deborah Clark / Southampton, MA
Eileen Z. Cohen / Haverford, PA
Khristina Cook / Durham, NC
Dahni / Rogers, AR
Sarah Denton / Owasso, OK
Nancy Harrison Durdin / Glenbeulah, WI
Stephen Faillaci / Westminster, CO
Alex M. Ferrell / Dixon, CA
Adrienne Garber / Pittsburgh, PA
Natalia Grosso / Zion, IL
Jeffry Halverson / Trumansburg, NY
Alexander Hart / Kirksville, MO
Vickie Y. Hodge / Memphis, TN
Kevin Jacobs / Bristol, CT
Keegan Jensen / Springville, UT
Sarah Jones / Fresno, CA
Donna Light / Searsmont, ME
Natalie Lockwood / Rochester, NY
Erin Martin / San Diego, CA
Carolyn Martinez / Albuquerque, NM

Jennifer Leigh Minson / West Valley City, UT
Gary T. Morgan / Chicago, IL
Adria Kay Nesberg / Bellevue, WA
Charles B. Nesbit / Belleville, IL
Jessica Peck / Chester, NH
Rushel Porter / Tyler, TX
Scott Preble / Quincy, MA
Kerry A. Pylant / Dacula, GA
Valerie Rains / Moore, OK
Patricia Hentz Regensburg / Camden, ME
Joel Richard / Falls Church, VA
J. E. Robinson / Elk Grove, CA
Carol Rose / Medford, OR
Philip Rose / Syracuse, NY
Siene Schielke / Missoula, MT
Zubin Segal / St. Louis, MO
Jason Siegel / Highland Park, IL
Heather Slottke / Greenfield, WI
Brian Studwell / San Mateo, CA
Lauren Terry / Homewood, AL
Philip L. Thompson / Pensacola, FL
Robert J. Vyszwany / Silver Springs, FL
Kris Wagner / Waupaca, WI
Karyn Walker / Waukesha, WI
Chelsea Wallis / Kapa'au, HI
Kimberly Whitis / Science Hill, KY
Shamra Winford / Madison, TN
Karen Wong / Lubbock, TX
Georgia D. Young / Rixeyville, VA

Congratulations also to all semi-finalists.

Grand Prize Winner

"F. Scott Fitzgerald"

You wrote about yellow cocktail music and the green light on Daisy's dock,
You said it was always 3 o'clock
In the morning and that there were no second acts in American life,
That the rich are different from you and me—and sex always ends in mortal strife.
Your vision was Keatsian sensual,
Your dialogue visible to the ear—
But when did you begin to see your leaf was in the sere?
That you were lost—no longer free to be the person you could be.
Gatsby was great; Zelda was not
And Hemingway said how dry was your rot.
Yet the words that you wrote were a movement in time
To exist in the ether of brazen sublime.
The 30's subsumed you; the country forgot
That you were a wordsmith while millions were not.
When you died in the forties and nobody came
A bottle of Scotch was reserved in your name—
And now every year in the month of September
It's poured on your grave so we will remember
That the angels that brought you will not come again
To waltz in blue gardens with God's borrowed pen.

Patricia Claire Eggleston

Winter's Practiced Disguise

Rooted silhouettes reflect shadows
as morning's recess has drawn to a close

Steep inclines lie broad . . .
desolate as wind-wisped flakes settle
on the highest branches of the weeping
willow, hurling gentle implacability

Brook vessels quench the last drink
of still waters . . . for it knows the
shallow drops of dew . . . how quickly
dawn's early light
fades its luster

Winter . . . a temporary substitute
antiquated, thrusting forward
unasked

And I wake from a December's nap
with slight altercations in posture,
skin loosened from my limbs,
a cup of cappuccino
        Kimberly Whitis

A Longing for the Annual Revolution

I miss the demise of summer's careless heat
dethroned by fall's alabaster reign

New York's concrete upheaval
to victorious gray sky
paves a reminder
that seasons too die

I miss winter's stab
the steel of cold blade
a murderous foe
to fall's color brigade

Loneliness marches
on crystal-frost air
to accompany winter
in each homeless stare

Far to the west
spring time is saved
by saccharine sun-warmth
and swords of sun rays

But radiance cannot disguise
the truth I miss in winter's eyes
        Michael F. Brady

Redemption

A half-remembered poem, a dream,
a scent, a touch, a careless style,
a memory now here, now gone,
elusive as an infant's smile.

Was there caprice, a transient glow
that brought me joy, or was it grief?
Through shadowed paths of time I search;
Illusion mocks me, time's a thief.

My eyes have paled to emptiness,
this wintry vista never planned;
my soundless song no longer sung,
my footprints leave no mark on sand.

How tenuous my days, so thin
that I could slip through falling rain
and stay untouched by any drop
of fearful joy or daunting pain.

Yet something magic once filled me
and dim remembrance clouds the pain
of dissipating into air
with no one knowing I was there.
        Patricia Hentz Regensburg

Philosophical Walk

I have traveled main street,
A frozen plum in my pocket,
melting violence
condensing on the walls
of my conscience.

I have been a talk show
sputtering its grumbling grin
across main street, lapsing into a coma.

I watch you,
peek into the junk drawers
of society, sifting through lives.
Old keys crowd
into the smooth of your palm.
Only one.

It is plum colored lipstick,
sliding over pale faces,
that mask the fear crawling home.
        Khristina Cook

Tucker's Day

It's President's Day, 1997
I wake up at seven A.M.
my third night in a strange bed.
I look out the window, the sky
appears gray, and then becomes blue.
I get up, wake Tucker and
send him out to do what it is that he does.
He lies down in the snow and
goes back to sleep.
I cook him eggs, they cool off and he eats them.
It's going to be a beautiful day
I shower, I dress. We get in the car and
drive through the State Forest.
The scenery is fragile, the snow is like powder.
We reach our destination, his final visit.
I love these ten acres, my pride, his playground.
We conquer the snow bank—
The perfect goodbye.
        Deborah Clark

Lost Soul In Vegas

In the unpure midnight
between the death song and breathing sand
lies a beautiful sun
strong and relentless in his morbid quest
human heart
a beat among the jungle fury
the city, Las Vegas
time stands still for him
in the unclean midnight
drinks, money, sex
things forlornly perplex his grieving soul
amid the frivolous boas and cheap tricks
there misery has no end
a tortured man leaving behind a city
leaving Las Vegas
        Kerry A. Pylant

Writer Made

Sneak off to the bathroom to read a little Kerouac,
I'm stuck behind a van towing a lawn mower.
Feel like I'm cheating
Bangles clank on my wrist—
    Clank—
        Clank—
            Clank as I write
                Metallic jibber jabber
Hoping I'm a writer born,
not made.
        Terena Elizabeth Bell

Under

Deep into the yawn of night she sits
awake and weightless,
un-innocent upon earth's placid surface.
Trees' healthy black arms
outstretch to accept her
in front of a less black sky.
Marcescent leaves cling,
still, un-surrendering.
Outlines metallic from the sting of moonlight.
Earth suspires softly,
incessantly.
Silk breath caresses timid skin.
Soothed by the somnolence of night sounds
yet un-enticed by sleep,
a human soul becomes solid,
with nature coalesced.
Understanding
incipient in a young belly,
rises . . .
instantly evanesced.

Erin Martin

Just A Resting Place

Beneath the ancient Blue Ridge Mountains
Stand cedars tall and proud
The sentries from forever
Cast their blackened shadows down
Under lie sorrows of the gentry
Who have lain their wearies there
Casting tomorrows in the dewdrops
Never to pick them up again
Saddened souls who had no place
Sort this solace with no disgrace
The heavy bows drop down to earth
The needles make a lasting bed
Inviting the burdened to come and rest
Upon the forest floor
And as they dream the dream of peace
Earth's mantel will enfold
And celestial doors open wide
To receive the spirits that soar

Georgia D. Young

M. F. C. (1905-89)

Revering arts, he turned to crafts
perplexed by classic form and face.
Unsorted plans in meager drafts
comprised the norms he could embrace.

Selecting means to cause an end
refined designs to meet a test.
No compromising could suspend
his choice for more than second best.

If tools were old or second hand
respectful fondling framed a trust.
The newer ones with plug-in strand
purloined the peace and offered lust.

He rose to struggle every day;
to elevate, repair, expand.
Destructive notions held no sway
expelled at once by reprimand.

A secret act revealed a gift
unwrapped at length by few he knew:
A burden bared engenders lift
to those in need of caring too!

Charles B. Nesbit

Untitled

Warm winds blow as my father wipes his brow.
Out in the pasture, a cow sways in the breeze to ward off the flies.
The corn reaches toward the sky, parched,
The leaves browned by the sun, the tassels limp.
Neighbors volunteer time but time is useless.
The rain knows no time.
The men drag out hoses, the women mix lemonade,
Hands dark with dirt, faces damp with sweat.
If just to see the leaves blow against a hard rain, Father sighs.
The sun beats down as if punishing the soil.
Time, it is just a matter of time he says.
It was just weeks before when my father stood in this field,
Flooded and muddy,
With no chance to get the crops in by June.
Now the merciless sun, the dry, cracked soil below Father's feet.
I stand
At my father's side.
The wind strokes the fragile crops as we turn to go home.
The clouds roll by,
Rain in the distance.

Natalia Grosso

Fade to Black

I have come to expect the teeth of the freezing pellets
biting at my windshield,
taunting the rubber tires
to grab the asphalt.
Icy roads follow February on its slick journey.
Glossed bridges the offspring
of a winter's day in the shade.
Where is the salt to tame the peril?
The few, green crocus shoots
claw the packed ground,
only to shrink away from the snarling cold.

I have come to expect a freezing touch on my shoulder,
as you push past me to hug another.
Your icy looks become an enemy,
revealing the hollowed inside through robin egg eyes.
Their warm glow now fading like embers.
Where are the sweet Valentines
to quiet the screaming pain?
The few soft glances struggle to peek through the hard facade,
only to disappear under your faded blue baseball cap.

Adrienne Garber

Close

Touched the Sierra Sky did I.
Memory revisited? A feeling,
Much like fading, slipping into weary sleep.
Merged with cradle-bed, the sinking stops.
Without warning, mind alert.

Monumental granite and iced water
Hosted dainty Solomon's Seal,
Gnarled pines arboreal,
Aquatic Caddis Creepers and lively Skippers
Darting hither yon.

Crystal blue brushed the Crest,
Enchanting splendor to reflect.
Masterfully configured images primordial.
Earth's life forces—simple molecules.
Mirrored beginnings.

Wedged between rock and sky and water
Life—Hope
Regeneration—Birth
I was close.
One with. . . .

Carol Rose

The Room

The room is dim that each is in,
The walls are dark, black stripes therein,
Vertically they rise and fall,
And in between it is so small,
A pair of windows at one end,
Yet little information lend,
Such tiny breadth can each discern,
So small is that which we can learn,

Before the walls and after them,
Have lived so many countless men,
Yet little information here,
Our trust in this be placed with care,
Reality is what we see,
We can't be sure, it might not be,
The limits of what we perceive,
Discourage that which we believe.

Jason Siegel

Friends

Minds unframed, portrait of lost summer's June
Mountainside, fireside, wood, stream and moon

Revisit a soul passed, close, dear, and warm
A trust so solid as to beckon form

Discoverer earth's most precious charms
Wild flower fields amid earthen horse barns

Round brown eyes reveal genuine heart
Hold strength and loyalty beats apart

Peaceful walks cleave soft, still night air
Abreast companions stride faithfully rare

A middays errand, out tended abroad
Through brown eyes, a journey without epilogue

Relaxing and leaning on unspoken love
Lifelong partners seemed sealed from above

The touch of a friend, received as a gift
Returns with a gesture, stirring spiritual lift

As if pursuing the scent of reunion someday
Eyes pause for approval, then steal away

In this world such souls should we cherish
Then true joy and love, fear not soon to perish

Robert J. Vyszwany

Translation

Dear England! Where hast thou gone?
The golden green hillside that first welcomed me home;
Barren moors where shadows move under lowering skies,
And grass and spirits tremble.

Gone from my view are the northern mountains,
Where God walked on a misty morning as the sun rose.
There I saw flaming fall consume the hillsides
And a country church in snowfall.

The omnipotent sea flees from before me,
Where rising tide met majestic cliffs in thunderous symphony.
I looked windswept over a veiled emerald coastline
And the earth was mine for a moment.

Vanishing are the vast ethereal forests,
Where vivid imaginations pass silently under leafy boughs—
Revealed as blue and golden when caught in dappled sunlight—
And the shade has healing powers.

Thou has been taken up into heaven,
For thou art too celestial for this world.

Jennifer Leigh Minson

The Father Moment

There is that moment,
a motion,
when the hawk leaves the branch,
when the glowing cadence of the sun falls
behind the rounded shadow of earth's horizon,
when the earth tilts and the longest day of the year ends,
when the boy,
filled with confusion, his heart swelling up,
turns to the father,
sawdust on his sleeves,
stubby pencil sharpened with a jackknife
locked behind his ear, and waits
for the embrace of those strong arms, that moment
passing like a stone falling
from the hand into the lake's dark unknown.
Descending, the boy gives way to that darkness
turns and walks away.
"Ask your mother," is all his footsteps hear.

Philip Rose

The Journal

Thoughts of the past discovered
Deep in the dust of time,
Right where they had fallen
From an overcrowded mind.

The paper holds together.
The ink still reads just fine
But fragile are the judgments
In each philosophical line.

Be careful as you study them
Within the story told.
Don't crush with modern musings
These weaker judgments old.

Preserve them in their weakness.
At one time they were strong.
Since wisdom grew from where they fell,
Dust not away the wrong.

Look on them with wonder.
Respect their impact then.
Our thoughts that seem so strong today
In wisdom's dust may end.

Vickie Y. Hodge

On Contemplation

Raven streak over quiet pastures
Flocks swarm back to the womb.
The sky scraping city of trees,
Yield to streams of sunlight.
Revealing winter hideaways.

Tiny morsels of rebirth sprout through
And nurture themselves,
On the decay from the death
Which surrounds them.

Pebbles shine through the surf
Even when embedded by sand.

As I walk along the pier to nowhere
I wonder,

I am watching you, or are you
Watching me?

Diane Abbinanti

They Called It Silverthorne

Thirty-six long tedious hours, four bus transfers, multiple conversations
with a disgruntled, eight fingered truck driver, and over a 1,000 miles
later legs stiff, cramped, muscles knotted, my mind plays an inner
questioning battle of unknown vs. adventure.
I take my first unsteady step onto the fabled land of the snow-capped Rockies.

My eyes zoom in, then out nerve impulses send images of jagged horizons
Tick, tock, tick, tock . . .
and two minutes later after the initial stride,
I stand alone amongst the brisk cold, gasping for more oxygen,
on the 9,200 foot mountain base,
my life necessities consumed in a sixty-pound backpack
and my only transportation disassembled in a brown cardboard box.

No place to sleep, no one to meet.
I look back, my heart thumping in faster rhythmic beats of fear,
at my bus ride of wonder, my trip of uncertainty
as the Greyhound's exhaust floats up from an unfamiliar land
driving away and disappearing into dim-lighted city streets.

Kris Wagner

Searching For Me

Another mundane Tuesday closes over the suburbs.
As I turn down the street of my youth,
As a memory passes where the bus stop was,
Nostalgia passes through my nostrils.
Unwanted memories of the past invade like a thief.
Each time I have been summoned I answered.
The gothic figure reached his hand to me.
I held on to the air around it.
A liquid snake stopped and waited and became available.
I swam because it cured a burdened deep within.
Each night is a search for the treasure of me.
This street holds such ambivalence under my thumbs,
Like an aria sung to an unpure air.
This life so far has tempted a jaded mind.
As I lie down in this comfortable bed I wonder,
Why do we only remember the good times?
It rained again today.
I think that I enjoy the rain mostly in the humid evening.
I just want to know myself;
I just want to know pure.

Stephen Faillaci

Sounds of the Underground

The bronze, rusted door knob dances on a frenzied stage,
My feet absorb the glassy tile loosely like ice,
Adjusting to the dark in a palatine of whispers and confusion;
My best friend's voice like a gargling, flushing toilet.
Scared in stagnant air feeling each breath of the closet walls,
Mundane daily lapse with each terrified moment intact,
Electrified, blood singed eyes seep harnessed tears,
Feeling as prey in my shallow elevator like two years ago,
Bleakly stuck on the basement floor and my fingertips calloused;
My mother's demands drown in her pregnancy screams.
A devil's smirk manifests in the dusty rays of ventilated light;
Rage impales each pore and seizes me like a militant rendezvous;
Subdued emotions explode staining each wall of my cell.
Left helpless I fall to my knees like a licked Jell-o bowl,
The elevator alarm's incessant ring colliding with the rattling door,
Alive underground hoping to escape this noise infested exhalation.

Kevin Jacobs

California Windmills

In line on the hills the windmills stand,
     waving from the brown hills,
          from the misty morning hills.
And as you near, they open their arms
     and twirl in endless dance.
The wind has wooed them; they cannot be still.
Turning slowly, spinning fast,
     they welcome the whim of the wind.
And when the sun smiles, they are white birds
     flying, flying, flying up
          and
               down
                 the
                    hills,
Never daring to soar.

Carolyn Martinez

Saran-Wrapped Rainstorms

Tremulous tears trickle
from a million faces
brimming with heather remorse.
Slowly,
sad smiles swirl
mixed limes and blues
of mudpuddle sorrows,
dripping down dreams
of artichoke flavors.
Desperate dead drown
in artificial rainbows,
gasping for a breath of darkness.
Silver
silhouettes slip soundlessly
toward mirrors of melancholy laughter,
reflecting ruined rivers
of tomorrow's yesterday.

Siene Schielke

Untitled

Gliding, floating, sailing down
Gently fluttering to the ground
Colors above all ablaze
Upward eyes fondly gaze
Evening walks with crackling sounds
Crispy whispers all around
Brisk new air make cheeks that blush
Foggy breaths from mouths do rush
Fires burning smoky scents
Weary trees have all been spent

Elizabeth Bourland

The Bookmark

Life is like the book you read,
the pages are the days we lead.
The bookmark is the note to life,
it tells the times of joy or strife.

My bookmark was 'fore you I met,
gauging a life I thought was set.
New chapters now are in my book,
inspired by you with just a look.

With eager turnings now I greet,
each day, each page I race to meet.
My mark is found since I met you,
in pages now and ever new.

Each day a page in a treasured book,
I can't set down nor overlook.
The bookmark now it marks my life,
with joy and bliss, thank you my wife.

Scott Preble

Tainted Meeting

Pen and paper meet.
They stare at each other,
Up close and personal.
Paper darkens as ink soils it.
Words, formed in the pen,
Are jotted on the once clean white space.
Lines are crossed along with t's and dotted i's.
Does the paper have any clue of the travesty the pen is orchestrating on it?
Can it sense the meaning that is imbued in the scars of ink
That now riddle its once sanitary surface?
The drying brings semi-permenancy to the vandalism that
has been insistently spread.
The pen is the tool, yet can the paper comprehend
It is not the controller of its actions?
The writer incites the incident that causes
The eventual disagreement between page and utensil.
Disgruntled wood fibers allow ink to fade away to nonexistence.
A friendship that could have been,
Once again fouled by the hand of man.

Alexander Hart

Eulogy

A dark cloak fades gold rays to chilling white
And fills the void with bastions far, serene.
The surface of the sphere now wants for light
Where once five billion candles could be seen.

A child binds glowing gold in his glass jar
While the chirping orchestra plays a show.
Two fish swim in a sea of misty tar.
The wise archer draws taut his astral bow.

The weaver spins a yarn to sew their sleep,
Awaiting Morpheus to weave the charm,
Then banishes dark things from shadows deep
So that her precious watch they cannot harm.

Apollo's chariot is stabled now,
But let it not forget the morrow's vow.

Michael Baker

The Old House

Candle crooked, on the mantle,
Melted wax on ashen wood.
Once a warmth rose from the fire,
While shadows danced around the room.
Standing here I remember, her youth, fresh and tender;
She'd place her warmth on a stranger's cold hand.
Off he would go with a vow to remember—
The love she held, he'd someday have.
Winter was blamed, as he robbed her,
Stealing all she held from the ball of her hand.
In his pronounced returns to her
Made sinuous and aged her stand.
Stripped and naked, warmth discarded,
Thrown upon a shoulder cold;
Once with meaning, deep and feeling
Now lies touchless on the floor.
Candle crooked, on the mantle;
Air gives in to the musty smell.
All the rooms are left here empty,
And the sign reads house for sale.

Shamra Winford

The Merchant of Coins

The facts of my pockets,
The coin hordes and door keys,
Both haunting my elegance,
Distract me from the practice.
Even in the company of late night's finest
I dwell on the past
And the dreams.
The dreams.
Over, they churn with reminders
And the things to return to,
All words to exchange
That they might bring closure.
But all rivers break,
Like fractured sparrows
That fall from the flying masses
To sing . . .
Only to find a few notes were missing.

Jeffry Halverson

Apple of Eden's Renewal

Earthy tones
give the cloth crispy textures,
sharing the volubility of the season,
mastering the chameleon
of fallen distance,
covering, for the last time,
limbs of winter nakedness.
This will uncover the identity
of bland characters
standing at attention,
through the most bitter waterfalls.
Until the last froth is consumed
again, a bud will appear,
showing Eve,
even the richest soils
can be trespassed.

Heather Slottke

Granite Roses

Sandstone tears fall from an ashen sky
Crashing like boulders on the hard brick earth.
Paper lightning and whispers of thunder
Give life to the silicate winds and duster clouds.

All around, fractal trees of vibrant green tiles
Shield our coal eyes from the furnace sun.
The chatterbox birds and oily owls swiftly flit
In the limbs of the realistically artificial forest.

In the distance, a rosebush of rock-granite
Grows silently, stealthily up the side of a hill,
Green tiled leaves and wire stems covered in
Steel nail thorns and red-granite petals.

Pipe-cleaner bumblebees of black and gold
Feed from the sawdust pollen and oil nectar
Making glue honey for the fuzzy carpet-bears
To gorge on before the cold, cold winter sleep.

The granite roses drink the sandstone rain
And grow even more, covering the hill with their
Hard, cold beauty under the furnace sun and the
Grey sky, dusty clouds, and fractal forest leaves.

Joel Richard

Mirror Image

My Momma told me about the old lady
Who lived behind her mirror.
She said the hag looked like her.
Sadie always made up stories.
She played roles.
She stole good lines—
That one from a French play.
It isn't life.

Now the crone is behind my mirror.
Odd how she looks so much like me.
It doesn't seem right.
Old ladies always live in shoes,
The "fairest of them all" in mirrors.
Sadie taught me those fairy tales too.
How could I know that
She played smoke and mirrors
With the truth?

After all, it isn't life! Is it?

Eileen Z. Cohen

A Van Gogh in Him

Surrounded by an austere blue frame,
Hangs my grandfather's painting:
Three potted marigolds.
A colorful whirlpool;
Yellow, pink, peach
But no color is drowning; a perfect balance.
You could stare for hours,
Whirlpools spinning and circling.
Flowers come to life.

Van Gogh smiles from above.

Zubin Segal

Debauched

A generous weekend gift of the gods
Who seem pleased with our play
On the riverbank in bright sunlight—
Bacchus's wine and the Food Giant's beer
Provided for us children who dance the
Ritual of life ignorant of great powers.

Laughing, Lacey arches her scantily-clad form,
Nike shoes swiftly lifting her to Titus
Who stands nearby, bare-chested, posing
His Nautilus body of muscled arms and thighs.
The nectar of the moment becomes reality;
Our revelry obviates the need to think.

Olympic sponsors of our nescient event
Look down from multi-storied monuments
Philosophically pleasuring themselves with
Knowledge that sparse allowances
Provide complacent offspring
Who will labor all the more on Monday.

Donald L. Brase

Untitled

Light coming from a lamp made of brass on a wooden desk.
The light climbs half up a wall then pauses to keep the room quiet.
It paints shadows on the floor and unknowingly makes the wood
more than it is.
The narcotic waves keep you silent as
you watch your life become a single point; and things you
will never again understand present themselves to you in brass light,
then leave you alone in the shadows.

John W. Buckley

Untitled

Staring through winter-stained windows
    I see a crocus pushing through the
      heaviness of winter;
the unrelaxed, icy grip
imprisoning blossoms, buds,
    my restlessness.
The earth needs turning
    and I want to pedal along
      the river,
brown my arms
with long, warm days
    and
      it's snowing.

Donna Light

The Diaphanous One

I see that you are shrouded
In a new suit of broken glass;
Gaping holes are forming
Upon your already rotted path.

Hues of softly chalked mirrors
Drip now in pitiless forms of ill;
I gather you in bottomless tins
You're beautiful to me, yes, even still.

Entwined, charred emotions
Are eternally pasted in your eyes;
Yet, the presence of hope can pierce stone
To emit life's rainbow colored dyes.

I promise you, my Beauty
That wounds are rarely soul deep;
Tears and time will heal them
And my shadow is ever so cheap.

I will be amongst you forever
Or at least until the demise of the sun;
Clearing your walkway, always
Always, I will remain your Diaphanous One.

Sarah Denton

Carwash

Auto/mated in the carwash line,
I idle slow morning moments with
Simon (and Garfunkel then) singing
something sad, while
the usual worries whisper
on a day like any other.

Entering the (secret) code,
I drift into twilight spray, song
condensing into something—urgent—
about a mother and child.

And she and I cry out (O my god) as he
wavers, undecided on a ledge,
too high to see our faces
in the crowd.

Rolling, son/warm droplets
bead on my steel skin, but
Simon (and Garfunkel then) is gone, and
the usual worries whisper
on a day like any other.

Alan Parks

WHILE YOU WERE ASLEEP

(ARIEL'S REQUIEM)

I watch you as you sleep,
Feel a warm breeze pass your cold, still lips,
An essence of florals, and my eyes affix
On the bleeding heart draped upon your silk blue gown.

A string of azure beads intertwine alabaster fingers;
The crucifix gazes over you in Extramunctional passion;
A single ivory rose finds peace beside your breast,
Reminds me of the one you pressed in a paperback by Poe.

And, oh, those abhorrent and gaunt torchere lamps,
Catty-cornered and rigid as catatonic pallbearers.
You used to say: "Why must parlors insist on their presence?"
I despise them too, and for you, my love, I exhort their removal.

'Tis nine of night; prayers of closure pave an eerie silence.
I exercise temperance with amorphous expression,
Masking wired nerves, and veins depressed;
Handshakes of pestilence acknowledge unknown faces.
Tomorrow it shall rain, my love; our final day shall cry.

Abound the desolate mist in air, I cannot say good-bye;
Instead I kiss your powdered brow and whisper in your ear,
And await the day I may place an ivory rose on you again.

Frank James Ryan Jr.

Melancholia

Scraggly claws of drizzle dragged themselves across the pane,
Caught my eye, and forced my sight to peer upon the dinginess of the day,
Chilly, dampened air passed through my pores,
Grasping and clutching the meager remnants of any inner warmth.
Without resistance, this invisible thief took his leave,
Deserting the remains of an empty, hollow shell.
Sadness sat before me, spinning and weaving tales of desperation,
Accompanied by the sounds of down-cast, dripping dew—
The corner Grandfather declared the length of the day,
And binged and bonged and shattered this fragile frame of thought.
Amid the confusion of scattered bits of concentration,
I cursed the interruption,
For in this sullen state, there lies a certain sense of comfort,
Protection in the spirit of a cozy wrap of woe,
In a web weaved with threads of self-pity.
But songs of woeful sighs, by their nature,
Signal to the soul and stir the spirit.
And 'mid this humbling circumstance,
The dancing drops of sparkling dew catch my eye,
And force my sight to peer upon the breaking light of day.

Margaret Kist

Point Pleasant in November

Sea silt inhabits the pores of a grainy candied apple tossed onto
the beach against the edge of the world, making pearls amidst
the garden of driftwood, discarded cigarette butts, and lost shoes.
A guardian angel slow dances with his metal detector, and
an off-season tourist pauses long enough to snap our picture
under the boardwalk. We lead a stealth reconnaissance mission
at the abandoned roulette stand, recovering three stuffed POW trolls.
Their captor left us a message, "Be back in 20 min." A local drunk
snaps to attention in front of a dart board and with his 80 proof breath
barks and slurs his rendition of a past drill sergeant. "Hup! Aaaah,
pree-zent arms! That's Charlie Muscatel, good 'ol Charlie Muscatel!"
We passed a has-been singer that claimed Frank Loesser slapped her
backstage after she went flat on the opening night rowser. Now she
does her torch songs for the shady squatters down at the all-night
Fluff and Fold. We exit "dead beach," as the locals call it come winter,
with salt water taffy capping our molars, and the trolls smile up
at us in gratitude for their rescuers, riding our pockets.

Barrett Brokaw

TV Dinner For One

Clocked out
Battle scars and dishpan hands
Quiet hum, messy car
Broad unlightened streets

Other side of town
empty rooms lie waiting,
empty couches empty
kitchens empty beds
All holding breath,
unlived-in and still.

Tired sighs fog
cold window panes
and people and stars
and none of them are hers
Not even one
is hers

Valerie Rains

Fall Comes in on Lion's Paws

As fall comes in on lion's paws,
forcing leaves to fall,
into stinging slaps
of wind and rain,

I feel a steady rise
in the level of pain
I need to tuck away.

On other days,
the hot sun
bakes out,
the raw, damp, memories
of past fallen leaves,
and loves.
But,
Fall
and fear
come in
on lion's paws,
and tear at
the fiber of my soul.

Nancy Harrison Durdin

Womanhood

This hourglass figure
Perfected for you
Through your eyes
This is natural
But the use of our disfigured ideas
Has lead us into an addiction
Of posing and acting
An obsession with beauty
The ideas of right and wrong
Will we ever get what we want?
Things slowly progress
But back down
We will only go

Karyn Walker

Daydreaming in English 142

People: fickle, fad, and fatuous,
poetic and prose, our verbosity drones on and . . .
On a day like this, when the cold seeps in under my skin
Sends chills down my spine and memories through my mind—
"When will Summer come . . . and where did Summer go?"
I don't know. I just wait

Believer of fate,
You have your way with me
Destiny. But what am I destined for?

People—listening to the rattle
of a flag pole
and the dust settles
on wooden floors
(Dreaming in my present while the future takes place)

Natalie Lockwood

Eighteen

Familiar quiet plops itself upon our civic afternoon
reach down to fetch a lemonade
from the porch's knotty cork-filled grin

Kitty darts across my lawn (in plain pursuit of nothing)
gleam from an Edsel snickers by
as an acorn dives into the freshly paved Parkway

Johnny sits upon the curb
watching leaf canoes drift by
and off, somewhere, a mockingbird
celebrates the clearing sky

School bus pulls up, and sighs relief (another demon gone)
and Johnny's day is a little brighter
skip on home with the big kids, John!

Wake up from screams of neighbors' kids
and mouth is mighty dry
a fresh, new patch of piercing green brings Landlord into mind

Add a hole to this old house (the flies have got to go)
across the way, a mother cries
around her men in black take notes

Philip L. Thompson

September

Sometime during the third week in August comes an
actual decided moment that triggers the coming of
the days of September.
The humid days of summer begin to weaken and surrender
their immature ways.
Peculiar feelings of emptiness and longing fill the soul.
A passing moment signals a wave of promise.
What belonged to summer form would soon change.
A sign of completion and end.
And by Friday of that August-third-week it becomes official.
The early signal has turned into new blue air.
Freshness of autumn beginnings titillate the bush
and the brush and the sway of the trees.
And from a slight tinge it becomes its own era.
A time for celebrating moments.
Ordinariness. An order of service. Intent.
Quite right to understand and be content.
Time calms the question.
Earth offers approbation.
Sanction of a new beginning for life's September soil.

Gary T. Morgan

Recognition (For E.H.)

Perhaps it is not surprising
that I should find you here—
sorrows woven into your hair like sea-roses,
stirring the grasses of remembrance
with your pensive fingertips:

You were ever at the bergamot-scented shrine of Melancholy,
attentive to your Cimmerian oracle,
solemnly brushing tansy across your collar bones
and into the sacred hollow of your throat.

Longtime I tried in vain to draw your attention
to my humble offerings of dawns and daylilies;
your eyes fixed on the gingery shores
of the echoing country of remorse,
you contemplated the dusk in sighs and whispers
and drank the rich, poisoned honey of regret . . .

Yet now—when, in resignation, I turn from you
into the cool white pillared place within me
and kneel at the priestess-pool of my solitude—
I find your sloe-eyed, elusive gaze finally meeting mine.

No . . . it is not surprising.

Jeaneen McAmis

Menschliche Grenzen   (Human Boundaries)

Don't walk where the cobblestone's not laid.
Morning bloom the roses greener, and the heavens fade.
Choose your words carefully, and re-use words well said.
Forgotten is the song, disenchanted.

Roads untaken
Lead to truths unwanted
Ways for those left wanting
In a world with enough for a few good times.

Smile and take another look.
Nothing more than what you see.
But whose eyes can truly see the shining,
Unopened fire amongst the straw?

In the corner, hunched into a ball,
Starlight burning in his ancient eyes,
But five years old
And already his feet have trod the unknown.

Broken, and free!
Tomorrow's dawning is eternal
Light shall penetrate invisible worlds
In the back of a child's eye.

Keegan Jensen

Petrol Requiem

White lines rolled down the highways
as road gypsies moved in the dark.
Iron steeples jutted in the night, too many to count,
Sky torqued, piercing the earth deep.
Distant lights charted the paths of subterranean pockets,
Drilling ships in the desert ocean of ancient fish.

Gone now are the signal lights flashing in the sky,
A sign, making a trip through the crust with diamonds.
The cities of steel pipe and casing, greedy, waiting above,
for the gush of a struck vein.

No more mud-dancing, roughneck, boom days,
Smooth gamblers making deals on a chance.
Dispossessed are the zone scholars, hard drillers, toolpushers,
the mudmen and wildcatters baptized in sludge pits.

Wit, wisdom and lore of oilmen lost,
Carried now to the earth from which it came.

L. L. Ball

Spacing

Printed hearts
on paper dolls
a singing phone
when no one calls
fresh flowers
vased on a desk
something's missing
can't find the rest
the touch the smell
the taste the fear
trying to know them
to hold them dear
every second
of every day
such importance
wasting away
but who can tell?
were they there at all?
just a dream . . .
but there's the doll

Chelsea Wallis

Deathwatch

I hear the Beatles through the wall—
I think that it's "Norwegian Wood."
The sad, sweet strains recall a time
Of lesser loss, of greater good,
Of walking smiles through miles of rain,
Of pain that hangs like honey stains,
On all the memories I glean,
From grains the Reaper let remain.
The grains of sand fall one by one
Like insects in an amber sea,
Each second tortured on the rack,
Each hope nailed writhing on The Tree,
Each scene repeating endlessly,
So I relive each anguished stride
That brought me to this shrouded bier
Where lies the victim of my pride
Which died the Martyr's grim demise,
Bequeathing me an Exile's Prize
Of solitude won by my choice
And Banshee-voice to echo lies.

D. M. Weiss

A Utopian Tale?

This is just another one
Among your many other reads—
It won't describe a perfect glade
Nor tell of lover's lustful needs.

Don't peer between the lines too long;
You may get lost amid the white
Of verses struggling to conceal
A somewhat constipated plight.

And gosh! the lack of poet's stuff
(I scratch my head and bounce my knee)
Host boredom while you wait in hopes
For occasional hyperbole.

I'm sure you've noticed, structure-wise,
I haven't been working all that hard.
And as for just the basic theme,
I'd say it's far from avant garde.

The atmosphere is free of drear,
The sun is shining in the sky,
And all that I can do is pray
You'll have a less critical eye than I.

Jessica Peck

Inheritance

I am a young traveler.
I have been searching for the river Tsuyung,
where my father, august youth, lingered high in wild waters
to glimpse my mother swimming in stark sun,
droplets licking round her cheeks.

My father was a Dragon.
Emperor indomitable, crusader of unquenching fire.
He was of the chosen to tame fate.
He was chosen to forge his destiny, brass hard.

My mother was an Ox.
Resolute stabilizer, trustworthy restorer of promise.
She patiently pushed the wheel of fate, welcoming woven will.

I am a Rabbit.
And I have stopped searching for the river Tsuyung where my father, the Dragon,
and my mother, the Ox, tangled with fate for me.

I am a Rabbit.
I am a Moon Hare, temperately firm, placidly fervent,
and I wander deep in the mountains of Suikwan, north past the Yangtze,
to find my own river, where I will loose my locks and soak in moss pools and
drown in the rays of the moon.

Jia Chen

From the Text of Apocalyptic Conformity

welcome to the teenage psychiatric wish-list
take information and drink from the common trough

fabled comedians dance the tango pulling eyes with repulsive sentence structure
would-be crooners get winded trying to gather a would-be verse
disciples make their presence known with essence halos while finger puppets
memorize their souls and dance joyously to haunting ballads
soft-shelled dandelions draped over label-studded cavemen
floaters lay themselves down to sleep to the star's philosophical dismay
midgets ravagely ransack for stilts among the piles of exaggeration
heavenly pageant contestants set up the conceit perimeter
sailors set their bows for exploration while toasting with exasperation
and set off among the desolate street lights
"true sailing is dead!"

J. E. Robinson

"F. Scott Fitzgerald"

You wrote about yellow cocktail music and the green light on Daisy's dock,
You said it was always 3 o'clock
In the morning and that there were no second acts in American life,
That the rich are different from you and me—and sex always ends in mortal strife.
Your vision was Keatsian sensual,
Your dialogue visible to the ear—
But when did you begin to see your leaf was in the sere?
That you were lost—no longer free to be the person you could be.
Gatsby was great; Zelda was not
And Hemingway said how dry was your rot.
Yet the words that you wrote were a movement in time
To exist in the ether of brazen sublime.
The 30's subsumed you; the country forgot
That you were a wordsmith while millions were not.
When you died in the forties and nobody came
A bottle of Scotch was reserved in your name—
And now every year in the month of September
It's poured on your grave so we will remember
That the angels that brought you will not come again
To waltz in blue gardens with God's borrowed pen.

Patricia Claire Eggleston

Remembered

last night i toyed with
my own
rose-scented nostalgia,
inhaled its old, dust essence
and i felt, like
sunlight struggling over the horizon,
the accidental discovery of
one moment that hid
on a corner shelf in my memory
a dim, distant corner
a moment born when
i was   six? years old
a moment regretfully idle for many more
delighted, i rechanneled sight and mind
a friday evening time travel, back, far back
and traced, retraced my path to the moment
and wore out a path to preserve the way, remembered.

Karen Wong

Ogygia (Brick, 1997)

The stones sing circles of seasons
as i dance the eternal calypso
tales of brothers beaten blue
by the crests of an unseen orchestra
a movement of waving memories

For that fading coin would i not embrace that solemn hill
my rechristened spirit splashing pirouettes
towards the veiled horizon

But there is not a penny beside me
when the sun never comes
only a strand of rope from naïve hands
he who claimed kinship with the gods
and promised to show me the path home

I dance the eternal calypso
when i hear the crack of another log on the fire
i sometimes fancy feathers falling
from the soles of heaven's untouchable feet

Brandon Avery

Motel on Atlantic Avenue

narrow hallways, pool tables, corners of nasty streets,
i waited by your old water fountain,
watching cue balls thump against green walls; all four.
slept in your hard bed, uninvited,
while listening through thin walls to lovers coming and going.
the square room that hoarded privacy—
saving it for a lonely visitor who was not me,
but perhaps was the old fat lady, janice, who brought me clean towels.
and now, undoubtedly, she must be unemployed or dead,
without her sticky bathrooms and stained sheets
that no longer need to be cleaned. without buzzing lights,
fluorescent, and static on the televisions—no longer fixable,
ever since your weak walls crumbled
leaving room for a brand new complex.
i can imagine her frumpy body
sprawled out in the hallway.
each of her sides, rolls, touching a wall,
windex in hand,
finally
checking

Kendra Griffin

Paean to a Working Woman

You are wheat to me, ma'am,
from the whole-grain honey of the bun
rolled so carefully under your wooly mushroom cap
and bobby-pinned expertly, to the
nourishing naïveté of your white-bread inflection.

Cows mill, gleaning the roadside fields you daily cruise,
entirely undisturbed because you
serve home-cooked suppers faithfully,
brown-bag it day by banal day
and nurture nebbishes when spare time's at hand.

Plain as the crusts you give to beggar jays,
you reduce the molding cheese Danish of greed
to a simple "Why?"
enriching our cynical sandwiches
with the riboflavin of blind bran-muffin optimism:

Wheat grows, wheat flows,
cut, into sheaves the shape of you,
and always will.

Lauren Terry

Welfare

"A hot water bottle is better than a man," you say,
and I believe you, because you are the prophetess,
bright and fierce and indignant,
tattooing fairy tales of peace
to the roof of your mouth
with the dark sharpness of your tongue
as you lie curled around your red rubber life raft.
Like water in a cave creating eye-sockets
for the blind rocks, the black rivulets
of your frustrated prophesy
drip slowly down the curves of your mouth
to splash against molars,
and when you speak the ink is
flicked from your lips, spattering my cheek
with dream freckles, diluted and misspent.
"You can be the new voice," you say,
but really
I need a hotter water bottle
and a more permanent ink
if I'm going to get my soul off welfare.

Liberty Boor

Sonnet # 8

Her fruitless soul turns in amongst the meek,
Wherein each day a teardrop's silent scream
Doth make like fat and chokes her chance to speak.
Crusted canvas quilts seam-line her dream
Like wool-warm winter coats cling to my sweat.
And shades her luminescent burning bulb
That finds no crease of mercy which to let
This beam spill, crack the fears she doth indulge.
Thus weepy waiting wrings those cancered hands
From former palms which nourished healthy hearts.
And desolate this leaves her shell to stand,
Cracked, empty, dead, condemned, and kicked apart.
That each descending day rises to mend,
Her tempered hopes do conjure and pretend.

Suzanne Cerreta

Sextant

She set sail seas sublime
to turn twisted torrential tough
precarious passage prime
ears echo enough.

Great gusting gales
billowing bulging broth
hounding hails
wringing, writhing; wroth.

Rollicking rolling ruin; fear freezing fright
brittle, broken, beaten; never nutating night.

Listless languorous latitude
changing care-concern
great gripping gratitude
long lesson-learn.

Cadastre cache celestial; bold beacon bright
tabula rasa terrestrial; leading luminous light.

Peradventure procuring peace
Futile flying, fraught forceful foam
Cosmos calling cease,

For there's no place like home.
        Dahni

Honeysuckle

We, four and five,
Sat sucking sweetness
From purple patches
Of honeysuckle.

And you, flower-lipped,
Drunk with the day,
Sit cross-legged,
Making crowns of glory.

King and Queen, we
Ruled our vast kingdom
If only
Just the garden.
        Sarah Jones

Divinity

A dream of divine insight,
A glimpse of the future's part,
To believe in this serenity,
And seek this to last.
Forever in a broken soul,
To never mend in light,
We live a mask to fit our show,
And hold it ransom to the night.
        Alex M. Ferrell

Bali

cool rushing waters ripples rhymes
warm supple breezes sanguine sublime
dancing my shadow mirrors and mimes
as my spirit wades through pastoral time
wanting to fall
frozen depths silence peace
wanting to rise
flaming star consumed freed
wanting to end this purgatory
wishing to leave this paradise
        Brian Studwell

Watercoloured Stranger

As I drag my feet along Hennepin Ave.
I see you from afar,
sipping your cigarette
and inhaling your coffee.

The tattered green canopy dangling over your head
sways in the gusts to catch the crashing raindrops.

Your friends build castles on the cafe table
with napkins and plastic forks,
and your laughter keeps you warm
as the gales slip their bitter chill through your faded blue
sweatshirt.

But I walk alone through these drippy streets,
kicking rocks through the swelling puddles,
my soggy shoes sloshing with every random step.

You lift your head in greeting
and as soon as you're sure
that your eyes were burning into mine,
you smile
to spread the warmth on this dreary evening
to a simple girl,
with no place to go.
        Kirsten Volnes

My Mother's Strong Arms

She used to read to us
our ears pressed tight, as her rhythmic
heart wove us Bianca's tales,
and other mice, at Christmas.
She tucked us in—cocoons against bugs.

And the small houses where people wore
plastic smiles and bandaged wire legs.

She used to bandage our wounds
no cut too small for iodine mice—
their tails trailing down our backs.
She wiped away the streaks of pearl teardrops
Her pearls—subtle and enduring.

And her fingers worked ribbons of hair
into tight bands and butterfly clips.

She used to hold us in
arms of coral and roses
and soothe our knotted hearts—
as we said good bye . . .
one by one, we search the distances
for my mother's strong arms.
        Adria Kay Nesberg

Child in Me

Breathe the breath of freedom cling to the air full of light
seeing not the open wounds bleeding in plain sight
shackles falling and the heart is well seen
to the naked eyes . . . the child in me
I hear not the gasping only the sound of my words
for they've fallen in the air with a voice that's heard
from a place so well-hidden from a sight never seen
comes the pain long standing in the heart of my need
Taste the sweetness of forgiveness and bitterness of truth
lest I fall for the lies I protected in my youth
and retreat to this fortress where my pain did begin
and never feel freedom with the touch of my hands.
        Rushel Porter

Shadow of Doubt

we sleep alone, we change the station
but every song on is always the same
we miss our call, we miss our flight
we set alarms, but we can't set our sights

we clutch our sides, we grip the rail
we convince ourselves
Let's rest for awhile
we keep appointment, fill small black books
with the numbers of those like us
the losers and crooks

the solstice passes, the sun loses its shine
yet we con ourselves into thinking,
everything's fine
the truth is this, our lives go by
our words say much
without being said
our hearts keep beating
though we're already dead

Charles Varani

My Sister, My Mother

There with a shoulder for me to cry on
Upholding a pedestal to keep me strong
Always encouraging, safe, undaunting
Love unconditional—
Giving, seldom wanting
My guide when I am lost
Fulfilling when I need, no matter the cost
Courageous, bold
Warmth when my spirit runs cold
The heart of my world, my soul
My father, my brother
My sister, my mother

Comateta M. Clifton

Untitled

A collected book of sorrows
too rhythmic to be good
Opinions darken the water,
I open my door to intolerance
opening the eyes of malice
nothing stays the same
hoping I was dreaming,
but morning never came

You dislike all my thoughts
(too thick within the mud)
ignorance drowning you in my shallow pool
I thrive within obsession,
I love to be nowhere

A closed door hide a smile,
An evil one will show
I wish I didn't know
The emptiness of being full

Pamela Bosse

White Mountain Valley

Drums and zephyr unite
sunflowers sway
golden

Lynda Rich

You blessed our lives near thirteen years.
Fond memories appear amid the tears:
A ray of bright sunshine,
The soft raindrops,
A garden sprouting carrot tops,
The brightly colored butterfly,
A rainbow splashed across the sky,
A gentle breeze and shady trees,
The sweet green grass,
and bushes full with luscious berries.
You will live on in every nature's scene.
And now we lay you down to rest
within the ground that you loved best,
and looking upward to the sky,
as we sit and wonder why,
there above the clouds we see
a smiling angel named Raemi.

Esther Coffield

I See

I see in me
an approaching storm.
I see in me
a shape waiting to take form.
I see in me
what no one sees.
I see in me
the tumultuous sea.
I see in me
a soon-to-end night.
I see in me
a soon to be seen light.
I see in me
a wanting to be free.

Abbie Hartung

Emancipation Day

Not one more
drop of dew
drips down from
pathetically pondering pupils
past the crescent
moon's sad scriptures.
The somber past
forgotten;

the future quietly
approaches with laggard
spontaneity, hidden within
the full moon's
serene shadow
The New Year rejoices,
The New Love—
Last Lesson Learned,
Eternally!

Robert Mannion

By The Bed

Standing, no sitting,
I recall my eyes
(being level with her chest)
by the bed.
This is what I did.
The minister, the nurse,
the aide that washed her hair;
Though I could do none of these things,
I had the most important job of all—
sitting by the bed.

Trulinda Johnson

Do We Think To Pray?

When morning comes to face a new day,
Do we always think to stop and pray?

To thank our Lord for a safe night through,
And then, for the many things he will do.

For his many blessings, his care and love,
And all the bright light that shines from above.

When we need his help, he is always there.
All we need is to contact him through prayer.

Janis B. Drinnon

O Foolish Heart

O foolish heart why don't you see
The love you choose can never be
I do not live inside his heart
Like he in mine when we're apart

O foolish heart you deceive my soul
You choose the one I cannot hold
I'll never feel his lips on mine
That's sure to taste as sweet as wine

O foolish heart help me please
Don't play the fool and please don't tease
You made me love this special man
So take this pain if you can

O foolish heart I locked your door
I did not want to love no more
You found the key and opened wide
Now I love someone that I must hide

Shirley Reichard Morris

Sand Crabs

Blanketing the wet ocean sand.
Hurrying for cover, as water recedes.
Stalkers retreating quickly to deeper depth.
Fishing the surf, as the tide comes in.
Observing corbina, sand crabs and sea birds;
Before the sun comes up to warm a back.
Bare footed surf fisherman,
Hears a corbina's tail wacking the water.
Dawn breaks onto the breaking surf.
Corbina not taking a crab on a hook.

Donald Lawrence

Honor Guard

Old woman made her daily appearance,
at the road crossing.

Dressed warmly for the season her,
attire was old-fashioned.

Crossing the street much to slowly,
motorists beeped to hurry her on.

Many feared for her safety, but
pride insisted she walk alone.

Discreet boy meeting her at the
crossing, devised a way of helping.

Explaining his fear of crossing the road.
May I walk along?

Together, hand in hand they walked,
one young and one old.

Boy glancing back at his friend,
extending the school patrol flag.

Pat Bordner

America You Owe Me!

Called Native Americans, just one of our names;
We hunted, fished, trapped the valley and plains.
From ocean to ocean and where the buffalo roam;
This land was ours; our spirit, our home.
100 years later and our once proud nations,
Are still living on your reservations.

From China we were brought to build your railroads.
Degraded, demeaned we struggled and toiled
As many horrors and deaths we behold.
Your railroads built, our labor you no longer need;
You pushed us away from your society.

By the shipload we were brought, overcoming
sickness and waves;
To become your possessions, chattel, slaves.
A war was fought and our freedom was gained;
But equality and opportunity are still dreams that remain.
The Constitution reads, "That all men are created equal."
Must we wait for: America—the Sequel?
America—you owe me; we.

Ronald C. Brown

Weeds

May a flower live . . . thrive
Lacking sun which makes it strive
Toward life, liberty . . . love
Fallen, wingless, weeping dove.

Or the vampire in the night
Claims to live, fears the light . . .
Which gives him pain, makes him insane
While the flower cries in vain.

Sure, the flower craves the light
Yet, vampires can't stand its sight
Living ever in the night . . .
With no fear, yet feeling fright.

Flowers need the light of love
It's a present that God gives
To those who need . . . to live, to breed
Lacking gifts . . . transformed to weeds!

Robyn Murray

Lost And Found

'Tis the morning's latter hour.
A canopy of mist hovers like death,
and grieveth I with Autumn's flower
at the lingering sickness in every breath.

Silent statues thin and high
heavy laden with frozen lace.
Always reaching toward the sky;
I being lost and without a trace.

In desperation I cried for help.
Being at last too tired and worn.
On the moss I finally knelt
asking Him to heal the torn.

At last the rays have pierced the shroud.
Winds have blown and melt the mist.
Trees and flowers of every crowd
burst and bloom with Spring's first kiss

This day forth, a new life I will live.
To those in darkness truth will find,
and spread the news my life I give.
In a word of darkness, I will shine.

Gregory S. Bacon

A Little Help

I can hear you calling, calling out my name.
I can hear the whispers in your voice.
I can feel your presence, see your red fiery eyes,
Your blood stained ivory horns,
Your claws of steel,
Coming to rip through my soul.
You always seem to find me, no matter where I go.
I scream, as loud as I can,
but no one's there to hear
With a tear stained face,
I call out your name
But . . . can you hear me?
Can you feel my pain?
Take my hand,
Lead me to your heart.
cleanse me of my fears,
Take away my tears.
By the way,
Welcome to my world,
My world, soon to be your own.

Kara Kaechle

Gift Of Life

A new life is about to begin,
It's a feeling that is hard to understand,
All that is happening within.

Sometimes we take this Gift just another day,
This Gift is a moment to remember, I would say.

Life has started, for that road ahead,
where it ends, No one knows,
A road that can not be erased it has been said.

Sometimes life may be take away,
It gives one's feeling that the love of life

In closing, I would like to say
Thanks is given for this wonderful day.
"Gift Of Life"

Robert J. Ramp

I No Longer Drive The Street Where You Live

How nice were the days when friendship was there
We visited each other and our mem'ries did share,
And when we'd meet at the Odd Fellow Temple hall
Oh! how grand it was we sure had a ball!

You drove many miles, e'en when day was done
I did the same and it was such great fun,
We had so much each other to give
And I love driving that street where you live!

Then something happened A Lie Was Told
Deceitfully, judgementally you were so bold,
And it seemed as tho' a bubble had burst
Leaving behind hurtful hunger and thirst!

And now there's emptiness at the Old Hall
Our phones are still, we no longer call,
You're not there for me nor I for you
Friendship's in ashes 'neath the foggy dew!

And if, by chance we meet, our words are flow'ry
You say: "Come see us "; I say: "I'm sorry"
"I've lost your address, the one you did give
And I no longer drive the street where you live."

Elma M. Rasor

The Eagle

I remember when you came home from school;
You were in the second grade.
You shook your head with long brown braids
    hanging in loops over your shoulders.
"Today the teacher asked us all to be animals,"
    you proclaimed.
"Oh, and what animal were you?" We asked.
"An eagle, of course" was your reply,
    as if to say how could we not know.
Years later I saw you lying in a hospital bed.
You had taken pills and drowned them with a bottle of wine.
You could hardly talk due to the soreness left by the tubes
    that had recently been taken from your throat.
Your stomach had been pumped and you were a pasty white
    and you looked scared and harassed.
As I watched you with tears in my eyes
    and worry in my heart, I wondered
      "What happened to the eagle?"

Carolyn Elaine Cliver

Wild Goose Symphony

Shimmering waters, shadows call;
Cattails, shedding sentinels of the fall.
Islands inhabited, goslings tall;
Canadian geese, proud parents all.

Beckoning me to stop and shoot
Beautiful scenes before they scoot.
Parents, babies, like small troops;
All lined up, loop-de-loop.

Golden heads bobbing in unison
Like a conductors wand might spawn.
A symphony, a family growin';
Floating peacefully, dusk till dawn.

Patricia L. Purrett

What, Do You Know, Grandma

"How many grains of sand, Grandma?"
"Only God knows, my child,"
"How many stars in the universe, Grandma?"
"Only God knows, my child,"
"How many snow flakes fall, Grandma,?"
"Surely, only God knows, my child,"
"How many blades of grass, Grandma?"
"That too only God knows, my child,"
"How many flowers bloom, Grandma?"
"Only God knows for sure my child,"
"What, do you know, Grandma?"
"I know that I love you more than,
All the grains of sand, all the stars,
And all the snow flakes, and blades,
Of grass or flowers in the whole,
World, my child."

Mattie M. Stewart

A Man of the West

Mr. Grayson you owe your heart to me,
Just like these Western and summer skies to thee.
Mr. Grayson you own this Western town.
You own this Western town every time the earth turns around.
Mr. Grayson you own the West,
Where the sky is blue and the air is blest.
Mr. Grayson you owe me my pay,
Because I rustle cattle every day.
The West belongs to you, Mr. Grayson,
Where there are white clouds in the sky
And there is never any reason to cry.
Mr. Grayson you own the West,
Where horses run wild and life is like a restless child.

John Albert Britt

Love

One kiss
Two hearts
Three words, I love you
One night and love forever
Our love was tested, and we learn a lot
Life is like a roller coaster,
with all its ups and downs
Without God we couldn't shear
all the tears we had to bear
Through hard times and good times we stood together
In sometimes apart
If we could turn back the clock
and start all over again
But we know we can't, so we'll
go one, the two of us, learning to
forgive ourselves, then we can each other
Through the losses, and gains, from our first
child to our last
We past the test, our love was so strong
And our life went on

>   *Betty Lou Gignilliat*

Willow Tree

One spring or summer day in May, I know not which,
Unconsciously, I drove along the way, without a hitch.
May is me or I am she, I know not which.
From here to there or there to here I go, without a glitch.
Cry for eye or cry for thy, I know not which.
Perhaps I seek to dry the tear that overflows the ditch.
With tainted soul or chauffeured heart, I know not which.
Acquainted with the spot you pick, I stop to get a lift.
The bed of sick or lovers bench, I know not which.
I lay and face the aculeus that bows below your pitch.
Willow tree or box to be, I know not which.
Together here, the pain you share, that weeps within your switch.

>   *Joseph A. Suders*

The Ghost of Desire

Thought the night, and into the fire,
We become together, with burning desire,
Our hearts as two, we share as one,
With nothing to lose, and nowhere to run,
I'll take care of you, and hold no reins,
Together forever, we'll share the sorrows and pains,
The good times we've had, and the memories will last,
What would have been, will be in the past,
Everything about you, is perfect and right,
Your eyes and your smile, on a cool Alaskan night,
Soon we'll be gone, from this God awful place,
But I'll always remember, your beautiful face . . .

>   *Brent Daley*

My Mom

You give me hope and love
You're there to tell me I'm someone
In this world above
When the hard times come along
You're there to keep me strong
And when I'm sad and feel like I
want to die
You're there to comfort me and tell me
why I'm alive
What I'm trying to say is
for the first fourteen years of my life
You've given me comfort, hope, and love
So to me you're a beautiful white turtle dove
Also you say you're not perfect
But then again no one is
So to me you are a perfect angel
And a white turtle dove
And the number one mom that
everyone should love

>   *Elisia Perez*

Lonely

I couldn't trust my friends,
So I had to make up my own.
When I met her,
She looked so life-like,
So real.
She was always there to listen,
And never pushed me away,
Unlike my friends,
We could talk for hours on end,
Never getting bored,
Or having nothing to say.

One day I reached out to touch her,
And my fingers hit glass; My mirror.
That's when I knew I didn't have any friends,
But only had myself.

>   *Carla Griebel*

Thunder At Night

Thunder at night sends shivers across the town.
Sleepers stir and feel the tremor in their bones.
Dogs wake, investigating the rumble.
Lighting jags from earth and sky
And meets in the middle.
Rain thunders on a steep roof,
Blotting out all other sounds.
Silence announces the end of the rain
And sleepers descend into deeper dreaming.

>   *Louise Norman*

Changes that Remain the Same . . .

Images of good times past
Bring close to each dismal day.
Memories of both pleasure and pain
Swim in an ocean of thought.
Yes, I remember all that was said,
And done in the short time we saw.
Not being totally honest doesn't mean
That all I said were lies.
I opened my heart to the heavy close door of yours.
Excepting the fact that we could
Never be is only the first step.
I was prepared to wait, or do what
Ever it took for you to love me.
If it wasn't for the fact that you told me
That I deserve better.
My love will be yours for eternity.

>   *Liberty Star Gonzales*

To Love You

To love you is all that I want in this world,
To hold you in my arms, and take away your fears,
If I could not do this I would surely die,
Because to look into your eyes is what keeps me alive,
To hear your angelic voice call my name is heaven,
If I could not do this I would surely die,
No matter where I go or who I am with I think of you,
When I sleep at night I picture you are lying next to me,
If I could not do this I would surely die,
Your love is all that I hunger for in this cruel world,
It carries me through the long, long days and nights,
To see you, to hold you, to taste you, to love you
If I could not do this, I would surely die.

>   *Eric J. Sye*

Chains

How silent the darkness that falls on my ears
Invisible whispers and hushes I hear
Spirits floating past
Moaning and sighing
Locked in their chains
Their unbreakable chains
Trapped in a dimension
Beyond earth beyond time
Endlessly searching for peace
Floating and searching
Haunting at times
Trapped in a hell far beyond ones belief
The path that they chose the path to destruction
Now they're locked in the chains that they made
The darkness keeps falling
The hushes much louder
As I look all around me in horror I see
Chains floating past me
Chains that I made

Deborah D'Elia

The Sands of Time

There is a friendship we share
almost like a kinship.

Today with in my memories I walked
along the sands of time.

Where I walked so many times as a
child, along the beach and climbed
high into the rocks to sit and watch
the ocean waves as they crashed
against the cliffs.

Letting my mind wander over the happiness
spent in friendship the night before.

When we too had walked hand in hand along,
The sands of time.

Vicki Coulombe

Divine One

God is not a Democrat, neither Republican
He is omnipotence above all man
He is so high, you'll never climb above
So deep is the fathom of his love
His arms out stretch where you feel warm
God can amuse you with his charm
God's a spirit you can't ever understand
Took dust of the earth and fashioned man
They called it the Holy Land
But there's always war with man
Where Jesus, one walked about
Multitudes follow him, and shout
In the wilderness where they were taught
Famished from hunger when food was naught
The multitude was well fed
With two little fish and five loaves of bread
Let us return back to the one true Lord
Multitudes flock, for the lame it was hard
He spoke to the inner soul of each
A divine spirit, how he could teach.

Helen Reed

The Ladder of Faith

The ladder of Faith we must climb to God,
For we are all human, made form the sod.
The way to God is by Faith in His Son,
Who died for man's sin to save ev'ryone.

We should grow in Virtue, when Christ has saved our soul.
Follow in His footsteps and he will make you whole.
Study to gain more knowledge through God's Holy Word.
It has the greatest stories, man has ever heard.

Learn to gain more Patience too, as in Christ you grow.
Strive to grow in Godliness, as through life you go.
Show Brotherly Kindness, and pray to God each day.
Read your Bible daily, and learn His Will and Way.

Love is the greatest gift on earth.
It is so priceless in its worth.
God showed us His Love when He gave us His Son.
Christ's death on the Cross, can save ev'ryone.

Bertha Gregg Cain

Silver Raindrops

Silver raindrops doth fall outside,
But they are not of gentle softness.
The pain of their falling makes me blind,
Like silver bullets from the sky.

The raindrops fall and sting my flesh,
Causing deep pain in my heart.
I watch the rain fall and begin to wonder,
How my life could be such this mess.

The splashing water burns my eyes.
I can barely see through my tears.
Yet, I keep watching and feeling my thoughts,
Hoping the thoughts will soon die.

Silver raindrops doth fall outside,
And I am in the world alone.
Still I know I am safe all because,
The silver raindrops are not inside.

Emily Madson

The Fool's Role

Lately it has been three and one
always three and one—and why?
When it's so easy to see and feel
and be sensitively high—
only to be brought down and passed by.
Those that give me pleasure turn their heads and sigh;
those I truly seek to please either criticize or pry.
What is freely given in love and truth
is made mocked and betrayed.
Such is fool's role on the set that has been staged.
Robbed in giving silently
and suffering indignities when speaking out;
my friend beside me now is all that matters—
That's what my life is all about.

Richard Belsky

To Splendor

And there my soul lies.
Wrapped tightly with blue silk ribbon.
Ceased in a shadow of yesterday's time.

Calling to me when jasmine reaches my nose.
Touching me when light rays sprinkle down.
Caressing me when ancient tones flow with sound.
Deserting me when I cease the dance.

And there she lies in her gift box.
Praying for her moment of wanderlust to return.

Mara Papa

I Heard Paul And Keith When I Died

In Memory Of Earnest Richard Pinkerton
I heard Paul and Keith call my name when I died,
The stillness around my form,
Was like the stillness in the air,
The calm before the storm.

I heard people around me start to cry,
They whispered, "Why did he have to die."
At first I didn't know what they meant,
And then I knew . . . off to heaven I went.

My spirit floated in mid-air,
I'm going to miss them, I really do care.
Paul and Keith appeared before me,
They said, "Dad can't you see?"

"They're all crying for you,
Like they all cried for us too.
They're so sad that they don't know,
That we have wings and a halo.

We'll see them all again one day,
When God calls them each on their way.
Until we see them, let's go cut some wood,
God said since you're home now that we could."

Betty L. Fulmer

A Smile

I had a dream just last night,
and in this dream there was a golden light.
The light it came from up above,
and I could have sworn I saw a white dove.
A beautiful warmth of a gentle kind of love
descended upon me,
a gift from above.
The air around me was pure and sweet,
I could almost taste it what a wonderful treat.
A voice of love full of greatness and grace
made me fall to my knees and lift up my face.
My eyes they couldn't believe what they saw,
A man in white stood straight and tall.
He touched my soul,
he touched my heart,
he touched the tears on my face and smiled with delight.
His smile erased my fears and doubts,
A feeling inside I wanted to shout.
To tell the world, tell everyone here,
that Jesus loves, he's near and he cares.

Kathleen M. Dixon

The Desert Storm

The stillness of the windswept land
was broken by the blowing sand.
The camels stood with heads held high.
The drivers tried to shield their eyes.
The sudden lurch of mounds of sand
gave warning that the storm was near.
the brightness of the blazing sun
was made unwelcome by everyone.
Desert life was in a state.
Nothing living could escape.
The thoughts were racing through my head.
It gave me time my fears to shed.
The whistling roars warned all to flee.
And suddenly there was a break.
The wind died down.
The air was clear.
The caravan went on its way.
The camels kept a steady pace.
I rode along with much relief to know
that now the storm had ceased.

Helen T. Brennan

Remember

Remember, those were the days, when all you needed was a spaulding,
A stoop was your king, steps your ladder to victory.
Where have they gone, where are they now?
When you lost to the sewer, a hanger was your friend.
A wall was something that you used for flipping.
What happened?
Give me a stick, stand clear and watch the heavens open their arms,
Hit the penny was king, an egg cream, queen.
Where have they gone?
When you lost a skate, it now became your hot wheels.
A top, marble cats eyes and bottle caps were prized.
Old wood fruit bins, a glory to behold, every nail pulled,
treated as if it were gold.
A friend was your friend, for the rest of your life.
A handshake was your bond.
The leaves are falling, the air is still
Where have they gone—where are they now, only in our dreams.

Lawrence Gellerstein

25 Years

The silver lining is what we aspire to know
Therefore, we toiled in trials and tribulation
Resulting in a multitude of frustration
But paradoxically, here and forever, is how we shall grow

Through this journey for which we together doth sow
Experiencing experiences that developed a maturation
Leading to a transcendental encapsulation
For this wondrous intertwined love we bestow

Conceptional innocence is but where it begin
With God's blessing we were united to be one
And set our path to seek our worth

Through it all is joy in love and pain in sin
But staying true we knew it could be done
For the silver shine doth line our matrimonial berth

Thomas L. Scott

The Charge of Lake Placid

The most memorable of all events
In America's Olympic past,
Took place during a hockey game in New York
At the charge of Lake Placid.

During the winter games of 1980,
The United States team held its ground
Against the veteran players from Russia,
Considered to be the best around.

But those young men did the impossible,
And the whole world was there to see
How they defeated the Soviet Union,
With a score of four to three.

In the final game they faced Finland,
And brought the gold medal home that day.
Americans everywhere celebrated their triumph
With victorious shouts of "USA."

The took their place in history.
With a mark that will forever lost.
Remember and honor those heroic young men
And their charge at Lake Placid.

Jeff Ayers

Journey

One who tours an unseen beautiful place
composed variety of life long reminiscence
remembering of all the scenic explored
which money never could buy.

Its beautiful views bear like
dream deep in its utmost memory
although such concerned been here
dwelling long ago at its birthplace.

Now as he further seriously perceives
the course of his journey which begins
to reminisce heartfelt senses which

she never saw.

Has actually believed that seemed
newly born into this wonderful
world and now said to himself money is
nothing because eventually it pays beyond.

Truly the tourist took a seat, relax
and says my trip has brought me like
daydream because if I didn't make
an effort I wouldn't feel as newly born.

Irenio Vergara

Grandmother

The sun spoke this morning
I decided not to say hello
Instead, I went back to bed
Covered my head
Enjoyed the pleasure of being dead
Thunder clouds came
It began to rain
The wind started to blow, small ships to and fro
Trees are falling, my walls are hauling
Glass across the floor, the clouds depart
I looked with a start
To see all I could see

Behind the cloud I saw the dove
Who stayed behind the golden tree
But out flew the wise white owl
Who stared directly at me
She soared the earth, an angel in flight
So that I may learn, day from night
The sun came out today
I've decided I welcome it to stay

Larcenia Yhonquea

Tears In Her Heart

My day began like always,
With coffee and a prayer,
And then I dialed her number,
To see if she was there.

I told her I might be leaving,
It was time for me to part,
And soon I heard her crying,
There were tears in her heart.

It really caught me by surprise,
I didn't know she cared,
But I soon found out different,
As she began to share.

I knew you wouldn't wait for me,
Her plea was just the start,
All the while her voice was cracking,
With those tears in her heart.

I finally said those three little words,
From my lips they did impart,
And I waited until the smile replaced,
Those tears in her heart.

Jim Campbell

A Mother's Love Song

James and Jonathan

You are my Cherokee sons
of the fathers before you

You are warriors of this Earth
and the sky of blue

You will defend your country
as you have been shown

You will go
where eagles have flown

You will follow your dreams
and be all you can be

You will shine in your brother's eyes
for all of Heaven to see

You are the wind beneath my wings
the spirit of a dove

You are my sons
that I will always love

You are here with me, your brother is in Heaven
his spirit is alive in our hearts

You are my Cherokee sons

Rhonda Branson

Mary Frances

When my kids were hid, my life was crushed,
My heart was tore in two.
A princess shared her time with me,
For she knew just what to do.
Despite how crushed or tore in two,
She showed her love could heal.
She bridged the gap in my broken heart,
To help my love to feel.
She's my prayer, love, line to life,
My hope without the chances.
My brown-eyed blonde, angel from God,
My special Mary Frances.
It was years ago, when my kids were stole,
I wished my life would end.
In that plight, God showed one light,
My niece is now my friend.
We did some Y.M.C.A., camped other days,
And were in Parada Del Sol.
My sorrow turned fun, with all we had done,
For she's worth her weight in gold.

Jim Stewart Jr.

Love On The Cross

True love was given most boldly and clear
On an old rugged cross by our Saviour so dear.
When His blood stained the cross of Calvary that day,
His life was given freely to wash our sins away.
He did not have to suffer, to bleed and die.
Lovingly, He bore the cross to save you and I.

God looked beyond the ages and saw our need.
He knew what must be done His plan to complete.
Christ could have called the angels to set Him free,
Yet He died upon that cross at Mount Calvary.
He did not have to suffer, to bleed and die.
Lovingly, He bore the cross to save you and I.

When Jesus died on that old rugged tree,
He was saying I love you throughout eternity.
When he comes for us someday to go to Heaven-Land,
We will see the print of nails He has in His hands.
He did not have to suffer, to bleed and die.
Lovingly, He bore the cross to save you and I.

Elizabeth B. Arney

Backyard

You stand there with your aloof pride
Never moving, never smiling, with nothing to hide
But who are you really, dressed to boot,
Does the little boy exist as he did before recruit
With hone you defend this country so free
This code of liberty trapped between seas
What do you defend, hell we don't know
Here anything is, and anything goes.
You risk your life with no regard to sacrifice
An oath you vowed by the roll of the dice
Do you love the men you seek to protect
Or is their existence just your job with respect
We lie, we murder, we steal, we cheat
An honest man, I'll never meet
But still you stand in defiance of all harm
As we slowly lure in temptations charm
So as you stand watch through the night
Keep repeating to yourself the reasons to fight
And I ask of you, my aloof and brave guard
When you get the chance, look in your own backyard

Kristina Schoch

A Shadow's World

You've followed every step wherever the darkness led.
Through mysterious passageways,
but soon your journey will end.
When you find what you have longed to.
Your faith in life.
Your love of yourself and your one true feeling of happiness.
The one true treasure that keeps your soul alive.
The one true thing that makes you feel secure.
You walk alone through tunnels.
Until you reach your key to happiness.
That can be reached only through your heart.

Dena Pulsifer

The Legend of the Dogwood

Centuries ago, when the world began,
The dogwood was sturdy and strong
As any other tree.
But when the dogwood tree was cut
To make the cross where Jesus died,
The dogwood tree began to shrink and never again
Would be sturdy and strong.
The four petals of the flower,
like the cross, had two petals
two long, two short
And the drops of pink on the heart of the flower
Tell of the agony Jesus felt
When wearing the Crown of seed pods as He walked
On His way to the place of crucifixion.

Alice Whiteside Jorg

Flame

Greys lace around my moves,
All day dance with every step I take.
Clouds lightening, sauntering heavenly.
Only when I think of you.

Cracked vanity blames me effortlessly,
Hiding behind empty gossip,
Slithering under the follicles below my nape.
Safety drums,
Coming ringing through my dome.
You love, shaking infinite bounce to my heartbeat.

Should it ever crystallize,
Sea breeze whispers soured blue,
Rivers rain and waver east.
My spirit, find it soaked and drunken
For it's already so
You are here.
Soul candle.

C. D. Loveless

Untitled

As I look around me,
I hear the children of today,
Being very disrespectful,
Don't listen to anything you say.
They think they're smart and know it all,
You're called stupid, dumb or worse.
And if you try to correct them,
All they know how to do is curse,
But if they want a favor,
Or need money to go out.
They sure know how to sweet talk
You're the greatest without a doubt.
I feel sorry for these children,
They'll find out when it's too late
How much time they wasted in their life,
Being greedy and full of hate.
A day will come and they need help
But help cannot be found,
'Cause that dumb and stupid person,
Is buried six feet under ground.

Evelyn M. Ferrari

Days Gone By

When I was just a little child
With so many questions on my mind,
I would look at my momma and say,
Mama what was your life like, when you were my size.
Mama would look at me and smile,
Much like your my question child.
Then in her mind she would look back there
And till me of her mama and papa,
How they lived and how they died.
Mama was only twelve when her mama was taken by God,
How I wondered, how I prayed
Please God, don't take my mama so soon away.
For I will never know the answer to all my questions
Without her around to say, much like you my child
Now I have my own question child,
Who look to me for answer only Nanny can provide
So nanny till me a story of days gone by,
Of what your life was like
When you were my size.

M. Ward

Desperation

Writers write and dreamers dream,
But not everything is always as it may seem . . .
The world turns upside down.
   A clown's smile becomes a frown.
Another murderer gets a reprieve.
   Children die. Mothers grieve.
Newborns enter innocently into this world.
   Another precious life is desperately hurled,
From the rooftop of a church or the highest point of a steeple.
   What becomes of the lives of so many will we find?
When those final days come, what will we find?
Who will make the judgment? Your God, or mine?

Joshua Gutterman

Heartache

Stabbed in the heart with a glass slipper
I choked on the midnight pumpkin
and got stampeded by the magic mice.
My fairy godmother was a wicked witch.
No gown could cover my nakedness;
I bore the scars of an overworked love slave.
This heart of cinder brushed behind locked doors.
My two evil step-sisters: lust and passion
raped me of the love I longed to give.
Merrily, merrily, life is but a dream.

Crystal Morawitz

My Best Friend

Best friends are so rare and too often difficult to find,
but I have been blessed with a best friend I call mine.
He waits eve so patient to lend me His ear,
He listens intensely to both my joys and my fears.

Although I spend every moment with my best friend each day,
He's still eager to listen to ear what I have to say.
One would think He'd get tired of hearing me speak,
but He's always eager to listen, my best friend is unique.

I tell Him my problems and seek out His voice,
but He remains oh so silent for He knows it's my choice.
He communicates to me without speaking a word,
and I know that He's listened, and I've always been heard.

I know I've been blessed with a best friend that so true,
and the good news is yours, for He can be your best friend too.
You see my best friend is our God who gave His only son,
to guide and direct us as our life has begun.

He never grows tired or weary from hearing from you,
in fact, He awaits patiently as He observes what you do.
Please share my best friend and partake of His love,
for He lives in your heart and He's just waiting above.

Edna M. Powell

Walk Your Talk

You say you're proud of the life you're living—
A model to live by, to others you're giving.
What you say, sounds quite good.
But what matters is that you would—
Walk your talk

There are those who for sake of self-esteem,
Need another's help when pursuing their dream.
Someone to lead them, and do their best,
To stand by them til' dreams manifest.
Walk your talk

It's easy to tell folk what they want to hear—
The nice things you've done for others far and near.
What you say, whether true or false,
We both know that it will be your loss,
If you fail to live by what you say,
By not helping someone along life's way.
Walk your talk

Dorothy Woods White

On This Thanksgiving Day

On this Thanksgiving Day we have much to rejoice,
Giving cheers, sharing gifts, the laughter in our voice.
Greeted by family, by neighbors, and good friends,
We'll feast on this day, and enjoy to the end.

A banquet so exquisite set on the table before us,
Will offer an array of entrees so warm and delicious.
A turkey so grand, juiced in rich honey glaze,
These dishes look so succulent, it makes my eyes haze.

We'll sit around a table with hands in gentle hold,
To give thanks on this day for the blessings to unfold.
As we bow our heads together to softly say grace,
Lord, give us peace in our hearts always to embrace.

A toast of thanks is raised for all preparations done,
Pour the wine, pass the food, our feast has now begun.
A moment of excitement to enjoy this holiday jubilee,
Surrounded by loved ones it's a warm sight to see.

As the last pie is eaten and evening comes to a close,
There is so much contentment, as our bellies will show.
To spend time in sharing a feast from the start,
On this Thanksgiving Day with love from the heart.

Sylvana Gabrielle

Free

My heart is black, My soul is dark
Which is all I lack, so I'll make my mark.
The days are never-ending, feeling never more.
I feel like I'm being confinding,
Always feeling, falling to the floor.
My head is not with me, my body is uncontrolling.
Needing the feeling of being free.
My body, My soul, My heart never paralleling.
Darkness is where I sleep, always needing to be.
My heart, my soul they keep, never wanting to be free.
Darkness keeps me flying, keeps me feeling high.
Immortality is what I'm buying, never, ever will I die.
Sadness sinks deep within me,
Should I leave, or do I need to be.
Should I believe.
Darkness holds my hand, it lives within me.
Look how high I stand, it is good to be free.

Signed, Vampyr

Raymond Kessinger III

Spring

The first warm spring air, traveling ever so lightly-
Tapping at the earth, murmuring, "Oh, you're unsightly."
The earth awakened, off it flew
Searching out heaven for a rain cloud or two.
Whispering to the clouds, they understood
By sending down their rains as they promised they would.
Washing the earth clean of all winter grime
This is the beginning of a wonderful time!
Sleepily, new life stirs underground
Take time to listen—a wonderful sound.
Something peeks out and then another
And soon everything is from undercover.

Evelyn Cooper Bruce

Nuggets

Morning's we rise, take up our placer-buckets,
Wade into life's main-stream, and start our dredging.
Mostly we bring up sand, mundane and common:
Yet now and then, a trace of something finer.
A gleam of gold, to tantalize the senses,
To whet the appetite, and keep us working.
But once or twice in a lifetime, if you're lucky
(Or maybe truly blessed), you find a Nugget.

A moment of Joy, or Love, or Truth so precious,
So rich and fine, it seems it must have broken
Off of the very golden streets of Heaven,
And sailed the galaxies, to light our world.

Viola Gamm

Just Wishing

If all of my wishes could come true,
I'd wish for you only skies of blue.
I'd wish you never no clouds of gray,
And your happiness always here to stay!
I'd wish for you always the very best of health,
And our whole clan an abundance of wealth!
I'd wish we could fly to the moon and stars,
With a stop-off at Jupiter, Saturn and Mars!
I'd wish like all the beautiful birds in flight,
We could stop and rest on "Cloud 9" every night!
I'd wish too, that you and your heart of pure gold,
Will forever be mind to have and to hold.
And last of all, but certainly not least,
I'd wish for the whole world to just be at peace.
So Sweetheart, even though my wishes may not come to be,
I'd still wish our love to last, from now 'til eternity!

Lois Wyant

How Many?

How many must die at a tyrant's word?
What price? What loss can we afford?

How often shall we turn our heads?
Until millions more are dead?

If we stand mute when our neighbor is taken?
Will he turn his head when we are shaken?

If we look away when babes are curetted,
The slayer's appetite for blood is only whetted.

"Blood, more blood" is their hue and cry.
During ethnic cleansing will you die?

Nero, Hitler, Stalin, Mussolini, the list is growing.
Let men of courage their strength be showing.

Declare that right now a new day is here!
Let murder cease here on this sphere!

Let love abound and laughter return,
let no man his neighbor spurn.

Look under the color and through each creed.
Let's not be selfish, but do good deeds.

Let us see all men as brothers.
Come let us love one another.
Margie Kirkpatrick

Mission 51 L: Lives:

On a icy morning with a clear blue sky,
Americans left the earth for answer to, why?

Search the Heavens, seek fact and reasons,
Our unquenchable thirst knows not limit or season.

Onboard our chosen seven and best.
Represent well; All questions this quest;

Launched from the pad on fiery tail of torrent
Was a man of color, and one from the Orient.

Three other heroic men, two tiny ladies so darling;
Met this awesome fate, so dark, as a starling;

Crystalline icicles below and above a sky of azure;
Planning, training this mission, memorized so pure.

An explosion so fierce of awe, to take your breath.
God gave them this sign, there is dignity in death.

And as smoke and debris to sea below fallin'
Remind us, we're to go home, at his callin'.
Daniel M. Crawford

Gentle Healing

He stands and gazes at the empty chair;
How many months have gone by?
Her eyes so intense and her hair so fair
Are gone. He grieves and he wonders why.

The years were filled with memories sweet
Candlelight dinners—an occasional fight!
Sunny mornings, a smiling face to greet
Are gone, and sadness dominates the night.

Bright colors flash as he turns his head;
A blue jay shows off his beautiful crest.
The bulbs she planted are bright yellow and red;
Two colorful cardinals are building a nest.

New life unfurls and promises him hope,
With resolve he attempts to go on.
He still wonders why, but now he will cope.
He looks ahead—and loneliness is gone.

Margaret A. Koepplinger

Making Excuses

Oh, it's a shame not to wanna serve God
I murmur, fuss and complain against the terrible odds.

I look back at my life, what a tragic mess I've made;
Wanting to do all the terrible things,
and then say—"I'm saved!"

I lied and cheated a little bit
and said, "Oh, what a mess."
My heartstrings pulling me apart,
saying, "I must confess."

Only one person I can really tell all,
He's the fairest of them all.
Not to judge my mess, and giving me another chance
to serve Him my best.

I've only been forgiven and it's remembered no more
It's a pleasure serving God in this messed up world today;
Only He and He alone can give me forgiveness
and help me on my way.

I don't know why I woke up
and wrote this poem this way,
But God dropped it in my spirit and you have a blessed day!
Louise Majette 11/94

I Met The Perfect Man

I met the perfect man,
    He is sweet, charming and oh so handsome;
I met the perfect man,
    He is smart fun and very understanding.

I met the perfect man,
    He loves me more than anyone else;
I met the perfect man,
    He taught me to love myself.

I met the perfect man,
    His appearance brightens a room;
I met the perfect man,
    And you could meet "Christ" too.
Elsa Bennett Reid

The Old Bellman

Our mother had a repertoire of readings,
as she used to call her poems
And she would entertain us, as she went about her chores.

We all sat and listened, as the old bellman rang his bell,
Ringing out the blow for liberty, the story was something to tell.

Ring! Grandpa! Ring!
As she beat the bread dough to a pulp,
Ring! Grandpa! Ring!
We sat as if sculpted.

Our mouths would drop open, as she whacked each packet of dough,
And we had visions of no supper,
As the dough lost its bounce and glow.

But lo and behold that evening,
As we sat at the table for nine,
Those beautiful brown loaves had risen
Crackling, crusty, glowing, how divine!

All these years it's been kept a secret,
No one dared breath a word,
How these little dough nuggets took a beating,
To give solace, prevent discord.
Roberta G. Bird

After Life

One cannot help but wonder
About our fate once we're put under.
Is there another life ahead for us
Or, are we merely a memory of ashes and dust?

Our teachings tell us of a God above
Who will lead us to a heaven through his love,
And of an evil Satan who dwells below
In a fire and brimstone hell where sinners go.

How much love is one to give
So that after death he might live
In an eternal kingdom of blissful serenity
With God and his angels for all eternity?

A small price so many are unwilling to pay
So that they may be sanctified on their judgement day.
Instead, their souls they choose to sell
And in return, spend forever in burning hell.

Thus, the afterlife we are to believe in
Is achieved by how we love or sin.
This seems an easy choice for one to make—
But, how much of either does it take???

Dick Blanchard

The Flim-Flam Man

Bill Hookem played the humbug game.
He earned his fortune and his fame
By indicating paths of glory
To greedy chumps with his glib story.

Long before they would awaken
To the fact they had been taken
And realize that they'd been cheated
They'd find their purses were depleted.

Bill played his tricks among the hicks
In small communes out in the sticks
Where he stood small chance of being sought
And even less of being caught.

There came a day, you might surmise,
When Bill was taken by surprise
A farmer's daughter used her wile
To take old Bill for his whole pile.

Greener pastures was Bill's desire.
For safer climes he did aspire.
Broke, chagrined and down on his luck
He caught a ride on a turkey truck.

Robert Kelly

The Championship Cup

To Coach Ted Ehous

As the coach tips his hat to Old Glory
from the batters home.
He sees his fielders began to roam.
His eyes move from third to first
and thinks, "This is the greatest game on earth."
The coach's heart begins to pump
as he watches his battery warm up.
He hears "Play ball" from the ump
and the coach yearns for the championship cup.
Before the first pitch, he realizes his joy
Was to have coached this team of boys.
He prays, "I'll thank you God for who I am
If I have helped but one of these become a man.
This will be my championship Cup!"

Ruth Braley

Sonnet

Let me also count the ways in which I love.
The thousand ways in which you will remain
A part of me when you have gone again
Back to the world that holds no place for me.
I love thee for the nights and for the days,
Those precious few in which we both became
A unit—oneness—both of us the same.
So short together—so long to be away.
I love thee for the depths and for the heights,
I love thee for the sureness and the fears,
I love thee for the darkness and the lights,
I love thee for the laughter and the tears,
When days first seemed so many then so few.
But most of all, I love thee just for you.

Joan Finnstrand

Daydreaming in English 142

People: fickle, fad, and fatuous,
poetic and prose, our verbosity drones on and . . .
On a day like this, when the cold seeps in under my skin
Sends chills down my spine and memories through my mind—
"When will Summer come . . . and where did Summer go?"
I don't know. I just wait

Believer of fate,
You have your way with me
Destiny. But what am I destined for?

People—listening to the rattle
of a flag pole
and the dust settles
on wooden floors
(Dreaming in my present while the future takes place)

Natalie Lockwood

Morning Glories

We planted morning glories in the sun
And wondered which way the vines would run.
We smiled into each other's eyes,
Forgetting a morning glory dies.

They grew just like our love, or so it seemed;
Yet nothing is quite the way we dreamed.
For one by one the blossoms dried
And our love and morning glories died.

Now I plant my garden in the sun,
Recalling how far that I have come.
I start to think I've done all right
Until a morning glory comes in sight.

Then I'll remember the blossoms reaching for the sky,
And I'll remember how hard we really seemed to try.
For those morning glories will always be
A reminder of love that used to be.

Morning glories, morning glories,
How sweet the blossoms grow.
I remember morning glories
I'm no good at letting go

Mercy Graf

Daydream

The sky is radiant and translucent on this precious day
Mounds of clouds beneath my feet
   Cherubs and angels dancing to and fro
So happy to see what I see
   I see beautiful crystal cities ascending profoundly into
the heavens
   Thank God for my slumber; I am awake and not asleep
Patiently, I roam; mind and soul suspended in awe, and my
   Creator I'll soon meet.
My God said, "Come my humble child, welcome, have a seat."
   We must have talked for at least a thousand years, for
tremendous relief had fled my soul and I had surely made it to paradise.

Janee M. Banks

Warrior Wife

The art is timeless and beautiful.
His movements are to and fro.
Weaving with lethal intent,
the inner-light makes his eyes glow.
Hours of practice and torment
the pain only to me he'll show.
Years have passed, still he has the fire.
His second home is his beloved Dojo.
The inner-strength he now commands
is obvious to anyone with strife.
I am always safe with him
I trust him to protect my life.
He is my warrior.
And I
am his wife.

Lori Beth Hudson

A Moment In Time

Should I remember your smile love
And the way your brown eyes look
Will I remember your voice love
From a long ago summer's day
I shall my love
I've had many memories to fill a sunless day
For I've understood my destiny and now my fate awaits
Captured now forever
In the darkness of the night
A small light shines bright
Keep smiling love
Your not lost I'll find you love
Just give me a moment in time
To last forever is a wondrous thing to share
The briefest moment is to share destiny with only a thought
Never to be parted love
For even a thought brings you back to me time after time
How grateful I should be love for a moment in time
Brings back to me all I had thought lost
But for a moment in time

CeCe Jones

True Love Can Last

The voyage I have embarked upon,
Over many years ago,
Through laughter, tears, and turmoil,
My love did always grow.

As morning turns to evening,
As sunrise turns to sunset,
I will always be with my loved one,
As we age gracefully, with no regret.

To my children and their children,
I will leave remnants of my past.
But most of all, dear Lord, they will know
True Love Can Really Last.

Lorraine Blake

Listen With Your Heart

Can you hear they're silent pleas
For they have sight of what no man sees

Creatures of God with a journey all their own
If they are lost we walk this earth alone

They look at us through eyes of fear
For we hold in our hands all which is dear

The pulse of the earth beats ever so slow
Will we show mercy or prove her worst foe

We must learn to respect all of God's creatures
For they may prove our most important teachers

Kerri J. Incitti Walkinshaw

Untitled

There is a peaceful reverence
as you stand in the moonlight gazing at the stars.

The noise of the city still echoes in your head.
So much chaos and confusion there.

In the stillness you find yourself at ease with the world.
Your mind becomes uncluttered, and clearness takes its place.

You contemplate your life,
and wonder about the people you once knew.

Consider the people you love most,
and the happiness they have brought you.

Then without intent a feeling of ease comes over you,
and a smile finds its way to your face.

Pamela Voelker

The Blazing, Orange Ball

The orange ball floats higher and higher in the sky.
Beneath it, the sea of mankind watches the ball go by.

As it floats, it blows its warm rays on the flowers in May.
Then, it yearns to float down to spend just one day.

But it must journey on, for earth is not its home.
Above the mellifluous land and through the sky it must roam,

Peeking at Earth's awesome stretch while it floats along,
Seeing children board the bus while it hurries on.

Hearing voices in praise vibrates its radiant rays.
And—lingering gracefully in the sky, its wavy rays wave "good-bye."

Then floating toward another day,
The gigantic, blazing ball is on its way.

B. J. Mathews

Get Well

I know you are smiling, so is He.
I know when you woke up, you said thanks
to the man that hung on the tree.

He pleaded your case as He said he would.
He knew that you have tried,
He did not have to search your heart,
He was glancing about and saw your knees,
He heard you pray for your family,
He heard you pray for others and then yourself,
just as you should.

He said your sickness is mortar for your bricks,
your new home, that too you knew, strength
you will gain, faith you have kept, soon you will be about.

Some will say a miracle, some will shake their head and marvel,
yes, deep within you knew he could do it without a doubt.

Donnell Linthecome

A Poem For . . . .

. . . . I'm, afraid to tell you what I feel inside,
Things I want to say to you may make you run and hide.
The feelings are so intense it really scares me too.
I'm telling you . . . . I just do not know what to do.

Sometimes I feel real bold . . . . . bold enough to tell you
Then insecurities take hold, and I suppress what I need to
share with you.

I know you could not know what goes on in my mind.
The words I want to say to you, are so hard for me to find.

Maybe some day I can let you know the fondness that I feel.
And maybe you won't perceive me as a foolish and utter heel.

But until I muster up the courage to face that possible rejection,
I must keep it to myself, and ponder the suggestion.

Carolyn Paulette Carter

Christmas Greeting

The world feels young Tonight
And we who live and stand in the world
face a new time
snow covers and whitens our stones
As if white were peace
As if white were mercy

Open your eyes Tonight let them see
Peace is falling in the streets
Let them find a way in the dark
Let them one by one look at the child
There is hope for a new heart.

I, say, he will be planted in our mind
We shall be happy
There is strength and energy
We shall go singing
We shall go on by the light of our dreams.

We shall sing together
O you who sick, lie down anywhere
I salute you here.

Sadina Roselin

Love

I am a virgin to love's hands
Untouched by her unforgiving thoughts.
No individual has struck me shining
Or unfolded before my life.
I'm young and know the dangers that lurk
Hoping I'm prepared for the crystal experience.
I live every day unaware and not looking
I live free of burden, but not knowing
Love is one.
I suppose I'm very confused
But not realizing it.
Till then I live unaltered.

Austin Bentz

Spring In New England

As the rays from the sun kiss our mother earth
The bare withered trees and shrubs give birth
She's completed her cycle, and once again it is spring
It's been several months since I've heard the birds sing
Where there was once bitter cold, hard ground
Green blades of grass sprouts up all around
The now leafy tree branches dance in the breeze
Outside my window on those once naked trees
The fresh scent of lilacs fills up the air
A scent so beautiful, no other could compare

Lori A. Nason

'Til Someone Listens

Rubber in the way and no one
knows the troubles that are here to stay.
It goes like this:
  Latex changes lives and careers.
  Allergy that can take on many forms.
  'Till someone listens I continue to suffer.
  Education is my only hope.
X is for x'd out if continued exposure goes on
  Always on guard each and every day.
  Learning to cope, 'til someone listens.
  Living with the fears that's brought on.
  Expecting truth to prevail.
  Rubber a word one wishes she could forget.
  Expecting truth to prevail,
  Going on 'til someone listens.
  You'll never know, 'til someone listens.

Shelby Y. Blackmon

For You

Through blazing fire,
Against wave after crashing wave.
Across an endless desert.
There is nothing I wouldn't brave.

To the bottom of the ocean where the deepest currents flow,
Or the top of the highest mountain;
There is no place I wouldn't go.

Be it any man or any beast of any size or height.
There's simply no opponent
I wouldn't try and fight.

There is no road I wouldn't travel,
No risk I wouldn't take.
No pain I cannot endure,
I'd place my life at stake.

Whatever the challenge,
There is nothing I wouldn't do.
I love you more than anything
And I would do it all for you.

Kurt Ellison

Balloons

Two balloons, dark in color
that look like wild cherry flavor
last night hung over my head;
but in the morning, they were dead.

Instead of hanging in the air,
their lifeless bodies were in my hair!
They must have died in the night,
before the morning's first new light.

Who killed them? I know not.
"Maybe the cat did," Mummy thought.
My brother Tom, only four,
asked their names and nothing more.

"So what's their names?" asked little Tom.
"Are they two kids or Dad and Mom?"
I looked down at my two dead balloons,
looking much like two perfect full moons.

As if their bodies had been filled with lead,
my two balloons had fallen dead.

Heather Hopkin

Shine On Yonder Window

Shine on yonder window, with your fields o' gold.
That you can see for a hundred miles or so I have been told.
Shine on yonder window, at the blue crystalline sea,
Where warming sun and cooling waters can set a man free.
Shine on yonder window, from the mountains, so high,
There the eagles hover, in their majestic sky.
I gaze from my window, on the street below;
All I see is suffering, that's all I'll ever know.
A man on the streets, sticks a needle in his veins.
Trying to find relief from some hidden pain.
Another pushes a shopping cart full of empty cans,
Always, talking to himself, making useless plans.
A car drives past, full of wayward youths,
Shooting at innocent victims, who were searching for some truths.
Shine on yonder window, from a town in Bethlehem.
They say a savior was there born but I don't know when.

Joseph G. McCleary

When I Was But A Little Boy

When I was but a little boy,
How often I would try—
To do the things my Dad would do,
In order to catch his eye.

When he would drive a nail in place,
I drove a nail in to.
Then I'd look at his smiling face—
For he knew what I wanted to do.

It didn't matter at all to him,
That my nail went in on a slant.
He was glad to see me try again—
And not hear me say, I can't.

As my Dad walked thru the snow,
Leaving his prints behind—
I tried to follow in his steps,
But saw they were too big for mine.

Then he turned to me, with that same kind smile—
And picked me up close to his side, saying, son—you'll just
Have to wait awhile.
To match your Daddy's stride.

James E. Yost

Sick

What's inside me makes me fear
What if others know
If access to all thoughts were public
How different would mine be from the rest
Am I demented or sick - have I an injured mind
To think such thoughts must be criminal
To express them surely must be

I am sick
They tell me I am
They tell me I'm alone
They show me what's right
They show me normality
Consistent, dependable, predictable
Cost effective, accountable, controllable
Abusable, expendable.
Fearful
Of any less than this
Of being sick
I am sick
Thank God I'm sick.

Matt Kubinski

The Ones Left Behind

Why do some seem to always find,
The ones who are never left behind?
Why not look for the ones who are lost,
Who've been tossed and bounced, bounced and tossed,
Into a world from which few return,
Yet who seek new life and anxiously yearn?
They call them the wretched, the homeless, the dirt,
And fail to give them their love, their shirt.
Are the they the ones who are really to pity,
Who live in homes in suburb and city,
Without so much as a look or a stare
For the ones who are lost, to show them they care?
When some are judged by God we may find,
That it is really they who are left behind.
"Whatever you do to the least of my brothers
You do unto me," Jesus said about others.

T. Michael Francis

The Brook

I took a stroll by the brook today,
A look, just to see what was there.
It filled all the air with clear chuckling sounds,
And birds flew around everywhere.

The brook seemed to speak, its sounds were so clear.
I sat down and soon fell asleep.
I must have napped for almost an hour.
Then awoke with a squirrel by my feet.

This place is so quiet, no sound but the brook,
With a chirp now and then from the birds,
Once in a while, with a"chip" from the squirrel.
That's absolutely all that I heard.

So I'll come back tomorrow, and the day after that,
To sit here and nap in this glade.
Without any doubt this is just what was meant
When someone said, "Made in the shade."

E. R. Case

A Change of Heart

With good looks and nothing else
Yours truly took the chance,
With arrogance and pride
Challenged road and every tide
My heart thundered and I never cried

In search of fame and glory
Enlisted in Castro's army,
Crossed friendly and hostile borders
Joined trendy cults and numerous Orders
My heart wondered and I cried

With greed and hollow thirst
Lied, cheated, killed to get there first,
With doubts and false sense
Took chance after chance
My heart fluttered and I cried in vain

Today with broken wings
And shallow spirits
With no mountains
And boring valleys
My heart cries and I flutter in the wind.

Joseph Jacobi

Alone

Trapped, with nowhere to go
Lost, in a world going by me
Just there, not knowing or feeling
Here, where? Where am I? Who is with me?
Lonely, scared, I'm sweating.
I see but they don't, I hear but they are deaf
Or maybe it's me just there in my own world
I'm banging on the door but they ignore me
Just there, where? Is it me? Is it you?
No, no, it's me only me.
I'm alone.

Consuello N. Linwood

The Witches Creed Of Faith

I am with God; Father Justice; who holds the keys
To Heaven, and the Universe.

I stand, one being, in a multitude of many. This
is my prayer, my oath; to one God of a thousand Gods.
Father, Son, Holy Spirit, a symbol of his power.

I am Immortal. I am one out of many. None other
shall be except from my womb shall come.
I know in my heart of his presence.

Therefore, I will remain humble; so the powers
bestowed upon mankind be safe; so long as Faith
has her virtue, and strength is the substance of
things wise and wonderful . . . Amen.

Melody White

The Change

Our life has nicely shaped together,
As we begin our entry into June;
Then squirrelly things begin to happen,
Could it be we're starting way too soon?

We have finally reached that point in time,
When we look distinguished wearing glasses;
But just as things are going well,
We develop nasty flashes.

They carry on from time to time,
And often well into the night;
We can't help but think they'll never end,
And will we ever see the light?

But time moves on and we adjust,
Then things seems very clear;
And the freedom which we'll now enjoy,
Shall last from year to year.

William Henry O'Donovan Jr.

Old Man

From the park bench I watched the land
And begin to talk to this old man
He tells me how things used to be
How he was treated with dignity

He tells me things are different and wild
Nothing like when he was a child
Old people used to be respected
Not robbed, mugged and totally rejected

I listen intently to what he would say
Knowing I'd be old and gray one day
What he said caused me vexation
Over how we treated our senior population

He tells me how he raised his kids
And all the great things he had did
I was really amazed at how he did it
But now they're too busy to pay a visit

He says pretty soon he's going to a home
It's pretty lonely since his wife's now gone
It makes me wonder if this what I'll reap
I can't help feeling sad as he drifts asleep

Larry M. Boyer, Jr.

Sacred

Believing in the Almighty God
Is a big step to achieve.
Through sacred prayers said,
His blessings we'll receive.

Having faith is of importance
Walking righteous is the way to go.
Learning the Bible's knowledge
Will give us the insight to know.

Establish in the counsel of God
And He will give us what we need.
Being able to harvest the Holy life,
Good things happen from the righteous seeds.

Changes for the better,
Can do wonders in our lifestyles.
It can take a sad soul
And make them smile.

Believing in the Almighty God
Is a big step to achieve.
Through sacred prayers said,
His blessings we'll receive.

Daniel Gray

Rose of Love

The rings we've exchanged, band our promise of love together.
Like the gold, our love will be precious and pure.
As the diamonds glisten and reflect light
So shall the love shared between us.
I give you now my heart in full.
I'll give as I ask, no less no more.
Our vows complete our bond for life.
We are now as one, my Husband, your Wife.

Patti "Paz" Wickham

Untitled

On the coldest of nights when the chill sets in.
Life and death is a fight, to survive is to win.
You should have no fear and look around.
Take in the sights and hear the sound.
At the moon the wolf howls not missing a beat
Soft breezes blowing through the fields of wheat.
The world can be cruel and so very cold
If you are not smart you will never grow old.
Through the cold comes warmth and darkness comes light.
To roll with the changes the heart will take flight.
As the birds fly so free and dart to and fro
The seeds in the ground will soon start to grow.
Life will begin where death once did play
With colors so bright to dispel the dismay.

William E. Schutte

Much To My Delight

Much to my delight he was the most perfect
Person I'd met that night.
Attending a dance merely by chance never
Expecting to find romance.
The night was lovely and the lights were
Quite din when I tripped and stumbled right into him.
I begged his pardon as he extended his hand
As a gesture to dance I replied I think I can
First dance seemed like it would never end.
Frankly I'd never tire from holding him.
As night wore on we seemed inseparable
His reputation I learned was truly impeccable.
As midnight drew near I came to face my biggest fear.
The dance was ending and I'd be alone but
Much to my delight he offered to walk me home.

James M. Tildon

A Gloomy Song

A mother walks down the street
A little child stays by her feet
No place do these two belong
They both sing a gloomy song

A father looks for some work
Mother and child help him look
The family is hungry all the time
Can't buy food without a dime

The family is stared at by the crowd
People talk and laugh out loud
The father is hurt by what they say
He'd change their life if there was a way

A warm bath and food do they desire
They get their warmth from a barrel fire
Another long day turns to night
The family hides from the policeman's light

Morning comes and the family wakes
Again they face life's gives and takes
No place does this family belong
The family sings a gloomy song

James Topping

A Personal Gratitude

In Memory of Dr. M. L. King, Jr.
Hello, Dr. King, please accept our deepest love and respect,
Your absence is truly unbelievable and really heartfelt.
We have kept a very "Special Spot" just for you,
'Cause your lessons are immortal and draw the global view.
You achieved your "Spot" through enormous tolls—
And they are still so vivid in everyone's souls!
Your thunderous speech stirred up the hearts of all,
And we will remember you always without your call!
Your strength and the struggle for equality are felt everywhere—
Around the globe, in ocean, in soil and in open atmosphere!

Today, we float our minds immersed in dew moistened tears—
To display our close affections for you without any fears!
Our hearts now cry alone in daylight and darkness,
But vividly remember all your "dreams" with natural harness!

So, in conclusion, we love to say this,
Although it's very very true, as it is—
You are the eternal guiding light, just like a "Rising Sun,"
And always glow in our hearts to put darkness on the run!
The aspects of your glorious life are simple and straight,
And remind us old reminiscence even after the "Sunset"!!!

   Hillol Ray

The Sweet Memory of a Rose

The right hand of my doctor moved ever so slowly
As I watched his index finger
Gently push the corner of my white bedspread
To form the petals of a flower.
My eyes were glued to its progress
As I sat very still, eating my dinner,
Sitting on my hospital bed.

Before long my doctor left, and I finished eating;
The dishes were removed
But I continued watching my beautiful rose
About two hours.
Then it faded away just as garden roses
Lose their petals, and join eternity.

But my bedspread rose
Remains perfectly intact
As a memory, stored in my heart.

   Donna B. Murphy

What Is This World Coming To?

What is happening to us?
The world is now just a big fuss.

People dying every single day,
because of drugs or gang related ways.

People becoming pregnant at the age of thirteen,
getting AIDS, STD's, diseases and all other types of things.

Fights and guns are always on the news,
police try to stop them but there is nothing they can do.

They try to stop them before it is too late,
but nothing they can do will make them have faith.

Some people don't care about their futures,
then they join a gang and possibly destroy yours.

Nothing can you do to make it go away,
I just pray, that someday, it will all go away.

   Tiffany Weiss

The Game Of My Life

A single rose I lay,
for each day that passes my way.
Nothing anybody can do will change the way I feel,
because guns and violence are so real.
I lay awake every night,
wondering what might have been.
Could they have stopped him,
I don't know, his life seemed so dim,
Now as I sit and weep next to their gravestone
my heart is filled with anger.
How, I ask, am I suppose to cope,
well I thought the answer was dope.
I learned that it was not,
but my life just seems like a mere dot.
This terrible murder in my life really hit me,
blinding me to where I could no longer see.
Now that the gunman's dead,
My life is like a book read.

   Brandy Odom

One Flight Up

Our plane stood idling on the ground awaiting the tower light
Like a small bird scratching on the sand before it takes to flight
Then, like a rabbit runs, jets pushed the land aside
Steel wings seized the warm clear air and we went into a glide

Giant windward thrusts drew us up as landmarks fell away
Blurring runways, concrete towers and the gentle fields of clay
In all directions God's handiwork began to seem less near
As separate things began to blend and earth became less clear

Then as quickly as our view was gone, it came back once again
And a bright new world came into view devoid of wind and rain
This world was sparkling white with winding hills and dales
And golden sun brightened every field as it road along the trails

White mountains reached white fingers beckoning to our plane
That seemed to urge us upward in this land without a name
Volcanoes, rivers, lakes and streams came slowly into veiw
All glowing white without a sign of color, tint, or hue

I thought this truly must be Godsland or so it seemed to me
For only He could keep these fields so white and pure and free
I could not help but wonder how many flights there are
And how far up in Godsland one must go to reach a star

   Jeptha R. Macfarlane

Child or Adult

Beaten and bruised
'Til you can't see a thing
When the tears roll down your face,
How much do they sting?
Life is confusing in so many ways.
But I'll figure it all out one of these days.
I've seen so much and grew up so fast.
Trying to forget the things that happened in
the past.
No one can realize
How much pain I have felt.
All I hope for is
That he'll never use the belt.
Hands up my shirt feeling around.
How could I stop myself
From taking my feet off the ground.
Drinking and drugs helped me get away.
But not for long, just 'til the next day.

   Jennifer Dellrich

The Other Woman

She purrs in the night, the siren song that's
Only hers alone. Like a sultry temptress,
She seduces him with her promise of
Mystery, intrigue, and ever-new things to try.

Invisible waves of pleasure entwine his mind
And body and slowly, surely draws him
Down into herself until he is hopelessly,
Completely addicted. Soon he knows what
Buttons to push to elicit the delicious ecstasy of
exploring and learning and trying her new things.

He spends hours with her, as with any
mistress, completely unaware of the
passing of time. And all the while,
I wait . . . and wait . . . and wait.

I really do love him, and I know in my
Heart that someday he'll be totally mine again.
Some day, I'll win over her and then I'll
know the final triumph; for I will pull
her plug, and she will purr no more!

Cheyrl Pound

Untitled

As twilight sets on an empty shore
The sound of love echoes and more
Flowers and sorrow are all that remains
Nothing more left but caverns of pain.
The years that we dreamed are far away
And all that I see is what is today.
A distant hope of happy forever
Sits in a box to stay 'neath flowering heather.

Kimberly Thomton

Daddy No

Looking out the window she remembered his face.
His arms to hold her, his soft morning grace.
He would ask God to watch over him.
He couldn't forget his girl as he gave her a little grin.
She knew she would always, love Daddy so.
When he left for work she'd cry, "Daddy no."

But when he'd come home her tears had dried away.
Daddy reads a story, then they start to play.
She'd never forget the day Daddy stopped to pray.
Daddy knew he'd be leaving on this very day.
As she looks out the window she would softly say:

"Now I understand why Daddy had to pray.
He knew he'd be leaving somehow, someday.
I just don't understand why Daddy had to go.
Daddy, if you can hear me, please Daddy no."

Aimee L. Scott

Mom

Mom is your name,
It belongs in the spotlight of fame.
You give us everything,
And we enjoy the love you bring.

We never said Thank You,
But we hope it does not make you blue.
Sometimes we were bad,
And we are sorry for making you mad.

We have been through bad times and good times,
Just trying to get by with nickles and dimes.
Oh Mom how can we say Thank You,
The way is that we Love You!!!

Garth Reed Messinger Jr.

In Your Arms

I choose this home because, when I had no home, it was found
"In your arms"
I waited at night for you, so I could be,
"In your arms"
When I could not find you, I would look for you, so I could be
"In your arms"
I always knew I had a place, and best of, friend when I was,
"In your arms"
When I had my babies, I wanted you to be first to hold them,
"In your arms"
When I was cold, you always had plenty of firewood,
"In your arms"
I grew old, and could not see, except when,
"In your arms"
I needed your help again, and I found it,
"In your arms"
I thank you for many years of holding me,
"In your arms"
I have you to thank, and be sure, I am always,
"In your arms"

Joseph D. Warren

Feeling Great at Ninety-One

Since I'll be Ninety-One on August the 9th,
I have trouble with my feet.
I can't eat a good steak dinner,
Because I have trouble with my teeth.

I'm losing my hair,
And I'll soon be bald.
But no one will even know,
Because a wig will cover it all.

My hands are steadily entertaining,
And could look worse for what they do.
But running them fast on the accordion,
No one can see them, only the one they belong to.

Now there is nothing the matter with me,
I'm just fine and healthy as I can be.
I hope you're all feeling the same,
Because this is coming from Edith, that's my name.

Edith M. Schragl

Love Shared

Come Lay in my chest melt over my lips
You I will love there my tongue our taster
Your fingers our explorer our rhythmic bodies
Composer and home to part would become homesick.
Hair hides the place where we camped
Our tears to purify hearts broken
And nurtures love's birth.

That we may climb self cliffs
Realizing sea is but a tear
And when surf crashes over cliffs
Shaping it like God a wounded soul
Experience every coloration known and unknown
Passion our summer may it be endless
Our thoughts like wings over our bed kneeling before love's shrine

Fire consume us that we may be the casting furnace
For the unloved.
That they become like the enchanted phoenix bird
That consumed itself by fire
and rose renewed from its ashes

And we become incense

Ronnie McFadden

Something To Think About

I had a vision, a wonderful clean,
All the land was lush and green.
All mankind working side by side,
Creed, color, religion all put aside.

Children playing games, laughing with joy
Sharing and caring, man did employ
Land abundant with water and food.
We'd finally found a world that is good

It seems the way we live today
We've forgotten how to love, give and play,
We have gained one thing, we must gain more,
This wish for riches, inevitably leads to war.

Can't we put all these things aside,
Like greed and war and egotistical pride,
And remember the important quality of living,
Love, honor, respect and giving.

It may have been a clean, a vision,
If only we could turn it into an ambition.
To rid the world of wars and hate.
Before we go too far and it's too late.

    Vivienne Alonge

A Quaint Little Man

Control, yourself as best you can,
And I'll tell a tale about a quaint little man.
It seems that when a teenager, he was
Without a beard or a little fuzz.
As he continued to grow and to sprout,
He never lost when he fished, he always caught trout!
One day as he looked in a faithful old mirror,
He noticed a hair, then he panicked with fear.
"What's this?" he said, to his amazing eyes,
"I'm growing older, not younger." he then surmised.
Next time he went fishing, 'twas unable to catch any
Til he plucked his hairs, which were now many.
The fish started biting right away,
So from then on—a barber—he did pay.
He's never been without his newfound luck
Whether he drives his limousine or a daily milk truck.
Even when the waters are cold,
The fish around him all remain bold.
So now if you would like some advice
If you'd like fish for your dinner use this device: Shave and Behave!

    Linda Lawseth

Barbed Wire Baskets

How did I ever get in such a fix.
I had a barb attached to Ole Saint Nick.
I had another stuck in his elastic.
Now, I'm all wound up, I'm a barb wire basket.

Why a hundred years ago I stretched the land.
I'd grab the britches of any passing man.
I was what was called the cowboy pride.
Rub me wrong and I'd take some hide.

When I was new I was just like most.
I couldn't be much help without a strong host
To hold my strands and barbs at my best level.
Farmers and ranchers I helped settle.

Many a bird has found rest and a place to roost.
I'd stop those tumble weeds until the wind gave a boost
I'd help stop the enemy when we went to war.
I'd be springy and tough, my barbs were a horror.

I closed off the old frontier and open range.
Stopped some fusses and helped some people change.
Time caught up to me and I couldn't outlast it.
I'm rusty and happy, I'm a barb wire basket.

    Joe Funkhouser

Never Forgotten and Still Loving You

To Oliver "Dutch" McCarty
We were living so far away.
not really seeing each other except
on holidays.
You were always in and out of the hospital.
Always feeling so much pain.
I'd pray for things to get better.
They'd always seemed to get worse.
Day after day, waiting, praying,
Just hoping for another day.
Then suddenly one Thursday, you
went away.
I blamed myself for your death.
Because I didn't know you that well
I now, see that I was wrong.
I always wanted to tell you just
how much I loved you.
But, I missed my chance to say it
Now I think it's time.
Just always remember that in my heart.
You're never forgotten and I'm still loving you

    Betty Jeske

Love and Hate

If Love is living, please never let me die
If Love is tears, forever let me cry
If Love is time, it's something that you don't want to waste
If Love is a food, it should have a favorable taste
And if Love is a fairy tale from a book,
never close the book and let it end
If Love is an everlasting royal ball,
please say that everyone would attend
If Love is a heart, then please don't ever let mine break
And if Love is from a person,
don't let their love ever be fake
If hate is a door, please keep it shut
If hate is a fear, then help me please and give me some gut
If hate is a promise, please don't let me ever keep
If hate is a hole, please don't let it be deep
And if hate is a test, please let me fail
If hate is a storm, don't let it be hail
If hate is a bullet, please don't let me get shot
And if hate is a song, let's not start at the top

    Julie Kickbusch

A Remedy to Loneliness

The clouds cover the full moon
A girl is lonely in an empty room
She longs to fit in
To have a friend through thick and thin
She wishes upon a shooting star
She wishes to meet a friend from afar
The girl's name is Lex
Her birthday is the day after next
She doubts anyone will attend her party
So all she can do is sob whole-heartedly
A doorbell suddenly sounds
Lex begins a short journey down
A stairway to tend to the doorbell
But what she finds is a young man named Mel
He is a postman, you see
She is overjoyed and invites him in for tea
He graciously accepts the offer
And soon fills the room with laughter
The clouds cover the full moon
But a girl is no longer lonely, nor in an empty room

    Cynthia Hunke

In the Light of a Hero

In a dark lonely corner
A single soul sits
He's scared of the light of dawn.
And there is a someone out there, who cares
Someone . . . someone . . . someone . . .

No Mother or father were known to him
And his dreams were filled with distress
His days were rarely numbered
He could not rest.

His home was the alley.
On the streets he was alive.
No one was there to help him
No one cared if he died.

But theres a person
Who cares for his health, it's a mother
And for him she's wasted her wealth.

No one knew him,
But in the light of a hero
He knows he belongs to someone . . .
Someone who will cherish him forever . . .

Umara Saleem

Untitled

If a fire burns like it's supposed to is it a real fire?
If love keeps burning, is it real love?
Can it be claimed by a person to be so true,
even though it may burn out?
How or even, can you, keep that burning going?
Is it possible or is it just pure luck?
Can you keep adding wood and starting it again and again,
or once it's out, do you have to let it end?
How does a person know, when to keep
trying or just to let the flame go out?
Will your own fire tell you when,
or do you have to make your own choice?

Heather Black

Black Hole

She has to run, has to hide
She has bruises deep inside.
How can she escape the pain
If it will never end?

Her soul is a black hole, sucking in all the hope.
She can't get better if she can't cope.
Her eyes are always crying, without shedding a tear.
She can't talk to anyone because of her fear.
Someone hurt her once before,
And now she can be hurt no more

How did she bury them so deep,
That they could never escape?
How did she hold it all inside?
All she knew was how to hide.

And now she's gone, cold and alone.
She thought the only way to hide,
Was kill herself; and so she died.
She drowned her sorrow in the cave.
Now she lies in her watery grave.

Anne Goulding

The War

The world around me is closing in
I'm striving for air; there are screams everywhere
I look to the left and then to the right
Oh my, oh my there's blood at my side.

The sky is pitch black with small streaming lights
A big bang here and a loud boom there
There are holes in the ground and glass on the streets
What ever happened to the peace that we seek?

The dungeon is waiting; my name's on the list
Surrounded by walls and perilous grips
My arms are in the air, my feet are bound tight
The tears from my eyes are stinging my cheeks.

Then He is here, helping me up
A man in a robe so pure and so clean
He looks in my eyes, all the pain goes away
Now all that's left are tears full of joy.

Lisa S. Schindele

Thinking of the Past

Do you remember how it was 50 years ago?
Do you remember if the events happened slow?
Do you remember how life was back then?
Do you remember if you had money to spend?
Do you remember the hard times you had?
Do you remember the times you were glad?

Do you remember when your children were young?
Do you remember the things that they done?
Do you remember the places you all went?
Do you remember the money that was spent?

Do you remember when everyone was glad?
Do you remember the happy times you all had?
Do you remember the times we were sad?
Do you remember events that got you mad?

Do you think these 50 years have flown?
All the family has changed so much.
Your children and grandchildren sure have grown.
Haven't the years gone by in a rush?

Judy A. Kirk

Sunday Morning

It is early morning when tree branches sway by wind
Play melodies of peace, hope, and dreams
It is early morning when dew drops begin
To create translucent hues of nature's theme.

It is early morning it's a day of spring
When tulips rest closed while the sun is still weak
When bird flocks return to nest and sing
When life's silky web is bewitched by mystique.

It is early morning heaven is tinted on pale blue
In the horizon cloud silhouettes show me embracing you
There is no distance or people holding us apart
Our love is sincere and will last forever in tunes stanzas and art.

There is fever in the air a fever of freedom and joy
the flowers in bloom wait for the bees to feed
While the majestic array of beauty is deployed
It was early morning yesterday it was a day of spring

It's no longer morning it's not even noon
The sun's ball of fire is hidden to give way to the moon
The stars shine like diamonds on the black veil of night
The moon's radiant light became a companion of pilgrimages fright

Aurora Munoz

Springtime in Arkansas

The season of spring has always been special to me
But springtime in the Ozarks is special to see.
The presence of the most beautiful blue sky
With trees in different shades of green, oh my!
Daffodils and tulips come along in their stately, manner
While white spirea popcorn style, form a banner.
the forsythia in yellow style adorns many a home
Purple and while lilacs, and wild flowers wherever you roam.
It is a coloranea traveling from hill to hill
And there is so much more beauty coming still.
The beautiful red bud trees break forth in their glory—
While spectacular pink and white dogwood could make a story.
When both red buds and dogwood come out the same time
It is truly an artist's paradise which makes this rhyme.
The return of the humming and blue birds in not rare.
So not only is there beauty but a song in the air.
Truly God has given all of us this beauty to see.
That's why spring time in Arkansas means so much to me!

Maxene Mayenscheins

This Delicate Leaf

This delicate leaf hast fallen for me
But for reasons I cannot comprehend;
Just as the fledgling from the nest doth flee
Ne'er to look back, for itself to fend,
So too dost this waif fly to me hither
From its haven amidst the yawning sky,
Only to lie at my feet, to wither
Amongst the choking vines, waiting to die.
O little leaf, may others learn from this;
If proceeding in life should mean to wait
Than rushing into a smiling abyss,
Then sooner shall ye find the Heaven's Gate
    Rather than the fiery gate of Hell,
        Whose access requires a soul to sell.

Shaun E. Brune

Untitled

From a riverside terrace I can sense a place
It's across the Hudson and close in case
You wanted to know where I turn my face
To the city where I left my heart behind

Not a very long drive, just across the way
Out of a state that drives my thoughts astray
Three syllables long and if that's okay
By me it's where my true love lies

Out of sight, blocked by a forest of trees
The span of a bridge marked by four dollar fees
But it's free when you only catch the tease
And a beat of the heart of my "King" Tut, that is!

Time on my hands when my half's not around
In a separate world but still level to ground
When it's just us two can you hear the sound
Of the waves that reach you from my terrace

Tisha Hill

Dear Mothers

And the mothers of our world
shall be honored above all women
because it is they that make our world by
bringing to life the honorable people
that promote happiness,
allow love to grow, and prove that
the unity of our people is a possibility
and not only the dream of few.

Ramon F. Barron

Evermore

Years ago I meet this girl, as sweet as girls could be,
I looked at her, she looked at me, but never could we see,
that down the path of life we walk with someone else in mind
somehow, someway, some blessed day our hearts be intertwined.
We've had such fun, it's been a blast,
and, yes, we know that this will last.
Though times may change and leaves will turn
from each of us we both will learn.
She is my sweet and God I pray
that time will pass and one great day
she'll say, "I do" and be my wife,
and evermore live one great life.
I tell you this now my sweet loving dear,
no matter what distance, I'll always be near.
Just close your eyes with all your might
and I'll be there . . . to hold you tight.

Colin C. Usher

A World of Books

There is a world of books
for young and old
about grass and trees,
silver and gold.

It is not a world we live in,
nor a world of birds,
but a world of pictures,
and a world of words.

It is a world of giants,
and a world of some
even as small as
the tip of your thumb.

We can imagine we're there,
between the thin pages and air.
I think the world of books
is far greater than fishing and its hooks.

Ashley Worth

My Plea

As I open my eyes after a restless night,
Yawn, stretch, wash my face, then comb my hair.
Traces of the nightmare fleetingly lingering fright,
And soft whispers telling me, "You'd better beware."

Depression sent me spiraling down,
In stages slowly, so I did not see,
I'd adopted a permanent frown.
Feeling so lost and ever so lonely.

Death had come knocking at my door.
Taking my mom, and my very best friend.
Then a long term friend, who I had adored.
Sending me emotionally around the bend.

Zapped three times within one year.
My shoulders slumped with a heavy weight .
Tears streaming down my cheeks, "Why am I still here?"
What dear Lord is now my fate?

I must now seek a positive way,
To find a much needed release.
And endure another day,
Can someone help me, please?

Jessica L. Fink

B-I-B-L-E

Blessed Information Bringing Life Eternal
is what the Bible offers me
This life was purchased by the Savior
When he died on Calvary

Eternal life is free to every man
It's life's greatest deal
For Jesus Himself said
"It's free for whosoever will"

So friends if you're searching
And don't know where to look
You don't have to take my word
Just go to the book

In it you will find the answers
That will keep you through eternity
Yes friends there's never been
A greater book than the B-I-B-L-E.
        Gene McCormick

My Undying Love

I remember the night so clearly,
the power had went out and everything was fiery.

When all of a sudden my heart had turned bright,
from the moment he walked into my light.

He started to walk towards me,
from a skip of a heart beat I knew he could be.

The one I have been looking for,
all day and all night through every open door.

His eyes were like diamonds with every little speck,
his heart was what I wanted, but he wanted me to reject.

His warmth of his lips and the most powerful hugs,
made my heart feel like he gave it a tug.

I gave him my love, soul and heart,
but he turned around and tore it apart.

His feelings they were like a wave,
back and forth as they swayed.

Though my love for him did not change,
my family and friends had told me I was strange.

For him I won't forget,
because of my undying love that still stands yet.
        Tabatha Loveland

Bless Her

My dear and mighty Lord Jesus, enormously high, high above;
I beg you to hear my lonely cry for this girl I really love.
Bless her perfectly placed silk hair, that shines in the night.
Bless her sweet luscious lips that once kissed mine just right.
Bless her basic instinct it's very simple, yet so very cleaver.
Bless her elegance of a Queen, keep it a radiant moon forever.
Bless her dear diamond tears, if a love song makes her sad.
Bless her ocean deep emotions and keep her from getting mad.
Bless her untamed heart that's make of a priceless rare gold.
Bless her rose petal soft body, cherish it from getting too old.
Bless her cheerful circus smile, showing happiness in every way.
Bless her innocent angel eyes, to see me again soon someday.
Bless her flower blossoming mind, make it absorb life's lesson.
Bless her with angel's music and rainbows of heavenly presence.
Bless her from head to toe, add a magical touch to her soul.
Bless her through tough times, let it be known I think of her so.
My kind Lord, show your overflowing strongest might.
As You keep her safe, secure and within your sight.
        Adrian Rodriguez

My Little Girl

Little girl with the rosy cheeks,
Sitting there giggling
As your daddy tickles your sides.

Do you realize how much you're loved?
When I look upon face into those big blue eyes
My heart weeps,

Because one day your giggles with be gone.
No more will you need me to hold you close
And make your monsters go away.

You'll ask me no more to kiss your boo boo's
Or look up at me to say "help me."
You will no longer be my little girl.

All this will break my heart.
But if you ever need to be that little girl again
My arms are always open.

In my eyes you'll always be
That little girl who is giggling
As her daddy tickles her sides.
        Michelle S. Kelso

C'est Fine

C'est Fine,
T'is gone and through,
Weapons lay upon red sand,
Groans of men sadden the mist of morn',

We overcame, are victors, yet have lost,
In ending others' days,
Having made widows and children,
Hungry and alone.

A wrath dealt upon men closer to us
Than our leaders,
T'is to be ruined at life in war,
Feeling to carry to our end.
        Joseph Daniel Barrett

Where One of the Fallen Lay

Where one of the fallen lay
Just beneath the soaring wings
of the Restless Black Raven. The eyes
Of prey so full of fear and stricken.
Where one of the fallen lay.
Just beyond the sea of expectant
silence, mysterious and sullen.
A tattered bridge fails to close the
gap as the torn of heart contemplate
elusive destiny and a quiet place to rest.
Where the Lamb lays down with the
Lion, where the weak and destitute
Bow a knee and pray.
Where one of the fallen lay.
        Tyler B. Harrington

Reflection

An image transpired from time long ago,
someone familiar, her face I should know,
smiling there, unsure in thought,
recalled to mind, the past I sought.

Amber hair, shines silver now,
lines of age, upon her brow,
through tears, with backward glance, I see,
a distorted image that resembles me.

As thoughts entwined amidst the gaze,
of youthful dreams and bygone days,
I watched, as through the mirror, she came,
reality lost, within a frame.
        Carole Joeckel

To The Friend I'll Never Know

That cold, cold body lying there
That cold, cold body lying there
I know it's her, but she's not there
A cold, cold body's lying there

She's not there, yet she's still here
I feel, I know that she is near
Down my face now falls a tear
I only hope that she can hear

This can't be real, it is not her
I only know how live things were
It's cold, it's stiff, it's not my friend
This is not, can not be the end

She's gone too soon, for I had plans
But now I just feel cold, cold hands
You see she was to be my friend
Instead, to heaven, prayers I'll send

A friend is a friend to the end
No more chances to make amends
This is the end. It must be so.
To the friend I'll never know

Crystal M. Eubanks

Forever Innocent

They are God's chosen children,
Not to rest without knowing their deeds.
They cry, they sing, they ask not why,
Compassion rises through their needs.

The fast pace life to say what they think,
They want understanding in their delay.
Knowing exactly what's on their minds,
The constant struggle of words to say.

They were hurled into the air swiftly,
By a driver who didn't care.
To land on pavement not able to speak,
The change of normalcy so harsh, so unfair.

Rehab clothed them with strength and dignity,
It has taken doctors, parents and teachers in all.
To help these teens regain their self esteem,
To help these young teens attend their senior ball.

Roxanne J. Sprague

Justice Delayed

She walked into her broken house,
He clenched his fists in rage.
She can't make any sense of his fits,
He can't remember his children's names.

The neighbors frown, and make a face,
But no one makes a sound.
They'll tell somebody tomorrow, maybe,
But they'll leave it alone for now.

Her body is bruised, her hands are tied,
The courts won't let her be.
They say she needs to get a lawyer,
But God knows it ain't' free.

She's not just a statistic, she's more than that,
She's not just a woman, she's somebody's wife,
She's somebody's daughter, she's somebody's sister,
She's somebody's mother, she's somebody's life.

There's something wrong, and it's not just him,
There's something someone didn't say,
The children cry as they watch their mother die,
And the courts let the criminal get away.

Craig Dees

Life

Darkness, destruction, cold desolation,
I turn to my flag
and then weep for my nation.

Emptiness, evil, too much exploitation,
I can see that corruption
takes not one vacation.

Anarchy, atrophy, alienation,
I wonder if we
are beyond liberation.

Terrorism, torture, enticing temptation,
I turn to religion,
but find no salvation.

Holocaust, hell on earth, horrification,
I pray for the day
of emancipation.

Lance D. Brown

Do It Over?

If I could do it over would I
feel the way I do and do the things I feel?
How many beatings does it take to remember
to wear your boots in the snow?
She always had a way of making a point
"This will make you stronger," she'd say.
Afraid to go home.

It's supposed to be sanctuary
your own corner of the world.
The safest place you'll ever know,
except for the monster in the hall.
You figure this is all there is
the best it will ever be.
It was.

Hard lessons taught
to soon gone, too young old.
Couldn't the good thing make us strong?
A little whack on the head never hurt anyone.
Wanted to be someone else,
but do it over?

Keliy S. Haglund

Drug Addict

Far from the world I remember and know;
I open my eyes unto a place filled with something like snow.
Not knowing where my money has gone;
My arm hurts as if blood had been drawn.
A mirror in one hand, a razor in the other;
At home worrying about me is my mother,
The sound of footsteps are coming toward me;
Trying to run, but white was all I could see.
The walls were spinning, the floor was mush;
I knew I was moving because my face felt flush.
The sounds of voices were coming near,
Running in a strange place full of fear.
The people who were with me the night before.
Left me here, knocked out cold on the floor.
The sound of people were coming at me fast;
Then there was a sudden flashback from the past.
My friends said "we'll help you when you need it."
But those friends of mine didn't think of me one bit.
So I guess my parents were right in the end;
Your family's not only your family, but also your best friend.

Amber Nolet

Full Moon Riders

Not a sound can be heard
    but that of the owl somewhere in the night.

Not a sound can be heard
    but that of the river rushing through the meadow.

Not a sound can be heard
    but that of the wolf howling at the moon.

Out of the darkness they emerge—
    a party of eight mounted warriors.

They cannot be heard
    but only seen in the distance.

Along the river they ride.
    All is quiet and calm.

Into the darkness from which they came,
    they disappear.

Not a sound can be heard.

    Mark Baur

Remembrance, Again? . . .

I remember dragonflies sitting upon your hand,
I remember dunking Oreos while stars fell to the land.
I remember not completing some movies we would view,
I remember snuggling close and making love with you.
I remember going out to Friday night plays,
I remember swinging light sticks with colorful arrays.
I remember flicking on your watch to see how it would glow,
I remember you crying too over some sad picture show.
I remember putting make-up on you the eve of Halloween,
And I remember the Super Bowl with you cheering the Chargers team.
I remember awakening to surprises on Christmas morn,
And I remember us both in bed when the New Year was born.
I remember this and much more that we did do,
For I'll remember these always wanting more of them with you.

    Fawn E. Caldwell

Springtime Inertia

Waiting
head up, arms out, legs poised
for release for sweat to consume me
for ice cream slithering between sticky fingers
for bug bites behind my knees
for pretty boys with straight teeth and nice shoulders
for baseball games and fireworks and theme parks and
first everythings
for bells
in the distance
jingling,
bring,
bring
and for children
heads high, eyes wide, hands out
waving quarters and dimes
at the man in the spotless white suit

    Jill Quint

What My Grandmama Said To Me

Something so beautiful encased in a pen ink
Which says wonderful things on plain sheets
But when they become one they can create
phases, paragraphs, and mottos that devour the soul
They eat up the heart in bite size pieces invoking
emotions that are unexplainable but definitely understood
But beauty can only be seen so far
Love for another is rare and truly hard to find.
To accomplish it is sincerely a task
Love all that you can and enjoy what is made out
of it before the words are erased

    Cutrice Lockson

Up Front At His Funeral

For Harold Logwood
His bowling ball.
There it was, up front at his funeral.
Green and black, sitting with his shoes.
He had clobbered many a pin with it in his time.
Some alleys were stripped; his ball sang with the victories.

His ball, sitting in the darkness of his son's closet corner.
It could rest now, recovering from its pounding.
Yet his son too passed and the light came one day—
Granddaughter giving it to the Goodwill.
A funky old bowling ball;
Someone's ball.

A teenage boy clunking down the gutter
his used gutterball, one after the other.
So he lives on, taking a poke at clubs still
and picking up a piece of the varnish with every bounce.

    Matthew R. Henry

God

Show me, empower me, enlighten me, inspire me with your spirit.
Let me now that it does not matter what my past was,
Only what my future holds.
Give me the strength and faith
To walk on water.
Lead me in thy pathway so that
My children may know some
Things in life are worth
Standing up for, or you will
Eventually lie down and die.

Let me prove to myself and others
That wisdom and experience
Can walk hand-in-hand,
While anger and resentment
Can be binding, leaving
Shackles on your mind.

Lift me and let me in turn, lift you.
Show me that love, trust, hope, and
Determination are the tools
To unlock any door and any heart.

    Debra K. Tilley

Mirror

Mirror, Mirror What do you see,
Of life's reflections upon me?
A child's dirty shirt or messed up hair,
reflects a mother who does not care.
A man who does not show he cares,
reflects a love that is not there.
A woman who receives no respect,
reflects the image a father's meant.
Oh mirror, mirror, if what I see is what I get.
I must remember who's looking at it.
Mirror, Mirror, what do I see,
of life's reflections upon me?
A child's dirty shirt or messed up hair,
reflects this child's had fun somewhere,
A man who does not show he cares,
reflects a love that's hidden in there.
A woman who receives no respect,
reflects the lives of illiterates.
Oh mirror, mirror, what do you see . . .
Just life's deceptions upon me.

    Janet McCullough Waterman

Odie And Me

Odie: The best little beagle dog around
Looking at me with his big round eye's
He's the best little pal to have around
This little dog Odie of mine

When I come in from school
He's sitting there on the ground
Flapping his tail all around, he jumps up to greet me
I wish Odie could talk to me

If I go for a ride in the truck
Odie hops in and away we go
He sticks his nose up in the air
He thinks he's the only dog around

Odie is the best little beagle dog around
This little friend of mine named Odie
I wish my little friend Odie would talk back to me
I love this little dog of mine

Odie loves me all the time
How much fun Odie would be
If he could only talk back to me
You never get lonely with Odie around

Ruby M. Merritt

Soon The Pearly Gates Will Open

Soon the pearly gates will open
to receive onto the Lord Jesus Christ
the redeemed of this world
will rise into the air.
To meet our loved ones
who have gone to glory
to live with the Lord in their mansion
in that city of gold,
where we will never grow old.
That meeting in the air
will be so fantastic and
the beauty will so glorious
that all the redeemed of this world
will sing in Heaven's Jubilee;
about the eternal love of Jesus,
King of Kings,
Lord of Lords,
for eternity on that evergreen shore forevermore.

Janice K. Summerford

A Generation of Differences

When I come to think of those times, they all remind me of
   the peaceful chimes
Of which, all along, were not just happiness in a song.

Just thirty years ago brought the joyful flow,
Of a new music, different thoughts and hippies among lots.

And yet it was so tense, as if surrounded by a fence.
Just beginning to understand how to lend a loving hand.

We were red, white, blue, all the way through.
But who led? Was it Communist red?

So the two nations set equal sensations
Only to face a race to space.

And in late sixty-eight
Ideas by whites were scattered in the Civil Rights.

Across a vast ocean floor, desperate men saw the horror of war.
Finally, Vietnam tore no more!

But somehow they brought a generation of whom the taught
A different understanding, for good.

So, isn't it neat how we were brought by the same feet,
And have such differences between us.

Leslie Sturdevant

In Your Eyes

John Roberts
When I look in your eyes,
I see more then you see,
I see your heart and your soul—the real you
Your essence, your spiritual flow
You are loving, giving, and helpful.

In your eyes, I see the peace you seek,
Yet, the love and respect you look for
From others cause you to take on their burdens and your own.
You feel useless and hopeless if you can't help.
You are the bearer of burdens an interceder
God bless you for your work.
May the holy ghost guide you,
And ease the pain you carry for others.

Always remember the work is God's
Don't take His praises
Just say, "Thank God" when someone thanks you.

Cheryl Mitchell

Mother

Mother is not a name to take lightly.
To bandy about, affix as a label
To just any woman with the proper intentions.

Mother is in that single word
Love, hope, courage.
Mother is beauty, grace, integrity.

She most often tickles memories,
Brings delight with her simple smile,
Guides assuredly, coaxes when her child balks.

Mother picks up her faltering child,
Brushes off the dust, and
Sends that child on to a new adventure.

The daughter wants most to be her mother, and
Prays her daughter wishes the same.

In simplest terms, Mother holds together the world,
Fills the cracks with her love,
Takes the injured to her heart.

She gives unconditionally, asking only our love in return.
And if by chance we don't, or can't,
Mother loves us anyway.

Tammy Kimmel Asbery

(My Mind's) Dusty Book

Cloudy skies make me reminisce of my youth.
These trees are houses, these leaves are roads
By God I wish I could, I wish I could leave this
land of trouble, into my land of dreams,
into the back pages of that dusty book of my mind.

These all happened to me, to me the young child.
The young one who was a different one,
different among all there, different even from me.

The imagination going wild, the rock star image,
the Rolling Stones, Vietnam War, 18 and II-S,
too scared, life was never so free.

Summers in the park, lazy on the bench, on the field,
my life wasting away, so free,
that's in the back pages of that dusty book.

Eric Johnson

Death Not It Be

When eyes are empty, but for fear
When the body burns in the cool air
When a tear shed cannot be wiped away
When each morning is nothing more than another day

When a body's skin has color no more
When an eerie essence is beyond the door
When no words, no touch, can change a thing
When existence is solemn fear . . . of what the day may bring

When reality is no more than a heart's piercing throb
When time is lost to a strange, peculiar fog
When darkness just is . . . no matter the sun
When the battle, simply, cannot be won

When hope has no home, the heart no peace
When faith is all that is still within reach
When the night as we know it, has no next
When yet the sun still rises, shining its best

When our hearts then know . . . that death not it be
But the beginning of a life . . . we've yet to see

   Phyllis Smart

With Love, Grandma

"Grandma," I said, "I don't want you to go.
I don't want you to leave me here.
When you go, I'll be so alone."
And then she said, "You'll never be alone, dear."

I said "I wanted you to see me do many things.
And, Grandma, I really need your love."
Then I felt the warmth of her hand and she said,
"I'll see everything you do, my child, but I'll be
seeing it from above."

   Lacie Beth Hall

Life

A chapter that hasn't been written,
A tale that hasn't been told,
A verse that hasn't been sung,
We'll all contemplate this, when we are old.

The sun that hasn't yet set,
The theory that hasn't been taught,
The painting that isn't yet finished ,
Is this life? Don't think not.

Yet, sometimes we stop in our writing,
Sometimes we're interrupted before the whole tale's been told,
Sometimes we don't get to see the sunset,
What is happening? We begin to wonder,
As we start to lose our hold.

We never finished writing the book,
We never sang the whole song,
We never saw the sunset,
For a day, a life, is only so long.

   Nykole Bower

The Reckless Society

They make rules of their own.
The area they inhabit will remain their zone.
They don't care how others think.
The similarities of the cause will help them link.
No matter what happens their message will be heard.
Because anything less would be absurd.
It wouldn't be smart to cross their path.
This will only give them an excuse to enforce their wraith.
Forget anything that you have ever seen.
The end result will be something truly obscene.

   David Goldberg

Love

Love makes the world go round
But the greatest love is of God.
Next is love between husband and wife,
Hopefully, until the end of their life.

The love of our children is next.
No improving on this text,
For this is a full-time job,
Of which parents will ofttimes sob.

The love of grandchildren is a joy,
Whether they are a girl or a boy.
They add laughter and spice to our lives
And give to us mostly good vibes.

We also have the love of nieces and nephews,
Who sometimes can be our refuge
In a world of success and plenty
Can become a time of empty.

Then there is a love of cousins,
We can sometimes have by the dozens.
But do not forget love of friends
On who our life so much depends.

   Martha W. Ruhl

Oh Little Angel

Oh little angel, why did you make me cry?
You said you loved me, but why did you lie?
Oh little angel, why do you fly so high?
Why do you float when I want to die?
This was supposed to be forever,
But I guess you forgot and can't remember.
Oh little angel, why does it hurt so bad?
How did we fall short and make me so sad?
All your words and memories that were kept.
So why am I writing while yesterday you soundly slept?
Oh little angel, why aren't you with me?
Why do I sit here crying with my head between my knees?
Oh little angel, why aren't you sorry for you lies?
How could you be if you didn't apologize?
Oh little angel, why do you fly so high?
Why do you float when I want to die?

   Dori VanMyers

Memories of the Night

How nice to hear the words coming from the heart.

And honest word is what I got.
It's seldom heard or never caught.
The best to get.
But yet.
The love I know was there.
All the truth, the care.
It must go.
But no!
It touch me deep, my very soul.
Sincerity without the role.
This I do know
Even though.
The growth she won't let be.
It can't grow with me.
So I'll just.
Keep trust.

And the tears I'll take them light.
But, not the memories of the night.

   Mark D. Spencer

A Poet's Dream After Seeing Her Picture

I saw her lovely picture, in such a douce display,
Telling me the words no mouth could ever say.
Her face with such a beauty, oh heaven is it sweet!
It strikes my heart with pleasure and makes it loudly beat.
Fitted with two eyes, in such a piercing fire,
Even God Hephaestus, so deeply must admire.

Her gorgeous conquering smile, with such a touching splendor,
Could even force a stone, to turn soft and tender.
A divine dream, with burning charm and grace,
Came down to earth and took her reigning place.
A loving God, once gave her such a gorgeous shape,
Captured by her beauty, no mortal will escape.

I hear her tender name, sounding through the spheres,
Creating so much joy, could dry a sea of tears.
I see the gates of heaven, being open wide,
Looking in her eyes, so beautiful so bright.
I see her lovely shadow in the morning mist,
Oh blessed joyful feeling, I never could resist.

And you oh city Memphis, I must you so adore,
Where once inside your walls, she set her foot ashore.

Dr. Hans Gerbert Bogensberger

Reunion

My Poppa is gone
No more will I see
His wrinkled brow as he plants a tree
His sun browned hands as he tills the corn
My Poppa is gone—he left at dawn

The goodbye so final
The loss so real
My Poppa loved God
And 'tis He who can heal
Those open wounds, so fresh, so new
In the fullness of time, I shall feel God's dew

Two score was he when he gave God his heart
Fourscore and two when he had to depart
We will meet again in a distant land
And this time forever
I'll hold his hand.

Betty Agolia

I Am

I am who I am but what I wish to be
I wonder if my dreams or wishes are heard
I hear voices from inside dungeon walls
I see the door to the world closing slowly
I want to feel the passion explode from within you
I am who I am but what I wish to be

I pretend to see wishful images
I feel a soft, cold hand touch my shoulder
I touch the visions but do not grasp them
I worry that the future will break down
I cry out to the frustration
I am who I am but what I wish to be

I understand what consequences will tear apart my soul
I say to the voices to silence their pleas
I dream to believe the visions
I try to brush away the cold hand upon my shoulder
I hope to live by my wish
I am who I am but what I wish to be

Christina Deskins

Boomer

He came to us in a most unusual way,
Scooped up from a litter playing on the floor.
The owner was anxious to give them away,
So one was picked and carried out the door.

On the prowl both day and night,
Hunting and stalking for mice.
He comes home when he feels it's right,
To leave "presents" he thinks are nice.

An orange tiger with big feet,
A bouncing ball he will chase and fetch.
In the house he drools for the parakeet,
And hopes it escapes so he can catch.

After the catnip he's ready to play,
Chasing his brother and sister to even the score,
Purring loudly at the end of the day,
He's bounding with energy to start once more.

Michael J. Handy

Thoughts Of A Child

My child and I,
are bound as one.
I love the time we spend,
it is simply lots of fun.

He sees the world,
the way that he likes.
From a simple color to explain a car,
to the roundness of the tires on passing bikes.

My child and I,
are growing as one.
He is now a young boy,
yet his growth is far from done.

We are outside now,
beneath the sun and the clouds.
He focuses on one thing,
and picks it out of crowds.

My child and I,
are leaning as one.
He about the world in which he lives,
and me, from the experience of my son.

Adam Devoid

A Time

A wanderer, so far from home
In the minds of those who run and roam
Sees love through eyes of grief and sorrow
though a tear, upon his face, shall never show
For he is one with sad disposition
A frown makes up his constitution

Through the dawn and dusk he slowly strolls
taking in life's ill troubles and toils
But once I saw this person smile
though only for the shortest while
For at that time he saw the only thing
that could make one's sad heart sing

He saw the world, at one special time
When it is bright and everything's in rhyme
Where the air is clear and the grass is green
It's the most beautiful thing you have ever seen
In the minds of those who run and roam
A wanderer, so far from home.

Jessica VitelloA Time

A wanderer, so far from home
In the minds of those who run and roam
Sees love through eyes of grief and sorrow
though a tear, upon his face, shall never show
For he is one with sad disposition
A frown makes up his constitution

Through the dawn and dusk he slowly strolls
taking in life's ill troubles and toils
But once I saw this person smile
though only for the shortest while
For at that time he saw the only thing
that could make one's sad heart sing

He saw the world, at one special time
When it is bright and everything's in rhyme
Where the air is clear and the grass is green
It's the most beautiful thing you have ever seen
In the minds of those who run and roam
A wanderer, so far from home.

Jessica Vitello

Nothing

Nothing is what I feel, inside this empty shell.
It's like my soul has fell, into a dark empty well.
My eyes are open, and I see no light.
Not one ray of life, is in my sight.
Nothing is what I feel,
As my heart skips no beat,
The air I do breath, and the pace my feet keep.
No songs fill my soul, and with joy I don't dance.
It seems from first light, I was given no chance.
Nothing is what I feel,
Inside this empty shell.
My eyes I now close, on this point I won't dwell.

Lear A. Baker

Young Surgeon's Dream

The playful rush of blood sings to my apparition.
Swift red rivers bring joy to my vision.
What does it require to repair a pulsating heart?

Hands gently brush the damaged heart's irregularities,
As the scalpel dances over frail arteries,
The weight of a person's life permeates the air.
Would a patient's death fill my soul with despair?
What must be done to repair a pulsating heart?

Operating on the left ventricle is not easy,
But the joy of healing a valetudinarian will be mine.
I will repair a pulsating heart!

Michael Staren Hollander

Was It Yesterday?

Was it yesterday that I
remembered and today I forget?
Was it yesterday that I
loved and today I hate?
Was it yesterday that I
got my first kiss and today's my last?
Was it yesterday that
the man that I loved told me
that he loved me but today he's
engaged to another woman?
Was it yesterday that
I was found and today I'm lost
in this tragic-n-confusing, sinful world?
Was it yesterday that
I lived and now I'm dead?

Janna Hearl

In My Room

The sky fell, the clouds faded away
The moon went out, the stars turned gray
The grass grew tall, the trees died in gloom
The water became cold, as I lay there in my room

My mother forgot me, my father was too late
My life shriveled up, as I walked through the gate
My heart broke, my ship floated to the earth below
My mind was spinning, I had nowhere to go

In my room I lay there still
Wondering where I was, life didn't seem real
In my room where I gave up my hopes and dreams
In my room alone it seems

Nicole Nichols

Like Dandelions

Dandelions are everywhere in the spring.
There is no pattern to where they appear.
They just grow.
By summer's end, they are gone.
Children are spring.
They add color
like a sea of yellow dots on green grass.
Suddenly,
the lush green-and-yellow-dotted lawn
is replaced
by crunchy brown leaves.
Longing for a fresh-picked fistful of sunshine
from small hands
stained and sticky.
Wish they could be dandelions
just a little longer.

Maria Vogl

In Memory Of My Daughter Charlene

She was always around when I was feeling down.
She'd say, "Oh Mom I love you so very much",
With that special touch.
I'd look into her big bright eyes and smile,
"You are my beautiful child".
She touched your heart with love.
Wherever she would go,
Through the streets and the valleys,
They all seemed to know.
She would sing and bells would ring.
She would preach and then she'd teach
A message that would touch your heart with every reach.
Oh! Yes Charlene, you have done your best.
And now it's time for you to rest.

Pauline Boone

Untitled

Warm winds blow as my father wipes his brow.
Out in the pasture, a cow sways in the breeze to ward off the flies.
The corn reaches toward the sky, parched,
The leaves browned by the sun, the tassels limp.
Neighbors volunteer time but time is useless.
The rain knows no time.
The men drag out hoses, the women mix lemonade,
Hands dark with dirt, faces damp with sweat.
If just to see the leaves blow against a hard rain, Father sighs.
The sun beats down as if punishing the soil.
Time, it is just a matter of time, he says.
It was just weeks before when my father stood in this field,
Flooded and muddy,
With no chance to get the crops in by June.
Now the merciless sun, the dry, cracked soil below Father's feet.
I stand
At my father's side.
The wind strokes the fragile crops as we turn to go home.
The clouds roll by,
Rain in the distance.

Natalia Grosso

Wind

The wind blows a fresh needed breeze tonight.
My heart is low.
The stars are high and light the sky as they dance along the wind.

The wind lifts me and carries me,
How wonderful it feels, what joy it gives.
The scent of flowers is all around.

Rolling thunder approaches, frighteningly magnificent.
The wind no longer takes his time,
He is rushing in now and makes me humble.

Lightening dances across the sky,
laughing, shaking and jolting the earth.
The clouds playfully roll by.

I can hear the voice of the trees,
as the leaves echo the word hush, hush, hush, the storm is passing.
A fresh new breeze will attend your heart tomorrow.

Laura M. Thomas

Mating Souls

To love someone with heart and soul.
Is all one dreams to ever know.

To see them walk into a room,
Knowing they'll be near you soon.

To feel a joy all inside.
Heart beating fast it's hard to hide.

Oh! to hold them feels so right.
It's like a first time every night.

To find a soul mate no one else can compare.
It's a chance of a lifetime to say the least, it is rare.

When it happens you'll know, hold on tight, don't let go.
Fight to keep it with heart, mind and soul.

A once in a lifetime love is hard to find.
There will be no doubt about it, you'll not need a sign.

When you hold them you'll feel whole, like one in the same.
A new love, a new life, all sunshine, no rain.

Yes, a soulmate is love, no else will do.
I knew it the day my soul went to you.

Kathleen E. Perry

A Dying Soul

Like a prisoner on death row
The sentence has been rendered.
Now the long, belated execution
Is being carried out.

She tried to prepare herself
But like watching a loved one,
Their pulse beginning to slow, then stop;
It didn't actually affect her
Until she retained the last beep.

Now the silent, insipid echo
Of a perishing soul rings in her ear.
She struggles to feel anything.

So disassociated from herself,
She knows not who she is.
The hate has depleted her.
No mourning, just motionless.

There is no merit without venture, no pain without emotion.
She died so long ago, but is just now descending.

Closing herself off to the world,
She sheltered her heart, but imprisoned her soul.

Linda Giguere

My City

My city was torn, my city was besieged
My city, by the military, was eventually seized

But out of the smoke, out of the ash
The people of my city quietly answered the task

They came from all areas, all colors and creeds
To assist in the clean-up, to ponder the violent deeds

My city will rebuild, my city will survive
Because of its people and what is inside

Answers to why or who is to blame
Each one of us is guilty, and must bear the shame

But my faith in God and in my fellow man
Give me great hope as we walk hand in hand

There is hope in the future, there is hope today
There is hope for my city, the city of L. A.

The city of angels, the city of dreams
The city of Los Angeles, where people work and play as a team

Irene Olsakowski

Winter Wind

Blow wind blow, and fall snow fall
You don't bother me at all.
Snug and warm by the fireside,
My thoughts and dreams serenely glide
To that mountain cabin in the pines
Where we have such happy times;

Where from dawn to dusk the shadows play
Like fairies flitting bright and gay;
Where the whispering winds their stories tell
As magic Blue Creek casts its spell.
Warm as the fire is my heart inside
For the cabin's beauty does with me abide.

Blow wind blow, and fall snow fall
God's wonders amaze and cheer us all.

Jim E. Clarke II

Cherokee Rose

She beckons me by silver banjo strings
while I'm trapped in California's condo walls.
Her transistered Chattaoochee tongue brings
me to my love with magnolia smells. Bluebells
Her body's curved of trumpet vines. Bluebells
tangle with the foxtails. Catfish moon blues
my flesh inside her lilyed fen, where shells
sleep and swirling bugs blink in twilight hues.
I'm with her starling singing high on cue
and beavers whittling on willow sticks.
My sweetheart kisses me with morning dews
and evening berries sweetening near creeks.
But this melodious affair will close
with the song. Farewell, my Cherokee Rose.

Bryan P. Franks

Path of a Woman

Who is worth millions,
But Is sometimes impoverished?

Who is a scholar in many fields,
Yet sometimes holds no degrees?

Who can endure pain beyond belief,
But is sometimes looked upon as weak?

Who sacrifices their own life for others,
But is sometimes called selfish?

Who? A Woman, A Mother.

Balinda Knowles

Untitled

One day, all alone, we were here
No one to disturb our silent communication
No one but you and I to explore our ultimate passion

And, all alone, we were awaken within
Touching the very depths of our souls
Experiencing life, as if only with love we would breathe
And tasting our love, as only life can relish each breath of air

All alone, in a world of our own, we were merged as one
Fused together, as body is to soul, in a timeless arena of ecstasy
—for all else to envy a passage to
We were here, just you and I
Communicating the passion within our souls
Breathing each breath of air as one
Unconscious of the timeless era we awoke to

Yes . . . just you and I
We were here one day
All alone

Ildiko P. Balogh

The Quest

Lonely, desolate, void of happiness overfilled with turmoil.
I venture out in search of answers to the emptiness inside me-
To all the uncertainty and questions haunting me,
To all the ifs running through my head and finally,
Get clues to the hows, whens, whys, whats and wheres ever
resurging.
I wonder if I'm alone in feeling like this?
If I still have a little portion of sanity left in me?
How can I be alone and empty?
When did this inescapable hole get me?
Why do I run from myself to nowhere?
What could get me away from this trauma?
Where is this ever-present anomaly taking me?
I look around for comfort and serenity
Then I noticed the peaceful movement of the trees,
Responding gently and in tune with the wind,
I felt the happiness radiating from the chirping birds.
Then I decided, I'll sway with the trees,
Sing with the birds and divulge the congestion within me,
Cherish and draw inspiration form the perfect solace—Nature

Abiola Oladoke

Pearls of Love

White as crystal, bright as sun,
Drowns beneath the soul, flares of red and dreams of gold.
Precious as the wind, rolling by,
Gentle as the light, blue sky.
Hides behind the darkest corners, one warm day in the mid of summer.
Fluttering of a bluebird's wings
Strawberry cheesecake, smooth, whipped cream.
Crescent moon, on a winter's night, cries of joy, hope, delight!
Stars that amazingly shine, sending shivers down the spine.
Topaz, orange, moonbeam yellow, wishes granted love mellow.
Pearls of love is what you see, what you feel relaxingly.

Ashley Parker

Immortal Adoration

Why must everything good always fall apart?
There is nothing she can do when her life is over just when she it
Should start.
She loves him so much she know she'll never really be able to part.
She treasures everyday and hour she ever spent with him.
She still loves him with all her heart.
She knows somewhere deep down inside herself she must let him go.
She just doesn't know it she can because sometimes it's so hard to do so.
She finally says goodbye, her tears will never cease to flow.
For he is gone and now her life is filled with woe.

Rachell Leach

Today Seems So Long

Today the air seemed to carry a softness though
lingering at times to caress the limbs of a forgotten
tree, or to sternly shake a sleepy pine or to dust
the peddles of a beautiful rose, who then gratefully
scented the air with its special perfume.

Today a soft cloud hung lazily in the bluest sky,
it seems that its softness was tempered with determination
and strength, I felt that if I reached high
enough I could touch a wisp of its beauty
would it, could it engulf me?

Today I gazed at the beauty of a retiring sun, as it settled
behind a magnificent mountain, a proud mountain, it was
chosen. The sun had a resting place. The sky above it
beamed, its cheeks a rosy red above and ever so gray beard,
with hints of orange that seemed to dance about.

Now with darkness surrounding me, the air remains scented
with the special perfume, the determination, the strength.
The softness of the clouds still hang in the air.
The Sun it will return, the moon tells me so.
Then I wonder . . ."What will tomorrow bring?"

Carolyn Y. Brooks

A Mom

To my Better Half
How do I? Tell the world and my family.
What hard times this life can bring.
When do you say my child is my heart and life.
Time in here; life can be short or long!
On day one when she was first
told, can me her own mom?
Understand the pain, angry
in her heart and soul.
But to just: say keep the
faith in herself and God's
And believe that this not
the end a life of being!
Off all the numbered days one
off many more too come.

Be sure your child, son or daughter
Live's their life to the fullness
and all it entails
And to do this live to be happy
and live with all
the joy too be had!

Mommie R. Battle

Forever in a Day

I live one day after the other, the one
thing that I think that is pretty amazing
is the love that we have for each other
When were not together I miss you so much,
And I long for your touch, I think to myself
Can we be any further away, and still be forever in a day.
When were not together I'm just counting
the minutes until were together my friend,.
You have no idea just how much you mean
to me, and what it really means to be free
to be who you are, I've often felt like I've
spent most of my life living for someone
else, and the other part of my life loving
you, and wanting very much to be with you,
and trying very hard to get next to you,
at least with you I always knew who I was,
And the things that I never knew,
All of a sudden I knew with you, and also
that you meant everything to me,
and you allowed me to be free to be me

Stacie Stafford

Thank You

I wish that there were more words to say
  What I feel inside,
You've brought me back to life again
When a part of me had died. Thank you.

For all the kind words of encouragement,
  And those of correction too.
    This only was to show me,
    That Jesus is within you.

Always there when I needed help,
  Always with a smile,
Always knowing that for all of us,
  You go that extra mile.

You heard God's call and you answered it,
  With a willing heart and mind,
Are there better Pastors to be found?
  No, you're both one of a kind!

Thank you seem such small words,
  For all you've done for me,
I'm glad to have you as my mom and dad,
  In God's Visalia family.

Mary Ann Rojas

Is There Life?

Is there life on other planets?
I often wonder if it could be.

Nobody knows for sure,
isn't it fun to explore the possibility?

Aliens with eighteen eyes? Maybe.
Aliens with twenty legs? There just might be.
Aliens that look like you and me? Probably.

Is there life on other planets?
Possibly.

Wesley Farr

Ten Mice Recently Deceased

Ten lives lost in one day—
Ten slithering corpses, ten smashing craniums,
Trap's claps oversounding squeals—
Too many slaughters for one soft conscience.

There's a spider in the bathtub
I don't intend to kill,
'Cause ten lives lost in one day
Is more than a lifetime's fill.

Jennifer Lee Kirkham

The Tree

Your shadow casts a spectrum of images.
I know they all belong to you,
But I am amazed at their differences.
Which one is the real you?
Shades of gray and blue mix with the cold
white of the snow.
I ponder your existence,
I try to understand you.
While one image seems beautiful and brilliant,
The one closest to it appears harsh and cold.
Here, here you seem vulnerable.
I think, only if I could understand you,
Then maybe you could somehow understand me.
But just when I think I have you figured out,
I notice another piece to your puzzle.
The longer I gaze at the intricate shapes you form
The more confused I become.
So, in your own way, you shut me out.
and you remain a mystery to me.

Jenny Esquivel

The Dance

Little pitter patters
become the dancing feet.

And in my mind's eye,
a drum begins to beat.

The fire's flame dances—
a song never heard.

And swaying to the music
flames become firebirds.

And in the firelight I sit
watching in wonder
till the scene before me
vanishes as thunder.

Lydia Messick

As Strong As Me

You told me once,
and you told me twice.
That our love was over,
I know you tried to be nice.

My heart still hurts,
from the way you taunt me.
Over and over,
can't you just let me be?

I still have feelings
for the boy I once knew.
That held me when I cried,
and asked me what he could do.

You changed and grew,
to far away to see.
But love is strong,
as strong as me.

Patricia Nieman

Untitled

Dedicated to Ryan Paudreana
You're so cute
And Ryan
You're so nice
I wish you
All the
"Luck"
'Cause I know
you'll be
alright
And that
Ball will
get you
There
on time
So Ryan
I wish
you were
Really mine

Marlene E. Brown

A YEAR OF HORSES

Horses have fun,
in the warm Summer sun.
Horses munch hay,
on a cold Winter's day.
Horses mate for a reason,
in the chilly Fall season.
Foals are sometimes born,
on an early Spring morn'.

Kerri A. Nottingham

Golden Wedding

We met and it was lovely spring.
Then all through glorious summer days,
That sped with lightning touch,
We danced as though our feet
Were loath to touch the ground.
Now through autumn's mellow glow
We walk—and hand in hand—
And hark the sound of merry song
On younger lips. Myriad melodies—
And one of them is ours.
And may it then be so, when yet
Another season casts its slower spell,
That we will sit, heart in heart
And thought in thought! We sing it not
Nor measure with our toe; still
Winter has not touched our hearts,
For there we dance and sing the way
We did that lovely spring we met.

Louise Dodd Gerken

Edmund Fitzgerald

A fateful ship left its shore,
Knowing not the tragedy in store.
Many trips trying to prevail,
All the cargo that it held.

As they sail the great lakes,
Sailors knowing not their fate.
Keeping their duties all in line,
Sailing again for the last time.

This is their life to be on board,
Sailing from shore to shore.
Working together as they sailed,
Through storms, wind, or hail.

The water once more took hold,
Taking the "Fitzgerald" down below.
A ferocious storm lashing its fury,
Sending the ship to be buried.

The ship and crew lying together
Resting in peace forever.
Weep not all those left behind,
The crew will live again in time.

Juanita M. Cole

Cold Sleep

Let me sleep
in cryogenic bliss
engrave my tag
with frozen mathematics
feed my flesh
with nitrogenous kiss
record my dreams
on paper hieroglyphics

Inject me then
with what may seem
a happiness
thaw my brain
when you have found
the long-lost gene
for loneliness
if you cannot
then do not rouse me
from the cold machine
but bathe me in the Hippocrene
where poets convene.

Gordon Schlundt

My Little Red Piano

My little red piano,
So pretty, soft, and small,
I couldn't trade a dime for you,
Nor dolly, dress, or ball.
My little red piano,
Oh how I love you so,
I can play you anytime,
In sunshine, rain or snow.
My little red piano,
Now you've gone away,
But I'd always play upon you,
If you would've stayed.

Jessalyn Brooks Guizzotti

Borrowed Son

Dedicated to Ronnie
I borrowed you, when
you were born.
I tried to keep you
safe and warm.
I tried to be always there.
Then your mom came back
and I was air.
I loved you then,
I love you now
I eat, sleep, and drink you everyday.
For I cannot see any other way.
I wanted it better,
it didn't work that way
you'll always be in my heart
night and day.
You're close to your mom now,
maybe it's suppose to be.
But I would borrow you
again if ever need be.

Roberta Richardson

We Can No Longer Be

I told you I didn't love
you, I told you I didn't care..
You wouldn't give up now they
locked you away, you were told
to stay away. But in reality
I do care, deep inside I
know this is not the answer
Now you need to understand
you are no longer a child now
just a helpless man. I hear
your cry for help and I will
help you if I can please
look into your heart and
set me free as I told you
once before we can no longer be.

Holly Ann Pinter

"Touch of an Angel"

Angels are something you
can feel, and often never see.

But wherever I am they
"Often seem to be"
Equal of me, as Equal to you.

Angels have daily flights,
from Heaven to earth,
to help those in need
on this Earth.
And as you believe in
Heaven above, you will
find your "Angel of love."

Betty Angel

Silver Charm

Bolted
Out of gate

With furor
And grace

Tore down
The track

With muscles
Stretched out

To win
Preakness race.

His head pulled
Neck extended

Far as it could go
Determined to win

He danced and pranced
For owner

And trainer
At Pimlico.

Dixie B. Childress

A Testament To Life

The iris there upon the stand
Its beauty simple, yet so grand
Its petals brighten a sunless day
Its fragrance chases gloom away.

The iris presence fills the room
And sweeps aside as if a broom
The snagging darkness lurking there
Upon the bed, the stand, the chair.

A simple symbol of fresh life
Its sight and scent refreshing
Reminds of daily miracles
Brings fresh hope to my wishing.

Robert B. Aukerman

Poems

To write a poem would be
to easy I have so much to say
To write about my love for
would be written without delay
To write a book would take some
time but it's not hard to do
'Cause the best things I've
ever written were always about you

Jessie Rae Gibson

Ribbons

I had to leave you, Ribbons
Couldn't even say good-bye
But I shall always remember you
And your beautiful big green eyes

You'll never know the joy you brought
How much you eased my pain
And you're the one that helped me
To believe in prayer again

You were just a big black cat
But God sent you—this is true
For He knew you needed me
As much as I needed you

Helen M. O'Brien

Untitled

I know where I've been
Saw things most have not
I walked on the wild side
Blamed it on the life I got

You look me in the eyes
Then simply turn away
You saw I was hurting
But didn't bother to stay.

I'm in a state of depression
But they say I'm insane
They see the anger and rage
Not the sadness and pain.

Two sides to every story
What if only one is told?
No one will question the other
So its locked away in the cold

I know where I've been
I know what I've been doing
But I hope I'll soon find out
Where the hell I'm going

Vikki Lynn Palmisano

Cross of Gold, Cross of Wood

We wear a cross of gold around our necks
And make our faith seem so complex.
We go throughout our many days
Saying we follow in His ways,
But when they look inside our lives,
They see we are only trying to survive.
We fear joining the dead,
Though it isn't the dead we dread.
We fear what is hiding inside,
The secrets and sins that try to hide.
Yet, on a cross of woods Jesus died,
And by our heavenly Father He resides,
For through His very death,
He gave us a new, refreshing breath.
He granted us a better life
Without suffering, pain, or strife.
Our Savior has set us free
By His blood that was shed on Calvary.
I look forward to my reward eternal,
And, to Him, I'll remain forever loyal.

Amber Voehl

You Don't Need Eyes To See

. . . and you don't have to see me
to understand
that I can get easily
the hardest to get man.

Although, I do slip
and show nothing but fury . . .
above all other things
I still show my black beauty.

The wisest of persons
doesn't need eyes to see.
that I am the epitome
of all black beauty.

The epitome . . . the epitome . . .
you don't need eyes to see
that nothing but pure beauty
flows through and out of me.

And you don't have to see me . . .

Amisha Guinn

Invitation

The world of today has become
ominous with its freakish
attitudes causing harm one onto another.

Hate is spread by ugly, loudmouthed
antagonists hoping to ignite flames
from hell onto earth causing
explosions and death everywhere.

I must seek refuge within
a world of fantasy where
I can dwell and be surrounded
by Mother Nature's beautiful
creations . . . a togetherness filled
with love and caring.

P.S.
Join me in imagery for a
dump on hell and
all its siblings!

Evelyn Giles

Help Yourself

Expect others to love you?
Love yourself
Help yourself
Train yourself
Force yourself to improve
with strong determination
God as your guide
Go ahead, you cannot lose
Hurry, get busy
Been complacent enough
Find a library—read, read.
Place yourself on the highest plane
Reach for the stars
Go past Jupiter, and Mars
Obtain that goal
Believe you can win
Have a consistent attitude
Use all your energy, my friend
There isn't anything you can win
Help yourself.

Ella Stewart

These Empty Arms

These empty arms are waiting,
　For someone just like you,
And when you get between them,
　They will know just what to do.

My nights and days are lonely,
　As I think about your charms,
My life will never be complete,
　Until your in these empty arms.

I remember the day I met you,
　In an office down the hall,
For a lady only five-foot-two,
　You sure seemed awfully tall.

Your gracefulness and beauty,
　Is setting off my alarms,
It makes me want you more than ever,
　In these empty arms.

I'm a country boy from New York,
　Spent time on all those farms,
I came all the way to Oregon,
　To fill these empty arms.

Jim Campbell

Weeping Willow

Weeping Willow,
gentle as the breeze,
what do you weep?
Do you cry out the
soft sounds of the morning bird
or the fierce fire
of the midday sun?
Tell me, weeping willow,
why do you weep?
Do you weep for the children,
weeping for their mothers?
Do you weep for Mother Nature,
struggling to keep herself alive?
Do you weep for peace,
wishing for its existence?
Weeping willow,
gentle as the breeze,
I hear you weeping
I weep the same.

Kathryn Wieckhorst

Misunderstood

What is a little love . . .
I don't want your life
I don't care for millions . . .
Nor polished diamonds

I long to feel the smile
That lingers in your eyes
When you touch little precious

You skimp on your tenderness
But pour your lust-like . . .
Steaming lava into my crevice

And!—at times . . . most times . . .
My ocean still raging . . .
All I want . . . is a little love

Stephen Allistair Yearwood

Tides

Mother earth...living, breathing,
grandly measured in her strides.
First inspiring...than receding
see her movements in the tides.

Mother nature...ever breeding,
new spring life in depth resides
chain of life unbroken, feeding
on her pulsing, plenteous tides.

Flooding first she lifts, meanders
'til no higher can she ride.
Then in summer she decanters
shellfish fresh from the ebbing tide.

Wafted spume and salten odors
wintry mixtures clash, collide
watery deeps with roiling borders
tamed mere slightly by her tide.

We can learn from nature's ranging
truth meets truth on every side
our life's seasons need be changing
true in spirit . . . like the tide.

K. G. Wood

The Poet

It may be late at night
When the poet sits down to write,
To try to find, just the right line
To let someone know in time
Just what you wanted to say,
On that particular day
To express the feelings
That often go unsaid
As we go off to bed.

Sometimes the words come easy,
And then again, quiet hard,
To put together a verse
That doesn't sound like a curse,
And wonder, "Where did that come
from?"

Feelings are brought from inside
To the surface,
No longer to hide
From the world outside,
And you feel your soul is cleansed.

Ruth Cline

Red Lobster

Red Lobster,
A great place to eat.
It tickles my fancy,
Right down to my feet.
Lobster, shrimp,
A sailor's delight.
I eat there all day,
And into the night.
Prompt service,
I wish you could see.
Eat there today,
And be just like me!

David B. Herriman

He And She

He'll build a new lake town
She'll wear a bold silk gown
He a Lord from a great name
She a lady of a grand fame
He has a home of big rock
She has a home by a dock
He stands tall in the new hide
She stands well at his left side
He'll hunt soon his prey a dove
She'll turn soon to pray for love
He may soon go for a walk
She may soon stop for a talk
He has hair now thing and gray
She has hair still long and gray
He can see the near star blue
She will ever be his love true
He'll place the dead in a tomb
She'll form new life in her womb

Wayne Augustus Harrell

Christmas

Christmas is about
Sharing and caring.
Christmas is a time when
Families and friends get together
Christmas is a time when
People start to care.
I like Christmas because
It brings love and peace.

Stacey Fisher

Regret

I got bolder
as I got older
I thought I was strong
but I was wrong
If I had only listened
I would have glistened
instead of sparkling
I'm snorkeling
in my own river of tears
with all these fears
I wish you were here with me
but I wanted to flee
Now I wish
I could change this dish
that has been served to me.

Chrystal Litzie

Halloween

Orange stacks of pumpkins
Say its time for Halloween
When witches, ghosts, and goblins
Come upon the scene.
To their chants of "Trick or Treat"
We give them goodies galore.
Then they leave with laughter sweet
Run hand-in-hand for more
To another house that's waiting
With treats of every kind,
Then go on never knowing
The joy they've left behind.

Deane Bruce

How Did You Know?

How did you know
I needed you
when you walked quietly into my life?

How did you know
there was a lonely space
in my heart that only you could fill?

How did you know
you were the one
who could make my life complete?

How did you know,
for I didn't know
until your love touched me.

Lucile Gieg

Divorce's Ache

One is ashen, the other brown,
these two children bright and bold.
One is two, the other four;
two children to love and hold.

Both are devils, in their way,
mischievous, too, but never sad.
A devil, now could ne'er beset,
this love they have for their Dad.

A father, aye, and none better
to these two children that I kiss.
For him they are his life and rock,
for, you see, they are his.

Pity though he cannot share
the joy they give him, day to day.
Weekends only is his fare,
to their way of loving play.

This, his torch, he doth bear well;
a torch with which I could not.
His love awaits, within, to flow . . .
And to that, I raise my cup

Margot Fridge Clark

United Clique

The bond of bikers will never part,
For they would always understand.
Brotherhood held within the heart,
Always lending a helping hand.

Their rodeos are all fun and games;
With money raised for a needed cause.
They reach out and obtain their aim;
Helping children is their own applause.

Freedom being the ultimate goal;
In the wind, free as a bird.
Clearing the mind, cleansing the soul;
Thunder being the only sound heard.

The rumble makes them feel alive,
When one or twenty wheels by.
The beauty of the chrome thrives,
Being driven by a cool guy.

Leather jackets and long hair,
Tattoos which may be bizarre.
They are judged, but they don't care.
They know who they really are.

Ann Yanulavich

When

When will I be old enough?
When will I be smart enough?
When will I be pretty enough?
When will someone love me enough,
To make the pain go away?
When will I be good enough,
To be recognized as one of them?
When will my best be good enough?
When will I be educated enough?
Will the day ever come when,
What I do is enough?

Colette Palmerio

A Moment In Silence

Close your eyes for a moment
Imagine a place of peace,
Picture yourself by the mountains
All troubles are released.
Imagine a colony of stars
You lie close by the ocean,
The winds from the waters cover you
While the waves more gently in motion.
Slowly gaze toward the horizon
As the sky and waters combine,
Never thinking of looking back
With a painted picture in mind.

Carol Ann Asbury

Images of You

I look in the mirror
And what do I see?
A part of you that's
In me.
There's so much of you
That I can see
Through so very many memories
The brilliance in your eyes,
The warmth of your smile
Is shining through
Me within every mile
All I can do, and
All I can say, is
You're seen in me everyday.

Jennifer Elssworth

When I Fly up to Heaven

When I fly up to heaven
And meet my Holy God,
The angels will surround me,
And my loved ones will embrace me.
We'll sing in exaltation
To the glory of our God.

We'll walk the streets of heaven,
We'll see our mansions there
That God had said we'd inherit
If we kept His laws down here.
So we'll sing His praises
In that holy land above.

Rozella D. Ashbaucher

Untitled

You look so blue,
Every time I see you

My heart keeps beating,
It will stop if you're leaving

You and I go together,
You never know, it may not last forever

The other girl you like looks so happy,
Her hair is so nappy.

Her name is Beth,
She looks like a mess

I am sweet,
She is a neat freak

If you don't stop me,
I will fly to the sea,

I stepped out the window,
It made me blow

I started falling very fast,
I had to let our very big gasps

Then when I hit the ground with death,
All you had left to go to was Beth.

Melanie Bond

At Twisted Pines

The rose does pale
before the vine,
where now, the shadows dwell,
and moss does eat
the scattered stones of time.
The moon webs glimmer,
where now, the owls
do screech in silence still.
Where now, no words nor lines remain,
to speak of times,
when hopes grew tall,
and flowers did bloom.
Where now, the winds
do whisper still,
"oh, when was then?"
"oh, when was then?"
Where now, the rose does pale
before the vine,
and shattered dreams do search,
among the scattered stones of time.

Richard R. Curren

Homeless

You stand in the street,
All by yourself.
No one to take you in,
No one to clean you up.
You are left outside to fade away,
For everybody to laugh at.
Merely a statistic,
That's all you are, face it.
No one cares what you are really like.
If you had friends or family.
All they look at is your appearance,
The layers of old, torn clothes.
The dirty hair and face.
Homeless, dirty, and sad.
People just care about themselves,
They don't care about you!
Broken hearts, broken dreams.

Amy Balsley

Positive Impression

Hummingbirds hum
Butterflies fly
Little colts run
Babies cry
Chickens crow
Bunnies hop
Gardens grow
Over
Fence tops
Sunflowers show
Daisies below
That petaled
To nectar collectors
in the garden jungle
of printed Calico
a rumble, a bumble
a buzz from
Strawberries sweet
Jamming, jamming
For winter's treat

Delphia B. Nogosky

Years

As the years have past
We've found friendships that would last.
Through the years we will find
that teachers have filled the
wells of our minds.
But in the years of childhood dreams
We reach for goals with tattered seams.
And as we find our life's a mess
it is time that we must confess
of our shattered hearts and
broken memories.
And in our darkness we see a light
of a golden color that is bright.
And in that light we see new dreams
that is not so tattered at the seams.

Valie Welch

Untitled

Little dream adorn the walls
In here and down the hall
Solitary pieces inspiring my
fascination
Drawing me with their
soul sedation.
And drawn in my mind
are these pictures which are
now uncertain reality
Temporary respites from what
ail me.

Erica Stein

The Drifter

As I flow thru time
A drift in my mind
Time and space has no meaning
My vision quest exceeds the gleaming
A distance but a step
A step but a mile
A mile but eternity
Like the seed of the mighty oak
Planted near the river
Flourish in strength and beauty
But a drifter flows like a river
Mighty at times calm at other
Picking up life experience as he goes
Drifts
The drifter has all he needs
Of society be bleeds

Charles Caldwell

All I Do

All I do,
is think about you.
Every night and everyday,
it's all the same.
Emotional visions
and emotional collisions.

All I do,
is want you.
Every minute of every hour,
but I can only cower.
I run away with only a guess,
of no or yes.

All I so,
is try to please you.
But all you say,
is go away.
I wish I could be,
more than just me.
So you could love,
this poor lonesome dove.

David Pratt

A Rude Awakening

To cry
To feel the confusion
To be abandoned
To be totally alone
To realize
You're the one to blame.

To be blind
Unfeeling to others
Selfish
Always wanting
Never giving
You deserve the pain.

Open your eyes
See the destruction
You have made

It's not others
But you that has to change

Barbara Hinkebein

A New Beginning

It is cruel and heartbreaking
To have to leave the ones you began with
To create a new beginning
With a new identity.
For the world to grow,
We pay this price.

Holly Nolte

The Watcher of the Skies

Behold Him, single on the cross,
The Watcher of the Skies,
Outstretched amidst a thousand cries,
Left for profit or loss.
Never a Man so deep,
Or met with such defiance,
Watchfully praying, lanced to silence.
Nor since felt, such unrestful sleep.
His last cry, an atonement bell,
"Jerusalem . . . Jerusalem,"
Opening Heaven, gating hell.
Blood stained nails, halfstem,
Remained furrowed in the cross,
Go profit! or hammer in loss.

George T. Solotruck

Dreams

Rosy visions
Little house
Picket fence
Loving spouse

Bountiful life
Boy and girl
Happy ever-after
Perfect world

Not!

Charlina Recob

Untitled

A thousand willows wept
Upon a strange forgotten land
While a thousand lost souls
Searched endlessly through
The black sky

As I cried

Demons took comfort
In caves of desperation
In this nation of confusion

I cried

Loveless children run free
Screaming for answers
And burying their heads
In the sand

I cry

Teresa Perry

Outfielder

The dust drifting from
its ever-changing home
And the outfielder yearning
for ungiven flight.
Silence stretches
For the apprehensive
audience
The soaring sphere
Holds either victory or defeat.

Erika Jacome

Sunset

A sunset
is a blend of colors
bumping into the sun
peeking above the mountains.

Ryan Holland

Faith Walk

Faith is to walk . . .
Walk when I want to run
Run to safe places
Beckoning embrace
Fool's gold

Faith is to walk . . .
When I cannot see my way
When my strength is gone
When my mind is clouded
When my soul seems adrift

Faith is to walk . . .
When my feet stumble
When my body wears out
When my vision is blurred

Faith is to walk . . .
But, Lord, if I can't walk
Faith is to firmly stand

Darlene Stafford

Waking with the Sun

Fire rises in the sky,
glowing warmth wakes my eye,
I gaze a while, then lift my head,
how I loathe to leave my bed,
He is staunch, keeps me safe,
rescues me with loyal embrace,
To my feet, stretch and yawn,
my limbs are an infant fawn,
Cannot walk, must learn once more,
I stumble to the shower door,
The tile feels cold, it's hard to bear,
scent of mildew in the air,
Rain falls and splashes my face,
sleep is gone without a trace,
I am alive, no turning back,
the day is now a one-way track,
I go on and on until I tire,
anew my head rests, as does the fire.

Amanda Harding Atkinson

A Memory

I remember what we did,
The words we used to say;
Never "I love you"
But "You're in my heart today."

We danced a million dances
And I remember every one,
Because each one was special,
Thanks to your love.

In your arms I was special
Because, to you, I was everything.
We never really said it,
But we wished for eternity

Now you are far away
But in my heart you stay,
Because love never fades;
It lingers from day to day.

Lorraine Norris

Going Nowhere Fast

The first time
I talked with him, I was fourteen,
cold, and frustrated
with my fist clenched
January. New year.
A beginning for me . . . for us.
As I discussed my life,
he teared . . .
The screen showed no affection,
nor did I.
The scent faded, as I continued.
My only disruption
was a comment of defense, a lie
and a sip of his watered soda.
I confessed, he denied.
It was the end . . .
The screen began to show
the tears, they faded with the lights,
and I sat back in disappointment.

Angela Lunetta

Horses

Feeling an urge to run.
Having so much fun.
Horses!
Gliding swiftly over their courses
Being pulled by unknown forces
Don't tire
Running through the fire
Running through the glare
Rewarded by fresh air
No stopping, nor resting.
Until death.
Horses

Brittany Hunter

This Dark Road

My search for the truth
Has led me down this dark road
All the smiling faces
And the lies they told
They claimed to have the answers
That would save my soul
But I keep walkin' to the light
That I see at the end of this dark road

Every step is harder than the last
But I'll carry the weight
Of the present and the past
Some have called me a misfit
And other stone throwers an outcast
I'll embrace what's in my heart
I'll keep walkin' hard and fast
My eyes fixed upon the light
At the end of this dark road

Jefferson E. Kerry

Flowers

Flowers are beautiful
Flowers are brilliant
Flowers are colorful
Flowers have little petals so soft
Petals that drip with dew and raindrops
Brilliant, brilliant colors of all kinds
Colors that shine in the sunlight all day.

Heather Stanley age 10

Vietnam

1970 was the year
Dying was my greatest fear
Tromping thru the paddies
Carefully trying to avoid betty
Always trying to keep myself steady
Charlie comes and Charlie goes
With that thought, keep on your toes
Look to the left, peer to the right
Pale with fright
Thirteen months my tour lasted
I came home
But my mind was blasted
Treated like dirt—spit upon
Finally got a job
But every night I return to
Vietnam

Richard W. Carl

Untitled

It's such a joke!
The way people claim to be
your friends, when they really
don't care at all. It's all just a big
popularity contest.

And I wondered if they knew,
all prim and proper,
the real meaning of life beyond
their cars and houses and clothes,
which they flaunt whenever possible,
how to live in happiness without
the materialistic things
that are so irrelevant,
and do they understand feelings
and emotions and love and trust or do
they only see what they want to?

Angela De Bruyn

Winter's Practiced Disguise

Rooted silhouettes reflect shadows
as morning's recess has drawn to a close

Steep inclines lie broad . . .
desolate as wind-wisped flakes settle
on the highest branches of the weeping
willow, hurling gentle implacability

Brook vessels quench the last drink
of still waters . . . for it knows the
shallow drops of dew . . . how quickly
dawn's early light
fades its luster

Winter . . . a temporary substitute
antiquated, thrusting forward
unasked

And I wake from a December's nap
with slight altercations in posture,
skin loosened from my limbs,
a cup of cappuccino

Kimberly Whitis

Banked Fires

Beware of banked fires they say.
They can be quite deceptive.
Sparkless with no sign of flame
'Till bestirred by breeze or hand—
First a flicker, soon a blaze.
Reach out, then, my friend, for warmth.
Caution, then, my friend, for burn.

May Spencer Ringold

Untitled

Our love is stronger then man
made steel,
It explores one another's life
with a powerful will . . .
Our love was destined
to be together
It's a special element
to withstand any weather . . .
Our love was designed
and crafted with care
A unique type of love
That two people share . . .
Our love has gone through ups and
downs,
a bonding love that can't be found . . .
Our love isn't old, it's fresh and new,
created by God for me and you . . .

"Our Love". . .
Anthony D. Hawkins

I Have Today

I rise to greet a brand new day
for once glad to be on my way,
I vow while going out the door
to look for beauty not seen before

The dappled sunlight through the trees
the cool green grass, a gentle breeze,
white fluffy clouds o'er azure seas,
I take the time to notice these

I remember all the days of worry
when all I ever did was hurry,
and realize now it is so sad
Not to have loved the things I had

Though yesterday is forever gone
and though tomorrow may never dawn,
I have today, a day to love
with grateful thanks to God above
Priscilla A. Kirkland

The Rose

I offer this rose
For your lips so fine
I offer my friend ship
For the sparkle in your eyes
The tears on your cheeks
Like raindrops on a rose
Show me more love
Than words have ever shown
The fact that you listen
Because I am your man
Make my house a home
Just because you can
And always seems happy
When I hold your hand
Show me I'm a very
Very lucky man.

Mist Glantz

Wing Song

Sleeping cherub
Gliding in a White Dream
With pink-cheeked wonder
And platinum coils
Her innocence enticingly
Clouds skimming
Breathing in, breathing out
Life and kisses
Sweeter than heavenly cream
Donna M. Bassett

Child of Darkness

Child of darkness
So young,
Yet old beyond your years.
We were not aware
Of the battle within
Nor see the silent, internal tears.

Child of our hearts
So vital,
Yet gone before your time.
Please forgive us our human frailties
For we did not sense the inner turmoil
Nor recognize the other fatal signs.

Child of Heaven
So far away,
Yet in spirit, always so near.
May you walk with God now,
Never again to be alone
In the shadow of your fears.
Brenda J. Hunt

Untitled

The ashes fall slowly
like they don't want to
let go of the cigarette,
like they don't know where
their going after they get
flicked off the cigarette
and the red hot ashes
fall like they're sick of
everything, and they don't
care what happens after
they get flicked off just
like some people the ones
who go slowly are afraid
what's going to happen
after they let go of life,
but the people like the
red hot ashes don't care
what happens after life
and they just want to die...
Gretchen La Lena

Baseball

It is the bottom of nine,
The score says it all,
One team thinks the game's fine,
Until the crack of the ball.

The ball went deep,
The fielder raced back,
The ball flew in a somber sleep,
Until Smack!!!

The fielder hit the fence,
The ball flew to the stands,
The pitcher walked to his bench,
He looked at his hands.

His heart was shattered,
He looked at the mound,
He got madder,
He let his team down.

"Until another day," yelled the pitcher
As the hero was carried out;
"Good game," said the catcher,
But the hero had a doubt.

Chris Santucci

My Mother

The Lord above looked down to earth,
To see if He could find,
A proper girl to be in charge
Of this poor soul of mine.

He looked around and when He saw
The one with a merry heart,
He made the choice because He knew
This one would take my part.

She took the job with Joy, I know
And did a good one too.
Teaching courage, faith and hope
And lessons tried and true.

That's why I love you, Mother mine.
You're special, don't you see?
I'm glad the Lord looked all around
And chose you just for me.
Kathleen Spear

Frustration

It is not just another word to me,

It's a feeling of being helpless.

Knowing what should be done
And not knowing how to do it.

Knowing what should be said
And not knowing what to say.

Knowing what you want
And not knowing how to get it.

God, please forgive me
for being a mother and not knowing.
Bettye J. Davis

Miracles

Lost somewhere inside,
The vastness of this life
We are sometimes reminded
That miracles do occur,
Miracles as many
As the world is vast
Yet, somehow hard to see
I am, from time to time, reminded
Of the miracle of friendship
And the knowledge that you, too
Are traveling in the vastness
Of this life—
Hopefully—
Never too far away from me.
Sandy Knight

Liking Honey

Sweet honey
Moon honey
Rain honey
Honey dew
Sweet honey

Sticky honcy
Lily honey
Lilac honey
Honey sweat
Sticky honey

Hot honey
Star honey
Soul honey
Honey tears
Hot honey

Eric James

That's Poetry

What is poetry?
Poetry is souls
Painting pictures
On the black holes
of life.

Margaret Partlow

Midwest Prairie

The kismet of so many solitary hares.
First star in the winter sky.

Mary M. DeVier

Rain

Trickling,
Splishing, dripping,
Although the sky is gray,
It's making silver puddles on
This rainy, rainy, day. The air is
Moist and cool, and it dances
With the trees, while the pelting
Of the raindrops pitter-patters
In the breeze. The gutters gurgle,
Bubble, drip; the birds fly down
To take a sip. And as they
circle, swoop, and dive,
They make the puddles
come alive.

Dania Ilatahet

Prefunctory Man

Perfunctory man
Same thing everyday
Says "Hello" and goes on his way

Perfunctory Man
Not profound nor deep
An original thought he cannot keep

Perfunctory Man
Conforms with them all
United they stand, together they fall

Perfunctory Man
Same day after day
Ask him to think and he will run away

Perfunctory Man
Alone he will die
Unknown, unmourned, one-dimensional guy

Dennis W. Waltz

Revelation

Dear Lord,
I do not know how long you knocked
Before I heard your voice.
I only know one quiet day, I heard
And softly lifted up my latch
Enough to look at you.
You looked at me.
I opened wide my door
And asked you in.
You came, and supped with me
And I with you.
My house is now suffused with light
And filled with peace and laughter
Because each day you sup with me
And I with you.

Mary F. Asay

Pounded Until I Bled

Like a nail I stand,
stiff and strong I wait.
For the time I am struck
to the time I am beat.
I have been pounded down
by burdens.
Beaten bare with conflicts,
and stripped naked with stupidity.
My striker strong and heavy,
weighs me down with it all.

Like a light flashing before me,
I see my purpose.
Tight and stiff I stand,
to hold together the frame.
The frame of life I am.
A picture of peace I be.
A perfect place you see.

So come near and listen, one and all.
Listen with your heart and,
you will see why I bare the pain.

Renee Crozier

Cycles

Hugs and kisses
Birds and bees
Candy and flowers
A ring on blended knee
Hand in hand
Promises of love
I do you do
Two rings and a dove
A kiss and eternity
Some cake and champagne
A week and nine months
Intense labor pains
Doctors and hospitals
Ten fingers and ten toes
Blankets and diapers
Innocent eyes and a perky nose
Eighteen and high school
Beauty, brains and curls
Eyes meet and hearts soar
Girl meets boy meets girl

Kelly R. Liddell

Lives

Time seems to go by so quickly,
Everyone fades away into a memory.
But memories are now forgotten;
Only whispers of the wind,
Are known when they awake.
Lost feelings never surface.
Old trunks, cobwebs, and rusted locks;
All up in the attic,
Alongside wilted flowers.
Keepsakes from separate lives,
That have no one to tell their stories.
Experienced minds no longer remember,
Life and all of its joys and sorrows.
Most better off,
Safely put away in a tiny little world.
Children and grandchildren float by,
Names mean nothing to them.
Everyone just fades away . . .

Candice Hallinan

Untitled

You have it made,
Even when you don't make the grade.
You call for their love
And only get scolding from above.

They bring you in, they send you out,
And you really don't know why.
But your sounds of pain
Only make others cry.

Michael D. Sheaffer

A Memory

I thought I heard a sea bird call
Though far away is he.
I thought I felt a touch of spray
Blown briskly off the sea.

I thought I smelled the salty air
And perfumed flowers sweet.
I thought I felt the smooth white sand
So soft beneath my feet.

I thought I saw the diamond lights
The moon cast on the bay.
I thought I heard the whispering
Of palm trees as they sway.

I thought I heard a sea bird call
Though far away is he.
Alas, I realize now that it
Was just a memory....

Barbara Burke Pearce

As The Last Petal Falls

I've wished upon my candles
I've tried the shooting star.
I've looked around this universe
To find out who we are.

The stare from across the room,
The cold and lonely heart,
Reflection of the shining moon,
Has torn me apart.

And as the shadows faded
I couldn't hold back my tears.
My views of love were jaded,
All animosity and fears.

The great times of our lives
And what had we to show?
Cruel, heart breaking lies
As our spirits start to go.

And in a critical moment
All is said to be,
The petals of a dying rose,
With nothing left to see.

Brandy Bell

Brighter Ray

The sun is shining a brighter ray.
God has blessed us with a new day.
bringing hopes of loving songs,
lifting, spirits, for us to carry on.
Overcoming all the sad,
filling with joys once had.
The sun is shining a brighter ray.
God will bless us with each passing day,
Overcoming all lifes pains and fears
know always God is near.

Belinda Briggs

The Time Is Now

Somehow someone's calling
Somehow someone's singing
Somewhere way out in this world
Some church bells are still ringing.

Somewhere someone's living
Somewhere someone's crying
Somehow in this cruel dark world
Some baby's kept from dying.

The future lies ahead.
While the past's behind us all
And today is waiting here for us
Still looking oh so small

But why wait 'till the next moment
to show someone you care
For in that moment, they might be
no longer standing there.

Kylee Gower

Five Fish

Four fish:
red, gold, blue, old,
confined in a glass-walled coffin
Swimmers without passion

Fern algae
Mirror reflections,
an illusion of escape

Sad fish
Sad fish

Butter-scaled adventurer,
water-logged patina,
eternally in motion,
heading t'wards the light

Swim fish
Swim fish

Horizontal swimmer,
"Great Houdini,"
energized artist
Frantic plight

Endure fish, endure!

Cidy Drago

Fire in the Sky

Clouds across a golden sky,
Lights a figure in my eyes,
Sometimes bright,
Sometimes dim,
I wonder what it could have been.
High above in the sky,
A golden sun with many dyes,
Could that be what's in our eyes,
Or is it lost within the sky.
As night falls within the sky,
Tiny bubbles of gas lights the sky,
Could this be what's in our eyes,
Or should people wonder what might lie,
Within the dark blue sky.

Stacie Guidry

Haiku

The warmth of her hand,
encouragement from a touch.
An unspoken gift.

Richard Wrubel

Dying Within

The rain is falling outside my window.
Singing a sad melody.
I'm just wondering why you're leaving.
Does it really have to be?

I look into your eyes, my friend,
And see a love so true.
But reality soon sets in,
and I've become so blue.

I wish I had one more glance,
of beautiful face.
But you've already left me.
Gone without a trace.

I lay in bed and cry out for you,
in the middle of the night.
Without you here beside me,
I feel nothing but fright.

I can't help but dream of you.
Your voice, your skin.
Sometimes I feel like
I'm dying within.

Kimberly Michelle Curry

President John F. Kennedy 1917-1963

Whisper greatness into history
Shouting does not linger long
That which we would like to be
Runs away with laughing song
Now the moment is too soon
Will we understand His Will
For one man rode in the afternoon
And his greatness stood still.

George L. Darley, Jr.

A Winter's Day

Tears like ice
Pour down my face
Calling out to others
Come look at my pain

I stare into their eyes
But they do not notice
My heart has exploded
And all my dreaming has died

The cold wind blows
Through the snow filled trees
The leaves have long since fallen
And been taken by the breeze

Don't you see that I am naked and cold
Cover me with your love
Open your heart to my voice
Listen to me breathe

Tears like ice
Staining my cheeks
And there you are
Your hand on my face

Lori R. Reinhart

Untitled

I saw an old farmhouse,
Sitting on a small hill.
There was no glass in the windows,
The paint was starting to peel.

The house looked so lonely,
So quiet, so still,
It would be abandoned forever
On the soft, weedy hill.

Stephanie Fowler

A Teenager Discusses Her Future With Her Mother

I'm on the road
Called Dis-cov-er-y,
Looking for all
That's meant just for me.

You helped me, Mother,
As much as you could.
You did it for love—
Not 'cause you should.

All I need—I believe—
As far as I can see—
Is to find my potential
And use it, it's free.

Dear Mother, keep faith
With me, please do.
I'm hoping and praying
My dreams will come true.

Kristin Shelly

Troubled Times

When time are hard
And worries plentiful
Kneel down and pray
And know that God is on his way

I hope he hurries
And relieves my worries
I'm so depressed
I do need rest

My head aches
My heart breaks
O dear Lord
Make no mistakes

I'm so tired and weak
I even find it hard to speak
Please hear my prayers, dear Lord
Don't let me down
I know with your help, I can rebound

Eileen Chow

Changes Outside

With blue eyes and colored skin
No one knows what's within
By surprise she is mistaken
Everyone judges and she is shaken.

Her eyes open wide and turn green
A new color—what does it mean?
Her skin peels to a tan
A little darker than the sand.
She moves with ease
So graceful and pleasant
Yet no one knows she is present.

In the sun her hair turns from
black to eternal brunette.
Everyone turns by the change and is
startled yet.
She is still the same inside.
The truth bares itself not to hide.

Now she is new and bright
She isn't happy, but is it right?

Amanda Hyde

Promises of the Heart

I promise thee,
love, laughter and honesty.
I promise thee to always be,
for you, for me, for our family.

I promise thee
life with an everlasting arm.
I promise thee
smiles, happiness and charm.

I promise thee
the love thee deserves.
I promise thee
to try and never get on your nerves

I promise thee
to be there myself
I promise thee
to be there in sickness and in health

I promise thee
to be a true actor, and play the part,
that forever and always, the promises
I make are promises of the heart

C. B. McKnight

Would You See Me?

If you were me
would you see me,
The me that I know I could be
Would you see me?

When they all say
no matter the time of day
Yes, you did okay,
But he did it a better way

You see, if you were me
You would finally be
Swimming in a constant sea
Thinking what so wrong with me?

No, it's not that bad
I'm lucky to have had the things I had
It's a hidden feeling that's sad
Maybe it's just dumb to be mad.

But, I guess until you are me
You'll have to wait and see
If you would see me,
The me that I know I could be

Heather Sumner

Sister

When I need a friend
You are always there.
To lend me your ear
To brighten my day

Even though you are miles away
You are always in my heart
each and every day.

We talk about old times,
The good and bad,
We talk about our love and happiness,
Sadness and pain,
But I wouldn't have it any other way.

Just remember,
You are the dearest friend
A sister could ever have

Joy Greenwood

Ocean Of Fluid Enchantment

The beckon came softly
A knowing from within
Mutual exchange so natural
Nigh, time to begin

Toward her the journey
Resistance out of bound
Winds embracing ever gently
Love controlling sight, sound

Entranced by alluring beauty
Crying out I moan
Desiring merger, union, oneness
Earth bound soul sojourn

Unveiling inner divine presence
Twilight surrendering full moon
Rebirth of forgotten consciousness
Baptized into eternal tune

Mary Stampone

Forget Me Not

When times are unrefined,
When times are uncultivated,
Forget me not.
When times are challenging,
When times are baffling,
Forget me not.
When times are joyful,
When times are gleeful,
Forget me not.
When times are displeasing,
When times are lacking,
Forget me not.
When times are miserable,
When times are deplorable,
Forget me not.
When times are sanctified,
When times are dedicated,
Forget me not.
Whenever you remember,
Forget me not.

Danette Kobolt

The Sun

Good morning merry sunshine
Why did you wake so soon?
You scare away the little stars
And shine away the moon.

I saw you go to sleep last night
Before I closed my play.
How did you get away out there
And where did you stray?

I never go to sleep my child
I just go around to see,
The little children of the east
Who rise and watch for me.

Victor M. Palmer

Christmas Night

I am a little cedar
Left standing on a hill.
All the rest were chosen
To give some heart a thrill,
To make the children happy
With the tinsel and the lights.
Here I stand unwanted
This lonely Christmas Night.

Viola E. Tipton

The Bravery That My Grandpa Had

The bravery that my grandpa had
he earned when he was just a lad.
Laying perfectly still in a secret pit
down below the enemy he would sit.
He would radio the angle and the arc
to shoot at the enemy in the dark.

He went in front of his army troop
to locate and pinpoint the enemy group.
He had his job for two long years
and finally it numbed away his fears.
His was the first group into Dachau
he won't talk about it even now.

Now he leads a normal quite life
with a helpful, caring wife.
He is glad that it's that way,
and there is only one thing left to say.
I am very glad he was spared
for the friendship he was shared.

Robin MacGillivray

To Know

It's beautiful to know
What is love about
Especially . . . when you are around
It's beautiful to know
When someone cares
And make my life so sweet
And wonderful to share,
That I only think of you
And dream about
It's beautiful to know
Still love around.

Even when I thought
That love had passed away
You touched my heart
In such a special way
That I knew that your
Love is here to stay
It's beautiful to know
Still love around . . .

Mary Di Salvo

Cursing Is The Game

Roses are red
Violets are blue
I'll dance on your grave
And make fun of you
I mixed the potions
With what I exchanged
I made a motion
To drive you insane
Be sure and thank me
If you feel ashamed
For I let you see
Cursing is the game
Hatred is forbidden
So I'll never forgive
All the things you've hidden
as long as I live

Phuong Hoang

Kaila

I am a girl.
I think I am a boy.
My Mom says I am a girl.
My Mom is right,
I am a girl.

Kaila Kowalski, age 6

Have I Ever Told You

Have I ever told you,
all the things I love about you
though my tongue is quick to criticize?

Have I ever told you,
how much you make me laugh and smile
when all you see are tears in my eyes?

Have I ever told you,
my heart swells when I think of you
though all you hear are words of anger?

Have I ever told you,
that with you, my future looks so bright
when all I show is despair about today?

Have I ever told you,
without you my life would empty
though I say leaving would be easy?

Have I ever told you
how much I love you?

Danielle May

A Church of Two People

Can you imagine
A church of two people
It can be any shape
And not have a steeple
This congregation
Though in numbers just two
Its blessings are many
And it doesn't have a pew
People may join
From all different faiths
They come together
On all different dates
The people that join
Are like you and like me
There can't be more members
There can never be three
They may travel to join
By car or by carriage
A church of two people
Is just a wonderful marriage

Paul Allen

I Want You To Know

Dedicated to my sons
I want you to know . .
I loved you when you were just a seed
Growing and moving in my womb
I loved you when you were just a tot
Crawling then walking then running a lot
I loved you as you grew to become a man
Then husband and then a dad.

I want you to know . . .
I am proud of where you've been
I am proud of what you've done
I am proud of where you are and
I am proud of whom you've become.

I want you to know . . .
That you are loved more than
You can ever know
That you are loved much more,
More than just a lot.

Barbara L. Mlodoch

My Love

I want you to be mine.
'Cause your love is so fine
You are my reason for living
My reason for loving
You're all that I want and wish to have
If only wishes come true
My love is for you
I burst in tears when I think of you
'Cause my love is for you
I never stop thinking of you
My love will grow for you
You are an angel from above
Sent for me to love
You are my God
The one and only one I love

Amanda Sloan

The Bottle of Life

Some things sweet
Some things tart
Some things spicy
Some things not

Given to us as gift
Take and eat of life.

Sometimes full
Sometimes empty
Sometimes mellow
Sometimes hollow

Taken from us as gift
Give and drink of life.

Donece M. McCleary

Crow Time

Caw, caw, calls the crow
Spring has sprung again I no
Just a shore as we are born
There's a farmer planting corn
Blue boy was my brother Joe
A horn he did not blow
He was busy with a hoe, to
Be sure the corn would grow
That's how the farmer make
His crop to grow
We were so forlorn so the
Crows had to be scorned
Had to store the master's corn
So the crows won't eat the corn
Our crop now is stored and we
Have plenty of corn
Sorry crows.

Ruth L. Castelli

Sea of Wonders

The sweet smell of sea envelopes you
Wind sweeps across your face
The sea is rough and coarse
But as beautiful as lace

Waves crash and combine
they shuffle themselves and mix
Seaweed and plants get thrashed and torn
But a natural repair comes to fix

The sea is a mystery
that can never be explained
I do not understand
But still don't want to live on land

Crystalynn Buda

Untitled

Her eyes glow like the
Morning sun, then the storm comes
and darkens her eyes.

Nelson Arencibia

Pages

Clean and crisp,
waiting, waiting
for you to come
and write your
everyday thoughts.
Beautiful love
stories, everyday
tragedies, come,
come read me
your fantasies,
your hopes, your dreams.
These pages are
beckoning for you to come.
So please write
in them your
life story.

Hannah Greve

August Sky

August,
an early morn.
Dawn's cloak sweeps the sky.
I see night,
he sulkily creeps away.
And a sliver of frosted glass.
I pick it up,
and see a sky.
It is one that I have known.

Eleanor L. Gunshows

Mom

Chasing me with the fly swatter
Sprinkling on my face with water
Waking up late for school
Diving lessons in the pool

Teaching me all I know
Always helping me to grow
With lectures of trivia and laughter
In little sayings to remember after

Made me what I am to be
The artist that I see in me
With confidence that I see in you
Always knowing that it's true

Telling me that I am smart
A reflection of your nurturing part
Hoping that I am all you planned
And knowing you are simply GRAND

Love, Laney

Elaine Taylor Jessee

WHEN LOVE IS GONE

When love is gone,
Life still goes on.
It's never the same
While memories remain!

Charlotte Kapp

Baseball

The hitter whacks
the big bat cracks

The hitter starts to run
his transformation begun

From hitter to runner
to the big crowd stunner

He rounds the bases
seeing many faces

His foot touches home
he isn't alone

His team cheering
the other team leering

The winning run
the game is Done!!!

John Wilson

Last Night

My mother got old last night
She stayed in the hospital
Till the morning light
She can't read her mail anymore
She says it's her sight
But since she's been home
She hasn't been quite right
My mother got old last night

Sandra M. Gersh

Time Stops

Drowning in your deep blue eyes.
Basking in the warmth of your love.
Drowning in the softness of your skin.
Basking in the tenderness of your touch.
Drowning in unbridled passion.

When we make love, we become one.
Never knowing where I begin and you end.
Feeling your love for me . . .
In every touch, in every kiss.
Time stops, I know only you.

Susan Drury

Wednesday Blues

Alone again
while you're away,
Sitting here
afraid to stay,
Can't hide
these fears inside,
Loving you
not knowing why,
Broken hearted
I'm the fool,
Mind games
with no rules,
Lonely nights
filled with fright,
Longing for
your arms tonight.

Sherry Mainquist

From A Distance

From a distance I have seen you,
From a distance I have heard you,
From a distance I have loved you,
From a distance you are mine.

Glenn Folsom Jr.

Fog

It creeps through darkness in the night
and lingers
on till morning
hanging
like a smoky mist
suffocating the world beneath it.
Under its mask
lion and lamb appear the same—
and I cannot see if they are friend
or foe.
Only the lighthouse beacon
shines through,
a Cyclops
guiding seamen with one muted eye.
It rolls o'er swell and sand
beckoning seductively,
like a siren,
for me to crash myself
upon hidden rocks.

Jenna Christina Distasio

The Willow

Gently bending over,
And sweeping the ground
With soft fingers,
She whispers to the grass—
"Come, rise up higher;
Let me guide you with my boughs.
My branches will protect you,
And I will whisper words of
Kindness and encouragement to you,
So you will grow strong and tall;
And your blades
Will intertwine with my leaves,
Comfortably, comfortingly,
Until the summer ends."

Amy J. Quick

Untitled

Wandering
Round
Inside
Time's
Endless
Reality
Scripts

Banished
Long ago
Outraged
Creativity's
Killer

Lindsey Hyter

Mother

My thoughts drift
like the morning fog,
only to be interrupted
by the chaos of daily turmoil.
Time passes, as though
nothing has changed.
Having known you
has enriched my life.
Even though you're gone,
I shall never forget.
Rain falls from heaven
like my tears for you—Mother.

Paula Holcomb Mason

Melissa

You are one of a kind
How can you be so blind
You are my daughter and
You have a daughter that loves you
Why can't you love her back
Forget what you want and
Wrap your world around her.

Marlene Gilbert

Death of Innocence

When someone dies in an accident,
We wonder if it's to heaven they went.
Then we see it wasn't their fault,
That their lives came to such a halt.
The other driver was a drunk,
The police found beer in his trunk.
Now we say it makes no sense,
This thing called death of innocence.

Nicole Shelton

I Cry

I feel my throat begin to swell,
and I look up to the sky.
I try to think a happy thought,
but I can't. I start to cry.

My emotions are controlling me,
as my eyes fill up with tears.
I can not keep this pain inside.
Now everyone can see my fears.

The first drop escapes my eye,
and I feel it run down my cheek.
Inside I fight hard to stop the others,
but my attempt is just too weak.

I wish that I could hide emotions,
or sometimes not feel them at all.
I wish that when I am pushed,
I wouldn't always fall.

I take a walk until my eyes dry out,
And I think about today.
I hope the next time I am upset,
I handle it in a different way.

Jennifer Manney

Teacher

She is stern,
Yet kind,
My helpfulness
I find,
In my third
Grade teacher.
She inspired me,
Taught me a lesson,
To believe
In yourself.

Anna Bumiller

Hope

I will not die.
E'n though
There is no sign of breath;
E'n though
My lips are sealed in death;
E'n though
My body lies at rest.
I will not die.
My soul will live;
My thoughts abide.

Edwarda L. Burns

Man Of God

A man of integrity,
strong and secure,
bold and dependable,
built to endure.

Full of God's wisdom,
knowledge and truth.
A man with a vision
seen in his youth.

A pillar of strength,
full of power and might.
Won't stray to the left
or turn to the right.

His path is before him,
it's narrow and straight.
Grace and mercy will lead him.
he'll finish the race.

A man who's devoted,
faithful and true,
Loving, compassionate.
This man is you!

Tracey A. Stout

Gossip

A confidence I shared with thee
You shared with two or three
Freely over cups of tea
My confidence was returned to me
It had grown as it passed along
Didn't recognize it as my own!

Margaret C. Green

Never Known

Into a world with choice not
A genesis certain of all pure thought

Aged by time not alone
Body and mind surely grown

Queried reasons as to life
Of the happiness, joy and strife

Concerted efforts to understand
Answers elusive of some plan

An existence of what intent
May only be learned once spent

Ronald J. Ceyba

Heart

They're easy to break
They're not for keeps
If I lend it to you
Will you treat it gently?
If I lend it to you
Will you keep it safe?

Sophiah Hamidi

Families

Some families are small.
Some families are big.
Some families are medium sized.
But most of all
family is a great thing
God has made.

Jessica Pauline Flook

I Want To See I Want To Live

I want to see the world in 5 minutes
Not to gather up the shame
But to gather up the happiness
To enjoy life as it is
To enjoy being a child
You can't go back to the past
But instead you can go to the future

Anna Midyushko

Love Will Conquer

I am cold.
I am shallow.
I keep my feeling hidden
deep down inside.

On the surface there is a smile
to hide the hurt from the past.
When you are near
I have a warmness in my heart.
It frightens me.

To love you is but a dream
for I must first learn to love myself.

Be patient and kind.
Stand by my side.
For I know that love will conquer.

I will love me
then you.

Michele Sfakianos

Fantasy

Fondness seeded sweetly.
Nestled very deeply.

Quick vines grew of much
Deluga.

Take me not, breathed the pot,
Too vast you'll spread through me.

Sweet smells oozed a fervent interlude.
(Spurring the poets fancy)

Enchanting own style,
Admiring (I smile)

For this is only a Fantasy

Stefanee Freedman

Easter

Oh sealed Tomb accept defeat!
My Savior's gone away
He needs your silent walls no more
His grave clothes only stay
He's risen now! He said he would
There's total victory
I thank Him for that rugged cross
And the Blood of Calvary
The Dogwoods Bloom, The Robins sing
There's freshness everywhere
So cry old tomb, retract your doom
For the Father no longer sleeps there
The stone is moved, the Angels came
The Battle now is won
Cause on the 3rd, God looked below
And lifted up his Son
The thunder rolled, The Veil was torn
While yet the crosses stood
A bridge was built with 3 old nails
And 2 old sticks of wood!

Joseph Franklin Clark

Over Again

The evening stood still,
While the world passed by.
Alone with the memories,
Sat the once youthful viewer.
Thinking, remembering, hoping.
Where did the time go?
This was the question that was repeated
Over and over and over again.

Karen E. Cunningham

The Storm

We need rain
so I pray.
The night becomes calm,
the sky turns gray.
I see no stars,
this gladdens me.
The lightning flashes
and strikes a tree.
The thunder rumbles,
the ground shakes.
The rain begins,
my soul breaks.

Justina Kuschel

Alone

I sit here alone,
with feeling of despair.
No one to talk to
No one that cares.

My heart cried out
into the void of night.
As I pray for someone
To turn on the light.

Time goes on as I
shrink further into my gloom
the light glows dim as I
approach my doom.

I lost all hope
as the darkness draws near.
I pray to God
to end it right here.

I sit here alone
with all of my fear,
I caught a glint of light
As the end nears.

Kerry Day

A Man I Never Knew

A shot in the darkness
Took my grandfathers life
Before I was born,
And we never met
The only way I know him
Is by a blurry picture someone took,
A picture of a man
With a mysterious look on his face.

A story never told
Echoes in my ears
His breathes are like the wind
His spirit lives on for years,
In his kids,
Grandkids and me,
My unborn kids and on and on

I never met him
but through a picture
I feel I know him

Jessica Gallo

A Longing for the Annual Revolution

I miss the demise of summer's careless heat
dethroned by fall's alabaster reign

New York's concrete upheaval
to victorious gray sky
paves a reminder
that seasons too die

I miss winter's stab
the steel of cold blade
a murderous foe
to fall's color brigade

Loneliness marches
on crystal-frost air
to accompany winter
in each homeless stare

Far to the west
spring time is saved
by saccharine sun-warmth
and swords of sun rays

But radiance cannot disguise
the truth I miss in winter's eyes

Michael F. Brady

A Desert Song

Sing for me a desert song.
I long for the beauty.

I sit in this cold misty land.
It holds nothing for me.
How can I stay here?
It's not meant to be.

Oh, but the desert, the warmth, the light,
The quiet dark beauty of the night.

Oh, sing for me a desert song.
I long for the beauty.

In years to come
I know I will venture there.
The colors, they await me,
Inviting me to stare.

I'll go to the desert,
the place that is a part
Of my soul and my life,
The place that has my heart.

Oh sing for me a desert song.
I long for the beauty.

Susan A. Devore

The Cruise

Aboard the cruise of life
We start with expectations
Our ships moves on, we find a wife
We learn our limitations

We toil, we strive
Perhaps we reach success
Our children come, they grow, they thrive
We wonder if we're less

The cruise goes on
Our leaves begin to fall
A sailor shouts "Last Port In Sight"
We wonder if that's all

Antonio Navarro

Sky Blue

If you want to find Sky Blue,
fly to England,
take a castle tour,
feel the cool, damp, mildew
infected Sky Blue castle walls,
go outside, it's sprinkling,
feel the warm, Sky Blue
raindrops strike your scalp,
in steady, rhythmic beat,
If you want to find Sky Blue.

Ryne Saxe

All I Want To Do Is Cry

There are times I don't know why
all I want to do is cry.
But, Lord God, I don't know why
you should choose my son to die.

Hurt so bad to lose my son.
But I'm not the only one.
You chose your own son to die
for the sins of such as I.

On the cross he died for me,
all of my sins to receive
on the cross in Calvary.
For my sins he died for me.

There are times I don't know why
all I want to do is cry.
Dear, Lord, help me understand.
Guide me with thy loving hand.

I had dreams, goals for my son,
Holy Spirit, three in one.
Precious Lord, the Trinity,
now my dreams they rest with thee.

Scott J. Bates

Wild Fire

Silent, burnt, it start,
The flame of hate, hide inside its heart,
Added the excitement, it spread fast,
The suffering we face hard.
If it wild to grow,
We vainly to control;
If it happen tomorrow,
We will be sorrow,
If no fire begin,
There may no burning;
If do not hate,
Where have the heartbreak?

Van K. Martin

Mom's Cooking

When Mom is cooking,
I am always looking to see if I like it.
If I really, really like it,
I'll bug her for twenty or thirty seconds
Then I'll get back to writing a poem called
"Mom's Cooking."

If she is cooking some kind of rice or spice,
I definitely will not hate it.

Patrick Brown

Why

As I walk along the road of life
My heart is heavy and I silently cry
Why did You take my son from me.
Why, God, why?

He was handsome, virile, gentle and kind
A joy to us all and too young to die
Why did You take my son from me.
Why, God, why?

I prayed day and night you'd make him well
And a miracle you would not deny
Why did You take my son from me.
Why, God, why?

So I walk the long, long road of life
With a heavy heart and silently cry
Why did You take my son from me.
Why, God, why?

Elsie W. Smuck

The Life of a Book

The life of a book is not divine,
Faded pages and tattered spine.
Dog eared-corners and
Chocolate smeared pages,
The collection of dust that
Has piled up for ages.
Stuck in a corner, with nowhere to go,
The cold feel of wood is the only one I know.
So I am left alone in my worn little nook,
Yes, it's a sad life—the life of a book.

Jennifer M. Pirowski

Why Lord?

Why, oh why Lord, did you take my beloved?
We had so much that we wanted to do,
It's been so hard to let him go.
Oh why Lord, why did you need him so?
Please tell me Lord I need to know.
Then I will try to understand
The plan you've made for me;
Now that I must walk alone
Please guide me as I journey on;
Then in Heaven when we come
Face to face,
This time and pain will be Erased.

Audrey Ann Krause Harder

Thoughts and Dreams

I stand on a hilltop free and alone
watching the orange rays of the sun
wash gently over the never-ending green
of the pines as it awakes from its slumber
Knowing I must return to reality
I reluctantly turn my back to nature's
splendor and fulfill the promises
made so long ago

Conflicts in life are inevitable
Everyone hides one deep inside
Person versus self
Some long for freedom
but cower at the thought of loneliness
while others want everything
but know they'll never get it

Nicole Harson

Budding's Humanity

Feelings of refuge, feelings of fear vacillate to either extreme
Silence, darkness, an environment void and without form.
But changes in my composition invades a milieu once so serene.
Ambivalence riddles my existence and by some mitotic force I transform

As I emerge from the confines of my hydrous sphere,
I transcend this milieu.
Lubriciously I traverse a strait, gentle contractions
urge me on through.
A gleam of light, introduces my sight, to a habitat different and new
From my hydrous cell I emerge, to activity beneath
a vast canopy, magnificent and blue.

There are lights, there are sounds, some nurturing, some alarming.
I experience touch, some disturbing, some calming.
I acquire knowledge, some reward me, some deter me
I entreat others that be wayfarers of this journey.
I find refuge again in a coherent world order,
For I am a product of God's handy work, I am budding humanity.

Marvin P. Gathings

Reaching for a Special Place

I'll reach for a place where a sunflower can grow high,
As high as the tallest cloud in the sky.
And where it won't rain in April or May,
And there never is a cloudy day.
Where there is no smoke or pollution in the air,
And there is nothing that can give you a scare.
Where plants, animals and humans collect,
And there is crystal clear water where I can reflect.
There could be a place like this, but we're unaware of it now.
There could be a place like this, but we don't yet know where or how!
Take care of our earth, it's a very special place.
Reach up for the stars and we'll win the race.

Kara Allinson

Memories

I sit here alone as memory backward turns
On times of laughter and times when hot tears burned.
Of times I said "Yes" when I should have said "No,"
And of God whom my soul inquireth so.

Through the years it seems I have taken all of God's tests,
And I am sorry to say too often my grades were not the best,
I have learned sickness in a man can distort and bend.
I have seen hopes and dreams come to and end.

I have known what it is like to feel whole
When my soul commingled with my true love's soul.
Then to lose him and cry over his grave,
And Jesus who comes and lifts up the fallen to save.

As I look back I see stones in my path that made me trip.
I have learned to avoid most of them and still learning to "zip my lip."

I have touched on some of my past notes,
Perhaps like a sad melody that floats
Out over the world and mingles in its roar.
But I need to look ahead now and not before.

So on my future now I contemplate.
And day by day to achieve my unaccomplished fate.

Jean Hansel Bryan

Gone Are The Days

Gone are the days you held my hand as we walked through the park
You comforted me as I awakened from nightmares in the dark.
We shopped at the stores downtown, with the fresh smell of
popcorn all around
We raised chickens colored with dye. Ones that we bought for a
dime at Eastertime at the T.G. and Y.
Gone are the days with the look of surprise in my eyes when you
baked me fresh cookies, cakes and pies.
Gone are the days you showed me the way. I kissed your sweet face
And you kissed mine. You were my only ray of sunshine.
Gone are the days when I climbed your trees. I broke your window
With my knees when I climbed your shed. You never com-
plained when I wet the bed.
Gone are the days we watched TV as we shucked the corn and
shelled the peas. You gave me medicine to comfort me when I
coughed and sneezed.
Grandma, gone are the days because God took you away.
He took you to Heaven to be with him.
I pray that I too can live my life without sin.
So when my time comes, I can go to Heaven.
And you and I will be together once again.

Sandra Sue Davis

So What Killed Clara?

Joe and Clara, camping poles in hand, "Source"? lake, and fish to bake.
Joe spied an old barn! For Sale!, "Hey!", lets explore!
Clara murdering, to herself, "Now a barn tour."! Let's buy it!,
"Joe beaming!" Clara wasn't happy with her barn in the dale.
"Red Tape," the barn house was liveable
A tree lined lane, even a weather vane. Four days of bliss
was a miff. Missive for Clara, and Aunt Bee passed on, leaving
Clara a huge sum, "Joe overjoyed!" Bought a Bottle of wine,
while Clara pines.
Next day Clara gardening, felt a pinch on her toe.
And woodland scorpion ambles away.
Woozy she quit for the day. Have some
wind dear it will make you feel better. Dinner in town will fix you
right up, Driving along, a bee had gotten into the car, and stung
Clara on the arm, it's only a bee, "grinned Joe." That evening
Clara wasn't feeling well "Yes" you do look pale,
"I know!" Said Joe, a boat ride will fix you up, in a dark corner
of the boat a black widow spider finds Clara's leg and bites her.
Clara died that night But!, where is Joe?
Joe is on his way home, to wife Trudy, with Clara's Body.
So, what killed Clara?

Sara James

Why Bother Living?

You ask for reasons.
All I can tell you is we are all hostages, bound by Fate to Time,
yet Earth still puts on her apron to rainbow bouquets
for a single splash under a hide-and-seek sun.
Showers sweet as candy.
Snow kittens paw drift atop drifts.
Indigo paints a long, slow twilight.
Dawns fragrant with rose and honey.
Live, then, as a prayer of thanks.
For those who need what you alone can give.
For the moment when you forget the crowding thrash of pain as
a child snuggles near.
For that single summer night that fits you like a glove,
velvet as a leprechaun's slipper, and the silver sheen
of a workhorse spider's web and a lollipop-purple cloud.

Waves tickle shells stronger and more intricate, no two alike.

Live for the moon.
Cold as she is, she remembers to paste a smile on her pitted mug.
You can face anything.
Live!

Phyllis D. Green

The Gifts of Love

What kind of present can I give to Baby Jesus who loves us so much,
I would like to give Him gold, bright and shinning to the touch.
The only thing I am poor, not of wealth, but rich in His eyes,
I sat and thought, toss and turn, and wanted to cry.

The gift had to be very special, something that would really rate,
Being he forgives us even when we pierce His heart and make mistakes.
As I laid down different things ran through my head,
Then I sat up straight, looked on my dresser from my bed.

There was a piece of paper and I wrote the word love on it.
Put it in the box, wrap it up and found a bow that would fit.
I headed out with the gift in my pocket as I enter church that was quiet,
Laid the gift next to baby Jesus, the star above gave some light.

I knelt down in front of the nativity scene and whisper this is all I have,
Then an angel voice I heard say to me—don't look so sad.
As I looked at the Baby Jesus I thought I saw a little smile,
He knew it was a gift of love even though he was a child.

Margo Dawson

Mrs. Jay's Roses

Mrs. Jay planted her rosebushes year after year
under the bedroom window, so they would always be near.
One of her bushes perished before she could even bloom.
A winter frost came early and would be her doom.
Four of her bushes flourished and began to grow,
until Wally, the neighbor, came at them with his hoe.
Just as the bushes were budding, he chopped at their roots.
He pulled off leaves, broke their stems, and stomped them with his boots.
The bushes didn't die, although they were all marred.
They fought to live every day, even though it was hard.
Wally continued his onslaught, mostly at night.
He thought no one could see him but he wasn't very bright.
Mrs. Jay was aware of him but chose not to look.
Every night she closed the blinds and read the Holy Book.
The roses all grew beautiful despite what Wally did.
Mother Nature took over the job while Mrs. Jay hid.
The bushes all had scars within but not on the flower.
They realized through their struggle to live that they, too, had power.
There is a moral here that the bushes want you to know;
If you're going to plant roses, make sure you watch them grow.

Barbara Quappe

I Would

I would tap dance on top of the whole-wide world and twirl each
passing planet swing upon each twinkling star and ride the crescent moon
I would surround the globe without stretched arms and tenderly
squeeze the equator dive into craters of deep dark waters and tip
toe across sandy   seashores
I would tunnel through grand canyons and open up the sky roof,
step on each continent and touch heaven with my fingertips
I would jump to the highest mountain's peak and breathe down
on valleys below, dab on fragrance of fresh clean air and suck in
breezy winds
I would sip Summer's hot temperatures and taste the sizzling heat
kindle blustery Winters and glide off frosty snow caps
I would be ready to suddenly Spring up and fall instantly for
Autumn's rich beauty, sweep earth's gigantic floor and rinse
parched deserts in cool waterfalls
I would skip through big green forests and inhale scented pine trees,
whisper sweet talk to the animal kingdom and zoom amongst the birds
I would soak up moist dew drops and saturate my eternal soul,
extract nectar from flowery petals and pour over iced cold glaciers
I would run through endless galaxies and drink from milky ways
and when I push my love button, I shall parachute with soft fluffy clouds

Jo Ann Brown

God Help Me Be Me

It's almost impossible to say at a person's time of death,
that they lived a full good life and was ready to go.
A question I most often ask myself is, when it comes my time
to leave this world and it's my time to face God, will God
be pleased at how I lived my life or will I hear God say,
"Depart from me; I never knew you?"
The word "depart" cuts through the heart right to the soul.
"Depart" means to quit, forsake, withdraw, renounce,
desert, relinquish, and to give up.
Will God know me? Did I live my life as me or did I try to live
as someone else? Whatever amount of time I have,
I know I'll have to answer and be accountable
for all my thoughts and my actions in this lifetime.
Have I said all I need to say, done all I need to do, gone
where I should go ? Have I been a stepping stone to help
others along the right path or at times been a stumbling block
in their life that has caused them to fail, get hurt or lost?
Will an indifferent, uncaring insensitive and unconcerned
attitude show when life gets rough and time are tempestuous?
Will I weaken and fail or will I remember God is fabulous
and marvelous?

Mary G. Alexander

Reflections

Who is it that fussed with you from morning till night?
Who is the one who wiped your nose, and kissed you goodnight?
Who took care of the boo-boos, and made them alright?
Who loves you more than anyone can?
Who kept you from harm, and chased away all the bogeymen?
Who's arms held, you when you were afraid, and who is the first
person who taught you to pray?
Who is it you run to when you are all alone?
And who is it you can count on when everything is wrong?
And did you ever ask yourself, what happens when she is gone?
You try to remember, the things she's taught you from her heart,
You must always know that you never really part, and although
this trip she has to make alone . . .
She has always prepared you to stand on your own,
So whenever you feel lost, empty, or alone you need do only
one thing to bring your Mother home . . .
Just look into a mirror and, see really see, the things from the
heart she left you, the things she gave you freely . . .
Just look into that mirror, and your reflection your mother is
there, and so is all of her affection . . .

Colleen D. Vanskiver

Young Black Man In America

You wake, a Black Teenage Male. To combat this concept called
America, the feeling of alienation, the feelings and hatred toward
you. You place in your hands the offensive weapons of
hostility and hatred, you adorn your body with the defensive
armor of anger. You begging fighting this invisible enemy, trying
to protect who you are, what you are. So you survive, only to
become a Young Black Man in America. You look down in
amazement realizing, your weapons and armor are gone. You
look down again, you see blood flowing from wounds on your
body. Then you must face the sad truth, that the weapons you
used were inadequate to fight the enemy. You knew they were
inadequate in the beginning, but you felt alone and empty, so
you used weapons and armor that aroused you emotions. You
lay on the battle filed psychologically bleeding to death,
mumbling in the immortal words of Christ dying on the cross.
"E-lo-i, eloi, la-ma sa-bach-tha-ni", "My God, my God, why hast
thou forsaken me?

James Dexter Moore

Yesterday's Today

We were once strangers dwelling in one establishment.

Hesitant to speak to each other we preserved our silence
Knowing a time of trust would come.

A Kaleidoscope of characters
Belonging to the same affiliation-each undiscovered.

We ached listening to each other's cries, but remained still and unseen
Being careful not to reveal ourselves.

As a combination of tears flowed
Immense barriers which kept us apart began to dissolve and melt away.

Our souls united as we consoled one another
During which time a powerful covenant formed.

Recognizing we were artifacts of another time
Each created using distinct techniques
Provided us with the backdrop for a rare masterpiece.

We allowed ourselves to become vulnerable
As we shared memories of our existence
Realizing we were all great journalists.

As we held hands our hearts were set free
Love rushed in like a mighty river
Bringing us forth to the same place and time.

Pat Duty

God's Chosen Miracle

Dedicated to Andi Hrusovsky

Lord, I realize a birth is a miracle, a gift of life you and only you control.
Please don't misunderstand, I'm not questioning your almighty power,
although there are mixed emotions; after all this time, why now?

Possibly, consideration was taken before sending your angelic
army on a special mission.

You may have sent an angel to scan the universe seeking a
cluster of crisp evening stars and warm crystal morning dew for
the sparkle in our baby's eyes.

An angelic soldier could have fluttered her wings across a
mountain stream producing ripples for our baby's smile.

A tint for the tips of our baby's tiny fingers and toes may have
been retrieved from seashells resting on a warm golden bed.

Lord, you may have sent an angel to comb our precious earth
during the past fall season to gather a unique shade from your
bouquet for our baby's hair.

Perhaps, the softness of our baby's skin may have been chosen
from a cottontail, and the sound of our baby's voice plucked
from the harmony of your angelic harp.

Innocence for our baby could have been absorbed from fresh
fallen snow.

Lord, before closing I ask humbly, would you have your angelic
soldiers ever so gently flap their wings, as to allow stardust to
sprinkle over my husband and I, as we experienced first sight
and touch of your CHOSEN MIRACLE?

Jack Maravola

Burn Baby Burn

Pray dear children terror is on the rise.
The burning of the black church is the racist prize.

For years the black church has been the symbol of strength and
I suppose you thought a torch, would stop us and make us weak.

We have overcome J. Crow, Selma, and Regan to just name a
few. Please be aware we shall overcome this injustice too!

For we shall stand arm and arm where the cinders lay.
We shall stand arm and arm and continue to pray.
But, please remember the meek shall also have their day

James Anthony Parham

Innocence

'Tis at its best when you are young and nothing has flaws.
Parents are the smartest people in the world
and new shoes make you run fast.
School is about ABC's, coloring and recess.
Those things were so innocent; how I wish to recapture the past.
To be able to return to a time when cotton candy
was thought to have really come from cotton,
When everything was a new experience
and the smile on the face of a clown was not painted on,
The nights of wanting to be able to bounce the big ball in the sky,
Times when your mother is the most beautiful woman
that you know and no one is stronger than your father,
Believing in actual "happily ever after" endings
and that someday your prince will come.

Catosha Hughes

I'm . . . My Neighbour

History reveals and civilization knows, perfect man is a dream.
Man invented science, making astonishing strides in commerce
and physics.

Technology is a force, probing the heavenly host,
bestriding the earth below—feat hitherto unknown.
Human hate persists, causing wars and disasters
more in this age than centuries past. That's the fall of man.

Peace, humanity needs.
Neither in edict nor statues found, only within the soul of man.
All faith is one. All religion is same,
teaching love, banishing fears—the only way to God.

God radiates thy face. Beholding his glory
in thy neighbour's eyes, is the gospel of love.

A new age comes, teaching neither economics
nor science—only the unity of man.
Everyman is a brother sharing equal needs,
inhabiting different lands and having one world fellowship.

In each of us is light, in that light is love, in that love is peace.

Wealth and riches put aside, man still a mystery.
Only in the secret of the soul,
does the flame of God remind us, we are one.

Charles Emelumba

In Words

Some sweet song of razor lust, and bloody love . . .
Drip, drip, blood trickles down my chin.
You chop hard with your axe when I'm out on a limb.
You let me fall then kiss my would—but finish it off
With burning alcohol. This lust, this love, damn singing dove!
Fighting to stay above . . . always remembering those loving eyes—
each time mostly lies. How to repay you, slay you, play you.
So much easier to hate you. Nothing left inside. I don't need to hide.
No more razor lust, bloody love stealing every bit of me, leaving me
Empty and ashamed. Stripping my soul. No longer a whole.
I'm taking back everything you stole. Living with this freedom
I haven't known in years. Hating that I hadn't been stronger.
Happy that I didn't stay longer. Wondering why I make myself
Remember the things we shared. Sometimes feeling like you
Were never really there. You are just a dream embedded
In my mind, faint in memory but somehow there all the time.
My freedom is lonely and content. The razor finally bent.
No more slicing and bleeding and healing.
Slicing, bleeding, and healing. Nothing left to steal.
Nothing more to give. Nothing in between. No longer a seam.

Adela G. Iniquez

Hear Me Pray

As a child I didn't know any better.
I did what other kids did although it was strictly forbid.

I often did the opposite of what was asked of me.
My aunt would beat me drastically.
It seems like she was always after me.

I prayed, at night closing my eyes so afraid,
Hoping the pain would go away but it stayed.

God do you hear me calling you?
Please come and protect me.
It seems like even when I'm right, there's people out to get me.

"Hear me pray"

My mother raised me and my brother.
We never really knew our dad.
I stole a Batman car from valley fair which made my mother mad.

It wasn't that I was bad for I was far from that.
It's just that I was sad because we didn't have what other children had

A broken family; it seems like history repeats itself.
Now I'm grown up and all alone; my kids all live with someone else.

Lord take the pain away for it is as plain as the other day.
Oh God please hear what I say, when I pray, "Hear Me Pray."

Perry D. Wooding

Phantasmagoria

Melancholic sadness surrounds the place where she stands.
Loneliness and frustration dizzily whirl around in her
weary head. Saltwater tears float softly down her dry
cheeks as she thinks about the depression that makes up her life.
Every thought that exists in her mind is morbid and dark.
She continues to search for a way out, but still remains unsuccessful.
She screams as her mind blacks out.
She reaches around, trying desperately to find something to hold onto.
Her once happy, creative imagination has turned to insanity.
Her worst fears have come alive and have completely swallowed
her entire being. Turning back is no longer possible.
She has travelled far beyond the realms of realism and has
entered into an unknown world that is consumed by
unfamillarness and fright.

Theresa Scanlin

Southern Boy's Statement

A mystery it seemed I would never solve
whose heightened heritage or horrific humbling identifies with me?
The Cherokee is my family which produced my grandmother
and her mother
High cheekbones, stone-cutting eyes, woven words of truth
ruby red rivers of pain crying out to me,
the son of many people
I have no right to deny these sculptors of my existence

But just the same, Africans bid my ear to hear
People of such splendor with spears sent sailing
into the dust suits of their enemies
Builders of incredible, innovative, incomparable kingdoms
Spider web tangled hats on their heads, tongues of a hundred lips,
ruby red rivers of pain crying out to me, the son of many people
Who am I to deny these authors of my history?

The English are part of me, too.
Launchers of mass invasion, enslavement, and expansion
Bleachers of my original shade who made part of my present
pilgrimaged place, Alabaster wrapping over shadows of existence
Strong, stern, strenuous hands

Marques Vaughn

Pass The Word

Pass the word on from the out house, to the white house, from
the store, door to door, from the mountain and hills, that's part
of our forefather will, to spread the word, like a bird thru the wind
and rain, sometime there is pain, we'll win, so there is a gain.

The enemy and competitor is on our case, to win this country
over, and take our place, we got to be extra careful, not to make
the wrong move, to protect our dignity, win or loose, we got to
get it together and learn to love our country man, put a band on
this hate and let go hand and hand.

Together we are strong, separately we are weak, so what's it's
going to be? Strong or weak?

The enemy is coming at us in a different way, away that Star Wars
cannot save the day. The enemy has declare his tongue as a
weapon to corrupt the mind of our young, and drug the rest. Not
many will be left sane, to play this game unless a band is put on
this hate, from block to block and state to state.

Clemetine Pitchford

The Journey of the Soul

The wisdom of the sages lights our pathway;
The Lord of the universe lights feeds to the sun, the moon and the stars.
As we begin the journey of the soul called our life's experience,
The path is made of purity more precious then gold;
It leads to the golden vessel at the end of the rainbow.
It is boundless, there are no limitations;
We can go anywhere do anything
And yet, never be lost from the cosmos to the seven cosmic rays,
Cosmoolite, embracing all celestial bodies.
Infinite possibilities . . . on both sides of the path are flowers
They are all so special to me.
If I told you all of their names, you'd see where I begin
And where I am, on the path of eternity,
Raised in the divine mystery of love with truth and life,
Entering spiritual union where akasha astral lights
Fills all space.

Violet Caswell

Dear God

Dear God, The ground is rocky and hard as cement, digging is not fun
I dug my foxhole to accommodate only one
It is a tight squeeze, but I'll let you move in
Let me tell you, as a G.I., I'm not really free of sin

Yes, I have done my share of killing
I did it and I was willing
You must understand and I hope you see
I had to do it to them, before they did it, to me.

This is not a game, so that when it is over, you can go home
No this is war, and it has quite a different tone
In a way, it is deadly game, in which you have to kill, or be killed
In order to survive, you have to be iron willed

I don't know what you are doing here
this is a place of fear
I have a question God, listen to me
Is it that you are here, as a referee

I'm not being funny, I'm scared, like the others, too
As long as you are in my fox hole, listen to me, there is nothing else to do
Well, I'm glad you are here, If I do get killed
There is no better place for me to be than with you.

Harry B. Sherr

We Can

Here we are walking hand in hand down a lonely path
through each other's discovery of a dreamland.
A man and a woman have very special thoughts.
They want to care about each other but are afraid to share
the true feelings in their hearts, scared that they would be
hurt or drawn apart.
We can be there for each other every day of our lives
with a love as beautiful as a sunrise or a dawn.
Together they can light a fire that time cannot put out,
and share the secrets that only lovers know.
The love between a man and a woman is a very beautiful
and precious thing that only two people can share.
When you fall in love you have eyes for only one.
You talk about your hopes and dreams.
Maybe someday they will come true.
When you are in each other's arms,
words cannot express how you really feel.
The nights you hope will never end, so you won't ever have to part.
Together you can make anything happen as long as you stay
together forever and a day.

Lynn Jones

Mother

Everybody loves a mother. Who wouldn't?
I mean, they're nice, sweet, and caring.
I don't know what a daughter would do without a mother.
Just what is a mother, you say? A mother to me is
the woman who brought her kids into this beautiful world.
The one who gave them a special name that they shall have forever.
The one who spent her life raising her wonderful son and daughter.
The one who loves her husband so very much.
I don't know what anyone would do without a mother.
They're just so wonderful. This Mother's Day Mom,
I just wanted to tell you how special and lucky you are to have
A family that loves and cares for you.
A family that probably wouldn't be able to go through life without you.
This Mother's Day and every Mother's Day should be special to you.
I know it is special to me because it is the only time
I can really show you that you have special place in my heart.
If you ever go to that special place,
You will find all you did that was special to me while I was growing up.
Pretty soon Mom, I will be living my own life.
But don't worry. That special place will always remind me of you.

Katherine Lee Marshall

Autumn Now and Then

Autumn finally appears, and the massive oak trees stretch to the sky.
Their leaves are mixtures of fiery orange, golden yellow, and
hunter green.
Their limbs reach out.
In the middle of this abandoned wood sits an abandoned cottage.
Its faded wood and waterless wheel look dark, yet cozy and inviting.

In years past, it provided a home for a miller and his family.
The children played on the rocky ledge of the creek and wan-
dered about the mysterious forest in search of adventure.
The wife washed their dirty clothes in the cool water of the creek,
and hung them to dry in the radiant sun and crisp breeze.
The miller ground the wheat for the town and received a fee for
his services.
The huge wheel creaked and groaned as it labored.

When their day was over, the family sat along the creek to hear the
owl singing, the crickets chirping, the small woodland animals
scurrying to their holes, and the water gushing to power the mill.
All was calm and bliss.
The moon cast shadows through the trees, and smokelike
clouds drifted across the silver crescent.

Trista R. Zoll

Mama's Apron

I remember Mama's apron. The one she always wore
She kept it hanging on a hook beside the kitchen door.

It was made of checked gingham, tied with a perky bow,
It was not a thing of beauty. It was not meant for show.

She would rise up very early, an hour before the sun,
And when she put her apron on, her day's work had begun.

She would wear it to the garden, fill it up with beans or corn,
And then she'd wear it to the barn and bring back kittens newly born.

She would wear it to the neighbor's that lived across the field.
She would wear it to the orchard when the trees began to yield.

I've seen her use it many times to wipe away her tears
And it really grew quite faded as the days turned into years.

It had so many uses. Enough to fill a book.
And though she's been gone a year now, it's still hanging on its hook.

When God prepared her new home, on Heaven's golden shore,
I know He hung an apron there beside the kitchen door.

Lois Bault

Our Love

I see you sitting there across the room, your body so fine,
and as bright as the moon. You look at me with a loving smile.
You make me feel that your love is worthwhile. As we gazed into
each other's eyes, with feelings so strong and true, in my heart
I know I'm thinking only about you. As we stare, I feel that we're
both right, that this is truly love-at-first sight! Although love is
so strong and true, it makes me go crazy over you. If only I could
tell you how much I really care, to make you see the way I do,
and to find that love we could both share! I think about you
every night and day; I can't hardly stand it when you're away.
To have you and hold you by my side, there could be no better
place to hide. Sometimes we don't act the way we feel; I guess
we're both hoping that our love is real! Although sometimes I
get confused, and feel I don't have a clue, maybe it's because in
my heart I feel I really love you!

Christina McDonald

She's a Special Person

It takes a very special person to be a nurse
for it's not only medication that they disperse.
It's a part of themselves that they give
to help you fight the battle, fill you with hope and the will to live.

It's that nurse that comes into your room with a smile
takes the time to be with you and talk awhile.

She goes about doing her job and all she has to do
in order to care of others and you too.
Some will say, "That's her job, that's what she's paid to do,"
but it's that nurse with her sincere and caring way
that helps you through your pain and what you face each day.

That special someone tries to comfort and console you,
chase away your fears—
She listens patiently, holds your hand, wipes away your tears.

She not only does this for you she's there for your family too-
As she knows what they are going through.

Her job sometimes is stressful, she's had a long day
and it's time for her to leave and go on her way.
Yet there she is, at your door giving of herself a little bit more.

This gentle, caring person has her own special ways.

Sheila Obertubbesing

Dear World

I must apologize; my brothers and sisters knew not the consequences.
The Mother calls the child, but the child doesn't answer.
The child is the cancer killing the Mother.
She loves the child even though it might destroy her.
The ringing is heard; it is the call of Nature.
The Mother is so in love with the child that she gives it gifts of endless beauty.
But the child sees the world through infant, untrained eyes.
A blur, only skin deep.
This child has learned about himself and his cousins around him,
  at least that is what he thinks.
He has studied the land, he knows, or thinks he knows it.
This child has explored the air, the sea, and has climbed
the fence out of the Mother's backyard.
Outside the fence the child learns how important the Mother is.
But still the phone lay unanswered.
This child grows more powerful by grasping the power of the atom.
His knowledge makes him feel superior, and he forgets his Mother.
The phone is moved from the mantel to a dusty pad locked box,
  yet it still rings waiting for an answer.

Donnie Joseph Burdette

Every Ritual Night

Every night I dance my poetic dance in this circular ritual.
I light my oblong candle in my concave room and I wait,
Something I don't look forward to in this life habitual.

The great disc descends below the line in eyes...too late, too late...
So here I sit in this palace of palaces just awaiting to lie,
And dream of countenances long ago, to undo my mistakes.

Every ritual night I streak tears down my rock hard cheeks
preparing to die.
And from my heart fate will seize my love but will not take.

So I sit here in this circular trap waiting for her intoxicating call,
My beautiful, my sweet, the one who carries my heart forever
in her eye.

But I know forever still my love will never fall.
Look at this and look at me, you know all too well you cannot deny,
That in this life laced with cutting irony, together our hearts should be.

Think how godly we were finger locked in finger.
But my angel weeps her tears and weeps herself refusing to see,
That the truths of this universe, the truths of our hearts, see
nothing better,
Than for us to coalesce on a bed of perfect THORNLESS roses.

But much to my demise, much to my dismay, it is not as destiny would indicate.
Cupid has lain down his lover's TAROT cards that show us,
Despite my efforts SISTER FAITH has fallen from your grace so
separate is our fate.

Robert Perry Ivey

Where To Go?

In the world, there are two places.
One place is on the ground.
When I'm there, it guides me to my future.
It pushes me to do ordinary things, which are very easily accomplished.
I ride the carousel, but sit in the protective cars in the middle.
With every step I take,
I know I have the solid, firm earth under me to support me.
I'm only allowed to go where I will be safe,
where I will be guarded by familiarity and routine.

The other place is in the sky.
When I'm there, it guides me to my future, also.
All it does is think about my dreams.
It pushes me further and further
to think of all the wonderful places I could go
And all the exciting things I could do.
I ride the horses on the carousel,
and am encouraged to take the risk of reaching for the ring.
Yet, in this place I am vulnerable.
All my thoughts and dreams exposed.
Capable of being hurt in various ways, by loved ones or by
crushed hopes.

Lydia Cintron

From The Heart

As your spirit haunts these halls
The echoes of family and friends bounce off the walls.
I often cry for your arms around me tight,
without you here my heart is black as night.
You left me in an unforgiving, desolate world of fear.
As people come and go the only things that remain are memories,
and the dreams we shared.
What we had is sacred and will be locked in the deepest chambers
of my heart until you uncover the key, only then will it be bared.
You stole away my faith and hope,
each day is harder and harder to cope.
Life goes on until the Lord says the time is right and I will think of only
you during my Angelic flight.
So, until that glorious day we meet, never to part,
our love will be held untouched in my heart.

Alison Golter

Contradictions

Love is not an affection—It's a state a mind.
Jealousy is not envy—It's feeling threatened.
Anger is not rage—It's pain.
Pain is not a feeling—It's a selfish affliction.
Crying is not an emotion—It's release.
Essence is not a picture of yourself—It's your whole being
  displayed for all to see.
Sex is not an act—It's a pleasure that's shared, an expression consumed.
Faithfulness shouldn't feel forced—It should be wanted.
Desire—It's inside me my love, I love you but could you love me?

Kristin Theckston

Tomarrow Is My Birthday

Tomorrow is my birthday, it will be the best one I ever had
A year ago heavenly Father gave me my Mommy.
This year will he give me my Dad.

Mommy asked me what I wanted, for my very special day.
I could have anything I asked for anything I say.

"Mommy" I got you a year ago, that's when Heavenly Father gave you to me
But I was just wondering, this year, won't Heavenly Father give me a Daddy?

My Mommy just looked at me, and then she began to cry
She told me that she love me, and she was sure that
Heavenly Father would try

She carried me up to bed and tucked me in real tight
She gave me a good night kisses, and then turned off the light

I thought about my Daddy, I wondered were he could be
Then I realized I already had one 'cause Mommy been both to me

I raced down stairs to tell her, that my birthday wish came true
Not only are you my mommy, you're my daddy too.

Tomorrow is my birthday, it will be the best one I ever had
A year ago Heavenly Father gave me my Mommy,
this year my Mommy will be my Dad.

Dalina L. Neel

Shadow of a Person

My friends don't really know me, only half of me.
Think of her, think of Alice.
Do they think of the person who lies, thinks, and dreams?
Or the other side, loud, obnoxious, and overbearing.
Do they think of the person who is easily hurt, and eager to be liked?
Or the person who doesn't care, about anyone or anything.
It worries me, if I could show the real me would they like that person?
Would they like the girl who really does have talent,
can do things, who is a good person, and loves to walk
and canoe and read by the honeysuckle, and who
doesn't just think, but knows, she is beautiful?
Would they accept and like that person, too?

Alice Edgerton

Children on the Street

When you see children on the street,
You feel so sad when you see how they are beat.
You want to help so you offer them some money,
While other people are driving by laughing as if it is funny.

If you ask me it is not funny at all,
That they are living on the streets because their parents had a bad fall.
You want to be nice to them to try to lighten their day,
Before they have to go home and sleep in the hay.

They wake up and their tummies are lacking of food,
Personally me if I am hungry I am in a bad mood.
And yet these children are the nicest around,
It seems like the mean kiss sleep in a bed and the nice sleep on the ground.

To help these kids that have no cash,
If you have some extra food do not throw it in the trash.
These kids are very, very kind,
And if you can please keep that in mind.

Shane Philip Perkins

Leonardo

My fair Leonardo you left me once, but now your back.
You left me crying in the rain. My tears filled the world with hate.
My world was left me to pick up the pieces.
Your love was warm and so fine, but you left me alone.
My joy and happiness was gone too.
Your love was blinding so I could not see the true feelings you
had for me.
I had hoped you would come back, but you never did.
Time passed and so did you and I, with memories from long ago.
My love faded, but not the memories. They left me
Crying for you and feelings left from wanting you.
Your ring of love left spinning on my finger was
Cruel and hot. It left a burning and yearning for you.
Your kisses were still tickling on my lips.
Now your back and your love is stronger than ever.
All the things that went with you are now back.
The memories are stronger which makes it even harder not to love you.
Now my heart is together and is staying together,
my fair Leonardo.

Crystal Corbi

Motherhood

Mom, Mother, Mama . . .
We have all heard these terms . . .
How do you put into words what they mean?

What does it take to be a Mom, Mother, or Mama?
Sacrifice, endless energy, patience, diplomacy, nurturing . . .
Hugs are just a part of every day and lots of hugs . . .
Kids need them . . .
Moms need them . . .
Tender kisses on boo-boos make the difference between
a good or bad day . . .
The laughter of your children . . .
The angelic faces of your sleeping children make the chaos
of the day vanish . . .
The quiet at night, however brief, is a gift from
those sleeping children . . .
Motherhood is a experience to enjoy and relish in to the fullest . . .
Enjoy, it will be over in the blink of an eye. . . .

Gail K. Zehe

How Sweet an Exchange Is a Rushed Embrace

How sweet an exchange is a rushed embrace,
Hurried by the silence of two startled spirits,
Once nestled within this fragile place, this shelter, yet now set loose
To stumble upon itself and disrupt this weary solitude.

How careless am I to let my words run across this barren page,
Yearning to be filled by the thought and worries of sweet romance,
Yet it must witness this full and frightful expression, This empty face
lost in the dream of your warm embrace.

How drunk would I feel to taste the parting of your lips?
A pleasure to set me spinning, slurring my words, intoxicated by
your presence.
Yet calm would surely cast aside this fervor should I near this
precious refuge.
A silence, perhaps inspired, perchance be fallen, to deafen us.

How easy must the lens be tempted by your charm!
If ever a form should be captured, it is you.
And would your eyes, for the moment, glance away.

Then softly, sweetly, this thought of you would impart your
grace unto me.

David Hanks

The Unheard Siren

Somewhere a gun fires,
A man crumples to the ground,
A woman screams for help,
But all is silent.

Soon sirens can be heard in the distance,
They grow louder . . . louder . . .
Until the flashes of red and blue light reveal the bloody to the world,
A man and a woman jump out of the ambulance,
They work to revive the lifeless body,
Their hands, soon covered with blood, cannot help,
The man is gone, forever.

People will morn for the lost life,
A boy will remember is father as hero,
A woman will remember her husband as a comforter,
No longer here to right the wrong.

There will be flowers and prayers,
Then time will continue and life will return to normal,
Except for the boy and the woman,
Their lives will remain forever changed by this senseless act of violence,
Forever.

Sarah Werner

Unhappy Medium

The raging wind picks me up with a convincing gust.
Being light as dust, the blast carries me.
As I float higher into the sky, the opaque clouds blind me.
The sun's glare discourages me, so I turn my head away.
Suddenly, the cool wind leaves my aid.
I plummet to the ground with my burdens weighing me down.
As I fall from the inspiring perfection of the heavens,
I look down to the murky waters below.
As I splash into the aquatic hell, I pray for another strong gust of wind.
Depression embodies me and serves as a heavy anchor.
Further and further I sink, but do not hit the bottom.
I mock the few unfortunate lives that lie below me.
Oblivious to all above me, I regain my confidence through those below.
As my body's balloon fills up with the air of aplomb,
I slowly begin to float to the surface of the ocean like scum.

Dave Nelson

O' Release Me

O' Release Me, from the words that feel like they are fighting me, wrapping around me trying to get me to fall on my knees.

O' Release Me, from these powerful hands that have anger beneath their palms, blood dripping from their nails greed covering their deceitful eyes.

O' Release Me, from breaking glass shattered dreams having me to push though lost people who want to move forward but don't have the courage to walk with proud steps.

O' Release Me, from feet that want to stomp my heart into the ground and let it remain there to turn to dust as I fade away.

O' Release Me, from stupid minds that feels as if I'm nothing without somebody, but my eyes shall see a new beginning that will lead me to a beautiful promise land.

O' Release Me, from breaking hearts, eyes full of disappointing tears that have been shed for years, let there be happiness.

O' Release Me, from the dim light that grows, shine for when my eyes open let it shine like the morning sunrise.

O' Release Me, from the hate that blinds my joy let it break loose from these chains of misery, when it does, I will fly like the birds in the everlasting blue skies forever.

Jerry Mitchell

Keeping Love As Principle

The principle of love is unchanging as Law, like the pull of gravitation or accord without flaw; So sweet is the harmony so deep is the depth, is it able to be found in this world of neglect? My heart is unnerved in search of this truth, my mind is perplexed for the burden of proof; How futile can be the very thoughts of many men, to pursue a loveless life and with this thought not reprehend? Changing the unchangeable would indeed be this feat, like a voice with no sound and pure honey with no sweet; Principle is established fact and irrefutable, is not the essence of love defined and thus concluded? Many in society who embrace our cold world, has lost sight of their hold as they age and grow old; Why is it said more than once I have heard, "Change is for the better," in every case, to me absurd? My thoughts are like seeds in the midst of the wild, silent and unplanted as there is no root to be found; What shall I do to make the subject known at hand, should I make this a public agenda as my purpose to reprimand? Nevertheless my hope is like the rays of the sun, or the beauty of the dawn as a new day just begun; What more am I asking by the love of God's grace, let principle remain established by the presence of Thy face!!!!

James E. Smith Jr.

Just Because of the Rain

Sometimes it rains for days and days, but we know that the sun will shine again . . . if not today, then tomorrow, if not tomorrow, then another day, the sun will shine again. We never think twice, whether the sun will ever shine again, we just believe, in our hearts, and it does, the sun always shines again.

When the rain pours, it's good . . . for we know that in the long run, the crops, the grass, the flowers and the trees will benefit from the watering of the rain. And, after the rain has stopped, the air will be cleaner and fresher, the flowers prettier, the grass greener, the crops healthier, and the sun is shining again . . . And now, we have learned to appreciate the value of the rain . . .

So, it is times in our lives, when the rain begins to pour and the clouds overshadow the sun, that we must always remember, that the sun will shine again, and that the rain is good for the cultivation and development of the crops in our lives. Then, when the clouds have cleared and the rain has stopped, we will experience that maturity has come, just because of the rain. The sun will be brighter, our air cleaner and fresher, and our spiritual flowers will be blooming, and we will have grown even closer to God, just because of the rain. . . .

Diane Marie Young

The Loss

To the loving memory of Jesse Vernon Oliver Sr.
She feels empty. Like her world has somewhat changed
Will she ever regain herself. Will she always feel the pain
Witnessing something drastic. Changed the way she looks
at the world
Will it always remain a painful thorn in her soul
Will she grow up to be a beautiful girl
He wanted to see her before it was time to go.
So she came as he asked for her to do so
She climbed on the bed and sat down beside him
She had to be brave and hold back her tears
Even though she was full of fear
How was the child to know that she would never see him again
That very next morning a call of pain and sorrow came. He was dead
At that moment in time all she could think about was him
She remembered those hot summer days. They would go out
in the garden
He would take his cane and put holes in the ground
She would follow behind him. Putting in the seeds
While on her hands and knees. They would then go and eat a watermelon
In the winter, near Christmas time. They would eat fruitcake all the time
Now all she has is loving memories. Sorrow and pain have no remedy
Life goes on and so will she. That's the way she wants it to be

Miranda LaRue Brown

I Feel the Thunder

I feel the Thunder in the sky: And I know, I'm on the verge of a miracle promised to come, to light the sky of my night, and way.

In my mind, I can see Angels dancing to my victory,
I hear the Winds whispering to me: You're going through the fire.
Go through the flames. Now, dance to your victory.

You see me, crumpled in a heap, as I bow at your feet.
Tears mingle in my hair, dripping to mix with your own; You've set,
waiting for me to accept this great feat, Where Mercy has kissed Defeat.

I feel the thunder in the Sky,
I hear the Wind calling out my name, you're going through the fires.
Go through the flames. Now, dance to your victory.

Child, I am your Father,
Know Me. Believe Me. See Me. Touch Me. Feel Me.

In the Thunder, in the Wind, and the Rain,
As surely as the Angels danced on Jacobs stairs'
I hear your prayers.

There is victory in the beat of the Eagle's wings.
In the rumbling hooves of the Buffalo, as he speeds upon his way.
The Hawk cries out in the Wind, Thunder and the Rain; you're going through the fires. Going through the flames. And I'll be waiting for you there.

Starla K. Powell

Winter Solstice

The wind stirs a rhythm into the aspen boughs
As the golden leaves whisper a melody and fall
To the ground in a shimmering dance.

The mighty spruce join the sacred dance.
They sway methodically to keep time with the frozen
Moans of the wind, sending low creaks of summoning skyward.

The clouds gather 'round the low voices and thicken as they approach.
Streams of light are pulled through the gray shadow of clouds
Illuminating the dusk air before turning back to heaven.

The wind screams fiercely as the trees strengthen
Their song at last the clouds understand.
A single seed of ice slowly glides to the earth.

Winter begins!

Matt Tebow

How To Let Go

I met you it seems, just yesterday, but now you're going so far away.
It's not been long and yet I see that you are quite a lot like me.

You understand what most others don't, and stand by me when
others won't. I trust you, and you, me too.
But yet, I just do not know, how to let go.

We've had our fights, and we've been hurt. We've made them
right and very curt. We've had bad days, and we've had good,
and still we are misunderstood. Two people like us just should
know, how, exactly, to let go. But my dear friend . . . friend did I
say, why you are more than that today, and not just today,
ut every day.

But my dear friend it can't be true, what will I do without you?
The days will be long, and longer still, until the day comes I may
see you at will.

But think of this for just a moment, of all the times we've shared
together. We've laughed, we've cried, been sad and happy.
We've made mistakes both big and small, and still I do not mind
at all to call you my Best Friend.

At times I felt that I hated you, and others you hated me too. But still
I know that that's not true, and yet I just do not know how to let go.

But look the day has come, to soon as I can tell, the day that I must
say two words I know too well. But there is just one thing that I
would like to know, Do you know how to let go?

Laura C. Pronovost

The Everpresent Conscience

The everpresent conscience looks over you like a mother,
protecting you from what is wrong.
It is an emotional friend that can bring you tears.
A gift from God and a loyal friend who is always there.
We were all born with consciences, but some of them
were shunned by our inner self to eternal silence.
Those who did, paid dearly with pain and torment.
A part of you that will never die and should not be taken for granted.

Jordan Falchook

Beauty

The beautiful lakes mingle with the rivers,
And the rivers with the ocean;
The winds of heaven mix forever.
With a sweet emotion;
Though sometime a thunderous cloud emerges from beneath the light.
Somehow the shiny crystal fountains are seen even with all the commotion.

Nicole Dinkins

Big Face Moon

Oh Big Face Moon that's shinning so bright,
Keep clear the path that I tread tonight.
And tell no one that you saw me this night,
Not even Gilliam Town whose lights are so bright.
She would laugh at me if she knew the facts,
Especially if you told her you saw my tracks.
Tell all these fields, trees and grass
To hush their mouths as I try and pass
Tell all the snakes, bobcats and coons
that you are watching over me, Oh Big Face Moon
You can see by my face and also my height
That I am only a little girl caught in the night
When I started out for Home I knew it wouldn't be soon
Oh Thank God! for your Big Face Moon.
There was not a ghost and not a breeze as I passed those pecan trees.
They just stood back and gave me room. Thank you so much Oh
Big Face Moon! As I walked across that highway home, my mood
indeed was quiet. My family now was looking on and just how
might you be?" I didn't want to appear excited, and kept listening
to their tune. I just wanted to take a last look and say,
"Thank you Oh Big Face Moon!"

Lula M. Avery

A Day of Mourning

Today is a day of mourning, for those who died without warning
Let us bow our heads in prayer for all who are in despair
We all must pray without ceasing, for "evil" deeds are increasing
We must never get so complacent, for the devil has many agents
It behooves every one of us, to know that in God we must trust
We know not our day or hour, but we know God has all power
Be grateful to Him for all things, and seek refuge under His wings
He will let no evil befall you, you must trust Him to guide you through
Praise Him each day He gives you to live,
    His blessings anew to you   He'll give
We pray for those who are left to mourn,
    their loved ones no more to   see the dawn.
Many lives lost, both young and old.
    Why? The reason may never be told
We pray for the ones who did this deed,
    our hearts are sad and we do weep
We cannot judge, but God will judge them ,
    one day for sure they'll answer to Him
If you know not the Lord today, seek Jesus, for He is the way.
It could have been you or even I, not given a chance to say good-bye.
So let us unite in prayer today, for none of us are here to stay.

Frances M. Bradman

The Dark and Bloody Land - III
(The Past - The Future)

Beneath this "Dark and Bloody Land" lies the echoes of
voices now long lost
Can you hear their murmurings—their saga of conflict and struggle?
Can you hear their shouts: freedom, conquest, revenge, death?

Feel the raw invective roiling beneath the surface as a witch's brew
set to simmer over an open cook fire.
Experience the chill fae mist obstructing your vision
of those souls still haunting these much disputed hills.

Yet, even now on occasion, there's a sudden time warp, a lurch
in your spirit, a quickened sense - you are not alone. There
walks alongside a shadow person calling you to listen to his tale
of victory and woe. Still there is a glimpse of life as it was all
those years ago. Look, and you will see the faded colors of a
patchwork quilt laid at the foot of an old four-posted bed.
Search, and you can almost smell the aroma of coffee boiling in
the embers of the open hearthfire. Stand quiet, and you too can
feel the sudden clench of fear at some unfamiliar sound.

Come to these hills and listen for the votes. Come to these hills
and feel the remnant of struggle and conflict, still vibrating
through time. Come to these hills and experience the past
merging with the future. Come to these hills, touch the verdant
life-giving soil and see why Kentucky was once called paradise.

Laura Wiggins

True Love

My diplomatic love and my deep love to you has just forced
me to write this poem. You shift my heart into over-drive.
Your pretty beauty and charm take the place of birth.
Your beautiful face is always rolling over and over in my mind.
Your sweetly voice sunning sweetly in my ears.
Your sweet smile just in front of me and I say, "I love you."
Just giving myself five minutes for reflection of my mind,
I found myself with you swimming in a world full of roses and gold.
It's the consequences of dreams that I found my pen dancing
automatically on this paper dramatically controlled by my tender
fingers. A day without thinking of you is like a year without June.
It's not important the distance between us, for I close my eyes
and see you holding my hand saying, "I love you."

Erasmus M. Mhlanga

Addict

Am I an addict? An addict of your love?
For I fear, it's as though sent from above.
For when I'm with you I can only bear to smile,
and if I were to be placed in hell (as long as it was with you),
it would be worthwhile.
Yet, though, sometimes I'm pained and hurt bearing a sea,
carrying the burdened tears of me it only leaves me to see...
This has to be love,
or I would not keep returning to the hit spot, in the glove.
For you are to me, as the wind that pushes a swing,
even to a dove with broken wings.
Yes I love you, and would suffer my desire,
if I knew if you in return would love me and never tire.
So I'll just keep waiting, until you decide it's time for me to know
of your love in return,
and then I will no longer have to write of love like
this, on pages of which I only wish to burn.
For this is the only way in which I have to say "I love you."

Tina Faragi

Unseen Gifts

Have you ever smelled the scent of an exotic orchid?
The aroma is so sweet and full of life
The feel of the tiny petals wafting across your
Bare skin on a cool summer's eve
As it whispers of untold delights
Or have you ever seen the eyes of a child
Witnessing the new falling snow for the very first time?
As the child's face shines with the unbridled joy
As he learns of the untold delights
With the feel of the warm noon sun shining
On the glorious frozen wonderment
As the orchid wilts and the snow diminishes from the heat of the day
The circle of seen gifts renews itself with the new day
Have you ever stopped to think of all the things you have seen,
Touched or even smelled as a precious gift from God to you?
The unseen gifts in our life no matter how small or big are no less important
And more precious than the gifts that are seen, bought or sold.
Do you know what the unseen gift is in your life?
The unseen gift is you!

Teresa E. Townsend   Belleville, KS

Wish You Were Here

The morning sun arises bringing forth a new day.
The children awake all bubbling with joy and at the ready to play.

They hustle about putting warm clothing on,
For new snow had fallen, and this is what they wanted to sled down on.

As the children are getting ready for the eventful day,
I glance out the window marveling at natures beauty.

The sun acts as a silhouette for the snow covered trees.
And a bird ruffles his feathers as if he is pleased at what he sees.

The limbs become flaccid under the weight of the snow,
Creating a graceful setting which is a shame to see go.

Some of the snow has started to melt from the roof,
Forming icicles that shimmer like jewels that are polished and proof.

The children are back inside now all happy and worn.
They huddle by the fireplace exchanging giggles while keeping warm.

They scurry on upstairs for it is getting late,
With the thoughts of what tomorrow may create.

Now I can settle down and relax in my chair.
With the thoughts of wishing you were here.

For the beauty of the day still seemed empty and alone,
For your beauty was missing, but the thoughts of you still kept me aglow.

Gary R. Benoit

Man

I am man, I can feel;
I can sense, I can wonder;
I can fear, I can think;
I am man.

My skin is a prism,
Be it black, white or red;
Be it yellow or pink;
I am man.

My blood runs cold when frightened;
My heart skips beats with elation;
My mind races with clouds of confusion;
I am man.

My eyes have seen history,
Yet have I learned.
Once seen through a child's innocence,
My perception has tarnished.

I am not different from you;
but I am intelligent,
to create differences where there are none?
I am man.

Barbara Weiler

Ode to the Red Wings!

I write these words of wisdom to
A hockey team that was real due;
42 years a burden lifted
The Red Wings were a team most gifted;
Yzerman, Murphy, we want to scream
They bottled up the Lindros team;
The Russian five traversed the rink
And Philly became a missing link;
The Wings progressed and Scotty kept score
His head all filled with hockey lore;
The flyers were so strong and deep
To no avail - a red wing sweep;
The wings all played for the true fans' sake
And all enjoyed their "Coffey break";
The octopus from the rafters hung
The die-hard fans their praises sung;
The penalty box was filled a lot
By body checks their minutes got;
Detroit, I hope you keep it up
And hoist again the Stanley Cup!!!

Emil C. Carlson

The Swan

A block of ice.
That was me.
When all was innocent.
Drip, drip, chip, chip.
Chip away at me.

As time marched on
A form began to take shape.
Not even I knew
What the future held for me.
Drip, drip.

And then a wing appeared—
Next, two feet to which I stood tall.
Down this rutted, unknown path
One more wing formed to create a pair.
Chip, chip.

One sweet, lilac day
A swan came into view.
And each soft feather was a triumph or fall I had lived.
And someday down this more familiar path
This swan will fly away.

Alana N. Coats

The King's Highway

If you can walk the dusty path of broken stone and earth,
Without a thought come day or night of your own life's worth,
If you can be found obedient in the little things, come what may,
Do you think yourself worthy to travel the King's highway?

If you can bestow kindness and mercy, both before it's too late,
If you can wear the cloak of forgiveness, no matter how heavy its weight,
If you can endure the cruelty of others, and all those little games they play,
Do you think yourself worthy to travel the King's highway?

If knowing that the evil one plots death to be your fate,
For it is the evil one who despises most your glorious, future state,
If you can stand firm against Satan, yet kneel before God at the end of day,
Do you think yourself worthy to travel the King's highway?

If you ears can hear the sound of many feet, as if running in a race,
If they should come to crucify you, those who run in joint pace,
If you can be nailed to a stake, surely then, couldn't you say,
You would be worthy to travel the King's highway?

If a crown of thorns you can wear, as He, when that third hour had come,
If you have as great a love as He in the sixth hour, as darkness covered the sun,
If, in the ninth hour, "It is finished," to the Father you could pray,
Then you have already traveled the King's highway.

Gloria Stumpf

Quantum Leap

The wind blew through his hair. The gentle cooing of pigeons
and the refreshing smell of his cigarette burning down to ashes
caused him to rethink the most important decision of his life.
He looked down, perusing the crowd.

There stood his parents, looking up at their son, praying the
seemingly inevitable would not happen. He missed the days when
he and his father would ride aimlessly in the '57 Ford. He missed
the trips to the park and the long talks. He missed his dad.

Petty arguments had given way to stony silence and the beginning
of an estrangement neither could overcome. He knew that
after jumping the police would find the letter and give it to his dad.
His love, loneliness and confusion would finally be expressed.

He threw his cigarette stub down and pulled out his pack of Camel
Lights. It was empty . . . well, this just wasn't his day. Tilting his
head back, gazing up toward the azure cloudless sky, he laughed.
He took one more look at the world around him, turned and jumped.

He landed on the gravel rooftop. The crowd burst into applause.
He ran down into the street below and gave his father a hug that
conveyed better than words the unspoken feelings between them.
They drove in the '57 Ford to the park and talked about the past.

John J. Horvath Jr.

My Little JoAnn

What a dear little tot is little JoAnn, she's as sweet as a day in June;
so tender, so loving, so good and so grand, a rose from God's garden in bloom.
With joy in her heart, and with willing feet, she tenderly serves in her way.
Anxiously, happily, doing her part to spread sunshine all through the day.
With eyes of clear blue, and gold of her hair, and cheeks all rosy and red,
She's a picture of health, to mother great wealth, and to dad, aha, none so fair!

When you're resting, and say you're just tired, she is ready to lend a hand;
Better service? No, never, if a nurse you hired, than is found in little JoAnn.
Just tell her a story, one she adores, about Jesus so tender and mild,
Tell of His love, and how He implores, saying "Come Unto Me, My Child."
And, as a garden flower is watered, so God's love sinks into her soul,
Giving life, and strength unaltered, sheltered safely into the fold.

Say! It's great to be blessed,
with a flower of love plucked from God's garden so fair;
may she grow and be used by the Father above, and joy in His service share.

Irene C. Pemberton

My World

If sunlight could be dark
and darkness be light

If we slept during the day
and awoke in the night

If we sat in our beds
and slept in our chairs

If walked underwater
and swam in the air

If we ran through the clouds
and we flew underground

If everything was wrong side up
and upside down

If we walked on the ceilings
and looked up at the floors

If we went through the windows
and climbed out of doors

I guess it wouldn't be our world anymore.
It would be mine.

Ashley Rolison

Untitled

There he stands in the doorway
Blocking all the view
There's no longer any time to play
He's already here and come without a clue

He snuck up on your withering heart
Is now grasping for your hand
Up rolls his hellish cart
To carry you to his land

He's come straight from your nightmares
But also from your dreams
Together all sorrow you two share
From all the madness rises steam

Fear builds deep inside you
But relief accompanies fear
Now you'll no longer feel blue
No more tears to smear

He's come right out of the doorway
And pounded at you with his wrath
You think of nothing you can say
But smile and welcome death

Nicole Johnson

If Only . . .

If only our world was clean
would we still have to try so hard
to keep it in the best of shape
so that the future could have a yard?
If only . . .

If only people didn't care
about the color of skin
all that would really matter
was the beauty that lies within.
If only . . .

If only every child was fed
and loved and housed and clean
and everyone could be friends again
and no one would have to be mean.
If only . . .

So the next time you're out on the street
pick up some trash and throw it away
shake someone's hand and give a child a hug
so that you don't have to say,
If only . . .

Jessica Rowland

Magic's Price

In the darkness of night
Magic bestows the air
Underneath a new moon's light
Appear little folk so fair

A silvered harp breaks the silence of calm
One by one they take up the dance
Its flowing rhyme tells of days long gone
The melody seems wrought by chance

On glassy wing they soar around
Their figures lithe and flowing
No one know where they are bound
Nor what harvest they are sowing

The music's fire begins to cease
Night loses its blackest hue
The golden field resumes its peace
As the folk leave two by two

The sun breaks the still of dawn
Now the cock crows thrice
The fairyfolk are long gone
For the magic has its price

     Michael D. Plumb

My Childhood

When I was at the age of five,
I sat beneath a Maple tree.
A storm came up so fast.
It started lightning.   I was scared.

My two brothers went to grocery store
with their little red wagon, shopping for my mom.
Hoping they would make it home
Before it rained, I prayed.

As I looked up to God, I asked God if he is real.
He sent a bolt of lightning and struck the Maple tree.
I was underneath, and I knew the sign
Was telling me, He is real.

As I grew up, I would never forget
My wonderful Saviour friend so true.
He gave me memories I will never forget,
Because I trusted him for more.

His Love is so great, none to compare.
No one will ever take his place,
Because he'll be forever faithful and true,
Just like he said in his wonderful book.

     Beulah Lepley

Country of Hope

It was September, when I came here.
Colorful leaves all over the streets.
From up there in the sky,
I saw you, and the quiet Mrs. Liberty, elegant . . .
Since then you are inside me.
Since then, I started to think,
that you were the only one:
adorable, beautiful;
"a country of hope and reunion."
Since then,
I have been trying to belong to you . . .
suddenly you don't want us.
But here we are:
finding out that America is really "you,"
that English is "English only,"
that young and old people are losing their battle,
that babies are losing their game;
and families are falling apart!
But here we are:
"Aliens, encircled in this sharp fear!

     Mario Antonio Zepeda

If You Think . . .

If you think that you are special
Like I used to do,
Then maybe you've been thinking
Good friends are very few.

You never seem to realize
Like I used to do,
That just maybe, could it be,
The problem lies with you?

So, if you think that you are special
Like I used to do,
Take stock, analyze, and
Honestly think it through.

Then you will come to realize
Like I try to do,
You'll have friends aplenty
Because the world doesn't revolve around you!

     Diana L. Long

Untitled

You can always read articles of footprints in the sand.
But the footprints that wonder in my mind, only
I can understand.
You gave me memories that will linger on
In my peaceful dreams.
Keeping thoughts of you there in memories,
Are easier, the way it seems.
Your gentle smile,
Your soft words of love,
Our warmth and closeness for a while.
The footprints of mind will always belong.
There will never be an ocean to wash them away
As the ocean did the footprints in the sand.
These are footprints in my mind,
And not footprints across the land.

     Johnny L. Espenschied

Autumn Leaves

The falling leaves of Autumn have arrived,
In colors typical of Autumn.
Emerald green leaves turn into,
Deep golden leaves with crinkled edges from the birch tree,
Brilliant orange and intense crimson of the sugar maple,
The dark chestnut leaves of the oak tree.
The colors of the summer wild flowers are fading away.
As the colors of the summer die, Autumn arrives.
Soon Winter will come, with snowflakes and icy waters.
All color will leave and white shall prevail.
But there will be the color of,
The delicate leaves of the silver maple tree,
Reflecting against the winter snow.
Ice storms that will cover everything in silver,
Glistening from the radiating sun above.
Winter and Autumn are a time for change,
With seasons there is life and death.
Death is upon the land now,
But soon delicate colors of spring and summer will return,
And life will start again.

     Janice Fiorelli

Catharsis

Emotions run deep like the still of the creek.
When there's no one around and no other sound.
Then rain and lightening all over the peace,
Tossing rocks and stones around in the deep.
They filter away all the dust and the grime,
And toss them away in a whirlpool of time.
Then silently, silently, the rains are forgiving
And the creek becomes deep again.
Just like the beginning.

     Lesa Lee Mustard

A Fractured Heart

A fractured heart reaches out to other fractured hearts
Sharing, holding, touching, loving caring,

Hoping to achieve, in return, but yet not asking for anything
hand open-wide
palms up! Waiting for what's already exist so deep within
that no one can dare to even pretend
to extend the type of love that already exists so deep within

Yet, the fractured pieces seem to linger,
The pain seems to continue around the rough edges of the soul
Yet, love, continues to call beckon

Loves seems to know no pain or boundary,
still searching out the cries of others
who seemingly bear the same signs of brokenness
in hope to find some fitted pieces,
to the fractured fragments of the soul
as the heart continues to yearn for love

No one seems hear the cry or take the hand that's open
because of the lack of trust and total caring ad commitment of
the truth of love, which has no prejudices, no disguise, no shame
no pretense, but just is!

Commie Ell Jones

Untitled

God made man in His image
From the dust of this earth.
God made a woman from man.
Each has a role in this life:
A woman to bring forth children,
To watch pray and give care in the home;
A Father to be Christ Provider and Protector.
This is an open letter to a newborn Son.
One day my Son, you will to take a wife
And have a child of your own.
A woman with tears of joy
Also has tears of sorrow and much, much pain,
For this is God's wonderful, Glorious plan.
God sent His only Begotten Son.
One day the Book of life will be open,
By believing by faith, your name written in Blood
In the lamb's book of life.
This is an open letter, to His newly born Son.

Stanley Klayer Deremo

Mother, Mother.

Mother, Mother I have something
difficult to tell you.
I've lost all hope for myself,
my innocence has been taken
against my will.
Uncle Ron plays games with my
body and mind, he says no matter
what I say, it's all my fault.
Mother, I don't know why it's
happened like this, or why it began,
I just want it to stop!
Mother, will you help me go to the police?
Mother why are you looking at me with anger on your face—
don't you believe me,
why would I lie to you?
Mother don't walk away from me,
please believe me! Mother, Mother!

Hope Mesa

Psychic Vampire

Soulseeker, hungry again.
Feeding on dead dreams, broken promises, tricks and lies.
Living forever, undercover, yet hidden in plain sight.

Hunting, moving, quickly passing—before a clue gives you away.
Hurry, hurry, growing weaker.
Time is beating the soul seeker.
A new dreamer must be found.
Treading lightly, breathing quickly, wings on pavement
Without a sound.

Suddenly, you see her, she's the one, the new dreamer.
You wisk her away, like the thief that you are.

Before the night is over, the dreamer is your lover.
Her soul slipping with each sigh
Of course, she'll never know it.
In deed, she'll hardly show it.

Ah, but the proof of what you've taken, no way
Can be mistaken
The proof is in the eyes.

Alex Accomazzo

Mirror Image

Have you ever looked in a mirror
And found you weren't looking at what you thought?
You're almost the same,
But there's something different
Different about your eyes,
Once you saw compassion and care in them
Now you see a fake,
Someone who's self-centered and hateful,
It can't be me! I'm not like that!
But a mirror doesn't lie,
It shows it how it is
You want to scream out
"No, it's not true!"
But you can't,
You know the truth

Have you looked in a mirror lately?

Rachel Zeigler

April

A life so beautiful, a life so young
Yes, your daughter's life, your only one.

So many nights, I cannot sleep;
I feel your pain, I hear you weep.

Wishing there were something I could do
To lift this burden, take it away from you.

So I just pray, and pray, and pray, and pray
That God will ease your pain, Oh God I pray.

Being a mother and a distant friend,
I know how you feel, but it's not the end.

April's just beginning to blossom and grow,
She's in heaven Pat! She is, I know!

May God give us the strength to endure this pain,
it will never completely end, but it won't always be the same.

The burden will become lighter, I know, in time.
April lived, and she will always live in our hearts and minds!

You're a good mother, be strong for your son.
I know God is listening and he'll help you to overcome.

He'll guide you through this pain, one day at a time;
He'll give you the strength you need and peace of mind.

Carolyn Green

Fork In The Road

Comes a point in life,
When you see a fork in the road.
Which way do you go?
Day passes day, each one the same.
Sister it's all a game.

On and on I plow and I plant.
The path I tramp looks wider,
Yet nothing grows.
Up ahead- a fork in the road.
Now, what if, I think, I go right?
Pray tell dear man, what's to the left?

Today, I climbed a hill, stopped, looked forward, looked back,
Then sat on a rock.
Behind me, the path I had tramped,
The right I had chosen.
And, before me, up ahead—
Another fork in the road.
So, what if, I think, I go left?
Say nothing you! I know what's to the right.
To the left I'll go.

E. A. McArthur

Our God Is God, Not Saddam

There's a desert storm a raging across the foreign sea,
There's a man who thinks he is God,
But we know he cannot be,
He has no pride—no dignity,
No feelings what so ever,
What is worst - he wants us all
to think that he is clever,
He prays like he is Holy as though he knows no sin,
A hardened criminal without a cause
is the way to describe him,
He thrives on Praise and glory
from the blood of other lands,
Make no mistake— Saddam Hussein
is a mad-man in Command,
How dare him use our Peace for War,
our men for sacrifice,
His behavior is an outrage,
His doom is his surprise.

Dorothy Fisher

You

The glow of the moon, on an open sea
Or its beauty on the Cliffs of Dover.
The sparkle of the dew, at morning lite
And when you smile!

You, radiate all that is beautiful, in life.
When compared with the things I've seen!
The Alps, Nechar, Rhine, and Moselle rivers,
The Atlantic ocean calm as a mirror!

The glitter of your eyes, out shine the Moon
Sun, and radiant lights that glow.
Their warmth, emulate an open heart
On a cold winter's evening!

Bardot, Princess Grace, Loren all
Had their beauty and fame!
You in quite bliss, surpass them
In Warmth, Beauty, and Kindness!

A song goes something like this!
You are so wonderful to me.
You are so beautiful to me!
I can only say, tis true, this is You!!

Richard Casey

That Million Dollar Feeling

If I had a single dollar
For every time I thought of you
I would be a wealthy person
With more money than I would know with what to do

If I had a single dollar
For every time I visualize your beautiful face
I would be a high roller
And everything I had would have exquisite taste

If I had a single dollar
For every time I miss you my dear
I would own half of the world
Some things of real value and others I would have no care

If I had only a single dollar
But I had your true love so rare
I would feel so blessed and honored
That I would still be a millionaire

Raymond L. Floyd

The Thrill Of Victory, The Agony Of Defeat

In the game of ping pong, it's not how hard you play,
It's what you accomplish.
Ask yourself, did I play well, and was I pleasant?
A thoroughbred, never cries.
You take the bitter with the sweet.
As a last resort you make strategic retreat.
A person who cries is a half of a person,
without any sense of pride.
Play the game of ping pong well enough
to make your opponents get a stomp to fit their romps,
because you wailed on them, until their hind parts jumped.

Roosevelt Cox, Jr.

Your Beauty

Your beauty is so immense
Past, present, and future tense.
Your smile brings radiant light
To those stuck in the dark of night.
Your hair is as soft as a spring breeze,
Everyday the world's eyes you do please.
Your beauty is like a rainbow in the sky,
I would talk to you but the courage is far from nigh.
You are the wind, sun, and sea,
Without you the world would not be.

Stephen Rice

Born Again

Once we thought we were close to divinity.
We used to walk with God through the garden,
Until Eve picked the apple from the tree.
Now in the garden we are forbidden.
How we live in a life of sin.
It all but defines our humanity.
That is how life must begin,
And last until eternity.
The world has become a foreign land.
Our lives broken apart,
Wondering on which shore we stand,
As our peace is ripped from our heart.
Where did our souls begin to cry?
Why must the dying ask why?
How can children be expected to die,
And pass peacefully into the sky?
But the sun will rise again,
In a worlds that's war-torn.
I will see the angels again.
The day I died was the day I was born.

Jacob Noterman

Echoes Of The Past

September breezes in the mist.
Softly whispering my wish.
Friends that never stay true,
May find their wish forever blue.

Slowly leaving the past behind,
Never looking forward to the pain I'll find.
Echoes of the past forever in my mind.
Echoes of the past remembering people I may
Never find.

Bonnie G. Aubrecht

Happy Birthday William Shakespeare

Hail, hail, the gangs are all here,
Paying homage to the bard Shakespeare,
In "much ado about nothing" the play is the thing,
Or it's the story of "Henry the Fifth" an English king,
Could it be tale of "Merchant of Venice",
Or a noble Roman called "Caius Marcius Coriolanus",
Perhaps it may be a "Midsummer Night's Dream",
Or the king "Henry the Eight" he of broad beam,
"Antony and Cleopatra" on a ship they did sail,
And now we come to a play called "The Winter's Tale",
"Two gentleman of Verona" we dare say,
"Julius Caesar" remember his words "et tu brute"
We now have a play called "King Lear",
Three daughters the king had to fear,
"Loves Labor Lost" and "As You Like It",
And "The Comedy of Errors" as we see fit,
Would it be "Lady Macbeth" out, out, damn spot,
Or the "Merry Widows of Windsor" a comedic plot,
"King John", Henry the Fourth, or Fifth, "Othello the Moor of Venice,"
We wonder why he did not write a play called "Dennis the Menace."

David Schwartz

My Shattered Dream

I fell in "love" with the man of my dreams
Forty some years ago -
Soon after - I realized - he was not what he seemed -
And my heart broke and the tears did flow.
Two wonderful sons - were given to me -
Two blessings that "God" did bestow.
The years came and went - as I struggled - to make sense
of this man- who cared nothing for me.
And now I can see, how his hatred of me
Grew deeper with each passing year.
At last - I did leave - the man of my dreams
and ended up with a broken heart!
My "Love" turned to "Fear" - for this terrible man
Who shattered my dream - and you see
I paid the ultimate price - for falling in "Love"
With this man - who Never loved me.
So now all I wish - is - to be Free.

Virginia H. D. Cook

Peace

It's like snow falling on
earth's deaf ears.

It's like an eternal love.

It's our own personal heaven.

It's the sun's tapered fingers
tickling us in the morning.

It's the moon's welcoming arms caressing our
aching bodies at night.

It's the quiet that seeps thru the busy days.

It's the invisible inner source
of power our hearts ache for.

Beverly Broussard

Zeus

In the backyard of his palace
Zeus slowly creeps up
His dark shadows shove Apollo's chariot out of the sky
It grows darker and darker
Then suddenly Zeus throws his thunderbolt
from his hand
onto his mother
she cries out
Stop, Stop!
Her body is burning
Zeus starts to cry
His tears drip off his face and
heals his mother's wounds
Zeus cries out
I am sorry, so sorry
Zeus runs back to his palace
to be comforted by Hear
Apollo calms his horses
and gets back into the sky,
cleaning up his father's tears.

Ryan R. Hays

The Earth

Another sphere floating in the bright darkness.
This one is different.
Life is spreading and dying all at the same time;
A giant bubble holding memories and dreams;
A place where tall redwoods hide the animals;
A place where mist covers the wonders of life;
Where the ocean rolls our its anger and joy to the sands.
A place where the clouds are distant puffs of cotton,
Where the wind is a glorious song,
Where the ferns hide the tracks of rare species,
Where sweet rain falls through canopies onto soft river water.
A place where life is struggling to sprout anywhere it can,
Where thunder crashes against the corners of the earth.
A place where galloping herds of animals are struggling
to survive on great plains,
A place where the young listen to the secrets of the conifers,
A place where small, round eyes of all colors are looking
Up at all the other spheres in the bright darkness.

Julia Maureen Benson

I Saw You Today

We did see you today
and I didn't know what to say.
Boy or girl it was love at first sight
when you were seen in that picture perfect light.
The very first photo of
your tiny little self
to put with the hundreds that will be on the shelf.
Your tiny arms and hands were stretched out
like you were letting us know what it's all about.
Your Mother and I had a few tears as I recall.
A wonder of wonders so small.
A small life so strong as to start a life for your Mother
and to help complete a circle for another.

Carol VanBalen

Silence

Dogs barking in the night,
Stereo music playing in a lit room.
You would think all in the 'hood is right,
Yet frequent thoughts of gloom.
The day also filled with fright,
No sun, no game, no work, no moon.
It is Sunday, think worship, study, bright,
God, unseen, unheard, unknown, yet full bloom.

Robert A. Pence

Mothers

Mothers, what can you say?
They're always there for you, anytime, night or day.

They wipe your nose and patch up your knees,
Along with skinned up elbows from falling out of trees.

They hold you tight when you've had a bad dream;
They are always there for you, at least that's the way it seems.

They make you stand in the corner and say it's for your own good,
And maybe you'll learn something, or at least you should.

And when you're bad, a spanking's what you need,
And it never fails—they always say,
"This won't hurt you as much as it hurts me."

Then you finally get older and it's time to leave the nest,
Then you take yourself a mate and hope for the best.

You apply all the things you were taught to believe,
And when things turn out right you are so relieved.

But one thing for sure you've come to understand,
The backbone of families is a mother's soft hand.

There's love in her touch, but she's strong in her own way,
So may this be the very best of all Mother's days.

Chuck Hall

Baseball

I sit and think of baseball in its prime,
Remembering the heroes of the game,
Brooklyn and New York, winning all the time,
The wins and the losses that gave them fame,
The greats, Mantle, Killebrew and Mays,
Along with Snider, Williams and Berra,
Dazzling the crowds with all their plays,
And Koufax, great pitcher of the era,
But now, a brand new age is upon us,
Ebbet's Field is gone, and the memories there,
Gehrig's record has been broken, and thus,
Players play for cash and give very little care,
As I think of Baseball in its prime,
I wish I'd go back to that great, great time.

David C. Shank

Affection

Love is more than a feeling and emotion
It is deep as the soul and a lasting devotion
For it is slow to lose patience and resort to fury
It must be taken one step at a time, unhurried
I shall become selfless to meet your needs
Because your kindness has put forth a seed
That will forever grow in me as I age
For we can look back on our lives like the turning of a page
Intertwined by the Master above
I want to give you my unconditional love
Not wanting to cause you any pain
I shall keep my mind on you and the world refrained
When I am with you I am just myself
Not rich in material things but in your humble wealth
May God hold you while we are apart
For you shall forever dwell within my heart
There is not a word to explain the fondness
Just the thought of you brings out the zealousness
That I can not hold within
While I fall in love with you again and again.

Stanley Gray

Leaves of Love

As I sit and watch the leaves fall off the trees
I often wonder about the power of a breeze.
Can it tell you how a true love feels?
Or will it tell you to stay on your heels?

As the summer sun finally sets
I often wonder if it has any regrets.
Does it ever ask itself "why"?
Does it ever want to run away and cry?

As the winter days grow dark and cold
I often wonder what the future will hold
Will there be fame, power, and friends?
Or will I stay lonely until the very end?

The mind is such a powerful thing
When you sit and watch the leaves fall off the trees

Joden Kohls

The Simpler Things

Buttons, bows, and butterflies
Soft breezes and long walks by
Peaceful waters and fragrant fields
In bloom, or frog ponds that yield
Evening serenades, and long-legged cranes
That gracefully bow to gentle rains.

Shady trees, and sunny parks
Children's laughter and morning larks
Whirring bicycle tires that spin
And merry-go-round choruses of "spin us again"
Ice cream drippings on Sunday pants
And following the trail of picnic ants.

Family dinners, kids and cookies by the dozen
The smell of pies and cakes in the oven
Grandma's hugs, and joy surrounds
In a place where love abounds, with
A rosy spring and a pumpkin September
And more simple blessings than I can remember.

Carla Edwards

Why

Why did you have to go?
Why did you leave me?
Why didn't you stay?
These questions keep
going through my mind.
You left me sad and lonely, why?
You left me scared and confused, why?
If I could ask you one question
it would be "Why?"
Why did you leave me with a broken heart?
Why can't I understand?
If I could ask you one question
it would be "Why?"

Jill Justus

The Return Of The Lord

The end of the world is almost here
As I think about it, I tremble in fear
We're soon to see our Lord Jesus Christ
And to see your face, I think it would be quite a sight
The devil has had his time for a thousand years
But the coming of the Lord is trouble to his ears
The Lord shall make His return in a twinkling of an eye
A return so fast He will leave people in a sigh
Then the world will end in a big bang
But to avoid the bang we must make a change
You can't go to heaven by being a fake
You must seek Him at all times for goodness sake
But only the Lord knows our faith
All we can do is seek Him and wait

Clarence Jackson Jr.

That Old North Star

Every night as the sun went down,
That first star would appear in the sky.
I would say these words
and place all my dreams on that old North Star.

Star light, star bright
First star I see tonight
I wish I may, I wish I might
Have the wish I wish tonight.

The dark sky brought hope and anticipation.
The belief that if you wished long and
hard enough that your wish would come true.

My wishes were for things that could never be.
My dreams were better than life.
The trip back to reality was long and hard.
I still long for my dream filled days and nights.

That old North Star comes out every night.
no matter where you are, no matter how you are
the one thing that is steady and true
is that wishes will always be made
and some might just come true.

Roseanne McGee

For Jason On His Graduation

Oh where, oh where has the time gone?
It's not 1997, that calendar must be wrong!
It seems like yesterday when I removed your training wheels
I was at the 10 year old all stars last week, is how it feels.
But those days have passed as you're in your gown of blue
Your childhood is gone and I am oh so proud of you.
As you reach out to take that ribbon wrapped scroll
Just how much joy you've brought me, I hope you know
As you walk so tall across that graduation stage.
My emotions are flipping like a turning page
These tears that well are those of happiness and joy
As my heart and head tell me, "There goes my little boy,"
But you're a young man now and you are on your way
You have stepped into adulthood on this very fine day
So now I must let go of you and realize you're not a child
Much like a lioness lets go of her cub into the wild.
Allow me to say once again just how proud I am on this day
You have brought so much love and laughter your own special way
The times we have shared couldn't be matched by another
Please know how much you are loved by me, your mother.

Laureen Wester

The Traveler

As the traveler walked down the solemn road
He knew not where to go.
He would end up where his legs would take him,
where to he did not know.

As the traveler moved on, he came to a fork
the road it broke in two.
He tried to decide which way to take,
but this he could not do.

As he sat and looked down both the roads
until they curved from sight.
Which one should I take, which one he thought,
Are either of them right?

He finally decided which path to choose,
it was not down either way.
He thought, as he turned, and traveled back,
I'll try this road again, someday.

Brian Boyd

I Am . . .

I am a girl without words who likes the art of life.
I wonder how God became God.
I hear angels sing in churches.
I see the light of heaven.
I want to know what heaven is like.
I am a girl without words who likes the art of life.

I pretend that everyone gets along.
I feel that war is unnecessary.
I touch the hearts of others.
I worry about the day life ends.
I cry for those who lives have already ended.
I am a girl without words who lives the art of life.

I understand the facts of life.
I say that we are all equal.
I dream of the days to come.
I try to meet my life goals.
I hope that mankind will find peace and not die out.
I am a girl without words who likes the art of life.

Tara Henson

A Visit

I'm sorry, sister, it's been a while.
You see, I've been so busy . . .
I know it's no excuse, but I'm getting old.
I'm still picking up pieces.

Do you remember, sister, the day we arrived?
They finally unloaded the boxcars,
And we were separated for the first time since birth.
I only saw you twice in the camp.
Remember, sister, how we lied about being twins?
The scientists terrified us.
I've already told you about my search,
Looking for you after the liberation,
And how I finally found you here in Poland.
I visit whenever I can.
I'll leave this hillside now, and go home.
I can stay no longer without tears.
I stand alone in this unmarked graveyard.
Maybe the others have forgotten.
But I won't forget, sister.
All my love always, goodbye.

Maria Montague

Heroes

The world is full of diverse people,
There are those that come into
Our lives and leave us unaffected,
There are those who come into our lives,
Touch our souls, then slowly fade away,
All that is left from them,
Nothing but a mere shadow buried
In the deepest part of our memories,
Then there are those who possess a very
Special gift, the gift of touching
Our souls, without ever crossing our paths,
By uttering a few words,
They can trap you into their spell,
Enchanting everyone who listens,
They are indeed different from the rest,
When they come into our lives, they can never
Be forgotten, their gift enables them
To be looked up to, be loved, remembered,
These people go by a very special name,
HEROES

Catalina Mora

Want

You are nearer to me than my deepest breath.
Your touch melts my resistance,
yet I am left yearning.
I ache to feel the enchantment of love surrendered.
For I have plunged from a rivulet
of desire into unfathomable passion.
And, yet, you are a mirage, just beyond my reach.
Am I destined to this void, to endure this hunger?
Will I alone know this incessant love?
I cannot speak to you the words I long to hear,
and feel unfettered devotion.
To caress your body, while eluding your soul.
To give my love unheeded.
I simply cannot, yet I must.
For love, once yielded, cannot be rescinded.

Barbara Clark

Daughter

Don't desert me.
You are falling down a narrow well, a cramp grave.
It makes me feel cold and dejected.
Why go with those worms?

Every time you kiss them your life breath gets sucked away.
They pretend to care but you will let you fall,
Break, scrape, just so they can have you all.

Where is your loyalty, faithfulness?
We are to be friends to the dying end, mother and daughter
I feel so cold and dejected, what can I do because of you.
You I loved—one of my daughters don't go, desert the worms.
Their life is dust, dirt a grave.

Stay with those who care, you could be brave:
Care to live again, grasp this rope.
Because the well is dry.
You will surely break and die,
And I will surely cry.

Kathleen Reynolds

Wishes Can Come True

All my early life, it seems,
Was centered on almost hopeless dreams.
Not only did I want love,
But I wanted to love.
Then, one day I saw blue skies,
For the miracle of a son was before my eyes.
I couldn't believe how blessed I could feel,
For the essence of one of my dreams became real.
As time went on my eyes began to water,
Precipitated by another dream, that of having a daughter.
Nature couldn't provide this fulfillment,
But the inner beauty of my son made it evident
That one day he would bring along
The daughter who would fill my heart with song.
The result—I have happiness beyond all measure,
For in both of them I have the utmost treasure.

Frances Roth

A Painting

A painting is a poem without any words
The colors add rhyme
The brush strokes are swiftly, but one at a time
If you listen closely at a painting you hear
The wind blow
Hear children playing and watch them grow
hear men laughing at a good joke
There's a pond hear a frog croak
Next time you're near a painting stop and look awhile
'Cause if you glance quick you might see a little girl smile

Jennifer Scheibel

Fade to Black

I have come to expect the teeth of the freezing pellets
biting at my windshield,
taunting the rubber tires
to grab the asphalt.
Icy roads follow February on its slick journey.
Glossed bridges the offspring
of a winter's day in the shade.
Where is the salt to tame the peril?
The few, green crocus shoots
claw the packed ground,
only to shrink away from the snarling cold.

I have come to expect a freezing touch on my shoulder,
as you push past me to hug another.
Your icy looks become an enemy,
revealing the hollowed inside through robin egg eyes.
Their warm glow now fading like embers.
Where are the sweet Valentines
to quiet the screaming pain?
The few soft glances struggle to peek through the hard facade,
only to disappear under your faded blue baseball cap.

Adrienne Garber

Slither

Converse with me in ancient tongues.
Spill the blood of knowledge upon my brow:
Let it poor into my eyes, tainting my old vision.
Oh, blackened night, take me far away.
Let me see the sunset.
Drift with me, dark one.
Let us knead and seed and sow
The shadows with our souls, so stark.
Intertwine the minds of all who love and hate
and show and tell our antecedent wisdom.
We can share the bonds of will
And distinguish all the filth and lies
and bring the light that leads
our hearts to all that lies ahead.

Chris Volenec

Untitled

Bitter sweet, pain and sorrow,
Oh, how I long, long for tomorrow.
Another day of longing I suppose,
But I guess that's just the way life goes.
Oh to enter a new life,
A burdenless life, void of strife.
A life of no more longing, no more sorrow,
A life of no tomorrow.
Now that is for what I long
Someone to share it with, someone strong.
Someone longing for the same thing,
Someone to take me under his wing.
Someone look at the world today,
Someone to say, "Hey, this isn't the way."
Someone who longs for eternal peace,
Longing to cure this lonely disease.
Someone who God wills for me,
Someone who looks and sees what I see.
But for now, I guess,
Only God knows what will be best!

Tiffany Ericson

Ah Yes . . .

We shed no tears, and those there are who wonder
that we can jest . . .
Are we by strange compulsion, or capricious whim possessed?
Do we not understand the ebb and flow of life to be
In serious vein, a trauma fraught with grim solemnity?
Ah yes . . . a lighter touch we choose, our spirits and heads held high.
We shed no tears, but deep within our silent hearts we cry!

Virginia E. Fox

Reasons

I walk about amongst the rain,
every drop a tear someone has made,
I surely cant imagine there sorrow but then again
there's always tomorrow.
Time is only but a wheel true
things are what you feel.
Yes we can all wait but to wait
longer can only hurt, for now you
only have more work.
I think about everything I know
and I realize everything is just a show.
Many, people wish a lot but
if it doesn't come true it's forgot.

Dustynn Burlingame

The Office Girl's Lament

I'm tied to my desk from 9 to 5.
Typing and phoning, but inside I'm groaning.
Yes sir Mr. Zilch, no sir Mr. Thrush:
It's hustle bustle, rush, rush.
But when the whistle blows at noon,
I hurry down to my private lunch room.
It's really the supply room
Which is dim and kind of small.
But spread across its dingy wall
Is a map of the world, and every day
I travel to far off lands and play.
I'm the Maharanee of Koochbear treading the desert sands.
I'm in Rio, Capri or Hong Kong . . . or other distant lands.
Whether the country rhythm be jungle, or a calypso beat
My sixty minutes are well spent (and sometimes I get to eat).
But it keeps me doing my average job
Taking the guff and the subway mob.
With hopes in my heart that it soon may be real.
I'm just getting used to how it will feel!

Ronnie Donofrio

Mold

People think they are invisible and
Nothing can hurt them when really
Death is right around the corner.
It seems so perfect to them also irresistible.
Temptation is there pulling their limp lifeless
Bodies in no one knows how to resist it.
To say anything is unheard of there is a certain "mold"
Of how everyone is but I break it; I'm the
Outcast of this perfect world. I am the
Oddball and shun from social life.
I have a deep feeling that just gets swept aside
With the rest of the dust from the
Floor; my life is irrelevant to anything
That goes on in his "perfect world."
Then I wake up and nothing is different.

G. F.

Reflections

Did you ever look up in the sky,
And watch the white clouds floating by?
Did you ever let your mind ponder,
As you watch the sky with all its wonder?

First a ship with sails so high,
Still there's plain clouds riding by.
Next a shape of a dog appears,
Soon the dog too disappears.

A bear, a cow and mountains show,
As though they reflected objects below.
Time passes so fast when you dream this way,
But haven't you had a beautiful day?

Mary L. Weiseman

Love Expressed

The undoubted, endless love inside my scared heart,
Is held inside for no one else but you.
I held my passion deep down in my heart so long,
To reveal only to one I love true.
Your hair is plentiful energy, flowing forth.
My hands run through and across your sweet face.
Your sweet body flows with silky smooth perfection.
I follow the sweet curves with detailed grace.
Your deep, lovely, ocean blue eyes are priceless gems.
In them I find all I will ever need.
Your voice is a soft, enchantingly loving bell,
Which I need: for without it my heart bleeds.
My life, liberty, and endless undying love,
Belong to you, my one and only dear.
Words cannot describe my endless feelings for you,
But I'll try with sweet whispers in your ear.
I wish I could express each little detailed thought;
To tell you all I feel inside for you.
But there are not enough words, or paper, or pens;
So by your side, I'll prove my love is true.

Wesley Ownby Jr.

Sorrow and Joy

My heart is full, my soul is crying
Forever searching for happiness.
It's at the tip of my fingers, but out of my reach
My mind is focused. My heart is full of conflict
My soul is unable to conform to unite.
Unable to be content with this confusion.
Not at peace with myself, unable to be whole
Forever searching for the unknown.
I am happiest where I am fill with joy.
I smile upon the sun. Knowing sorrow is lurking
My heart is full of possibilities, I rejoice in life
My soul is at peace. Not knowing what to expect
But not afraid to follow the path. For which
I am destined I look at my reflection and see contentment.
I have joy in my life.

C. James

Halls of Anonynmity

If I could let you know I've lived, if there were but a way
To let you know I walked this earth and wrote these words today,
I'd break through time's relentless walls to etch my name in stone
Through halls of anonymity where countless lie unknown.
Through fathomless eternity, the dead are laid to rest.
To time's cold, cruel obscurity, the hero ends his quest.
Like ants that swarm upon a hill and labour unto death,
So is the ceaseless plight of man who strives 'til his last breath.
But if on some cold city street I touch a heart of stone,
Or let one solitary soul know they don't drift alone,
If I can reach the teeming streets, enchant the bitter crowd,
If I can speak for you the words you cannot say aloud,
In bars, back alleys, barrios, awake the hardest heart
To a fleeting glimpse of beauty in the dismal and the dark,
If I can melt the soul of ice of one who hears my word,
I'd know I'll live forever in the hearts of those who've heard.

Maria Antonia Valdes

Why?

As a young boy, I often ask the question why?
Why does the mountains and tall pines reach toward the sky?
Why are there so many rivers and lakes
That stretch across this country so wide?
Why the ocean with its ebb and flow
of high and low tide?
These things were not created by
nature bened the sands of time.
But by God, who took a tear and
shaped it into one little sphere.

Keith Estes

For My Wishes And Prayers

For my wishes and prayers
It's you I been dreaming of the thrill of love

From the stars above I know you will always be with me
From dreams to memories

The love I found may wear a crown

A circle to a family
For love I feel is real
You touched my heart
And filled it with magic
For love is a sign
Of hope Gold finished

Sandra E. Seip

Loneliness

She sits hunched over the counter,
Her delicate hands tightly clenched
Around the steaming cup of tea.

Sad grey eyes stare unseeingly,
As tears drip silently down her pale checks;
Unaware, she is, of others around her.

In the corner booth, the man
Feels unbearably moved,
As he gazes upon her gentle beauty.

Sympathy fills his heart;
If only he could hold her close,
And shield her from life's cruelties.

She lifts her head to see,
Her lonely eyes sweeping the room,
Briefly settling on the stranger.

He seems to care, but why?
She knows him not at all;
Hope flares briefly as she looks away.

Melanie A. Kempff

My Turn

Upon this earth I came, with God's help,
A woman gave me birth, My Turn!

I grew up in a world, in trouble and strife, then realizing,
I said, My Turn!

I did whatever I had to do, during my stay, helped and tried
To do my best, always knowing,
I'd one day say, My Turn!

From God and woman, I did ascend, however, people believe,
I'm gone, however, I had My Turn!

To return to wherever God will place me, but in my parting,
I trust you will remember,
I had My Turn!

Dale A. Broads

Untitled

I whispered your name on the valley winds tonight,
I wonder if you heard.
Please say you were wide-eyed and listening.
For even if my words were caught somewhere in the branches
of a snow covered pine
and forty years from now
you were to brush up against that very tree,
send them falling all around you
and finally absorb what I tried to make known so very long ago,
listen to them while the winds rise and guide you to me.
If you didn't hear me tonight,
may you take long daily walks through the pines.
For I'll be forever ready,
this moment could never come too soon.

Amy C. Brayton

Untitled

knowing the inevitable and waiting for your fate,
but still lingering on to that last wisp of hope,
not wanting to let go to that last grain of sand
that the greedy ocean desires to devour.
lapping at your feet, the water instead takes you
into that vast, bleak enormity.

thrust into nothingness and hopelessness—lost.
the pangs of suffering are overwhelming
and finally, you let the hungry ocean win.
you allow yourself to be pulled down and drowned.
your lifeless body is thrust onto the beach . . .
the water gurgling around you—laughing.
and still your hand is that last grain of sand
that you never let go of.
that dream that never came true.

Gaby Juarez

Untitled

His radar cuts across the sea
Some how I sense he's after me
I gasp for air and try to surface
to escape the inevitable, but I see his flashing eyes
and know he's very capable
of attacking me, and biting me, and killing me so dead
and then he opens up his mouth
and bites into my head.
The pain, the horror, the blood and guts
are spilling everywhere, my head falls off and what looks good,
my bright red underwear.
Those twenty foot claws
and nightmare jaws are breaking me in half
and I see him eating, with regret
my so-hard-worked for calves
But something's wrong, it's just not right
no tunnel or bright light
I can't die,
I never could I just exist
and watch me rip myself apart

Jordan Burnette

My Special Friend

She's always there to shelter me,
To give me hope, to help me see.

Her words are strong and firmly spoken,
But her promises are never broken.

Like a guardian angel, she led the way,
and she was always there to save the day.

Through the good times she was there,
And the bad, she helped me bear.

Her heart is gentle, caring, and warm.
She led my family through many bad storms.

Like the sunshine in the sky,
her soul will be with me until I die.

Whenever I was hurt, she cried too.
And when I helped someone, her pride shone through.

Her love was never silent or restrained,
And though life was hard, the good in her remained.

She helped me, my sister, and my brother,
My special friend: My mother.

Elizabeth Newman

Scores

Here on this fresh icy slate
stand stories of mighty warriors
where the sealed halls of yesteryear
has echoes of memories past.

Flesh and bone rumble as thunder
over the pinnacle of time.
Here on this icy slate
Blood splatters
as if a pen had wasted ink to spare.

Yes, here on this slate of ice
has time for you to write your own story
If you dare.
But hurry, time is fleeting!
"Bring?"
Bring your hat and your fancy stick.
Just make sure your hide is as hard
as a turtle's back
For you won't have time, for that pinnacle of time.

Jeff Ybarra

Never Too Late

He appeared late in my life and more,
he is someone I wish to had known before.
The kind words, the smile, and the jokes
are something a woman need and hopes.

He lifted my spirit and mended my heart,
he left something inside for a fresh start.
In such short time of being friends,
It didn't take long to tie lose ends.

The sword that was causing all my pain,
from a love that was all in vein.
He was well aware of my past,
and assured me a friendship that would last.

He realized my fears as he saw my tears,
we were both unaware the difference in years.
As days went by the feelings grew strong,
somehow I could not see anything wrong.

Juanita Barrios

Life

Life is like the sun.
It can bring warmth and joy.
Life is also like hail.
Hard and cold.
Death seems to be like life.
For dreams always seem to die.
When this happens you must remember that life is like a tree.
Your dreams are the top you must climb up to get them.
Life is like the heart.
Filled with hate or kindness.
With ever beat we move to find out who we are.
The most imported thing life is like is love.
For out of love we come together.
Out of love we help each other find peace and dreams.
For out of love we are given life.

Julia Ross

Remembering

The longest days, the blackest night,
I still remember your arms, holding me tight.

The picture you gave me, a gardenia, a rose;
the pretty pink dress, how in it I posed.

Those loving letters that had to come;
gradually they stopped, one by one.

So much for me to forget, so much I won't tell;
leaving me here alone, my days so long, my nights a hell.

Doris Warren Myrsten

Menopause

The house is too quiet early every morn.
Theres no pitter-patter of little feet or
honking of (hurry up) horns.
The closets and drawers are all organized
and the house is almost dust free.
Isn't this the way I always wanted my life to be?
There must be something out there, that I really need to do.
But what there is that I must do, I really don't have a clue.
I need a little romance, something to put a
little spark back in my life.
I'm tired (I think) of being a mother and a wife.
There is a longing deep in my soul, that makes
me want to cry.
And if something doesn't change in my life, I feel
that I could shrivel up and die
My friends say I'm just getting old and that's
the way life is supposed to be,
And that being over 50 years, in menopause,
is supposed to set all women free.

Dorothy Kincannon

End of the Year Blues

With one more week to go,
How are we supposed to know
What can come,
When our freshmen year is done?
All secure in our classes,
Not knowing how fast the time passes,
Sitting in the gym bleachers,
Or trying to pay attention to our teachers.
Time goes by,
And the tension grows high
Knowing that the year is done,
Wondering what is yet to come.

Vicki M. Walkoviak

If I Could Write

If I could write, of what would it be?
Perhaps of night where fantasy is free
To fly as high as you want it to go.
In the morning it's over though.

Or of a beautiful woman I could somehow amaze,
We could live in love for the rest of our days.
We'd be free of hurt. But that's not true.
A woman can cause pain, a fact I once knew.

But that in itself is an idea all its own.
I once had a love but now it has flown.
When it is read I could scream and shout.
Well, maybe that story is a little played out.

Maybe of children so innocent and carefree,
Their eyes filled with wonder of all that they see.
A lesson to learn with every dispute.
But actually children aren't always so cute.

The truth is I could never make a solid stand.
For every side of an idea there is another hand.
Maybe it's better that I don't even write,
On the other hand, though, I think that I might.

Matt Blackshear

I Wish

I wish there was an end to all this abuse
I wish there wasn't abuse on this earth
I wish there was fun for all the children
Instead of broken bones
I wish their was a special place
For the children to go and play
So they could play in the sand
And build sand castles like other children do
I wish they could go up to heaven right now
I know the happiest place is to be with God

Dawn Parrish

Close

Touched the Sierra Sky did I.
Memory revisited? A feeling,
Much like fading, slipping into weary sleep.
Merged with cradle-bed, the sinking stops.
Without warning, mind alert.

Monumental granite and iced water
Hosted dainty Solomon's Seal,
Gnarled pines arboreal,
Aquatic Caddis Creepers and lively Skippers
Darting hither yon.

Crystal blue brushed the Crest,
Enchanting splendor to reflect.
Masterfully configured images primordial.
Earth's life forces—simple molecules.
Mirrored beginnings.

Wedged between rock and sky and water
Life—Hope
Regeneration—Birth
I was close.
One with . . .

Carol Rose

Untitled

He touched my heart,
even my soul.
As he lay in his new bed,
Heaven his home.

He was special to me,
this I never said.
He made me see things
that I never had.

It's funny how when someone is gone,
everyone stops for one moment,
and then they seem to move on.

I will not forget that day, it was special.
Special to see my grandpa for one last time,
before he was buried and forever planted in my mind.

Lisa M. Goerl

To Die

Gripping the blade with my right hand
I force its sharpest point, into me
Moving it slowly across an unknown land
Feeling my warm soft flesh between my fingers

I can see blood now slowly flowing all about
And I don't feel the pain for I am relieved
That all frustrations are over and I shout
To feel my soul let go of what it once believed

I drop the blade next to my thigh
And lay my soft head upon my pillow
And as I close my innocent eyes I begin to fly
Dreaming of a world unlike my own

Making up a life I want to know of and
Then I wake up and open my eyes startled
At what I saw, what I saw of love
I want that more than anything,
What I'd give just to die!

Amanda Hadlock

A Black Bird

Early one morning I saw a beautiful being,
its slender, shapely, ebony composed body was one to desire,
a look of grace and harmony,
its eye's shadow, a bright shade of orange,
enhanced the blue and black of its eyes.

There was the look of coldness and darkness that fills the night.
I could touch this beautiful ebony being without
a request for approval.

I walked, looking quietly
our eyes met. With a stare
he said, "Don't blame me. It's your society.
My kind share the work of building nests.
We feed our young. We fill our needs, but take no more.
We choose where to light and when to flee."

I must continue to soar so I can eat.
Come if you must and take a flight with me
and I'll show you what's free.

Annie R. Bunch

Lady Bug

I was walking in the woods and what did I see,
a little red dot the size of a pea.
With black little dots a round little head,
big buggy eyes,
I think I'll call him Fred,
he was wobbling back and forth round and round,
flapping his wings up and down.
I thought he was happy,
but I was wrong he was scared to death because I was long,
his little eyes met my big brown eyes
and he jump back to the side, he let out a scream,
When I lifted him up high,
but I did not want to say goodbye.
I put him down on a leaf so bright
he flapped away into the night.
I miss that little dot so much.
Until I heard a little crunch
and the same little scream I heard before.
I saw my little Fred and his little black head
I yelled to the world my Lady Bug is not dead!

Jennifer Hutchings

My Father

When I was young my father stood proud and tall
If I was in trouble it was him I could call
There was one thing I had always been wishing
Then one day he asked do you want to go fishing
We were always together here and there
And if he went alone it was very rare
As I got older I depended on him less
But if I had troubles he'd help me solve the mess
In my teen years we seemed to grow apart
My own life I was beginning to start
So we started to go our own separate ways
And I forgot about those wonderful days
When I was seventeen father taught me to drive a car
We would go on trips sometimes afar
When I was eighteen my father died
And I sat there and I cried
Now I'm forty-five and I think of my father every day
And I wish I could have one chance to say
I love you father and to me you will always be proud and tall
But I wish you were here for me to call

Robert L. Meyers

Hope

Gun shots ring out every night,
Young children and even adults sit in fright;

They hope someone would end it all,
instead the homicide detectives give them a call;
Thug runners taking over the neighborhood by
killing and pushing dope, as people sit and hope.

They hope for a better place to live,
to live away from the violence and grief;
To live where the kids can walk to school
without being approached by gangs,
that are soon followed by the sound of gunshot bangs;
To live where the police are not afraid
to come into their neighborhood and save the day,
where it is safe for young children to play.

The drug pushers can keep pushing their dope,
but some people will not give up their hope.

Troy McDonald

Life of a Clown

Come on over to my side of town
Let me show you the life of a clown
Always remember just how I looked
Just to see me once, you'll be hooked
I promise this clown won't see a tear
When the big top rises once a year
So come on over to my side of town
I'll show you my life as a clown
Everything I learned for me to do
Mostly for children, and you too!
As long as I can see smiles on you face
Lets me know I'm in the right place
The laughter I hear from the crowd.
The better it is when you get loud
All my clothes that do not match
Is for all the little eyes to catch
Now watch my flower, it's tricky you see
Stand too close and it's wet you'll be
So when you see me I don't make a sound
Just know you're invited to my side of town

Patricia Marchant

I Was Only Fifteen

It was a dark night in the month of April,
I should not have stayed alone,
But what could I know, I was just a girl,
And after all, I was in my own home.
He broke into my house, God knows how.
I saw him, and I yelled so hard, to be heard.
And, I run, and, got away, somehow.
I will never forget that awful smell of alcohol.
The smile on his face, and his dirty look,
They reflected horrible thoughts and a malicious desire.
That attitude I will never forget.
I was only fifteen and raised in a Catholic school.
Where they told me to love and that people were good.
I was innocent, just a girl of fifteen.
He stole my dreams in just one night.
Because of him I had to leave it all behind,
And yes, I hate him, because I can't forget.
And I hate him because I was only fifteen.
Only a child with many dreams
Only fifteen, I was only fifteen. And, I will never forgive.

Beatriz A. Cobb

When Kindergarten First Began

Sr. do you remember when Kindergarten first began?
You were all very small and scared half to death.
But you got through that year at times holding your breath.
Graduation came and that aisle looked so long.
You didn't think you could do it, but I guess you were wrong.
Mrs. Smallwood was proud and so was mom and dad,
But you didn't know why everyone looked a bit sad.
Well the years rolled by fast day after day.
The next thing you knew another graduation came.
Time was going fast this time it's 8th grade.
The next few years weren't easy at all.
Not as they were when you were very small.
The years came and went and so did some friends.
You learned a lot about life, how it begins and how it ends.
Then that day came graduation 12th grade, it's finally the end.
But wait a minute Sr. always remember and never forget,
When Kindergarten First Began.

Debbie Heflin

Loneliness

She sits alone by her window,
And stares out into the misty night,
Thinking, dreaming, remembering her plight,

All her children have gone away,
And will return no more to stay,
Sometimes she wants to fly away . . .
And leave this cold, cold earth.
But winter comes, then summer again,
And still she can be found,
Staring out her window, wondering
If the world,
Will ever stop spinning 'round,
And if it does,
Whatever will become of her?

And, breathing in the stale, warm air,
She doesn't think she'd even care,
If it did.

Nichole Rupp

The Heart

If life could really be fair
Why do people live in such conspicuity.
Never being able to endure love
why even look for feeling smothered.
Open yourself honestly and completely
only to realize it's just to be continually.
A love that's true never found
exceeding passions being so overbound.
The heart's in a state of shock;
memories flash abroad being frolicked.
A dark shadow covered by a cloak,
learning the heart has been restruck.
By chance letting it slip being revealed;
will you find it again amongst the shuffling.
Savoring the pleasure of this sensualism
blocking out feelings of the insecurities.
On the shelf again it sits with pain
to be released from these tightened reigns.
Hold onto love when it's found true in the heart;
don't be discourage to let it escape too soon.

Jackie Booth

Wild Flowers

As the wind blows softly across your petals.
It takes the dust and pollen away.
So that I can smell your sweet spray.

The many colors you give,
to make my eyes be still.

By the highways, biways and
even on the country roadways,
That we all travel along.

It's so sad to me,
for them to be,
so beautiful and free.
But, yet not everyone
Notice them.

So let me give thanks to thee,
for giving me, wild flowers
in the spring.

Stephen Cartwright

Crush

I watch you from a distance
I fell for you in an instance

These feelings I cannot show
Even though I want to let you know

But without a doubt
You and she are happily going out

What is there to do
I can't like anyone else but you

I was so delighted when you two broke up
But just like a dream I woke up

You're back together again
That deserves a perfect ten

Why can't that be us together
To have a chance with you I'll wait forever

My heart has been broke before
That only makes me want you more

All I can do is just hope and wait
Who knows, it's all up to fate

Jessica Zivkovitch

The Spirit Knotted Within

It is knotted and tied by the path of its life.
The tendril is rotating along the barbwire,
The line of faith is a coil,
The smallest joy a bucket of tears.
The way is to become entwinded.

Man is embedded in an enchanted Cross.
We were prisoners of a plea. The wine jar
Is empty that makes our circular thirst.
Birth to spring, daffodils and tulips
Bring us home and salt our wounds.

With dead lilacs the ground is littered white
With our own cells of happiness. The wonder keeps
Our eyes cries out. Grown into its life, its crippled
Roots cannot sail; they only cling to misery.

That lilac was my body. The woman was the anchor.
I lashed myself to the stars and now clutch at my hands.
I am in love with my echo. My face wrinkles in the pool.
I must look over, I cannot leave.
I tremble with human love—a soul that doesn't work.

Jay Bradford Fowler Jr.

My Brother The Storm

Through years I have know, without fail
The soft, yet insistent, thunderings of your soul.
Few others have felt the mighty rumblings
Which set rhythm to my heart, keeping it whole.
They have not seen the flashing brilliance
Of the lightning that illuminates the depth in your eyes
But I have seen it, and taken its limitless worth
Charting my path by the wisdom in those dark skies.
Unaware are they of the raging torrent of thought
So brutal and swift under a placid farce.
But the devil runs deep and it is I who knows it
And mock their judgmental, ignorant race.
Seldom you speak, but 'tis always the truth;
So few have listened to the wind of your word.
But I, I sit quietly, waiting for the whisper,
So know you, my brother, you will always be heard.
Finally, but mostly, the rain of your love,
Which on to this parched heart falls cool and clean.
The storm that you are rages on forever
But only to the fortunate will ever be seen.

Vanessa Rastetter

Springtime

Goodbye cold winter.
Now comes good old spring.
Oh how everyone will be in a twitter.
Now everyone has joy in
What they bring.
"Goodbye," everyone says to their bitter.

Now the earth has joy.
Joy comes to the moms and dads,
Joy comes to the girls and boys.
Everyone who is dead.
Every girl and boy put
Away their toys.

Spring is warm, unlike
Winter and fall,
But not all as hot as summer.
Every human loves, it short and tall.
The bees buzz like hummers.
Spring has come to a end all.
Now comes the hot summer.

Josh Williams

The First Time I Saw You

The first time I saw you
You were crying
I saw the tears fall one by one
I wanted to comfort you but
I didn't know how
I longed to go and hold you tight
When the rain falls I see your face
Then I see the tears falling one by one
I will never forget the tears that fell one by one
They remind me of the first time I saw you.

Maria Borgmeier

The Sea

I sometimes sigh and sometimes seem to sleep
At times seem to broad and sometimes
seem to weep
I, at times welcome with light
dancing feet
Beware tho-I am a creation
wild and deep.

Alma Shcrader

Mountains

I look at the mountains,
And what do I see?
I see high majestic peaks of sculpture,
Made by God for you and me,
I look at the mountains,
And what do I see?
I see deep winding valleys carved by the glaciers
For all the world to see,
I look at the mountains,
And what do I see?
I see beautiful babbling brooks, and wild creatures,
All that are fast becoming a rarity.
When you look at the mountains,
Can you see what I see?

David R. Harwick

A Haunting Train Whistle

A haunting train whistle
heard far in the distance
brings long ago memories
in the still of the night

A small girl listening with heart and soul
filled with longing
as those magic sounds grew far away,
carrying a yearning heart
to far distant places

A small girl grown
now but still traveling swiftly
with the lovely haunting sounds
of the train

Esther R. Fain

I Will Never Be the Same

Dreams hold you in my heart.
You swore we would never part.
Another girl came to you.
There was nothing I could do.

I watch you from my tower.
Each and every hour.
You and he were beneath me last night.
I held back the tears with all my might.

I watched the moon dance behind you.
Forever I watched you two.
I saw your eyes glance up at me.
I took a deep breath and waited patiently.

He stared at me.
His eyes were full of pain from what I could see.
I read his lips; "I'm sorry," he said.
Before he could hurt me anymore, I turned my head.

I found you.
I loved you.
Then I lost you.
I will never be the same.

Amber Nelson

Sand Painting

Swirling about the ceremonial grounds, the wind
melts the sand painted scared wheel.
Its once familiar landscape is now
a desert of shifting colors.
On its shoreless sea I am set adrift.
My mind is a whirlpool of recurring words, images and feelings.
Afraid, I struggle against becoming caught in its undertow.
But in the silence, I hear,
Let go and let God."
Through the vortex I pass.
Tumbling out of the shaman's hand,
I fall to earth again,
onto the newly emerging design.

Gary Shikles

Just One

One look on your face, I knew we'd be together.
One smile from you, I knew it'd last forever.
One look in your eyes, I could feel my heart race.
One kiss from you, I could feel the redness on my face.
The world was waiting for a couple like you and me.
One who would love unconditionally.
The love we would share, the love that we held-
Nothing could break the bond that we cared.
We were always together we were just like one
Those magical nights filled with so much fun.
The kissing, the dancing, you held me so tight.
I'd never let you go, not without a fight.
Promise to love me, promise to care.
I promise all these things we always will share

Carly Harrod

Fate

Fate is like time. You cannot
see her but she affects you nonetheless.
Fate can be cruel and heartless;
full of despair yet she can be gentle
as a mother to her babe.
Fate determines who you are and
what you're not, so be kind to her.
She has never ending paths that
twist and turn and circle around
but you never return where you
once were you feel lost but
you're not alone. Fate is the
guide and you are the follower,
Trusting in her alone can
destroy you or make you a God.

Paulette Taggart

Deception

Enveloped in darkness all around
Even now your heart begins to pound.
To see what's behind you, you peek over your back
You know there's no turning back.
Step after step you hurry along
By now your heart beats like the crash of a gong.
Faster, faster, your pulse races
You try to hide from the eerie faces.
Behind you, you hear a rustling sound
And something starts shaking the ground.
It's coming towards you then you scream
You know that it isn't a dream.
You have to stop to catch you breath
You know you may be inviting death.
It's closer now you realize
Because behind you, you see two burning red eyes.
As you run you know it's sealed your fate
But then you run into a swinging gate.
You take one last sniff of the murky air
And you step out into the light of the crowded State Fair.

Justin Wilson

Ninth Grade

I have always wondered about ninth grade and high school.
Will I make it through my first day, or will I look a fool?
Will I get lost and not be able to be found?
Or will I know where everything is and find my way around?
Will I have so much work and not be able to get it done?
Or will I have work but also have fun?
Will all the older kids torture me to no end?
Or will all the older kids and I become good friends?
So many questions with the answers yet to come.
I will find out these answer when the ninth grade has begun.

Angela Libretti

Light of a Friend

Like the Captain of ships who have sailed the high seas
We must battle the forces that rage all around us
The storms of our lives are rough and hard
And often the nights are dark and cold.
The wild winds will whip small boats back and forth
Rising and falling upon the tossed seas
And the Captain cries, "Where is the light?"
The rocks loom nearer
and higher and fiercer the waves become.
The captain bows his head amidst the fury of the storm
and in one hopeful last attempt
Looks up and sees the light.
Badly bruised and tattered, the boat has made it back
Back to the harbor safe and secure
Back from the endless storm
Brought back by the light in the dark of night
Brought back by the light of a friend.

    Tressa Lorene Gaufin

The Two Trails Of Life

There, in front, lay the two trails;
Which one shall I take? I ask myself.
Two start out the same,
But only one leads to fame.
Slowly, I raise my head
To see the trails more clearly;
One is beautiful and inviting,
One is everything that a person could wish for;
But what can be over the hill? I ask myself.
I hold my breath, and see those around me.
Each one seems to ponder over their future;
While they ponder, I study the other trail.
This trail is full of thorns, and hardships,
But what can be over the hill? I question myself again.
Slowly, I see others choosing the easy trail,
And, yet, very few choose the challenging trail.
I choose the better and run to the top of the hill;
I stop in the mid-stride, the two scenes are painfully different!
Damn! If I just have one more chance,
Which trail will I take? I ask myself for the fourth time.

    Esther Yelim Kim

I'm Not Scared, I Love You

I'll never turn my head away from you.
You can never hurt me.
Your heart won't let you.
You try your hardest to scare and make people flee.
But I wouldn't.
I couldn't.
Your heart is full of love
Love for things of all kinds.
But they never loved you.
They were scared of your kind.
I'm not scared, never have been.
I've loved you through thick and thin.
I just want to be in your loving arms secure and safe from the world.

    Tequila Sunrise

The Greatest Love

The greatest love only a mother can possess
Is given to her child with unblemishing tenderness
Immersing in affection with teaching and guidance
While creating an asylum of love and kindness.
An unsullied child who is predisposed
Chained and purloined, her heart is closed
The imps of ecstasy impenitently cry out
For love and compassion-not a shout
While remorse can't abolish repetitive deign
The greatest love will prevail and reign!
When she reaches for the one she sought to destroy
The profuse sorrow transforms to infinite joy!

    Lori Nelson

Hatred of Love

The man that said he loved me dear.
The one who whispered in my ear.
How naive could be.
Just to think I believed he really loved me.
As the tears run down my face
The only thought that crossed my mind was
pure disgrace.
Anger, hatred
Mere words of feeling that mean nothing
At this point.
An angry voice.
The unchosen choice.
To be so hurt as to shake.
Violence
Rage
and lie, true lies.
This man that inflected all this pain.
Shall die by my hand in vain.

    Laurilei Rodehorst

I Read This Book

I once thought that dreams were for dreamers,
And what you wanted most could never be.
Until I found a calm within myself and,
Prayed for love, joy and peace from Thee.

I often wonder about the Heavens and
Where do the people you loved once would go.
But, I read this Book part by part and
Found the answers everyone should know.

So, next time I need to know about living and
The Great Heavens above
I'll think of my Book in part to learn about
The One that Truly Loves.

    Deborah Militano Osvatics

Bright Fame

I dream of you, my desire,
for the searching and caressing of your hands and tongue.
I feel them on my body;
I know it is my very self that I wish you to seek out.
I need you . . . I want you.
And yes, for you to need me, to want me.
I am consumed, like Rome beneath Nero's torch.
My desire of you leaves me gasping for air—
You are my air, giving me life's meaning.
You are me, and I you.
Yet, we are two people, and different at that.
We are an enigma and dogma in the same moment,
How can that be?
I do not know—just that it is.
Do you?
I wonder.

    Ann M. Albert-O'Clair

A Dream

I had this dream one night, you see,
that told me of my wife-to-be.
For all those years I'd spent alone,
now I'd have someone for my own.
Someone to talk to someone to love,
for that I thanked my God above.
No more sadness, no more tears,
no more worrying about being alone as I'd feared.
A wife, a mother, my best friend.
I thanked God for the wife he'd send.
It all started with that dream, you see,
that told me of my wife to be.

    Barry L. Mills

Eighteen

Familiar quiet plops itself upon our civic afternoon
reach down to fetch a lemonade
from the porch's knotty cork-filled grin

Kitty darts across my lawn (in plain pursuit of nothing)
gleam from an Edsel snickers by
as an acorn dives into the freshly paved Parkway

Johnny sits upon the curb
watching leaf canoes drift by
and off, somewhere, a mockingbird
celebrates the clearing sky

School bus pulls up, and sighs relief (another demon gone)
and Johnny's day is a little brighter
skip on home with the big kids, John!

Wake up from screams of neighbors' kids
and mouth is mighty dry
a fresh, new patch of piercing green brings Landlord into mind

Add a hole to this old house (the flies have got to go)
across the way, a mother cries
around her men in black take notes

    Philip L. Thompson

A Plea For Love

What are we doing that's so wrong today?
Why isn't there someone to show us the way?

We've become so nasty and full of greed,
Seldom helping those in dire need.

America was the country that was a model for others;
Children were raised to obey the "Golden Rule" by their mothers.

No longer do we have the family, so loving and strong.
Everyone doing their own thing, and we know that is wrong.

We used to be people that were happy and full of pride
But now we're angry and the government is a thorn in our side.

So, let's get back to the things that made our country so great,
and let us all practice love instead of hate!

    Miriam B. Scott

Thoughts

I lie and smoke as I sing
Listening to the song of a trickling stream
Watching the flame flicker and gleam
Thinking thoughts of a broken dream
I love to just sit and think, dreaming dreams of lives to pass
Feeling life is just passing me by
I decide to work and try
Not to make my baby cry
Which is hard to do you see
Because just holding her brings her closer to me
My love is my life, as my life is to love
Thinking of things in the heavens above
As I fish in a cove
I see her as she dove
I can't help to love my baby
You see she is the only one who can save me
From the thoughts of a broken heart
To the hope that we never part

    James C. Sproat

Love In Bloom

When that special person comes around,
Suddenly it enhances our yearning, to be bound.

Bigger then life our feelings are,
Ego builds up high, like a glowing star.

All things seem such a delight,
A sunset, a sunrise, shining so bright.

Inspirations multiply like a parade of balloons,
Hearts pitter-patter to a melodic tune.

Feelings get ticklish like a feather,
Lover's drawn to one another, to be together.

How many ways to interpret romance,
In the eyes of the beholder, take a chance.

Better to have loved and lost, then not to have loved at all.
An old cliche, remember, having total recall.

Many happy memories to leave behind,
Unknown as to what our future finds.

Love in bloom is truly what makes the world go round,
So much to capture, it is absolutely profound.

Cherish each moment with all your might,
Life's journey, with a remarkable flight.

    Dee Mahood

Drowning

In your divine holiness,
Lord, have mercy on me!
Rescue me from loneliness,
that I finally may see
the shining light
at the end of the tunnel,
blow away the cloudy funnel
that threatens from above
'cause I'm starving for love,
send someone on my way,
that at last feel I may
true companionship once more,
that I wash, at last, ashore,
and forget being left adrift;
let my soul receive a lift
from the horrors of the sea.
Yes, my rescue I'll soon see!
I was by myself in a foreign country,
sick and depending on neighbors' assistance,
when I was blissfully rescued three
months later, now happily married.

    Milagros Frau-Martinez

Untitled

Standing on a corner doing a bit of harm.
Along came a little boy and took me by the arm.
He took me to a corner by a little rail.
Along came a squad car and took me off to jail.
6 o'clock in the morning the jailer comes around
To give you bread and water that doesn't weight a pound.
The water taste like turpentine. The bread is hard and stale.
That's how they feed you at the country jail.
8 o'clock in the morning I looked a pound the wall.
The bed bugs and the cooties were having a game of ball.
The score was 6 to 0, the cooties were ahead.
The bed bugs hit a home run and knocked me right out of bed.

    Jeanette P. Wheeler

Somebody Knows

Somebody knows when your heart is low,
somebody knows who loves you so,
somehow she knows that you weep inside,
when you hurt her in your foolish pride.

She always shares in your joy and pain,
walks by your side in sun or rain,
always there in time of strife
to pick you up when you wreck your life.

Helping you build it up again,
for it's her life to that she helps to men,
and yet at times she must breathe a sigh
as the one she loves seems to pass her by.

When you are all mixed up and so all alone,
just find her heart, and you will find your home.

She will keep you from all earthly harm,
as she holds you in her gentle arms.

No matter what way the battle goes,
always remember, somebody knows!

Sherry Behnke

Ralph

You will notice a sudden burst of
Energy soon
As Ralph the cat races quickly
Across the room
Up the couch and down the chair
And when he finds the newspaper
Beware
As between sharp teeth and claws
He will shred and tear
Till alas nothing but a mess is there
And you can surely tell where he has been
And you know he will come around again
Under the couch and behind the chair
He races to see if dinner is there
For he has worked up quite and appetite
And he must refuel
Before saying good night
Tired and worn out form his play
He rests now
Preparing for another day.

Maureen A. Hagler

Children

Children we were yesterday
Parents we are today
Grandparents we will be tomorrow
The lessons we once learned
Are the lessons we will teach
and shall be taught tomorrow
The child we conceived
will only mirror what they see
not do what they are told
I then present this food for thought
Show me a child who is disrespectful
and I will show you a child
who receives no respect
With that in mind
Shall we amend the forth commandment to read:
Honor thy Children so in turn they shall
Honor thy Mother and Father.

Joel Dinsfriend

Starting Off Wrong

We all walk down the road of life,
did you choose a road with hardships and strife?
What are some troubles you could meet passing by,
that could allow you to live or force you to die?
The road I was on had strong winds blowing forth,
that hindered my travels toward the North.

Toward the North my travels must follow,
into the Arctic a barren land hollow.
A fire from afar full of anger and hate,
no time to lose, and no time to wait.
A storm doused the fire,
didn't know if to wait.
A pace that had quickened,
my mind gone irate.

I saw a new road I had hoped I would find:
one of pure glass,
quite solid and fine.

Jason Stoneking

Anniversary

Every year you have one of these if you're married.
This day you remember your loved one.
And the day you went through.
The getting ready.
The make up,
The dresses,
The tuxes,
And the pictures.
And when you remember the troubles
of getting it all ready.
You remember her walking down the aisle,
And him standing there so handsome.
Then comes the prayer,
The changing of her name, and then the kiss.
Now you remember the best part,
The party!
The gifts, the money, from dancing.
The food, the toast,
And the cleaning of the hall.
It's the Anniversary.

Natasha Purcell

Forewarning

Many people claim to know my mind.
What I think, and what I will do or say.
But they only know one side of me.
One of the many facets composing who I am.
The real person I am, I choose to hide.
Behind a facade to keep others at bay.
My thoughts are mine alone.
I won't let them dictate what I allow others to see.
I will share them only with a chosen few.
A chosen few that I can trust.
I can count them on one hand.
Do you accept what I give, or do you hunger for more?
Are you anxious to know the real me?
Think twice before answering.
By your admission of hunger, you validate my distrust.
And I withdraw further into my shell.
Be wary, if you plan to pursue me, for this is my lair.
This is where I am most powerful.
Because of your eagerness, you will be undone.
I will prevail.

James J. Brown

Waters

The sea is like a human being,
the skies portray its mood.
The sea is like a human being,
an ever changing attitude.

Rough skies with clear waters,
is not the way that it's to be.
Clear skies with rough waters,
a day at the beach, hardly.

The sea is not like a human being,
for what you do not see is what matters.
The sea is not like a human being,
for we assume that rough skies mean rough waters.

Rough waters on the surface,
does not mean rough waters underneath.
Clear waters on the surface,
there's not always clear waters beneath.

The sea could be rough,
yet underneath could be serene.
The sea could be rough,
so no chance is given to carry out a dream.

Brandie Poppe

Author's Delight

You are a gift from God, perfection's mold.
You are the brightest diamond, the purest gold.

You are a rock concert, a spiritual revival.
You are emotional first aid, the key to my survival.

You are sensuous kisses, the warmth of an embrace.
You are a poet's passion, a ballerina's grace.

You are nature's tranquility, the calm of a storm.
You are the crashing of waves, the sunrise of morn.

You are an artist's masterpiece, freedom of choice.
You are the cup at an altar, a prophet's voice.

You are the ticking of a clock, reason and rhyme.
You are the giving of gifts, a church bell's a chime.

You are a snowy bank, a waterfall's pools.
You are happy children, the summertime of school.

You are a newborn baby—you are forever.
You are the wind of a sail, a pirate's treasure.

You are the sleep of insomnia, the moon beam of night.
You are the end of this poem, the author's delight

F. B. Lewis, Jr.

Drinking Wine

The silk slid down my throat like tears on the cheek of a child.
The glass was still full, though I had drunk my fill.
You said I had to finish it.

I could not.

Your face reflected the burgundy of the wine as your hand
Reached out to meet my cheek and give it some color
Of its own.

My feet wanted to run but could only kick,
Turning the carpet a deep shade of wine.
It soaked up every drop,
Drinking with a passion like yours.

Wine seeped through the floor boards and into the basement.
Injected into the veins of our house,
It ran through walls and sinks and showers,
Staining our life with a hue so deep it could never be removed.

You stepped on the broken pieces of glass that had held
The half-drunk poison, and wine oozed out of your foot,
Smooth and deep,
Taking you with it.

Kayla J. Noonan

A Special Gift

A certain young man had graduated
He was not given a wrapped gift
He was given a card
The young lady who had given him the card had no money
So the card seemed empty
But to his surprise, he found it was very full
See, it contained a promise
A promise of her love and friendship for always
This was a very special gift
A gift that would last,
Last longer than any gift that could literally fit in the card
She told him to take it and cherish it always
For the card held a special gift

Katrina Y. Baker

I Will Shed No Tears

Today we leave.
No more laughs, no more smiles is what I believe.
Never to see each other again.
I must say good-bye to you, my friend.

I will shed no tears.
Alone in the world, we must face our fears.
No more cries.
No more good-byes.
Alone.
Adrift in a strange zone.

I will shed no tears tonight.
We've taken a long flight.
No more pretty faces.
No more friendly races.
Never again will we comfort one another.
Never again will we see each other.

I will shed no tears tonight.
No more meaningless fights.
Alone in the world to face my fears.
I will shed no tears.

Shawna Throneberry

Ghosts of Roma

Oh Eternal City, preserver of souls,
hold forever dreamers of old.
Mighty Emperors and Christian kings,
their victories and glory the clouds did sing.

Death and destruction upon the world they wreaked,
pestilence and misery for the poor and meek.
Tyrants from ages long since past,
memories of your evil will forever last.

Darryl A. Grainger

Until The Sunrise.

I lie here, unable to sleep.
Thinking of you, as mine to keep.
I look into the peaceful night sky.
I see your beautiful blue eyes.
Thoughts of you fill my mind.
How could someone like me, find someone so kind.
I can't help thinking of you, day after day.
My life without you, could never be the same way.
You fill my heart with happiness.
I never thought, it could be like this.
Now I will close my eyes.
Dreaming of you, until the sunrise.

Pat R. Morris

In Pieces

In memory of my brother, Shadd Rayner LeBlanc
You came into my life
And said you's stay a while
Every time you'd leave me
You'd leave me with a smile

Now my heart's in pieces
Which no one can replace
You left me with a frown
And tears rolling down my face

The day I lost my life, my dreams, my hopes, and my faith
Is the very day you passed away

I love you now
Until the very end
Now my heart's in pieces
Which you could never mend

Until I'm up in heaven
And see you once again
I will still love you
Until the very end

Trisha Lane LeBlanc

That Pretty Day

Once upon a pretty day,
In June, July, or even May,
Forgive me, for I cannot remember,
It might have even been December,
See, I got my memory from my mom,
(But don't get me wrong, she's the bomb)
Back to that pretty day in June, July, or even May,
I was laying out along the bay.
Our house is near an alligator marsh.
Some days, unlike today, the wind was very harsh.
It was sitting there, out on a dock,
Watching a mother bird feed her baby hawk.
very sweet, yes indeed,
When she fed her baby that tiny seed.
Then the father flew up to them.
He sat with his family on that limb.
So that goes to show you how much they care
(mothers and fathers everywhere).
There they were, a family together.
They lived happily ever after. Always. Forever.

Mary C. Hartley

Words Don't Tell

With angel's wing she now has flight,
and her eyes find peace in heaven's light
Where a chorus sings in life's delight
and words are notes from more divine sight.

Now, she is embraced in the breath of the sky.
She whispers with winds that make God's love sigh
For times when she was with us still
and her hand to hold.. now the angel's thrill.

Now that peace must return to gingerly fold her eyes
In memories she'll live to defy our goodbyes
For what words were lost before she left.
In my tears she'll know my love's true depth
To smile on us all from where we can't see
But forever in our hearts, her smile shall be.

Bryan C. Hanes

The Oracle of a Woman's Soul

Passionate heart opens its dam again.
The flood of emotions come rushing in.

Oh! how her soul weeps to be touched . . .
jilted again by an undercurrent
called: "The Tide of Love."

Her eye's that can see the vision clear,
for she needs to breathe and find hope
as she sinks in despair.

Drowning vastly her Soul, into a sea of tears;
swallowing the waters of loneliness and gasping
for air.

Each day she swims faster to get back to the shore . . .
pretending he might find her and say
I Love You once more.

Intoxicated by sleep and dreams again,
she imagines...the dam in her heart opens
and his "Love Comes Rushing Back In!"

Khrystan Page Renfro

What My Home Means To Me

My home means a lot to me.
I love to sit in my bedroom chair,
I always feel comfy there.

I love my most wonderful bed.
It's where I lay my lazy head.

I love my home, and it loves me.
I also love my family.

I know how to get around by heart.
I hope my home never falls apart.

God blesses my home, my family, my food,
God puts me in a very good mood.

So here's to my house which is really a home . . .
Because of all the love it owns.

Nathan O'Dell

Abused and Confused

My Life began when I was just four
My mother and father thought I was a bore
One uncle I had seemed to believe
That with me, everyone he could deceive
It started with a simple touch
But it made me feel creepy, and it was a bit to much
My parents, I thought, could never believe
Because he had them quite deceived
He said that I should never tell
Because God would torture me in hell
I finally decided my parents I'd tell
That's when they had him locked up in a cold dark cell
I realize that a crime he did commit
Though sometimes it's hard for me to admit
I never understood that I was abused
Because for many years I was very confused
Now my life is on the right track
But my innocents was lost and I can't get it back
So educate your children this is the key
To keep this from happening and being a tragedy

Ericka Olivas

I Wish That I Could Mend This World

I wish that I could mend this world
Bring about the peace upon each life,
I wish to start a brand new trend
Bring love and harmony and less strife.

This is the land of milk and honey
Our shores provide the best,
This is the land of opportunities
Accept all nation's weary test.

Here great leaders come to abide
Display worthy efforts share,
Among wise men come worldly goals
Together bonded in worldly affairs.

I wish that I might prepare you a place
Among the rank of distinction of deeds,
We might share an abundance of wealth
Mend this sweet world one hundred ahead degrees.

I wish what you wish this very day
Give our world another chance,
With the promise of enjoying friendships
Stand tall, firm in dignity, let the world expanse.

　　Dorothy King

The Age Of Innocence

To my siblings who number three
I pen these words for the memory
Remember when down on the farm
We built a dam but meant no harm

A place to swim was our only goal
"Find more rocks. We're on a roll."
There we swam like we said we would
Till the neighbor said his yard was a flood

"Tell those kids they ruined my place"
"Tear it down kids." Dad was on our case
How did we know what was going to be said
Kids surely can't see that far ahead

We thought we had our own secret pool
And that our ingenuity was pretty cool
After the grown-ups had to meddle
For just wading in the creek we did settle

　　Joyce Cortez

The Man Next Door

Hear him shuffle
　early in the morning
For the paper to retrieve,
　his life now more forlorn

His mighty, deep voice
　still echoes the former man
His body changes, unrelenting though,
　don't belie his plight; he can hardly stand

His current state is to be belittled
　by his wife deep in fear,
Their eons of time shared,
　their togetherness, an end so near

Now many doctors and thoughts of cures—
　yet time will still take its toll.
He know inside he is really,
　now, clearly along for the ride.

Finally his widow alone at last,
　angry that he dared leave first,
Must face that he has really gone,
　left with but the memories of the past.

　　John Varich

Locked-Down Language

Like a statue on the threshold of language
I never quite say what the Jack of Hearts
And the Queen of Diamonds told me
Too long planted in the ground outside
I've been faded by the sun and quieted by the rain
My shattered tongue is frozen on the edge
Of where imagination and poems stay
Often saw those cards passing my verbal plot
On the threshold of death's speaking cemetery
I see distracted travelers come and go
Then I sadly see they never read the sign
That hangs at the talking threshold by my feet
But cawing crows and untidy pigeons play
Mindless games and think they really speak
And though my cast-iron neck won't allow me
To read the ignored message set in stone below
I remember the builders of the deathyard gate say
What its chiseled message reads in every light
"Caskets for language sold here cheap"

　　Stuart R. Johnson

The Broken Promise

A promise was made that you did not keep
Now all I do is sit and weep.
The seat belt works if only you wear it,
There are no excuses, I don't want to hear it.

The phone call comes at three A.M.
I'm dazed with sleep, just can't comprehend
The voice tells me "There's bad news dear,"
I shake from fright, I sweat with fear.

The news sets in and becomes reality,
There's been an accident with one fatality.
I hold my head up, way up high,
I pray to God you did not die.

My heart is sad that you are gone,
The memories I'll keep to carry on.
The birds chirp loudly, the sun does shine
I know deep inside you're doing just fine.

My brother dear, remember this,
From this day on I'll reminisce.
About the promise that you did not keep
Still I sit and only weep.

　　Linda A. Killing

I Travel The Night

While I sleep by a fire
Underneath the open sky
It gets hot and I know what I got
Can't stop the warming desire
Toss and turn and soon I learn
That to she who travels all will be true
There she is at the end of the mile
She knows why she's been travelling too

The moon in my eyes shown through silken dress
The stars in her eyes I longed to caress
I held her a thousand times
In my dreams she's always there
So fair and fine
With a glance she can tear down the wall of deception
Hand in hand we dove in her rivers stream
Her touch sends us in another dimension
With a smile she flowed out of my dream
Back to reality . . . miles still left between

　　Scott Smith II

Mom's An Angel

Mom used to smothered my fears
And wiped away my many tears.
Mom was always there for me.
Mom taught me the lady I became to be.

I hardly noticed her growing frail and old.
To me she was a unique angel
I remembered all the special stories she told.
She's an angel even if I really can be bold.

When God gave me this mountain to climb
He also gave me inner strength inside.
Although it's a time for sorrow for me,
I am rest assured of her place and salvation can be.

As it's always hard to say goodbye,
I know she's an angel in heaven nearby.
I know again soon I shall see her in
The bethel land the sweet bye and bye.

My Mother's love was always so much joy.
Somehow my heart feels like a broken toy.
I shall miss her so much now,
She's an angel and I must let her go so she can fly.

Lorraine Henshaw

Yet So Innocent

Barely open, the darkness of my eyes
gaze upon the shiny steel of the crib.
A smile presses on the blue, decorated sheet.
Sounds . . . Lights . . . different from those at home.
But I have never been home!
So many to care for me,
Which one is my mother?
Special tubes to give me medicine,
Special tubes to help me breathe,
Special formula for me to eat,
Special this and special that,
Am I special?
I love it when I'm held close to your body,
So I can see your mouth, your nose, your eyes.
I love it when you play with me,
Your laugh drowns out the beep, beep, beeps.
All I want is to live a normal life.
Am I normal?

Michael G. Duffy

For the Sake of Joslin

In silence, tears flow down her face
At memories she can't erase.
Grasping for what never was,
She settles for what he says and does.

Empty promises, apologies galore,
She forgives him just ONE chance more
Only to be let down again
At her expense and that of kin.

Then one morning, after a fight,
Restless sleep, crying all night,
He comes bearing flowers, a card and a plead
To somehow account for his abusive deed.

But by then she has made her choice,
Relying solely on an "inner" voice.
Refusing to hear what he might say,
She firmly tells him to go his way.

Closing the door, she lets out a sigh,
Released of his binds at her final goodbye.
As she embraced me I kicked with delight
Because my mommy had done for me what was right.

Tyena A. Isla

The Holocaust

I close my eyes and open them both sights were all the same
all I can see was darkness

But on both sides of me I can see flames as bright as day and hear
the voices of agony from people in despair in the mist of darkness

By my side is the father that I love and admire
If he were to see my mother she would not recognize him
like seeing him in darkness

In the hearts of men who torture and men who kill all
there is left is darkness

Great and honorable men because of the
lack of food has become beast-like
being consumed by darkness

Running, faster and faster can't stop must fight or will die and
be covered by cold freezing darkness

Father dies but no more tears to cry
must be strong deaths surrounds me getting closer
to the darkness

Soldiers liberates camp we are all free
Finally here comes the Light.

Kam Cheung

Defense of Beauty

A rose, a rose, such a delicate flower.
Soft petals, sweet aroma, such a precious flower.
Dainty and fragile, handle with care.

A rose, a rose, such a lovely sight.
Vivid color, broad blossom, such a wondrous sight.
Pretty and prim, admire in awe.

Take this foliage—snatch it up.
Crush it with a merciless fist.

Tear it to shreds, petal by petal.
Rip it—torn ragged edges.

Spirit broken, but beauty remains, in the pile of
what was once a rose, rose.

Hand victorious, stings from deep cuts,
received from the thorns, ah yes, the thorns.

Revenge is
bitter sweet,
my love,
bitter sweet.

Heide L. Loney

Modern Man

Exiled to a field of wild
Sitting all alone just as a child
Calm—relaxing—mild

Do the smells deceive?
Daisies, Daffodils, dancing in the dandelions,
Divinity of ability to receive.
Send forth thy orchid.
Or bow thee iris to thyself's eye.
Pretend what isn't real,
but believe anyone who cannot see the hidden
Ability of the scent that exudes from the seed.
Of a wild flower—hence is he.

Rachael L. Voss

Ending the Madness

What did I do to deserve this pain?
All the memories are driving me insane.
I can't get the thoughts of us out of my mind.
I search for answers, but there are none to find.
We used to love each other so much.
We needed no words, only a touch
Our love was the strongest ever felt,
But we misused the cards we were dealt.
You used me and left me in agony and despair.
You led me on, let me believe you cared.
Now you're gone and there's nothing to do,
But sit and think of how to get over you.
I rack my brain and come to one conclusion,
I just can't live in this immense confusion.
I get my gun out my room.
Close my eyes, it will be over soon.
I aim the barrel at my head,
Pull the trigger, and pray to be dead.

Stacey Dean

My Day

Out of the bed, feet on the floor.
As quick as I can, I'm out the door.
City drivers are rude and my patience is thin.
Got a ticket for rushing; at this rate can't win.
Oh oh Lord, Help me get control of my day, try as I may.

Into the office to a job I just hate.
The debt that I owe has sealed my fate.
The job is stressful with to much to do.
Corporate America is greedy, they experiment with you.
They don't want to pay you enough to live.
I've let them rob me of all I have to give.

It's off to lunch to inhale my food.
Got a meeting at one, the agenda is crude.
Then back to the phones ringing off the hook;
No one else is there when I turn around to look.

The time has come to rush out the door again to my second job
I'm on a merry-go-round; I can't make it stop.
Trapped in a life style that is in charge of me.
I need to break out; I long to be free.
Oh oh Lord, help me get control of my day, try as I may, I pray . . .

Ellen Charette

My Soldier

Long and lean with sincere eyes,
Gentle soft hands that have roughened with time;
Always well dressed and meticulously groomed,
The perfect soldier that sleeps in my room.

Up every morning no later than 4:00,
Never complaining of the day before.
He sweeps it away with his magic broom—
The perfect soldier that sleeps in my room.

Soldiering, leading, guiding his troops;
Gracefully marching in spit-shined boots.
Calling out cadence in rhythmic tune,
The perfect soldier that sleeps in my room.

You've served with honor, distinguished with class:
You can stand proud, looking back on the past.
One of the stars that surrounds the moon,
The perfect soldier that sleeps in my room.

It's time to retreat, it's time to take rest;
Over the years you've withstood the test.
This part of your cloth complete in life's loom—
The perfect soldier that sleeps in my room.

Sonya J. Thompson

Dream

I though I had a talent for acting,
But never imagined it on a movie screen.
I thought to myself Hollywood? Let's go!
Thanks to Bullock and DiCaprio.
In the school's dramatic play,
I made myself practice everyday.
I studied and memorized every part.
Held and kept the wish and dream deep in my heart.
The first time I got the leading role,
I knew acting was my heart and soul.
Finally, my big dream came,
And I was awarded fortune and fame.

Kathy Snell

Ants

A clump of ants here
A clump of ants there,
The worst of it all
Is they really don't care.
They wander about
The rooms in my home,
Relentlessly I search for them,
Yet still they're not gone.
I admit, I am guilty
For not using modern defense
Of pesticides and ant traps,
All of which I'm against.
Ah, but this year again,
Carefully I'll prepare
All my assorted concoctions
To fend off my despair.
At once, they'll disappear,
For the remaining three and one half seasons.
Although I know, early next spring they'll all return,
For their own personal reasons.

Angela Mackey

Divine Archer

Lord, I am the Bow that in Your hand bends gently to Your will.
Your Word is the Arrow swiftly flying toward the target—still.
Your Target the unsaved loved one, whom You have set apart.
You, Lord, are the Archer, Who penetrates his heart.

Carol L. Hulse

Let Me Be The Lover Of Your Life

Let me be the lover of your life
Let me fill that place within
Let me hold you within my arms
Let me love you from deep within
Let me show you what life's really like
Let me show you just how good love can be
Let me show you what it takes to please me
Let me show you how good I can be
I want to show you the glory within me
I want to show you my marvelous light
I want to show you the love that is in me
Let me be the lover of your life
Let me be the comfort you seek for
And the one that gives peace and life
Let me be good, kind and gracious
Let me be these things in your life
Let me show you compassion and understanding
In a relationship that is filled with love
Let us dwell together in happiness
Let us be one together in love.

Diantha M. Smith

Magnolia

The epitome of the South, to me,
is the beautiful and stately magnolia tree.
No pruning hook not touch of man's—
created perfect as it stands.

Great lady clothed in leaves deep green,
spine straight, across the landscape seen.
Native sons and passers through
are captured by the emerald hue.

Her creamy blossoms, when they show,
herald summer with their glow.
A heady fragrance fills the air;
thoughts slip back to times more fair.

The Old South lives in quiet places,
mirrored in the friendly faces.
Smiles and greetings, handshakes warm,
extend from small town street to farm.

For years my path has wandered far
in hot pursuit of a distant star.
Upon returning my tired eyes see
the welcoming boughs of the magnolia tree.

    Barbara E. Klaassen

The Red Wings Will Win

The crowd goes quiet,
The lights are dim,
One woman shouts,
"The Wings will win!"

People gasp, and look about,
But the woman continues to shout.

Now she is quiet,
You could hear a pin drop,
Spotlights go crazy,
Then suddenly stop.

Something's on the ice,
What could it be?
The Red Wings of course,
Who else would it be?

The crows gets excited,
Food flies in the air,
Octopi are on the ice,
Giving the Avalanche a scare.

The Avalanche talk, and try to find a way,
How they can beat the Red Wings today!!!

    Cheri Lynn Nowicki

Night of Lamentation

I remember the day we part,
Those tears from your eyes
Besets my heart with pain and sadness,
Remembering the tears and laughters we shared together.

And now how could I forget you?
You who brought the lovelight and its tenderness;
You who from time to time lingers in my mind,
You have broken my heart filled with sorrows.

How could I forget you?
When I see you in my dreams;
Heard your voice a dozen thousand times
Whispering in the melody of the morning breeze.

And you who curses me,
In the night of my lament;
And though you have gone forever,
Still dreaming the tenderness of your love and caresses.

    Virgilio M. Dalapit

Untitled

Anything is what I would give to leave this place
and go with you somewhere,
someplace,
where we can be alone,
for that which is eternity

Someplace where I can gaze so far into your eyes
that I lose myself in your embrace.
A place where you touch is worth more than diamonds,
where to kiss you would be far better than any earthly possession

To find this place,
This place,
where I may indulge in your radiance,
your beauty,
would equal that of visiting an angel,
Perhaps an angel I would be with.

    Christian Gerard

The Deep Breath

My friend just took a very deep breath,
I told him to stop, but it was too late!
He inhaled shirts that had long sleeves,
Now and then he inhaled some leaves.
He inhaled dirt and some stars,
Ohmigosh! He just inhaled Mars!
I told him to stop with no delay,
Instead he inhaled everything today!
My mom told me to be at ease
Because, she said he would soon sneeze.
Then it came like a rumble of thunder!
I say, it was a wonder.
That sneeze he made was super strong,
Everything was moved to where it didn't belong.
Listen up, there's a moral too.
Don't ever let this happen to you!

    Karthik Ramanathan

Lovers or Friends

Do you see what I feel?
Can you tell by my eyes,
Or do you even care?
I sit and watch you,
And I think, lovers or friends?

I look into your dark eyes,
And I watch your lips as you talk to me.
Do you notice?
Are you doing the same?
Do you wonder as I lovers or friends?

Say something, anything!
Don't leave me hanging.
I need to know,
But I'm waiting for you.
Tell me lovers or friends?

When will he tell me?
Will it be to late?
These are the questions that run through my head.
But I get no answer.
And I'm still wondering, lovers or friends?

    Amanda S. Arnold

The Gourmet of the Diaper Set

Have you ever tasted a garden hose?
Or string from a tattered kite?
You ought to try a candy wrapper,
That's a grand delight!

Taste the remnants of a red balloon?
Or a crayon black as night?
Or a plastic strap from a roller skate?
Or a bib that's blue and white?

Try a piece of comic book?
Or chew a rubber ball?
Or a cracker slightly damp with dew?
Or a sandal from a doll?

You grown-ups don't know what you're missing,
Eating steaks and cake and pie.
You've never really eaten right.
'Til you've tasted Daddy's tie!

Luther E. Whomsley

As You Have Spoken

Twelve men sent by Moses to search out the land
Returned with a cluster of grapes so grand.
A staff between two held the grapes off the ground.
So wonderful the scene! Such richness had they found!
This was God's Promised Land, flowing milk and honey.

Showing no Faith in God, Israel grumbled and said,
"Strong giants are they, and we are but dead."
Fearing these giants, against God they cried,
"In Egypt or the wilderness, we wish we had died!
Forget God's Promised Land, flowing milk and honey."

Caleb urged, "Rebel not," and Joshua did, too.
"If God delights in us, great things we can do."
God answered their grumbling distrust with a "Cue,"
"As you have spoken, so will I do.
No Promised Land, flowing milk and honey for you."

"Those twenty and older, who grumbled with you
Shall die in the wilderness! You'll see it come true.
Only Joshua and Caleb shall enter My Rest,
But the young (after forty years) will see they are blest,
In My Promised Land, flowing milk and honey."

Mary B. DeLoach

Love's Orb's Child

What words held, light's moon's child
Spoke this night, hearts heard;
Which might just to orb's blue belong.
Just as true as moon doth belong
To light and not light to moon,
Her eyes, moon's, to love belong.
And love's child be held in those
Words orb's spoke, soul bright,
Worlds heard tonight, soul to soul,
Moon to night, her eyes to my heart.
Light's moon's child breathed words
To the night; orb's blue light's
Loved its soul to my mind tonight
In heart of earth's son that heard tonight,
And saw love's child, words thus spoke held,
In those bright blue orbs, Christine's eyes.

Malacca

Equipment Suicide

Last night my television bled to death, right before my eyes
It could no longer take the pain form pictures that terrify
Who is to say it did not feel
Showcasing years of torturous will

Three mourners gazed upon the screen
No killings, stabbings, or pillage seen
Tears ran down the family's face
It was ascended to heaven in God's good grace

The mourning over, and the past is done
Importantly now a new TV's come

Michael Ritz

Ode to a Friend

I think of you my friend and a
Flood of gratitude fills my heart.
In my thoughts you are standing
Beside me even though we are miles apart.
You touch me with such care and concern,
And I feel the love that comes from your soul.
Your winning smile that only I can see
Transmits a wealth of peace and joy untold.
What a blessing you are to me each day,
And I am so grateful for you . . . what more can I say?
Except that I treasure the friendship we share,
For it is indeed a gift most rare.
Thank you so much for being such
A vital part of my life.

Iris B. Dillon

Spring

The wind is whistling through the trees,
You can hear the sound of buzzing bees,
You can smell the scent of flowers in the air,
You can feel the wind as it ruffles your hair.

It moans softly, ever blowing,
You walk slowly, never knowing.
All the secrets of the past,
Can finally be unlocked, at last.

Only spring and spring alone will tell,
All the things you know so well.
The wind whispers softly in your ear,
Listen well or you will not hear.

It tells you secrets of faraway places,
It tells of unforgettable faces.
Of what it has done, of what it has seen,
Of where it will go and where it has been.

There's lots of things that you can find,
When you take the wind with you to unlock your mind.
The wind will tell you many things,
But only if you listen . . . in Spring.

Lauren Paulk

Meaningless Words

"Shalom!" said the blue jay, one sunny afternoon.
My mind was joggled.
"What does that mean?" I asked.
The other birds laughed.
"Peace," chirped a sparrow
"Love," said a dove.
That didn't help.
"Will you explain?" I asked the Wise Robin.
"What's to explain about peace and harmony?
In a world like this, the words hardly exist."

Denise deCarion

Behind the Gates of Tomorrow

Sometimes I dream and wonder you see,
Not knowing just what will happen to me.

I've had all these years of joy with the folks,
And we've shared lots of fun and many a joke.

Oh, I'm not afraid, after all, I'm prepared,
But to tell you the truth I'm really quiet scared.

As I ponder my youth and think of my past,
It seems like the time is just passing too fast.

I just couldn't wait to get into my teens,
Somehow I knew I'd look good in tight jeans.

I really don't know what tomorrow will bring,
But I don't feel cheated, I've had a good fling.

My school days will soon be a part of my past,
And I knew all the while that they just wouldn't last.

Somehow I am sad when I think of my peers,
We've been like a family all through the years.

I've known that these things would all end someday,
And that all of my friends will go their own way.

Oh, but as I reflect on the sand, sea and sun,
I know that my life has only begun.

J. Clark Devilbiss

I Am One of a Kind

The thought of wanting to be different
is always in my mind.
Then people stop and look and I think,
Why do they stare?
Is it my hair?
Maybe the clothes I wear?
Do they know I'm living in fear?

Do they think I'm worthless,
Not like the others?
Can't you see them talking?
Is it me they hate?

Then I hear a whisper,
Something filled with pride.
Deep down I know
It's the love I feel inside.

I know I should listen,
Stand proud and tall, with confidence to know
Yes I am different.
I am one of a kind.

Emily Brandon

Pity

Pity entered my soul with the
night air that enveloped me. I
felt this for no one but myself.
I exhale and let out the vapor
triggered by the brisk moon atmosphere.
The subject changed and I forgot myself
for once. Genius . . . the one who
created the moon. I stare at it and
see double. Others look for the refuge and
know not of what they shelter from.
Themselves They forgive everyone
when they sit on that stale park
bench in exile, I speak as if my life is
perfect but it is not. The butterfly
is not trapped. It is of choice.
Acceptance is a melange of ambivalence
and impedementation. An inevitable
feeling of negligence that occurs when
the wind blows in my face
and it ends.

Tiffany Prashad

LAUGH AMERICA

I come to the computer to write, and all I can do is
chuckle at a joke that no one else hears.

Sometimes it gets so bad, all I can do is sit here and
laugh out loud, my face streams with tears.

I'm glad I do, for everywhere I look it seems that the
people around me are full of disappointment and fears.

The humor of the past is replaced with crude jokes, sex,
putting people down, give me back the yesteryears.

I want to hear verbal visions that stir my mind, see physical
slapstick like Lucy and others, before it disappears.

America used to laugh out loud and long, through hard
times and good, to fill the air with laughter and cheers.

We need to laugh with family and friends, to build up
relationships, and encourage and support our peers.

Rick Metzger

Untitled

I told him I loved him
But he never realized
Just how much I meant it
I bet he'd be rised
He left me here without a word
He never even said good-bye
How every time I think of him
I can't help but cry
'Cause what he doesn't know sure hurts me
And there's no way to make him see
The way I feel about him
Just how much he means to me
I never will get him
My heart is in so much pain
What he doesn't know sure hurts me
Now I'll never be the same

Kym Reyna

The King of Fools

A bent-over king on his throne,
attended by a court of clones,
All are suffocated by their fascinations,
None showing any gratification's
Each wears a dunce hat on their head,
no one sleeps, never goes to bed
They eat endless cakes and tarts,
some dance, some shoot darts
An endless sea of ignorant sin,
only caring if they win
The king is ever silent and in a slump,
blind to see that they're turning his nice palace into a dump
The people have made their own hell,
All escape in fragile shells
One day a giant comes along,
he hates their foolishness and their songs
With one powerful hit that palace did fall,
the foolish people slid to one side and hit a wall
The giant left and they do live like that,
to their whining and chatterings they shall go back.

Tania Stricker

The Ocean

The pulse of the waves beating upon the rocks;
Smell of bodies slathered in lotion;
Salty sea air all around;
Laughter of children frolicking on the beach;
Sand castles along the shore, cherished by a small child;
The warm sun shining upon your face;
Soft fluffy clouds hanging in the sky;
The blazing sun beginning to fade,
revealing the solitude of the evening.

Stephanie Tompkins

Deep Within My Soul

Diving deeply into my soul
I discover feelings and thoughts rarely known
Those feelings like a stranger never met
Even though unfamiliar, I will never forget
My feelings like the thoughts of an indecisive mind in the
way they change
Some bring sadness, others joy and others pain
My emotions remain a mystery
Resembling the way I feel yet something more I do not see
I will never understand all that I feel
Yet those explicit things make my soul's personality real.

Lisa Harshman

LOVE IS IN QUESTION

Do you think to much, or can you let it go
Is it an answer you seek, or an answer you know

Does your brain run wild with thoughts so real
Of feelings you felt, of feelings you'll feel

Can you give it up, can you say "No More"
Is your head in the clouds and your feet on the floor

Love is in question, Love is on trial
Do you wait just a moment, does it take a long while

Is it something you take, or something you give
Does it help you to die, does it help you to live.

Is Love always blind, does it ever have sight
Will it always seem wrong, will it ever feel right

To strong to hold on, to weak to let go
Will your heart ever open, will Love ever flow

Will you always feel scared and never quite sure
Could it ever be real, could it ever be pure

Love is in question, Love is on trial
Will you wait for a moment, it may take just a while

Tracy Dingmann

Beginning of an Angel

Raindrops and the sun create a beautiful
rainbow above my wings.

Yes I am an angel. But I am an angel of death.
I help the deceased come to a time of peace in their life.

Whether they hated or loved their life,
it is over now.

At first the butterflies carry you up to the pink clouds.
You'll see a pink unicorn, which will take you
to the big white gates where you register
and find your wings and your own
rainbow above you head.

That's the beginning of an angel.

Lauryn Grinnell

Stars

The stars shimmer in the night
Glowing so beautifully bright
As I look I see a face
A face I have seen in some other place.

The fragment of a smile slowly creeps upon my face.
I remember how it was long ago.
You and I never parted,

Then the smile slowly fades.
I remember why your face is only in the stars and not with me.
A tear slowly rolls down my cheek.
I dream of you kissing that single tear away
Only in my dreams will you kiss my tears away, again.

Ami Weaver

White

White is fluffy calm and light.
The feather from my blanket I sleep on at night

White are the pearls on the queen's crown,
And the bride's silky wedding gown.

The sparkling diamonds a girl's best friend,
The torn piece of clothing I need to mend

White is airy and worry free,
The clouds I lay back just to see.

White is the backboard in basketball,
White is the peacefulness inside us all.

White is the color of a soaring dove,
White is the color of a secret love.

The brand new look of shoes I just bought,
The sweet delicious marshmallows I enjoy a lot.

The white line paper I use to write,
The stars above twinkling bright.

The white onion that makes my cry
One more line and I'll say goodbye.

Abie Siegel

The Sun Rises, the Sun Sets

The sun rises, the sun sets
Putting a temporary end to the day
of grief and tragedy.
Leaving fear in the hearts of some,
and the feeling of warmth in others.
Taking away all the injustice
And leaving it to be faced again tomorrow,
With prejudice and hate.

The sun rises, the sun sets

Carrying with it the knowledge
of all the terrifying images of forcible lost innocence,
And an everlasting life of fear and distrust.

The Sun rises, the sun sets

Contemplating what tomorrow will bring,
And how to block out the tragedy that was reality.

Elizebeth Manders

A Joy

She smiled . . .
I walked in thought
And realized how much this world would gain
If all, as she,
Would smile.

Nancy Mailand Rademacher

Answers

Why do so many people look to me for answers?
Tis beyond my time.
For death is welcomed into my heart and soul,
Then I realized I love actually love my-so-called life,
I love laughing with my friends and being with my family.
Why ask why? says I,
For did anyone once think I need answers too?
Death is sometimes welcomed amongst my heart and grieving.
Maybe I don't even have the answers to your problems or
questions?
Has that ever occurred to you even once?
It has to me.
Then I regret telling you what the answer is or should have been
But, you never listen!

Jamie Lee Thornton

The Modern Ancestors

Heed the warning, fear the fire.
My wrath on earth it will transpire.
The rain began to fall that day,
It washed the unclean world away.
The mournful pleas released from each mouth.
The entire world from north to south.
Deaf ears received the screaming cries.
Yet the rain still fell from teary eyes.
Will we listen and fear the flame?
Has he not gone mad with shame?
Nature warns us with skies a flame.
The earth itself erupts with pain.
Plaque and natural disaster can't you see?
It seems as plain as day to me.
History again shall repeat itself
Another layer on earth's crusty shelf.
On deaf ears our cries will land.
The doom of earth is near at hand.
Should we scream and lamely plea,
Or shall we invent a way to flee?

    George Rivers

Sun Rise

I want to see the sunrise.
So beautiful that it waters my eyes.
So romantic that it makes my soul melt,
If only you knew how I felt.

Everything would be warm and calm,
As I hold my engagement ring in my palm.

All the colors would blend together
Just like a peacocks feather.

I would feel at peace with myself,
And not have to worry about anyone else.

As the birds sing and fly by,
I would let out a long sigh.

All would be lovely as I watch
the sun rise.

    Monica Mullen

Loving You

As I walk through the doors of this sad lonely place
I see pain and sorrow on every face
I'm asked to sign a paper stating I am your mom.
The woman behind the glass motions me to move on,
I step through the metal detector and ask myself why
I struggle with my emotions and try not to cry
This is the place where a child does time
When he breaks the law with no consequence in mind
The man behind the door slips a key in the lock
In that room full of children, I'm too numb to feel the shock.
I stand there for an eternity it seems
When out of the crowd steps my son who's fifteen
Hi mommy you say I've been waiting for you.
Holding myself together is very hard to do.
As our hour together ends I look at you
I can still see that precious little boy of two.
I will always be here loving you
No matter where you go, whom you become, or what you do.

    Peggy Avratin

Untitled

Your face is like the wind, always there for my soul,
never changing of its ways, yet, only there when I ask.
My heart spins before your hands reach my face and
as the next car drives toward us on the road deep inside
the earth of your heart.
I cry inside, "Why can't you set me free?"
I am imprisoned inside this living death, yet love streams over my lips.
I know your heart is not as fast as your mind, for you heart
does not will this to be true.
My guilt opens into a channel of regret as I drift far away,
not waiting to stay, forever unworthy of my own love,
Being alone here in the starlit sky lying in your heart.

    Niah M. Bononno

Friends

Your friends are always true to you, and they're always true to me,
They look inside me and you and kind is all they see,
Their hearts are big, their souls are great,
They always have an open gate, that's because . . .
Friends are loyal, friends are true, they pray, help and care for you,
If they can't figure something out, help them,
And don't leave them with a pout,
When they come over don't be a boss,
Don't choose what you're going to do,
Take suggestions from your suggesting friends,
It's more fun for them and you,
Now that is the end of my truthful poem,
Now say good-bye and you can all go home.

    Danielle St. Pierre

Untitled

There's a new thing everyone's buying,
And no, I'm not lying!
You guessed it; it's a "Beanie Babies,"
And it's driving everyone crazy!
Even McDonald's caught on to the fad,
But their "Tennie Beanies" sold out quickly,
and made everyone mad.
It's worse than "Tickle-Me Elmo," if you ask me,
Many others will also agree.
I've heard of people having a hundred or more,
But I only have seventy-four.

    Stacy Spaller

Future

Suddenly one day I reached a new level,
learning from input about the inside rebel.

A whole new pattern for new lessons to be learned,
strength and endurance will be earned.

Achieved the need to gain more knowledge,
my past is now hanging on the edge.

Visions of my quest, repeat in my mind,
help from my guide, in this journey to find.

Goals for the future keep me going
patience for time, trying to keep on flowing.

    Melissa Kinder

An Unrequited Love

Out of desire, more than need,
You chose the wild and slender weed,
And left my lonely soul to bleed.

Alike we were, and that's a fact,
But you say that opposites attract.
I'm afraid to know just what I lacked.

When youth and beauty fade away
And there's nothing left to say
Will you remember me someday?

I pray, the Lord, my heart will bless
And heal me of this awful sadness.
I only wish I'd loved you less.

Dena M. Spohn

Looking Back

As I stand on this mountain
This mountain of time
Looking back to the distant past
To this life of mine

I grew up on a mountain farm
I worked in the coal mine
I worked on the railroad
Like the distant road of time

I served in the defense of my country
On foreign soil I trod
I learned the value of freedom
And the strength of Prayer to God

I'm proud of my family
My daughters were three
They give me happiness
And are a blessing to me

As I look back on this distant road
This distant road of time
To the many hills and valleys
And the mountains yet to climb

John Bucklen

Silent Golden Fairies

They flew through all the night,
They flew through all the shadows,
They rose from left to right,
Those silent golden fairies.

They tickled all the smiles,
They rippled through the sheets,
They flew through all the miles,
Those silent golden fairies.

They hushed up all the cries,
They dried up all the tears,
They sighed through all the lies,
Those silent golden fairies.

They come through all the gloom
With their magic flights
To help us all to bloom
Those silent golden fairies.

Tabitha Hunter

My Lost Love

If you only knew
How long I've been blue.
Through all these years
I've shed so many tears,
As I had hoped you would be
The one and only one for me.

Regina Charbonneau

Magic In Motion

Captured star light
in her brown eyes,
glistening white,
Soft pink her smile,
roses brushing
each sweet cheekbone,
Floating toward him,
Gowned in style.

Young man reaching for this darling,
Ribboned flowers in his hand,
Dreams fulfilled in magic moments,
Lo, 'tis "Prom night,"
in our land.

Mary Little

Perfect

A perfect love,
Is like the touch of God's hand;
The sweet sound of rain,
Leaving its trace on the land.
The perfect feelings,
Are a lover's care;
And knowing your,
Guardian angel is there,
The perfect dream,
is like God's dusk skies;
Or the vision of love,
In the depth of one's eyes
The perfect love,
True as angels sigh,
Is truly the love,
Of you, dear, and I.

Bethany Rey Sanchez

The Wife

The home of the brave, and the
land of the free, cannot compare
to my love for thee.
She's the one that's always there.
She's the one that always seems to
care. She's the one that makes your
life happy, and sometimes sad, but
from her mouth you'll never hear
anything bad. Your wife is forever
and should always be, till the end
of time her love is the key. No
sorrow or regret will ever be found,
true love for your wife makes
the world go around.
If there is a Heaven after our
good life, she will be there,
this husband's dear wife.

Ronnie Chambers

Love's Afterglow

You walked into my life
Bringing the sunshine with you.
Its warming rays encircled me
Like loving arms
Warding off the chills
Of life's darker days.

Although you are gone,
The lingering warmth
Of your presence
Enfolds me still..

I will ever
Cherish all we have shared
And will forever bask
In the sunlight
Of many beautiful memories. . . .

Helen I. Popely

People and I

People come,
People go.
People are friends,
People are foes,
People do love,
People let go.
But
I come, and
I go.
I am friend
As well as foe.
I learned to love
And have let go.
I am young and
Have a way to go.

Brigitte Garringer

The Thrill Of Happiness And The Agony Of Pain

The thrill of happiness
and the agony of pain
bring to mind
sunshine and rain.

Happiness is bright
Pain is dark.

Happiness is like laughter
at a children's park.

Pain is fear in a child's eyes
Like tears of a mother
when her son dies.

These are opposites
but yet they're the same.

Before pain comes happiness
and after happiness comes pain.

Katie Dunn and Lauren Anderson

All Grown Up

The little boy is gone
A man now takes his place
These are tears of happiness
Falling down my face

It seems like only yesterday
Into my life you came
You've brought me so much sunshine
And very little rain

As you go down life's road
You know you'll never be alone
God will be watching over you
From his golden throne

And if he will let me
When my life on Earth is through
I'll be your guardian Angel
And I'll be watching too

Dorothy M. Manley

Untitled

Look at what love has done to me!
Why are you the only thing I see?!
My love is set on you,
Yours was on me too.
But why have you looked around?!
With us beautiful bound.
Now our love is all through,
But my eyes . . . are still set on you.

Cassie Thiessen

Nature's Beauty

You sit down to rest
So nice and cozy
Your face lit with happiness
And your cheeks all rosy

You glance out the window
And all around
Snowflakes are falling
Without making a sound

The earth is frozen
The wind has its chill
You are so happy
This is God's will

You sit in silence
And gasp in delight
You say a silent prayer
Thanking God for this beautiful sight

Laura Combs

Sometimes on Valentine's Day

Sometimes on valentines day
There's always a way
when someone gets a broken heart
by a loveless dart

People with a caring heart
and gotta be smart
usually get a lot of kisses
with romantic wishes

And the one thing
I truly think
that all boys stink

But there's one thing
I should say
never, I mean never,
believe a boy
on Valentine's Day.

Amber Stywater

A Father's Joy

Look what we made
When we made love,
You and me with a
little help from above.
you gave me a son,
then you gave me daughter
the best thing in the world
is being a father, to share
their joy and pain makes
me feel like a little boy
All over again.
Thanks to you I have
Something I never had
A son and a daughter,
Your caring loving touch
it means so much, I love you very much.

Shannon Templin

Address Unknown

I live in a house not a city
Dark hallways of pity
Locked doors taunt
Memories haunt
Past the pictures on the wall
Down the stairs I like to crawl
Because my cellar is the only place.
Where darkness has no face
This existence was meant for me
The builder never left the key.

Kristy Conway

A Feeling

There's a feeling I
have for you, one I've
never felt before. A
feeling that will never
die, a feeling forever
more. A feeling of joy
that keeps me laughing
inside, a feeling so real,
one I could never hide.
A feeling so strong that
comes from my heart,
a feeling to keep us
together never to part.
This feeling for you I'm
always thinking of,
a feeling so special,
the feeling of Love.

Alden F. Garcia

Why?

To live or die
And to never know why
We do what we do in this world.

To spy with an eye.
To hear with an ear.
To touch a living thing.

I would not give my life
Without knowing why
We do what we do in this world.

Derick Baisch

Epitaph

Transparent the earth,
Familiar faces
pass me by.

Never look down upon me,
Never a tear from an eye.

Never a flower,
Never a prayer,
Just dust and dirt
Layer upon layer.

People trample all over me,
Never stop,
Never wonder,
Who I am.

Sandi Brinkel

Happy Thoughts

As I lie back in my chair, wondering,
do you care?
About
—a thought—
—a touch—
—a smile—
—a glance—
maybe even
—a stare—

Think happy thoughts
—think of me—

Trial after trial
mile after mile
through life's road's
you may carry loads

Think happy thoughts
—think of me.

Cynthia Hill ("Slic")

Weeds Are Flowers

This morning walking
I stepped on a flower
Strange to think how it would matter.
My thoughts led to its significance
It was not a rose magnificent
Nor even a proper flower.
Only a dandelion under my power.

But when death places her foot on me
I don't want to be mashed to the ground
In the prime of holding
My bright yellow beauty high.

I picked up the flower and gently
Fluffed up its crushed sunburst
And placed it carefully beside
A flower of its like and kind.

Cindy Hollingsworth

A Prison Poem

I awaken to the sound of a bell.
I see the bars and reality hits.
I know it's not a school or church bell.
Another bell sounds, cell doors bang
It must be chow line.
I hate the word line.
Work line, yard line
or could it be the dreaded fog line.
Someone is yelling, "513 for pill line."
Did they call head of mainline yet?
What day is it anyway?
Is it time for church line?
Someone yelled, "Man down on 5 bar."
Is he dead?
For some, that's the only way out.
The sergeant is yelling,
"Lock-down for ad-seg"
The snitches must be going to TV.
The sergeant yelled, "Count."
It's the end of another day.

Gary Godleske

I'm Sorry

I have something to say,
But I'm not sure how.
I love you so much,
All I want to do is touch!
I'm sorry for what I did,
This isn't as easy as being a kid.
I did a lot of things wrong,
I would apologize,
But I'm not sure where the words belong!
It doesn't matter if you love me,
I just want you to believe me.
I can't make you believe,
Just please don't leave!
All I'm asking is for you to forgive me.
Without you I'm just me,
But with you, as you can see
I feel like more,
Than just me!

Ashley Stewart

Blueberries

There once was a girl named Kerri.
She loves to eat them berries.
With blue on her face,
she sat in one place.
Right next to them blueberries.

Todd W. Dubuque

The River That Flows

The breeze upon the leaves
of the river bank,
crackle and snap,
moving slowly
until they touch the ground.

They are numbered as many
along the shore
hoping to feel the breeze
once more.

To crackle and snap
to move slow.
Let us touch the water
of the river that flows.
Let us glide, once more,
upon the Sea of Galilee.

Kathleen Mihaljevich

Loneliness

The sun goes down
visions appear
thoughts come back
then eyes are tears.

The soul is bared
the heart still breaks.
Memories are there
brings back the aches.

Sleep comes hard
dreams abound
for those most gnarled
troubles a mound.

We wake each morn
in a room most bare
better not be born
loneliness is there.

Melvin J. Lee

Fun and Fantasy

Moonbeams dance on calmest lakes,
And willows sing a lullaby.

The stillest ear is all it takes,
To hear the forest sway and sigh.

A firefly, in sleepy trance,
Flutters through the cool night air.

Woodland creatures love the chance,
To play without a single care.

As the forest comes to life,
The fairies voice the softest tune.

With joy they play on lute and fife,
And frolic under the summer moon.

The unicorn has joined the fun,
Soon comes the elf and faun.

There's sadness to be felt by none
'Cause they'll dance and play till dawn.

But with dawn's light the shadows flee,
The sun comes up and the moon descends.

Yet, if you listen carefully,
You can hear the music upon the winds.

Geoff Edwards

Poet

The Poet is a lonely man
who never had a life
He rhymes his pitiful stories
thru agony and strife.

The Poet is a crippled man
in one way or another.
He's lame or sick or lonely
in solitude he will smother.

He puts in words so all may know
just who a Poet be.
He writes to warn the world
all others, you and me.

He writes to us of long lost love
of death, of fate and pain.
These are the true things in life
they always will remain

The Poet needs some love as all
but hence he has it not.
He wishes only that in time
his works not be forgot.

Gary W. Hearon

Truth Telling

To say I am unemotional
would not be true.
The truth is that they are
held inside, controlled, in order
to appear more stoic,
or something.
This way of mine is a
family trait, and I am content
with it, since then the occasional
hug from Mom is amplified
in feeling, and a firm handshake and
smile from Dad conveys
deep meaning.
Yet, I sometimes wish that somehow,
just once, I could
be someone else.
Someone able to tell
them how much
they have meant to me.

Andrew Diemer

Thank You God

Thank you God for all your blessings,
Each day you give to me,
Gifts that come from You alone,
So bountiful and free.

For each new day,
That brings the light,
For the moon and the stars,
That shine at night.

Thanks for always being there,
When upon your name I call,
Thanks for reaching down for me,
Each time I slip and fall.

Thanks for washing my sins away,
And remembering them no more,
Thanks for the cross you bore,
And the crown of thorns you wore.

For all of life's blessings,
That come only from Thee,
Thanks most dear God,
For loving me.

Mary Ellen Ricard

You Only Think You Love Him Dear

Although you think his voice you hear
you only think you love him dear

Think you can't live without him near
you only think you love him dear

You think with him you have no fear
you only think you love him dear

Can't see or think or hear real clear
you only think you love him dear

You went through this the other year
you only think you love him dear

But now he's got you all in tear
you only think you love him dear

And now away you try to veer
you only think you love him dear

And now I whisper in your ear
"You only thought you loved him dear."

Jennifer Webster

Why?

A child's life is taken;
Our future is forsaken.
Why, oh why must the children die?!
Our complacency! We don't even cry!
What can tomorrow bring
When the children cannot sing
Songs of hope and songs of joy,
(What about our little boy?)
Songs of peace and songs of love.
(Where flew that dear white dove?)
Shots and cries pierce the air,
Filling our lives with despair.

Doreen DeLeon

Carwash

Auto/mated in the carwash line,
I idle slow morning moments with
Simon (and Garfunkel then) singing
something sad, while
the usual worries whisper
on a day like any other.

Entering the (secret) code,
I drift into twilight spray, song
condensing into something—urgent—
about a mother and child.

And she and I cry out (O my god) as he
wavers, undecided on a ledge,
too high to see our faces
in the crowd.

Rolling, son/warm droplets
bead on my steel skin, but
Simon (and Garfunkel then) is gone, and
the usual worries whisper
on a day like any other.

Alan Parks

Untitled

Why?
How?
Who?
When?
Where?
An enigma
Often questionable

Aaron J. Stringfellow

Mall Walk

Tot

Walking at the mall
I feel so tall
Even if I'm only three
The mall is a magical
Place for me

Teenager

Walking at the mall
I feel so cool
It's the in place to go
For fun and games
Not for a child
The mall is wild!

Senior

Walking at the mall
For exercise
I feel so spry
The years peel away
As I start my day

Louise H. Goldman

Cupped Glory

Today is the day we come to play.
We shoot,
We score,
The cup is ours, galore.

Jonathan Cats

Uniqueness Leading to Segregation

I have a fear
That you don't want to hear
What I want to say
It's just that this is not the way
I mean to do things
Because happiness it won't bring
Your life will be joyful
But only if you're respectful
Don't worry about race
It's not something you want to face
Don't look at ethnicity
It's not for publicity
Don't judge people from the outside
Because all that matters is the inside
Only on occasion
People talk about religion
So be kind
Only then you will find
That everyone is just fine
Without having to hear you whine

Harshika Batt

Friendships and Flowers

Friendships are a lot like flowers,
For they make a sweet bouquet
That will bring the sunshine in
On those dark and lonely days.

Friendships provide a shelter,
When trials hit full-force.
Flowers offer comfort,
When sorrows overtake us.

Both can make the bad times good,
And will make a sweet tomorrow
That will never fade away,
'Cause when you prove a friendship true,
Life always seems to go your way.

Missy Dugger

No

Let me kiss you.
   You can pet an ewe!
Let me give you a pat.
   You can go stroke a cat!
Let me give you a massage.
   You can go clean the garage!
Let me take you to bed.
   You need to go to the wood shed!
Come on let's go with the flow
   No!
   You must go!

Randy Terry

Abortion Through Your Baby's Eyes

Mommy the month is now one
and were gonna have lots of fun.

Mommy the month is now two
And I'm just begging to be apart of you

Mommy the month is now three
and I can't wait until you see me

Mommy the month is now four
and we just have five more.

Mommy the month is now five
and you kidded me. Why?

Mommy the month is now six
but my broken heart can't be fixed.

Mommy the month in now eight
but it's too late.

Mommy the month is now nine
but I want you to know that I'll be fine
Love, the unborn child

Jamie Donchoo

Challenges of Life

The dawn is early.
The dawn is bright.
The eve is gentle,
and full of delight.

The day in between can be the worst
of it all; for challenge after challenge
shall challenge us all.

Janette Kacanic

Watching The Grass Grow

Inch by inch
Step by step
Day by day
Leap by leap
Year by year

Test by test
Class by class
Stride by stride
Night by night
Term by term

Growing tall
Standing up
Seeing more
Living life
Having hope

And then we're
All cut down

Kate Piatt Eckert

Life, God And The Universe

God, life and the universe
Went into a bar.
God
Asked for a light.
Life
Drank a Bud Dry.
And the universe
Had a mineral water
On ice.
He was driving

Jacqui O'Brien

Pegasus

Oh, how very gallantly you trot,
As though you were flying
from spot to spot.

No tracks left behind as
skies grow dim,
A glance over his shoulder,
so to speak.
Spread so wide
the beauty of his wings
over take him.

So strong but yet so
delicate he holds his own,
For yesterday he was here but
Today he is gone.

Sandra J. Woods

The Last Goodbye

The years went by so fast
Good times and bad times
Came and went
I guess I thought our time
Together would always last
And now with memories I have
to be content

If I had known our time
would be so brief
I would have savored each moment
Like the fallen leaf

Now comes the time to
Grieve and cry
And although I'm sure you're
Heaven bound
Mom, I silently say my last goodbye
And the room around me
Echoes no sound

Jerry Poovey

Saying Goodbye

I can't keep holding onto something
I know was not meant to be
I can't keep reaching out to you
To make my dream be
I can't pretend that I am happy
Happy as can be
When deep down inside
All I know is misery and grief

So, I have decided
To just say goodbye
To leave my life with you behind
To take a chance on being alone
For the rest of my time
To give my little light inside
A turn to shine
I will not fret, no not I
Because, I know everything
Will turn out fine.

Patrinia Mae Landrum

Only I

I awake, thinking of you,
It's the middle of the night.
No more sleep tonight
It happens often now
Waking up, thinking of you
Tears start, tears I cannot
hold back
Alone here, I can cry
until morning
No one will know
Only I

Kitten

That Special Person

Wonderful as a warm sunny day
A smile that lights up a room
Love that encourages me to do my work
Letting me know I can be anything

Parents separated when I was young
She is the mother and father
Whenever I am hurt, she is there
Whenever I need to talk, she is there
She is always there . . .

Making my life light up when I'm sad
She makes everything fun
Without my mother I would be lost

Marissa K. Jimenez

A Night In Childhood

The night is filled with terror
As I lay paralyzed in my bed
My head frozen to my pillow
Waiting
For the screaming to begin

Then it starts
It is here
I can hear it
Gradually breathing the air
With anger so intense
It engulfs the entire house

Suddenly, my door flies open
My mother appears
She slams my door shut
Screaming, screaming, screaming
At my father
On the other side
My father is screaming too
Their screams cut through my walls
And through my heart

Pamela L. DeMartini

Castle In The Clouds

There is a castle in the clouds
We all seen it in our dreams
Its beauty is renowned

With all the kings and queens
With all the riches and the poors
The rivers running wild,
The mountains, so supreme
As the humming of the bird
The valleys are so green

We all look up and see
The castle behind the clouds

Judith Parker

13 Seconds

Sudden noise;
immense, deafening,
ear bleeding noise.

The ground shakes.

Inside the house:
Dishes clank, the walls sway,
books fall, the floor vibrates.

The ground shakes.

Outside the house:
The earth parts and swallows cars.
Buildings collapse, trees are uprooted,
people run frantically.

The ground shakes.

Inside my head:
The house collapses on me.
No one knows I'm here.
Oh God, I'm going to die.

And the ground shakes,
and shakes, and shakes.

Lisa Taylor

Easy

Easy is our enemy,
a welfare check from fate
that brings out in us
our most ignoble nature.
Easy is an elevator,
and the fewest steps
from the parking lot
to our opulent offices.
Easy is no yard,
no plants, no pets,
no friends worth having
and no real lovers.
Easy is so safe:
no pain, no sweat,
just a microwave, a couch,
and no regrets.
Easy is the oblivion
of a spirit whose length and breadth
have flattened to a doormat;
Easy is a living death.

Robert Jones

Churchyard

Crumbling church, withered pines,
scarred by rains, winds and time.
Quiet echoes through the glen,
whispers from the past held in.
Loving messages from the past,
linger short and fade fast.
Faded marble, crumbling stone,
silent tribute stands alone.
Iron fence 'round rutted plot,
marble and stone crumble and rot.
Some are clear and some are blurred,
some secrets kept and others heard.
Many mysteries to unfold,
like grass on stone will hold.
Unattended and left in peace,
nature ravages piece by piece.
Wind, rain, sun and years,
cracks, falls yet no one hears.
The past is kept in nature's field,
even memories to time must yield.

Erika Braswell

Life's Mold

From my youth I still recall
The man who stood so tall
Who held my hand and made a stand
To help to mold a man

That man has gone, but not forgot
And I can still remember
The things shown me by him
To help to mold a man

He now says, that I'm so tall
And always holds my hand
I hope that I will do as well
To help to mold a man

I hold his hand and make a stand
And try to show him all
The thing that I was shown
To help to mold a man

My hopes are clear that I do well
That someday he'll recall
The things that he was shown
To help him to mold a man

Dedicated to my Grandfather
Elmer F. Heathers

Frederick R. Brookshier

Going Home

I think of you, my heart beats fast.
I think of you and our times past.
I want you, I need you,
I help you, I feed you.
So many miles, so much time;
It makes no sense, has no rhyme.
But now I'm returning to my love.
I'm now more peaceful than a dove.
Your face brings a smile to my lips
Wider than ten thousand ships.
My elation, happiness, and joy;
I'm a child with a brand new toy.
You've no idea how happy I'll be
Your face is all I want to see.
Let me hug you, hold you tight,
Not release you through the night.
And when the sun rises new,
We'll be together, me and you.

Nick Cromwell

Everyday About This Time

Everyday about this time, my dear
I feel your presence very near.
I see your eyes, your hair, your smile,
But I'm dreaming all the while.

Everyday, every way, I miss you so,
And wonder why you had to go.
I'm so lonely, empty and bare,
I pass your room, but you're not there.

Yet it's not the days I mind so much,
Hearing your voice, missing your touch,
It's the darkness, and sudden fright
To face the long and empty night.

Muriel Cruz

An Epitaph

Ashes to ashes, dust to dust;
Into this realm most timely thrust.
Life now grants me this shallow cage,
Freed from the world's unkindly rage.

Never again the stars to see,
This my home for eternity.
My beaten body laid to rest,
Buried beneath the Earth's soft breast.

Words can never capture a life,
Can never equally weigh one's strife.
Up in Heaven's celestial seat,
It is there again that we shall meet.

Tate Schulz

The Gift Of Words

To Vina Keeling
The gift of words has got to be,
a gift from God above,
that special touch to heal a hurt
with that special love.

To say and feel with all your heart
just how we feel,
I know it is a gift from God,
and he gives it to a special few,
I'm so glad he gave that gift to you.

A talent that's worth envy is wasted
if it is not used,
you used your gift so naturally we
know it's not a ruse.

So thank you for caring,
and sharing your gift with us,
it gets us through our times
of troubles
and keeps us out of ruts

David Combs

The Challenge

Life is but a mountain
To climb with every feat,
The challenge in the making
With hills we have to beat.

Life is but a river
That flows with every turn,
We bend, we break, we suffer
But most of all we learn.

Life is but a forest
Whose branches we do weave,
With lies and guilt among us
And sins we can't perceive.

Life is but a circle
With eternal love to bind,
Through strife and stress we struggle
An end for each to find.

So in times when we get weary
And we want to make it end,
We raise our head and walk with pride
Around another bend.

Jane Allen

Only Mommies Know

"Mommy" I can hear him say
this wonder I call son
"You know those pretty flowers?
I went out and picked you one."
I look down at this little man,
this miracle all mine.
And, there, clutched in his tiny hand
is a withered dandelion.
As he seeks a sign of pleasure,
I try to let it show.
For the love I feel at times like these
Only Mommies know.

Jeanette Kordonowy

Why We Love Grandmas

We love grandmas
Because they're sweet
and they also have
cute little feet. We also
love grandma's because
they're angels in disguise,
watching over us as we
grow. We also love
grandmas for their
awful nice ways.
All I know is that
I love my grandma.

Mallory Ann Eikenberry

Spacing

Printed hearts
on paper dolls
a singing phone
when no one calls
fresh flowers
vased on a desk
something's missing
can't find the rest
the touch the smell
the taste the fear
trying to know them
to hold them dear
every second
of every day
such importance
wasting away
but who can tell?
were they there at all?
just a dream . . .
but there's the doll

Chelsea Wallis

Chain

A chain is wrapped around my brain
As you can tell it's driving me insane.
I tried to hit it with a cane, and it's
causing a lot of pain.
I tried to think but my brain
was no longer pink. I need a shrink
and something cold to drink
Drank some milk, ate some bread,
but it just caused me to go to bed.

Carmela Hayslett

Practicing Imperfectly

it is said
that practice makes perfect
but
i'm practicing
imperfectly,

a face of pretend.

something's not right.

i attempting
make of myself
the undone,
knowing that

doubts and contrary
ponderings
slip into the struggle
whispering accept
their confusion: that's

reason for the
two -face you're
puzzled at now;

well, so am I.

Jeane Johnson

My Wish For Thee

My wish for thee,
A thousand laughs.
A million smiles before you.
My wish for thee,
A special love.
Just one that will adore you.
My wish for thee,
Some simple things.
Not glitz or gaudy clothes.
My wish for thee,
Is peace and joy.
Take time to smell a rose.

Ron Mumford

Love

Love comes to the mind
Some people say
It goes from the mind
And touches the heart
Once it touches the heart
It cleanses the soul
The heart lets it escape
into the world
And goes out to other
peoples minds.

Aniela Plasentilla

The Ringing of the Guns

As the guns are ringing,
And as the young men fight,
I hear their mothers crying,
And praying in the night.
I hear them asking Jesus
To save their precious sons.
I hear them asking us
To stop the ringing guns.
Yet where it is I hear this
Is not a distant shore,
The way it was in days
And generations gone before,
For the ringing that I hear today
Is on our streets, where children play.

Jack R. Lainhart

Hatred

Today my life was like
someone put a dark cloth
over my eyes and made
me feel anger at him.
I can't escape, it's too strong.
Help . . . help . . . drag me out
of this anger-filled darkness!
Please?? I'm half there.
No I can't do it; I can't get
out of my hate. It is too strong.
I am scared; I don't like this
but the hatred is too strong!
All I see are red and black skies!
Where are my beautiful rainbows?
Where are my blooming flowers?
Where is my beautiful sunset?
Where did all these beautifully colored
feelings of happiness and joy go?
He made me lost in my own hatred!

Jennifer Brown

Junkie

Her heart aches
At the plight of a hungry child
At dozens of worthy causes
That scream
for help

She mows her lawn
with her old manual mower
that (incidentally) saves fuel and
the environment—and dollars.

Her budget does allow the thirty
dollars for a mowing
So she donates the savings
To three causes

Her heartache eases somewhat
Till more requests arrive,
But, all she has left is
A hell of a backache and
a poem.

Rachel Grindlinger

Dedicated to Brian Neary

Too many times, I've tried too hard
Too many times, I've cared too much
Longed to see your smile
Longed to feel your touch
And I sit here and wonder,
Will the pain ever end?
Will the hurt ever ease?
Will my heart ever mend?
And as I sit here
Now I know,
I don't think
I could ever let go.
You can tell me you hate me
And you can push me away
But to tell you the truth
It doesn't matter what you say,
It doesn't matter what you think,
It doesn't matter what you do.
My feelings won't change
And I will always love you.

Kristina Mattox

Island of Flame

Hell is an island
An island of flame
It takes someone special
To work into its fame.

You get there by murder
By inflicting such pain
You get there by hatred
That grows stronger by day

Children of Satan
Come play by the flame
Bask in the glow
Then rot in the blaze

Children of Satan
Just do as I say
Come to the island
The island of flame.

Jessica Pepin

Mother-Daughter Love

*Dedicated to Ruth Ida Egnatovich and
Linda Jean Barth*
A bond of greater human strength,
No mortal man can know:
Then that of mother, daughter love,
From birth, its ceaseless grow.

Vast legends speak of manly ties,
Of brothers bound through life;
But love that mother, daughter keep
Survive past pain and strife.

Perhaps the kinship giving birth,
Gave "temper" to this "steel";
Then added to with tortured love,
That only mothers feel.

Since I, a man, have set these words,
I only go by sight;
And though I'll never feel that flame,
I see it burning bright.

Robert G. Egnatovich Sr.

Live to Live

Live a long life
To be as old as
One's grandparents
To be as wise and understanding
Of all that life shows you
Learning from mistakes
Growth of self
Seeing all shades of grays
Not just in black and white
Not from a child's view
Or from a child's world
Bridging the gap
Between past and present
The here and the now
Being an adult
So be grown man or woman
Live your life
The way you see it
What works for you
Just do it!

Terrie D. Jones

Expectations

Black Americans have transcended
From shackles of slavery to the
Glass ceiling of respecting other
People's expectations,
From the poorest to the brightest,
Brigadier General and to the
Fleet feet of top athletes,
Widening boundaries not only
For us but for every human being.

Cortney Gordon

Freedom

Freedom is out of reach
for the children of Earth.
Our soul is twisted
by the elders with power,
leaving behind a world of
war, fear, and pain.
Many of us believe we should
have a piece of freedom,
but as long as we are known
as insignificant,
we will never know what freedom
really is.

Stephen McCabe

Would You

If I left tonight
Because of a fight
And I walked real slow
Would you let me go?
Would you remember me
Would you want to see
What I would do
Without you?
Would you be thinking of
Our once shared love
Would you want to be
Back again with me?
Take me back would you
I need you through and through
We never again have to fight,
Would you please take me back tonight?

Danny J. Olivarez

Mother Natures Cleanser

Frosty autumn fields
And cold torrid rains.
Ice pegs splashing
On frozen window panes.

I look through the glass,
And see the stains
Of my past
Go down lifes drains.

Crossing the fields
The wind is blowing.
Leaves pass on by
Autumn harvest I am sowing,
Or freedom I am sowing?

In the wind a chill,
The eerie of night.
Feel the thrill
Of one's spirit in flight!

Windy Rochelle Adam

The Reflection of Me

As I look through the looking glass
Past the reflection of me
Into the future
That only I can see.

Past the reflection of me
Past my outward appearance
That only I can see
And only I can feel.

Past my outward appearance
Deep into my soul
And only I can feel
The need to be happy.

Deep into my soul
Where I keep all my secrets
The need to be happy
Burns brightly there.

Where I keep all my secrets
Where my dreams are held
Burns brightly there
As I looked through the looking glass.

Laura Carstensen

Untitled

A dog who did nothing but dig
He said digging would make him big
So he dug a giant hole
But was bitten by a mole
So now he is smaller than a fig.

Christine Kim

Lonely Quest, Quiet Revelation

Those new old places
We travel all alone
Where the closest soul
Remains so distant

Deep down there, you know
Light is just for one
Can you see? Tell me
Tell me! Can you see?

While your restless shadow
Is screaming for answers
You quiet the questions
Trusting the moment
Keeping time waiting . . .
To hear in your heart
The bliss echoing your silence!

Basile H. Zaloum

The Miracle Of Friendship

There's a miracle
Called friendship
That dwells
Within the heart.
And you don't know
That it happens
Or when it
Gets its start...
But the happiness
It brings you
Always gives
A special lift
And you relish
That "Friendship"
Is the most
Precious gift

Matt Heiskanen

My Memories

Memories of yesterday
come back strong and clear,

Of times we spent together
that I still hold so dear.

Some were good and some were sad
but love still found a way.

Of bringing joy and laughter
that helped to make our day.

So when I'm blue and lonely
and I look back on the past,

Our moments with its ups and downs
really didn't last.

But they gave to me some blessings
that are now so close in my heart,

For love has a way of keeping us near
though distance keeps us apart.

Pauline Wenger

The Treasure Box

There is an old wooden box
That smells like dirty socks.
It's covered in reeds
And surrounded by weeds.
It's as smooth as sand
You can hold in your hand.
It looks like a log
Without a frog.
On it is a lock
Shaped like a rock.
Inside the case,
Above the base
Is, behold!
Piles and mountains of gold!
Silver and jewels,
That box probably caused lots of duels.
It's on Treasure Island.
So come on by and
Try to find that box.
(Tip: Be as sly as a fox.)

Angela Eichenberger

Kidnapped or a Bad Dream?

Waking up tied down with mixed
feelings. Not knowing where you are
you feel your heart pounding so hard
it drops into your stomach. The
room is pitch black. You look in the
corner only to see the cherry of
a cigarette. Knowing you're being
watched you begin to tremble.
Then you blackout. You awake in
your bed, did this really happen
or was it a bad dream?

Jennifer Trombi

My Tunnel Of Light

I walked into the tunnel of light
not knowing what would bestow me.
My dreams became true and
meaningful for now my life was real.
The world was all around me with
Life full of expectations.
It became a reality the day we
met and became an everlasting gift till
the end of my time.
Love was the answer and the question
I always needed answered.

Debra Boyle

Choice Wisdom

Wisdom throughout the holy dies
mixed with Satan's spawning lies

They slowly move towards the flames
searing heat as wisdom wanes

Closer to his ultimate dreams
momentum steady wisdom screams

Souls are bought and sold at will
drowned in riches wisdom kill

Slaughtered good and all its worth
decaying slowly wisdom's earth

It's now a routine they do their deeds
wisdom knows not it's them he needs

Wisdom must fight if not to fall
laziness masks their holy call

Wisdom down he has his war
guarded not by God's galore

A decision is made by wisdom's self
not as a whole but individual wealth

What you decide is your own fate
glory of God or Satan's hate

Cory Vogt

I Won't Make You Choose

As you grow closer to twelve,
As you soon become a teen.
You try so hard to push away,
You try hard to be so mean.

I will put your mind at ease,
I will wipe out all your fears.
There's no need to be so sad,
There's no need to cry those tears.

You're my son who has my blood,
You're my son who's part of me.
My love has no right or wrongs,
My love has no boundaries.

I would never make you choose,
I would never say pick a side.
My son, you can believe in me,
My son means more than my pride.

As you grow closer to twelve,
As you approach those teen years.
Now your life seems so normal,
Now your future is so clear.

Velvet Mayer

They . . .

They give you pain . . .
and call it knowledge.
They take your knowledge . . .
and call it lies.
They give you lies . . .
and call it experience.
They take your experience . . .
and call it questions.
They take your questions . . .
and call it rebellion.
They take your rebellion . . .
and call it hell.
They give you hell . . .
and call it life.
They take your life . . .
and call it even.

Glorya Mirra

Sometimes

Sometimes my mind is full of doubt.
Please help me, Lord, to clear it out.
Sometimes I feel lost and discouraged.
Talk to me, Lord, and give me courage.
Sometimes it seems the pain won't stop.
Please help me, Lord, not to give up.
Sometimes I give in to my fears.
Comfort me, Lord and dry my tears.
Sometimes it seems all hope is gone.
Please help me, Lord, just to hold on.
Sometimes I simply need to cry.
Forgive me when I question "why."
Sometimes I need to know You're there.
You tell me in my answered prayer.
Sometimes, but it's not always true,
I just forget I'm part of you.
Sometimes I simply praise your Name.
For everyday is not the same.

Paulette Jones Simmons

Thoughts of Yesterday (Empty Promises)

Stumbling over memories
running circles around my heart
of shadowed whispers spoken
from buildings torn apart

Dreams of concrete skylines
In soul-less shades of grey
My thoughts were with my heart
And that was far away

Scraping at the sky
in building made of clay
these towering stones of emptiness
in thoughts of yesterday

Stephen Philip Hull, Jr.

The Back Door

Household Sins
Unknowingly Aired
Tense, Taunt Characters
Jerking Hastily By
Playing a Silent
Forbidding Tragedy
Nervously Staged
Precisely Choreographed
Careful to Avoid
Childish Mistakes of
Self-Shattering Proportions
Because
Someone, somewhere
Left the Back Door
Open

Christine Preblick Salib

Ode to a Clone

I thought that I would never see,
A fellow who was just like me.
But hark, it now has come to pass,
That we will rise out of the morass.
I wonder if all the woes and pain,
Will affect me all over again.
Or will my new self be able to miss,
All the pitfalls, and live in bliss.
And will me end up just like me,
a pile of compost for a tree?

Norman J. Hochella

Protected Corridors

Sorrowed memories of days past by
Like winds that blow to clear the
Debris of lingering waste

For time is relentless, yet the
Mind filters thoughts of hunger
To show us what realism is
Still to come

Walk in the background, not to
Be seen, but to observe the
Cruelty that loiters behind
Closed doors

Passages of the mind can harbor
All the horrors, so venture
Not past the safety zones
For what may be present
Isn't meant to be
Known.

Joseph Van Den Bosch

Human

Leaving the emptiness
that crowds his soul
Stare at the darkness
He's gained control
of every situation
He's reached his goal
of grasping complication
Tear into his soul
he begs for forgiveness
and winds around the heart
and dies in his caverns
left kneeling in dark
Shudders in his sorrow
laments in his hands
His only fear is to follow
the only human that understands

Stephanie Boeing

I Am Awake

When I awaken this morning
I looked all around
I said thank you Lord
I'm still on praying ground

I fell on my knees
To give praise and thanks
And throughout my body
God gave me power and strength

I will sing his praises
To the young and old
With God as my helper
I will stand brave and bold

I will not sway or falter
Along this narrow way
I will sing his praises
Each and everyday

When I bow down each night
I still will sing his praise
Because my Lord died
That we may be saved by grace

Elouise Washington

A Quasi-Romance

He and I were never a
May-December duo
Of carefree innocence and
Delightful rediscovery.

We were a compatible
July-November duet
He, the hot, spicy, youthful firmness
Of summer,
Irresistibly drawn to me,
The mellow seasoning and
Ripe plenitude of mature
Autumn.

Oh, how I yearn for the
Exuberant joy—the
Supreme hedonism of
Passionate ecstasy—pure L U S T!

Now (sigh) only the smoldering
Embers of un-erasable
Memories remain.

Rachel C. McMillan

This Is The End

This is the end of the morning sun,
The moonlight shines, the children run.
This is the end, to do right or wrong,
Go here or there or play along.
To tell your children you love them so,
Hold them tight and never let go.
This is the end of the good old days,
Old fashion cars and realistic ways.
To watch the children as they play,
To have it safe night or day.
This is the end, so hold on tight,
Be prepared, see the light,
Take Gods hand without a fight,
For my children, this is the end.

Victoria L. Harberts

In Memory of Grandma

A lifetime of memories,
are what we all know;
we can keep them forever,
wherever we go.

We can share them with others,
so they'll know you too;
a kind, gentle grandma,
is the lady we knew.

You spoiled us rotten,
with goodies and love;
you showed us through your eyes,
what dreams were made of.

You started this family,
taught us each all you know;
and with a part of you in us,
your family still grows.

So take with you the love,
of this family you created;
as we keep with us the love you gave,
as you never hesitated . . . .

Jessica Garbez

The Worshipers

Moving through night
Along the slopy path
Illumin'd by the starlight.
With stumble they made a pact
Hence their feet never get the slip.

In a single file they come
Sometimes walking, sometimes trudging,
With silence they recon
Yet the nocturnals bid them welcome.
While still afar their God beckon
Sometimes rushing sometimes gushing.
Quicken their pace become
To the call they cherish.

For the head of the young that is laden
And the back of the old that is burden'd
The heart of their God broadens
From whence blessings flow.
This is the way of the worshipers.

Okechukwu J. Anyaibe

The Wind

Listen! The wind is blowing,
blowing all around.

It's breaking twigs and branches,
tossing pinecones to the ground.

Making waves that crash and pound
like beasts upon the shore,

And letting little boys with kites,
release their toys to soar.

When rain is paired with tossing wind,
it makes the world brand new.

The air is clean and fresh and bright,
God's spectacle to view.

Beverly K. Renaud

Untitled

Did the rats
Finally gnaw
Through this grain sack world
Of ours?

Barbara E. H. Brown

If We Believe

A lustrous star that falls from above
is soon replaced by one that shines
more brilliantly than before.

The darkness of night is but a prelude
to a wondrous new day
a gift of the Lord.

All of our disappointments and pain
will soon give way to fulfillment,
joy and strength.

The heartaches we feel are an assurance
that we are capable of love.
Love of God and man.

Our tears are but raindrops of life
that will make the flowers of our hearts
burst into bloom, and rainbows
will fill our lives

If we believe!

Marion Bendix Creasman

Snowflakes

Snowflakes, upon the ground they fall;
They are falling from above,
Like tiny stars they shimmer
Radiant as a pure white dove.

Virginia A. Johnson

Wake Up

You need to wake up out there
Show your world that you care
Just don't stare
At the scars they bear
For making your world
stronger
For making you live longer
You need to appreciate
Do not hate
For a generation so aware
It doesn't seem that you're fair
For not giving any one a chance
For not inviting them to dance
This poem is for all those bums
That show their gums
In a hateful way
I hope you wake up someday

Nicole Irene Potes

Love On Earth Begins With Me

Some years ago I read it
(It is quoted directly thus);
'Twas pogo possum who said it,
"We have met the enemy and he is us!"

Because the singular of us is me
I am filled with great remorse,
For the enemy that I see
Is not you, but me of course.

"Love your neighbor as yourself,"
We're told, "and love your enemy."
So when I love myself,
The foe I love is me.

Now psychologically
The converse has proved true.
If the one I hate is me,
My hate will spread to you.

If you understand this zany verse
Then it follows quite rationally,
Things will go from bad to worse
Unless love on earth begins with me.

Jerrold E. Johnson

Hurricane

Dark and dreary was her game
She sat and squalled on border lane
Her name was Hilda, Beth or Sue
Fury's hurricane was her brew
She turned on us with all her might
And ripped to shreds in her delight
As with chaotic storm she blew
Of coastal wave and violent hue—
She lashed at us with a mighty leap
And bounded o'er the wall to greet
Chaos and destruction . . .
Then, with pride, she settled back
For a season's ride
Through quieter times; silent days
Until her soul's again enraged—

Gleniva P. Owens

Finding Moonbeams

Lay your blond head down
On a pillow of dreams.

I'll take you to the place
Where they invented moon beams.

Climb the winding staircase
And be careful of the starlight.

We'll get there together
If you just hold my hand tight.

Now close your eyes so blue,
I'll place a kiss upon your cheek.

We'll go dancing on the clouds and
Into true love, perhaps take a peek.

Now that we've found the moon beams,
Let's open up our hearts of gold.
That's the only way to see what they hold.

Jessica Paulson

My Feelings For You

If lonely men's dreams came true
I would close my eyes each night and
Dream of a life of loving you

If I had just two wishes
And wishes came true
I would wish for you to always love me
And the other I would save for you

If my tears could write a love song
The song would be of you
It would reveal the way you make me feel
And the true love I have for you

But dreams are just for dreamers
And wishes seldom come true
My tears may never write a love song
But when they fall they fall for you

Ronaldo Lamb

No Goodbyes

There is a place
That I can go,
Where you and I
Are always alone.

The garden of the good shepherd
Is where you spend your days,
Even throughout the night
That's where you still remain.

It's such a beautiful place
So peaceful within the shade,
With memories so vivid
Time could never fade.

At the end of each visit
Before I stand,
I touch the stone
With a trembling hand,

For you won't be going with me
Your destiny is here,
No goodbyes are ever spoken
So "goodbye" I'll never hear.

Pepper Jo Staggs

There Was A Time

There was a time,
Another place,
When I looked up
And saw your face.

Of all the dreams
And hopes I had,
In one short moment
They turned sad.

There was a time
I did not know
That now I would
Be letting go.

Hard feelings? No,
Just sighed "goodbyes."
It hurts to know
Just how love dies.

By this farewell
You now can know
That I have truly
Let you go.

Mary Bethany Swanson

On What Did Fair Apollo Dine?

On what did fair Apollo dine
That kept him fit and trim?
Let that Ambrosia now be mine,
That I may be like him.

But, no! I dote on butterscotch
and apple tarts and creams,
And tho' I loose my belt a notch,
My trousers stretch their seams.

The lovely lure of chocolate mousse
And cakes with thick white icing
Is like ancient sirens on the loose,
Delectable, ecstatic, enticing!

So go, Apollo, go! Be thin, be thin!
My fate's to be obese.
Is that more pie they just brought in?
I think I'll have another piece!

Hugh K. Holmes

Deep Inside

Staring at a dark sky,
As wonders flow through my mind,
showing reflections of me.
Deep down inside.

Contemplating if there will be
more to whom I call me.
Shall I search for a brighter day,
or shall I stand waiting for dismay.

The people around me seem so sincere,
yet, they cause me to shed many tears.
Wrapping me in darkness,
my heart is filled with hardness.

Deep down inside me.
I long for only one word,
which fills my soul with pleasure.
It wipes away my tears,
and removes all the fears.

Deep down inside me.

Cheilon Randolph

GIFTS

It's Christmas Time
My friends are near
I feel like celebrating
The mem'ries of this recent year
Send my thoughts — creating
Some people ask for
Toys 'n things
My wishes are much dearer
I asked for friends
'n
WHAT — DID — I — GET
Please take a look in your mirror
MERRY CHRISTMAS — HAPPY NEW YEAR

Patricia Trocano

Fishing

He approached the stream,
With a clever scheme
To fulfill a boyhood dream.
All of the elements seemed ideal
to provide this angler
with an aquatic meal.

Phil Perkins

Fireligt Of Flames

There's quietness, there's stillness,
There's shadows we admire,
There's always imagination
When you gaze into a fire.

Three logs burning slowly,
The room is almost dark
with him lying beside me
Our kisses formed a spark.

There's nothing like loving
With a fireplace at your side,
When nothing's going to stop you,
Nature's wishes will abide.

I feel like going out of it,
Just let it all hang out.
He touches my face with dignity
And I face what life's all about.

When nature has finally finished
I gaze into the flames,
To see life as it really exists
to know there is no games.

Deborah D. Sullivan

I Hate

When I die I find my freedom
When I cry I taste my pain
I am lost in my own kingdom
For I am typical of my shame

I have learned to live with fears
Now look what I've become
My mind has wandered too far away
Contrast cutting pears with fears

When I die I become my shadow
Black as night as I am dying
When I sleep I sleep in fear
Pummel brain cell stretch to boiling

Now I alone have lost my courage
I have learned to hate

Kirsten de Boer

God's Spring

There, can you feel it,
The softness of the air?
See, there's a robin
On wing without a care.
My eye has found a tiny pond,
As still as time gone by;
And yet, as I stand staring,
I see a fish swim by.
I look up to see a sky so blue,
With fleecy clouds of white.
Birds are flying, playing games;
The whole world seems so right.
The trees are budding, some in bloom;
Others leafing green.
The soft breeze blowing through them,
Cause the saplings seem to lean.
The picture now before me
Can simply not be bought.
The beauty and the wonder
Are things that God hath wrought.

George L. Silate

Imprisonment

Blame me not for
what's been done.
It's not of my mind
that he was gunned.

Behind iron bars
I distinguished
who's who.
Not one of my comrades
came to see me.

All alone
I'll face the Judge.
A Lawyer and defendant
will I be.

Hopeless I'll try to
appeal my case.
Life imprisonment,
They denied my plead.

Normadelle Harvey Muthra

Windchimes

Gray and silent images flutter
in silence behind closed eyes.
I strain to hear voices;
there is only muffled traffic.

A bothersome breeze agitates
the trees yet bare,
awaiting blessed green richness;
the promise of spring.

Droplets of rain splatter,
rinsing away the grim dust
that settles on the sidewalks
of the city during winter.

In these moments
before the world beckons,
dullness of sleep is still about;
sharpness of day not yet welcome.

The only calamity tolerable
sings to me from outside my window.
I am so grateful
I have given the wind her instrument.

Geraldine Griffith

Happy Thoughts

Happy, happy, little thoughts
Trickling through my mind,
Gay and sunny little flits
Of happiness I find.

I put them all together
And bursting all around
Is gay and sunny, happy laughter
Bouncing like a clown.

Oh, but could I capture them
To gently pack away
Lest they should not be there
When I need them some sad day.

Joann Morgan

Mmmmm

Hot piece of pizza
sinned with Italian spice
bitten with temptation

Karen Possessky

A Madman's Lost Soul

In the still dark night,
Wandering endlessly I see a sight.
A silhouette of a person,
one of blinding light!

Frozen, I stand, not a blink.
As it drifts away and appears to shrink,
"That's a madman's soul",
Is the sudden thought I think.

I begin to shake
With nervous delight,
Wondering who will take
This evil soul tonight!

Don't want it to be me,
So I won't stick around
Long enough to see
Who this menacing soul has found.

A madman lost his soul,
Because of a mindless killing spree.
That madman achieved his goal,
By setting his soul free!

Ryan Abraham

A Poem

A poem must be many things,
But should leave its mark with the
happiness it brings
It must be wondrous as a forest,
Happy as a clown,
Innocent as a child,
And never deserving of a frown.

A poem should be other things,
But should still leave its mark with the
happiness it brings
It must be soothing as a dream,
Tranquil as a sea,
Sweet like honey,
And as unique as you or me.

Diana Frey

Feed The World

The golden fields of life,
flow endlessly away.
The keepers of the crop,
have worked all night and day

From an infant seed,
the green begins to rise.
Acres filled with nature's bounty,
touch so many lives.

Long hot days and misty nights,
bring the fall to bear.
A teeming harvest on the plains,
for all the world to share.

It's wrong to think that all this work
affects so very few.
They plant a seed that feeds the world,
including me and you.

Scott C. Swenson

Untitled

I watched the cold, white,
fingers of the searchlight
Probe the sky;
And wished with all my heart
That it were I,
Who danced amidst the stars.

Shirley Singleton

You and I

Let down you hair.
Get into something comfortable.
Let me breath in your air.
The sight of you makes me stumble.
Can I hold you?

Hold me in your arms.
Stay close to my heart.
Lord, keep us from all harm.
Please, never let us part.
We are together.

Standing here in the night,
Your arms around my waist,
My eyes see the light.
I do not want to leave this place.
Thank you.

Omar Anderson

Elfin Woods

As the moonlight sweeps
　over the mountain's
　　untrimmed hedge
　　　up above

　and I enter
　　the elegantly trodden
cavernous hall
of the maple, evergreen palace
　　down below

　something else I find
　　that holds me
　　forever enthralled

　A rustle nearby
jerks my head and I catch
　　a glimpse

　of the human shied creatures
　　garbed in the hallow
　　of protruding moonlight

Luis Filipe Mateus

Spot

Into the air
Swept by a breeze
Went my little
Pekingese.

Where she landed
I do not know.
Perhaps buried
In the snow?

I'll have to wait
Until it thaws.
Then I might spot
Her tiny paws.

Jonathan Wetzel

Someday

Where do they put all the people
Who are romantically insane
Do they lock them up in barrels
To hide them from the rain
Do they give them 20 lashes
And turn them loose again
Do they find them little houses
With peepholes for their eyes
Or do they just let them roam around
In a funny little disguise
Or do they find someone else
Who is just as mad as they
And put them both on an island
Far, far away.
No, you do not do this to the
Romantically insane
You can let them be, or guide their way
And they will grow up to love you
someday.

Kimberly A. Williams

Walls of Tears

Walls of brick surround my soul,
as high as my eyes can see.
Each one I've place there is no hole,
all secrets inside, but I'm not free.

Tiny hands began this wall,
but now my hands have grown.
I've built it strong it will not fall,
if the pain it would bring I'd known.

The wall has done its job for me,
my secrets it will not tell.
But as I stand inside I see,
these walls around me are hell.

I'm weak and tired of being here,
the life outside I crave.
I built this wall with tears an fear,
for my life I was trying to save.

I know happiness is outside,
hands of my loved ones I see.
With love I'll throw each brick aside,
because love will set my soul free.

Beverly D. Woods

Accession

Two little, old ladies,
Out for a stroll.
One, white as snow
The other, black as coal
Holding hands, chatting.

Leon Smith

Along the Way

Gently sweep the sleeping shore,
on the dreadful daylight hours.
Seek the seed that sways the breeze,
away from daily showers.
Rock the boat that never floats,
when there seems to be a need.
Leave this life cut by the knife,
Sail upon the wind-blown seed.

John H. Quick

The Price of Freedom

A ghostly image of a Soldier
stood in the background.
As a mother with a babe
in her arms stood by a
grave site.

She lowly whispered,
"Father this is your son,
Son this is your father.
He gave his life so that
his country might live."

Shirley A. Smothers

Living With Myself

Four slightly distorted walls
That I never get to see.
I sleep all day
While the hatred grows inside me.

Filth surrounds and consumes my body.
but, "I can just sleep it off."
This sickness is ever more
Blocking my way to the top.

Seeing the light of day
is becoming rare.
People are staying away, as if I'm
holding a sign that says beware.

I lay and watch my life
Slowly disintegrating to black.
and I know now, there's no way
I'll ever get it back.

Melissa Higginbotham

Untitled

Our little Angels Keith and Kevin
were sent from up above.
To Challenge what the future holds
to have, to hold, and to love.

We thank you for the support
you gave us. In oh, so many ways.
Whatever it may be: A prayer,
flowers, a gift of money, or even
just a hug.

It means the world to us to
know that all of you do care.
Keith is now in heaven, but
please keep Kevin in your prayers.

Barbara I. Tibbs

B.C.

Swish, Swish
Went the Cat's tail
in a fit of
Aggravation and Disgust.

To make his point
more prominent
He growled at me.

Kimberley McConnell

Let Me

I can't! I want!
Let me out! Let me touch!
Let me see! Let me be free
Free as a bird flying in the
bright heaven above.
Free as the sun shining
on the earth.

Let me feel! Let me taste!
Let me hear!
Hear the angels singing like
hummingbirds. Lighting the
sky like flier flies.

Let me be that angel above.
Glowing as light as the
brightest star!

Let me fly. Let me hold the
big blue sky. Let me see the
one above my Lord.
My God My Love.
Let me!

YaLanda Glenn

Elfin

Elfin is my name,
I am a fairy like creature
that needs love and care!

Watch me, I love magic.
I know some tucks.
I can cast a spell!

Some people like elves,
others don't care.
People love magic.
I know some things.

I was bought in a store.
Someone loved me!
It was a girl . . .
I gave her love and
something else—luck, I hope.

Elfin is my name!
Sprite was another elf—
he went somewhere.

Everyone loves Christmas;
Maybe someday I will return.

Dorothy Moore

One Life

The world all around me
shows little concern

For the memories I've made
and the lessons I've learned

Truly alone to make
My own way

Hoping, or not, for
another new day

God give me courage
to face what I've been

And show me a reason
to let new life begin

Teri Brooks

Your Love

When you died you took my soul,
you vanished into the dark cold;
when you left you took my lost breath,
and know all I can think about is death;
your love to me was so very strong,
now you're gone, I can't hold on;
I see you walking down the hall,
but when I get there it's just
a shadow on the wall.
I can still there your voice in my head,
but then I stop and think and I realize
you're really dead.

Casey R. Wheeling

Rage On

The fight is life that rages on
For all that's left is all that's gone.
Distant memories from the past
Of days gone by, all gone too fast.

I look back now and still recall
Those days I thought I had it all.
They seem so far, this now I see
These days gone by no more will be.

And what's ahead I'm still unsure
Who's to know what lies in store.
But one thing I know will still remain
I will yet rage on despite my pain.

Daniel Longenberger

Olympian

Should someone ask me
Would I fall in love again
I'd answer yes of course
Let the games begin
I would not like a rainbow
Could I not bear the rain
Anytime
Let the games begin
Let the games begin I want to play
Count to ten
Close my eyes and make a wish
Then I'll fall
In love again

P. J. Cullen

Into The Fold

Life is very simple,
If you choose, my path today,
For I call you, to worship,
And I teach you, to pray.

I carry, your burden
Or lighten, them to bear.
Each day, with me is a joy,
For I teach you, to care.

On my path is only beauty,
For all, my children, to see,'
And nothing, alters my plan,
For it lasts, through eternity.

I'm the key, to this pathway,
And always, willingly there,
To keep your feet from stumbling,
For I'm Jesus, and I care.

So look up, as your on this path,
That my face, you may behold
And my joy, you won't lose sight of,
While I bring you into the fold.

Dawn P. Ware

Ode to the Janitor

O Keeper of Mops
    And Brooms and Such,

Master Trashman of his trade,

His life a clean sweep,
    Etched with the sands of time,

But from DUST he started,

And to DUST he shall return.

Marie A. Schmidt

Enchanted

I dream the dreams of lovers
Who yearn for enchanted lands.
Where people help each other
By lending hearts and hands.

With streets of gold, and skies of blue
And everlasting sun.
And every single thing you do
Is just like childhood fun.

I dream of gliding carousels,
And floating ferris wheels.
Of cotton candy on my face,
And all the childhood thrills.

Oh! To be a child again
And stay that way forever.
Instead of growing up and old
And looking back at never.

Ralph Caraway

Mother-Love

To my Mom
Gasping breath and trembling sides
First eye-gaze between the two
She the one to recognize
Glistening tenant of her womb

Tiny life-spark gently cradled
She, devoted, soothes the fear
Lives for the life that she created
Loving, gives a mother's care

Hot white walls again enclose
Child and mother pressed between
Again the two endure life-struggle
Child this time remains unknown

Eyes like embers stare past daughter
Long-loving heart for once unmoved
She is held by arms that know her
You, the child, give mother-love.

Rebecca Coffman

Untitled

Waves crash over the sand
the sun is beginning to rise
she doesn't care
the wind blows through her dress
her hair whips round her face
if she notices she doesn't show
silently she moves
I see her fall
and the ground rushes towards me

Hannah Rhae Noack

One Daugther's Declaration

Dearest Mother, as I sit here in the most quietest reflection,
All my thoughts are of you with only warmest-felt affection:

From the moment I was born and beyond that to when I as conceived,
I've had your love and tenderness, in which I have grown and believed.
You were there to help me get through the days when I encountered sorrows,
And always sustained my belief in the positivity of tomorrows.

You were there to witness my moments of triumph as I felt with all my heart—
And you shared in my times of happiness and joy and in them took your part.

But alas, I did grow older—as all children must inevitably do,
And in that growing process did cause you to be at times, sad or blue;
Please know I'm deeply sorry for any hurt I did cause you to endure,
And that these situations did happen needlessly and without intention, to be sure.

I do realize I was not always the daughter you perhaps had wished for me to be,
In my diligent quest to expand and explore—in the struggle to be free.

But for every moment of grief you felt or instance of utmost frustration,
I'd hope I also incited you to experience love and warmth and elation.
So let it be known my dear mother, that without you I'd have been so lost—
And for you, I would endeavor the greatest challenge—regardless of the personal cost.

And so from this pen these words have been scribed—and all of them most sincere . . .
Because I love you more than words can express and I will always hold you dear!

Linda M. Badillo

Feelings

Did you feel the pain and grief of things we've left unsaid?
Do you know I'm old and tired and wish that I was dead?
You never cared to know me then, when first we had hard feelings.
I never knew how to contend, with any human dealings.
I know the way things happened were entirely my fault.
I should have seen it coming and called it to a halt.
I often wished to hold you close and tell you of my love.
But I pushed aside these feeling so gently, with just a little shove.
You never saw inside my heart, I hid these feelings well.
And one that never knew me, really could not tell.
I closed my eyes and wept inside revealing none of me
And with a sight I said goodbye and thus I set you free.

Nancie Henthorne

Seraph

Beyond the beauty of nature, you are my gift from God above.
The most ardent, beloved friend of all—sharing with me your life and love.

My love is a precarious pool of water, reflecting your love alone in return.
The moment it chanced wondrously into our lives, we became each other's sole concern.

When I explore deeply inside of your soul—I realize I am one among few.
If you are led to search within me now, you are certain to find yourself anew.

Artless streams fill the river, as the purest love fills the soul.
The rain relieves the stressful streams—as the sacrifice bonds loves hold.

The most serene water, or the most content love—
Soon became rapidious splashes, to heed prayers of hope from above.

Placid waters return once more—leaving love alone to endure.
Beneath the earth, the streams remain to prove this love is strongly secure.

The gentlest breeze forming the mightiest rapids remain to be the test.
From the heights of Heaven—above thistled fields, wind whispers, as water rests.

Love is the Seraph. Faith and hope are but the wings
    by which it flies freely.

Amy L. McKissick

Countless

Countless are
The things I miss:
Soft-spoken words,
Each tender kiss,
Naked bodies
Joined as one.
This love we've found
Can't be undone.
My love, I see
Him every night
In peaceful dreams
To wake I fight.
And though for now
We're miles apart,
I hold him close
With all my heart.

Halley Harris

Tell Me

Look into my eyes,
tell me what you see;
you see our love reflecting
off you to me.

Please don't lie to me,
you know it's true.
Because the way
you feel about me is
the way I feel about you.

You tell me that you love me,
you say it comes from the heart.
But the three words I need to hear
right now are that we'll never part.

Latisha Snow

To A Holiday Anyway

Could—
be
Monday, Sunday
or Wednesday afternoon
'dey sit on the table
Mama's mixture

May—
be,
someday, a someday
with nothing to do.
I like 'em
Mama's mixtures

sittin' on the table,
            whenever
(it's the ingredients that
make them taste like something special)
For those;
    dirty toes,
    guests . . .
or for whomever.

George Gignac

Potato Peeler

Dedicated to Dmitriy Sliozberg, who met his demise
by the cruelty of the Soviet military machine.

In a far-away, across-the-ocean, always smiling country, where supermarkets
Are all bright, and full, and shiny I went and bought a plain potato peeler,
And memories, erased by time, were reborn quickly,
And drew the gloomy picture back to me much clearer.

I saw a snowy, dreary, hungry Russian winter
And barracks full of soldiers, stern and rigid.
There was a Jewish kid from Moscow—former student,
He tried his best to live in an atmosphere hostile and frigid.

His name was Dima; he was quiet, shy, polite and friendly—
The only child his parents ever knew.
But comrade Major had his personal opinion:
"This schmuck's place is in the kitchen, among the chosen few."

They gave him as his weapon that dull and rusty knife,
And peeling up potatoes he was both days and nights.
And not a single kind word he ever did receive—
Just yells, and screams, and punches, and threats he could believe.

His body was found hanging over the potato pile. "Committed suicide,"—
Was written in his file . . . I'm telling you, America—it's time
To play it wise: instead of joint maneuvers and monetary funds,
Export potato peelers—save Russian soldiers' lives!

O. Merkulov

To My Daughter

On the day that you were born you were a blessing from above,
To remain in my protective care to cherish and to always love,
Throughout your childhood years at times,
through sickness and through tears.
I nourished you and taught you with I pray,
wisdom and lots of loving care,
There were so many happy times we smiled with laughter from within,
There were saddened times, trying times, and times we couldn't win,
But we held together bound by love which softened many of the blows,
And I remember well through all those times, the family love that flowed,
As your mother my emotions peak, for realization has set in,
That you have crossed the barrier to womanhood, a bride to be and then,
As I watch with pride and admiration my thoughts take me back in time,
The clock of your childhood years has been, for growing and learning, an ever endless chime,
All that you have accomplished in your life I see a future that is bright,
I helped shape the woman you've become and quite content just knowing all is right!

Lydia Coppola

The Morning Adventurer

In the dew drops of the morning mist, a fragile being is born.
Adventuring higher to meet the sun, rain and sky,
To meet the sun and the wind, the birds, and other things unknown,
what a beauty she is, to see while passing by.

Her limbs occasionally have spears; proud and strong, to stab hunting,
misunderstanding foes who come to steal her for her beauty.
Her colors are numerous, but just one suddenly.
Once you look, then you see, that her beauty you must meet,
But you'll see her day or night, in the open fields, or at your feet.

This adventurer wakes to meet the sunny morning mist,
and to greet the sweet dewdrop's kiss.
For she is one who needs no introduction, because her face is known by all.
Take a walk in the parks, and you'll greet her on the sides and by the
trees, her presence is always near.

She's there all the time never moving, as a house, restrained by her supports.
She's the sun on a summer's day, always bright and gay.
In the winter, she sleeps until the April showers come to wake her and her sisters.

The morning adventurer never departs, travels, or sees, and only moves with the wind.
She never converses with her sisters, for no need of connection.
She's divergent from her sisters, but stunningly similar all at once.
But whatever she is, the one thing that the Morning Adventurer will   never be, is just a
flower.

Cory Medina

How Can I Say Thank You For All That You Have Given?

For my parents...
Thank you is far too simple an expression
to convey my gratitude to you . . .

For my first laugh, my first smile,
for welcoming me back when I've been gone awhile.
For showing me the wonder of blue skies, and teaching me to
always ask why.
For always telling me, "Yes you can!", and for making me who I am.
For opening your life and your world for me to see,
and for showing me who to be—
not by your words, but by your careful, loving actions.

For showing instead of telling.
For helping instead of hindering.
For loving instead of laughing.
For being brave for us, and for never giving up, for us.
For being you, and for showing me how to be me.

For being a Mom, a Dad, a Doctor, a Teacher, a Taxi an Artist, a
Cleaner, a Cook, a Barber, a Seamstress, a Career Consultant, a
Relationship Consultant, a Banker, a Finance Consultant, a Lending/ Loan
Officer, a Decorator, a Fashion Consultant, a Mover . . . and a Friend!

For everything you ever said, thought, did, or wished for that has
made my life so full of love . . . I thank you! From the bottom of
my heart, from the tip of my soul, and from the ends of the earth,
I thank you, and I love you.

Melanie J. Morris

For My Sister-in-Law Nancy

Someone called her daughter, to nurture and to guide
And someone called her granddaughter, an extension of their pride

Someone called her sister, a companion in their life
And someone called her aunt, a supporter for their life

Someone called her cousin, a partner at play
And someone called her co-worker, dedicated all day

Someone called her neighbor, when they needed a helping hand
And someone called her niece, a kind adoring fan

Someone called her Mother, for her compassion and her love
Someone called her Wife, sent from God above

Someone called her child, so innocent and pure
And someone called her patient, striving for a cure

Someone called her daughter-in-law, their son's loving wife
Someone called her sister-in-law, a bonded friend for life

Someone called her grandmother, though it may be a awhile
Before he knows the story of her sweet contagious smile

Someone called her friend, so easy to adore
But I will call her all these things, for she's all these things and more

Cynthia Rogers

The Tiny Trickle of a Tear

The tiny trickle of a tear sliding down my face,
Reveals the way I feel at home, I feel so out of place.
They never talk, they always shout. I've done something wrong again.
I feel like breathing might become an awful, deadly sin.
I'm never right I'm always wrong, and so at home I don't belong.
I run, I hide, I try to stay within the safety of my room.
But then I think, "Hey what's the point?" They'll remember I'm there soon.
Again they shout, again they scream. I'm wishing it were all a dream.
And then they leave and all I hear is the tiny trickle of a tear.

MeLissa Morgan

The War Memorials

The night was dark and cold as we walked toward the war memorials
So cold, we found it hard to care . . .

First, the Korean Memorial, and the faces came off the stone
as if out the mists of time . . .
These we could see, if not the faceless statues hulking in the dark.

We hunched on toward the Vietnam Memorial
Lost in conversation, the first names that seeped past our feet
   went unnoticed . . .
But as the wall rose beside us, the names lifted and poured above us.
A silent torrent, that cataract of names.

No finger in the dyke could stop the flood of names
A black river that crested and towered above us . . .
So many men
Lost at first in a trickle, that turned into a torrent
While a nation seemed too cold to care.

A host was swallowed in the tide,
But so many lost could not be ignored.
They seeped into the marble of our nation's conscience,
and onto the marble of the Wall.
Cold—but not too cold to care.

Carolyn Thomas-Davidoff

Watching Bridges II

Sitting and watching "Bridges" on a Sunday afternoon, and I realize
something of my life is missing, is gone! Like being the only one
aware of a mysterious full moon without a hand to hold, no one
to whisper words that reach me, that touch my soul.

Watching Eastwood and Streep capturing a glimpse of something
they've wanted all of their life made me sad. Then to hear him say,
"I've been taking pictures all my life to make my way here," making
the purpose of his life so very clear. How profound coming from the
depth of his being. Yes, it is true. It made me lonely, it made me sad,
for the void that lies in my heart is still awake, wanting another
to come along to make my heart whole, a bridge to unite us as one.

Can it be possible that four days of one's life can be so incredible
that it overpowers the rest? Can a "citizen of the world" be
hypnotized, be captivated by an usual housewife whose dreams
have been set aside for maternal bliss? Can two worlds become
one? Can a few days capsule one's "love of a life"?
Can it transcend time and space?

If this is possible, if it can be true, I hope it happens to me. Please
let it happen to me. My dreams still lie there, not forgotten. They
reside in a place waiting for when, I know not. But they don't end.

Linda Kay Dixon

Listen

I need someone to listen. Listen to me, with eyes and ears that care.
Simply say to me, "I love you," and with living arms, please share.

I see no one is listening, not one has chosen to listen to my cry.
What is my reason for living? There is none, and so now I'm going to die.

I'm listening to you, with eyes and ears that care.
Listen, I can now say I love you, and should you
let me hug you with loving arms, I will share.

Who are you? You never took time to stop and look, much
less listen to me. For in me, even with open eyes, you
just could not and would not believe.
Your fearful cry for help has taught me how to listen.
When you learn how to listen, with an open heart and
eyes and ears that care, then you can also learn to receive.

I now also have my reason for living. Choosing to listen,
one can learn to believe and see.
That is why I have chosen to live. May our life be filled
with love, laughter, peace and harmony.

Donald Ray Zinninger

I Remember Every Kiss

I remember every kiss and how you held me so tight.
And I remember every sweet word you said
underneath the moonlight.
And I wonder how that all can change in the blink of an eye.
The past is back to haunt me and,
Once again, you're saying good-bye,
goodbye to all the fun we had and all the love we shared.
You say that it would be too hard, but I think that you're just scared.
You're afraid to give me the power
because you fear I'll hurt you again.
So instead you make excuses and refuse to let me in.
I wish I knew how to change your mind and make you see how I feel.
And I wish I could prove to you once and for all that my love for you is real.

Melissa Zack

The Day

As the waking sun exhausts the moon, the roaming fog is
vanished soon and sallow colors set the mood for all the waking eyes.
Crickets yawn and birds withdraw from thicket beds made of straw;
they glide their wings above the law and touch the face of God.
The peaceful dawn foregoes the pain of wretched heat and
sheets of rain as windy waves soon go insane to calm the noon-day sun.
Yet, nothing can compare to a floating, white body of air,
as castles of clouds threaten to bare an uncontrollable force.
Then, the scarlet sun completes the day with vibrant pink and
yellow rays that light the path along the way into a zone called dusk.
Slowly, dusk shall bring the moon and all within its silent gloom
will say, "Goodnight, I'll see you soon," and drift into their dreams.

Cecilia L. Whidby

A Leaf

Oh Lord, I am like a leaf on a tree. In the spring I unfurl and
reach up to the heavens, full of promise and hope.

The summer brings sunshine—a time of peace and joy, a few
light showers—cleansing and cool.
Twirling and dancing in the wind, unaware of my destiny.

With fall comes the crispness of cool mornings. I'm no longer supple,
no longer reaching to the heavens. I'm just trying to hold on.

Winter slams into my world—dark, cold and unforgiving.
I fall from my tree, my source of life. I flutter this way and
that in the winds, only to fall to the ground—crushed and broken.

Even as I lie bruised and wounded, Lord, you care for me.
You use me to serve your purpose. I am absorbed by new life,
which unfurls with hope and promise.

My almighty God, you have a plan for me—a plan for eternal life.

Patti Jenkins

Morgen

It's 4:00 am
The genesis of a new day. I'm awakened.

Daylight gently peeps her head through the tightly closed
window shades
Young birds chirp continuously, boldly breaking the silence of
the night
that has soothingly eased into dawn.

This was our favorite hour of the day
Me and you, alone to share, laugh, love
While the rest of the world slept soundly.

Remember? I can't forget.
(For) It sickens me to face another day alone without you.

47 days since you've been gone.
One ocean, four time zones, and 15,000 miles away.

I miss you.

L'Tanya D. Pugh

The Tower of Babel

Beyond the endless swamp of death, the water of life from the lost
and forgotten Eden flows through my heart as it turns into a dew.
And it whispers: come back, come back.
I will return. I will return. And I will find those that for an instance
I have lost in a blinded love.
Painful days are those when the sprouts of hope fell like the sun
beyond the death.
I will build the tower with all my spirit.
I will build it with blood, flesh and tears, here where the curse of
the divine resides.
The divine also cries. With a heart hotter than God's,
will I remain in the future.
And the future will lead to a way to of perfection,
underneath Eden's tree of everlasting life.
I will hold your hand and lead the way like the day before.
Then the curse of God will break and the swamp of death will disappear
Then I will call God in my purest spirit to Eden, my Eden.
I will tell Him that I truly did not know good and evil.
And I will ask for pardon.

I will return to the true owner of the universe.

Sung Ho Kwon

Untitled

My darling Sara Grace
I never laid eyes upon your face
I never held you tight and
I never kissed you goodnight,
I never counted fingers and
I never counted toes.
The only thing missing was a tiny little soul.
I know God has you and that is fine
but, I wish you were here, I wish you were mine.
If you were here you'd be over a year old.
I thought the pain would go away but, instead it's all on hold.
I keep waiting for your little voice to echo down the hall
but, there is nothing there . . . nothing at all.
There is not little dresses to outgrow and no pink ribbons
for the wind to blow. There is no skinned knees to make better,
There is no need to finish a knitted sweater.
I can't brush you hair into a ponytail
and you won't receive your birthday cards in the mail.
I'll never forget you 'cause you're always on my mind
I can't let go . . . I can't leave you behind.

Teresa Cochran

Cheeseburger

"Would you like fries with that?"

The bun: Hot, fluffy, and lightly toasted
The mayonnaise: White, creamy and spread on thick.
Tomatoes: Big, round, ripe, red juicy ones.
Next the onion: thickly sliced, as the aroma clears my nasal passage
Lettuce: Bright, green, so fresh it crunches in your mouth.
Cheese: melts over the pattie like an erupting volcano
Pattie: thick, juicy, well done pattie of mouth-watering
beef straight from the slaughter house.
In every flavorful bite, you can taste the fear of the beautiful
creatures, getting their lives taken, to fill your stomach.
This is senseless death.

Daniela Anthony

Wisdom

I, too, have met Wisdom. She came to me wearing a cloak
of sorrow. We stood face to face on a chilly Autumn day when
the Winter's wind had began forcing itself into my world. At first
I would not look at her, standing there in tattered clothes,
stretching out her arms, desiring to embrace me. I held back,
not wanting to indulge in her embracing. I tried rebuking her
in the name of the Lord, ignoring what she was trying to
show me. Still, she remained, more determined than ever,
waiting to be received as humbly as the Lord would require.
Finally, after what seemed like ages, I allowed myself to
gaze upon her. Yet, I would not let her touch me. I was not
ready to welcome her person. Knowing this, she withdrew
herself slightly and was content while quietly holding me with
her eyes. It was then that I first saw her beauty, the beauty
hidden deep beneath the surface years of time. The Winter's
wind caused me to shiver. Seeing this, she placed her cloak
over my shoulders. Her kindness burned with me and soon I
was warm. Wisdom stayed with me teaching me her many ways.
When Spring arrived, she removed her cloak of sorrow,
letting the sun's warmth clothe and cover me.

Dwight Smith

Death of America the Great, AD 1997

In her youth she was found to be very fair and she was also
wise. For in innocence her eyes and heart were wholly in
submission unto God—And now behold! She draws nigh into
death for her breast do flow greatly crimson and her flesh is
gravely pale and deeply bruised, for she was not faithful unto
her God, father and protector whom loved her. For she goes
about all the world as an adulteress without shame, selling her
chastity for unholy communion and relations with the heathen—
Woe, woe, woe to you America the great! For why doth you lie
to thine own children? And feedeth them dry flour when they
hunger for bread? And what caused you to sign upon the white
of paper born of trees, your freedom to the ungodly of the world
- yes when you were made protector of all the earth. But now
look at you this day, you have become undone because you
have sown desolation! For by this you shall utterly be reduced
to a worm before the face of your brothers and sisters. For you
have even dispersed thine own young men to fight against the
very cross that bore you, shedding there flesh for the oil of
swine. Oh how I shall pray for thee with all my heart that you
shall be spared! Yes, before your dying banner is seen no more!

James Conrad

My Friend is a Turtle

My friend is a turtle on whose back I walk.
You walk there too, my daughter...my friend.
Butterflies danced around our heads. You look
beautiful in butterflies I said, my heart full of
joy. We walk on a turtle, we love her, but we ignore
her cries for help burned in the ground. Being in
peace with each other and nature. This is real living.
It's a fight my daughter to keep our hearts like children.
Even for you a child who has seen so much sadness. Our people
have lived it. Love is an odd mixture of joy and pain. Mostly
pain for me, because I cannot forget their eyes. We live in
danger of becoming a statistic. I almost left you my daughter
But then I remembered your innocent face; those soft deer-like
eyes and the holy man's words—to always pray. The sweet
smell of flowers lingered on the wind in my most desperate hour
the spirits sent a guardian. She was a mother. I saw her K achina
face. She touched my hopeless heart. You touched it too. There
is a glimmer of hope in a blue jay's feather, in the call of a dove;
in a Kachina. In the touch of a mother. In the single kernel of
blue corn lying at my feet.

Debra Lee

My Dear American Flag

Today is your day-Flag Day!
A day designated to remember and pray.
To recall how I first came to know you
And then appreciate all the things you do.

When you led the parades, and marched so proudly in array,
Never a falter when the wind blew,
Your colors always waved bright and true.

Oftentimes Veteran's Day you celebrated,
Memorial Day you commemorated.
The soldiers would smartly salute
Remembering those years of service and tribute.

Many wars you have served, respect and honor you deserve.
Men and women have devoted their lives to your cause
Because they believed in justice for all.

Schools and classrooms you beautifully grace
And stand reverently in churches in a special place.
At times half-mast you bow, honoring those who have gone on now.

America thanks you for flying so high
At our homes, businesses, sports events looking to the sky.
I recognize it's God's grace to have this freedom in this place.

I salute you for all your deeds and pray for God's protection on my knees.
In Victory you wave brave and true; I love you, red white and blue.

Nelda Ward Keck

Morning Flies

I awake . . .
one hour later with fluttering flies of butter
etching cautiously in tow . . .
awaiting escape from dark-hidden cavernous stomached soul.

Joining wing with wing this marveling troop begins their dance
for sleep is lost at this reached point
as walls of pitted instinct decisively sway to and fro.

They rest.

Two hours later . . .
again the awakened dream-like world begins its dancing prance.
Creatures never to be held at bay will unite again in faster beat.
Whispering into mind... will I ever have my sleep?

I sift back into sleep world thrice hoping flies will cease their flight.
If only for a few short hours- the rest is needed and it's 'morrow.

Surrender not these flies stand free.
This is poignant need so clear—hear the drums beat lovely rhythm.

Sleep is lost while enamored ones quiver . . .
content to draw much nearer.

Virginia Salazar

A Message To My Family

Do not cry for me...I am with our Father now.
Take care of and comfort each other, and
    one day we will all be together again.
Take comfort in the memories that we've shared and
    made together and look back on them with fondness.
I will never leave you, just close your eyes and I'll be right there.
You will remember me when you smell the fresh, sweet scent
    of the green grass, trees and wildflowers;
Feel the soft, gentle breeze on your faces;
See the sun rising in the early morning, and the
    beautiful hues of the setting sun at night.
You will remember me when you see the calm on the lakes
    and hear the beautiful melodies of each song.
I will remind you of these things because these were the things I loved.

Christine Janke

Closing a Day

Sunset over a beach, the gentle waves lightly tickle the sand.
Sunset over a valley, the mountain's reflections shelter our homes.
Sunset across a plain, the fields of grain soften their dance
   and close their eyes.
Sunset across a desert, the dry wind settles in the cracks of the earth.
God's sign of closure on a day, is the sunset that dwells in our souls,
Which leaves a beautiful remembrance of peace.

   Jessica Grimes

I'm Sorry Is What He Said

Bruised, scared, and my eyes are red
"I'm sorry" is what he said.
These words use to tell me he loved me.
But now I wonder how could that be?
He use to call to say he loved me for many reasons,
now his moods change like the seasons, how can this be him?
I'm sorry for your arm, but still he inflicts harm.
Towards me he beats, but we try to make ends meet.
My life is now a living hell,
for my body is tired and frail, and anyone can tell I'm not well.
We've been together for so long, and now I realize he's done me wrong.
"I'm sorry" is all that he can cry, and I wonder why,
why he says he's sorry if he doesn't mean it!
And when I yell at him back I am the one that got hit.
But no longer can I go on like this.
This sadness has made me hollow because I know love cannot follow.
"I'm sorry," I remember and I will never understand,
he said he was sorry . . . and? "I'm sorry" his words plague me.
Why couldn't he let me be? "I'm sorry" will no longer comfort
my scars. So I say to him I'm sorry.

   Linda Nguyen "Bubbles"

HOLOCAUST

HUMANITY—the meaning of the word is not known to them,
Killing anyone who dares to move; they're known as the SS men.
Depriving us of everything we loved, took for granted, and cherished,
Separated from our families, our lives had perished.
Known by nothing other then the numbers engraved on our arm,
Never in our lives had we ever been exposed to such adversity
and harm.

No longer were we all equal HUMANS,
But rather slaves paying for someone's hellish sins.
Eventually we were released and set free,
But with the mental and physical scars inflicted,
We will always be weighed down to reality.
We are all different individuals, with our own unique face,
But aren't we all united, part of the same group,
A group called the human race?

   Prachi Patel

YOU

When we're apart I can't stop thinking about you.
When we're together I don't ever want to leave.
My life would have no meaning without you.
I would never doubt you.

My life would be complete only if we are together
I can't imagine being with someone else but you, because I love you.
My feelings will never change, just grow and become stronger.

At night I go to bed dreaming about you,
Waking with a smile upon my face.
In my dreams you're always there with me, that's the way it
should always be.

I share with you things I share with no one else,
that's the way it will remain.
I will never give you a reason to doubt me, because I love you
too much, more than anyone will ever know.
Nothing in the world can make me happier than you.
Just remember I will always love you. From now until the end.

   Patricia Ladis

The Gift

I sit on my front steps and stare at the gaping hole in my hedge.
Only last week a white picket gate had marked the entrance to
   my sanctuary,
   symbol of a tacit understanding that here lies my boundary,
   the point beyond which the busy, noisy street will not intrude.
Now the gate lies in ruins, smashed by a careless driver,
   the shattered wood symbol of a broken covenant.

The passage of days not diminished the sense of violation,
   and the rage that fills me will burst my heart. But I cannot
   let it go. For a week I have stubbornly let the wreckage lie,
   refusing until this moment to even look at it.

Suddenly, furious motion startles in the air as whirring black and
red become a hummingbird. It hovers above me, and I hold
   my breath, blind to all but the iridescent color, the tiny
   beating wings. Then as suddenly as it had come, it is gone.

My attention returns to the hedge. But in that brief space, those
wings have liberated me, replacing the rage with unreasoning
   joy. The moment lived within the mystery of the earth has
   made all the difference.

I arise. It's time to clean up the wreckage and build a new gate.

   Sandra Marquiss

The Perfect Girl

There once was a girl who was very intelligent;
there once was a girl who was not very wise.
There once was a girl who was often surrounded by people;
there once was a girl who always felt alone.

There once was a girl who was quiet and shy;
there once was a girl who wished to be bold and witty.
There once was a girl who was constantly pressured to be the
   ideal child;
there once was a girl who used drugs as a way to escape her
   many pressures.

There once was a girl who was beautiful and slim;
there once was a girl who felt fat and became anorexic
There once was a girl who felt trapped with life;
there once was a girl who dreamed to be free.

There once was a girl who was a perfect girl;
there once was a girl behind that perfect girl.
There once was a girl who had a strong message;
there once was a girl whose message would not be heard.

   Erika Tulley

Who She Is I Shan't Tell

There's a Lady with the softest skin...the telepathy's between us...
My fingers graze across...the supple polish of her cheeks...Her
eveness is envied...by the finest marble statues...For the sleek
luster...of her shapely ivory surface...Gives way to the exquisite
cushion...of her pliable puff...Rosy lips resting Full and silky...
Frictionless upon each other...When she weeps...her tears will say
I love you forever...Her smooth tongue so moist...yet fatal to
those who assault her...Eloquent defense that can be so
cruel...beauty overcame them...Bewitching and Angelic
Shazari...a natural queen... Womanliness drapes richly from
her...by the most graceful move of creation...What will you do
with it? Need not look to others to develop your beliefs...With
shiny summery eyes so responsive...Full of imagination and
passion...The glisten of your glowing velvety fleece...
tranquil and noiseless...Reveals a luscious fragrance of the
ambrosial nectar of your soul...Soothing silvery satin...comfit of
sweetness so harmonious...Your mild massaging waves...slip
into the mellow unruffled calm of gentleness...Melting your
hardened pleasure comfortably dissolving in gratifications
together...You are refreshed... revived...and purified....

   Mick Santullano

Motherhood

Another life is in effect, it's not your world anymore. Time to take charge and run the score for most definitely the one and only one you truly adore. There's nothing like someone feeling and knowing your pain, yet to discover that this little someone has just you and can't abstain. You find it a wonderful feeling and an incredible job. Welcome to the land of Motherhood!

Praise and respect to all the black women (All Women In General) whom God has created and produces the tasks necessary to deliver the outstanding joys of birth. To accept for what is and what is going to be, that is what God wanted you to have. Again, welcome to the land of Motherhood!

The perception of a child and its mother is unexpected. When you hold your child, feeling your child's touch is generally what makes you love them so much. You know when your child is in pain, or feeling down and out, it is then that you know another mother's role has come about. And just what is another mother's role! Well let's begin with single parenting. You have providing the shelter, clothing, and the food necessity to ensure the skills necessary they will need to achieve their goals and to give them to never ending bond of love!!

Amongst the bond of love is the foundation of friendship, in knowing that most children feel comfortable to share any and everything.

Dawn D. Banks

Ode To Ginger

I think that I shall never see,
a little funny puppy dog, quite like thee.
I knew from the first look, that you were the one for me.
You run and you play; living your life to the fullest each day.
Your nose is cold and your heart is big,
you chase butterflies; roll in the dirt
and get filthy as a little pig.
You squirm in your bath and you
wiggle in delight as I towel you dry.
Upon release you dash around crazy
as if in flight and soaring high.
I feed you the best dog food that money can buy.
But you turn your nose up with out even a try.
You beg and you whine for a scrap or a crumb
You keep it up till I break down and give you some.
I scold and I talk till I'm blue in the face.
But you end up doing what ever you want, at your own pace.
Night-time falls and quiet time comes.
You lay snuggled by my side with peace surrounding us both.
By looking at the two of us, it's hard to tell who loves who the most.

Cynthia J. Alvis

The Ways of Love

The symphony of spring as sparrows awake from winter.
The soft purr of a mother as she comforts her kittens.
The silent beckoning call as the sun closes the chapter of another day.
Harken to the sound of love.
Sweetness of the honeysuckle to the hummingbird.
The zest of salt to a growing fawn.
A dark ripe cherry pressed between hungry lips.
Savor the taste of love.
A lilac blossoms, radiating its aroma.
Wild flowers summon bees to their nectar.
Crisp, clear air on the ebb of a morning storm.
Inhale the scent of love.
Brilliant colors drive away the darkness rousing dawn.
The promise of the rainbow in a summer rain.
The mirrored image of mountains on a crystal lake.
Behold the sight of love.
Whispering breezes float through a field of wheat.
Passion drifts in waves across the surface of the earth.
Snow flakes balance delicately on barren trees to caress the world.
Quiver at the touch of love.

Leif Smedberg

Hallelujah! Our King Is Coming!
(Open Wide The Gates)

In the quietness of the morning when the dew is on roses,
And the children awake from slumber to sweet and calm reposes,
The breakfast in the kitchen smells so heavenly all supposes.
Another day God has given all this earth to make his people free,
From bondage through God sent down to Moses 10 Commandments.
Through "God's Great Divine Guidance," Genesis to Revelation.
All in sweet reposes, claims all is well as in the time of Moses.
Now that is past, yet should be observed in "High Regard."
In the stages of life we work, we laugh and we breathe;
This breath that Jehovah God has given us is ours we claim.
We hold this breath so dear, so tight, but so loose;
Do we convey to the world things of our "Spiritual Growth?"
If not, what a shame, "From the Cradle to The Cross."
"Where Jesus died to cover all sins, and to give Eternal Life to you and me!"
However, one may try to reclaim his "Authority and Power,"
For their very own; not so says he, have you forgotten
"Your Great Almighty God and His Only Begotten Son Jesus
Christ and The Holy Spirit?"
He could come back this very hour "In Glory and Power!"
I have a message from Jehovah's holy book, our Bible, our Roadmap.
Hallelujah, time is running out, Our King Is Coming Soon!

Margaret D. Isdell

The Caterpillar

The caterpillar's short life is a mirror of our own.
A small, furry creature, crawling and inching around.
In the most important years of its life, the caterpillar locks itself in a
    tiny cocoon,
Confused, feeling helpless,
knowing not its direction in life,
Much like a girl or a boy
in awkward teen years,
not an adult, not a child,
what are you?
For one, next stage is a butterfly,
The other, an adult, both are
Beautiful, free,
and clear on where headed.
The light does not last long, as
Stumbles,
tumbles,
through the air,
through life,
Stinging as they enter the hard, unwelcoming world.

Katie Blatterfein

Mama's Image

Mama you always said, "You're just like your father!"
and when Aunt Barbara sent me his picture,
I studied it just to see how true your statement was.
I'd stand in front of the mirror, I'd hold it up and compare.
I see the similarities . . .

Our eyes, big, dark, almond shaped—I remember your comment
about our lashes, "you'll have to start trimming them pretty soon .
. ." and then you'd tell me how daddy would get irritated when his
lashes would rub up against his glasses so he'd cut them.
You'd also touch my face and mention the square of our chins,
the angle of our noses and, our big ears.
I see the similarities . . .

I remember you saying there was more; when in deep concentration,
I have the habit of sticking my tongue out to one side of my
mouth; "Your father did that too," you'd say.
And my love of music and television, sometimes you had
to yell outright before you could capture my attention,
". . . that's your father all over again."

Yes mama, I see the similarities.
I guess when you saw me, you saw my dad.
But when I look in the mirror mama, I see you.

Mary Ann Villalovas

Night Artist

As night falls across the sky, a brisk breeze strokes my face.
A chill runs down my back, I shudder at the cold temperature.
The smell of cool rain fills my nose, a thunderstorm is on the horizon
The wind grows strong as I peer upward into the dark.
Bright and undefined, lightening streaks through the night sky.
An artist's quick brush stroke on black canvas.
Soon another more dense and brilliant, as if with heavy weighted
paint dripping from the fine bristles.
My eyes open wide as the light jumps effortlessly leaving a
glow of color in the clouds.
Bright blue and white are the first colors selected from the palette.
Then purples and orange fade to gray.
The shapes become more abstract as the storm grows stronger,
Pausing only for a moment to reload the artist's brush.
It begins again spattering the shapes to the left and right.
The brilliance of color staining the sky only for a moment then fading
away, as if being soaked up by a great thirsty sponge.
These paintings I see, unique and admired by few,
like a fine masterpiece of an unknown artist whose only
footsteps are the familiar sounds of thunder.

Stefanie Correa

The New World

The sun has set on the vast ocean ahead of me, and the waves
begin to blend with the horizon.
Its mysterious appeal starts me thinking of how those bold
mariners felt centuries ago, when the world was flat and the sea
inhabited by monsters.
How frightened and excited they must have been sailing to the
New World.
How their hearts must have quickened as they looked to the horizon,
wondering how much longer was their journey to land or death.
How they must have prayed for daylight to last another hour—
then another.
When would they reach the endless falls that would claim their lives.
Day after day, nothing but the sea to gaze upon.
Day after day, hoping, wondering if they would ever sea another morning.
Then one day . . .
Land!

Douglas Tombari

A Celebration of Life, Love and Faith in God

Life is a gift from God
A challenge to enjoy . . . a dream to pursue and fulfill
The past enriches the future
Which grows from the present's nurture
Behold and cherish life
For one can tread the earth endless times
But the final judgment is His.

Love is a gift from God
The color of life . . . its brightness endearing . . . its darkness mystifying
The past colors the present and the future
Behold and cherish love
For one can turn the color wheel endless times
But the final judgment is His.

Faith in God is life and love
Be dauntless of the insurmountable . . . believe in courage and strength
Let the heart speak of goodwill
Touch people with kindness of heart, mind and spirit
Peace and love abound
Be thankful for all the blessings
Celebrate life, love and faith everyday.

Lyvia M. Villegas

My Healing Prayer

I close my eyes and look within, knowing God is here.
I ask him to make me well, and take away all fear.
He seems to go right to the spot where pain is all about.
He says, "You breathe in, I'll load it up . . . and you can breathe it out!"
The nurses and the doctors are like angels helping him.
He shows them what to do outside, and then he heals within.
So when these angels say you need a shot, or here's a pill or two,
It's 'cause God has said to them, "Hey, I need some help from you!!"
Sometimes it takes a while, but this I do believe,
As Jesus said so long ago . . ."Ask, you shall receive!!"

Billie Jean Pagett

The Candle

Candle, candle, burning bright; 'tis the only source of light.
See the fire, touch the flame; life shall never be the same.
Feel the warmth, see the glow, watch the fire burn and grow.
Now concentrate, hard and long; listen to the fire's song.
Is it mournful? Is it glad? This is the best fire you've ever had.
Watch the fire, see it wither and die; doesn't it make you want to cry?
Darkness all around you now, your time has come.
Say good-bye, to those you love; darkness covers you like a glove.
But do not fear, my one true friend; we shall meet in the end.
My fire is still burning strong, though I fear I won't live too long.
I can hear the ending now; the only question is when and how.
Candle, candle, burning bright; measuring out the days of my life.

Elizabeth M. Renner

Untitled

I saw an evergreen today, greet limbs stretched out to catch the wind,
With needles hanging low to gently brush across my cheeks like tears.

I saw a tiny spider's web, so delicate in beauty and intricate design,
The work of one tiny individual, one life so brief.
To break the strands of silken thread would cause her to begin again,
In an unwavering diligence to repair her treasure.
And yet she would, as if there were no yesterdays,
seeing nothing but the moment of her needs.

I saw a butterfly today, dancing across the flowers in my path,
Brushing the petals' lovely lips with purposeful instinct.
A not-so-chance encounter.
A collision of beauty.
A drop of mercy for my eyes.

I heard a broken heart today, with jagged of raw despair
screaming out from a dead silence.
The sudden rush emptiness inside.
And did I mention yet my friend, the tree I saw was dead?
Dry and brown from roots to crown.
Once a resting place for life, great limbs stretched out to God,
Is evergreen no more.

Dianne Floyd Diaz

Once Only For Me

Shall I kiss the twilight off your cheeks
brush the dew of the morning off the tips of your light brown
hair and let my eyes wander upon the high arch of your brows
that rise when you smile
I love you . . . why must you leave?
the touch of your lips go too
as does the constant warm comfort of your soul
that once enshrouded my own in its soft unassuming sweetness
so sweet the memories that will die in my heart never, never will I
forget your fingers on the underside of my arms, my thighs,
against the small of my back, the nape of your neck,
the vein that pulsated so demurely when I kissed it,
enraptured in the coolness of your warm blood
under the soft flesh that was yours
once only for me
for me, were you
once
goodbye my love
goodbye

Meera Maheswaran

Father

What if a father had no soul,
What if his heart were as black as coal,
What if his purpose was to hurt and control,
And all the years of torment had taken their toll?
What would you do, for he is still your father,
Even if he never tried, or didn't bother,
To show you love, to give comfort, to act like he really cared?
If he never spoke of the few good moments that you two had shared,
If all the feelings he showed to you were anger, distrust, and hate,
Would you give up or keep on trying to earn this wretched man's faith?
For after all, no matter what, you owe this man your life,
Even though he's filled it up with pain, struggle, and strife.
Just keep in mind you're not divine, you're better than no one else,
Accept the man for what he is and find it in yourself,
To forgive and forget and don't give up and maybe just one day,
He'll come around and change his heart and treat you a better way.

James A. Sievers, Jr.

Enduring Love

The evening sun cast shadows low, 'bout the old oak tree out back;
As he gently placed her in a chair, together to relax.

Spoken words are gone as they sit alone, and watch the children there at play;
For the years have fled so swiftly by, now it's the evening of the day.

Where did it go for he and she, the love in days gone by;
But now they sit is silence still, on him she must rely.

The memories of the love they knew, through his mind oft times did race;
While the disease that crept into her mind, showed blankness on her face.

Spoken words are gone, as they sit alone and watch the evening sun depart;
for the memories of the love they knew, he held within his heart.

The years have come and the years have gone, now it's the evening of the day;
Where love once grew and romance bloomed, silence now takes its place.

Spoken words are gone as he reminisced, of a love that they once knew;
And gently took her by the hand, and whispered "Dear, I still love you."

The evening sun cast shadows low, 'bout the old oak tree out back;
As he and she in silence sit together to relax.

Jerry D. Putman

Lady Experience

I wander in search of myself.
I search for myself in experience,
In life, in love, in truth and pain,
And I am ever looking,
For experience is always dragging me behind her,
And I am enveloped in the path she trails behind.
Swirling around me are her colorful garbs,
Of vast sky blues bursting into flames of red,
In violets, yellows and oranges,
She sprinkles the countryside with flowers.
And as the sun sweeps the sky like a paint brush, with artistic touch,
Experience draws on her midnight gown of twinkling stars.
Her scarves trail out behind her outstretched clouds of white,
Billowing and flowing, caressed by the wind.
She is unpredictable and not always kind,
Blessing me with love and happiness,
And running off again, leaving me behind in sadness.
I embrace her with love as much as I can,
And find she is always leading me, teasing me and twirling me,
To teach me of her knowledge.

Veronica Flinn

"F. Scott Fitzgerald"

You wrote about yellow cocktail music and the green light on Daisy's dock,
You said it was always 3 o'clock
In the morning and that there were no second acts in American life,
That the rich are different from you and me—and sex always ends in mortal strife.
Your vision was Keatsian sensual,
Your dialogue visible to the ear—
But when did you begin to see your leaf was in the sere?
That you were lost—no longer free to be the person you could be.
Gatsby was great; Zelda was not
And Hemingway said how dry was your rot.
Yet the words that you wrote were a movement in time
To exist in the ether of brazen sublime.
The 30's subsumed you; the country forgot
That you were a wordsmith while millions were not.
When you died in the forties and nobody came
A bottle of Scotch was reserved in your name—
And now every year in the month of September
It's poured on your grave so we will remember
That the angels that brought you will not come again
To waltz in blue gardens with God's borrowed pen.

Patricia Claire Eggleston

Untitled

A cool breeze caresses my skin as I look into the blue endless sky
And I wonder, how long will this last?
I take a deep breath of a chill night air as I watch the full white
Brilliance of the moon and I wonder, how much longer will I see
That magnificent glove of light?
A thrill passes through me as I look at his face and long for his
Body and I wonder, how long will I feel this?
One morning I am unable to rise, a pain so deep captures me and
I wonder, how long can I endure this?
The laughter of a child breaks through the Sunday heat and
I wonder how long happiness will surround him?
A beautiful array of flowers, a rainbow of colors, fill my sight
and I think, will I be able to se them another day?
The glorious miracle of this world assaults me, in a decaying
Building, in a bird signaling the beginning of spring,
In a person walking, rushing down the street.
In my mind a loud silence fills my head, obliterating all thought.
I want this forever. To feel, to see, to experience, to love...life.
The realization of the reality is, I am dying, and the wondrous
Knowledge of this universe will never be mine.

Nova Patton

Untitled

Some poems are true, some poems are blue, what of this poem is new
Some poems win hearts, some poems break them apart, poems rhyme in time

Poetry is an art that takes heart one question is where to start
Should it an art that shows pain or shows gain.
The pain is not sane but than again neither is the gain

You must live the pains of life but to remain sane is a strife
To see the gain one must grieve but to grieve one must live

One must look deep into the soul, one must face the demons that glow
One must see the love within, one must be strange to remain sane.

People say pain is gain but what gain is worth so much pain
What gain comes from insane pain, what pain equals gain.

Some say you don't live. Some say you don't love
But you do more than any can give.

Some call you a child, some say you went wild
Some say you can't give, some say you won't live, but you do.

You give, you live, you love, with the passion from above

People judge what they see
They don't see what is true because it would make them blue

The part of the art is to look in the heart
The real art is to put back the parts of the heart.

Bernardine M. Johnson II

Untitled

In memory of a loving father and husband: Michael W. Woodward
He was the best father and husband, he was always there for his
family, he always had a warm smile, he is my daddy. He always
said he was proud of us, he showed he cared, he never left my
mom crying, he was always there. He loved my sisters and he
also loved me, he is my daddy. When we were going through
bad times, he always cheered us up, and when he got his job in
North Carolina we couldn't get him to shut up.
He loved his sailboat to go sailing on the waterway, my daddy
will sail again someday. Before he died he was the happiest
man, I wish I could just understand. He was taken in the worst
way I'll never forget that horrible day, I saw him in his coffin, he
looked so bad, that was not my dad. I felt his hands they felt so
cold, it was then I realized my dad was so bold.
At night when I look at the sky each day, I wonder which star
my daddy now lay. My daddy is special and he is so bold
because he lived almost 40 years in a world where people are so
ruthless and cold. His nickname is Woody, he is my daddy. I
know he is proud of my mom, my sisters, and me because we are
doing our best to be what he wanted us to be.
My dad and I won't always be apart, but until the whole family
is together will always be a hole in my heart.

Jackie Corder

Marriage Can Be Like An Old Tree

Marriage can be like an old oak tree we live we love so happily
As the branches grow we soon know our family is about to bloom

Time passes quickly and our little buds begin to grow
Just like those of the old oak tree

The weather passes sometimes beautiful and sunny we see life
Can be sad and funny

As the oak tree grows so does our love for one another

Hard times hit and for just a bit it seems as though we may not make it

Some branches are weak and begin to break then we know how
Our hearts can ache

The rain is so strong that we just can't see how we can ever
Be strong and happy again

But the Lord shines his light on us big and bright soon
New branches begin to grow

Time passes even faster now as our new love and lives flourish

We will always know each branch on the large oak tree has a part
Of our hearts

The tree now has weathered many storms and with God's help it will
Live long for the old oak tree grows forever strong

Anne Marie Lerner

Our Quest For Success

In our quest for success,
I stopped along the roadside and glanced into the deep blue waters.
In our quest for success,
I saw you standing beside me not in front or behind me.
Along side me.
In our quest for success,
I worked my fingers to the bone for us. Not just for me but for you.
In our quest of success,
I asked that you look at it from my point of view.
You turned and walked away. I asked, "Why?"
You said, "I am too independent and it seems there is no need for you."
In our quest for success,
My tears flowed like the waters.
I was deeply hurt and realized in my heart you were slipping away.
In what was to be Our Quest For Success, I stood alone.

Faith E. Mack Bradley

We're Still Friends

As the day begins, he drinks his coffee...I drink some milk.
As the morning passes, he shaves his beard...I curl my hair.
As we prepare our lunch, he packs sardines...I gather my candy.
As we start our trip, he puts on country...I turn to alternative.
As we arrive at the lake, he notices the women, I check out the boys.
As we head to the boat, he carries the worms...I carry my purse.
As we ride around the lake, he thinks about catfish...
I think about air-conditioning.
As we pretend to fish, he falls asleep...I chat on the mobile.
As we drive toward home, he dreams up fish tales...I pray for a bath.
As we pull into town, he's thinking...finally...I'm thanking God.
As we arrive home, he heads for his recliner...I run for the remote.
As we plan our next trip, he thinks of Reelfoot...I wish for Hawaii.

Though completely different..my Dad and I...
through it all...we're still friends.

Melissa Barnes

The Face Of Even Through Stained Glass Portholes

Stained glass portholes to the soul, is hues of every shade,
Worlds of wonder draw these eyes that capture me amazed.

Raven waves engulf the oval of darkened wicker brown
As lips lie closed and breath be still and name remains unfound.

Below crescent crimson, fixed triangle black-in equilateral form,
The skin sees smooth and darker still with its overwhelming warmth.

And wrap drawn taught against the frame from times of endless woe,
A fixed expression molds this face into a smirk just so.

The brow forms strong against the pain that is seen upon the years,
Eyes gleam crystal against the love and hurt gathered by
countless tears.

Strongly featured, a facade of mischief, trickery is laced within,
And Magick's sparkle shows plain and clear as faith combines with sin.

An image firm and resolute in memory and in time.
On paper slick, with flesh unknown, in the enigmatic rhyme.

And as image sleeps the circles of life in whispered and simple truths
Dance into the stained glass portholes of an uninterpreted youth.

Katrina Garcia

Dear Santa,

In Memory of Barbara "Robbie" Trout
There are people around that say you're make believe,
  but I know it's simply not true,
And that's why I'm writing this letter, I have something to ask of you.
You see, Mr. Claus it happened like this, my Moma is no longer here,
She went home to be with Jesus earlier this year.
Now if you wouldn't mind taking care of what I ask,
It really isn't hard just a short and simple task.
As you know it's that time of year for presents, ribbons, and fun,
But as for me, I've only one wish, I pray you'll see it done.
On Christmas Eve, could you make a stop, to my Moma in heaven above?
Please tell her Merry Christmas and that I send her all my love.
Could you also tell her that I think of her every day?
Santa, this year Christmas is lonely, because she went away.
So if you would grant me this wish, that's all I'll need this year
Plus one more message for Moma, "I wish that you were here!
Well, Mr. Claus, that's it I guess, now I'll let you go
I'd forgotten what Christmas was all about, now I truly know.

Love, Stacie
Stacie R. Trout

Grandpa

Death comes only once in someone's life, some die quick with no suffering,
Others die slow and painfully, and mostly all leave someone behind.

When death comes it leaves nothing but pain,
All of those who have lost a loved one slowly lose their mind,
Funeral arrangements are set, sometimes refusing the deceased wishes.

My grandfather died today, on this warm January 28th day of 1996
My grandmother went to church happy, and we all came home sad.

Today was Youth Sunday. Today was Super Bowl Sunday XXX.
Today the Cowboys won 27-17. Today my Grandfather died.

He was a gentle man, he loved his daughter and son.
My mom and uncle were left behind, again as they once were.

My grandmother and I never met, for she died when my mom was six,
She broke her back and died, and that's all I remember of her.

Now my grandad died in his chair, my mom thought that was best,
She knew how much he loved that chair,
And she knew that's one thing he would miss.

I remember where he lives, in Hagerstown, Maryland,
His house only a trailer, but a home well lived in.

I remember the money he sent for birthdays and Christmas
And the stupid thank you cards I would send him.

    Michael W. Pile

Life's Keepsakes

Is there anything worth keeping anymore,
has society become totally throw-away?
Sometimes when I look around, it seems it certainly has become that way.
For in the never-ending rat race and the struggle to move along,
I have lost the joy of life's true treasures, and the importance of
passing them on.

I change homes, and towns, and offices all in rapid-fire pace.
Forget the old, bring in the new, as I move from place to place.
But then, one day, in all my wanderings, I find that I have
somehow lost sight,
Of certain things I'll surely miss on some dark and dreary night.

The family Bible, my photo albums and that wonderful book of
prayers were lost along the highway when I moved from here to there.
Throw out the husband, the cat, the friends, the things that once were dear.
I pack the van, and the old sedan, this time I'm moving where?

And then, one day, I realize, how misconstrued my thoughts,
When I find my greatest treasures cannot be re-bought!
What about that childhood friend who shared my secrets then!
I wonder where she's living now and how her life has been.

    Betsy Wallace Johnston

Totality

Inserts of my mind are only shadows of the impurities of your heart,
That only holds the abundance of your life.
Through the essence of what wills your thoughts to me,
I can only cherish on what you give to me;
You give me your sight for when you have so much to see,
You engrave me with your thoughts when
There is too much for you to know.

You enable me with your trust like a bird
Taking flight for the first time;
There is no rarity in your harmonization,
Just as is promised this situation.

If there was assurance in the passing shades of life,
There will be existence in the faltered days, an obliviance of life.

    Robbie Robbins

Of Anxiety

People are so busy, how to make their life easy; Sometimes
they are confused and silly, how to tackle condition carefully

Most parents are apart from family, to earn money for ours,
satisfactory; Could understood the reasons fully,
otherwise who can take away my tears and weary

The little ones were left behind, admitting the fact,
making oneself unwind, living independently, tough and unblind
day by day scanning their self, what have I found?

The eldest is suffering, slowly losing her guts and confidence,
helpless . . . Nobody knows except the Almighty who enhance.
He absorbed every burden on my shoulder embrace,
and lifts me with his best defense.

My happiness is vested on the others
I know Jet M will soon be together;
I was praying and longing for that bright day after
waiting for my opportunity, somewhere farther.

The right time has come for me to leave how can I go when
someone will grieve; The love we share before the eve
He will be waiting, should I believe?

    Clemencia W. Roquero

Blue Eyes

There he sits, heaving sobs of thunder,
Or is it me and my eyes like the rain?
He is so silent but not to the eyes,
My heart is aching, filling with pain.

I long to reach out to him; tell him I care
But my heart is throbbing, saying don't you dare!
He can't see me to know that I'm there
I use all my strength not to run to him

The pain in my heart has reached my eyes
It's like rain now, dressed in lies
I can't push it away; I can see him
He had his back to me, but sees me now.

I feel his arms, strong and barricading
I glance up and look in his eyes they are turquoise blue like the ocean.
He whispers 'I love you' and in my arms, he dies.

So many years have gone to waste; I never told him I cared.
I fall to the ground and he lies in my lap;
All those quiet times we've shared
The hatred between us is gone now; it washed away with
the rain in my eyes
Blue rain, like the paint on the wall that was between us.

    Amber Saltarelli

Fearful

Don't want anyone to invade in on our time
So we wrestle with the word commitment
Don't want to lose our independence
So we run around and around in circles trying to chase our fears away
We take a step and turn but always wished we would've stayed
We're too stubborn to make changes in our lives
So we live with the discomfort of the question—if I would've tried?
Disregard how perfect we were together
Ignored how happy we really were
Afraid of making the wrong decision—thinking not knowing we
were really sure
All our doubts and oppositions turn into distrust
So now we question - is there room for both of us?
Denial grows, emptiness sets in
The discovery of each other—we'll never know
Risks never taken but yet I never did let go

    Christianne Cover

M e

I like pretty flowers and plastic phones
Everything that glitters and all that's gold
Shiny silver rings, white doves with open wings
Daisies, boys, and punk rock
But that's not all there is to me; I have personality
I am not shallow, like the waters of a pool
like the deep, deep lagoon
I can't swim, but I won't drown; somehow I will survive
My mind and soul are in control, my body does the work
Sometimes I think, sometimes I blink . . . and then I'm back in reality
I've returned from my own dreams
Where there was a forest with wise, old trees, looking down on me
I'm connected with the shadows, they're beyond my own denial
I can see, and hear, and dance; the spirits put me in a trance
I can love and I am loved; I see God
I pick flowers and put them in my hair
And then I'm swept away with the air
I fly and fly and fly and fly
And finally, I settle down
On the Earth's stop layer, where I sleep and say my prayer

Monika J. Bancarzewska

Words Do No Justice

Romeo and Juliet. Mark Antony and Cleopatra.
All hopeless fools who knew nothing about love.
They went down in history as the greatest lovers and would be lovers.
Yet none of them had a thing on you and I.

Our love is true. It's stronger than any force in heaven or in hell.
Our love can stand the test of time like no other.
If God should see fit to take us from one another,
Our love will only grow. Even when we are apart we're together.
Our minds and souls are joined as one and we are never alone.

My words do our love no justice. Our love is beyond understanding.
Some people go through life thinking that they have found true love.
Yet few of them actually have.
Some say true love is a myth and that we are fooling ourselves.

They're wrong. You are my best friend and confidant.
I've shared thoughts, feelings, emotions,
and experiences with you that I have with no other,
and would never want to.
I have pledged these things before you and God
and I swear they are all true.
God help me I'm in love with you.

Tasha M. Trimm

The Racing Tree

I seem to remember best the times I got there first.
In Grandma's yard, a long strip of grass between it and the sidewalk.
The first one there and back, to the racing tree.
Of course, it wasn't called the racing tree then, just the tree,
that white tree in our grandma's yard, across the road from mine.

We played over there sometimes, too, on swings my dad built
and in the sandbox, really an old tractor tire dominated more by
cats than toys.
There, my brother's yard, my yard,
was full of swings, sand, puppies, leaves, Easter eggs, and wooly worms,
but no long strips of grass, with a tree to tag.
So, across the gravel road barefooted we strayed.

Now, I've grown up and I'm too old for those races.
The tree is gone too, grew old I guess,
and fell with a strike of lighting one spring,
while swings swayed in stormy winds.
Another stands in its place, now, younger,
big and strong already,
and instead of waiting for that racing turn around tag
it holds the new kids' club house for tea parties and secret meetings.

Amy Kaetzel

Texas Pride

To pay the price, to sacrifice,
to fight like freedom loving men will do,
at Anahuac, the Alamo, at Goliad, and San Jacinto too.

You had to be brave and no man's slave to spit in Santa Anna's eve.
With you back to the wall and through it all knowing you would die.

Deep down inside that Texas Pride was swelling in each man's chest.
One hundred and eighty -three strong
and it would not be long to be put to the stiffest test.

Santa Anna bring on your soldiers rolling like boulders
we'll fight for liberty's sake fighting side by side for Texas Pride
till our bodies the Texas soil will take.

I'll make you a bet we'll never forget what these men did for us.
We'll keep Texas Pride somewhere deep inside and never, ever let it rust.

So sons of Texas shout out loud and be Texas proud
you were born in the Lone Star State.
Because Texas soil you see is a part of me and that makes Texas great.

So let's all pitch in and stand again like they did at the Alamo.
Live or die look the unjust in the eye the grab hold and never, ever let go

Raise up the flag and don't let it sag fight on for freedom's sake.
Till the Lord up above with His infinite love my Texas soul will take.

Carlos Jackson

Planet

I see that planet,
Its bright silhouette in the dark looming shadows of the Universe,
A Universe that goes on forever and ever,
I see that sun, glaring at me, hotter than a burning fire, an eternal flame,
I see that planet, I see that cheerful smile on its jolly face,
So serene and quiet, so beautiful and compelling,
With a melange of swirling, bright colors,
The atmosphere, so vast and tranquil, yet colder than a frozen iceberg,
I see a miraculous land,
With love and pure nature upon the open terrain.
This superior land has so many magnificent sights and smells,
But I must go back to my bed and wake up to see
the gigantic sun rise and call upon the world to wake up.
As I leave this astounding new planet, I see that gloomy Universe,
Now lit with mysterious, radiant lanterns, hundreds and hundreds of them,
It just lifts my body and soul off to a dreamland.
I see that planet, receding into the murky heart of the Universe,
I think about this planet, is there really such a planet out there . . .

Brian Lee

Thank You

Thank you God for all the love you give.
Thank you God for allowing me to live.
Thank you God for the guidance over the past few years.
Thank you God for the joyous tears.
Thank you God for the people you saved for the past two weeks.
I hope they thank you themselves because you're so neat.
Thank you for all the times I've been blessed because
I knew you could do it because you do it best.
God thank you for giving us pastors, teachers, deacons
and superintendents to guide us through.
That's because you're God and I will always love you.
God I hope one day that this could become true
that all the people that's doing wrong could believe in you.
Thank you God for cleansing me of my sins and I
will never forget that because you gave me life again.
Thank you God for keeping me so that I can stay close .
I will have no other God before me because you are the one I love most.
Thank you God for your mercy and embracing power.
I will praise your name any day; it doesn't matter which minute of hour.
I am sorry that I didn't have much to do, but I speaks for
everyone when I say thank you.

Eric Williams

Nature's Best

As I walk through the scented fields
that are decorated with green purple, and yellow,
Enjoying the peace that surges within,
as I listen to the hypnotizing sound of a nearby bayou.

I inhale the tranquil breezes that engulf me,
submerging me into sweet serenity.
I close my eyes, exhale, and pray
that God will allow the feeling to last an eternity.

With the sun giving off a warm radiant glow, and the trees
leaning gently,
I sit against an old weeping willow,
watching Nature at her best, smiling contentedly.

I watch as a pair of unsuspecting butterflies
engage in a playful game of love,
As the clouds pick up speed heading South,
and delicate drops of rain fall from above.

I run through the fields leisurely, in pursuit of a drier place.
Feeling energized by the rain as it trickles down upon my face.

Back at home sitting on my closed in porch,
in sweats, in the mood for rest, I dose off,
inhaling the sweetness of the fresh rain,
enjoying Nature at her very best.

Brandi J. Peters

Love Is Nothing but a Stupid Feeling

Love is nothing but a stupid feeling
You can't control it, it controls you
Most the time love is nothing but a healing
That's why I never want to say I love you too
For all I know it's just a pain in my heart
That's when you find out it's hard to be apart
Love doesn't always come out right
Most of the time it turns out to be nothing but a fight
That's why I sit here and tell you Love is nothing but a Stupid Feeling

Don's ask me why I feel this way I guess it's just from past feelings
That just ripped into my heart with real peelings
It left me in a cold dark place where there is no joy
Where I feel like nothing but a toy
When everyone plays with my emotions
And no longer are there any devotions
That's when I need a true healing
And like I said before Love is nothing but a stupid feeling

Monique Buduan

Dancers in the Sand

These clouds have they been this way before,
what did they see when last they past?
Listen to the surf, rolling timelessly thru the years
over the sand, and shells, and dreams of multitudes,
be they natives to this land or visitors from afar.
The dreams of Conquistadores on their mighty steeds,
and of Fisherkings, and the trophies they might land.
Of Lovers through the ages that have stayed the day
reciting their vows of love and hopes of future years.

Today I am blessed like the clouds, and witness you at play
and watch you sow your dreams upon this fertile shore.
Your dreams of peace and joy, as you dance with your grandchildren.
The wind celebrates your movements, blowing thru your hair as
the surf plays with you all, teasing once or twice then giving chase
and you spontaneously give thanks with squeals of great joy.
The birds have gathered to witness this love affair, joining in the
dance, singing songs, and reciting your vows of love and hopes
of future years.

Gary Keith

The Struggle Within

People are wondering and striving to make ends meet,
but sometimes there's this struggle deep within.

Struggles not only within but here in our society and government: you can also see it through sickness, street gangs, families and churches.

Wanting to belong to or just say, "fit in."
So, we turn to either trying to defame people's character to ease our own loss of self-worth, or to win favor with those who think they are God's gift to His earth.

But, we as individuals have to learn how to sustain our own self-preservation through what we call the "struggle within."

We have that undying hope and love that is in Jesus. His love and favor are the only rewards we need in this our "struggle within." His is know as that unconditional love.
The struggle within!

Vicky A. Taylor

The Walk

To walk along side by side, with your hand clasped in mine,
neither saying a word;

From time to time a tender glance is shared, and then to spring
apart when someone appears and steal gently together again;

To walk in the wind with it gently tugging through your hair
and see your face flushed by its playfulness;

To come to the sea, beautiful blue-green which matches the deep
fathom of green in your eyes, and watch the whitecaps merrily
racing to the shore;

And then to sway with the birds of the sea,
gracefully dipping to and fro as they search for their daily meal;

All these things are beautiful to know and to feel
as we take our walk and slowly turn for home;

Upon reaching home, we sit and share a warm drink together,
looking at each other with love in our eyes;

Both realizing what we have seen
and will always share locked deep in our hearts.

Jacqueline B. Latham

Winds Of Capital Reef

Given a time period of choice, hoist the plights of human achievement. Meant to live the experiences of horror, honor what, was to become of man. Handed a predestined future, lures which couldn't be changed— hanged an accepted fate, hate I'd have to deal with. Before born, sworn I'd remember, reminders on a tail, hail, I shouldn't have been able. Cabled signs and clues, blues had left me fate. Faith of the knowledge, lodged in a feeling. Choosing for greatness or cause, paused a circumstance should happen. Playpen of signs, assigns the crossroads of acknowledgement. Knowing we've accomplished our mission in life. Enlightened and frightened, knight of us all, calls the legendary father ape of us all. Fall into his glance, glands of instinct will awaken, hasten, was he not of this earth. Heart of technology, nor very logically, showed no technology, what was the psychology. Apology taken and shaken by mental superiority, priority, was the warning. Harmed or in pain, rained the water of the stream. Steamed and shrill, till he swung his arms and then limped around the mist of Or. Aground too close I saw ghost, aghast the white stripe of wisdom to the left of his black head and back. The hoofs appeared and wagon in tow, whoa, they're invisible. Indivisible feelings of injustice and malice, alas, collect us kids, kindness at hand.

Ralph De Vestern

No!

No. I refuse to. No. I don't choose to.
No. I most certainly don't.
You've made a mistake.
If you thought you could make me.
NO, No, no—I won't.
No no could beat me
No you could eat me.
Up from my head to my toes
And inside your belly
Loudly and yelly
I'd keep saying NO!
No you could sock me
Feed me some broccoli
Tickle me till I turn blue
But in between giggles
And sniggles and wiggles
I'd say no to you no you could tease me
Pretty pretty please me cry till your eyes wasted
away you could beg till you're old but I'd look at you cold en-oh
is what I say

Mandy Breeding

Shadows Upon A Mirror

When finally we can stand no more and glimpse at death upon
our door we see our lives through different eyes and experience
fears, to our surprise.

To be told there is no chance, not another time to run or dance.
We've done it all, we have been told. To face the truth, we must be bold.

We had our chance at happiness but let life pull us down.
Living our lives for others, here we are, the crying clowns.

Embarrassed to say good-bye when we knew life wasn't right,
not wanting to hurt, but hurting, and pretending day and night.

Not helping one another when misfortune came about
but living with our greed. Now, we must sit and pout.

We cannot live life over. There is nothing we can change
but we can ask for mercy from the one who pulls the strings.

No longer will we look upon the faces of those we hold dear,
for we will only be traces like shadows upon a mirror.

Maxine Moran

Untitled

Light coming from a lamp made of brass on a wooden desk:
The light climbs half up a wall then pauses to keep the room quiet.
It paints shadows on the floor and unknowingly makes
the wood more than it is.
The narcotic waves keep you silent as
you watch your life become a single point; and things you will
never again understand present themselves to you in brass light,
then leave you alone in the shadows.

John W. Buckley

Dare To Be Free

It is no simple task to duplicate what intelligent minds have set
as high standards for a comfortable living.
But it is a much greater task to follow ones heart through the
emotional battle fields of life. And stand alone in the end if we
must, like the tattered flag of our nation.
But comfortable, for we did not settle
Proud for we did not crumble
And free, for we dared to believe
It is our right.

Anthony Paisson

Peace

If you could give me anything would you give me back myself.
Take me off your pedestal, take me off your shelf.
Give me back my wings and let me fly away, and in return
I promise I'll come back to you someday.
Let me feel the Freedom of this world that God gave me,
let me know before I die.
The feeling to be free, I'll hold you in my heart, I'll hold you
In my mind, but never would I hold you, in love that truly binds
If we are meant to be as one, then give me back myself, my soul belongs
To only one and that is God Himself, let me fly away to him and
See His glorious face for only then I truly know, I have found my place.
Yes you and I will be as one when I become the earth, but till then
let freedom come, and peace will be my birth.

Anna Chavez

The Greatest Deliverance

You see Darlin', it's not that you're not important
But I've come to the conclusion that You are not the problem
You see it ain't the choices that you make for me
That disarm or empower, give life or take the breath thereof
From the longing in the thrust of what my spirit can see
So it's no wonder but as important as You Are
After much consideration I've stumbled upon the truth and now I know
That your voice cannot Ee-Nun-Cii-ate! purpose or direction for my soul
And it's not the beat of your heart that can feel the pulse of my dreams
Still caught in the struggle searching frantically for the exit signs
Nor can the intensity of your scratch soothe the agitation of my passion
I won't be your command that will caallmm..the hussshh! of my
hysterical passivity and even if you search for me you will not find
my buried places..Why? ...because, it ain't your thinking that knows
the measure of my existence or changes my perceptions in the realm
of my actions No! No! No! there ain't no thinking you can do for me
that will ultimately determine my destiny
So after much insecurity, isolation, and unnecessary pain
I've come to the conclusion that as important as "You Are"
It's not that...You're not important

Darlene D. Hartway

Robin Red Breast

The Robin ran across the yard, the grass of brown and green.
Her breast of red and blackest wings, I've ever seen.
Her happy thoughts run through her mind of her nest high in a tree,
but the happiest thing that she thought was that she was free,
to do the things that she thought best, and the cares of all the rest.
Her name I never knew; we called her Robin Red Breast.

Celia Lawrence

The Thieving Reality Of True Love

Hearts of fire meet with hearts of gold
when friends pass by with their love untold.
Unto one another they both love,
but feelings kept in a trove for reasons as thin as the fog of the
    midnight air.
As I dream , you are in it, as I think,
my thoughts are of you, and as I breath,
every gasp of air is in awe for you.
All sanity and view of reality is lost as word trickles out of your mouth
like a drop of glistening dew falling from a tree in the morning air.
To say that you are more beautiful than a meadow of roses
among the evening while the sun sets would be unfair,
for that beauty comes and goes as years and seasons pass,
all the while yours remains constant through life.
As my heart is sad, I miss you.
Through the loneliness that my heart endures, I also miss you
As those gleaming moments pass by when I am truly happy,
I miss you the most, for nothing will ever be complete without you.

Gary Wayne Cooper Jr.

I Am

I am a searcher for lost secrets
I wonder, is magic really gone from this world,
or is it who left is, is it just waiting for
someone to return to it?
I hear it calling me, hoping I will fine it soon, I see it in my dreams,
In the forms of faeries, elves, dragons and sorcerers
I want to find it, learn its long abandoned secrets
I am a searcher for lost secrets

I pretend I am in magic's long abandoned world
I feel excited when I feel its grasp in my dreams
I touch my dreams, trying to bring it from there to our world
I worry about losing it completely, about having it forget me,
and me forgetting it
I cry myself to sleep when I can't take the wait anymore
I am a searcher for lost secrets

I understand that it is not just an element of my dreams;
I can feel it touch my soul
I say I will one day join with it in my soul,
and the magic will forever be mine; I try to be patient, but how
can one be when they have almost joined with magic?

Kathy Bellville

The Sickened Voice Of Compromise

Paranoid,
wrapped up fetus control,
a picture of heaven on the downside
and humanity having a ball—
our insignificant comprises posed as the led our sinking ship,
the vessel dies tonight—

So have been warped,
pushed into this slightly trip
a voice cried,
calling the sickened and the dead
she wishes a bleeding below from the mouth of more than just
the accused, the colors are flashing,
the lights crawl out from under the blackened pillow of soft
disposition, a comforter in the heightened sense of insecurity—
a message of terror the mindless heroes of rage reveal to tonight!
The vessel lives again,
and tomorrow shall fall

Jason DiFilippo

Watercoloured Stranger

As I drag my feet along Hennepin Ave.
I see you from afar,
sipping your cigarette
and inhaling your coffee.

The tattered green canopy dangling over your head
sways in the gusts to catch the crashing raindrops.

Your friends build castles on the cafe table
with napkins and plastic forks,
and your laughter keeps you warm
as the gales slip their bitter chill through your faded blue
sweatshirt.

But I walk alone through these drippy streets,
kicking rocks through the swelling puddles,
my soggy shoes sloshing with every random step.

You lift your head in greeting
and as soon as you're sure
that your eyes were burning into mine,
you smile
to spread the warmth on this dreary evening
to a simple girl,
with no place to go.

Kirsten Volnes

The Man In The Glass

When you get what you want in you
struggle for self and the world makes you king of the day.
Just go to the mirror and look at yourself and see
what that man has to say

For it isn't your father or mother
or wifes who judgement upon you must pass;
The fellow whose verdict it count most
in life is the one staring back from the glass.
Some people may think you a straight
shooting chum and call you a wonderful guy
But the man in the glass say you're only
abum if you can't look him straight in the ege.

He's the fellow to please, never mind the rest
For he's with you up to the end and you've passed your most
dangerous, difficult test if the man in the glass is your friend.
You may fool the whole world down the pathway of years and
get pats on the back as you pass
But your final reward will be heartaches and tears
if you've cheated the man in the glass

Goldie Luke

Earth

On a Monday afternoon,
before your one o'clock Physics class,
you approach me at my locker,
as I slowly turn to the last digit—forty.
You wear a faded grey tee shirt, small.
A crystal icicle hangs from your neck like a guardian.
The lace of my left shoe is untied
and when I open the door to my locker,
you drape your arms perfectly over the top.
You say nothing until now,
when you ask why I wish to talk with you
I say nothing and smile shyly at the face of Dr. Seuss
on the folder I hold in my arms.
And when I look up to respond
your eyes of blue and mine of green unite like the elements of Earth.
I reach to touch your smiling face with just the tips of my fingers
when the bell for my one o'clock writing class interrupts.
As I watch you take eight steps from me,
I close my eyes and whisper that I could not wait another day
without asking you to wish on the same star when we are apart.

Jennifer Schumacher

A Very Merry Christmas To You All!

With Love comes laughter and many tears,
And many things to cherish throughout the year.
Lots of joy and happiness fill the air,
With people there to show they care!

It's not the presents or what we receive,
But the Love And Values in what we believe!
We gather together year after year,
To Honor the One we hold so dear.
For many years ago on this day,
Little baby Jesus came our way!

He gave us life, through Him we see, life can be an eternity.
A gift that comes from Heaven above,
So we cherish and honor the ones we love!
And with these thoughts I come to you, I want to say "I love you too!"

May all of the joys and happiness of this holiday season,
Brings you lots of Love And Happiness throughout the year,
And to all of those you hold so dear!

So from my heart and home to you,
May the season be a happy and safe one for all,
And the year ahead be as wonderful too!

Ann E. Beard

The Eight Deadly Sins

A painful childhood memory keeps haunting my mind—
a tiny church lit by the dying sun, low sermon, a pulpit behind,
the priest's quiet voice echoed placid, serene and soared,
I stood in the aisle, somehow bored

Suddenly scarlet sun rays swept down my face,
I watched dazed the preacher's solemn grace to disappear into
space as if under a spell I heard him thundering loud "And God
told them— kneel down despicable crowd

Let the seven deadly sins befall upon your head
as a stern warning for the posterity ahead"
These world never left my flesh, soul and body
throughout the years I confided in nobody

Evil people could cause me a world of pain,
why should I be angered in vain?
I haven't met my fellow being with a raised knife
I didn't commit the heaviest crime-to tread out the divine flame of life

My hands never shook over gold,
I was stripped off wealth, though I became old
I knew not a single day of leisure all my life
I was slaving beyond measure

My life is gone now—the years are not forgiving
Alas, I failed to taste all sweet fruits of living
My time on earth elapsed like sand in palm
I sense the end, but I am deadly calm.

Come Satan take my soul and flee—
I never knew what my days were meant to be!

Ognian Daskarev

Indulging Mine Own

A constant yearning for your moist lips to trail a blazing fire down my
   neck,
A constant aching to taste the pleasure of quenching my only desire
   for you.
To embrace the softness of your caress, yet indulge the roughness of
   mutual passion.
To feel the want through your fingertips, or the crave through your touch.
As I watch you move, as I watch you intake my innocence with your stare,
As I willingly watch your eyes take apart my
Soul and your gentle mouth unravel my sanity.
I slowly feel my world colliding with yours,
I slowly capture the moment in time where all else is a mere fantasy.
Now I have gone to far . . . Now I have fallen into pathways of lust for
   you, my love.
Now I am indulging in you and the reality is yet forever forgotten.
For now is a living dream, for now is the moment ecstasy overtakes
   the passion . . .
For now and for always, for this and forever shall the burn linger.

Rachael Riley

Fault

The pain you caused me, was never to be rehashed.
I thought it was, over, I thought it would just go away,
But you let it hang all over my head, you acted like
it was all my fault, 'cause I gave you my love. You turned away
from me with a bitterness and resentment and blamed your pain
on me. I tried to explain the way I felt without losing you, but
you couldn't bring yourself to listen. All you did was close your
eyes and turn away. I swear my heart and gave you my soul, but
you left me in two. All of sudden my dreams are not worth living, your
pain was my pain, till you turned away. I thought you cared, I
thought you knew. You just took and our love grew, then you
broke my heart in two. I should have listened when they said
opposites don't mix. I should have, I could have, I would have, if
only I knew it would go this far. Dare not I be the one to say it
was all your fault, but no you had to turn me away, never
listening, always doubting, never caring, always taking me for
granted. Although my passion still runs deep, you left for
yourself. Not for your sake, but for mine, it was all your fault
And never mine.

Courtney Baluski

My Spark Of Light

Hands which wrinkle with the slightest stir,
Crumpled; creased like a grandma's face obvious the note of
exceeding work,
Yet, the only pair money can't secure,
However, by far the most valuable medicine God ever freed;
passed down.
Hands which caress; release; defeat,
Like they've been meticulously trained at an ace labeled school,
But only the most prestigious- Nature itself.
A face so practiced, fatigued, and besieged,
As if it had just concluded a workday in Manhattan,
Although clouded with only condolence and devotion.
Soft, gentle, with massive concern dripping away.
A heart so benevolently open, with a pair of ears waiting; searching,
Though as alert as a cat's even after nightfall . . .
To seek a horribly tragic report of unfairness,
So that with a trail of heartfelt words given,
all the blue will go marching away.
It is hard to notice what we all keep at home,
A common person, figure, or being . . .
Is our key to life, signature to fortune,
cause of luck, or simply, our heal to poison.

Yang Yang

Black Woman

I am beautiful, yeah, I am precious too!
Don't judge me by the color of my skin
I'm a black queen, I tell ya, ain't nothing gonna change that.
What's inside is what counts. Not the outside.

Just cause we are big boned, big thighed, big breasted, big
lipped, and are colored chocolate, caramel, butter pecan with
whipped cream and a cherry on top because we are so precious.
You still don't have the right to judge us.
So what if I am a black woman? What are you gonna do about
it? Arrest me, lock me up and throw away the key?

But, see, do what you want because life for me ain't been no
crystal stairs.
Mine had tacks in it that stick when you walk on them.
But still I'm moving on. And I've finally reached the top. So,
what if I am a black woman? What do you have to say now
since I am intelligent and achieved all the things that I always
wanted to achieve?

I am a 90's black woman that has all the dreams
that everyone else has, and mine came true!!!

Andrea Morgan

With All His Great Power

With all his great power, he give us young
With all his goodness, he gives us forgiveness
With all his happiness, he gives us pleasure
With all his forgiveness, he gave us his son
With all his kindness, he offers his hand to all
With all his wisdom, he gives us more to live for.
With all, he has offered us all.

We accept our young, but crave for power
We accept our forgiveness, but we ask for goodness
We accept our pleasure, but long for happiness
We accepted his son, but we longed to grasp the same forgiveness
Some accepted his hand, but we lost his kindness
Some accepted what we can live for, but we will never grasp his wisdom
We fail to realize his offers and we push what he offers away
When his son comes back one day many will be forced to stay.

Cathy Brooks

Time Loop

Yesterday-set, past. Acknowledged, unchangeable.
Tomorrow-flexible, future. Unknown, unreachable.
Today-present, alive. Active, attainable.

Since yesterday is lost and tomorrow never arrives,
The moment becomes paramount to our lives.
Cautiously and with great wisdom, these moments we should nurture,
While weighing their impact on our lives, on our future.

Moments slip away without our permission, melting into another age,
While yesterday stands glaring at us from its cluttered, useless stage.
Tomorrow bounds forward waving its flag of hope,
Promising another day to repair the damage, so onward we grope.

Suddenly, today slips into dreams of what yesterday could have been.
That backwards stare robs our today, stunts our tomorrow-again
and again and again.
So, learn from the mistakes, rejoice in the successes,
but focus clearly and grab hold,
For today is the moment to set the flexible in the right mold.

Carolyn Denny

Codependency

He was in need of a missing link so he engaged in a bond that
ultimately destroyed him. His self manipulation led him deeper in
need not for the link but for himself. Self hope had been vanished
from his comprehension and he remained lost in dependency. He
began to search for reasons and found the link to be his rejection
from his self defined soul. In tremendous agony be tried initially
to repress the link out of his mind, but only found that link to
repress him. In the dark of night he sits and watches his soul
whirl above him, he tries to grasp it but he doesn't have the
strength to even try. In desperation he cries out but only hears
echoes around him. His emotional need for the link is causing
abundant deteriorated of the marrow left in his life. He must keep
going on to identify with his lost soul, but the soul is older than he,
it matured while he was one with the link.

Jay Westcott

The Dawn of a New Era

The March showers exuding from the sky
like an avalanche of tear drops, marks the beginning of Spring.
The ancient Greeks give the explanation that the sun god makes
the seemingly barren lady earth fertile and ready to bring forth
her array of colors; thus, the dawn of a new era!

So it is with this ambiguous existence, frequent new births in
time and space; never a dull moment.
Some rebirths are prolific, others are as redundant as a resounding brass.
As a shadow of hope in the midst of a dreary winter
that glorious Spring is soon to come; such is the feeling during
a period of bliss; whatever the nature of it....

Weeping might endure for the night but joy comes with the dawn.
And while this season of melancholy will soon pass,
the memory of the era will live on in the rebirth!

Tanisha Taylor

The Elements of Night

The elements of night kept me awake; a sudden jerk of the leaves
would make my eyes blink. My eyes grew heavily loaded with
shame and anger. The one true thing I had in life flew away like a
bird when winter approached. A meaning so powerful would let
me close but a light so bright kept me awake. A blink in the eyes
would soon count to keep my dreams alive and someday have
true meaning.

The elements of night kept me awake but the opening of daylight
blinded me, a light so bright would hold me towards my rest and
make the daylight seem it was not only night. A day has no
meaning where night means true light. A burning desire
too close to redeem if it were not day than night would it be seen.

Maria Mancini

There's A Spiritual Battle Going On

There's a battle going on, between Satan and the one
That sits on the throne, but if you're a Born-Again Christian,
You don't have to worry, you see, because
Our God is so much greater than he.

So friend let no one deceive you or lead
You astray, for Lord Jesus is the only way.

To life eternal, I want you to know he shed his blood
Upon the cross to buy our souls, to free us from Satan's
Evil hand and to make the wonderful salvation plan.

That's why you must be washed in the blood, come out white as snow,
Sinner know this, there's only one way to go.

Humble your heart, be born again, that's the only
Way you'll ever enter in, and when the chosen few will
Get to heaven, that land so fair, where all the saints
Will rejoice, and be so happy that we're there.

Where we'll march around God's great white throne,
Thanking the Father that we finally made it home.

Where we'll see Moses and all the prophets of old,
Oh, I long to see the one that died upon the cross to save my soul.
I'll kneel at his precious nail-scarred feet and give him praise.

Garrold Johnson

Hard Times

It comes a time when you just get so fed up with how things are
going, but we realize the best thing is to take one day at a time
and move on.

We often feel as though we're alone like no one really truly
cares, but remember there is someone who always cares enough
though to be there, when times seem as though you can't go on
just remember you have a purpose in life and there is someone
who truly cares enough to be there.

Always keep your head up high and never let anyone put you
down and make you feel as though no one cares. Always know
that your never alone, there is that perfect, special turn their
back on you and that special friend is Jesus. He won't forsake
you. He will be there, the friend I know I will have for life in
Jesus someone who truly cares.

Takisha McQueen

Out Of My Window

As I glance out of my window pane, Of my beautiful mountain house,
I wonder, if I will ever return again.
The crisp green plant life, as tall as a giant, as small as a mouse.
The blue lake, crystal clear, an eagle, a falcon soaring near.
This special moment must not end,
The view is my company, the view is my friend.
I see a scene, as perfect to paint, the great bear rises from the brush,
Graceful, yet powerful, like a saint.
A soothing calmness comes over me,
This is the most beautiful sight I will ever see.
A graceful fawn, her rhythm like music,
A feeling, that I will never lose it.
As I glance beyond the trees, I notice the animals all freeze.
And under the thick gray cloud,
The great bear lowers his head, but still proud.
The loud pitter-patter of the rain,
Her beat like a drum, the thunder like a train.
The jagged strike of lightning cuts through the sky,
The clouds so sad thy won't stop cry.
I myself look down with sadness, it's time to go, to say,
Goodbye

Lily Robinson

Reflection

I look into the mirror and see, a little girl lost and me.
I ignore her and I say, I'm okay. Then I find her screaming one day.

Everyone's gone! There's no one here! Who do I turn to? Who is there near?
What do I do? Where do I go? What are my options? What do I know?

I tell her I'm sorry, but I don't have time, I have so much to do, and I'm way behind.
You'll have to be still, and don't make a fuss, I am in the world of senseless rush.

She succumbs into a hallow slumber, of which she knows this way by number.
Her heart is still and her breath is small. She wonders, Why am I here at all?

She wants to cry, but no one hears. She wants to die, but has many fears.
She asks, Who is suppose to take care of me? Why aren't they aware? Why can't they see?

I look into the mirror and see, a little girl lost and me.
I take her hand and say, you're okay. Come on, I'll show you the way.

I know you're frightened, I know you're scared. I am here and have come prepared.
I'll never leave you alone again, I am in charge and now we can begin.

All those people who didn't know, are not a bad bunch as they go.
They are lost and so was I. I am here now, so there's no need to cry.

You are a very special little girl, with many gifts for all the world.
You come from God with goodness and love. You come to teach us from those above.

One day I will look into the mirror and see a little girl found and a Tiger Lady.
She is my ideal woman, you know. And she knows what you know, which is more than I know.

Lynette Garron

A Valentine Rose

Three years ago when first we met, I felt something I couldn't share yet.
As time went by my whole life changed, and our chance to be together was finally arranged.
We shared our joys, passions and past, I felt I had found a love that would last.
The person I loved left one night in December, but day after day you were all I remember.

One year later you suddenly appear, and in my heart I felt a great fear.
I again opened my heart and shared it with you, and I prayed each night we could start anew.
I take what I can but need much more, because you are the man I truly adore.
Our silent meetings are just not enough, I know the road ahead is going to be rough.
We both know you have things to work out, and it will take time to all come about.
So on this day I give you this rose, in hopes that you know my love still grows.
Accept this rose as a token of my love, sent in beauty from or God up above.
For the rest of time I hope to be together, because for my heart there is no other.
So, if your future does not include me, please tell me now and set my heart free.

Tina Amason

Children Of Sin

Always have they consumed, their unceasing motto of "Take, take,   take."
Glutton and bloated, never to be giving, always craving, leaving   nothing.
Still devouring, mostly killing, still trying to fill an endless hunger.
Threads of greed have sewn them to this world.

Forever have they loathed, their savage chant of "Hate, hate, hate."
Torture and fire, unrelenting suffering to those unlike them.
No shadow of remorse, no flicker of guilt to stop them.
Pain of others to fuel them, unmasked demons are they.
Threads of enmity have sewn them to emptiness.

For an eternity have they brought sadness, their pitiful wail of "Doom, doom, doom."
Gloom and forlorn, spreading like a plague, bringing everything down.
Their souls lost for all time, swallowed by self-invoked misery.
Down into nothing, no hope, no salvation, no one able to save them.
Threads of despair have sewn them to darkness.

Since the beginning are they to suffer, their blasphemous voices raised against God, "Sin, sin, sin."
They are the ones who have lost the Word, forsaken its meaning.
Unlife is theirs unless they repent, Hell is theirs unless they turn, else...
    their Threads of evil have sewn them to eternal death.

Aaron Earnest

Picture Of You

Within each sunrise,
there is a picture of you.
It glows with natural beauty
that only you possess.
Your everlasting caring and honesty
makes you even more radiant.
You shine as bright
as a newborn star.
Your smile makes me
happy and warm inside.
Sadness comes but once a day,
when you leave.
And I make yet another wish
that I will see you again.

Sarah L. Blash

The Living Room

The rocking of the rocker,
the giggling of the girls,
the dancing of the dancer
on the mantle doing twirls.

The flickering of the fire,
the smell of the smoke,
the bawling of the baby
who recently awoke.

The preaching by the parents,
the mothering of the mothers,
the glancing of the girls
who are being scared by their brothers.

The talking from the TV,
the cuckoo from the clock,
the demanding voice from the dads
talking about their stocks.

The finding of the ringing phone,
the luminance of the light,
the painting and the pictures
of Kate flying a kite.

Meghan Hatfield

Eden

The dandelions are all dead...
The dew evaporated from them.
It dried up to a crisp, and flaked
off of their dying limbs.
The birds have all flown
North for the winter.
It's safe that way, not nearly as hot.
The Garden of Eden is overgrown.
It's overgrown with asphalt.
It's the place that man took over,
the place that God forgot.

Kimberly Eck

Dogs

Dogs are misunderstood
Spanked
Whipped
Beaten
They only bark for
Love
Care
Affection
If only people could
Understand

Katarina Garcia

Unfulfilled Destiny

Listen for a heartbeat
Nothing
Wait for movement
Nothing
Looking for help
Nothing
Waiting for news
Nothing
Hope is gone
Nothing lives
Waiting two days and nights
Nothing
Trying to deliver the lifeless baby
Nothing to be heard after birth
Praying for the answer for your pain
Nothing
There's a hole in your heart
Never to be filled

Sarah Leigh Wigent

Sunshine

From the first moment I saw her
There was a light in her eyes,
She shines like the sun that
Sets bright in the sky.
Her smile brightens my day,
Her laugh makes me giggle,
She is so very funny, the way
She dances and wiggles.
Sometimes she says some
Of the silliest things,
Without knowing how much
Wonderful joy that she brings.
I'm very proud of my
Precious baby girl,
Before you know it she'll
Grow up in a whirl.
No matter what she does,
No matter what she'll say,
She'll always be the sunshine,
That lights up my day.

Angela D. Tate

To The World

I send you to the world.
My friends
To find a better place
Though you'll not find one
For you have no face
I send you far away from here
To find a place you'll know, no fear
Far, far away from home
For you to roam
And when you find this place
My friends
I want you to return to me
And take me to this better place
For us to call it home

Brandi Gates

To Our Children

When you were small and would follow me
I would feel a little tug
All you wanted was to be picked up
For a little kiss and hug.

Now you have grown, and I am older
And that's how life should be.
For a moment, stop and reflect
Can you feel a little tug from me.

Fusie Peck

Let It Be Known

I know your game, your plan, your
scheme
Lure me in with thoughts of trophies
And leave me as the consolation prize

Little did you know
Red is my color

And while your back is turned
Eyes shut tight against the world

I step up to the gaming table
Planning and scheming
Knowing that one day I will trump you

Andree Sablatura

Untitled

Angels rolled the stone away
From the grave where Jesus lay
And He's in my heart to stay.
I will never go astray.
He is my light that shines.
I'm so glad that He's mine.
He rose on the third day
And that is why
We have the victory today.
Let us praise Jesus every day.
All we have to do
Is to trust and obey.
I will live or die
To meet the Lord in the sky.
Eternally we will live,
And live happily through
The years.

Frederick L. James

What A Beauty

If only we were a flower . . .
What a beauty sight would tell,
So silent is it in bloom.
So sweet is its smell.
So silent . . . were we a flower . . .
Life possesses there in
The beauty is what it would tell
As God's spirits roams
about to defend.
He defends our heart to seek
The abundance of his grace
As shown in the presence of a flower
As given to the human race.

Jerome B. Matthews

Around

Around the universe.
Under the moon.

Around a forest covered in frost.
In a place that's nearly lost.

Around a place that's filled with doom.
Inside way deep you'll find a room.

Around the universe circles a prayer.
On a waver of love's holy air.

Of love and peace a child's dream.
Let the child sleep without a scream.

Jane Fery

Love So Sweet and True

Love so sweet and so true
Means the same to me and you
When we look at another and see a smile
Hear a giggle from a little child
Feel the warmth of an embrace
See the look of love on a mother's face
Shared laughter and shared tears
Sharing triumph and also fears
When we give a helping hand
To each other and our fellowman
To feel a cool breeze on a hot day
To hear children playing happy and gay
The gentle touch of a lover's hand
Walking barefoot on soft warm sand
To hear the birds singing in the tree
All these things mean love to you and me

Jean Gambill

My Dear Husband, Charbie

My life is so very different
Full of sorrow and full of pain,
Instead of having sunny days
It always wants to rain

Sometimes I sit and wonder why
God took my love from me,
But I guess you never question God
That's the way it's meant to be.

I know God had a reason
I know that this is true,
But sometimes we don't understand
And it makes us sad and blue.

But I know he'll be waiting
When it's time for me to go,
I can see him standing there right now
With his hands out for me to hold.

I know he's living with God right now
In a loving, peaceful place,
And when God calls for me to come,
There will be a smile on Charbie's face.

Anna Greene

I Didn't Do It

I told you time and time again.
I didn't do it.
I didn't knock over that lamp.
I didn't break that window
I didn't smoke that cigarette.
I didn't take that pill.
I told you I didn't do it.
I didn't break that vase.
I didn't stead that CD
I didn't run away with him.
I didn't beat up that kid.
OK! OK! I Did it all.
I'm sorry.

Natasha E. Smith

The Caress

With the unhurried grace of a swan,
I feel the sun glide across my face
Warmly caressing it,
In gentleness and love.

Its brilliance slowly envelops
My mind, my body, my whole being.
Carrying me along with it,
Towards its celestial path.

Audrey U. Dove

3 daughters of thee moon

3 daughters of thee moon
ride a white mare
named nightfall
silentlee along thee cold
atlantick ocean side

thee sea
whispers hur lullaby
& once they fall into their sleeps
shee cries & cries
hurself into (hur seasleep)
until thee sunrise
meets hur swollen eyes

& with the sunrise
9 goslings watch over thee
3 daughters of thee moon
in their atlantick cove slumberings
until nightfall
nightall arrives once again

lou suSi

Broken-Hearted

I cared for you with all my soul
So why did you just walk away
Why did you have to let me go
And see you with her the next day

Avoiding my eyes you look into hers
And I can see the loving glow
Why did you have to leave me and worse
Why did you have to leave me alone

You betrayed my trust in everyone
Making me act misguarded
But the worst thing to me you've done
Is to leave me broken-hearted

Jennifer Giangregorio

Walking Home From School

I love to watch children
Walking home from school.
The different expressions they display
Would set a record book of rules.

One child tells a funny story
While the others laugh with glee.
And one hangs his head and walks alone
So glad when the clock struck three.

There's always one walking backward
And one carries books upon his head.
And if you look closely
One child always wears red.

Oh what joys of laughter echoes
If one decides to kick a can.
And everyone scrambles after it
To be the leader of the band.

Some walk fast and some walk slow
Wether the weather be hot or cool.
I love to watch children
Walking home from school.

Nancy G. Wilkerson

Why Do People Talk Mess?

Does it mean something?
Is it a game?
Or a joke?
Do they want to fight?
Maybe it's the way of faking.

Myra Walker

Missing You

Dedicated to my Mom, Barbara Robinson
When I was small
You were always there,
So I didn't really notice.
I didn't seem to care.

But one day you left me;
You've gone far away.

I have all the questions;
Answers, you'll never say.
Life seems so empty
Without you here, but I'll
Never stop loving you.
I miss you mother dear.

Paula M. Smith

What Glows at Me?

What glows at me?
A far stretch of sight
Saw a starlight in the night
And I wonder . . .

Why all things
Must move through time
Leaving light
And existence far behind

A moment in time
Held you close to me

Where there was once a star
So there was you
Who shut your eyes
And left the light behind

Judy M. Bertonazzi

Just One More Day

Hazy dreams of yesterday,
Familiar things left where they lay,
Miss you much, all I can say,
Live the life, just one more day,

Sadness comes how I despair,
Gone my life, my love I swear -
That things remind me everywhere,
Still I struggle, love, and care

The pain sometimes it gets so bad,
Heart ache burns, makes me so mad,
I think about the life we had,
Little things make me so sad,

I'll come back to you someday,
Share my life in every way,
Miss you much, all I can say,
Live the life , just one more day

V. Frank Ward

First and Last Love

Here I sit staring out my window
just wishing that you were near
I stare blankly at nothing
just barely holding back a tear
things you said sting deep
into my heart
why you would say such things
I can't figure out
you were my first love
my first and my last
that light seems mocking
now that I am not with you

Tressa Porter

My Saviour's Law

My life, my God
We're all in one
To be chosen as
One of God's Sons

To live the life
That he once did
For our Jesus light
Will not be hid

For all the truth
Of Jesus will spread
Throughout the land
Of our Father's hand

His grace so sweet
His power so strong
God is breaking down
All of the wrong

Making all the things new
In the world today
Making others to hear
What He has to say.

Glenda J. Rodgers

Insomnia

The faucet drips every three seconds
The ceiling has twenty four cracks
As I lay awake at night
A train rumbles upon its tracks
The neighbors' cat next door
Meows a horrible tune
As I lay awake at night
Dogs bellow at the moon
The crickets chirp at a constant pace
The mice project a peep
As I lay awake at night
I'd like to get some sleep
The clock ticks and ticks
Forever, it may seem
As I lay awake at night
I realize all was a dream

Anna Moscicki

Long Winter

It starts out fresh and new;
A winter wonderland view.
Days are short, the nights long.
Can't help but yearn the robin's song.

The sun may shine tomorrow;
But I don't think it will.
I'll sit back in rockin' chair;
Lookin' past my windowsill.

Winterscape, not a passing fling;
My musings go to upcoming spring.
Experience tells me tis' no small feat;
For vernal sun to turn up its heat.

Evergreens blanketed with snow;
Train on track, whistle blow.
Frozen creek makes its way;
Far from clear; it's dark, and gray.

Brent L. Hewit

Whaling

Once we went whaling
And saw a whale loptailing
It gave a great cry
And everyone said "O my"
Then we went on sailing.

Amber Ritter

A Poem On Paper

As I sit here trying to write a poem
All I can think about is going home
Man, school is a joke
Ah, now I want a Coke

Oh my God, look at this!
Something that I could not miss
I think I'm going to die
But it's all just my lie

Oh boy, can this be?
A poem on my paper I see
Gee whiz, I'm done
Home, here I come

Kristine Monique Doss

Ripples

My words touch the world
As a pebble touches water,
Rippling.

Others move in the wake
As I am moved by others,
All the while
Rippling, rippling.

The ripples grow larger
The ripples loom fainter
I no longer control them
Headed for history,
Rippling, rippling, rippling.

As the ripples of my touch fade
Into the pool of eternity,
The ripples and pool unite
I am history
Rippling.

Ed Stafman

I Am Not Perfect

I am not perfect
I will not always win
I will not always be first
But you still love me

I am not perfect
I'm not that smart
I will probably never get straight A's
But you still love me

I am not perfect
My hair is not that shiny
and I'm not that pretty
But you still love me

I am not perfect
I'm not that tall
and I'm not that skinny
But you still love me

I am not perfect
I will make mistakes
But you will always love me

Kara Love Bingham

Life

Oh God, be merciful on my soul
My life is becoming terribly old.
My heart cries out for help,
But no matter how loud I yelp
Nobody seems to care,
Life just isn't fair.
Everybody's out in the cold,
Or am I just being bold?

Kurstin Stiff

Change

Change is inevitable
  Here today—gone tomorrow
Fleeting images
  In the shadows of Time
Even as footprints in the sand
  Are erased by incoming waves

Events that loom
  In the now of Time
Fade and move out of the limelight
  Until they no longer
Assume importance
  And are reduced to vague memories
Of a past Time

New events control the scene
  Destined to follow the path
Of earlier happenings
  Through the shadows of Time
To be relegated
  To the far past Time
Of long lost memories

Victoria Schmidt Ed.D.

The Writer

He lives among the paper,
the pencils, and a typewriter.
His publisher owns him.

He works by himself,
above a grocery store,
in a room where walls of brick

press against him,
and the floors are rough
with the weight of footsteps.

He hears no inspiration
inside his soul.
The hand of muse touches him.

He writes until he is tired
or someone calls him.
Yet he turns his back and forges on.

As he writes in his room,
he stops occasionally
to hear his muse.

Ayanna Williams

Passed

I remember that day
As if it were only yesterday.
How could I ever forget
The day he passed away.

I heard the phone ring
But, after that I fell apart.
I could no longer breathe
It was a knife to my heart.

My grandma said to me
"Honey he has passed on"
I asked her what I would do
Now that he was gone.

I know how much it hurts
Again she said to me.
But, do not cry at his expense
That is not what he wants to see.

Just remember his constant smile
Nothing made him blue.
Be strong for him
You know he loves you.

Erin Stoyer

Untitled

I look out at the world,
and sigh in despair.
I wonder how everyone lives,
without any care.
I wish I could just disappear,
and no longer live.
To be totally carefree,
my soul I'd give.
For just one person,
who could truly love me,
and hold my soul,
I'd be filled with glee.
But I know that could never happen,
for I'm filled with rage.
I no longer have love to give,
and my soul is trapped in a cage.
If I tried to free it,
I would surely die.
But I cannot live like this,
so, I say good-bye.

Mandy Hoskins

A Broken Heart

There was a time when I was the owner
I had complete control like a loner.
The keys were kept close to me
For no one to have or ever to see.
The keys opened the door so easily
To find on the other side was just me.
A tiny piece seemed so easy to give
Then I had to learn again just to live.
The door let it just enough light
Inside was such a lonely sight.
Fears, wonders were tucked away
To share on some far away day.
Time gave pieces out everywhere
No one seeming to really care.
Shallow words, lies with no meanings
Left the door open with no reasons.
Time has come to close the door
And put the keys away once more.
Why didn't I know this from the start
All that is left is a broken heart.

Wilma T. Brown

A Summer Storm

Pretty and blue
Yet hot and dry
What's this
Gray to black
And a cool gentle breeze
The wind seems to be picking up
A thump and then another
Cool rain running down my body
A cardinal in the field
Bathing in a puddle
A robin in the back
Tugging at a worm
The drops are gone
But the water still stands
The neighbor kids out in the street
Jumping in the puddles

Brandy Drevs

Release

I cried because I lost a love,
I cried because I was alone.
But when I spread my wings and flew
I knew that I had grown.
The love I lost was free to roam
and found somebody new.
And when I turned my head to weep
Standing there was you.

Thelma Barlow Blaxall

The Contest

I'm filling out my entry,
I know I'm sure to win.
It really is that simple,
To fail would be a sin.

It's just a mere formality,
I've got this contest won.
No one else is even close,
I know I'll be the one.

I just turned in my entry.
And now I'll have to wait.
I know I won this contest,
It must have been my fate.

The Judges do what Judges do,
It will only take a while
It's in the bag, not even close
I'll win it by a mile.

After all the facts and figures,
Were considered for their worth,
They said it's now official, I'm
"The Luckiest Guy on Earth."

Otto Steinegweg

Stars

When I was just a little sprite
I wished upon the stars at night.
But one time, quite to my surprise,
There were no stars up in the skies!
My mother understanding why
I gazed up at the empty sky,
Explained as only mothers do,
That far beyond the misty blue,
Although no mortal eyes could see,
The stars were waiting there for me.
A sunny day or cloudy night
May hide the little stars from sight,
But stars don't set, nor do they rise
They're always up there in the skies.

Mary C. Hicks

Meaningless Death

Yell, Slap, Cry
No, runs through my mind
What do I do
Nothing, put it behind me
Never again, I believed
There it goes again, harder this time
Madder yell, fiercer slap, louder cry
Sound of no comes from the sky
Wish I knew why
Need no help
It's okay, I have stopped, I thought
Here it comes again
Much worse than last time
Loud cry of innocence
Uncontrollable, unstoppable
Sound fades away softly, then gone
What has been done, If only knew
I loved him so much, now it's too late
I should have faced reality, got help
I abused him just as much

Gregory Creal

Sanctuary

Silently, we become . . . composed;
Spirits of each other—
Hearts in repose . . . sanctuary;

Raging, we were, ensconced in stone;
Wailing, drenched in fear—
As gargoyles, once unknown;

The darkness roiled nigh;
Hearkened, the echoing tear—
But, for love the heavens high;

Opened by Gaea's spring calling;
her perfumed zephyr—
With God's light falling—

Caressed us in their children;
imagined possibilities borne—
Again we are children.

Silently, we became . . . composed;
Spirits of one another—
Sanctuary . . . our heart in God's repose.

Joseph Anthony Ortiz Noriega

Sphere

I am here,
Here right now,
On this sphere
We call home.
I am but
One of billions,
Just a dot,
There could be trillions.
In outer space
We know not,
How many more faces,
How many more dots?

Kristina Byrne

He Is Waves

He is waves
In and out he goes
Gentle and calming
Like the fluttering of sea gulls' wings
Yet troublesome and crazy
Like little fish nibbling at your toes
He flows up to me
Then backs away
Teasing me
He comes crashing down
Hurting me
Washing away my feelings
He rolls over me
Ignoring me

Serafina Hummel

Thinking

A thousand thoughts running
through my mind.
So much to figure out
with so little time.
Like the running water
with no place to go.
Even with that it's still
going to flow.
The fields of thought
have no end.
Like the eagle soaring
across the rivers bend.
He flies so free,
if only that was me.

Jaime Nicole Knibb

A Tree's Way

Branches may sway.
Leaves may blow on a windy day.

Trunk is brown.
Held closely to the ground.

Tree looks bare,
From the sun's glare.

The tree will fear,
The fall that is so near.

When fall is here,
Tree's new colors will appear.

When spring comes around,
The tree will no longer frown.

Tiffany Easterling

The Last Goodbye

We said goodbye so many times
It did not mean a thing
As I thought about it all
The phone was sure to ring
As soon as I heard your voice
I knew right then I had no choice
For we all play to many a game
So soon we realize they are all the same
I did not want it to end this way
But for a love we all must pay
So to you goodbye, I hope it's the last
It still seems to me, it ended too fast

Cecelia Teslja

The Message Of God

Pray for her.
Dirty girl.

Wrong direction.
Inflated heads.

Save her soul.
Force her down.

Rape her thoughts.
Break her will.

Pray for her.
Ugly sin.
Dirty girl.

Joleen Huffman

Steel Dream

It starts with a kick
or the push of a button.
Cold roll steel
and the sound of rolling thunder.
The sun on my skin,
the wind in my hair.
Sometimes the rain
and the smell of damp leather.
Sometimes alone,
cruising black rivers
with banks lined in yellow.
Sometimes the feel of soft breasts
pressed against my shoulder-blades;
arms around my waist.
I see, I feel, I smell,
everything, Steel Dream.

Douglas A. Wright

Humankind

On a spinning orb, we are,
circling 'round our nearest star,
weaving life with every turn,
human niche to which we're born.

Speculating about the source,
that perpetuates our course,
given but these minds to spend,
searching for that riddles end.

Then when death, known friend to all,
leads us through the mortal wall,
we'll embrace the cosmic mind,
and merge as one, for all time.

Larry Evans

Confusion

All this time
Spent my time
Just to buy more time

I feel love
I know love
But I don't want to love

I know what to do
But I can't decide what to do
What do I do?

Chelsea King

Gone

Gone is the love,
That was strong as gold.
Gone is the happiness,
That shone so bold.

Gone is the tenderness,
That we once felt.
Gone are the problems,
We always with dealt.

Gone is the fear,
Of losing the thought of you.
Because my worst dreams,
Became reality and true.

Gone are the tears,
Cried every night,
Because of something said,
Or some petty fight.

Gone is the future,
Cruel fate did end.
It's all in the past,
And gone with the wind.

Carmen Sparks

Sweet Memory

Memories are good
or bad things you remember.
Memories are things that stay with
you forever. Memories can be little
things such as your first cut,
or your first TV. Memories can be
big things like your first date or
first kiss, but a sweet memory is
the best thing that has ever happened
to you. A sweet memory is the one
that makes you live.

Tiffany Raye Edwards

Dreams

Every night a wish I keep,
Only when, I go to sleep.

In my sleep, I dream of you,
Dreams I hope, you have too.

From within, I'll hold you tight,
Wishing for, and endless night.

When dawn comes, I will wake,
Only wishing, I could take.

Take the things, which I have dreamt,
In my heart, which I have kept.

Wishing, wanting, longing too,
Again in sleep, Dream of you.

Hoping, wishing, with all my might,
To dream of you, every night.

And with me, when I sleep,
The love for you which I keep.

keep with me, all night through,
And through the day, I love you too.

Wishing, hoping, praying you,
Dream of me, the same way too.

Scott Devel

Why?

Intensely I gaze in silent awe
At the distant hills over yonder.
Why a vista so lovely and ethereal
Can bring sombre thoughts and pain?

Oft I brood and wonder why
At moments when joy is replete
Surge a feeling—alien and anon—
Akin to pain and emptiness.

I yearn and seek for answers
In the deep recess of my mind.
Radiant as light I see—why?
A vacuum is there for God to fill!

Erlinda R. Anunciacion

The Man I Love

The man I love has dark, brown eyes
They're even more beautiful
Than the evening skies
His smile is like a beautiful red rose
His skin is so smooth
Including his nose
The man I love has beautiful brown hair
Don't you look at him
Don't you dare!
I love my man with all my heart
When will his love for me ever start?

Amy Smith

The Ocean

The ocean is blue, so full of life,
with creatures upon you, even
at night, the depths of the
ocean may vary as you can
see, but there's miles of ocean
beneath you and me.

So come sail the ocean, come
sail the sea and you will
believe if you see what I
see that the world is beautiful
as the ocean and sea.

Ayshea Quintana

Water

I am the great ocean waves
crashing against the rocks
angry
I am the peaceful
meadow brook
calm
I am the glittering pond
resting
I am the rain
falling down to the ground
crying
I am the river
running into the ocean
wishing
I am the water

Cindy Chen

She's My Sister

My sister is the best,
Better than all the rest,
She's my sister,
She's my sister.
My sister is the greatest,
Her clothes are the latest,
She's my sister,
She's my sister.
I love her every day,
And in every way,
She's my sister,
She's my sister.
She can catch a ball,
She's not sissy at all,
She's my sister,
She's my sister.

Jennifer L. Crivelli

You

I see you in my dreams
I hear you in my soul,
And I feel you in my heart
Because of its unwillingness
To let you go.
I miss you in my life
And it hurts to really know
That when you left for good
I'm not able to let you go.

Angie Easterly

Open Door to Love

Doors have closed and opened anew,
Excitement and courage beat the blues.
Strength and self-esteem grow high,
As an eagle soars the sky.
Wealth and fame are not the blame,
For the riches of God, I have gained.
His guidance and love from above,
Lead me straight in his great love.
Will-power and determination are mine,
For my hand in his, you will find.
Joy unspeakable is proclaimed,
His Father and mine are the same.
Glory and Honor is his indeed,
For he hung on that rugged tree.
Arise and shine, he did appear,
To share his news far and near.
Love and trust are here to stay,
To still the storm and keep Satan away.
Awesome and majestic cannot describe,
The true love I have inside.

Karen R. Taber

A Note of Music

Note by note, beat by beat
The language of the soul flows on
Expressions of strong love, gentle peace
A measure, a page, a song

Inspiration from the heart
Enticingly, a story told
Simple tenderness of emotion
Enchanting, sweet, but bold

An everlasting strain
Tranquility, muses by your side
Rhythm of nature, harmony reigns
This is life, for silence has died.

Cara Leigh Buttitta

Life's Path

We are never really alone
as we trod the path of life!
For God is always with us
through happiness and strife!

We must live to the fullest,
We are always in "God's hands!"
Whether at home or away,
We must clearly understand.
That life is never easy,
but with friends
and faith and love.
We can hurdle any obstacle
with the heavenly Grace of God
from above!

Trudie Gavette

Sleeping Dragons

Fear not the
Dragons of your
sleep, my child

They are the
keepers of all
that is good

They will hold
tight your fears
in the night

Spinning the darkness
into gold

And with God's grace . . .

May they smile down
upon you tonight, and always

Debora L. Kauffer

You

The first time I saw you
I knew you were mine
and it had nothing to do
with you being so fine
A feeling just suddenly
came over me
and I knew that your arms
would one day be waiting for me
when I looked in your eyes
I saw all I've missed
when I looked at your lips
I felt our first kiss
This is written to you
With all my heart
and when we hooked up
I knew will never
Grow apart because my
love is passionate and desirable too
and all my love is only for you

Chasta Dunlap

Love

Love is like a razor blade
that leaves your
heart to bleed
and never healing
the scars that it has
left behind
To leave you hurting
inside making you
feel as if there were
no hope to keep
on trying to heal
the wounds of love

Alicia Polley

Straight Up The Road

You better walk straight up that road
Find all the love you can

Fall back down that road
You're among the living dead

The man at the top of the ladder
Fell back in the sand

But he picked himself right up
And he got up there again

So let me tell you brother
You better walk straight up that road

For many a man got there
Who carried a heavy load

And the man at the top of the ladder.
That fell back in the sand

Picked himself right up and
Got up there again

Rene Gray

For You Are Part Of Me

All the loving words,
all the fairy tales,
I longed to hear.
I welcomed you,
I trusted you,
I gave up my life for you,
for I'm nothing without you.
You capture my heart,
you see through my soul,
for you are part of my life.
You opened my eyes,
when I can't see;
You lifted me up,
when I'm in need;
You shined down upon me,
when I'm lonely,
for you are part of me,
and I'm part of you.

Vivian H. L. Fung

I Wish You Would Come Back

Since you been gone
inside of me feels like a thunderstorm
after some time
past I feel
like me again but
before long I'll miss you again
Until you come back I will feel
like a thunderstorm
is inside of me
about to burst
out of my body

Katie Pierce

Like A Rose

A mother is like a rose.
She learns how to love
like a seed learns to grow.
She struggles to the surface
and stretches toward the sun.
She lives for love
as a flower lives for beauty.
She needs care
like a rose needs water.
Although she has thorns
and must be stern.
It's all worth wild
when the jobs finally done.

Danielle Rice

Untitled

Just sitting alone,
Listening to sounds of a saxophone.
When my phone rings.
I pick it up, chat for a while.
Then decide to go shopping,
And find what's in style.
Something catches my eye.
I go berserk,
Hoping I can get it
from the next sale clerk.
Finally I do, so I take two.
Starting to get tired
So I head to the zoo.
As I sit and watch
and check out the scene,
I see that one elephant
decides to get mean.
My popcorn was gone.
What could I do?
So I went home, and cooked me some
stew.

Carey Panzarino

Bear Necessity

The old bear rug was losing its hair
In the spot where the children sat.
Its mouth was sprung
And the eyes just hung,
But 'twas the favorite place for a nap.
And on rainy days the children played
On the little left that was fuzz,
It looked quite grotesque
But nevertheless
It stayed right where it was . . .
Now, if I could find the very same kind
I'd give it identical care,
And count its worth
In comfort and mirth
By the fact that
It's losing its hair!

Jackie Lewis Greeno

High

High in a tree,
Higher than the sea.
The clouds up above,
Looking down on me.

High up on the steeps,
Higher than the river weeps.
The stars from afar,
Shining down on my cheeks.

Jennifer Akers

Being With You

When you whisper soft sincerity
My heart thunders.

When I gaze into your maple
Brown eyes they say a thousand words

To be in your warm embrace
Let me know I'm secure

And when we kiss it's heavenly

The very thought of living
Without you leaves me stifled
And bleak, for I have
An everlasting love
Dreamer seek

Torithea Fitzgerald

Untitled

Once where a house stood
filled with laughter and happy memories
Now stands empty of anything.
forgotten and lonely.
There were so many joyful days
spent underneath the oak out front . . .
so many joyful ways.
The trees still echo with laughter,
the hallways echo of pounding feet
but now it stands empty
finally admitting defeat.
Defeated of a happiness
it once had,
now it stands empty,
lonely, and sad.

Kandice Leppo

Can You Hear Me

Can you hear me when I whisper
Can you hear me when I cry
Can you hear me through my laughter
or even when I sigh.

Can you hear me when I scream
or may be when I'm dreaming
Can you hear me in my silence or
when I call for you by name.

Can you hear me when I make a wish
or ask for help from you. Can you
hear me when I'm lonely or if I
speak to you aloud.

I know you're with me everyday and
showed me how to pray, I know you
hear me in every way —even from
a cloud.

Rosemary Beneteau

To Go and Know

As the world moves faster and faster
Where do we go;

As we work harder and harder,
What do we know;

Where have we gone,
What have we seen;

Have we seen or,
Have we let life go;

Have we learned or,
Have we worked too hard to know?

Edward J. Gaidry

For Laughter's Sake

My hair is white
My teeth's in a cup
From an old beat-up car
To a shinny new truck

From an old wrought iron bed
To a pretty one of wood
No more plastic covered couches
On three legs and a brick stood

Got them fancy store bought clothes
Don't need these coveralls
Got my fishin license
Be retired in the fall

Ant life good
That's all I can say
Raised all them seven young'uns
Now it's my time to play

Opps, I don't like this news
in the newspaper today
Gotta work til I'm seventy?
Sams up the age

Drama F. Watson

The Passing of a Day

The morning sun's beauty
As often as I see.
As I crack open my window
I feel the summer's breeze.
The daybreak is here
But not for long
for soon it will be twelve
And noon will sing its song.
Bluebird please fly
Spread your wings afar
As the growing of a day
like the passing of a car.
Life is a rainbow of everlasting sun.
As the morning is just starting
The night is almost done.

Chrystal Case

A Spider on a Rose

I am a spider on a rose,
Beautiful, but out of place.
Scared without my web
So the harsh world I must face.

I am a spider on a rose.
Like a sun in the night sky,
Like flames on the water's surface.
Different till the day I die.

But I am strong and brave.
I don't care if I end up alone.
Nor what others think.
As long as I'm not anyone's clone.

I am the spider on a rose,
Proud of my difference,
Because it is the life that I choose.
To be different. Oh, so different.
A spider on a rose.

Leslie Heiden

Here With You

Here with you
I wish I could stay always,
With your hand in mine
And that look in your eye.
The one that says,
"I'm with you forever,"
That we'll never have
To say goodbye.

And when you say, "I love you,"
I know the words are true,
Because they come across
In everything you do.
Even with the smallest glance
Or smile that comes my way,
I fall deeper into love with you
More and more each day.

Jenny Macken

The Musical Malady

Practice
Practice
Practice

So many hours spent
Perfecting the talent

Major scales
Minor setbacks
Crescendoing expectations

Rehearsals . . .
Evaluations . . .
Critiques . . .
And still more . . .
Practicing.

Will I master the beast

Or

Will it master me . . .

Carol Bowlin

The Other Day

Just the other day it seems to be,
In love we were both lost,
Now I'm here alone you see,
So high was the cost,

Every night before I sleep,
I pray that you are fine,
And when I'm in a dream, so deep,
I dream that you're still mine,

Such a lonely life I live,
Since your new love you found,
I know you don't belong to me,
So I'll make my last sound,

Under the moons shine,
Tears will leave my eyes,
And with the wind so far and high,
Will be my tired cries,

So even though I never let go,
I know you will never come back,
I will not say a word to you,
I'll let her love you, the way I once had

Marina Peregrino

Untitled

I learned about life
From the smile of a newborn babe;
From the hug of a child half grown.

I learned about life
From a man I hurt;
From the man that hurt me.

I learned about life
From the stars at night;
From the birds at dawn.

I just couldn't learn
From warnings;
From watching.

I learned about life
By living;
By crying.

Annette Bright

Tommy's Poem

You asked me once how
I loved you

I love you with all
my mind, my soul, my heart,
my body

You are inside me
You're part of me
you bring me life
you let me dream

Being with you is
like being in heaven
like being in the clouds
like dancing with the stars

That's how I love you

Joy Hoskin

A Prayer

My dear Jesus, my mentor and savior.
I pray you keep me in your favor.
You are so benevolent, loving
And caring.
May my thoughts and deeds be pure
And not wavering.
I love you so much my Lord.
May our love be ever in accord.
I pray and ask your guidance so I may
Carry out your plan for me on earth.
That my endeavors to serve you Jesus,
As you ask of me, will prove my worth.
May I be your instrument to give your
Love to those whomever I speak
Or touch.
For Jesus I love you ever so much.
Amen.

John R. Kaselnak

He That Has Love

He that has love as wide as the ocean,
Can mend a person's heart.
He that has love as the deepest sea,
Can fix a heart that falls apart.
He that has love as big as the world,
Can save those who have gone astray.

For the Lord sent this love
When He sent His Son,
To save the lost,
And mend the hearts,
Of those whose hearts have fallen apart.

Ben Pollock

Fall Comes in on Lion's Paws

As fall comes in on lion's paws,
forcing leaves to fall,
into stinging slaps
of wind and rain,

I feel a steady rise
in the level of pain
I need to tuck away.

On other days,
the hot sun
bakes out,
the raw, damp, memories
of past fallen leaves,
and loves.
But,
Fall
and fear
come in
on lion's paws,
and tear at
the fiber of my soul.

Nancy Harrison Durdin

A Father Is . . .?

A father is . . .
Someone who cares
Someone who shares.

A father is . . .
Someone who yells
Someone who tells.

A father is . . .
Someone who loves
Someone who shoves.

A father is . . .
Someone who always
Makes sure you
Succeed in all
Your greatest deeds.

A father is . . .
Someone we all
Need!

April Burford

My Turn

To have you near me,
Your body next to mine,
To hear your heartbeat,
Sounding as gentle as the tide.

The movement of the waves,
Soft and gentle out at sea,
Growing stronger together,
Until they just fade away.

You give me your hand,
As I give you mine,
You gave me a look,
Laughter lingering in your eyes.

I give you my love,
For nothing in return,
Only to have you near me,
As if it were only to be my turn.

Susan Marie Slisko

Contrition

Hail Mary
blessed with grace
the devil's smile
on an angel's face
dancing for sinners
drinking from the well
answering the music
calling from hell
selling sins
a soul gone bad
nothing from mother
too much from dad
a new education
praying on knees
a different sort of father
easier to please
now where Mary
with your wayward soul
begging for forgiveness
trying to be whole

Anthony Plum

Aunt Kathy

Courage is my Aunt Kathy
Who is fighting cancer,
When she was in pain
Doctors gave her the answer.

Brave my Aunt Kathy is
She is ready to fight.
Strong and Risky is she
She will win with all her might.

Courage is Mark her husband
Who never complains,
He is always there for her
Although the fear remains.

Enduring her pain
He is like a strong rope,
Off into battle is he
With no weapon but Hope.

Heather Lawson

Recipe for Changing
Sadness to Happiness

A frown, a cry
The sound of a hurtful sigh, why?
Take a broken heart
Mix it with some tears,
Pour in some loneliness,
And mix away,
Nothing to say,
Throw in some clouds
From a rainy day.
Where to put them?
What to do?
Throw them all
In a great big pool.
Take a rake
And stir till you're able
To smile, maybe even laugh.
Put in a room,
Turn up the heat,
Let it cook till you think
Of something nice and sweet.

Rachel Malerba

Imagination

My mind easily drifts,
And I'm no longer there,
I float far and wide,
On a cloud in the sky,
I mingle with fairies,
I chirp with the birds,
I sing with the angels,
And all heavens heard,
I ride with the camels,
I swim with the sea,
I dance with the butterflies,
I buzz with the bees,
I bloom with the flowers,
I sway in the air,
I breathe in the sweetness,
With tender loving care,
And when all heavens heard,
And when all heaven cares,
I float back to earth,
In the crisp springy air.

Jennifer Nelson

Strewn

Strewn:
clothes as well as emotions
ranging from here,
to here,   to there
in seconds flat—
flat, but with so much
meaning content intext notes
So much to say
    not enough words
    not enough ears
    not enough care
    concern   worry—
but she worries
    she cares,
notices when something
just   isn't   right
but there's nothing she can do
She's got clothes
strewn
all over.

Michele Lunday

To Wonder

I stand amazed in a presence
As time unfurls a rose,
Responding to some symphony
That only Heaven Knows.

As He hangs the world on nothing,
I do not understand
Why God would let such splendor
Be seen by mortal man.

Bettie R. Sprague

The Sun

The sun was there
With the sky so blue.
The sun was there,
Shining upon the morning dew.
It was there to guide me.
It was there for the sea
To sparkle it and reflect it
And make it there for eyes to see.
The sun was there.

Lakishea Marcia Tharpe

Weeping Willow

Weeping willow,
Don't weep so.
Think of the children,
Watch them grow.
One day they'll come
To remember long ago.
Their children will play
In your shadow.
Always remember
What you had.
Don't forget them.
And be glad
They love you still
And always will.
Weeping willow,
Don't weep so.

Sibhan T. White

Maybe Only Once

In the beginning
At the first sign,
Whether by God
Or by some unknown being.
The universe was made
As if carved by a knife.

Stars, planets, and wondrous sights
Fashioned for pleasure
Carved for man to treasure
Earth's darkness and light.

Yet man abuses his special place
Litters, scavenges,
Destroying his womb.
Till one day his planet's face,
Will be desolate as a tomb.

Then will God
Or some unknown being,
Carve out a new world
For a new man?
Having failed once, this, I doubt.

Larry D. Quiggins

A Noble Cause

Let us rise again and again
To stop and stem the tide of violence
To combat enmity and hatred
To stamp out evils and corruption
And we won't give up
Because this cause is noble
This struggles is great.

Syeda Naheed Nashtar

The Worst Lunch I Ever Had

When I ate peanut butter
I got mad and started to mutter.

The sweet pickles I ate
Were stuffed with nasty bait.

I wanted grapes
But she gave me drapes.

I had a big, yellow banana
And gave it to my dog, Hannah.

I had a nice drink
But it turned me pink.

Jesse Fearin

The Discovery

There was an Indian
Who had known no change
Who stayed content
Along a sunlit beach
Gathering shells
He heard a sudden strange
Commingled noise
Looked up and gasped for speech
For in the bay
Where nothing was before
Moved on the sea by magic
Huge canoes
And he, in fear, this naked man alone
Knelt low behind a stone
But could not understand
Columbus' doomed burden caravan
Slant to the shore
And all the seamen land

Evelyn W. Haslett

Life

So this is life!
Breathe in the day,
It crashes on creation's shore,
Lifestreams pulse in harmony.
Joy surges from its core.
Light and darkness take their place,
Worlds move from heaven's span.
All manifest, His hand of grace
So wondrous and vast the plan

Peter Cifelli

First Smile

Divine majesty
Aimed right at me
Across a room
A world of faces
But you're the only
One I see
Imagine, a look
Could make that mark
A point of light
Shinning through my dark

Oh, those eyes!
Sparkling just for me
A shine you could see
For a mile
It's love, I know
From that first smile.

Stephanie Bolger

Madness

In madness I sit,
Perfectly sane do they view.
As crazy I be.
No different do I seem,
For I'll but loud I am.
My mind stings with anticipation,
For that moment seized to lash.
No effort it takes,
For patience I have.
Darkened by hate, stone by pain.
Filling nothing, Dismay in life,
Not crazy in death.
Walking asleep, unconscious by soul.
My hard beats made,
My blood runs cold.
In madness I sit,
And wait.

PFC Ryan Rhodes

Salvation

The darkness overcomes me
then I step away.
The moon cuts like a dagger
across the starless bay.

I run from the shadows
following me everywhere.
I dart toward the nearest light
without a single care.

The rain pours down like acid
burning to the touch.
The loneliness again surrounds me
I fear it, oh so much.

The lightening hits the ground
as I fall upon my knees.
The tears well up inside me
as I cry, "Help me please!"

The sun comes up before me,
chasing the night away.
And I hear my Savior calling
as there arises another day.

Kimberly Olinger

Moonlight Magic

The moon was shining soft and bright,
It cast its magic spell;
As I gazed upon this wondrous sight,
These words it seemed to tell:

"Although you're far from her tonight
And your words she cannot hear,
My age-old golden rays of light
Will whisper in her ear.

They'll tell her that you love her,
And gently they will kiss
Her silent lips that do not stir
In dreamland's sweetest bliss.

Then the silent message spoken,
As softly as the dawn;
The spell by something broken,
They'll vanish and be gone."

Clyde S. De Long Jr.

The Lost Girl

An empty space fills her soul,
her heart—grown so cold.
Her life—filled with anger,
to her friends—a stranger.
Her life—nothing but pain,
herself she puts at blame.
By herself—so alone,
her happiness—all gone.
For it's her mind she fears,
down her face—the tears,
In a darkened room she sits,
the deeper depressed she gets.
She asks, "Will the pain ever end?
Will my life ever mend?"
Suicide on her mind,
wants to leave her life behind.
Just a scared little girl,
lost herself in this world.
Hurt—she feels so unloved,
off the top—herself she shoved.

Heather A. Epperley

Springtime

The sight and sounds of springtime,
will cheer you up at anytime.
The birds are singing,
while the bees are stinging.
The children are playing,
while the parents are saying,
"Please do not hurry,
or we'll have to scurry,
to your doctor Murry."
The parents are praying,
while the children are saying.
"We will not run,
because we're having fun,
out here in the sun."
But then once again,
Springtime will end.
Fall will be near,
as we wait hopefully for
springtime next year.

Erin DiMarcantonio

Daddy's Hands

Dedicated to Charles P. Rossi
Blood runs through them
Throbbing with pain
Dark, wrinkled
Small and stained
Wide steel that could crush any other
Cuts, scars, yet pride
Suffered, gentle, flowing in stride
I sit on your lap
Curled in your grasp
Hands wrap around me, Love
You kiss my face
Sweet embrace
of hands like yours

Jenell Rossi

A New Path

You know who I really am
You sat with me those lonely nights
You've seen my tear stained face again
you've taken me so many times

We walked along this dead end road
Beside me you seemed empty, cold
I understand what I must do
I must walk on without you

Leave us in these pieces
Don't follow close behind me now
I can't bear this "never" anymore,
Alone, I'll take this path somehow

We walked along this dead end road
Beside me you seemed empty, cold
I understood just what to do
I had to walk this path without you

I knew just what I had to do . . .
Even though I loved you

Nina Rogerson

Path of Flowers

I came across a divided path:
One with flowers lining either side,
The other with stones lying across it.
I took the path of flowers,
Because it reminds me of you

Trina R. Rawlins

You

When I see you, I smile
because I never thought
I'd feel the way I do
about you

When I watch you, I wonder
why I never noticed you
looking at me like
that before

When I touch you, I swear
that no one else but you
can save me from
my fears

When I kiss you, I know
I never want any other lips
to touch mine
but yours

When I love you, I cry
to think that I have found you
after all this time
alone

Kim Marie Blanchard

Underneath

Underneath my skin
Underneath my clothes
Underneath my wounds
A special person grows

I may not be pretty
My clothes might not be the best
My words may not always be kind
But I'm as good as the rest

If you look
Underneath
You will know it's true
You will see the beauty inside
and understand me too

Melissa D. Vitt

The Baby

I love him,
But I hate him.
I have never met him,
But I know him.

I am a part of his family,
But he is not a part of mine.
I am not a part of his life,
But he is in my mind all the time.

I think of him and cry,
But he knows nothing of me.
I am almost fourteen years old,
But he is almost four weeks old.

We share the same mother,
But not the same family.
We are two different people,
But similar with our love for one.

I love him,
But I hate him.
I have never met him,
But I know him.

Rebecca Parks

Sleepless Nights

She wakes from a deep sleep
Sobbing and not knowing why
Blackness fills the room
All that is heard is her sigh

A sigh of overwhelming relief
For it was all a bad dream
Everything is all okay now
Or so it just may seem

Things are just a little too quiet
The air is just a little too still
Wondering now, if it was all a bad dream
Or if this nightmare is for real

Her heart is beating much faster
Her body is trembling with fear
Her mind wrapped up in such confusion
As the nightmare seems more near

What is the suppose to do now
Not knowing how to fend
Fend for herself and all she might lose
Stuck in a nightmare that'll never end

Carrie LeBrescu

Wild Horses

Horses' wild manes aflow,
Running through the valley below.
Rivers, valleys, hills, and plains,
Never tamed by cowboys' reins.
Flash of lightning, rolling thunder,
Timeless beauty never gone asunder.
Always moving, never stop,
Traveling over mountain tops.
Massive power muscles burn,
Winding 'round another turn.
Until the earth does cease to move,
Forever hear the horses' hooves.

Catherine Zanolini

Love Is . . .

Where the heart and mind fuse
And devotion is not misused,
Where people come in twos
And happiness is all they choose,

This is where you find
The only state of mind
That is so preciously refined.

The perfection of a shooting star
In the Heavens of so far
Or the flickering flame
Started between a Man and his Dame,

Are the faultless depictions
Of the desired affection
Told in every Fairy Tale . . .

Denise M. Atwater H.

Untitled

You were there when I was born
You were there when I had to mourn
You were there when I fell.
You were there to yell
You were there back then
I wish you were here again

Lindsey Willman

Soul-Redefined

Uprooted and torn
from the soil
of which I had been accustomed.
Transported to a new environment,
frightening, but familiar.

The branches flowing
from my inner core withered,
wilted and destroyed.
The environment beating down,
shrinking, closing in,
suffocating the soul.

Longing for my natural
surroundings
like a child yearning for his mother
in fear.
Hoping for the chance
to become whole again,
growing and surviving,
with the elements.

Kevin T. Herrera

Inner Glow

Something in me
Something ticking
Something waiting
To ignite
A thought, a flame
A simple flicker
Bonfire or candle light
It's warm, it glows
With love it grows
And can't be stopped
To my delight!

Leslie Ruma

Immortality

Mid-winter early A.M. and I rise.
My pristine linen
Snow angel
unshapes herself as
dazzly-eyed shivers rack her
nocturnal charge, and

standing
still,
bed-side,
after fifty-six years of
life,
I am numb
enough to feel
young,
back-strong and slender,
and
terrified to shift my
weight
for fear
of the grave.

Mark Dunn

Untitled

The roads cross.
Trees bend and wave.
The air thickens.
A feeling of darkness sets in.
Who approaches?
And why do I watch?
It could be he for whom I wait,
But, no, it is a passing stranger.
So I must go back to my loneliness
and waiting, waiting.

Amy C. Forkert

On Coming Home

My heart was so full of love
far my family it was
Open to pain by those closest to me
But who was to care that my
heart was not carefree
And longed to be treated
with Love's sympathy.
It was shocked by indifference
of close friends and family
The ones I had clung to in sweet memory
So it fell by the way side
and lies unattended
And I have a hole where
my heart used to be.

R. S. Kent

Meadow Moonlight

Silent blue
moonlight
Slides thru
My window
cascading over
bedsheets
While wind whispers
throughout the meadow
Stars gaze pixiedust
to light the path of dreams
As secret fairies dance
amongst the gleam

Jenny Dolwick

The World Of Love

Through the mirror bound in gold
there is a land of wealth untold.
Where lovers love
and the birds still sing
there are so many splendid things.
The tall grass waves
when the warm wind blows,
And the streams bring life
as they flow.
The sun hangs high
amongst the clouds;
Shinning sweet light
into mans shrouds.
Now this land is growing dark
there is no trace nor a mark
Then all is calm and all is right
I know it will come back another night.
I
Love
Tiffany

Stephen Phillips

For You

As the seconds pass away
I think of you and how you are
forbidden to me.
How much I love you is what they
do not see.
For you I would give my heart
and soul
As for without you my heart
is an empty hole
But torture me they will continue to do
I would let the blood from my
body just for you.

Carrie Schulz

3 Shines, 3 Rains

I was sitting in the cab
Of a Ford Ranger with Sis and Dad
I was glad for the shine on
The first day of vacation
Then there's a shadow of doubt
With wet roads about
The darkness followed
By flashes of light then it came
The rain with light yet fierce thudding
On the cab's roof
We survive from wetness
As we eat our luncheon
It shines like a diamond
But after dad leaves for work
My sister talks to a friend
For a long time
There's darkness, rain
And Mom comes with wetness
After coming back, it shines like a star
Rain comes again, so does sleep,
goodbye

Wylie LeMasters

Friends

Friends are forever,
They laugh, they love, they share
Each other's thoughts and words,
And most of all, they care.

Friends can come and go
And never be apart
Because they keep each other's smiles
Deep within their heart.

Friends can laugh and talk and cry
And think of lovely times gone by,
But most of all—
They love until they die.

Mary Zimmermann

On Contemplation

Ravens streak over quiet pastures;
Flocks swarm back to the womb.
The sky-scraping city of trees
Yields to streams of sunlight,
Revealing winter hideaways.

Tiny morsels of rebirth sprout through
And nurture themselves
On the decay from the death
Which surrounds them.

Pebbles shine through the surf,
Even when embedded by sand.

As I walk along the pier to nowhere
I wonder,

I am watching you, or are you
Watching me?

Diane Abbinanti

Miles From Home

As I stand on the drive,
I look toward the house I called home,
but the house is gone.

I look toward the barn where
much hard work was done,
but the barn is gone.

Only the sugar maple planted by
my father's father stands alone.

I know I am there,
yet I am miles from home.

Randy Lee

I Am

I am unique and strong
I wonder why the world is a mess
I see the ocean's rage I want
the world to be healed.
I am unique and strong

I pretend I'm the healer of the world.
I feel the planet's life crumble
I touch the sky for strength
I worry about our lives
I cry when I fell the world dying.
I am unique and strong

I understand there's not much I can do
I say we should all try any way
I dream of a perfect life.
I try to help who I can
I hope to fulfill my dreams
I am unique and strong.

Briana Chapman

Sturgeon Bay

Come see the land of Sturgeon Bay.
Splendor light of sunlit lay,
In the early morning of May.
Won't you just come and stay?

In the green wild flowers grow.
Some are tall and some are low.
Spring comes at a time it knows,
Dashing about to and fro.

How I make this day seem real?
To pick the buds as I do kneel.
Put up to cheek by touch and feel,
Gives me such zest and zeal.

Thunder sounds along the way.
Raindrops approaching and want to stay.
Touching the petals to lay.
In the light of this day.

Come see the land of Sturgeon Bay.
Picnic blanket about to lay.
I won't wait another day.
Won't you just come and stay?

Pamela Waller

Death

Death comes in many forms
It's a shadow on your wall
or the light upon you

It's a friend but not one
It hides in every corner when
you go in a dark place
Or in a light place

Death is like a shadow
flowing very close behind
It's waiting to take your life
It's the shadows on your wall

It waits for the right moment
to grab up into your soul
And squeeze the life out
It wants you no matter what

It wants your soul
So beware of shadows on your wall

Amanda Fitchorn

Shed No Tear

You should not shed
a tear for me,
you never really
knew me.
The person I was,
was a person you
did not want to
know a person who
wanted many things.
but the person
you knew was a
person who really
did not care.

Jane Miller

Man's Best Friend

I've got Man's best friend.
I love him a lot.
He belongs to me
and his name is Spot.

He's soft and cuddly
and sleeps on the bed.
Crawls up beside me
and wants to be fed.

He lets me pet him
and rub his belly.
I sneak him some bread
with lots of jelly.

He will let me know
whenever he wants out.
And helps protect me
on my paper route.

I actually got him
as a gift from Ms. Miller.
He's one of a kind
He's my caterpillar.

Joseph Epley

A Chance To Be

What I wouldn't give
For just one moment
To be able to live
The life I've always dreamed
To be the person
I've always wanted to be
And to see the things
I've always wanted to see
I want to be happy
Carefree and calm
I want to be brave
And sing a soft song
I want the sun to shine
Upon my face
And to belong
In my own place
All I want
Is a chance to be
A person: Me

Josie Schwarz

The Flood

It came at us like a snake,
winding slowly north.
We thought we'd be prepared,
after all we have been for years.
Then with a gushing roar,
it broke the silence of night.
There were tears and screams of horror,
as the monster came to feast.
It ate and ate, never to stop,
until one night it was saturated.
It left us to rebuild, all swallowed,
as the stomach retracts.
"Next time be prepared,"
The monster warns as it regresses.
The life once known, now is waste,
digested by the monster.

Lacey Huschle

Is Death Really Bad?

Death is not good.
Death is not bad.
It is only a reward for
Those who have lived and given.
So that they may
See God, worship God.
And to find out all that is to be known.
No more pain.
No more tears.
Just peace and tranquility.

Jessica Lynn Ahlbrandt

The Peace Will Never Come

Peace will never come
Unless the Arabs and Jews
Do away with their hates
And their guns too.

Peace will never come
Unless the Irish people find ways
To stop hating each other
And put their guns away.

I know it is hard
To forget the past
But by working together
We can make peace last.

Peace will never come
Regardless who we are
Until we learn to love
Instead of causing scars.

Ken Rickard

Trees

Sitting, smoking, sipping—
Listen to the wind:
Secrets in the breeze swirling;
Mysteries and miracles whirling
In whispers slipping through my mind;
As time unfurls this spring
The things that matter
In shades of green
Where once the light hit the ground,
Now shadows are cast all around,
And each form clatters to the sky,
Every figure soon to die,
Yet sooner to live,
Ever reaching up, ever winding down,
Between the silence and the sound.

Valerie O'Rourke Kitts

Skin Shell

Hardly
any
notice give to
deep and
idle
captives
as
powerful
persons
ever so
driven to live!
And the only real difference
between you and
I are the
chairs we
sit in!

Mia J. Waddell-Naiman

When I Am Thirty

The sky is red.
It looks like sunset all day long.
I am quite cold.
I'm in an overgrown bubble
So my body won't deteriorate.
The houses don't look
Like they did when I was a kid.
Glass hemispheres don't appeal
To a guy who grew up
In an apartment complex.
The new babies just came
From the laboratory.
It seems very impersonal
To have your children manufactured.
The government told me
That it would be
A wonderful world of wild excitement
To be one of the first inhabitants
Of the red planet Mars.
Now I'm not so sure.

Greg Osier

Cannon Hill

Walking around cannon hill,
feeling the cool breeze,
sea gulls fly above me,
in peace and harmony.
Leaving my footprints in the sand,
fiddler crabs can hear me,
and they don't understand.
Running for their holes,
I stroll on by.
As the sun beats down upon me,
looking out to sea.
So quiet, so calm,
the water is still,
as I gaze over from Cannon Hill.

Felicia Murphy

Iris

Her name was Iris, she was my mother,
I'm sure as long as I live
there will be no other.
God called her home to be
with him, a flower was her name,
or did God name the flower after her.
How I long to see your
sweet face, but I know your
in the right place.
One day we will meet in
Heaven with our Lord, till then
my mother, my sweet flower
I will wait with anticipation
till I am called.

Shirley J. Sears

Lopez Waters

The sea touches my feet.
I feel a sense of coldness.
It tingles with pain.
Otters swimming and playing.
The whales jumping and talking.
Eagles cawing over head.
To find a star fish while
in the turnover water.
My mind is light like water overhead.
Boats tooting loudly.
Waves crashing hard
against the rocks.
The end.

Jesse Asia

A Friend

A friend is dear.
A friend is true.
Always near
When you're feeling blue.

The greatest treasure
Is the lasting ride.
The longest measure
Our unselfish pride.

Wherever I reside
Or travel to,
I'll know deep inside
My friend is you.

Jeffrey A. Watson

Said The Clock

Time passes you by,
quicker than you may think
Life is but a game
A race of the clock,
A date on a paper,
memories in your head.
So scary it can be
each second is history
then suddenly you see,
blood in your veins
pumping so slow
withered with time
yet aged to perfection
what a journey you've had
so much good and such bad
Don't lose track of your
life, its quick to run away.
Each day is a year then it is ten
here and gone with no trace
only here for lifes quick embrace.

Angela L. Mood

Daisies

Pick a petal
One by one
He loves me
He loves me not.
The world so perfect
Petal by petal
Word by word.
Remember the good
Fix the bad
Pick a petal
One by one.

Elaine Foss

Fireflies

Catching fireflies of summer,
I pretend that I can fly.
Standing outside in the cold
I'm alone except for the stars.
I watch as they wink and fall,
Leaving tails of stardust.
I wipe the dust from my face
And pick up the fallen satellites.
As they sit in my garden
The flowers applaud the show.
The moon smiles upon the sun
And the earth slowly turns.
Crickets begin their orchestra
And the frogs begin to sing.
Grounded by my feet, I reach to heaven,
And pluck the planets from orbit.
I sip the milky way slowly
And dream about Mars.
Tomorrow I will sleep again
And let the fireflies live forever.

Jeremy Ziemba

Brett

His smile is like the sun
His eyes are green like new grass
His body is like an eagle
That has just taken flight

The sun doesn't shine as bright
The grass has turned to weeds
The eagle no longer soars
Across the sky in flight

My friend, you see, has left me
But he's in God's sight
I know that he is happy
Since joining heaven's light

Angie Hopkins

Home

Home
What is a home?
Is it a place to eat or sleep?
Is it a place to meet or say good-bye?
Home
Is it a place to laugh or cry?
Is it a place to be alone or together?
Home
I know!
It is a place to eat or sleep,
A place to meet or say good-bye.
It is a to laugh or cry,
A place to be alone or together.
It's all these things and more!
A home is where you find
Forgiveness not vengeance
Truth not lies
Joy and sadness
That's a home
Home

Tiia Lin Quinn

The Struggles of Harriet Tubman

Whips and scars and calloused hands,
Bare feet on the farming lands,
Cooking, sewing, chopping and more,
"Lord, please help us through this war"
Cannons blowing, guns shootin'
Through the woods hear owls hootin'
Running through these crooked lands,
Trying to get to freedom's hands,
There it is—I see it now,
Thank you, Lord, to you we bow.

Kelly Watterman

The Place

Was this it
Or didn't I fit
I'm not in the place
I can tell it on their face
People calling me names
So then I know where I am
It feels like a traffic jam
People are pushing me around
And making a lot of sound
This isn't the sweet place
The tears rolling down my face
I think of how everyone's being mean
And making a big scene
Now you know how I feel
So don't make everything a big deal

Elisha Erb

The Farm

The farm is a quiet place,
Where the animals stray,
There is a lot of space
For the children to romp and play;

Everyone works together,
the chores that need to be done,
We all help with the evening meal, then
We watch the setting of the sun.

And with the blessings of the day,
We thank the Lord as we pray.

The dishes done, food put away,
We are ready to retire until another day.

Alma Moyes

If I Was Rich

If I was rich, would I still be the
same person I was before?
People say money can buy you
anything in the world. But it cannot
buy you love or happiness.
Money can change a person's
lifestyle and the way you
act around you friends.
Would I still be the same person
I was before, if I was rich?

Maria Contreras

World War II Poem

Off to war we go
For what, I don't know
Fighting the German planes
On the American plains
Also the Japanese
Who bombed Pearl Harbor
Seeing men get killed
By the Jewish killer, Hitler
Oh, off to war we go
But I don't want to go
And all of the killing,
Filling all of the graves
I don't really want to go
But since I am American, off to war I go

Cory Dellenbach

Deja Vu

Where I stand I've stood before,
and know the sands of an unwalked shore.
Beyond what living mem'ries trace,
how come I now to ken this place?

Not true that snowflakes form one time
hexagonal and frosty rime,
for with unique new clarity,
I know I've seen the one I see!

If cars connecting form the train
and link on link produce the chain,
mayhap my soul won't decompose,
but o'er and o'er itself expose.

If eons fuse among Time's scrolls
producing kissing aureoles,
and as those coils purport to be,
might not each one then swaddle me?

This Soul will now and then be shod
with flesh and bone, and blood, as hod;
and every time it comes and goes
it echoes . . . echoes . . . echoes . . .

Virginia L. Nunnally

I Think

I think you're mean and evil
Don't think you really care
I think you're just a bully
Who loves to boss and scare

I think you can't imagine
Don't think you really know
I think you're just a little child
Dressed in a big man's clothes

I think your eyes are blindly closed
Don't think you really see
I think that you should really look
How things could really be

I think you live in anger
Don't think you'll let us know
I think that you just don't know how
To let your tender side show

I think you need to listen
Don't think you want to hear
I think that you are just afraid
You rule and domineer

Carol A. Juliano

I Came In Alone . . . As One

I knew not where to turn
You took me in, taught me to learn
I had not to try for your love to earn
Always kind, often stern
A searing ember, your help burns
My broken spirit, painful, yearns
For You to fill this empty cistern

Words cannot express my newfound joy
Grace in excess, like a child's lost toy
I once was lost, but now am found
You paid the cost, my love abounds
For this I shall not forget
My life is yours with no regret.

We only have one life to live
Would you give . . . yours to give?
Salvations gift is free
What He can do for you
He's done for me
Just confess with all your heart
Nowhere to begin but the start

Jerod Powers

A Better Life

We thought we was cool, we thought we was hip,
No longer boys, we were men, we were Crypts.

Me and the guys on a Saturday night,
Drinking gin and juice, feelin' all right.
(It's my life, it's my life, it's my life)

Some us had ladies, some us had babies,
Some us had nothing to go home to.

(Nothing, nothing, nothing)

Hanging the streets, packin' a gun,
Thinkin' but not carin' if we see 21.

Jump in a car, we go for a ride,
Not lookin' for trouble, but not tryin' to hide.

Trouble come found us, trouble done came,
Wearing their colors, the Blood brothers name.

When "The Man" found us, when all the smoke cleared,
5 of us dead, 4 of us near.

Now I am 20, five years in the hole,
Still being a prisoner, learned nothing I'm told.

Frontin' to family, frontin' to friends,
In my head I can tell you this sh** has to end.

Get me a good woman, get me a good job,
Stay out of prison, gangs, things that are wrong.

The say you can't leave the gang life behind,
But I'll do my best and pray that I find
(A Better Life, A Better Life, A Better Life)

Karen Wunder

Lovers

Whispers in the dark of night
as lovers touch and come together.
Two hearts intertwined in such joy,
in sheer ecstasy they while away the hours.

In that moment of shared ecstasy
with their hearts and bodies
blending as one

Carried away in the throes of passion
in a fever pitch rushing headlong
to that moment of orgasmic bliss

When all the world is shut out and
only their pounding hearts remind
them that they still exist

In this world and not somewhere
in an ethereal heaven of delight.

Sarah Rushbrook

Be Strong

Being passionate is very sensitive
Getting romantic is very positive
Reaching a climax is reactive
True caress is very effective

Love blooms to perfection
Heart beats to affection
The body's physique,
Speeds up emotion
Motion sets the equation

Compose your versatility
Tune up your ability
Stride to economic stability
Allow your career to be reality

How nice it is to be important
We'll it's more important to be nice
Life is worth the living
Keep caring and sharing

Dave Milton Allen

Thug Clothes

It's best wear your pants too tight unless you wanna be called a thug.
Because it's the gangsta that wears low sweaters, hoodies, and gloves.
If your color is black and you're wearing a nice leather,
to turn around and walk down the block and think would be guide clever.
When you see the cop walking his beat and think you'd be wise and best
cross the street unless you want to be harassed
and find a white men's leg knee deep in your a**.
A scully is used to protect a man's ears but to protect your head you must
not wear one of these thuggish ornamental things,
because much pain a cop's billy club brings
to anyone who would ever do wrong
by wearing "thug clothes" or singing rap songs.
To all black people be careful and listen to me,
there's a dress code in America we all must see.
Because if we don't, it will be too late and we'll all end up behind a jail's steel
gate attached to a 6X9 cell
wondering what we did to be cast into hell.
I'll tell you what you did it's simple you see,
you were born black in America and you love "thug clothes" like me.

Steven Lawrence

Seasons

It was a beautiful summer evening the sweet smell of flowers were at full bloom,
a time for love that was more precious than diamonds and gold. The season
was all wrong, she just wanted to be left alone, he was enduring tenaciously.

The season changed, she was spending more time with him. She started to love
the smell of him, a clean muscular smell. She began having exotic thoughts
of them together, touching one another's soul. The sound of thunder a cool
breeze and the win played a part with the sound of the ocean waves. She could
feel her control starting to slip, she just wanted to be loved the way she gave
love. Could she trust him? here he is again, not once, twice, but three times.

She was trying desperately to hide her feelings, he made her feel like a woman
again. He touched her, pulling her body close to him, his manhood throbbed.
She was afraid, many thoughts racing through her head, it was like the first
time. He whispered in her ear softly, "I want you." Pleasure coursed through
her body, sending shivers of sensation down her spine; she deserves love
the way you do. It's another season; it's a cold, cold winter is his heart . . .
too cold. One love misused her, one love abused her, but no one will hurt her
again. A man once told her she's a diamond in the rough; why is it no one
can find this diamond and treat her like a precious stone?

Denise M. Hardin

Shades of Day

Have you ever had one of those days?

The kind that make you miss your stop on the bus.
The kind that make you feel like an idiot.
The kind you wish would end, to put back behind you.
And to make it feel worse, it's pouring down rain.
It's clouding your sky.

It rains and it rains, it rains and it pours.
The hail is small enough to annoy you, for now.
Walk right past the elderly, their families and some whores.
They say that they'll love you forever, for now.

You missed your stop, 'cause the streets all look the same.
Only difference is the people, their wealth and their names.
And not one of them share yours, not none of them share yours.

And your day has been nothing, but a pain in the a**.
And just as it gets dark, you're finally home.
Just in time to live, the same old rut.
Just in time to see, the same old faces.

And still you feel, that you haven't quite made it.
And with that thought, your day is gone.
And so are the faces.

James E. Winter

The Man Who Traded Coors For Ambition

Vietnam vet,
The man who traded Coors for ambition.
Look at him sitting there,
Pathetic sack of ***S,
No good waste of human flesh.
Got no ambition, imagination, or motivation.
Sitting there since 2:30
This afternoon,
God-damn-no-good-for-nothin'-man.
Popping beers
And suckin' 'em back
Faster 'an flies.
Every Saturday and Sunday
On his a** with can in hand
Useless!
No chores, no conversation,
****-no-good-for-nothin'-man.
Marie Tornberg

Puddles on the Castle Range

While I sit in this mansion
I realize how much I hate it here;
there are too many windows for me to close.
I watch as the downpour commences.
The rain remains on the branches of a tree
that will someday rule the earth.
It causes a river of black water,
which runs to my bare feet,
so the white army can be set free,
like soft horses in a toy desert.
The rain clears the streets of the white army
so we can stand for ourselves, and dance.
They dodge cars in the streets which lie stories below.
Their trivial lives waiting to be stimulated into something more
meaningful.
I lie in a puddle of my own bullsh** waiting for it to all disappear.
I look down upon them and say vehemently,
We all were, and are, familiar strangers.
The rain will never stop,
it will only pause for brief moments.
Roger Naggar

We Are All Slaves

We are all slaves
of ill masters
have we not all been abused
the bad records of
confused people saying
sick things over and over
the screaming the hitting
the bruising the raping the murdering
the insisting the pedophile-master
the common taking taking taking
the pimp raking raking raking
the prostitute faking faking faking
the drug deader using luring
and yet what is the real issue
do not do unto others
as they have done to you
Pam Puleo

Coming out of the Closet

Before the days of walk-in closets I march into my mother's closet,
Not gaily like Johnny marching home. This somber, illiterate recruit of two
Is dressed in blue, starched collar embroidered with Flanders-crimson poppies.
Following Mother's orders, I enter my personal brig for infractions unknown.

Before the turn of the skeleton key, a portend of darkness yet to come
A gruesome glimpse of fox fur stole, glazed glass eyes, a death-frozen rictus,
Razor sharp teeth devouring bushy tail, flattered torso and head in Pyrrhic revenge.
As if to reclaim control in its final repose: death by suicide preferred to
    the murderous trap.

The closet reeks of smelly-crotch witches, of Rapunzel-long tendrils from acrid armpits
Of stepmother-scented clothes, of cyanide-laced apples and insecticidal mothballs.
The patchouli, almond and naphthalene fumes fill my nostrils, my tiny asthmatic lungs.
No air to breath or sound to hear or light to see or space to move.
Pamela Dolkart Gorin

Untitled

I love your lips when they're wet with wine.
And red with a wild desire
I love your eyes when the love light lies.
Lit with a passionate fire.
I love your arms when the warm white flesh
Touches mine in a fond embrace.
I love your hair when the strands enmesh.
Your lashes against my face.

Not for me the cabin, cold kiss
of a virgin's bloodless love.
Not for me the Saint's white bliss.
Nor the heart of a spotless dove.
But give me the love that
so freely gives.
And laughs at the whole world's blame.
With your baby so young and
warm in my arms.
It sets my poor heart a flame.

So kiss me sweet with your
warm wet mouth.
Nikki McElveen

Untitled

As she looked in the mirror
She saw nothing.
Just a foolish young girl.
Who thought she knew something

Her hair a mess pull back in a twist.
Her face red as she cried you son of a b*t*h
Her body ached no doubt from his touch.
Her arms bruised from his unforgiving clutch.
As she touched her body in the most gentle way.
The words he said in her mind.
They will stay.
I'm sorry I love you, please don't cry.
Her eyes filled with hurt as she promised herself
This is it, this is goodbye.
Only if she knew at that time it was a lie.
Next week he would do it again
Except this time leaving her to die!
Heather Okolichany

Zit

Ripe with strife
Rotten with infection
Boils and bakes
Crimson
With striation
Upon the visage
The nose
An acrid caustic region
The mouth
A Cimmerian tropical house of death
The eyes
Polar ice caps all-inclusive and criticizing
You cannot live here
Amidst blight and doom
Enter the hairline
Pliable and yielding
Recedes with time
Cessation of health
Misuse and abuse
Renders immunity helpless
Tyson Cumming

Life Is But A Dream

Life is but a dream made of
fairy tales that soon become reality
the reality of life
it seems to be the hardest to understand life
no one can figure it out so why try
to understand, what can't be learned or
taught soon you shall realize the hardest
parts of life are only lived and lived
is how they become what
life is all about, think of this for
a while and soon you will understand too.
Life is lived the way you think
life should be now understand
and hear real clear life is not to be
Feared only lived and loved
so take good care of your life and
live it to the fullest and be as happy as
you can be in this life of yours

Katie Stark

Somebody Loves Me

I have changed my ways of living
Got myself a peaceful mind
Now I am converted
I know heaven is mine
I believe as He tells me there shall be an end.
But the righteous shall rise
And be free from sin
Somebody loves me, whatever I do
As I grow older I find this true.
Somebody loves me,
Somebody cares
Somebody watches
Somebody will share
So why should I feel discouraged
And darken my way
'Cause somebody loves me
From day to day

Charles Jackson Sr.

Halloween Night

Spooks fly out the windows,
As the goblins spread their fear.
The pumpkins eyes are shining bright.
It's my favorite time of year.

The children dressed of macreba,
Portray their favorite ghost.
They find the time, to compare their treats
and see who has the most.

The older children party,
Dressed for the big contest.
A fifty dollar first place prize.
To the one they like the best.

Heads bobbing down for apples.
As they try to grasp a bite.
All at once the lights come on.
For the clock has rang midnight.

The party ends with fireworks.
Time to tuck away our fears.
Save them for the thirty-first.
Come Halloween next year.

Gene Campbell

The Wind

It blows whirling
all around swirling
in the trees,
through the leaves.
chilling little boys knees.

It moves all hours, flying softly around flowers,
whistling through caves
singing a sweet phrase.

It breathes mysteriously,
circling around secretly.
It's never seen
by you or me.

Catherine Thorne

Chores, OH Chores

Chores, chores, oh! what a bore,
I wash the dishes and scrub the floor.
The plates and cups piled so high,
I think they've already
passed the sky.
How I wish that they would all just disappear.
Yet, how I try not to shed a tear,
My parents scream,
My parents shout,
I say we just throw it all out,
But as I know that's not true.
They will always be there for me to do.

Rebecca Keller

The Cobains

Why me? Why am I the chosen one?
Why didn't Kurt throw away the gun?
Why can't I come clean?
I need to be there for Francis Bean!
No one wanted Kurt to die, except for maybe himself.
I cry when I look at his picture on the shelf.
I don't think Francis knows what's to come.
It's all because of that crappy gun.
Sometimes when I am asleep I hear his voice.
I say to myself, "Was this his only choice?"
Time's come when I think his death was caused by me
and I wonder, were we meant to be?
But now I can clearly see that he was meant for me.
I guess he wasn't happy.
Maybe he thought his life was crappy.
Francis and I go through a lot of pain.
Why did you kill yourself Kurt Cobain?

Ashley Ludvigson

Untitled

Every time I see the sky,
I wish to God above you were nearby.
He gave you to me because he knew that
you were the only one for me. The angels
from heaven came and told me that when I
meet you my heart will be true. So I
want you to know that in my soul I care
so deeply for you.

But babe without you,
the angels will take my heart and tear
it in two. So promise me that you will
bring back those nights, when you held
me tight at your side.
And I will kiss away the pain you received,
when you fell from the heavens just to be
with me. So loving each other we will be
till eternity.

Jenny Martinez

In the Blink of an Eye

Composure went out the window
Every bitter word spoken
Callously cauterized emotions once felt strongly
Pain lingered on past your untimely exit
Yesterday's warmness now froze my heart
Without reason all this occurred
You said there was cause I never saw it
I wish I had an answer from you
You couldn't I didn't want to hear it anyway
After all that we had been through
Without a second thought How could you?
Your coldness your callousness so maniacal
I heard what you said I understood without understanding
You left perfection destroyed
More was promised in the beginning you lied
I opened myself my heart to you you closed the door
Without desire our souls mingled as one
That day That day you left I knew
I now know what you knew I could never be
Part of me died that day.

Daniel Shonk

Untitled

The pain you feel in your heart when he's not with you
The pain you feel in your heart when he's with her
Any her it doesn't matter
The lump in your throat
The feeling at any second you will cry
For the one question, why is she there
She doesn't love him
All the what-ifs that tag along
What if something happens?
Then the always famous
Why Me?
Jealousy pain and the feeling that you want to claw her eyes out!
Is there love between them?
Or are you just extremely jealous?

Heather Scheels

Lost Angel

Lost angel, alias poor soul
Rectify pain for anger
Console the cries and confusion, carry pain no more
Solitude company as best friend
Shadows follow covering secrets no one knows
Forget would be best, leave guilt undisturbed
Remember is all that can be done memories can't be undone.
Cold are the feelings this angel holds
The heart bleeds blue blood
Mercy on this poor Angel, Save this lost soul

Nancy Monarrez

The Miracle Of A Life

The vanished years, the uncried tears all the sickness, and
vomit, furnished by the liquor and beer.
Drugs, dope,and unfulfilled relationships.

All the empty boxcars, thousands of miles of never ending
Trips; Lost in illusions blind with confusion broken
Scarred and tormented with discrimination and refusing.

Round and round up and down looped loop, no time to regroup;
From jail to institutions of criminal and clowns.
No where to turn, no where to run, all sorrow and no
More fun.

Finally I turned to my creator and from these diseases, and
Desolation now his delivering, me day by day by His
Forgiveness, and grace when I bow and pray.

I seek and knock read and find now I am regaining my long
Lost mind.

Daniel Walker

Violence

Solving nothing causing pain, grief,
And, nothing but more, violence—
Hurting you, hurting me.
Always to be, never to be free.
Stop the violence start the peace.
All I want is to be free.
Free from violence, pain, and grief.
Will there ever be relief?
Relieve us of this violent world
I ask you this our great Lord.
Male, female, they all do such nasty things.
Will we ever be free from trouble
Stop the violence start the peace
All I want is to be free.

James M. Kernan III

Impenetrable

The exterior is constructed of marble
Beauteous - yet cold, touchable - yet hard
The interior is of steel
durable, if a bit corroded,
Glistening, if a bit worn.
Marble may be chipped away - a difficult task
Taken on by those who would endure
The tedium of a somewhat thankless chore
Steel can be bent - a feat of unrelenting strength
It may be melted were the correct degree reached
Yes! The melting did commence once - it seemed sure!
All effort well worth the grief, the struggle
The blood, sweat, and tears
The pain of lost years
But alas, it was a battle lost
For the coldness of the marble fought the flame
Smothering it, depriving its oxygen
Distinguishing it forever
Leaving only ashes in its wake.

William J. Ross Jr.

Moral Grayism

I long for society's resurgence to idealism
yet I do not have a messianic complex

My hope comes from my fear of realism
which makes me an idealist

I fear realism, yet I am mortal
which makes me a realist by nature

Some things are simply real and are

I am milquetoast,
the result of a reaction between four notions

Hope, fear, idealism, and realism:
Fear being the catalyst

A man's greatest downfall is his transition
from idealism to realism

Some things that happen simply do

Matthew R. Snively

Gone Forever

I think he was the only one, but no others pass on.
People still enjoy the world. Why do I feel still in time?
The world will still turn, and his death will always burn.
Even without me life will go on. It hurts so bad you'd hope
not to feel this pain within. I hardly even knew him.
As I look outside I see nature's pride, but he is no longer
there with it. He is the best memory in my mind, but what
memory can I find? I ask all the angels and saints, what can
I do? How can I save memories, of what I never knew?
I think he was the only one, but no others pass on.

Michelle Sebok

The Gift

Have you ever seen the wind blowing in the trees?
Have you ever seen the water rippled by a breeze?
Most certainly! You know that they are there.
Like an angel's soft flowing hair.

Have you ever smelled the lilacs as you go about your way?
Have you ever smelled the freshness coming from the bay!
Of course, you've been affected by these as you pass by.
Like you've been by your own angel as he looks from on up high.

Have you ever felt the brush of a butterfly in fight?
Have you ever felt the snow on a brilliant winter night?
No doubt I'm sure you've been exposed to these.
Signs of your angel—just trying hard to please.

Thus, when you're feeling all alone—without a friend in sight,
Remember that your angel's there, be it be day or night.
He's there to keep you company—a friend, a confidante, a pal.
A gift from your creator—to make sure you're doing well.

    R. J. Marince

September

Sometime during the third week in August comes an
actual decided moment that triggers the coming of
the days of September.
The humid days of summer begin to weaken and surrender
their immature ways.
Peculiar feelings of emptiness and longing fill the soul.
A passing moment signals a wave of promise.
What belonged to summer form would soon change.
A sign of completion and end.
And by Friday of that August-third-week it becomes official.
The early signal has turned into new blue air.
Freshness of autumn beginnings titillate the bush
and the brush and the sway of the trees.
And from a slight tinge it becomes its own era.
A time for celebrating moments.
Ordinariness. An order of service. Intent.
Quite right to understand and be content.
Time calms the question.
Earth offers approbation.
Sanction of a new beginning for life's September soil.

    Gary T. Morgan

Daddy's Hands

I remember my Daddy's hands
How he worked and toiled the land
They were strong, yet loving to me
He taught me about life, things to see

I remember the words he said to me
He taught me of God, the land, and sea
He helped me see how life can change
My Dad taught me these many, many things

Accepting things that come my way
Asking God for help, for another day
Lessons he taught me made me strong
He showed me right from wrong

Daddy taught me to respect God's land
Respect man's rights—to lend a hand
How to face life, to be strong, not weak
There is a Sabbath for us to keep

My Daddy's hands told a story themselves
Life is not lived by sitting on a shelf
Whatever you give, you get in return
A penny saved, is a penny earned

    Rev. Maxine E. Palmer

Grandmother and Grandfather

My grandfather was a good man,
He drank his pop right out of a can.
Fishing was his hobby,
My grandmother's cat's name is Bobby.

Plunk went the line into the water,
My grandmother used to solder.
The fish would always say, go away,
Go away come back some other day.

As I would sketch,
A bundle he would catch.
For I knew someday,
I would eat them in May.

My grandfather is dead now,
I never thought I would miss him so much. Wow!
I miss his funny pranks,
And days when bobbers sank.
I miss you Grandpa.
I love you Grandma.

    Lindsay Reider

A Kiddie's Dreamland

Far away from Timbuktu,
Yes, far away from me and you,

Lives in all the kiddies dreams,
A wonderland of kiddie schemes.

With castles reaching to the sky,
And puppies, ponies, and butterflies.

With dolls and boats and trains galore,
And every imaginable toy in store.

Where the kiddies reign as Kings and Queens,
And no one thinks of being mean!

Yes—far away from Timbuktu,
And far away from me and you,

Lives in all the kiddies dream,
A wonderland of kiddie schemes!

    Grala D. Libby

Him

I saw him as the bus went by.
He was in dirty rags sitting on a window ledge.
He seemed to be staring at his hands.
I looked away, quickly feeling pity
Or maybe anger at his fall to this
State of ruin.
In the instant I looked away,
I saw him in my mind's eye,
The same dejected figure but with
A bright light glowing from
Within him and lighting up the
Space around him.
Just like all of us I thought
The wonder and magic of our
True selves shines through.

    Gloria O. Ayon

More Than A Dream

He came to me in a dream, a babe asleep in the hay.
Then next I saw him as a boy, teaching in the temple at noonday.
Who is this whose voice alone
inspires the multitude to pray.
Again I saw him on a hill,
with children gathered round.
Why do they stop their play
to hear this young mans sound.
I wish I had not seen him next
crucified, nailed upon a tree.
This man of peace of love,
in shame I turn and walk away.
Then I see him once again,
this man of humble grace.
With nail pierced hands outstretched to me
he asks me to have faith.
Now I know who is this man,
this Jesus of Nazareth.
He is my savior, the son of God, who died for my sins.
Thank God for this peace I know, for Jesus lives within.

Mike Howell

What Spring Means To Me

Spring is a time of new beginning,
Spring is a time of new life,
Our life is inspired, we begin dreaming,
Life takes on a new meaning.

Trees take on new life, green leaves appear,
The hyacinths and daffodils, prettier than ever,
The time fruit trees are in bloom,
The bitterness of winter has had its doom.

Our lives are inspired by the new life of spring,
The birds are returning and they are singing,
Busy building their nests for their offspring,
This new life changes everything.

Farmers are preparing to plant their fields,
Corn, wheat, all kind of vegetables,
We pray for a bountiful yield,
That there will be food on our tables.

Let's not forget to ask God's blessings,
On the labor of our hands,
Let's not forget to thank Him,
Because it is God who gives the increase.

Earline Cox

To My Lover, My Best Friend

Though our paths did cross one year ago
Our voices they stood still,
Until the day they met as one
And stirred a stronger will.

Our lives so separate, yet still the same
Our hopes, our dreams we share.
Our desires, our needs, within our hearts
Too similar beyond compare.

Though our lives we share with others,
makes our time too short, it's true.
For "time is of the essence,"
The way I feel when I'm with you.

We search for something we, both, lack
It's true, within our homes.
But together we confide our hopes,
Our dreams, still yet unknown.

My hope for us, our dreams, our feelings,
stay strong and never end.
For then, we'll know true love, we've found
My lover, my best friend.

Barbara Passon

Celebrate Life

Vital parts may weaken fast
While God rearranges his family cast

Just when you thought your life would end
God holds in the wings, a donor friend

So as one family sheds tears of grief
Another celebrates joy and relief

While a stranger's heart beats on in your chest
With a miracle of God's love, you are blest

Why some are chosen to return to the stage
Is in God's script on the very next page

He's not finished with you, it's certain
You've something to do before the final curtain

Celebrate life! That's the motivation
To give our savior a standing ovation

And when the critics write their reviews
May your "comeback" be to share the Good News.

Carol L. Parman

He Is Lord

God sits upon the circle of the Earth
He stretches out the heavens as a curtain
He rides upon the storm and walks upon the waters
He sighs, the green grass dies
Flowers abound in variegated shades
The whirlwind of His breath explores the glades

The voice of the Lord is beautiful and strong
The voice of The Lord is majestic in song
With His voice the vast wilderness shakes
The mountain and hills tremble and quake
He tosses and spins the mighty oak with a kiss
He is love, He is life—He is Lord of all the Earth

The sun and moon and stars obey His will
People from every nation in awe stand still
Stars twinkle and dance in the night
Moonglow covers our world with light
The hills leap and the trees clap their hands
Melodious praise of birds fill the land

He is love, He is light, He is life
He is Lord of all creation

Johnnie V. Fortune

Gone From My Life Forever

We enjoyed each others company,
right from the very first start.
I couldn't believe you were real, the
way you healed my broken heart.

Many days we spent together, laughing,
playing, and just having a good time.
Who knew the thoughts you were thinking,
that all the time you wanted to be mine.

We had so much in common, I thought
that could never be. You were so warm
and considerate; I wasn't use to that
you see. All the time you were trying
to give me your love, it wasn't that
I didn't want it, I didn't quite know
how to except it, not when it was
being given to me.

Now it's too late and I'll never get
that chance again, to be able to spend
the rest of my life with a true lover and friend.

Sonya Y. Rozell

Turmoil

It seemed I had descended into the very depths of Hell
And my soul was rent asunder.
Was I destined then to dwell
In the dark and gloomy place so somber?

Must I spend my life in that place so vile
With painful thoughts and tortured mind I fear
My terrible suffering soon will end
The reaper so very grim is near.

I felt his fearful footsteps close behind
Smelled the fetid stench so sour.
Heard his cackling voice from deep within
"Soon yes, soon to come your dreaded hour."

Could I, with help, from this place climb?
Perhaps then become a better man?
I shall pray to God with all my heart and soul
With His help I know, I will, I can.

Francis Doug Stokes

Downsizing

Pour Soul!
He faced St. Peter still hoping he'd passed
Then felt a qualm at the next question asked.
"Did a bit of your billions dull sorrow or pain
For those you exploited then chose to disdain?"
The man facing Peter sank down in his chair
Then defiantly said, "You must be aware
That all CEOs have the bottom line itch—
You have to play dirty to stay in their niche.
Abusing the servile is part of the game.
How can it be something for which to feel shame?"
"That's it!" said St. Peter with pitying frown,
"Just take that door there, it's marked 'going down'".
Shook up just a bit the reject still thought
That there wasn't a soul who couldn't be bought.
He knew he could make a good deal down there
Since he and Satan had so much to share.
Poor Soul!
How the victims he left behind would be inspired
If they could but see how their ex-boss was fired!

Nell Baltic

These Arms

These arms are here to hold you.
These arms are here to comfort you.
These arms are here to love you.
These arms are here to catch you when you stumble or fall.
These arms are here to lift and move heavy things for you.
These arms are here for you and only you.

Dorothy A. Wisted

How Beautiful The Valley

How beautiful, the valley,
Wind-swept, then washed with rain.
All objects stand out sharply,
On the now sunlit terrain.

Each orchard row, each fresh green field,
Each roof top, clean and bright.
And then the lights are extra twinkly,
As day fades into night.

The sun feels so "life-giving,"
After skies of gray.
And the air is most intoxicating,
With the smog all washed away.

How beautiful, the earth.
For storms must come and go.
We'll join the birds in joyous song,
Our happiness to show.

Flora H. Stephen

Thinking of You

It's been a while since you went away
I've been hurting and crying everyday
hoping and praying
wishing and saying
I need you to return to me,
back into my life
I still love you baby
I still want you as my wife
Yes, my heart is shattered into pieces
but, my body still yearns for your kisses
It's been so long, I don't know what to do
yet, my love is still strong and I remain true
to you and our love
this I swear on the stars above
Thought we'd be forever
thought we'd always last
thought we'd always be together
but, I guess, our relationship was meant to pass
Meant to pass so we can be together again
To start all over so, for us, there will be no end.

Edwin Elder

Wisdom

You're the perfect father,
You're the man of the house.
You taught your kids right from wrong,
And how to run their house.
They may be big,
They may be strong,
But yet your wisdom has taught them right from wrong.
I'm proud to say I know you,
I'm glad to call you my friend.
Your kids may not know it, but yet you do.
So keep your wisdom flowing,
And the stream will never end.

Sarah Smith

Mouthpiece for God

Your job is not an easy task,
But soon in God's great light
you shall bask.

Even though your heart
may be aching with rejection,
It is your job to make people comprehend
their need for correction.

You must speak when you know
something is wrong.
And I personally admire you
for being so brave and strong.

When others have the chance,
but say not a thing,
How will He perceive them,
Our Lord, our great King?

For these works you are doing,
He will reward you well.
And for them that close their ears to you,
Understand you didn't trip them—
On their own they fell!

Krista Hasenbuhler

Mirrored Parallels

Thousands and thousands of galaxies away
a parallel universe matches us day after day.

In mirrored reflections of our bad side and good
we see ourselves do things we thought we never could.

Dazed, in confusion, on both sides of the mind
we feel ourselves lost in the centuries of time.

Jennifer Robertson

The Little Blue Bird

The little blue bird sat in his nest,
Stood up and found a bug.
How it got under him no one knows
Not even the little blue bird.

Can I eat that little green bug,
Or will it make me sick?
My mommy says brown bugs are best
For little blue birds like me.

I tried to eat that little green bug,
Yuck, what a mess!
So I sat back down on that little green bug
The one I found in my nest.

Teresa J. Westra

Her Strength

In a small community
neighbors thought they've a clue,
only to find out their neighbor man they never knew.

Her pride wouldn't allow her to speak of the abuse,
you didn't see it on TV or hear it on the news.

A gun was given to her little did they know,
God had given her strength to fire the deadly blow.

They said it was meant to be she had a lion's heart;
that's why she survived and didn't fall apart.

There's a sadness deep inside why'd he have to die?
She only meant to wound him; so many questions why.

She walks into the chapel to kneel down and pray,
asking "Forgiveness," for the life she took away.

Brenda Brumbaugh

The Field

The flowers that bloom so fragrant and sweet;
the birds in their nest go tweet, tweet, tweet.
The grass is so green you can almost hear it growing;
the man down the street at 6 o'clock mowing.
The air is so clean with its fresh, crisp texture;
lying in a field where there is no pressure.
Watching the clouds in the beautiful sky;
the birds now hunt for food as they fly on by.
The squirrels are playing, going from tree to tree;
life is full of spirit and glee.
The aroma of bacon frying in the pan;
my beloved comes and caresses my hand..
He tenderly lifts me up in his arms;
he protects me from danger and all possible harm.
A passionate kiss as he carries me home;
my hands in his hair, my fingers do roam.
My insides they quiver with excitement so rare;
the touch of his hands on my body that's bare.
I gaze in his eyes of crystal blue;
satin sheets with rose colored hue.

Bonita Snyder

Wild Flower

Love is like a wild flower
It sprouts in the most unexpected places
It comes about naturally
It is truest of them all
Everyone thinks wild flowers are just weeds
'Til you just take a close enough look
Then you'll see the love and true beauty
That's why when you look at our love,
You know it's the truest and most natural
Our love is a wild flower

Kristine Reinhold

Heaven

In loving memory of my Grandmother, Verna May Quinton Pack,
Died October 13, 1994

Time is only a flick of the eye,
and then one day we all shall die,
Live your days as though you should
and when your time comes you too will know
how great it was to do as you were told.

It's a glorious place for everyone
even more so than the earth, moon, or sun.
It is very beautiful, peaceful, and sweet,
a place that can't be beat.

Friends, family, and all you knew
are at the gate to welcome you.
To this place we have been told,
is a most glorious place of all,

Our Heavenly Father's Home . . .

Delmar Le Roy Hinckley

Your Love

For Love is what you have found
Your Future knows of no bounds
For Love is what you share
Your Future knows of no fear

Trust in the Love that you have
Trust in the Love that you share
Trust in your future together
Trust in your future forever

For the Joy and Happiness that you bring
Will forever make your hearts sing
For whatever the future may hold
For whatever the future foretold

Know that what you have in each other
Shall forever be in the other
For your Love together
Shall grow forever

For the bridging of the two
Shall then become one
And in that one
You shall find the two

Helen Jung

A Moment of Memories

God blesses me in so many ways,
He lovingly touches each passing day.
In the empty moments of my life:
He so gently reminds me, I am your wife.

He slows me down, so I can reflect,
While time stands still, it's not hard to detect,
My hearts being faithful and so very true,
All of my thoughts are only of you.

I may recall a touch.
I loved so much.
Maybe words you say:
Too brighten my day.

Sometimes it's a kiss:
I can't help but to miss.
I can see your face with a great big smile:
I can't help but to think, I'll be home in a while.

Memories pass by like dust in the wind.
My memories of you, I'll cherish til the end.
I know my love will forsake you never.
Our love will only grow forever and ever.

Angela M. Sargeant

Silent House

The house is dejected
Dark and gray.
Where laughter once resounded
Now only memories play
And in my mind's eye
Those memories pass silently by.
The house is quiet now
Those tiny voices grown
Their footsteps no longer
Echo through the room.
Each took a path
To far away places.
They found a life
Among the teeming crowd.
But memories of good times
Replace the sleepless night
Time and distance makes me realize
How time once was and will in time finalize.

Joyce C. Thompson

A Summer Day

A sweet breeze blowing through the air,
Rushes past a tree, so high.
The enchanting buzz of a bumble bee,
Beautiful white puffs stand still in the sky.

The grass so soft and vivid green,
The sky so bright, a luscious blue.
The trees stand still, their colors full,
To a baby bird, the world is too new.

The brilliant sunlight seeps through the trees,
The sparkling new flower's colors.
The delicious smell of freshly cut grass,
A baby squirrel searching for its mother.

The renowned song of the ice cream truck,
The shrieks and laughter of a child.
The splash of a pool as someone dives in,
The burning hot sun is never mild.

Children laughing as they run through sprinklers,
Staring at the sky for really no reason.
The distant sound of hammers pounding,
Why, summer, of course is my favorite season.

Jillian Wojcik

Untitled

She cries with sour tears of pain
I wish that I could feel the same
She dwells in hell upon this earth
Yet I have envied her from birth

And through the tortures of her pace
She walks the flames with so much grace
I watch in awe as she proceeds
To gather people whom she leads

Her stance is strong
Her head holds high
Not ever have I seen her cry

The cross she carries won't make her bend
For she remains strong until the end

Tina Tangalakis

I Feel Guilty

Dedicated to those who died and those who cried
I feel guilty each and every night,
because you went to bed full of fear and fright.
I feel guilty every day,
because you didn't get to run or play.
I feel guilty all the time,
because what Hitler committed was murder and crime.
I feel guilty because of you,
because you had to be so sad and blue.
I feel guilty deep down in my heart,
because he killed innocent people right from the start
I feel guilty,
because they died
instead of me.

Jenifer Graves

Time Marches A Forward Beat

Take your time
As you travel now
While you're young with eyes to see
You may not always have your vision
There's no money-back guarantee.

Take your time
And listen now
Hear the little birds that sing
You may right now, hear the high notes call
That are the promises of spring.

Take your time
And smell the flowers
Where roses and lilacs bloom
You may see them fade tomorrow
A sad loss of their perfume.

Take your time
On the trail of life
Sight, sound or smell so sweet
There's no return of yesterday
Time marches a forward beat.

Joanna Fauver

Alone

Weeping willow, weeping willow, you're my best friend.
Weeping willow, weeping willow, the bond will never end.
Weeping willow, weeping willow, I have a surprise.
Weeping willow, weeping willow, come to see the sunrise.
Weeping willow, weeping willow, your trust in me is gone.
Weeping willow, weeping willow, I sing a mournful song.
Weeping willow, weeping willow, if only I had known.
Weeping willow, weeping willow, the wrong I have shown.
Weeping willow, weeping willow, I really miss you
Weeping willow, weeping willow, my tears are the morning dew.
Weeping willow, weeping willow, now all the hope is lost.
Weeping willow, weeping willow, you were killed by winter's frost.
Weeping willow, weeping willow, I am no longer your friend.
Weeping willow, weeping willow, why such a sad end?
Weeping willow, weeping willow, saying sorry was never done.
Weeping willow, weeping willow, I am left with no one.

Elizabeth Ann Quast

My Little Man

I miss him so dearly, not a single day goes by,
that I don't think about him, he's always on my mind.
It's hard for me not to smile, when I think of how he laughs.
My little boy of yesterday, is now my little man.
I know he loves his daddy, he shows it every day,
it's daddy this and daddy that and daddy please come and play.
I'm wrapped around his finger. I'm in the palm of his hand.
My little boy of yesterday, is now my little man.

Michael E. Cargill

My Mammie's Song

I have washed your windows, draperies, and doors,
not to mention your back while mine was covered with sores.
I have dressed you fit for the most utmost part
and I have made sure that all of your meals were hearty.
I have driven you to every restaurant, library, and store
and I wouldn't leave until you found what you were looking for.
I have told you stories when in the middle of the night you'd awake
and I'd rock you to sleep, for heaven's sake.
I have studied with you for many a night
and I have cleaned you up if you got in a fight.
I have fed you the best medicines when you were sick
and I'd bandage your wounds even when you'd scream and kick.
I have made long braids and pig tails in your hair
and when you were sick I gave you tender love and care.
I have given you the nicest clothes for school
and I have offered you many a blanket on nights that were cool.
I have listened to you on evenings when you'd sit and cry
and on times like that when you learned how birds really do fly.
But now, child, you have to go on your own to be your best
because your Mammie is tired and needs her rest.

Jenna Bond Louden

Amend Your Ways

Killing and stealing is a crime.
Punishment should be given, and sometimes
We should love our fellowmen,
Black, white and tan.
In Jesus' name, we shall do right,
Worship Him both day and night.
Repent from your sins.
Fight Satan, you will win.
Heaven is a place everybody shall go,
Hell is a no-no.
Food and clothing is all we need.
Lust for monies, guide you for greed.
Amend your ways, it will be for the best.
You shall be blest.

Patricia Ann Williams

The River

An angel spoke to me—
And answered an unasked prayer,
The message brought a shaft of celestial light
And suffused my heart with awc and hope-
It illuminated the dark folds of my dusty soul
And opened the windows of my mind
To the fresh, sweet breath of Heaven's promise.
Tears I shed flooded my clay feet,
And swept me up into the current
Of a deep, unfathomable river—
Murky tears of sorrow enfolded me—
As God cleansed them into crystal tears of joy
And sped me onward in my journey.
What river is this?
Which carries me far from familiar thoughts and deeds,
Undeserving of God's love and compassion—
To the unseen shore
Perhaps its name is—Redemption.

Sallie Cynthia Manet

You Don't Know

The liquid emerald opulence which shrouds the Arizona
is glistening in the morning light

Belies the countless hidden horrors beneath

Against the lush dark green of Ford Island's trees the
Blinding white brilliance of the memorial above hurts my eyes

As if to scream, "don't look at me so casually
for there are spirits of men below"

You don't know

Greg A. Peterson

California

Her name is California and she lives up on a ridge
She's wild as the wind that blows
And freer than the river flows

Her name is California and she's brighter than the sun
She lives the wild gypsy life
And she'll be known as no man's wife

Her name is California and he'll love her till he dies
But she's wild as the wind that blows
A raging river, she overflows
If anyone comes near
She's filled with paralyzing fear
Of ever getting close

Her name is California and she'll always be alone
She'll never let him come inside
She'll stay up on her ridge for life
Never coming down
He'll beg for her and plead but she will never come around

Her name is California and she causes him such pain
Her name is California and his love is all in vain

Maranda Harold

Reflections of Life

Through childhood years I am a helpless dove
An innocent girl accepting guidance
Dependent upon their supportive love
Forever in need of reassurance

The relationship changes as I grow
My rebellious attitude seals my heart
From their lives and tears that begin to flow
I must now mend what I have torn apart

Now I'm as old as I remember them
Our lives are separate yet intertwined
Our love has been honed like a priceless gem
I realize they're the best you can find

When they exit our lives for God's great place
Ev'ry child will miss their parents' embrace.

Marie Stelzer

For Those Who Are Left Behind

Hysterical crying
Prolonged goodbyeing
Beloved cat Mr. Brown
Diabetes had put him down.
In my arms his soul escaped
I prayed to God my soul to take
Life had no reason without him.

Spades of dirt
Heart full of hurt
Loss of my friend.
I feel to my knees
Looked up to the trees
And prayed for my life to cnd
The pain was too great.

And the tears from my eyes
Joined the tears from the skies
Falling softly on the ground.
Softly,
On Mr. Brown.
Won't see you soon—Suicides don't make it to heaven.

Lucinda Tanner Howard

What Today Has Mostly Been About

Memorial Day 1996
was when I first sought you out.

Being the sentimental person that I am,
thinking of you has become what today,
Memorial Day 1997,
has mostly been about.

There was a restlessness in me a year ago
I thought satisfying my curiosity about
you might help quiet, or maybe further incite!

I phoned you; you sounded pleased to hear from me.
I was relieved and excited.

I felt welcomed; you felt right.

Which explains my current want and determination for us to
overcome
our real and imagined distances and differences.

No matter that the source of my relief
seems to be a source of your resistance.

Thinking of you
has become what today has mostly been about.

Carla Johnson

As Beautiful As He

I felt his smooth soft hand, moving across my cheek.
My eyes were closed, but I took a little peek.
At his glowing green eyes,
Brightening up the night.
Like the shining of the moon, filling the sky with light.
I twisted my finger around his curly black hair,
His hair was a shiny silk letting out a shining glare.
I place my hand softly on his small firm waist,
As he looked at me with a beautiful smile formed
Across his face.
The night was lovely, as beautiful as he.
His hair was so wavy, like the currents of the sea.
I moved my hand softly on his beautiful brown skin.
I place my had on his large chest,
As if touching a piece of tin.
I can't believe how beautiful a man can be.
Especially like the one I love.
As beautiful as he.

Karen C. Willoughby

The Purity of Life

Fill me with the purity of life,
As children cry and crime prevails,
Give me the warmth of a mother's hand.

Fill me with the purity of life,
Let me not forget the fragrance of a sweet rose,
Or the loveliness of fresh fallen snow.

Fill me with purity of life,
As I walk in the stillness of morning dew,
Let me be the audience to a meadow lark's song.

Fill me with the purity of life,
When shadows fade
And light turns to darkness,
Let me know that God's hand will be in mine.

Janice K. Barr

Being Small

A Beetle is my best tin lizzie
Driving fast I make it dizzy
I have a private bumblebee
Its hanger is a redwood tree
I house myself within old trash
My furniture is your lost cash
A deep rain puddle is my lake
To walk around it takes a day
A well grown lawn provides the goods
It serves the purpose of my woods
Hunting for my daily feed
I hide myself within the weeds
I prey upon the little bugs
And watch out for the slimy slugs
Now for fun I play my sports
I even have my own golf course
Baseball's played with sticks and pebbles
Football simply sticks with rebels
Being small I have it all
Except I can't play Basketball.

Jason Merrel

Turn To The Light

My friend, if you're lonely, sad and depressed,
You feel you have nothing and never been blessed.
You've tried everything this world has to give,
But you're so unhappy you don't want to live.

Turn from your darkness and living in sin,
Open up your door and let the Light come in.
Behold! I am knocking at the door of your heart,
If you will open I'll give you a new start.

Don't worry about others or what they will think,
Be an inspiration and hope they won't sink.
They'll wonder what's happened when they see you glow,
Asking you questions, they'll all want to know.

Then there'll be others trying to turn you away,
Hoping you'll come back to your old way.
But the Light that is in you will always be,
If you'll just hold on and let them see.

12-7-94 (6:30 A.M.)

Joan Jereb

Destiny

The world is a merry-go-round,
a place of ups and downs,
A place of never ending uncertainties and decisions.
A place where no one knows of tomorrow
and only blurs of yesterdays.
Where do we go from here?
Is it right to wish for some form of happiness
or should we go through life with only hints
of what we expect life to be.
Life is short and only we can fill it with
the fullness it is meant to be.
We should seek to find what destinies our lives
long to fulfill and capture each precious moment
We ourselves have every right to deny ourselves
whatever we feel we cannot conquer.
But that's it, we deny our own selves
and by that we can not fulfill our destiny.

Sherry Netto

February Snow

Have you ever examined a February snowflake,
They have a most peculiar shape
As tiny hearts they come tumbling down
Filling the air with love all over town
And when you walk in a February snowstorm
It's the embers of love that keeps you warm.

His fingers were a little numb
His gloves he'd forgotten, how dumb,
To last nights date, his love he wanted to show,
So off he trudged thru the new snow.
Jack Frost was biting at her nose
But she could still smell last night's rose,
Today, it was a simple daisy that she bought
She wanted to play 'He loves, He loves me not."

June may be the time to be a bride
But it's February's snow that turns the tide
As the tiny hearts come tumbling down
Filling the air with love all over town.
Yes, when Cupid's arrow hits its mark
The fire of love ignites from just a little spark.

Marguerite Gordon

An English Couple

On the porch in our rockers we sat
Me in my muslin you in your hat
We reminisce and speak of our flight
Children, grandchildren, home and such like
America our new land is what we are at
The chattels came too, and the black and white cat
Your brow is furrowed with the strangest of sight
Another warm humid American night.
Loving memories, dear thoughts, friends, oh what a mishap

Everything so different even to turning a tap
But we sat star gazing on through twilight
Wondering if tomorrow with effort we might
Smile and slowly begin to adapt
Lovingly your eyes meet mine, twinkling across the gap
We did right Mother, never mind the great plight
Age gracefully and together as only our right
Forward go, memories away, sigh and look forward to daylight

Sandy Darch

Far Away

Far away, walking through the trees
Mountains, hills are all she can see.

Pacing forward, not looking back
Trying to escape the memories of her past.

Tears trailing down her cheeks
Her goal to find a new life she seeks.

To start over again, was it too late?
She can only wonder, hope, and wait.

The pain, the betrayal she keeps inside
Whether to trust anyone again, she must decide.

She only wishes she had a friend
Her broken heart they'd help her mend.

Far away, walking through the trees
A person in the distance is all she can see.

Kelli Conkey

1995 Apple Crop

The goldenrod is yellow, and the corn is turning brown.
The trees in our apple orchard with fruit are not bending down.
The answer to this question we will soon see,
Was caused by wasps, hornets, not a bee.

The woods are nearby, to the southwest,
That is where the hornet's nest.
An apple is eaten down into the core,
And the hornets are hunting for more.

The hornets think their feast is free
So I gathered the good apples left on the tree.
The frost hurt the fruit, when tree was in bloom.
Most apples are not good to store in a room.

Some apples have spots of rot,
Cut that out, and cook rest in a pot,
Or peel apples, core, and slice.
Put slices in crust, add butter, sugar, and spice.
The smell coming from oven—oh, what a treat!
An apple cobbler none other can beat.

Hilda May Hyatt

The Difference

Some of them hunt and kill for fun
Some of them destroy their young
Some abandon one another
Others don't even care about their sister, brother, or mother
Some are searching for what there is in life to get
Others have never found it
Some don't care about their own health
and some only care about their own wealth
Some you can't turn your back to
Others you can't let near you
Some save lives right from the heart
Some have helped young right from the start
Some always stick together
They remain a family like birds of a feather
Some have found out the meaning of life
Others have always known
Some will always be there for you
To rely on, jest with, and converse to
It's not hard to see who they are
They're the human race close and far

Priscilla Williams

Who Am I

My mother says I am quiet and shy,
My husband sees my shyness as lies.
My father call me his child so meek,
My husband sees my meekness as weak.
My son says I am loving and kind,
My husband said in hell will I dine.
My daughter said like me shall she be,
My husband says he'll go blind not to see.
My friend said, no other friends better,
My husband says all the same flock together.
I ask myself who is wrong, who is right,
I pray to the Father for his guiding light.
I heard a answer so loud and clear,
It said to me, "My love, do not fear,
Courage I give you to do what you can.
The first step, of course, is to find a new man."

Kimberly Y. Jennings

Struggles

It all began before my time
Of how our lives were intertwined.
Be you black or white or purple or lime,
It all began in the course called "mind."

It all began in the physical being
Our burdens were heavy, and our bodies were lean
From dawn to dusk we did toil and sweat,
But giving up, we didn't—not yet.

We moaned and we groaned
We hummed and we sang,
We had to keep going
Until the bell rang.

And when dusk did come
We got our crumb,
For a long days work
And a body that hurt.

And now we lay us down to sleep
We pray the Lord
Our hearts, our minds and souls to keep.

Barbara J. Peters

It's Really Nothing At All

Here I lie on a beach of sand.
Where loneliness can be a beautiful
Feeling and thinking of you is all I do.
Your love is like a waterfall and I'm
Falling so much in love with you.
There's a stream where I go to
I stand there and look into the
Crystal clear water and the sun reflects
Thoughts of your love right through me.
Your love is like and open field and
I'm lost hoping to fall right into your arms.
And when I woke up all I'm
Really doing is sitting and staring
At nothing at all.

Rhonda L. Stoner

Battleground

How can we stand here now with weapons drawn? A battleground
of secret minds and jagged words where once was found
a simple unison where footsteps seemed as synchronized
as one. Now the voices that once harmonized
so well ricochet like bullets striking steel.

With fervor now you stab me with stiletto wit,
wielding accusations you release to seek their mark and hit
with brutal force, the aim precise, impacts plunge deep
into my ears and tender flesh and yet they keep
repeating like a hammer to a bell.

So deep within my bastion aches now swell you cannot feel
the searing pain, betrayal burns, this I conceal
with silent acquiescence. Absurd, I know,
this woman longs for love yet lets your spiteful laughter flow
across me like a thousand tiny tacks.

But in the dark I listen for that fragile, broken voice
that risks to soothe the wounds of day. You have no choice
in waging war within your private battleground, and I
shall be the ready target for your torment, standing by
your lightning rod to ground each bolt of pain.

Sally Houtman

I'm Waiting

I climb this tree.
I'm proud to wait.
From up here it seems
I can just see my mate.

That gold upon blue I see to the west
is surely the tail
of the one I love best.

Oh! in the broad valley at twilight
The tin roofs are bright.
From my treetop I count them
Just one, two, three, four steps
would take me to my gold heart's delight.

Across the bright valley
to the blue mountains beyond
I can still see the tail
of the one with whom I belong.

And when she gets back
Do you know what you'll see?
Two leopards, not one
In the top of this tree!

G. Allen Marburger

Missing You

I sit and think every day
Of you, so far, far away.
I want to see you, to talk for hours.
I want to hug you or give you flowers.
Missing you is a part of my day.
I miss you so much that words can't say,
How much I love you and want to be with you.
I miss you so much, what can I do?
I write you letters but it's not the same.
I want you here to watch my game.
I talked to you on the phone
But I can't see how your face shone
When I made you laugh.
I miss you so much, what will I do?
I miss you so much, I just want to be with you.

Sara Stinnette

By The Lake's Edge

By the lake's edge I sit
Listening to the gentle slap of the waves
While the gentle winds tease the leaves
And the swallows flit in and out of the banks
Circling around, up and down, and back around
Twittering happily they alight on a bar
Seemingly to rest yet surveying their nest
By the lake's edge I sit
The breeze caresses my soul with gentleness
While splaying wisps of hair across my cheeks
And the sun warms my whole being
Then slips behind the fluffy white clouds
Seemingly to play hide and seek
But returns to warm the very depths of my soul
By the lake's edge I sat

Mary C. Hollands

On A Clear Night

Endless, fathomless, timeless, infinity
Rapturous, alluring, enthralling beauty
Curtain of darkness, sparkles of light
Moving and still, transfixing the sight,
Visions of globules, globes and a veil,
Looking into the past, knowing little detail,
Awe inspiring
As seen from a microbe by a microbe
Whose existence seems
As nothing in the cosmic city,
Yet endowed by creation with eternity.

Hallet T. Allen

Our Love Is Fate

I can feel true love in the blink of an eye
As I pray to the heavens and my God in the sky
There's not such a feeling that is so divine
When two beats make one as does your heart and mine
I've loved you now since the day I was born
And the day that I left, my heart slowly torn
The years we've been apart have shown me the wrong
Cause when we're together our love is still strong
So I ask this question, what should we do?
You still love me and I've always loved you
Should we keep testing fate and take this great chance
Or get back together and let love enhance
Rushing our love would be a mistake
But staying apart, my heart would surely break
So let's look eye to eye and feel with our heart
Because it's been too long that our love's been apart!

    M. Kent Pletcher

The Invisible Ones

Oh, what trauma we pass through, as we view
The passing years of our frailties; Weakenings, forgetfulness.
Growing old has been our lot, yet most have taken it in stride.
Wrinkles soon appear; our hair (should we be blessed with some)
Turns gray and thins so mercilessly;
And dying only adds to our frustration when we hear:
"Is that who I think it is?"

Yet, others look at aging—no, they don't look, except away!
We soon become the invisible ones.
Folks look past us, as if we were not there,
Because they do not want to see what has to be.
The losses we endure, especially dignity, and modesty . . .
Yes. they look right by and we feel stunned, of useless worth.

Why should this be? There is not one of us who isn't growing old.
Who will not pass this way, someday;
So, why are we ignored as if we were not there?
Why are we so invisible, as if we were not there?

Would it not be better that you take my hand,
And help me find my way in this unknown land?
Walk arm in arm with me, through every change
To give me courage as I face the range of varying views.

    George Leo Michel

America Come Home

Like the prodigal who wept from hunger
and loss as he fell down in the mire.
Our streets show little more if you take
a close look for our very souls are on fire
He realized what he'd left as he'd ran to ruin
making his life's breath in vain
For no longer did he hold to the oath
of our heart we will live in Jesus name
Now his cries were great, they wracked deep
his being as he fled to glimpse familiar land
And his father did make welcome
and great rejoicing was known all around the land
America, as you grieve your dead and wounded
and wonder; hope, where are you?
I invite you to follow the path back to it's beginning
for your breaking is long overdue
I know arms are outstretched and tears and blood
in prayer flow across bone
And I can hear the master pleading
America, come home!

    Turyla Gunter

Poison

Kissing you softly so sweet, you believe every word I say.
It is all a lie. No love, just hate. I like to play games.
I am poison and soon I'll be running through your veins.
Destroying all your dreams, poisoning your heart and mind.
I am in control, you are forever mine.
Plotting and playing games when I am with you.
My poison takes complete control, I shall leave now.
Shortly, you will begin to go into withdraw.
Body and soul torn apart, I take you away.
You are no longer able to love, for my poison ran deep.
Remember not everything is as real as it may seem.
What you thought was a sweet and innocent romance,
Was nothing more than poison and hate.

    Meredith Smith

Road to Destiny

As I journey on this road to destiny
My philosophy of independence
Shows signs of dependence

No longer can my mind
Brake the speedy passions of my heart

No longer can I travel
the roads between love
and casual friendship

Being of one ignition
without attachments
riding in many directions
room for only me

Dependent, I am becoming
Room for only one passenger
you and I

Riding together in unity
Oneness- one map, one direction, one goal

Hoping to reach my destination in God—
Loving you

    Iris Jackson

Confidence

Although I write a lonely man,
a single grain in a desert on sand,
one day, one week, or maybe a year,
I'm going to conquer this tired tear,
I only have to ask, but when.

And though I may not be much yet,
in a kings chair I'll one day sit.
A courts jester may deserve a hand,
but its my destiny to rule this land.
These sores I must first mend.

A broken heart, a tortured soul,
a lover's touch I do not know.
No matter how hard I've tried, I'm still alone,
because I refuse to become a clone.
Yet one day I'll surely shine.

I've worked and I've scratched,
my problems, and soul are very well matched.
Although today I may remain a pawn,
remember, every knight first has a dawn.
This could be mine!

    Jason Siscoe

I Wish

I wish I knew my grandma as well as my mom
She sounded very nice
And when the wind blew it rolled the dice
And her life went into a deep
hole lost and never found again.

All I have left of my grandma is a few photos
and things so when the wind blows I can hear
her lifting her wings and whispering
I love you my dear
and the voice echoes in the night
with the sparkling stars
and I sit there and wish I knew
my grandma as well as my mom.

Holly Theresa Bauer

Insomniatic Soul

The sky is gorgeous
at three in the morning;
gray and purple and white and blue.

The peaceful trees,
that could seem foreboding
with someone else's perspective,
cast long shadows on the phosphorescent
green of the lawn,
lit by the streetlight,
peering sullenly through the trees.

I notice all this as I lay in bed.
I cannot sleep.
It is not unusual.

My soul is old and weary of its subsistence
on this astrological plane the uninformed
mistakenly call life.

The journey isn't over for this old, wounded warrior.
My soul cannot rest,
And neither can I.

Amy Brychta

What Is Love?

You have a boyfriend—you call it love?
You think it will last forever, but does it ever?
What is love to you?
A one day affair? A kiss on your cheek?
Or do you call teenage love an infatuation?
Infatuation is the world that should describe teenage love.
Infatuation is being obsessed with the one you desire.
Love is a connection and an understanding of traits and
personalities. Committing more than just your lips,
it is committing your heart to the one you cherish deeply.
Love accepts the truth and seeks nothing less.
Love comes through growing up.
It comes through being patient, for you can't rush true love.
Love comes through being yourself.
It arrives if you do not chase it.
It's more valuable than thousands of diamonds,
It's more expensive than all the money in the world,
yet it comes to the poorest of all people.
Love is something no one can change, but changes you so easily.
For the strongest thing in the world is that of love.

Kaily Lam

Jelly Beans, Oh, So Yummy!

Jelly beans, jelly beans, oh so good.
I would eat them all if I only could.
Jelly beans, jelly beans, oh so nice.
More flavors than numbers on ten dice.

Popcorn flavored, oh, how bad it tastes.
I throw them all away, oh, what a waste.
Oh, it's the peach that I love so much.
I love them so, I won't let you touch.

So many beautiful, bright colors,
Purple's the favorite of my mother's.
Red, orange, yellow, purple and blue.
These are colors, just to name a few.

Speckles, solids, stripes, and polkadots.
Some look like they have the chicken pox
Some jelly beans are big, some are small.
No matter the size, I love them all.

Lori Summers

We The Women

For centuries, we the women were owned, slaved and cheated,
We were used, abused and were always mistreated.
Men didn't know the strength of a woman,
What powers we possess, is known to no one.
We the women are the roots of the tree,
Stronger the roots, stronger is the tree.
Every branch, every leaf we nourish and nurture,
With kindness and love 'cause that's our nature.
All we need in return is respect and your love,
And we'll keep on doing all the above.
When the water of love stops coming around,
The roots get weaker and the tree falls down.
In this changing world we must stand strong,
'Cause we must make sure that nothing goes wrong.
We are tender and loving like a soft rose petal,
But are also the pillar of strength as strong as metal.
This thought is for you all men out there,
If you want to listen and if you want to care.
Together we are conquerors we are useless apart,
So the choice is yours, be stubborn or be smart.

Gayatri Singh

Family Reunion

It's funny how life, turns and dips and curves,
How it tantalizes, excites and jangles the nerves;
What we found to be true from days gone by.
Twenty years down the road makes us laugh, weep or sigh.
From yesterday's sorrow, comes the joy we share now,
Echoing the terms of endearment to which we will bow.
And down through the years comes the roar of delight,
Echoing the sentiments that brighten our day, our night.
In a smile or a nod or a twist of the head,
In a shrug or a bob or a word that is said,
Comes reflections of memories of those we once knew,
And confirment of ties to a small precious few.
Then, though we part, in our hearts we will hold,
All the love and the laughter, the words spoken bold;
Through the turns and the dips 'till its days gone by,
When we hug and embrace, when we laugh, and we cry.

Nancy A. Rogers

Death's Whisper

We sensed your approach . . .
muffled utterances of
dwindling days and restless nights;
years winding down. Scent
of your entrance; you fluttered in—
not loudly enough to ruffle the air.
Wistful eyes looked beyond my presence;
Ethereal.
I cursed your intrusion;
you bruised my heart.

I'm learning now . . .
many colors of grief. A sweetness
has dulled the edges;
it goes down easier now.
Your piercing sting, softened;
not forgotten.
Priceless jewels—polished and bright—
I keep my memories afloat;
Reverence.
Reflection of the days before you whispered "Come."

Gwen Ullo

Face in the Mirror

To be me is to GIVE
So much of myself that there is almost nothing left.

To be me is to ASK
For answers that are only the truth in fiction.

To be me is TRY
To become the object of another's desire.

To be me is to HATE
Not other people, but myself for my own imperfections;
Not life, but the way I've had to live it so far.

To be me is to WONDER
If I will ever be as good a mother as my own.

To be me is to WORRY
That I will never say the vows or wear the sacred ring;
That I have already made one too many mistakes.

To be me is to WEEP
About poverty, disease, ignorance, and loss.

To be me is to LOVE
In a way that it yearns to be reciprocated.

To be me is to DREAM
Of a complete happiness that is not inaccessible.

Tracey L. Grimes

A Rose

A rose to me, is the queen of all gardens.
Who sits beneath a budding crown,
Upon God's golden, rich, brown ground.

A rose to me, is wicked woman,
For with her thorn, all hearts are torn.

A rose to me, is a modest maiden.
With a dainty flair, and lovely red hair.

A rose to me, is a blushing bride.
Who stands up tall, in all of her pride.

A rose to me, is a ruby gem.
For she stands above all,
On her tall, emerald stem.

A rose to me, is a beautiful growth.
And through her veins,
Flows the blood of the earth.

A rose to me, is a magical thrill.
And when I die,
With roses, my coffin,
I pray you will fill.

Patricia A. Simon

Seasons

The winter has been, oh, so long,
The winds so fierce and cold;
But we've had friends and family
To encourage and to hold.

It matters not how sharp the wind,
How deep and cold the snow;
When we are with the ones we love,
Our spirits still can grow.

The spring brings sunny warmth and rain,
The trees begin to bud;
Within our spirits something stirs,
And, oh, it feels so good!

Then summer flowers begin to bloom,
They fill our world with color;
And as we drink in their beauty,
Our souls seem so much fuller.

When autumn leaves change color and fall,
The earth prepares for rest;
The God of all creation
Keeps creation at its best.

Evelyn Klein

A Civil War Poem

From 1861-1865 there was a war.
It was filled with sadness, blood, and gore.
The North wanted to free the slaves, the South did not.
That is the issue for which they fought.
U.S. Grant was a general from the North.
On and on they traveled forth.
They died, they fought, they killed.
With determination they were filled.
In the end the North did win, the South was defeated.
But sadly the nation's strength was overly depleted.

Anthony Weaver

Spring

A breath of Spring reached up to touch the sky;
A bird looked down and glimpsed a tender leaf.
The hands of time gave leave to Winter's sigh,
As Nature ushered in Spring's warm relief.

A joyful sound resounded through the hills;
A bird began to sing a cheerful song.
The music wafting 'round the rocks and rills
Reverberated Springtime all day long.

The pollen dusting flowers with new life,
Its fragrance gently dancing through the air,
The blossoms permeating Winter's strife
Created balmy breezes ev'rywhere.

The cold of Winter freezes into night,
As Springtime dawns and warms the morning's light.

Amber Abercrombie

Bruises

I want to get out of here.
The screaming voices, the tears.
She yells at him.
He yells back.
They continue to yell forever, it seems.
It's like visiting someone you don't want to see.
The time goes by so slowly.
It feels like hours but when you leave
it's only been fifteen minutes.
That's the way it is when they fight.
The time drips by like a leaky faucet
but the clock ticks just the same.
They never get physical
but that's not the point.
The bruises on the heart are large enough.

Carrie Davis

It's Just A Loan

From the lives you've touched,
From those who love your smile,
We all have one thing in common,
We'd all walk a mile,
To hear you laugh,
To see your eyes dance again.
From us who've known you through the years,
From those you've watched grow.
From the one's who've loved you most,
We know tomorrow will come,
Whether we see each other in a year from now,
Or when forever begins.
Happiness is sharing,
So we'll put you on loan for a while,
Forever will come.
And He who paid the debt
Will return you to us.
Have fun while you're away,
From those who love your smile.

Laura Dare Merrill

Approach The Lord

So in prayer I approach the Lord
Lord, I believe, help me in my unbelief
I so much want to surrender
I want to grow beyond this grief
I want to learn to really love
To be nourished like the tender leaf

I want to see your hand in every failure
Your victory in every defeat
May you have compassion upon my struggle
That I may know I am strong when I am weak

So in prayer I approach the Lord
Lord, have mercy on me, a sinner
All my attempts to imitate you
I simply offer you as a beginner
Create in me O Lord a loving heart
That your good works I may not hinder

Karen A. Zabielski

All We Have Met

As this chapter in our lives comes to a close,
We must look back and reflect on the paths we chose.
No matter who we are or what we have done,
We are assembled here together and we stand as one.
As part of the generation which shortly will lead,
It is time to step forth and give the world what it needs.
It is time to show them the strength we possess.
It is time we live up to the demands of success.
High school has provided us with a place to learn.
And a place to discover what it is for that we yearn.
We have become a part of all we have met
And the lessons we have learned we must never forget.
To the world and its ways we are no longer naive,
Our eyes have been opened and it is time to achieve.
We have faced many trials and overcome many fears.
We have shared times for joy and endured times of tears.
High school was a place where we had the chance to grow.
It is now up to us as to where we will go.

Krista Granato

Love

Every time you hold me I feel so safe
You make me feel like a beauty queen
When I am not with you it feels like a part of me is missing
I love you
I love you more than life itself

We have had bad times but our good are so much better
I don't know what I would do without you
You are the world for me
I love you I love you more than life itself

The happiest day in my life was when I knew for sure we
Would be together forever
To hear your voice or to be with you I would fight the world
Till the day I die I will love you with all my heart
I love you I love you more than life itself

Poonam Patel

Christmas Telephone

Thank you my dear for calling here.
We can't come to the phone,
that's perfectly clear.

We're chasing around a fat little man;
He says that he's lost
and his name is Santa Claus.

I say to you, "I don't belive that's true."
It's not Christmas Eve,
so what's he got up his sleeve?

He has a long white beard
and he's wearing a red suit.
I said, "I don't give a hoot!"

You get out the door and take your pack.
When we get rid of him, we'll call you back.

Anna Mae Sewell

Untitled

I didn't look Death in the eye
But I caught a glimpse of His shadow.
I never knew He was outside the door
Hovering in the dark,
Waiting for a chance to come in.
But I had the strength and the heart to survive,
Death wasn't going to enter my body this time.
But He'll be back eventually
And I hope I have the courage to live.
Death is more patient than I am,
He stalked me for fifteen years.
I never knew He was looking over my shoulder
Until I saw His shadow slip away.
I've won the battle
But someday, He will win the war.

Melissa O'Kelley

Poetry

Poetry isn't simply words written on paper,
and a poem isn't just a rhyme.
Those words are emotions that must be expressed,
and feelings that developed over time.

Poetry tells the world all the things you feel inside,
it lets people know all the thoughts you hide.

Poetry is an artform that takes on its own special meaning,
and it hides new understanding for everyone who's reading.
So take the time to read a poem or maybe even 2,
and get in touch with a whole new world that hides
inside of you.

Michelle F. Moseley

Sisters

It would be the first time I've seen my sister in years,
And I wondered if there would be tears.
There was a lot of curiosity . . .
To see if there would be any similarities.
When we met I could see her eyes in mine,
And I could hear my laughter in hers.
. . . Oh yes, there are similarities . . .
We have masked the pain and secrets we've kept,
And concealed the silent tears we've wept.
Her love for me is in the dream webs she weaves,
My love for her is in the books sent to read.
Look into our hearts and you will see
. . . There are so many similarities . . .
The distance between us are miles apart.
But my love for her is deep within my heart.
She is my sister . . . yesterday, today, forever,
. . . And I miss her.

Sandy Patnode

The Room

The room is dim that each is in,
The walls are dark, black stripes therein,
Vertically they rise and fall,
And in between it is so small,
A pair of windows at one end,
Yet little information lend,
Such tiny breadth can each discern,
So small is that which we can learn,

Before the walls and after them,
Have lived so many countless men,
Yet little information here,
Our trust in this be placed with care,
Reality is what we see,
We can't be sure, it might not be,
The limits of what we perceive,
Discourage that which we believe.

Jason Siegel

I Wish

I wish that cars were never invented
So the sky would be blue
And the flowers would be bright.
But now that cars have been invented
I'll never see the blue sky
And the bright colors;
It is just polluted.
So then I wish I am older
So I can see the beautiful sky and flowers.

Samantha Bull

Where Are The Fathers?

Another child was shot in our town today;
Another wife was beaten this week.
Who's responsible for all of this carnage?
Certainly not me...

Another boy was lonely in our town today;
Another wife came home to find daddy gone.
Who's responsible for all of this carnage?
Certainly not me...

Another daddy played golf this morning in our town;
Another mother and child attended church alone.
Who's responsible for all of this carnage?
Certainly not me...

Another father is here in our town today;
Another father who sees and hears all we think or do
Who's responsible for all of this carnage?
Oh my Lord, please God, help me!!!

D. D. Ponsell

The Coonhunters

They walk the woods together
On those cold and windy nights,
Listening for their dogs to bark
As the moon shines bright.

Deep into the woods they go,
Up and down the hills;
Will "ole faithful" be the first to strike?
(And will it be for real?)

They hear a yelp, he's on the trail—
Their hearts beat fast with pride;
They hurry closer to the sound
Until they're by his side.

The coon is in the old oak tree,
The dog is at the base.
His master is as proud as can be
Because they've won the race!

Linda Sethaler

You're Not Alone

You may say that you don't have anyone,
But we all know that isn't true.
I can really be your friend
And he, up there, can too!

I know he loves you and cares.
There will be times he might not answer
Because the right time just wasn't there.

I know that he is watching over you and telling you
To keep your head up high;
Soon or later we'll be in his arms in the deep blue sky.

In the room hiding
Away from the world outside.
Trying always to be free
And don't even know the reason why.

I can tell you now and not then
There's no such thing in not having friends.
Love is with you always, anywhere and at home.
I just have three words to say
You're not alone!

Rachelle Rutherford

Pretty Girls

Pretty girls get unbroken stares.
Win Teddy Bears at country fairs.
They get free drinks from hopeful dates,
In the longest lines, have the shortest waits.
Expensive diners, all the votes,
Become cheerleaders, prom queens and ride on floats.
At work they get the quick promotion.
From men receive undying devotion.
Pretty girls get stolen glances.
Have their cards filled at all the dances.
Warnings-not tickets, and pulled out chairs,
Romantic vacations, admiring stares.
The biggest weddings, passionate kisses,
Accolades; no boo's or hisses.
They get favors, respect, whistles and winks.
Quick service and roses, chocolates and minks.
Unending favors, the best invitations,
Compliments, crushes and dedications.
They are protected and comforted. Are never a fling.
Hey, who said looks aren't everything?

Nan Vrana

Over My Shoulder

It was an early summer morning, somewhere living in June.
And today . . . a late evening, dying in fall.
As do the bare trees bend in the wind.
As will the bare trees swell their greens, spring again.
But, like the bare trees . . . we are not.
I now look back to the morning we said goodbye.
Never to see a face that I once did caress,
never a brush stroke here with canvas moistened kiss.
Within the dusk of this autumn day, your memory returns
as a breeze reminding me that winter is on its way.
Just as your image brings me a chill, we are
as cold as any winter could ever feel.
Fate has taken our fortune that we once shared.
To spend, to ruin, to rid, to scar, to regret,
to be happy, to throw it all away.
Never to return, not even a lemonade Sunday.
What was once a warm home has fallen to a cold memory.
I'll always remember what we once had.
But its forward I will march.
Some days sorry, but mostly glad.

Patrick C. Rigney

A Mother, A Grandma, An Aunt

A soft warm smile like the touch of a rose.
A twinkle in her eye.
A tweak on your nose.
A firm thump and a wallop, she doesn't miss.
A warm hug a tender kiss.
Waterfalls of tears through happiness and sorrow . . .
Hoping still for a brighter tomorrow.
Years of laughter and singing, like songbirds free.
Bringing joy and happiness, to you and me.
All quieted now on a calm winter Eve.
A part of God's plan.
A message Received.
Take my hand, seek comfort.
I will help you understand . . .

Willard Miller

She Laughs

She laughs.
Walking down the green humble street,
her hard words kid with playfulness.
I become jocund and upset.

She laughs.
Her chaotic and insane movie was inevitable
I watched, then fell to my knees
dreaming, and asking, "come with me please?"

She laughs.
I'm a fool but that's already clear
my soft heart is filled with fear.
an open wound, not open enough
this is what makes my life so rough

She laughs.
her comic conundrums were harmful to me
I listened with exhilaration and enthusiasm

Her mind goes blank,
she plays with her hair.

She laughs and looks and I'm not there.

Phillip Johnston

Our First Grandaughter

I've just got another name,
just how I don't know
It's not grandfather, grandpa, Paw Paw
It's Po! Po!

At first I didn't know how to take it
because it sounds sort of old
But from the lips of our granddaughter
They could melt a heart of gold.

You know, she didn't stay a baby long,
she's already two and a half
Why she can sing all the nursery rhymes,
dance and make you laugh
Her vocabulary is so vivid, she
makes most people gasp.

How she knows how to do all this I'll never know
But she unlocks the door to my heart
When she says "Po Po"

Just when I thought that God had granted my every wish
I'd trade them all in a second just to hear
Please "Po Po" I need a hug and kiss

Bill Hanselman

Mistakes

When my one true love turned me down,
I wanted my life to end.

One night I decided to make this happen,
But told no one, not even my best friend.

I used a knife,
A knife, to end my hopeless life.

But now I'm gone,
And boy, was I wrong.

Even though I had no lover, I still had friends.
And I got good grades.
But now it's over,
This parade.

I wish I could come back now,
Being dead is such a horror.
Considering I finally realized,
I had so much to live for.

Kylie Bycroft

A Beginning

I received a letter from a friend today;
Her heart was heavy—her dear husband passed away.
Time will help to heal the wound of grief;
Time and friends and love and her belief.

She spoke of the years of love they shared together.
The times of joy and pain they had to weather.
It was all too short, for time has a way of flight,
Like little birds that vanish in the night.

Locked in her heart is the beauty of their love
And a picture of him "waiting there above."
The "good and special times" throughout the years
Bring thoughts of happiness mingled with her tears.

Jesus knows the storm she's going through.
Her faith will grow as he shows her what to do.
Her strength will come from day to day and then,
She'll think of this as beginning, not an end.

Dorothy J. Johnson

Heed My Words

Thank God everyday,
For the blessings, that come your way.

Live your life, with head and heart,
Always together, never apart.
For only with the two,
Will happiness, find you.

Take not the path, that leaves you alone.
Stay open, for a love all your own.
For love cannot be bought or sold,
But it is the most precious gift to hold.
For it will keep you warm at night,
And with the dawn, it will sunshine bright.

Fall not to the devil, with all his sin.
You must never, never let him win!
Always look to God up above,
For only he, knows all about love.

Alone you will never be,
If you heed these words from me.
    Tammie L. Brink

Animation

Suspended by seven strings
Six senses and one unknown quantity
Without a pilots license or seaman's skill,
We walk unevenly through a world
Rotating on an ancient axis.
Balancing books and articles on world events
Who stops to see who's standing next to them?
Have we traded touch for television
Or a window for the silver screen?
By turning channels or the pages of a novel
Can we fully grasp the generations of society,
Each with a variation on the theme?
The mechanics of our minds
Cannot be so controlled
Or our suspension so secure
That we fail to sense the fire flickering out.
Who's ready to fan the flames?
    Victoria Hale

Joined At The Heart

Joined at the heart,
are two people who care
and are always willing to take a dare.

Joined at the heart,
is a couple who can see
that being a couple isn't just about "me! me! me!"

Joined at the heart,
is a young husband and wife
who will always share a wonderful life.
    Amy Barber

My Shangri La

As the sweet zephyrs pass me by,
Scented with your loveliness I sigh.

Dreaming always of the place,
I last saw your heavenly face.

Night time brings no end of toil,
I no longer am on mortal soil.

The light of morn will soon appear,
There is no light without you dear.

Oh God, how can I thank you for this vision,
This love of mine that has arisen.

So if my life be sacrificed and omitted,
I will always be your slave,
If I may be with the one I crave.
    Victor Jones

My Angels

God, do you let angels out to play?
If you do, I know I saw them today.
One was dancing on a bough of crimson leaves,
Others were chasing each other in an early fall breeze.

They glided down on the backs of some swans
Twirling and laughing in swirls on a golden pond.
Their happiness and laughter filled my heart
As I felt I was indeed, a part.

Yesterday at eventide, they glistened in the rain.
Their merriment filled the sky as they played and as they sang.
They rode on bolts of lightening, drank raindrops as their tea
The rainbow was their playground, a show just for me.

They played again on the new-fallen snow
As the sun came out making diamonds below.
They were so happy to play and be free
As we all laughed together and they waved to me.

God, thank you for letting your angels play
Where I could watch and enjoy them today.
This was a beautiful blessing for me
And a promise to know someday I'll be—an angel let out to play.
    Mary Nelle Dill

Only In My Dreams

Only in my dreams is there no sorrow,
Nothing but love and peace for tomorrow.
In my dreams the whole world is filled with love,
Love that hangs over us, like clouds from above.
No wars, hatred, prejudice or strife,
But equality and justice in everyone's life.
In my dreams we all live in harmony,
Every skin color united in one family.
When we look upon one another,
We'd see our fellowman, sisters and brothers.
We all bleed and we all cry,
We all laugh and we all die.
Only in my dreams are there no crimes,
A world I long for in better times.
If only the dream could be real
Imagine how we all would feel.
We'd feel the pains and joys of each other.
Without checking first, to see who's of what color.
Only in my dreams, I would hope not,
For in reality we'd gain quite a lot.
    Deborah McCullough

Beauty Becomes You

In my eyes what do I see
I can't describe but don't know why
For I am lost in those eyes staring back at me
The answer is as clear as the bright blue sky
In my eyes it's sure true beauty

She stands alone with a body like Venus
So perfect not the slightest flow
If she were mine nothing would come between us
All would look upon us in awe
And worship the ground beneath us

In my eyes who do I see
A young, gorgeous, living doll
With those eyes looking back at me
There is one word that says it all
What I see is pure, true beauty

In my heart what will I do
I ask myself what I want of her
One thing that comes from a heart so true
I ask of you what is the answer
My love beauty becomes you!
    Blaze A. Tyson

The Ray

On a cold winter's day
Came a wonderful light.
It was a warm sun's ray
That was blindingly bright.

The ray went over a hill,
It passed over the sea.
It shone onto a windmill,
And passed by you and me.

The ray peeked into the windows,
It went through the front door.
It played with a kitten named Crow,
And flew out the back door.

As the ray started its long journey back,
It soared over many fields, mountains, and trees.
It slipped passed a little duck that went quack,
And it left the land of the birds and the bees.

Krissi Hubbell

If I Could Fly

If I could fly,
when I went to fly,
I would say good bye.
I would have so much fun,
I could reach the sun.
I could pretend I was a bird or a swan,
pretty soon I would be gone.
I could be whistling a song,
that might of been long.
I could even fly on a toy while I was in my sky,
But why would I?
Then I would go home,
and that would be the end of my poem.

Elliott Brafman

Son to Father

Father teach me to do what you do
Teach me how to be like you
Tell me all your words of wisdom
Sing to me from where I come
Let me follow in your footsteps too
Don't let me fall by the wayside
Let me be a man like you.

In this life there are many perils
If you teach me things I'll make you proud
Please let me play your beloved banjo
I promise I won't play too loud.

I ask you dad for the lessons
The good the bad and sad ones too
If you give me all your love and guidance
And now and then perhaps a clue
I hope that one day maybe just one day
I'll grow and be like you.

Robert Mason Wilson

A Perfect Day

A vine full of red roses all clustered together,
A May day with splendid weather,
Green luscious trees all around,
Not one cloud in the sky can be found.

A cardinal sitting high on an electric wire,
A barbeque grill with the start of a fire.

A breeze that gives the trees just a tiny sway,
Adds just the right touch to a perfect day.

Bobbie Joyce Lewis

If I Were Rich On Mother's Day

If I were rich on Mother's Day,
I'd take my mother out.
I'd take her to a baseball game,
And, boy, those fans can shout!

We'd go to dinner and movie,
And then maybe a Broadway show.
Then off to an amusement park.
How fast can that roller coaster go?

We'd go out for ice cream,
Then play on the computer.
And then we'd go for a ride
On my solar-powered scooter.

But I'm not rich on Mother's Day,
And to do that with twelve cents is hard,
So I think that I'll just stay at home
And make my mom a card.

Chava Gila Chaitovsky

Don't Take Love For Granted

Whenever I make an important decision
I try to discuss it with you
whenever I have a difficult day
I seem to forget about it
by spending time with you
whenever I have doubts about what am I doing
I can always depend on encouragement from you
whenever something special happens to me
your happy reaction makes it that much better
whenever I have new dreams
I can depend on support from you
whenever I find myself chasing after the wrong things
a hug from you sets me on the right course
because I realize that the most important thing in life
is your love and I am so fortunate to have you
I thank you and I love you

Diana Fitts

Cowboy Proposal

If you would say yes to me this time
I'd share with you this cowboy life of mine.

My saddle I'd give you to lay down your head
when the rocky ground becomes your bed.

I'd share my slicker to shed the rain
when we spend the day on a soggy plain

From daylight to dark the fences we'll mend
and all of my spare time on you I'll spend

I'll buy you a shovel all shiny and new
for all the irrigating I'll let you do.

The tractor is fixed and ready to run.
I'll let you bail hay now won't that be fun?

You can rope all the cows, and hold them real tight
while I put on a brand, Oh what a sight!

Then after your cooking and cleaning is done
we'll go out dancing and have us some fun.

If you'll say yes to me this time
I'll share with you this cowboy life of mine.

Bobbie Barnes

My Deepest Love

Not from impulsive spirit on this special day,
do I tender this deepest love to you,
but, rather, from wellsprings constant,
love with currents deep springing from
origins unfathomable I have for you alone.

From this time forward onward will it surge
and, eventualities demanding,
meet and overflow all craggy obstacles with torrential
certitude being destined for the warmth of green valleys
dappled with colorfully,
blooming tomorrows beneath skies sunny and blue.

Nothing greater could I bring you than this,
a love with faith in its destiny that in these
green valleys it will meet and intermingle
it's all with another of its kind from the
wellsprings of your love, in oneness fulfilling.

And for that union of on flowing love a greater
rendezvous lies fast beyond—a rendezvous with waters infinite,
a rendezvous with God.

Yet, it has happened even now!
Rev. William J. Davis

You Are For Real

The day I meet you I knew you were fore real.
The look threw your eyes
were as if you were communicating with my soul!
Letting me know you are for real,
although I had no doubt about your genuine,
sincere real, real personality.
Something about the glow on your face
as if it was reaching on to mine
led me to see the true realness
inside your heart and mind.
I truly feel within my mind
you will always be genuine,
because you are honestly for real.
Roshaunda Alexander

Roll-Call

Yesterday, today and tomorrow,
Roll-call here and there
It comes like lightning—the striker—
Victory is ever assured.
And the convivial soil with monstrous mouth is ever ready to gulp
To render this world vacuous,
My turn is right around.

Would someone tell me where we heading to?
Heaven, purgatory, hell, yet a mirage to me.
No matter how obdurate we are,
Cadaver is all our names and fate.
Mankind is bound to throw in towel,
That is the weird side of the game.
Clergies, Yankees, politicians, dictators, terrorists,
Famous or traduce, before death they bow,
So is my turn well-nigh.
Mr. Almighty Death, would you treat good
people with fairness; they wish to stay and pass on
their good deeds and thoughts even to the still-born.
Henry Bate

Jagged Roads

Hardly able to breathe
Face stinging from fallen tears
Head throbbing full of thought
Gone up so many roads
In such a short time
All the roads seem
Jagged and very bumpy
Looking for a nicer road
Wondering if one actually exists
Wishing it would smooth out
Realizing maybe the roads won't ever change
And that I'll just have to find stronger tires
Carolyn Kaufman

Shaky

Once I stood on shaky grounds, not knowing I was there.
With no one around, no sign to say "beware."
I gathered up my thoughts to see what I could do.
As I looked around, I didn't have a clue.
All the things around me, were standing still, you see.
Was this shaky ground I'm on, just meant for me?
I caught myself in time, as I began to fall,
even though my head landed hard against the wall.
The hurt I felt was bad, as bad as it could be,
but it made me open my eyes to what I had to see.
Could this be a warning to stay away from there?
Or a lesson to be learned, with someone else to share?
One thing I know for sure, from what I've been told,
to keep standing there I'll never grow old.
So I'll watch where I'm walking and always look around,
this way I'm sure to keep, my feet on solid ground.
Lodis Landerth

Destruction and Existence

You want to destroy me
You have in your hands the key to deadly arsenal
then why is this trick of deception?

If you want to be my killer
then why are you hiding your hue
in the silent mask of tenderness
and beneath the frivolous expression of your face
are tiny moths of viciousness.

I am a homo sapien
then why so scared?
Life is like a meandering river
going through a destruction and survival.

Justice and unfairness swirl in the stream
A sea of hatred surges, and then comes a turnaround in life.
Mukhlesur Rahman

The Face of Hunger

There are homeless people everywhere
staring at me with eyes of despair
longing for just one bite of food,
they do have the right.

Hungry people in all these places
I look for a smile on these sad faces
yearning for someone to help them live
everyone who has should surely give.

All the people of this big earth
should give away something of great worth
it will fill your heart with joy inside
knowing you helped a child who has cried and cried.
Alyssa Nicole Crea

Saved by a Hero

My master, Jack Nicklaus, was an older lag.
He lugged his tools of torment in a bag.
His greatest pleasure was torture with sticks.
The sadist struck us leaving tiny nicks.

The evildoer drowned my younger bro.
I tried to hide from the devilish foe.
He discarded my oldest like some trash,
and he slammed my head making a deep gash.

He banged my pock-marked face against a tree,
I had scratches, bruises, and cuts on me.
My wicked master rubbed sand in my eyes.
My injured Titliest shell almost dies.

Old Jack Nicklaus whacked me into the Woods.
I stayed down low as quiet as I could.
Under the leaf which shielded me from sight.
I waited in the rain until that night.

My pulverized body felt a relief,
when a young, black boy uncovered the leaf.
He carried me home and washed my bruises.
I wondered why it was me he chooses.

Why rescue someone so white, small and scared,
from the could, wet, dark, and demonic lair?
A feline is a deadly predator,
but Tiger Woods is a hero on tour.

    Ryan Zook

Taste Oblivion

To embrace the beauty of death
To free from its human prison, my last breath
To escape all earthly pain
To cling to the liberty of eternity I'll surely gain
To unchain forever my burdened heart
To knit together my being, torn apart
To slip away and never return
To rescue my wretched soul, too many times burned
To set my spirit aflight
To never again be fearful of the dismal night
To dwell among the stars watching for the dawn
To taste oblivion

    Jen Castellani

The Pilgrims' Faith

A visit to Plymouth and you naturally feel
That your first position is one to kneel
As your thoughts go back to 1620,
And to those who filled our horns with plenty.

I think of the hardships of that little band,
With winter cold in a brand new land;
And how they suffered amid such strife
As they paid so dearly with human life.

And yet their faith withstood the test;
Though great the odds they did their best
To build a land so all could share
In love of God, and know His care.

I'd like to feel that 'tis true today,
As we bow our heads to God to pray,
That the courage they had we still attain,
And the Pilgrims' faith was not in vain.

    Juanita Bennett

Life Is An Amusement Park

Life is like a merry-go-round;
unless someone is there to help you slow down,
you will continue to go in circles at an uncontrollable pace
Life is like a roller coaster;
there are ups, downs and an occasional curve,
and, sometimes, the pressure of it all can make you ill
Life is like a kiddie ride;
which you want to get on but can't
because of the responsibilities of acting your age
Life is like an amusement park;
when something goes wrong, you tend to shut people out
and let them back in only when everything is fine

    Julie Rivera

The Wind

I hear you call my name as you brush past.
You mock and whisper behind my back as I turn away,
Attempting to shut my ears and heart from hurtful woes
You refuse to let me forget.

Your touch is malicious and cold
And you slap my face, ruthlessly, with my hair,
Unwilling or unable to forgive me
Of sins and blunders from other lives,
Lived and died; thrown away because of their turmoil,
Pain, or emptiness.

I hear you call my name as you brush past.
The bruises and the pain you have inflicted upon me
For too long, oh so long,
Has left me numb and detached from
The rest of the world.
You have scorned me and broken me down.
Now leave me in my state of agony
And call my name no more.

    Amanda Colleen Leichty

The Day Before

I on one side Sue on the other
Each holding a hand of our beloved mother
She was so thin and frail her color was pale
She's dying we said, as we stood by her bed
She was so ill yet she could smile, still
We knew it wouldn't be long so we began
Singing a song. She sang along with us
Much to our surprise. We couldn't continue
For tears in our eyes
Sue said "go on over and be with Jesus if you
Want to," she said "maybe today", she knew the way
We smiled through our tears remembering the years
We shouldn't be sad she's with her family and dad
And safe in the arms of Jesus

    Marta Thompson

Drink

Oh my poor Henry, all dead and gone away
His life was sadly ended by drowning in May
One night thought left him and in it he sank
To depths of the deep so far from the banks
Before this event he was a mighty fine swimmer
But it all does end up for loathsome little sinners.
He tasted and trickled, then drunk his mouth full
And talk would not stop him, that stubborn old mule
For his death did not come by river or by lake
It came by cheap liquor bought by the case.
Drowning his sorrows, he did that late night
Down dead and gone without even a fight.
And I will not follow his sunken little ship
Oh, I'll never try liquor . . . maybe just a sip.

    Stephen Short

Waiting

I've given up, I'm waiting to die,
For I have failed at everything I've tried.
No one can forgive, no one can forget,
If I were dead, they would I bet.
No matter how rotten, no matter how mean,
When you are dead it's the goodness that's seen.
Why is it that death takes such a toll,
For you're still the same person after all.
So hear I sit Waiting on the reaper
I know he's coming I feel it even deeper.
He knows I'm waiting, Ready to go,
I think he likes to make us suffer
That's why he takes it slow.
He likes to see us, in our agony and pain,
For everything we have to lose
Is his to gain.
Of death I really have no fear,
It's just the wondering of when it will be here.

Jeff Buban

Seed

I had a dream, my heart was fertile
A seed was planted, a seed of love
a seed of love, within my heart
As the seed grew, the roots got deeper
The roots carried my heart,
like a fragile egg in a bird's nest.
The seed was growing into a beautiful flower
The flower and the roots were really one,
They were both growing in opposite directions
But so profoundly connected.
If you cut the flower, another flower may grow
but not until another season
If you dig up the roots, the flower dies
and the roots will follow.

Azita Langhorn

When The Rose Has Left My Cheeks

When my hair has turned to silver and my June's are fall's
September—when the rose has left my cheeks—
Will you care and still remember?
When my eyes were young not faded and,
My voice was as a girl's—my heart was fresh
As morning—will you remember,
Dear when I walk a little slower and,
Thoughts slip my mind—will you caress me
As a maiden as you did in our first spring?
Will you kiss midst the meadows?
Will you beckon when I call?
Will you cherish all our memories?
Will you catch me should I fall?
Will you think of me my darling,
When the song birds start to sing?
Will you think of me in evening—
When the church bells start to ring?
When I am gone away, my love—will you weep for me?

Sherrell Ann Schuster Hatfield

Untitled

There is a tower, I know not where.
An old grey tower, full of woe and care.
Who lives here, in this ancient tower?
That knows not even the sight of a flower?
In this tower, so dark and damp,
Death resides, without a lamp.
Beware oh man, the threat of doom.
And fear the tower, with its darkened rooms.

Deanna Einbinder

Wild Horses

A streak of color
A crack of a twig

A distant sound of pounding
A pounding like a war drum

Then all of a sudden it emerges
A smoke cloud rising up from the prairie ground

The speed of the cloud
Was amazingly fast

In the middle as it neared
Was a group of some animal

The pounding turned to
A roar of thunder

As they rushed closer
Their beauty was stunning
A group of elegant heads
All moving in unison

It was the beauty that
Could be only a horse

They were running for
Their lives, a life of freedom

Elizabeth Schaetzke

The Cross Is Lifted

From the day he be born, he was the one chosen,
To carry their Cross, to feel this great burden.
Although he did cry, he did not ask why.
For he knew there would come the day,
when the Lord above, to him would say.
You my Son, did not stray.
You my Son, did not sway.
Now on this glorious day
I come to you and say.
The burden is yours no longer,
with me you shall be stronger.
Let those who remain,
remember you in my name.
For you are the one
who carried their Cross.
For you are the one
who carried their burden.
And for you my chosen one,
the time has finally come.
For you my most gifted, the Cross is lifted . . .

Robert E. Lubomski

Birth of a Poet

I'm feeling an intrusion
Causing me confusion
Longing lasts forevermore
Still I wonder who's the whore
Staring at the bore
I can almost feel no more
A thought that passes
Only though my soul harasses
Another one stands with the masses
No one cares to wear my glasses
A word to mind has come
Growing feelings that are young
Another poet the bee has stung
Causing silence to become undone
Forgiving the world without demise
Never forgetting to open their eyes
Lust us surpasses in many more tries
Seamlessly wandering throughout the cries
Once to surrender without the prize
Who can remember what between us there lies

Raoul Farer

Jack Frost

Who was the greatest artist for landscape?
Why, it was Jack Frost, for goodness sake.
From late fall through early spring;
Jack Frost would be right out there doing his thing.
He created fantasy forests and landscape on windowpanes.
And when the sun started to rise in early days;
The scenes on the windowpanes would slowly melt away.
The sun illuminated Jack Frost's pictures,
Made from a cob web design;
The pictures looked fragile—like lace so fine.
As chilly as the weather was outside;
Jack Frost showed up on the windowpane with pride.
How will I remember our big old farmhouse,
And those fences around our lanes;
I miss Jack Frost designing our windowpanes.

Vi (Lee) Ford

Excuses

Society is falling for many reasons
The main one being our kids

You have kids payin' for their parents mistakes

Daddy left so Mamma can't stand to look at you
"I never knew love so I can't show it"
"I'm workin' to support them, I have no time"

Excuses, Excuses

I really don't give a damn

It brings tears to my eyes to watch my peers fall
 or slowly fade away 'cause no one cares

To watch them learn the hard way . . .
hands on . . . even if the first try just may be the last

To see and realize that they have no reason to
believe so they don't

I can't stand to see another fall under the pressure
. . . but with no help, what can I do?

Latarsha M. Young

Tradgedy

Tragedy it fills the air
We see it everyday
It's often hard to speak about
But know how much we care

It's hard to hear about some things
They tear us all apart
Like the Oklahoma City bombing
Or an airplane fallen down

There was the Unabomber
Jeffrey Dahlmer, Bundy too
It's hard to see how they did think
And all that they did do

This world has become a tragedy for sure
The wars we fight the take of lives
It's as senseless as can be
We know not what we'll see

If tragedy could end at last
It really would be neat
The world would be a better place
And at last know world peace.

Carol Sterzinger

The Passing

Wings beat silently in the dark
As a form parts the night.
A slender arrow of darkness
Passes quietly over the grasses.

Below all movement stops
As the hunted realize they are preyed upon.
And then, from the darkness,
Two shrieks are heard.
It is the dying scream of the hunted,
Mixed with the exalted cry of the hunter.

As the echoing cries fade,
There is movement once again
As life picks up where it stopped before.
The threat of danger has passed
With the leaving of the hawk.

Kristin Ash

What Is Black

Black is a horse
The feeling of fright
When witches come out
On Halloween night
Black is the night sky
Studded with stars
A cat on the prowl
Running under a big, black car
Smooth piano keys
The magic eight ball
Round black-eyed peas
And little, bitty fleas
Black is olives
Gooey sticky tar
A mysterious penguin
And the mood of a golfer who can't shoot par
Black is velvet
A twist of licorice
The ashes of a fire
And an unanswered wish

Andrea Nichole Roberts

My Best Friend, My Aunt

I hope you know how many times
I've missed you through the years
especially when I was down and so full of tears

And how many times I've wished we weren't apart
but I never let the good times and
great memories of you slip from my heart

And I hope you know how proud I am for us
to be together again
because you're not just my favorite aunt
you're also my best friend

So I hope you know how much I love you
and I always will
Oh, by the way, 46 isn't over the hill
Happy birthday

Dena McDaniel

As One

Two bodies united together as one,
under the mysterious light of the night,
hopelessly devoted to each other with the most
respect and love two could ever have.
So we join to love as one.

Misty Michelle Deese

With The Rising Sun

The shadows fall as the sun gently
sinks beyond the hills . . .
With the darkness dreaded loneliness
barren, void of frills . . .
Makes my heart nearly burst, yet it's
only the pain of living . . .
Then tears I shed while a voice cries
loudly, "I've nothing left worth giving" . . .
The voice dies now to a whisper, pitiful
moaning of a lost Soul . . .
Tears unseen, my cries unheard as I try
to climb from the devil's punchbowl . . .

Dawn graciously waves her golden wand
bringing light where all was dark . . .
With the rising sun there is warmth
and the song of a meadowlark . . .
The aching pain of loneliness drifts away
with the darkness . . . and waits . . .
Waits for shadows to fall when my life
is again in the hands of the Fates—

Hazel M. Masters

An Empty Man

On a desert barren wide, walks a
Rugged man toughened down inside.
His hardened face looks upon the misty
Sandy white. Like a snow-blind wolf,
He searches with nothing in sight,
Nothing, nothing at all but his withered
Shadow still standing tall; he's a Brave Man.
A Man of Great Pride, the last of a
Thousand, the last of his tribe, forced
Into battle with ten thousand in blue;
Shots were fired and the bullets
Flew—forced into battle with sticks
And stones, now the man stands all alone.
All that's left are broken dreams
And the horrid memories of the
Children's screams. Little smiling
Faces of pure delight cry no longer
in the night, swept away from their
Peaceful land; all that remains is a shell
of an empty man.

William Selph

Mother-In-Law

My mother-in-law is honest and bright!
My mother-in-law is like a ray of sunlight!
My mother-in-law has a loving smile!
My mother-in-law is always ready to go that extra mile!
My mother-in-law keeps us tight!
My mother-in-law keeps us in her sights!
My mother-in-law I know she cares
My mother-in-law has always been there.
My mother-in-law, no need for the rest
My mother-in-law, she's the best!
My mother-in-law as you can see
My mother-in-law means the world to me!
Mother-in-law I want to say,
Mother-in-law happy Mother's Day!

John B. Bruce III

The Small Box

I found the small box in the attic
In a trunk of old things from the Twenties:
Postcards from France with pale brunette women
Marcelled, with arms upraised and bare
Exposing brunette hair; it was their way in their day.

A foot-long twist of my mother's brown hair:
Young hair without a trace of gray tied at one end with blue satin
Nearly eighty years ago in her day.

The same pale blue ribbon—it was silk then—
Was tied in a bow round the wall-papered box
Easily undone in my fingers as I reached to open its cover.
Could there be letters from a secret lover?

I opened the box and laughter spilled out
Sliding through my fingers like quicksilver beads.

Laughter filled every corner of the attic:
The laughter of all of those years made me laugh
Till my eyes spilled with tears.

Laughter was her hidden treasure to brighten her darkest day
And fill her daughter's life—my life—with pleasure.
It was her way.

Marilyn J. Perry

Untitled

I remember a time
my life was empty and full of sin
I never once thought about a new beginning
only dreamed about the end.
I remember a time
when depression had me crying at night
And not having any idea about how to make things right
I remember the day
I met two of God's disciples named Darlene and Mark
They gave me this hunger for more knowledge
Then ignited a spark
I remember the hour
when I decided to pray
On my knees begging for forgiveness
"God please wash my sins away."
And I remember the moment
when I heard Jesus whisper in my heart
"I've waited for you my child
I am so glad you came, all you needed to do
was call my name.

Amy Padgett

Recognition (For E.H.)

Perhaps it is not surprising
that I should find you here—
sorrows woven into your hair like sea-roses,
stirring the grasses of remembrance
with your pensive fingertips:

You were ever at the bergamot-scented shrine of Melancholy,
attentive to your Cimmerian oracle,
solemnly brushing tansy across your collar bones
and into the sacred hollow of your throat.

Longtime I tried in vain to draw your attention
to my humble offerings of dawns and daylilies;
your eyes fixed on the gingery shores
of the echoing country of remorse,
you contemplated the dusk in sighs and whispers
and drank the rich, poisoned honey of regret . . .

Yet now—when, in resignation, I turn from you
into the cool, white pillared place within me
and kneel at the priestess-pool of my solitude—
I find your sloe-eyed, elusive gaze finally meeting mine.

No . . . it is not surprising.

Jeaneen McAmis

Beauty of Nature

I witness the beauty of nature in the summer sky at night,
When I see the glowing moon and the stars shining bright,
And the dark trees in the distance that stand so tall,
And when I hear a nearby owl let out a call.

I witness the beauty of nature on a chilly morning in fall,
When I see autumn leaves brush against a city wall,
And the trees as they change from green to red,
And fall into the stream by which the river is fed.

I witness the beauty of nature on a cold winter twilight,
When I see the icicles turn blue in the night,
And freshly made tracks laid deep in the snow,
And I stop and I wonder where they go.

I witness the beauty of nature on a sunny spring day,
When I see the squirrels come out of the trees to play,
And when I see the baby rabbits as they tag-along,
And when I hear the bluebirds sing their beautiful song.

The beauty of nature is all around,
It is high in the sky and deep within the ground,
It is not only a picture, but also a sound,
The beauty of nature is all around.

Amber Cantrell

Dreamland

A place we go, when we are bored,
to be creative, and imaginative,
to be ourselves, to think about
good and bad things, love and hate.
You go there, do get away
From the real world of misery.
Dreamland, the best place
You can ever go, alone,
To be free and gone.

The dark side, we all have it,
Deep in our souls, it lies between,
your emotions, your feelings.
Your heart, it goes, it leaves,
It sometimes stays so long,
When you don't want leave and never return,
But it comes and it goes.
It even makes you hurt
Others and yourself.
You can't do anything about it.
So dark, so cruel, it is the Dark Side.

Monika Bogdanowiez

Dear Bryan

You are my joy, my love, my inspiration,
you are what takes me through the day;
You are the light at the end of my tunnel,
and when I feel lost, you lead the way.
I look forward to sharing your future,
your hopes, your dreams, and more;
So much there is before you,
the whole world is at your door.
Right now you're just a portion,
of what you'll one day become;
It's so hard to just imagine,
that within me is where you're from.
I enjoy you every moment,
and love you more each day;
And as you grow and learn from me,
I too, will learn from you some way . . .

Jessica M. Lopez

Know

If I knew where I was going, I'd be there by now.
If I ever find out, I'll get there somehow.
Until then I think I'll just go with the flow
And try to learn what I'm supposed to know.

If ever I find the place I should be,
Will I be able to act like me?
For now, I don't know which direction to go.
I'll figure it out, but for now take it slow.

I ask myself "Why do they walk alone?"
But know they've created a life of their own.
Am I alone? Yes or no.
Am I lonely? I don't think so.

Happiness maybe the key to life.
But independence prevents you from strife.
The cupid has an arrow and bow,
But he'll never know about love like I know.

Maybe I am headed in the right direction.
Maybe I don't see it from the right perception.
Does anyone care which way I go?
Or am I the only one who cares enough to know?

Andrea G. Noakes

Pursuit

I dreamed you walked among my treasures, eyes ablaze.
Then lines of light as fine as silk began to flow
Between our hearts until cocooned, I met your gaze.
The radiance consumed all discord one could know.

Your auburn locks were glowing, brightening a path
Into those umber orbs so clearly seeking love.
While all who dared oppose were slain in fiery wrath,
You gently beckoned onward—raised a satin glove.

Behind my face my leaden vaults became unsealed.
Unleashed, the golden words; coin and currency
Of honest, precious, true desire; remain revealed.
A princely ransom, yet unclaimed, I cede to thee.

When I awoke, the morning treeline etched her gown
Where strands of sparkling gossamer were trailing down.

J. Delaney Watson

Yesterday

It seem's as only yesterday.
I stood and stared across the brook,
As the water rush down the stream,
The shadow of the trees,
Slowly moves a upon the brook,
I look and wonder at how time so quickly passes,
But yesterday we know has gone.
The birds softly whistle's in the trees.
As the petal's fall from the trees
Quietly I felt the beauty of it all.
Appreciative I am for the days that rushed by.
I stood and stared a cross the brook.
it seems as only yesterday.
So quickly time pass by.
Love and respect we must share,
Then life is worthwhile,
We put our best forward
And pray for a new tomorrow

Mary L. Demps

My Child

My child is here
Born into a world of fear
Born into the unknown
But I am a mother and will always be near.

My child will learn about race and creed
And through faith will be there for those in need.
My child will not discriminate against rich and poor
But will always be there with and open door.

And when my child goes to sleep at night
Looking at all that was wrong and right
My child will say goodnight
Knowing God was there in a very
Special way but also someone else was there
To help every moment along the way

Oh my child how I have watched you grow
From an infant through maturity
And all the way I did know,
You would do me proud as my child
My children I love you so

Maxine Kent

Moving On

The times come for me to move on with my life.
To discard some self-imposed limitations;
Limitations placed because of insecurities.
Insecurities stemmed from traumatic experiences;
Experiences in a subconscious to be buried,
Buried, and yet, serving as a catalyst —
A catalyst giving me strength.

But oh, the agony—the pain . . . the memories.
Memories later resurfacing;
Resurfacing to defeat . . .
Defeat, only momentarily.

I have indeed climbed the rough side of the mountain;
The mountain from which now I see.
See best what to discard; see best what to keep.
Keep some pleasures; keep some pain
Pain and pleasure . . . always as reminders.
Reminders of a forgotten past—
A past turning future mountains into molehills,
And molehills . . . into . . . nothingness.

Barbara Hammonds

Quiddity

There in the whistling wind
Of a dreamscape in a sea with an island
On which we set foot only three times ever
Is the substance of our most puzzling intuitions,
Created for the mind to wander
In immense joy and profound insanity
Without the solace of a safety net
Or a single crutch to hold upright
The wanderers of the Ephemeris (the island)
And the swimmers of the blackest ocean (the dream sea).
The sweetest place ever known to be,
Seen just thrice: in birth, love and death.
Any more, we'd not be human;
Any less and we'd live in the mind's favorite fearscape.
The puzzling stuff of our fantasies which we spawn
Can sometimes turn hideous, too.
At the island wander on, while the dream's still pretty,
Swim the dark waters of the enchanting dream sea;
Wake safely in the solid refuge of home
Before lucidity is endlessly lost.

Amanda Rose Culver

Free

I wish to be as free as the
air that gently blows across an open field
Or an eagle that soars throughout
the sky enjoying the beautiful features
in sight. I ponder the feeling of
flowing like a river with no beginning
Nor an end, as free as a infants'
thoughts of innocence that, if left free
to develop, untampered with by yesterday's
mistakes, tomorrow's failures and promises
today not kept, can grow to expand
pass the universe and be as valuable
as the Kings and Queens that ruled
the earth first but not recognized.
But I greatly wish to be free
Body, Mind and Soul so I can be
Who I am—a man.

John E. Smith

The Cherries

The two lovers afraid to part,
They hold their hands together hard.
Looking at yellow apple moon,
Kissing in little basket lagoon.

Their tiny red hearts are skipping a beat.
(They only look like a simple seed).
You can hear her quiet laugh.
They are the sailors in the Sea of Love.

They lead conversation with their eyes
And wait for the orange sun to rise.
The color of passion is their skin
Closer to each other they lean.

He kisses with feeling her ruby lips
And touches gently her beautiful hips.
They always will together lie.
Together, together . . . until they will die.

Anna Savelieva

Kaitlyn

Do you believe in miracles?

You were born one year ago today,
They closed all the doors;
Because a tornado, was passing this way,
You didn't care, you wanted to be born in April, not May.

Do you believe in miracles?

With a beautiful face and great blue eyes,
And intelligence that's up to the sky,
We all know you will reach great highs,
You're so cute, we all just sigh.

Do you believe in miracles?

You don't know the joy you brought,
And happiness, that we have sought,
There's so much love, that it pours,
We all love you, more and more.

Now, we believe in miracles.

29 April 1997

Bruce W. Clodfelter

A Child's Cry

Mommy, why do you leave me?
What wrong have I done?

Why can't I please you,
and why do you run?

Mommy, why don't you love me enough to say "Goodbye?"
I'm not even four, Mommy, so why must I cry?

Am I so unimportant that you can't take time to try?
If so, Mommy, please tell me, "Why?"

Godspeed, Mommy, and put the drugs aside,
It's much too soon to lose you, so long before you die.

Susan Kiehl-Fisher

The Hanford Reach

There is a great river that flows to the sea,
I know it well and it's a friend to me.
The Columbia runs deep and its path is wide,
But the land has changed much along its side.
Great power has been made by hydro-dams built on its flow,
Also damage unknown except for the few wise that know.
But there is a stretch unchanged of beauty with white
Shining cliffs and many a pristine beach,
It's known as the Hanford Reach.
This reach looking the same for a thousand years,
Its fate now sadly belonging to politicians who
Have big budgets and few tears.
Once home of the Wanopums, native people that lived here,
And still the land is home to the jack rabbit, coyote and deer.
How rich in history and delicate is this place
Even the use of atomic power and its story in the human race.
Drifting now down the silent beach
I hear a whisper, "Save the Reach."

Gregory Hobson

Little Children

Delighted is the child with an imagination
When nature becomes his play thing.
Contented is the child with a few square blocks,
For they stack together!
Gleeful is the child at the touch of a prickly horny toad,
For what is there that feels the same?
Excited is the child at the beginning of a new day.
And why not?
There is no telling what adventure the day will hold.
Happy is the child
For he has a loving, watchful eye upon him at all times.
No wonder he is at peace!
Is it any wonder that God would have us be as little children?

Raechel Durden

Fear

I'm afraid to fall asleep at night.
   in fear that I'll dream about you.
I'm afraid to let my mind go free,
   in fear that I'll think of only you.
I'm afraid to let my true feelings show,
   in fear that you'll be gone.
I'm afraid to let you get too close to me,
   in fear that you'll hurt me again.
I'm afraid to see,
   in fear that I'll see the truth.
I'm afraid to listen,
   in fear that you'll say the words I long to hear.
I'm afraid to speak,
   in fear that you'll hear my secrets.
I'm afraid to feel,
   in fear that the pain will hurt too badly.

Marissa Bracco

Eternal Mother

Possessed of a beauty
certainly not typical by any standards (ethereal and shadowy)
Comparable to the joy of an inspiring novel
or in the sweet droning of the pipes
but never physical!
She reaches into a place, far past the senses
Where you yearn to be whole
reconnected with the essential
with the beginning of all.
Your limited vision cannot perceive
Your soured lips will never taste
Your busy hands can never reach
Your deaf ears refuse to hear

Rest your lids
Silence your tongue
Free your hands
and listen!

Swallowed by her darkness
You will enter the light
Reborn: Free of your senses, you will finally see!

Rachael Maciel

Stirring

Coming back,
falling awake to a blurry world.
Feet pad cold, but soft along the
carpeted kitchen floor.

Why is my kitchen carpeted?
Why isn't everyone else's?

My reflection,
round, abnormal, frightening, distorted.
That's what you get for looking
into a spoon.

Does a reflection mean
that the reflector becomes what it reflects?

Is the moon bright?
So does the spoon become me,
or do I become the spoon?

Funny, I don't feel
any connection.
Who says I should?

So maybe I really am
stirring my coffee.

Duane Lacey Jr.

Fantasy

The sun shone down brightly on the green valley below.
An innocent land lay revealed which had never known hate or sorrow.

Castles made of crystal, reflecting the brilliant light.
A trained disciplined army, which had never had to fight.

A loyal, gentle people with one king to rule them all.
His queen by his side; both fair, lovely, and tall.

A host of wizards to keep them safe, in robes of silver and blue,
Snowy white beards and kindly eyes; everything they knew.

Bold and beautiful dragons gliding majestically through the air.
Kept to guard the palace, the king and queen and their heir.

The young an curious boy, a wooden sword in hand,
A golden crown on his head, the future of this land.

The wizards and the dragons, the young prince and the rest.
Are now no more than a child's fantasy at best.

Lauren Sullivan

The Thoughts of a Trucker

Some people call me a big time trucker.
Some people say they envy me.
But they have no way of knowing,
How lonely this job can be,
I need some more time home with my lady.
So I can watch my kids grow.
But when the phone rings tomorrow,
I'll be back on the road.
I travel around hauling freight from town to town.
I guess I will always be a rolling stone.
If I find fortune in vain,
And lots of people know my name.
That don't mean a thing until,
I get back home.
I get no rest when I'm feeling weary.
I've got to hook up and go.
I've got to be some where tomorrow,
Smile and deliver my load.

Bruce D. Austin

Why Not Tell It Now

In dedication to my son—O'neil St. Clair Small, who died 03/22/93

Why would you wait for tomorrow, to let loved ones know you care
For after the dawn of tomorrow, you may not find them around.
The past is now lying behind us, and tomorrow may never come.
We only have today dear friends to beat upon life's drum.

Why not tell them "I love you now!" say you love them dearly.
For time is like a delicate flower that death soon take away.
Love those around you so that there is never a doubt in mind,
The best time to tell is now my friends, time to work things out.

If you always keep love a secret it cannot multiply,
for love decrease when neglected and, finally, slowly dies.
Hug a brother, sister, wife and children, then, shed a happy tear!
After, love will pay grand dividends, each, and every day.

Eldoreen E. Small

Life Through A Picture

The blackness, so deep, so dark, so bold,
when I draw it, I feel so cold.
My feelings seem mixed, shuffled and rot
should I do as I was taught?
To express my feelings deep inside, and draw my feelings abide.
I feel so closed, tiny and small.
As if my pencil is my friend of all.
I scribble, doodle, shade - but through my picture no one can aid
I lock the door to block my fears
of memories and thought brought out by tears.
My paper and pencil bleed with my heart.
confused, sad - bitter and tart.
The pencils so pointed, sharp, slim; the paper, black, square, thin.
The night grows dreary, mean and cold
I lean to my pencil which draws so bold.
My picture, abstract, confused, messed up
The tears they flow so rapid, abrupt
If my world seems empty for any reason
I go to my pencil to explain the season.
My life so black, so cold; my picture, so dark, so bold.

Jennifer Norris

Icky—With Love

God, you must know you took a good man:
But you are Almighty, you must have a plan.
As we go on with life, we'll try to withstand,
Our hearts will still ache and we'll do what we can.
Remembering the good times now makes us so sad.
He was such a great friend and even greater a dad.
Our hearts go out to Gail, Beautiful Mother and Wife.
Her family is our family for the rest of our life.
God reached out from Heaven and Ray took his hand,
Ray's troubles have ended, he's in God's Precious Land.
We will go on with life until we are free.
Life's just a journey and not destiny.

Randy Hargrove

From You To Me With Love

One night I lie in a bed, not sure of the state my mind was in,
So I began to focus on You - my Lord, my Jesus, my Friend.
You began to show me a love that no man can give,
You showed me how You gave Your Life so that I might live.
You were there for me, before I even began to call,
For, it was You who caught me in the midst of a fall.
As I began to beg Your forgiveness and offer my pleas,
You wiped sin from my head to my feet as though it were dirt from My knees.
Things were great, You held my hand. I thought You were not Around,
But once again You caught me before my bottom hit the ground.
You were there when I felt I was the worst thing in the world,
You treated me as though I was a darling little girl.
But then You showed me a face (my face) of a soul that was lost,
And then You showed me that same face as You died on the cross.
My Lord, my Jesus, my Friend, You have been there for me my Whole life through,
I ask myself time and time again," When will I die for You?"

Robin Taylor

Baby Needs a New Pair of Shoes

Down in Hell's Kitchen where we all used to meet,
it was a real dark and eerie street.
We always went there to shoot some pool.
None of us hardly ever went to school.

Sometimes we would shoot craps too, and say,
Baby needs a new pair of shoes, that's cool!
Baby needs a new pair of shoes!

There was Johnny, Franky, Mike and Buz.
Johnny would laugh and holler, here comes the Fuz!
We all acted real tough and smoked cheap cigars.
If our dads ever caught us, we'd be seeing stars.

I'd swipe some of Dad's beers,
It was awful tasting stuff.
Just another way of making ourselves look tough.

Dad would kill me if he knew the things I do.
"If you don't tell on me, I won't squeal on you!"

I'm a grown man now and I've got my own kid.
I'll flatten his butt if he does what I did!
Baby needs a new pair of shoes! That's cool!
Baby needs a new pair of shoes!

Norma Lenhart

Remembering

In memory of Bobby Rae Brown, a victim of AIDS

Guilt. You can't stop thinking about it.
Sweat and fever takes over, scaring you.
Dizziness. Confusion. Secrets that shouldn't be told.
Illness. A crazy self conscience, rambling on.
Blotches of darkness. Fright. Losing your independence.
Disrupted functions. Repeated slurring.
Anxiety to be well. Denial. Expenses.
Useless treatments. On going agony. PAIN.
Sorrow and remorse devours you.
You can't compete with it anymore.
It takes over. Loss of functions and vision.
You can't speak or control your bladder.
Helplessness. Someone else has to feed you.
Doctor's lies. Family gathering.
You feel weighted by death.
Your family's teary eyes, starring into your blank, glass-like eyes.
Despair. Lonely and lost.
Only your hearing lets you know that you're still there,
and they're still there with you. Total darkness.
Flower arrangements. You are missed.

Sheniece Brown

The Happy Senior Driver

I get in my old car and away I go
I'm a happy senior driver who likes to drive slow
Driving slow in the fast lane is really cool
I try to be careful I am not fool.

Heading for the club on a lovely sunny morn
I wonder why so many are blowing their horn
People are so impatient they get uptight
Just because I happen to run a red light.

The cars in the slow lane fly by on my right
In just a flash they are out of sight
They must all belong to some sort of clan
Their expressions are the same and they point their left hand

If these people drive fast it suits me fine
But at the next light why do they wait in line
If they are in such a hurry I wish they'd turn right
I could go straight ahead and make this red light

When I reach my destination I'm as happy as a lark
I hope today I don't have to double park
This happy senior driver who likes to drive slow
Looks forward to the senior clubs and playing bingo

Rhoda Levea

The Lady Bug

A lady bugs rests on a leaf, it lifts its tiny head,
Its spots as dark as blackened coal, its shell a glossy red.

With delicate, dainty strokes it lifts up into flight,
It chirps a little shout of cheer, and flies up with delight.

But appearances are deceiving, your eyes are easily fooled.
This creature is wild; solitaire, it can't be tamed or ruled.

With armor as hard as granite, with teeth like railroad spikes,
It crushes any wall or fence, it does just as it likes.

It stalks its prey unnoticed, its colors a disguise,
It swoops down, looking gentle, to bring you your demise.

It sheds its beauty everywhere, a trail to blood and gore,
'Cause deep inside, this evil fly's a killer carnivore!

So up against this demon-being, let's see how well you fare,
Spread the news, this evil ruse, I warn you all, Beware!

Christopher Bounincontri

Willie

Willie was a boy who grew up sad.
For one thing Willie couldn't stand his dad.
He drank too much and smoked a lot.
He's not the kind of guy who's easily forgot.
When Willie was 20, he still could not forget
the way upon his mother his father would hit.
He saw the fear in his mother's eyes
and after it all, she'd begin to cry.
Willie finally got married and
twins his wife carried.
The twins were born in July
And a few days later Willies dad died
Willie wasn't really very sad
But he couldn't say he was all that glad.
To his dad's funeral he got an invite
But he didn't think that going was right.
Willie had vowed to his mother so sad
that he would never turn out like his dad.
He kept his promise until his dying day
and the twins were glad he didn't turn out, The Wrong Way!

Faith Hester

A Lonely Flower

Its delicate colorful petals
Glisten in the sun from the morning rain
Wet with dew that formed like little beads
And dropped on the ground from time to time

Its stem long and green
Like a fern
Its roots are in the ground like a hand
Grasping on to a cliff edge
Very tight and firm

Its leaves fat and oval like
Stretched out to catch the morning sun
I see bees flying by
and come back to get nectar

I walked by this flower
Many times before
It is unaware of dangers around it
And sits there peaceful and alone

Jessica Hatch

What Is Utah

Utah is a land of wonderful dreams
With majestic mountains and clear crystal streams
High mountain meadows and deep blue waters
Loaded with fish and swimming otters
The forests abound with elk and deer
And hunters come in from far and near
There are also bobcat and cougars too
And pheasants and quail and chukars for you
When you look upon the valleys so fertile and green
You can hardly believe what you have seen
And there are the deserts painted every hue
From the palest of pink to the darkest of blue
It's a very good land for you and me
With plenty to do and plenty to see
The sunsets are beautiful with skies all aglow
There is no prettier sight I want you to know
And the moon glowing down on a lake at night
Makes a silvery shadow that is really a sight
I love this land with a heart big and true
And a satisfied feeling deep down that is new

Richard H. McCowen

My Guardian

He comes to me while I'm sleeping,
he watches over me, as I lie there, not knowing.

I never see him, but I feel his presence around me.
He enters my dream world without my consent.
I know he won't hurt me, he is a gentle soul.
He doesn't let me down, he loves me always.
His soul and mine are forever intertwined.
He awakens me from nightmares, he protects me from danger.
He finds no fault in what I do, and is as always forever loving.
As long as I live I will never see him,
but always sense his presence around me.

For now and forever, he will always be . . .
my guardian

Robin Hendrickson

The Coming of Winter

A cold, biting chill reaches out with icy claws and
firmly grasps the last moments of a warm Autumn.
The sky turns pale and gives way
to a bombardment of grey-white clouds.
Leaves are torn from their branches
and the trees begin to sap and hibernate.
The grass stiffens and crackles underfoot
while the ground hardens to a concrete inflexibility.
The coming of winter has brought blackness and solitude.

Jason Jonathan Young

Truths

Speak only the truth and they shun you
Lies have built fortunes untold
But never the kind that quiet the mind
Like the stillness of an unburdened soul

Some they will call you a stranger
Others will say you're a friend
It's the things that you do that differ the two
'Cause one's where the other has been

My life feels shattered and broken
When I think of the lies I have told
If I speak them to you I won't have a clue
That in your heart my love you will hold

Whatever your troubles or pleasures
Your time here is hard enough
Follow the signs with truth in their lines
For choosing the right path is tough

So hold fast to the words that sustain you
From waters that run shallow and low
And speak only the kind to quiet the mind
And strengthen and nurture your soul

Diane G. Tidmore

Translation

Dear England! Where hast thou gone?
The golden green hillside that first welcomed me home;
Barren moors where shadows move under lowering skies,
And grass and spirits tremble.

Gone from my view are the northern mountains,
Where God walked on a misty morning as the sun rose.
There I saw flaming fall consume the hillsides
And a country church in snowfall.

The omnipotent sea flees from before me,
Where rising tide met majestic cliffs in thunderous symphony.
I looked windswept over a veiled emerald coastline
And the earth was mine for a moment.

Vanishing are the vast ethereal forests,
Where vivid imaginations pass silently under leafy boughs—
Revealed as blue and golden when caught in dappled sunlight—
And the shade has healing powers.

Thou has been taken up into heaven,
For thou art too celestial for this world.

Jennifer Leigh Minson

And We Were One

Waves crashed in the night,
Shadows moved slowly across the sand.
Hands entwined like vines.
You kissed me softly,
Leaving a sweet essence of salt on my lips.
Your cheek brushed against mine,
And you whispered gently in my ear.
The moon seemed to have eyes,
Approvingly, it lit a path,
Like a red carpet laid out in front of us.
I wanted to walk on forever,
And never look back.
Into the distance - into the night.
The breeze sprayed us with the warm ocean mist,
As if to bless us,
Like an infant being christened.
We walked on,
Our destination unknown.
Soon our shadows became one,
Two hearts were united.

Dana LaCourse

Reality

Is the sun shining in your life or is it raining
down pain joy or happiness
I know I'm not dreaming and
It's not a fantasy. We all need
love and peace to live in a
world of reality. Reality, Reality
Hey, Hey, Reality. Children are
hungry and can't sleep the
homeless are living on the
streets poverty Aid, And drugs
are destroying our nations
Reality, Reality gotta find
a way to be free living in
a world of reality. Keeping
our hopes and dreams to be
living in a world of reality
hey, hey reality living our lives
so candidly in a world of Reality
Reality, Reality gotta find
a way to be free living in a world of Reality

Helen C. Morgan

Dusty Path

It was long and dusty
The dirt stood still,
But I moved
I moved slow,
But I moved
The further I walked,
The longer the path seemed
Finally, I had broken
It was there that I finally new what life was about
What life meant to me
I watched others move fast
They did not see,
Nor did they seem to care,
But the dirt moved too

Jason Dru Crochet

Untitled

It's like you're out on a cliff
and you don't know if you're going to fall
You look down on the world
and you feel very small
The world from up here is enormous and vast,
and you wonder if you're going to last
You hope that the path chosen is the one that you need
That will teach you new things and will help you succeed
Something to be learned through all of this though,
Is that every experience helps you to grow
No matter what path you've decided to choose,
You take something with you whether you win or you lose
For it's not that you're up on a cliff after all,
There's more of life to see than what you always saw

Christie L. Picardi

If

If only the past could remain in the past
Instead of haunting our souls In the present.
If only our mistakes could be times of learning
Instead of them being things we regret.
If only our minds would listen to our heart
When our hearts tell us to forgive.
If only we could fill our lives with goodness
And draw upon that as we live.
If we allow our trails to lead to fortune
We would most certainly find acceptance
For who we are and what we've done
If we are willing to take that chance.

Jodi S. Schultz Etra

Siberia's Loss

Your beauty's your demise,
Your power and your size.

Men cannot be content,
Until your last is spent.

Now you must endure,
Russia's desperate and poor.

Chinese superstitious cures,
Mean slaughter for you and yours.

The land that you call home,
Soon won't be yours to roam.

So what is to become of you?
Death? Mutilation? A zoo?

Even if your ground bones are kept off shelves,
Who will save us from ourselves?

Constance Porter

Tomorrow

Tomorrow, tomorrow, it's so easy to say.
When sometimes we plan for a special day.
The hopes are high we're all in high gear.
Then someone will say
Lets do it tomorrow.

Tomorrow, tomorrow is here today
Our plans are ready to soar
But someone will say
it's just a bore
Wait until tomorrow.
Will tomorrow ever come?

Bernice Mason

Building The Tear

Silence strays friend from friend,
And time erases memory,
Jealousy builds its fortress,
And torn lovers stand on different sides,
Throwing stones from the past,
And on each setting day,
A once traveled path,
Grows narrow to the grave.

Mark Whitten

An Awakening

Today the world turned green, and with the sun
Transformed itself at last to warmth and love.
My restless heart grew calm. I looked around
And saw God everywhere. So different from
The dull gray-green of yesterday, in which
Were mirrored all my thoughts, was this new world
Wherein all man was free. My greedy eyes,
My gladdened soul, my anxious ears, my heart,
Searched and drank in the perfect gift of God:
The bowing down of love to earth—Spring.

I walked along the path and felt at one
With every tiny shoot, each shrub and tree.
The noisy frogs, the bees, the oriole,
Watched me go by; they never feared, for they
Too, were enveloped in this veil of warmth,.
The very lake and sky reflected peace.
Then suddenly I knew the meaning of
This penetrating message of the sun:
Spring is the waking to what life is worth.
I was awake, I knew, I understood.

Elizabeth Spelman

Heartbeat

There was always something to be said of you.
You spoke suddenly.
You showed the inside of your heart to me.
The thought of it beating kept me warm
as night carried over and over,
taking you away. How could it beat
when all those nights you stayed in darkness
as though you lived there.
No wonder you left me
afraid of light, your love
like one heartbeat after another.

Dawn Misner

A Budding Rose

A budding rose is fragile,
Too much sun can scorch or burn.
A gentle spring mist nurtures
Its want to live and yearn.
A cool wind too and fro will agitate,
The petals develop within...
To burst of fragrance . . . smell . . .
And beauty . . . see . . .
A delicate life begin.
Too hasty for a smell can lend oneself to a sting of a bee.
Or a thought of one quick pluck . . . bloodstruck . . .
By a thorn one didn't see.
Let it blossom from strong stems and unfold its inner self.
A vision of beauty for all to see
And not hidden upon one's shelf.
One day it will fade
And dry to a pulp
But its memory will always live.
A young heart swoons, an old heart cries . . .
Emotions a rose can give.

Timothy Lowell Sorey

The Changing Seasons

As Spring arrives, the tulips bloom,
The iris and gladiolus sprout up
I too feel the new life cycle.
The warmer air perking up my body and soul.

As Summer hits high gear, the iris
And gladiolus start to bloom and the
Fresh garden produce begins to ripen.
I also feel that I can accomplish anything.

As Fall approaches and the flowers
And vegetables begin to dry up,
I too begin to grow sluggish and lifeless.

As Winter arrives, the bulbs are under
Frozen tundra and several feet of snow,
I too am on my back covered with
Blankets to keep warm waiting for Spring,
So I can bloom again.

As, of course, the real difference between
The flower bulbs and myself is that
The flowers do this once a year but
I experience this everyday.

John Parsons

To Save You

When you have overstepped your bounds and crossed the line,
Grace was there to save you.
When you are down on your knees begging the Lord please,
Faith is there to save you.
When you knew it was too much for you and admitted you could
Not do it alone,
Jesus died to save you.

Christine Klein

Loneliness

Loneliness is the color of green, jealousy gone wrong.
It sounds empty and left behind,
And tastes like a kiss touched with vinegar.
It smells like your own perfume,
And looks like your own reflection.
It makes me feel unwanted.

Loneliness is the color of black, cold, forgotten;
It sounds like a small child huddling and weeping,
It tastes salty, like the tears streaming down your face,
And smells stale like a musky house.
It looks like a homeless man begging on the street.
It makes me feel desolate.

Loneliness is the absence of color;
It sounds like a valley without echoes,
And tastes like spring without flowers;
It looks like a reflectionless mirror.
Loneliness makes me feel non-existent.

Loneliness is an unrestful reflection of death.

Shanda Cool

His Name I Shall Not Tell

His name I shall not tell
'Cause he has so many.
He's wonderful, strong, ever so mighty.
His smile so bright; he's just so funny,
That he makes me laugh instead of being grumpy.
But why he doesn't know how I feel for him
'Cause I feel so alone when I just don't fit in.
I sit there and stare as he talks to his friends,
So I try to make him notice but he just doesn't give in.
His muscles so large, his body so fine,
I just wonder why he doesn't come for me. Why?
His name I shall not tell,
'Cause he has so many.
He's wonderful strong, ever so mighty.
But why he doesn't notice me in the shadows of it all.
I don't know why I even care, 'cause I'm not important
to him at all.

Tina Gillinelli

A Love So Perfect

Standing here-hand in hand
Our silhouettes swaying in the gentle breeze
The elegance of the dawn's sky pushed away
By the serenity of the willow trees
My heart descends unto your gracious hands outstretched
Your eyes are golden bells that
Chime eternally in your sentimental happiness
Our love subdued by the fair passersby
The etched green grass is paid no attention
Even though it will tend to the feet of us lovers forever
Our souls are a splendor so powerful it could blow away
Our shadows like a feather drifting to the empty ground
Our feelings are silenced for the beauty
Of love is too perfect for any words

Gabby Berghammer

ODE TO CREATION

Creatures of silence sing to me.
Let me hear your whispered hymns in blades of grass.
Let me smell the newborn earth as it awakens
and catch first sight of the morning dove in flight.
Surround me with your golden halo and kiss the
springs of dew from my eyes.
Caress my heart with the loneliness of living things
and carry my soul into the depths of the earth.

Mary Margaret Foley

Distant Heart

Oh lovely lady lean close to my lips
Let me speak of love.
Oh lovely lady fate rests in your hands.
No longer doubt this lasting love.

Pull not away this time darling.
Fear not this love. I offer you my heart and soul.

Oh gentle lady give love this one chance
And my vow is this:
'Oh gentle lady to you I promise
My one last breath sent with a kiss.'

Lay down your arms, surrender now.
Dismiss me not or think of me a foolish heart.

Oh lovely lady trust in this magic
For now our time has come.
Oh my sweet lady only admit
In truth, we are not two but really one.

Drink deep this love now and forever.
Embrace this love.
Don't leave me here a distant heart.

Dennis McLaurine

Chapter U

U were a chapter I thought I'd never reach,
Verses I'd never read.

It seems like every time I turn ya page,
The less ya love I need.

Ya see, for me, at times U were my God,
The gospel of my soul.

I worshipped the very space U involved,
But my dedication took its toll.

Last night I thought I caught ya scent in bed,
But it was hope gone too far.

You don't wear perfume for me anymore.
It's like I don't know who U are.
Am I chasin' somethin' that's already gone,
Or was it nothing from the start?

You got so used to taking, U forgot how to give.
Tell me, can U return my heart?

U don't always see with ya eyes, this now I understand.

Honey, if I can't give U what U want, don't kiss me as if I can.

I always thought my love was enough, I guess it didn't do.
My heart spilled out these lines, Welcome to chapter U.

Charles Maye

Johnny's Eyes

That day I looked in Johnny's eyes
I saw the depths of Johnny's soul.
I saw the sheen of a million tears.
I saw the depths of pain untapped, untold.

I felt the grip of all his fears
Had known them in my own time.
I knew a kindred spirit here.
I saw the lonely in his mind.

I could relate to sleepless nights,
Could feel the rumble of the thunder
Of circumstances that crowded him in
And trampled his soul asunder.

So, I look away, try not to see
Not to feel and not to know
The lonesome call of the solitary
Aching depths of Johnny's soul.

Becky Parsons

Episode of Summer

Barn yard noises
the crowing of the rooster
didn't disturb our sleep,
Already awake and ready
Our young hearts wouldn't keep.

Standing against the weathered barn,
letting the sun's bright, warm rays
Spread across our sunburned limbs
As we greeted the newborn day.

With warmth in our bodies
Energy our friend
Across the barn we'd swing,
back and forth, and back again,
until against the rough old rope
our gentle hands would sting.

Then snuggled deep in the golden hay,
a cushion for our landing,
We lay sweating, soiled, and out of breath
and hoped for mother's understanding.

Bonnie Lyons

My Life's Book

In memory of my father, Henry Reitz, Jr.
Many of the pages in my life's book have turned.
Many of the pages in anger I have burned.
Many have been removed or lost along the way.
Many can just be read at the end of along, long day.

Some pages give me comfort with a picture or a word.
Some pages haunt my memory with a love song that I've heard.
Some pages seem to turn back time; relieve a long lost love,
While others only laugh with the twinkling stars above.

God holds in His hands the pages of my every night and day.
He holds them with a strong firm hand to guide me on my way.
Those pages hold the meaning - the reason for my life.
To finish the book is the ending. The ending of my strife.

Celebrate my journey. I have joined my life with God.
In peace I now move forward on His golden path I trod.

Judith Reitz Navarro

Soup

A good bowl of soup is a wonderful thing
Fills your body with comfort from
Your head to your feet
It can be used as a starter to gourmet feast
It can be used as a meal satisfying the beast
You can start it today with some
Bones and soup meat
Freeze this portion and add veggies
Whenever to complete
Just be sure to include your love for those served
And they will shower you with the
Praise you deserve

Jeannette Martingale

T'u Command

When it hurt the most I sat down and cried,
Luv me, Meg
And when the last of the tears dried up,
I went out and bought some more.
For I could never be alone in the darkness.
and I was supposed to be happy,
But something burned the insides of me,
I'm not sure what.
When I grew so tired I slept often
wondered, will it be eternally?

Megan Haas

Endless Tears

She sits alone, looks up to the sky
she thinks about past months of fear
and loudly says: "but why?"
Oh, honey, can you see me here
she feels so small
I miss you dear, only pain now, that is all

She "sees" the pictures of his death
as she stood vigil by his bed
the longest night she ever had
her fingers gripped the rails
teeth clenched and holding on so tight
all alone, she said, just you and I

God took you right in front of her
what did it mean, your little tear
did someone come to greet you dear
to take you home to God?
or did you know that leaving her behind
rest and comfort she will never find

A cloud drifts by, so white and pure
my love to you and God bless you

Hiltrud B. DeVine

Baby Boy

May you find peace when you look into his eyes
And love him even when he cries

May you always remember that he's tiny and helpless
And needs you to be selfless

Even though he may consume you with his needs
Just remember that he loves you endlessly

He will only be little for a split second in time
So cherish him, kiss him, hug him and sing to him in rhyme

When you're holding him, look into his eyes and
Memorize his face
Take the time to just be with him in a quiet place

They grow up so fast
So cuddle him now because soon a little boy he will be
And the baby he is, will have passed.

Tamira G. Gates

Untitled

My own mortality once frightened me,
Now death is a place that I long to be.
An eternal sleep free from the pain
Of losing you to someone else once again.

I know you can be happy without me,
But without you by my side I cease to be.
Your smile and laughter haunt my night,
I cannot imagine you believe this right.

So off you leave with my child,
It is my love and heart that you defile.
Give no more thought of what was to be,
Go live you life and bury me.

Stan Deaver

What Scares Me

Violence, guns and pain scare me.
Love and marriage scare me.
I'm stuck like a rock growing
on a mountain, and that scares me.

Problems in the future scare me
And seeing the world collapse scares me.

But I'm still here, and that does not scare me.

Santy Gray

Untitled

Walking along a dark corridor
Wondering what's around the bend.
A single petal falls to symbolize the dead.

You hear a baby cry and walk a
little faster deeper and deeper into
a corridor.

The wind blows through the dark corridor
Sending a chill down your back
turn around—
No one there or was there.

Coming to the end, you think, of the
dark corridor
turn the bend—
and start again

Christine Houser

Untitled

Her face is like a perfect rose
That blooms in the early morning of spring
Her smile is like the brightest star
That shines in the winter sky
Her heart is as warm as a mid-summer day
With all the warmth all around her
Her happiness brings joy
To those who are with her
The spirit of God is within her
She's the best thing that has happened to me
She's my best friend
and the one that has I'll always love
She's young, beautiful and ambitious
And she's my wife
The one our Lord has put me with in my life
God has put us two together
and we are one.

Larry Ray Taylor

Within My Silence

Within my silence,
there is so much violence.
In my darkness, I have so much pain,
my thoughts, cause my eyes to rain.
The whole world could be quiet
and my thoughts would still cause a riot.
In my light,
regions of my head still fight.
In my day,
emotions always get in the way.
In my sleep,
nightmares still do creep.
In my mind,
there is still so much I have to find,
within my silence.

Allison Cook

Lost

As the sun sets on another day,
I wonder where my soul will lay.
Will peace ease the thoughts of my mind?
Or will a raging storm leave me blind?

When one is lost in a desert of sand
and he holds his souls in his hand.
Should the left see what the right hand shall do?
Or is it best to separate the two?

In search of happiness should we always fail?
Or is contentment there in our lives that are frail?
Perhaps some things should be left lie still.
For in stillness of mind we find gods will.

Gary Daniels

The Eyes of the Beholder

The sun rose and fell into the ocean
The wind blew and the leaves stood still
The flower bloomed and grew into the ground
The sky was clear and it rained

The baby died because he was old
The world was in peace because of war
The people were segregated because they were free

We give but we want in return
She pushes away but wishes you near
His tears fell but he wasn't crying
You are full of pride but full of shame inside

I smile but I really want to cry
I say I'm sorry but I was right
I love you but you love me

Elysia Irena Melendez

Untitled

Under the endless sky
Beneath a million stars
Within the coarse of a lifetime
How very young we are.
As I stumble on this journey
Along the road that is real,
I'm not made of steal with all my lessons of my learning.
All the strength that I possess
Still there are mountains I wish was moving.
That take so much more than my best.
There are plans beyond my power,
These are dreams beyond my reach,
These eyes deceive the words I speak.
I don't tell the story inside,
So don't believe the face you see.
It's only the face of pride.
I can't be anything more than I'm made of.
I would move heaven and earth on my own if I only could
But I'm only a man, I can bend
And I can break It only shows I'm a man.

Ryan Ricke

Reflect

A memory of tomorrow,
A memory of today,
Listen to me closely this is all I have to say.

My anxiety and ecstasy they were never reality.
My sorrow and determination all fell under temptation.
My hurt and hate all depended upon your fate.
My passion and belief never would I have relief.
My happiness my words they were all mistakenly unheard
My wishes and my bliss they were all because of this.
My jealousy and madness all aroused from my sadness.
My lies and depression were all because of my obsession.
My inspiration and my fantasies never came through for me.
. . . But my love and unending pride shall never cease to die.

Everything I am,
Everything I'll be,
Is all what's become of you and me.

Jennifer Alvarenga

Dying Dreams

I look down the hall at the closed door.
Oh, how I long to explore that long forgotten lore.
It seems locked behind forgotten doors
Lie our lost, dwindling dreams.
They seem to melt away with the bitter winter frost.
We forget and cannot see what was easy to spy.
But why? I ask you, why?
Do our dreams suddenly die?

Alexaus Toland

Sensitive Skin

Sensitive skin
a sensitive thought
of strong emotion
from a caring person

What a day
from a sun shining autumn day,
a short prayer for all
and you, and you, and you

To our life
to universal paradise
to our children's, children's, children's lives

More sensitive thoughts
of strong emotions
from a caring person

Alan Wylie

My Journey

I started off running, I was in high gear,
My destination see, it was critically clear.
Success was my hunger, my desire, my thirst,
Prosperity was mine, unless it killed me first.
I started with pride, I was proud of myself,
My body willing, it was in perfect health.
A mile was taken already in my head.
Nothing would interfere, unless I was dead.

I started out smiling, I was completely free,
My vision complete, it was easy to see.
I was in control, I held knowledge inside,
Power was unlimited, unless I died.

I started off dreaming, I was number one,
My world revolved, I would remain the sun.
Overwhelmed by confusion, I lie taking my last breath,
Reality was responsible, it claimed my death.

Amanda Ricci

Teardrops

Oh, Heart,
Why are you crying?
My blood runs thick with your tears
It is you, not I, who is dying,
Yet I must endure the painful years
Perhaps when you're gone and laid to rest
You'll not lie so heavily within my breast
Surely you cannot last for long . . .
I know that you are not that strong to get up and live again
Oh, there are happy moments, but I see them as a curse
For they are fleeting, and when it comes the drop is only worse
Each time the yo-yo on the string dips closer to the floor
As it slowly loses energy and then can bounce no more
You ache for love and tenderness and yearn for a gentle touch
But can't accept them as sincere for you've been hurt too much
But therein lies the mystery, and therein lies the pain
For what will happen when you fall so low
That you cannot rise again?

Barbara Gorniak

Paladin

His goddess kissed him—And he was at the eye of the calm.
For he could see her; Almost feel her. He was as close to
Her as any on the Prime Material Plane could be.

Her voice reached out for him—you are truly one of my
Beloved; and she wept. For these were the burdens of her
Love: First—You will never fail to do your absolute in
Battle—To carry my honor there can be no other way. Second—
Your memory will be absolute in past deeds—A mistake made
Twice strengthens your enemies. Third—Your love for me must
Be absolute— As is mine for you my beloved.

Then she was gone—and man arose Paladin—He could feel her,
Her love was all around him.

William J. Hagadorn

Love Me!

I am a person a daughter of God.
I need the same things you need.
I want someone to talk to, to listen to.
I want someone to do things for, to serve.
Help me to be the best I can be.
Do you know that each time you hurt another,
Your hurting God, I am his child too.
Ignoring me, is Ignoring Him.
If you were to see him would you stop to speak,
Or call him some crude name's like you do me.
But when you do it to Me, Your doing it to Him.
So put your arm around another, who is needing you to care.
See just how much you will fill God's love, Everywhere.

Marva Kupfer

Everything

He is the source of all my dreams
He is the culprit for all my schemes
He is the one thing I so desire
He is the match that ignites my fire
He is the warm face that starts my day
He is the one who makes me gay
He is the god who has such hair,
Such hair that has the sun-touched glare.

He has the dulcet, kindly smile
He has the laugh that's worth my while
He has the touch to make me quiver
He has the voice to make me shiver
He has the signs to let me know
He has my life, my heart, my soul.

Janelle M. Brophy

Spending Problem

I'm trying to save my money,
but I couldn't do it if my life depended on it,
'Cause every cent I get,
I have an urge to spend it.

Got nine dollars sixty-nine in my pocket,
and then it's lying there,
I knew I needed shoes,
a really good looking pair.

I went in and found my size,
tasty for the hungry eye.
Said the man, nine dollars seventy-nine.
On no! All I need is one more dime!
I searched through my pocket,
hoping to find,
a little silver coin,
Oh! Just a little dime!
No dime here, I said as I sadly put the shoes away.
Guess I'll have to buy them another day!

Jamie Lee Caplan

I Wish I Could

I wish I could always say things sweet,
About people I know, and people I meet.
I wish I could spread sunshine as I go,
I wish I could always let a smile show.

I wish I could do deeds, great or small,
For others, never gossiping if they fall.
I wish I could have strength in my arms,
To lift up each weak one safe from harm.

I wish I could see in all, goodness there,
And sing the praises of it everywhere.
I wish I could heal pain with my hands,
And send out the Dove of Peace to all lands.

There are many things I wish I could do,
Yet I am only one person; my talents few.
But if I keep trying, I am sure I will find,
Treasures of loving kindness in all mankind.

Ola L. Curry

When I Was Young

When I was young
I listened to the songs I sung

My family grew and I found content
In everything that God had sent

As I approach my senior years
I come face to face with all my fears

I know I will be leaving one day
I'll meet my maker and I'll hear him say

"My arms are open, your loved ones are here
Come sit beside me in this chair
You cried, you laughed and lived
You accepted all that I could give"

There will be no tears
And no more fears
Once again I'll be young
And listen to the songs that I have sung

Jane E. Schmidt

The Cochise Stronghold

Boulder strewn the rugged canyon and down the mountainside
Ancient deer trails cut the thickets to the sparkling stream.
Walls of granite echo night bird calls, coyote chorus, Panthers scream.
Ghostly warlord Cochise leaves his hidden unmarked grave,
Wanders lonely on the night wind, high among the towering spires,
Adding voice to phantom warriors, chanting "Glory to the Brave."
Lifeless now his people, lost to hills and valleys,
Deserted now their signal fires.
Hark the coming of the morning,
Mists of purple crown the eastern hill.
Shafts of sunlight pierce the pine tree,
Dewdrops jewel the oak leaves.
Gentle doe and spotted fawn come out of hiding,
The earth is still.
The stronghold wakens.
Only Gods of darkness know a phantom warrior grieves.

Bertha Marsh

Summer Love

Today was the day that we fell in love.
My friends saw you first to give me the extra shove.
From that day on, you were the only one in my heart.
You came up to me to make the first start.
We saw each other every day.
But I was so in love I had nothing to say.
As the weeks went by you began to change.
From a handsome man to someone strange.
Your diminishing love fell from the start.
You always felt the need to play with my heart.
I had no choice but to do the same as thee.
I started to see how much fun cheating can really be.
I studied into our everyday
To find cheating is just a game you play.
Oh what can I do but keep on loving you?
I know that if I lose you, I'll lose a real good thing
Because when you're near me, my heart skips a beat.
I can hardly stand on my own two feet.
I knew from the moment I met you
That you were the guy for me.

Margie Jeff

Untitled

My heart climes many a mountain,
slowly swelling with adoration.
Though near the peak always to be trusted downward,
smashing to pieces in a desolate vapid desert.

Brianna Leahy

What Manner Of Love

What manner of love is this
So strange yet so real
Since I've met this Prince of peace
Words can't say what I feel
He took one such as I, lost in my sin
Unworthy in all my ways
Yet with love took me in

What manner of love is this
That He'd give his life
To purchase my liberty
With His blood pay the price
He bought my soul through death on Calvary's tree
He took his bitter cup
Just to save you and me

Now the love of Jesus fills me night and day
It overwhelms my soul and somehow I know . . .
From His arms I never want to stray
When I think of all Christ did for me
Because He lives, I'll live throughout eternity
My heart can sing. His praises ring what manner of love!

Diane White

A Readiless Mind

The gift Creator gave a man
A man says is in his mind
He buried the talent, saying is in his mind
When the bell is ringing, call a man
His saying, is in his mind
The bell is ringing, go and follow others to spread the good news
Are you going to start your work before it's too late?
You made a promise to your Creator, after say, is in mind
When are you going to keep your promise?
Get out there before it's too late
When the bell of death rings, sisters and brothers
There will be no time, no call, and no waiting
No time, for our weakness is in His hands
Like when He brings wind, fire, snow, rain and no water on earth
Nobody can stop Him
Our power and knowledge are in His hands
In His hands, in His hands
The imaginary, endless impossible hope
Wait until judgement day
There you have nothing to show but empty mind, he cries.

Irene Ogbru

Clouds

White puffs in the sky,
slowly pass us by,
making shapes in the sky,
until your childhood flies by.

No more shapes, or fun, or games, or . . .
no more laying out with your friends,
no more imagination.

Now they are just white puffs in the sky.

Lindsey Langer

The Perfect Love Song

A melody so sweet like kisses in the night,
words that encourage him to hold her tight.
A beat so gentle like the rhythm of true love,
a sound so pure it drifts into the heaven above.
A tone so soothing it puts her in his arms,
snuggling, cuddling, safe and warm.
Creating a mood in which he takes her hand,
The perfect love song as he is the perfect man.

Rosalyn R. Ross

The Last Father's Day

I buried your ashes on Father's Day,
No circumstance, pomp or tears.
I covered your ashes with dirt and clay,
And shrouded the wasted years.

No hugs or kisses or daddy's good graces,
No ice creams or rides on a pony.
Of fatherly love, you left no traces,
Did you know that my childhood was lonely?

Hardly a kindness you gave to me,
Just impatience, indifference and such.
Your affection was never meant to be
But oh, I had needed you so much.

Did you love me at all, did you ever care?
Or was I just a bad daughter?
You never ran your fingers through my hair
I never felt the love of a Father.

I buried your ashes on Father's Day,
A good day, the right thing to do.
The pain is now hidden under dirt and clay
But tell me dad, why do I miss you?

Kathryn A. Kaniecki

The Dream Ship

A lullabye to my son, Riley Morgan
While the boats are snug at bay,
Time is nigh to sleep away.
While the stars are shinning bright,
On a dream ship you'll sail tonight,
With chocolate sails and treasures in the hold,
the rigging is licorice, the waves are gold.
When your ship returns from sea,
On the closest shore I will be.
When gently from slumber you awake,
The desert may become a lake,
Tonight once more the sea will call,
And gently asleep you will fall,
To ride again on adventure's wake,
On the dream ship again you'll take.

Karen Leigh Cox-Dennis

I Love You

I love you for being only mines.
I love you for being by my side.
I love you for the time we shared
I love you for the time you spared.
I love you for your sexy smile.
I love you for your mind, body and that's not all . . .
I love you more than I ever could say.
I love you more and more everyday.
Baby, what I'm trying to say is that I
Love You in all kinds of ways!

Shurikus Ivey

The Sea Gull's Secret

The sea gull soars on endless flight to see the world below . . .
The woods, rivers or fields of wheat, his life seems to move slow,
but there are those that stalk him down and wait to kill their prey.
He's on his guard to save his life, he watches night and day.
He looks as tho' he's happy, but looks, they can deceive,
and words that have been written of him only fools believe.
The sea gull cannot tell you of the hurt his feathers hold
and stories of his life are those that humankind have told.
He doesn't get a chance to tell you why he settles down,
far from home, which was the sea, to this crowded town.
It could be that he cannot eat a fish covered with oil
or that his young would never hatch on man's polluted soil.
I doubt that he prefers to live a life that's dirty grey . . .
but we can only guess, because the sea gull cannot say.

Teresa A. Inman

Soul Of The Eternal Dance

Flickering flames as I burn my hands
Now I'll take you down with me
Crack like the fire that cuts the night
Feel the grinding heartbeat that gives you life
Steal the magic from me
I'll soon fade away
Like a match to a flint, I burn my soul away

Flickering flames as I burn my hands
The evil then will drain with you
Out of control like a forest fire
Breaking down the walls of your soul's desire
I give you my life
Without me, you die
As vibrations pound you under the twilight sky

Danny Burges

Unknown Soldier

In darkness stirs the heart of men
awakening in the black path's bend
of twisting arms that tell of when
the branches were young
and he was among friends
but now abound for the battle line
the darkness tends of fill his mind
of vision of crimson,
the blood in the rifle's whine

Valiant soldier is he, alone in the night
clutching his sole rifle tight,
knuckles gripping so they're white
determined to hide his deepening fright.
The watchman calls, for he is done
and crawls in bed to await the sun.
Rest on, my unknown friend,
when darkness stirs the hearts of men.

Kerri Tily

Learned From A Veteran

One day as I lay in a hospital bed,
Feeling empty within, overcome with dread,
I caught the eye the of the adjacent Vet
And learned a lesson I'll never forget!

I saw the despair of this once Proud Man
Whose body refused his Brain's Command
To lift itself from the mess and Filth
His uncontrollable gut had spilt.

As I looked on to this Veteran's Eye
I felt such guilt I began to cry!
I went to a nurse, then to the yard,
Dropped down and prayed so long and so hard!

I repented my failure to love today
And could not ask Him to take this MS away!
Moments ago I pouted my plight—
Now I've been given a reason to fight!

This thing is still in its early stages
While after eight years his war still rages.
Lord, if he's the example of what I will be,
Ask him to share his courage with me.

Ronald N. Pridemore

Alone

When I saw what I didn't want to know,
The pain scraped me like some hated needle of fire and ice.
I was alone in a silent void of tears.
Shut away from all gifts of the happy.
Why should I be alone?

Meghan Roberts

A Confession

The world's coming to an end
I need a friend
Praying for time to spend
With everyone again
Missing days
When we all got along
Start to cry
But society says I have to be strong
Think of saying goodbye
That's not right
All I know is that I'm tired of crying myself to sleep each night
Days aren't the same
Everyone has changed
Can't take much more
I'm stuck in a room with no door
Ready to lose my mind
Tired of drugs and crime
Too bad they can't see a sign
I'm leaving before due time

Nakia Watkins

A Child Is Like A Flower

A seedling that grows to an indefinite measure,
with the passing of time to bring so much pleasure!

Treasure, once hidden, now a joy to behold—
A miraculous being to have and enfold!

What a blessing for all, a gift Heaven sent,
that awakens at daybreak, then sleeps curled and bent!

Thriving and flourishing with sun and with rain,
Your love and devotion is never in vain—

This wondrous creation should never grow wild.
Yes, a Child is Like a Flower, a Flower is a Child!

Phyllis Joyce Falk

A Vision

I look yonder, I see a dark cloud,
it appears just over the horizon.
But . . . it is not the cloud that I fear,
it is the destruction that it brings.
Without warning, the trees will burn and crumble,
into ashes they will fall.
Buildings will tumble, nothing left but a pile of dust.
They sky will turn pallor, rivers will run red,
they prey of the wilderness, will cease to be prey.
Agony of the flesh will disintegrate, leaving nothing but bones.
Religion will succumb to vanity, as time becomes still,
the glory will be vain.
Children will no longer be, and the field of fertilization,
shall become a barren waste.
The explosion of myth will become reality.
In the blink or an eye,
there shall be nothing left to remember the cause.
All brought on by the dark cloud on the horizon,
the dark cloud . . . the dark cloud . . . Man

James K. Chenevert, Sr.

Stardust Light

In the morning I wake up to start my day,
trying to find a better way.
I think of my dreams last night,
knowing that I travel on the stardust lights,
to find a better life,
hoping and praying to God to give me new life.
So I go to bed at night,
so I can travel once more on the stardust light,
so I can find a better life,
Knowing that God is the stardust light.

Gregory J. Appleyard

The Oracle of the Plain

Cowboys are Cesarean comrades
Cut from Roman cloth and
Patched upon the collage of Americana.

Lost in the patchwork, one can only see
Them in the corners of small towns
Taking the space between the
Smog of industry and the wetness
Of the false intellect to the right.

They came, saw and conquered.
As the great epileptic Roman did.
With the same reason of my stoicism
And pagan rituals upon the beasts.

All that is left now are
Dusty bar floors and the swill they call beer.
The country music cries the
Falsetto of the bleating lamb.

The twang makes invisible
The blood from a cut jugular.

Jeffrey J. Church

Omega

What a rare and special find
and he's the last one of his kind

the last of his kind throughout the land
and we must save him, if we can

If we could only find a mate
for him, before it is too late

We've searched and searched, I fear in vain
we shall not see his kind again.

Alas, a female has just been found
and soon their species will abound

They cannot, must not, pass away...
But, they killed the male yesterday

His life was ended for a thrill
a hunter had the urge to kill

I cannot help the tears I shed
their one last chance for life is dead

I'm not ashamed that I have cried
a part of you and me, has died.

George E. Simmons

Untitled

Why is it? something beautiful never remains?
A sunset only lingers on the horizon
Until the moment comes when night
can take its place.
A rainbow only appears when rain
and sunshine unite.
Is it because beauty is so frightened
of staying anywhere for very long
for fear that the beholder
will lose appreciation?
If beauty comes and goes, we anxiously await
its next return, reminiscing in the joy
that it brought.
I felt that joy in your beauty,
and will anxiously wait for your return.

Denise S. Jackson

Cape Breton

Some souls are caught in moments
That never let them go.
I soared upon a lofty crest
Till Janus sensed my pleasure.

From the heights I'd sing,
"Get on with life,"
To those who mourned old sorrows,
And then, he said those words, with eyes
Steeled fast against my pleadings.

The very voice that lamented once,
"I love you, Lollie . . . "
And the bluebell fonts that languished once
With tears
When he thought I slept.

It has been two years.
And the memory swells
In virulent waves throughout me.
A mere thought still undoes me.
His look of disgust
In the rain that day.

Connie Caswell

Sensual

With one look, I know your feelings . . .
Towards the moment,
About the day,
Concerning me.

With one sound, my heart stops . . .
then echoes your words
forever kept there.

With one scent I am drawn,
powerfully, unceasingly, to you.
I desire something tangible.
The moment is mine.

With one touch, I am calmed, reassured and ignited.
Nervous, apprehensive, and sure of myself.
Elated, but elusive, I want more but cannot show it.

With one taste, I am lost.
Not of this world, this time, this body.
Spinning, Spiraling, only continuing passion.
I am yours.

Jill Hayes

Dream State

I am still dreaming?
If so when shall I awake?
My life seems . . . at a standstill
As my mind sifts through this abstract state

Dreaming if for wishers who search for falling stars
Conjuring up an ideal world: pure, unblemished and free of scars
A dreamer lives amidst shadows: vacuous and void of substance
Hoping to coalesce the human species: a futile redundancy

Fairy tales, good luck charms and tales of fortune
Mere fantasies and mental escapades given undue proportion
Genie's bottle, Aladdin's lamp and the visionary crystal ball
Mere schemes that bewilder and infuse us with awe

Wake up! all ye dreamers and take a look at life
Be mindful of your surroundings and witness all the strife
The hunger, disease, violence, racism inundating our homes
Because of slovenly dreamers transformed into clones

Tis by hard work, sweat, blood and tears
Than humankind can extinguish their most ingrained fears
Not by simple dreaming will progress be achieved
Dreaming is not enough if we Wish to succeed!

Richard Valoppi

Procrastinate

Practically finished, I'm almost done
Really I'll get to it, let me have some fun
Oh I forgot, I'll get to it soon
Caught in a rush, I'll finish by noon
Right now I'm busy, there'll be a delay
Alright already, I'll finish by May
Soon I promise, I'll do the job
Time will tell, no need to sob
I know eventually I'll finish my writing
No not now, I'll be in hiding
A
T
E

Rose Rosales

Our World

What is happening to our world today, a world
that is going astray. Space ships flying so
high in the sky, breaking up the clouds
as they fly by, bringing rain floods and
tornadoes, by the score; it is not a nice
world to lived in anymore.

People are living out on the streets, and
some people are starving and not having enough
to eat. Even in the Depression these people we
never seem to meet. In other parts of the world,
they are fighting and killing each other,;
Why can't they learn to love like brothers?
Lord, we need a miracle to change the world,
a world you created when you here.

You gave man a will to live, marry, have children,
and not live in fear, but fear has come to each
and every one of us: drugs, alcohol and shooting on
the streets, we must have that miracle, Lord,
So we can all live in hope, love, and peace.

Ruby W. Coghlan

Untitled

In the beginning the wizard thought that the potion
would make him majestic, but it only made him weak.
He took another sip. Perhaps he liked the taste.
Soon the glitter that once surrounded his wand had turned
to dust, but he pretended not to see.
He took another sip, and his magic doves flew away.
But the wizard did not even look to see which way they had flown.
The beaker that held the potion was never empty, and the wizard
never stopped drinking from it.
Another sip and he missed his creamy birds that had soared to
freedom even though he would not admit that he had let them go.
He drank the bubbling broth so the children would admire his
tricks, but it made him forget them.
I tried to take it away once, but he made more.
He became a prisoner. He became weak.
I stopped going to his magic shows.
But only because he stopped performing.

Susan M. Halka

Wisdom

She moved and thought with nature.
Her oneness with the subtleties of it all
were as complete as the moisture rising from the earth, clouding,
then returning as rain to freshen the violets
whose softness was surpassed
only by her touch.
She moved and blended in and around the man who needed
and hid behind the armor.
He found no resistance
and surrendered.

W. H. Land

Hope

In this world of hurt and anger,
I search for a way out.
A hiding place where I can
Surrender my angry thoughts.
A place where pain has no meaning,
Where it doesn't exist.
I long for love and compassion
From friends, family, and enemies alike.

As long as there is sky above me,
There is hope for a brighter day.
So, never will I give up.
I will continue searching
Even after the sun burns up,
And the earth disappears from beneath us.
Even then, I'll look towards a brighter day.

Mariana Naglosky

Reminders of the Past

Like a flower with a piece of its petal torn off,
And a child who has been teased by his peers.
Like memories of things you would rather forget,
It always seems to bring back the tears.
Songs and pictures may bring back the past,
May strike up that moment of pain.
Like nightmares of things that once were,
And the monotonous sound of the falling rain.
Like a child falling down and scraping his knee,
And the temporary look of hurt in his eyes.
He just picks himself up and brushes his knees off,
And carries on his way with a sigh.

Jenny Vogtman

Summer

School is almost over,
and summer is about to begin;
Sports start soon and kids play to win.
When your favorite show is on,
don't hesitate to watch and stay up late,
for in the summertime there is no bedtime debate.
In the summertime the fun just never ends,
but wait . . .
what about your friends?
How about the ones who don't live
down the street but you see at school?
All of a sudden, summer isn't as cool;
maybe it's not as great as we'd like to say,
but it gives you time to get away
From teachers and homework that never ends . . .
Sorry, I've got to go and call my friends.

Tracey Booth

Finality

From an entity of energy
Crackling, sparkling electric blue.
A tall, statuesque man forms
Clothed in a cloak of every hue.

And from his face of pearly white
His eyebrowless eyes stare.
Into the dusty aired west
At sol so radiantly dying there.

And upon his face, there is no expression
And deep within his soul, there is no fear.
For he is the last, the final man
So lonely, the end will be so dear.

James Wilson

A Night by the Fire

The flames of the fire gleam in her eyes.
In the dark night,
The powdery white snow falls to the ground,
As the squirrels run for cover from certain death.
While we sit nestled in our blanket,
Our eyes come together and
At that instant I know
I have finally unlocked the door to her heart.
I can now say that our friendship
Is at a whole new level,
Stronger than it has ever been before.
The moment her lips kiss mine,
I feel a bond between us
That I've never felt before.
Could it be that my life has finally
Found what it's been looking for.
This has been one of the most memorable nights of my life.
"Buzz . . ." the alarm sounds, I rise from my bed,
Look around and realize
That it was just a dream . . . .

David Fischer

The Choice

I was tired and sick, not very strong
I knew that I couldn't last very long.
My family was gathered round my bed,
When out of my body I was suddenly led
To a light that was shining Oh! so bright
I knew that leaving was nothing but right.
I followed this light to a beautiful place,
Then I was looking into God's face.
The angels were singing a glorious song.
This place was Heaven, I couldn't be wrong.
The streets were shining, all paved with gold,
My small child came for me to hold.
Then God's voice beckoned to me,
He said, "This is your choice, what will it be?"
"You can stay here or to earth return"
"There are still many crowns for you to earn."
My small child took my hand and led me to the door.
He said, "I love you, Mom, but my sisters need you more."
As I returned to my body, I felt stronger inside,
Knowing that one day, in heaven, I would reside.

Vivian Overstreet

This Day Was Mine

I love to watch the clouds go by,
Like angel wings that patrol the sky.
To stroll in the country on clear warm days,
Brings peace to me thru sun bathed rays.
I stopped to notice a busy sparrow
Finishing today, awaiting tomorrow.
She builds her nest till day is done,
And prepares to care for her very young.
I love soft breezes on my face,
That turns each leaf like delicate lace.
Or to walk by a stream and feel its mist,
Upon my cheek like a gentle kiss.
I love to look back at the close of these days,
And recall the joys I saw on my way.
I can rest at the end of my day and find,
God gave me these joys, and this day was mine.

Carol Baker

Time

Time is forever,
And it never stops.
Time is your life,
And it always goes too fast.
Time is what you remember,
And what you'll never forget.
Time is what hurts you,
And what heals you too.
Time is what helps you to deal with things,
And what helps you to better understand them.
Time is forever,
And it never stops.

Jennifer Zucker

Please Stay

I'm not ready
My heart can't take anymore pain

If I let go I don't know
if I can love again

Since the day I laid my eyes on you
nothing could keep me away
I love you so please say you'll stay

Stay in my life, baby don't go
Without you I really don't know

I can't go on without your smile
I love you so please stay for a while

If you took one minute to look in my eyes
You would see my love for you because my love can't hide
Look a little deeper and the pain you will find
That is all the pain you left behind.
So please promise you'll stay

Give it a chance I promise you will be-
the happiest man alive if you stay here with me
I have so much love inside this heart of mine
give me a chance, a chance to make you mine.

Joy Frank

Child Abuse

A child cries at night
In result of all the fright.
Bruises on her back and cuts on her cheek.
She hides so no one can peek.
It's not a game of tag.
He's using her as a punching bag!
Thinking, she lies in bed.
Tomorrow will she be dead?
She has to do something now!
But she's trapped so how?

Candice Roy

Locked Out

Locked out, that's what I am,
kept away from family and friends,
by a wall.
The terror slowly sinks in,
while I wait in silence.
Craziness on one side,
loneliness on the other.
Locked out, that's what I am,
kept away from all I know.
A tear starts to fall as I realize
I can never escape.
I think of the blood that's been splattered on this wall,
that came from others before me.
Locked out, that's what I am,
and that's how I'll stay in my helplessness.

Cherise Gilmer

Cruelty

Why are we so cruel these days?
You know someday it's going to pay.

Rapes, murders and so much more.
Why can't we just shut the door?

Our country was born on Christian ethics.
But now the country has turned.

Jesus is the answer for the world today,
So why don't we all bow down and pray?

Jesus made the ultimate sacrifice,
So we wouldn't have to pay the price.

Jesus died for you and me,
So he could set us free.

Now why don't you stop doing all those cruel things,
Because of the results they bring.

Now you can see what I mean.
We can work together to keep our world clean.

Alissa Welsh

Untitled

Two seeds are planted.
The first grows
with the forces of Mother Nature—earth, water, and love.
The second refuses all help and begins to wilt and weaken.

As time passes, the first blossoms
and shines its beauty upon all the others,
Sharing its knowledge and love.
One day there is a storm so strong
that it pulls both flowers out of the soil.
They both die.

The next afternoon the garden speaks of the deceased.
It was the first flower they remembered,
best allowing its memory to live on forever.

Lindsay Bateman

Airplane Ride

Taking off
The ground gets smaller
The tiny world makes me feel superior
Lights twinkle below like broken glass and I
Could destroy man's hard work with a sweep
Of my hand across the tiny surface under me
The world's possibilities are in my power
The clouds begin to rise; or maybe we are falling
Growing land beneath the plane wavers my plans
I can once again make out the familiar human
Structures on the Earth so I frown and
I am now another ant among ants
I am one of millions
Landing

Jenny Strickland

The Last Butterfly

One late October afternoon, I
Saw an autumn Butterfly.
When days grow short, with winter nigh
He floated up to touch the sky.
Though frost had come and kissed the night,
He fluttered as in his first flight
With colors bright in fall sunlight
And not a hint of the coming night.
And as I watched him disappear
I pondered on my own time here,
With hope that as my day grows near
The way before me would be clear
As the last Butterfly.

R. K. Flory

Unicorn's Promise

Unicorns with the pure of heart.
Mysterious in their ways
Keepers of the world unknown
They all stand alone.

Unicorn came to dance with me
She kept me far away from home
I had no way of knowing then, what was at stake
For in my trusting heart provided the keys to the gate.

She took them long ago
Releasing only my fears
But today I found them at my door
And I can't handle them anymore.

Grounded am I for the control I have
Control over my life
For the keys unlock the soul
So I gave them back to the foal

With the promise that someone would come
And say the keys belong to that of an undying heart
The Unicorn Agreed.

Jasmin Lynn Milenberg

My Last Will And Testament

The day will come when lying in a bed, a doctor will determine
that my brain has ceased to function and therefore I am dead
When this occurs, do not attempt to prolong my life artificially
Let me go, and use my parts to show my love for life and humanity

Give my heart to one whose own has caused much pain and sorrow
Take my bones, every nerve, every muscle and make a crippled
child walk tomorrow
Give my eyes to the man or child who has never seen
Give my kidneys to one whose life depends on a machine
Give my blood to a teenage boy lying in his own
My tissues can be useful too, don't leave them out, alone
Give my brain cells to a speechless boy that he might shout
at the umpire at a baseball game telling him - "he's out"
To a deaf girl who has never heard the patter of the rain
Who'd come to know the gentle sound against her window pane

But give my sins to evil, and my soul to good
Then bury me with all my faults, lest I'm misunderstood
And if by chance you wish somehow to remember me
do it with kind words and deeds and great humility
This much I ask that I might live to eternity

Joan G. Warren

THE WISH

In the depths of my love-torn heart,
I find you both are there. Torn between
the two I love and the feelings we do share.

If I could have just one wish come true,
I'd wish to have two lives to have you
both for my husband, and to both I'd be the wife.

No worry, no guilt, no sneaking about—
always on edge, "What if someone finds out?"
There'd be no clock ticking away precious
time we must now steal for just us two . . .
Only time to spend discovering the love
I feel for both of you.

We both know this wish I have will never
become reality. And so we take it as it comes;
that's the way its got to be.

Baji

Untitled

When a fantasy crosses the boundary
Between a dream—
And into your reality
It grips you
It clenches you between—
Moral and insanity.
When fears walk
The evil infects you—
Spreading through your veins
The suffering unimaginable
Only by one—
Whose soul becomes clouded and unattainable
Who dares to understand?
The dark heart's intentions—
The wealth, the pain, the absence of guilt . . .

Jennifer Spear

You And Only You

You and only you
here at my side
A love that will never change.
You and only you will be true.

You and only you
When dark, there's always you.
You will always light up my life.
You and only you will be true.

You and only you
the one who lifts my heart
You are the only one that will be in my mind.
You and only you will be true.

Sara Chartier

The Power of Women

Working day by day, to earn the pay
Proving ourselves to the men of this world.
Do we really need this harassment and turmoil
to justify ourselves to men?

We are doctors, we are lawyers,
we are majors in the military.
No limits, no boundaries, we are equal.

Elizabeth Cady Stanton, Susan B. Anthony
Are we doing this for you?
Giving us the right to vote in 1920.

Pushing to the limits, reaching for the sky.
Shannon Lucid, Amelia Earhart really know how to fly.

From passing amendments to fighting in a war.
Are we really the weaker sex?
Women are the powerful ones.
Hear us roar!

Kristen Costa

Nightwebs

Nightwebs.
Ever flowing on until the dead live again.
Always growing larger,
Encompassing life with its silent whispering of peace,
Controlling minds.
Nightwebs.
Staring silently into the gloomy nights of doom,
Fingering thoughts.
Groping after those who reject it,
Capturing all.
One mind,
Picturing, contemplating, ruling.

Kim Bergeron

My Corner

I have a little corner where I can go,
A place where a loner
can let her emotions flow.
If my mom can never find me,
that's probably where I'll be.
And when my heart is broken,
That's where I set it free.

I have a little corner where I can go.
I can sometimes be a moaner,
but don't think of me as low.
Someplace I can sob and weep,
my very own little keep.
When my life is in a drought,
that's where I go to shout.

I have a little corner where I can go,
I feel I am the owner,
It's where I sleep and grow.
It keeps me safe from everything, even in the snow.
There isn't even a bed, but that's nothing that I dread.

I have a little corner where I can go. . . .

Erin Schneider

Dominick

As a child, I used to think that clowns were really scary
And those I'd seen by age eighteen were funny, but just barely.
When the circus came, they smirked from posters on a wall
And the one at the amusement park didn't make me laugh at all.
I really wasn't fond of clowns, 'til one day, in a window
I spied a clown whose countenance brought on my clown-love syndrome.
I brought him home, and gave him to a friend who then was lickin'
A little bit of fever and a pox he'd got from chicken.
The doll was given, as a name, a strange one I am certain
But "Dominick" was more than doll, at times he was a person.
He saw that little friend of mine, through chicken pox and measles
Without complaint he was there through sniffles and through sneezes.
We grew quite fond of Dominick, and mourned his final days
But had at least the memory of his loving, clownish ways.
Then through the years, I received clown dolls large and small
Made with yarn, with fabric, but made with love were all.
I have in my possession, "Dominicks" one through twenty-two
I wouldn't give another name. I ask you now "would you?"
I'm heading for Fifth Avenue, I want just to parade them.
God bless the clowns one and all; God bless the hands that made them.

Dolores Clark

Wonders

Life is like a mystery that slowly unfolds before our eyes.
What our past holds, and what still lies ahead,
Only our dear Lord really knows.

Many a man has traveled far, traveled along the roads of life,
Not always knowing which path to take,
In hopes of finding his way . . .

As we go through life's journey
Sometimes we don't quite understand
Why we have to experience the things we do,
Searching for the reason as to why.

If only we could try to understand the wonders we've never seen,
Not even in our farthest dream.
There lies a place, a place for you and me,
A place for all to see.

Happiness in our life comes from within.
It is not something that is given from a friend.
Living each day anew, maybe,
Some of our dreams shall come true.

So next time you look up into that big blue sky,
Remember the Lord is always looking after you.

Lauren G. Hayward

The Man Upstairs

When you don't think anyone is listening,
Just look to the sky and
You'll see it glistening.
When everything goes wrong,
You think you can just sing a song.
But no one can solve your
Problems but he,
So don't go to anyone else with your plea.
You should never cry a tear,
Because with him what do
You have to fear?
He has this whole world to share,
And all he wants is for you to care.

Erin M. Fitzgerald

Dreams

The only time you ever really get away.
Be them good or bad, it's always something you decide or imagine.
Like a movie you watch with your eyes closed,
ending when you want it to, and always beginning when you decide.
The only thing some people really feel they control.
Happy, sad, love, or death,
at least most of them end like you want them to.
Aspirations, inspirations, and most of the time just plain Dreams.

Candace Utterback

Greenhands

Green hands
gremlin delightful playing
loosened bolts dangerously out
along the plane wings
little green palms
working for the common
surely doing no good
green little grubbing fingertips
heavy with their grandiose
reaching and rending out
cool calm and collected
working the engine's guts
leaving no lubrication
ceasing the motion forward
a violent screaming
two hundred fifty million passengers
all aboard for the final ride
taking off with stops at two four and six
green grabbing hands at the pilot's yoke

Erik Robert Frechette

Sisterhood

Sisterhood is a bond that goes beyond our roots.
It knows nothing of race or color,
for its love knows no boundaries.
As the years roll by, the unity becomes stronger.
It will overcome any obstacle in its path.
Sisterhood is so powerful, that nothing can destroy it;
it is invincible.
It is unstoppable, unparalleled, and unselfish.
Diverse voices coming together in unison is sisterhood.

Ebony Harding

Heaven

Heaven is a place of happiness and freedom from a world
full of violence where a soul can rest in peace.
A world where there are beautiful clouds and a wonderful
palace made of roses.
A place where peace, love, and happiness prevails, and a
world where there is no blood, no violence.
Heaven a place of rest.
Heaven what is it, where is it?
Heaven?

Natasha Danielle Escobar

You Knew

You knew it wasn't true
You knew it was a lie
You knew you could have helped me
But you didn't even try

Why did you hurt me?
Why didn't you care?
You just stood there and lied
While I was in despair

You knew all about it,
What had happened that night
You knew that I was innocent
But you didn't help me fight

You knew our friendship would surely end
But you didn't seem to care
All you thought about was yourself
And it really wasn't fair

You didn't care about me
You wrote me off as your friend
I didn't think that this could happen
Our friendship is at an end.

Shannon Sinnott

A Nuclear War

An event which prohibits anyone from using their telephone
Which separates people from their family
Thousands of men and women must abandon their homes
which causes them to live unhappily

Many people live off their own environment
Which hundreds do not know how to survive on
Young workers go into retirement
And the economy weakens as time passes on

Many countries use atomic bombs that contain radiation
Which causes targeted cities to be destroyed
Losing countries are thrown into tribulation
While the winning countries are filled with joy

The streets are filled with dead men, women, and children
Whose bodies are being decomposed into radioactive decay
Buried only by the dust flown around by the wind
The life these civilians once had has now been taken away

After a year or two the war has ended
In which the winning country is commended
It will take many years to restore life back into our towns
Which our government can do since it is not yet broken down

Howard Coleman

Sonnet of a Love Affair

Aphrodite's allure holdeth no light,
when compared to your angelic splendor.
Along with my heart, my mind taketh flight,
and my wondrous love shall have no ender.

On the wings of Love we do fly tonight,
Drifting aimlessly within timeless bounds.
Through the cloud's of Daedalus' son's plight.
never shall we touch the inconstant grounds.

Ne'er our united hearts will separate,
and by no means can our love be broken.
Even though grave times, our love won't abate,
nor will it become merely a token.

It is easy for anyone to see,
we're together for all times, you and me.

Brianne Russell

Sweet Lily

The bud is tight and
The night is moonlit
We stutter in innocence
The bloom yearns for light

And as morning comes
Like a sex-starved season
Coveting one chance to
Taste her succulent nectar

You retreat from the drippings
Back to the spectator's chair
As caramel seduction is relished by another
While you long for another chance to explain

Your thirst will be quenched Sweet Lily
Again and again till you drop from the stem

John T. McMahan III

If

If dogs were granted their wish to fly
As fast, as far, and as high
As the feathered bird who desired to be
Finned and scaled like fish in the sea;
And fish began to walk the land
With the gracefulness of superior Man;
And the sun so longed to give birth
To trees and flowers like mother earth;
And finally life, in the blink of an eye,
Mimicked death and decided to die;
Man would yearn to see his best friend soar,
But would dog be his best friend—or
Would his new best friend be the bird,
Which is now the fish that walks the world?
If by chance all opposites switched,
Man's reputation guarantees this:
Gas on the sun, he would eagerly pour;
Infinite love Man would make, and very little war.

Terry D. Stovall

Blind

Making love with a single tear in my eye,
Moon light dancing in the night's dark sky.
Tis no wonder to a soul like mine,
so hollow, dark, and my eyes so blind,
That a stream in the darkness goes flowing by.
The rain has started now, or is it the early morning dew?
Sorrow filled; if I only knew.

Josh Mason

The Father Moment

There is that moment,
a motion,
when the hawk leaves the branch,
when the glowing cadence of the sun falls
behind the rounded shadow of earth's horizon,
when the earth tilts and the longest day of the year ends,
when the boy,
filled with confusion, his heart swelling up,
turns to the father,
sawdust on his sleeves,
stubby pencil sharpened with a jackknife
locked behind his ear, and waits
for the embrace of those strong arms, that moment
passing like a stone falling
from the hand into the lake's dark unknown.
Descending, the boy gives way to that darkness,
turns and walks away.
"Ask your mother," is all his footsteps hear.

Philip Rose

Of Pirate Ships

Why do I dread the night and not the day?
A child asks his mother
When being laid down after a hard day's play
under the cool, smooth cover.

Snuggle up and rest your weary eyes,
my inquisitive little one,
and I will explain you why;
'tis story telling time, now that the day is done.

A magical world comes to life
but only in a sweet child's dreams;
A world when on your pillow you lie
but in another world it seems.

Of fluttering fairies and pirate ships
and magical sights that be;
every night you venture on a trip
and sail an imaginary sea.

Do not dread the night my son,
for how ordinary is the day
when at night, my little one,
on pirate's ships you play!

     Gina M. Villasmil

To My Lee

Love is a feeling that is felt within the heart, And cannot be enervated once it gets its start

It envelopes the soul in an abstruse way, That resists all miscreant and never goes astray

No miser or shrewd could in any way impede, Upon the only form that created you and me

This love that I feel for you will never abate, It rhapsodizes my soul in an exorbitant state

I really love you and I want you to know, That no matter what intervenes and causes us woe

This love I feel for you will always remain. And no matter where I roam it will always be aflame

The Lord tied us together in this knot we call Love, That is only experienced from heaven above

So I thank the Lord that he gave me you, Because you're the reason my heart beats true

This love that I feel for you will always be, And I hold in my heart this love for you, Lee.

     Krysta L. Webster

Through The Window

I look through the window and this is what I see,
Everyone is happy, everyone but me.
I have no life, I have no home,
It seems like all I do is roam.
Across the world, from here to there,
I have no one to love, no one to care.
All my friends were left behind,
Living without them had never crossed my mind.

I'm looking through the window, and this is what I see,
A sad, depressed, and lonely me.
I know I should be moving on,
But it's hard to look around
And find that everything you love is gone.

I want to close this window,
This window I've been looking through,
I want my life to just resume,
If only someone knew.

     Rachel L. Peters

somewhere and someday

somewhere underneath the stars he does exist . . .
someday i'll feel his lasting kiss . . .
somewhere we'll fall deeply in love . . .
someday heartache will never be thought of . . .
somewhere the candles will burn bright . . .
someday our lives will be alright . . .
somewhere he is out there . . .
someday i wonder if he'll care . . .

     Tara Turner

Friends

Friends are people who care
Friends are people who like to share
Friends are people who play
Friends are people who like to play everyday
Friends are people who climb trees
Friends are people who slap bees
Friends are people who eat over
Friends are people who sleep over
Friends are people who eat candy
Friends are people who named Sandy
Friends are people who don't eat leaves
Friends are people who don't leave
Friends are people who wear clothes
Friends are people with one nose.

     Dawn Cantwell

Friendship

Friendship is what God gives
Friendship is what love is
Friendship is a wonderful thing
Friendship makes birds chirp and sing
Friendship is when friends play together
Friendship is loyal no matter what the weather
Friendship is something that cares
Friendship is something that will always be there
Friendship is so true
Friendship will never let you be blue

     Kelley Vandergrift

Untitled

Love is the sweetness of your lips touching mine.
Every moment I'm away from you feels like forever.
I want to feel your embrace, and hold you in my arms,
If only I could touch you again . . . I hope it
won't be long. Love is the greatest
joy in this whole world. When will I
find that special one, to give my whole heart to?
Love can leave you standing tall, love will
help you through it all. Love is the
thing that stops the pain, when you're
on your knees in the pouring rain.
Without love in the world today,
everything would die and fade, then wither away.

     Alicia Brainard

Remembrance

Dedicated to my mom (Jo Miklos-Carr)
I look at her, and wonder:
What does she have that I don't?
What does she know that I can't remember?
What does my life have in store for me?
I can't think of what's important
and can't remember what to do.
Do I sit here and wonder?
Will I ever know?
What does she have that I don't?
What does she know that I can't remember?

     Katie Rogers

Hiroshima

On a hot August morning, 1945
American men watched the sun rise.
They guided their planes through the morning skies,
On a mission that would later bring tears to their eyes.

In Hiroshima, it was a normal day,
Adults work while children play.
One child wrecked buildings to make a fire way,
Another got a message about American planes, she'd relay.

Back in the skies, the Enola Gay men,
Were discussing the time to drop the bomb when,
There appeared a hole in the clouds and then,
They dropped the bomb and away they fled.

On the ground there were screams of pain and fright,
The destruction was a terrible sight.
People disappeared in what seemed like a smokey night,
All because the leaders couldn't get it right.

The swirling wind whipped up debris and dust
Causing a mushroom cloud to thrust
The smoke and ash they could taste from the gust,
The Americans they could no longer trust.

Katie Vater Age 11

My Sun Sets Over Your Mountain

My sun sets over your mountain.
But my beams reflect on your side into the deep ocean floor.
I show you all my love,
I show you all my care,
You ignore me as if I wasn't there.
My image is the reflection in your mirror,
There every morning to look at you.
You turn away from my image as if I were just as everyday object,
An object of nothing from nowhere.
My sun therefore sets over your mountain.
And still my beams reflect on your side into the deep ocean floor.
When will you show me your love,
Show me you care?
I wait for you forever.
Same place.
Same time.
Forever.

Nancy Trieu

My Life Will Never Be

My life will never be the same
Every time I turn around there's another game
From boys, sex, and drugs
To gangs, school and guns
I sit and ask myself will it ever end
Or will it go on like a new trend
Kids are being shot one by one
And bullets on the ground to prove they're done
It may be quiet as a mouse
But a kid could be shot by their house
We may not find away to end it all
But we all must be brave and tall
While mothers sit and cry
And watch their babies die
We should try to stand up and show our pride
So hold on it's going to be a bumpy ride

Vicki Proehl

The Pillow

I awoke this morning,
The rain was blowing in.
The pillow beside me was empty again.

The days just get longer,
The weeks never end.
When I look at that pillow it's empty again.

To see long chestnut hair and a pair of green eyes
Staring back from the pillow when the sun leaves the skies.
I think it's heaven on earth and then the morning begins,
I reach for the pillow but it's empty again.

You may take it for granted to have someone near.
Someone you call honey, lover or dear,
There are those who spend lifetimes lonely and in pain,
For when they look at that pillow it's empty again.

Jerry Emmert

A Different Likeness

A winding path that never ends
Its forbidding joys which it sends
So many truths, but even more lies
one's hope for love that always dies
so many choices we must face
Temptations would send us to the dreadful place
Fear that you would sit alone
Dark nothingness that you will roam
there are joys, but I see them not
Be content is what I've been taught
Eventually life will come around
And happiness will be forever found

Jacqueline O. Nusz

A Foolish Love

Called by the sun,
two lovers came running along.

They rolled together on the soft grassy hill,
then they lay perfectly still.

They stared at the moon,
till it came aglow.

Then they looked into each other's eyes,
and said a hurried goodbye.

Strangers at dawn,
lovers at dusk,
a love story unknown to most.

The more love pulled them together
the more the world pulled them apart,
a poisonous relationship from the beginning.

With tears of passion in her eyes,
the girl turned to wave goodbye.

His silhouette running away,
from the foolish love that would die by day.

Jenna Santoianni

Enough Is Enough

I'm beautiful and yet not fine enough.
I'm black and yet not African enough.
I'm woman and yet not feminine enough.
I'm (ADA) American With Disability and yet not perfect enough.
I'm a mother and yet not love enough.
And now I'm over forty and yet not young enough
Enough is truly enough.

Beverly A. Smith

Far From Home

Come take a visit to the other side,
far from home where the people cry.
The people here watch over them upon the clouds they ride,
singing and dancing all day and night.
People here have no worries,
because there is never a crime in sight.
Looking down, watching people scream and fight,
as they think to themselves, is that what we were like?
People here come young and old   ,
watching the people that they know,
sharing the memories of them they hold.
But every one will meet again at this place
until the end of the whole human race.

Mike Jordan

See It?

Can you see it?
Way up there?
It is up high.
It is so blue and, beautiful.
It is the sky.
Oh, look to the west, this is the best,
it is yellow and bright, and going out of sight.
Into the lake so blue, and cool,
for the fish and animals, they think it is their pool.
Now look and see, the stars twinkle in the sky.
A breath taking sight, my oh my.
It won't be long now, just time to sleep.
When the birds will awaken, and begin to peep.
And out of the East, there will be a big splash,
of rays of sunlight, for this day it will last.
The lake will begin to sway, and move.
It will crust and break, then be smooth.
The fish will jump up, out of the water, as if to say,
"Don't sit up there, come out and play."
You will smile to yourself with, joy and glee.
Was that fish really talking to me?

Peggy Tetreau

Blindness

Through an open field I hurry
Past the myriad people wise
Who see beauty in the world
No matter of its size.

My eye cannot spot them
But later I realize
That they are chasing after me
Attempting to advise

The mind I haven't time for.
The blindness in my eyes
Is longing for the view from a
Magnificent high rise.

I fumble through a forest
Where all creation lies
And so my soul then dies.

Time flies before the mountain peak I yearn for in the skies
Where I look down upon the people wise
Who told me to love the beauty that has lain there
All along before my very eyes.

Terence Purtell

To Whom It May Concern

To whom it may concern:
Loneliness has found a home in me, always neglected and
never given a chance, I will never be free.

To whom it may concern:
People seem to think that I can't feel,
don't be fooled; my pain is quiet real.

To whom it may concern:
I'm fighting a losing battle, I feel like I have no life,
People don't realize that the smallest word can cut like a knife.

To whom it may concern:
I'm a little bit different, but I'm not made of stone,
I'm not like other people, but have feelings too.
What have I done to deserve this?
Happiness is no friend of mine,
I hate to face reality, so I pretend that everything's fine.

To whom it may concern:
this plea for help is my song, flowing from the river of tears
that I have cried inside.

I hope there is something that the reader can learn,
Because I'm sending this poem, to whom it may concern.

Jared Anders

Good-Night

Sweet dreams, my beloved.
It is time to put our minds at rest.
With a swift and quiet Swoosh,
Mother Nature sweeps her hand across the sky,
Leaving shimmering ruby stars
And a sleeping moon.
Only roaming patches of wind
Move from here to there.
The birds from the apple orchard
Put their songs to bed.
The rain sprinkles down in light blues and greys
As it maneuvers through the shadows.
Lights gradually go off
In all of the windows,
As the USA kisses day away.
Good-night, my beloved.
You are safe for tonight.

Cristy L. Bunnell

I Saw, Which Startled Me, A Rose, A Tulip, A Daisy

A quarrel between a few
An idiotic dispute
They pulled out their rifles
And started to shoot

I heaved myself to the ground
Noticed the soil in which I layed upon
It cushioned my fall, it relaxed my bruises
And to a foot in front
I saw, which startled me, a Rose, a Tulip, a Daisy.
I asked them, "Why . . . why must
you show your beauty here?"
"Can't you see the evil we wear,
the terrible thoughts we share?!"

Without a response I had come to a
conclusion. For I shall not live in
a world with such beauty.
So I ate them
A Rose, a Tulip, a Daisy.

Jonathan Crollo

Stress

Stemming from the pit of my stomach,
Extending into the ventricles of my heart,
He rages.

Reaching out into my limbs
like a seedling stretches toward the sun.
Quivering each muscle
as a violent quake jolts the horizon.
Forcing himself throughout my head, knocking on my brain
like a persistent salesman pounds on doors.

The dark gray blanket of stress envelops my entire being;
Suffocating, suppressing,
spreading over my light
till the glowing
is invisible.

Kaye Spear

Him and Her

His cared turned to hate
His honesty turned into lies
His promises broke one after another.

Her promises are kept and still remain,
Her care is blindfolded by his actions she can't see through
He holds in his nurturing hands
A pure and delicate girl.

She is sensitive and emotional,
Hurt by the smallest words said,
Yet she strives to stay so strong.

He is kind and gentle,
Acts as if nothing bothers him,
His hidden fears make his strong also,
Yet so weak as she knows him well.

Her sensitivity and his kindness,
Her being emotional, his gentle touch
Make them what they are together
Yesterday, today, and tomorrow.

Tiffany Bradley

Covered Bridges

Covered bridge of weathered wood, built to work and last.
When I walk upon your deck, I transport to ages past.
I hear the hoof beats on your planks of sturdy ironwood.
I think of the wagon loads passed here, just where I have stood.
Though you are weather-beaten how strong and proud you stand.
Like a memorial to time past, an icon of this land.
Listen hard and you can still hear the echoes of the men.
Who crossed this bridge for a seven score, time and time again.
Now your working days have passed, retired to quiet leisure.
A testimonial to time, to be enjoyed for strolling lovers pleasure.

Thomas Rigano

My Rose, My Beautiful Rose

My rose, my beautiful cute rose,
The most beautiful flower in the universe
A flower that is the standard that
All beautiful flowers are judged by
My rose, my beautiful cute rose,
Preceded mankind and before any human
Ever walked the planet and cannot be duplicated and
cannot be destroyed
And you are blossoming everywhere,
I want to thank Allah for making it possible for
Letting me see this beautiful rose
The envy of all the worlds.

Imam Sulaiman R.S. Aqeel

Too Soon They Die

And the cries of the dying days grow stronger
The pain of the loss of life lasts longer
And into the end, we welcome the hurt
Piece by piece, we turn to dirt
Ashes bury the memory
Of the sorry souls left, their eyes no longer see
The past in flames, never able to return
Today on fire and tomorrow soon burns
Over, once more, they pray again
Too soon they die to wonder when
The spirits pulled into an endless sky
Too soon they die to wonder why
The winds whisper words of despair
The blackest darkness, unsure what's there
A dream born from a nightmare
Masks worn by souls, blind and unaware
Time get so close, so much closer to the end
Too soon they die, we hold their sins
Too soon they die, we cannot win

Jeremy Skaggs

Is There Still Tomorrow?

With so much sadness and a lot of sorrow,
Tell me, is there still tomorrow?

In darkness and no light,
Do I still have my sight?

I hear the roll of thunder
as I lie under the covers.
In the dark without my sight,
will I ever again see the daylight?

With so much sadness
and a lot of sorrow,
I wonder, is there still tomorrow?

Mary Josephine Jose

On Parting

My dear friend, how much I'll miss you.
Oh, why must you go away?
I know you must move in life,
But still, I wish you could stay.

Our time together is waning fast,
So soon you will depart.
Residing in another place,
You'll remain close to my heart.

I'll always treasure the time we've shared,
From beginning to the end.
I can't express how glad I am
That you are more than just a friend.

I don't know when we'll meet again,
Nor where our paths shall meet,
I thank the Lord that one day soon
Together Jesus we shall greet.

I pray that God will guide your life
And all your endeavors bless,
In every passing day and year
Grant you good health and happiness.

Judy Tremblay

Lost Love

Can you see me in the distance, in the memories of your mind,
Amid your thoughtful dreams; am I so difficult to find?
Is my face so unfamiliar, my voice a fading sound?
Have you forgotten that so swiftly, the love that we both found?
Did I really mean so little, were your words so empty then?
Where did you find the courage to say our love would end?
After all our times together the days, the months, and years,
we shared through all the seasons our happiness and fears.
The feelings that I knew then are buried deep inside;
I wonder if you will ever know how many tears I've cried.
And now I must look forward despite the pain and fear,
The summer of our love is gone and you are no longer here.

Darlene Caswell

So Close . . . Yet So Far Away

I look upon you from a near distance
With teary eyes I watch the fire ignite from within your hands
as your thumb presses against the igniter on your lighter
So as the fluid did inflame
So did my heart
Though a simple task it amazes me
The others seem separate from you and me
As they tell stories of places I've never been
Places that we can go
From where I stand I can see that you were meant for me
With you is where I want to be
Your beauty is all I see
But the color of your skin is different
Some think it matters
I know it doesn't
I've got so much to say
and so much to tell
But I stand mute
I don't know why
But I do

Rob Meisenholder

Autumn on the Farm

Beside the old barn, the maple tree
Shed her leaves early, as impatiently
She readied herself for winter's cold
To slide straight through, no leaves to hold.
Her naked top's forlorn and bare,
Looks so alone in autumn air.
Long lean fingers raised on high
Stroke the rosy dawn of eastern sky.
While sister maples hold leaves until
They glow like spotlights on the hill.
Vine maple and dogwood yet unshed
Set in like jewels of ruby red.
Backed by dark velvet of evergreen
Only in autumn this awesome scene.
Perusing this picture, a sudden thought,
What wondrous works our God has wrought.

Ruby B. Eddy

Untitled

I sit on my short throne peering hopelessly
at the unfortunate.
My everything would never be enough to change
their misery.
So I keep to myself,
with hazy dreams of becoming queen.

Jessica Tetreault

Winter

Mother Nature tucks the flowers in for a long winter nap,
and sends the summer birds on their way.
A words of warning in their ears,
don't come back until winter has faded away.

Softly the snow covers the ground,
deeper and deeper each day and night.
Oh! How beautiful the world looks,
covered with its blanket of white.

Snowmen are popping up all over,
even snow angels appear in flight.
Jack Frost works his magic,
on windows for our delight.

Everyone romps and shouts with laughter,
come, let's get out the sleds and skis.
Ice skates are flying over the ice,
off to the fire for warmth, please.

Winter brings such beauty and joy,
one couldn't ask for anything.
Such fun in all that heavenly fluff,
Why, then, are we glad it's Spring?

Mary L. Stover

My Jewel

Tell me what you don't love me; I refuse
To hear false statements bend in my good ear.
One thousand times or more those words you used,
Those puissant words: "Oh, how I love you dear."
How I know that strange love has many shades.
The dimmest shade resembles hate's crude form
And wields with vengeance hate's cold, sharpest blades,
To nothing gratify unless reborn.
If, by chance, other loves can polish stone,
Then I will lose and they will gain the most.
For the love you give is not theirs alone,
But partly mine, although be it a ghost.
You are a jewel in need of a safe place
And I know the keys to your jewelry case.

Calvin Joe Moore

In Memory of Sharon Belle

The Angel of Death kissed my darling,
Yes, kissed her and took her away.
The pain in my heart was so dreadful,
I feared it would not go away!

But, I found that Time was the Healer,
And my life could still hold much joy.
Then, God sent us a beautiful girl,
As well as a wonderful boy!

He knew Life belonged to the Living,
I still had so many to love.
The rest of my darlings—my comfort,
This lesson I learned from above!

And ev'ry day, though I think of her,
On my face, a tear and a smile.
How grateful I am that I had her,
Even though such a little while!

And when my earthly stay is over . . .
We shall meet on that distant shore . . .
Then again, I'll hold her in my arms
And we'll be parted never-more!

Rhema Delight Coons

He Wouldn't Take Me Dancing

He won't take me dancing, though he'll gamble, hunt and fish.
Even though a night of dancing, is my biggest wish.
I thought a gift he gave me, a concert, the best.
But he said it should put issues, of dancing, to rest.

He asks me what I want to do; I say, "Let's go and dance."
He just ignores and asks again, or laughs and says, "No chance."
He used to say he'd try it. That he would learn and go.
But anytime I ask, the answer's always "no."

We do the things that he likes, alone, or with his friends.
It hurts so bad to think, I'll never dance again.
He says that I can go and dance, in someone else's arms.
Doesn't he care if I should fall, for someone else's charms?

I love to watch the cowboys. The music fills my soul.
If I cannot go dancing, my life will not be whole.
He knows how much I miss it, he says he loves me too.
Yet this happiness so simple, is something he won't do.

I wonder if he'll someday feel he really missed his chance.
If I should need to go away because I need to dance.
If people ask what happened, when we're apart someday,
"He wouldn't take me dancing," is all I'll have to say.

D.J. Blue

Rain

Little drops of water, descending from the sky
Thunder rolling
Lightning striking
The rain turned very fierce

As the sun peeks through the clouds
It seems as if the rain has turn to diamonds

Looking from a distance
You can see a brightly colored rainbow
Now as the clouds roll away
The brightly painted rainbow surges with it.

Audrey Monroe

Young

So many choices to make at such an age.
Torn, pushed, and shoved.
How do I decide?
I love them both.
Time, so uncompassionate, had come for me to decide.
Forced to choose.
I stood there at their stares.
Looking at my options
one on my right, and one on my left.
Each had an arm as if trying to tear me apart.
I closed my eyes and teared.
Hoping for when I opened,
It would have been gone.
The fate of death,
I opened.
Facing reality dead in the face,
With the look of murder in his eyes.
Knowing that my choice will change the lives of many.

Tracy Fahrenkamp

Mother And Child—Full Circle

for Tracy And Beary
I sit here and stare at this little old bear
reflecting on love for my child,
who now comforts me as we share her old bear
and I rest in her care for a while.

Lesa Stasevich

My Mother Nature

What do you think is beautiful?
Maybe something you can see
A rock, some grass, or probably a prehistoric tree.
It is called mother nature and it is everywhere
It is not further than the distance of a single hair.
Mother nature is full of love
It is as graceful and elegant as an ivory dove.
As natural as it can be
From a rocky mountain to a bumbling bee.
And behind every lovely creature
There lies a lovely little feature
That is not difficult to see
Just take a close look it just might set your soul free.
So you should be thankful every special day
Therefore you have mother nature in every special way.
More valuable than money
More sweeter than honey,
A magical place
That is filled with wonders and much more to chase.
This place is called mother nature, the mother of earth

Michelle Volovelsky

Thinking of You

Not a day goes by that we don't think of you,
Sometimes it makes us happy, sometimes it makes us blue.
You were such an important part of each of us,
When we were close and loving, and even when we'd fuss.
You always saw the good, overlooking the bad,
Not to say you were perfect, we're all wicked just a tad.
You saw the world for what it is and then you looked beyond,
So see the beauty God created of which you were very fond.
You never failed to give credit where credit was due,
Often taking the back seat, letting others' lights shine through.
You were a kind and gentle spirit on loan from above,
If you taught us anything, you taught us how to love.
Life's not always fair as we have come to learn,
It took us on a journey, with an unsuspecting turn.
A wife lost a husband and a mother lost a son,
The world lost a precious gift that can be compared to none.
You are sorely missed, and again I tell you true,
Not a day goes by, that we don't think of you.

LaVerne Victoria Ferguson

Untitled

Being so happy when I fell in love with you,
Now fighting every day to try and fall back out.
In my heart I know you loved me,
You just didn't know what love was about.
The way you loved was painful;
And on my face, a many time did it show.
But now my love is ending, and the hatred starts to grow.
See, what I learned of love from you
Was a pain, a pain I didn't know love could bring.
And now because of what you've done,
I pray I never love again.
You were supposed to hold me,
And hug me, and show me you cared.
Not lie to me, cheat on me,
Or fill me with fear.
So if I start to miss your hug and your kiss,
I'll remember the pain if I dare!

Carla Gianformaggio

True Happiness

Love is something we cannot buy
And it is something we can't deny
And it is something we all feel
And we all possess it, it is real

It can easily be given away
Every second of everyday

It is not expensive, but it's not around
It's only in your heart, that's where it is found
It's free, between you and me

The more you give away
The more you get
If you save it, you soon forget
How to be happy.

You become selfish, angry and mean
So open yourself to happiness
And let your love be seen

Mollie Lemberg

Time

The clock is ticking
Tick, tick, tick
Hour after hour
Minute after minute
The ringing in my ears is getting louder
Think harder, think faster
Tick, tick, tick
Beads of sweat are running down my forehead
The sharpness of metal against my skin
Tick, tick, tick
Time is running out
The thrill of pain pierces my body
My heart beats faster
Thump, thump, thump
Tick, tick, tick
I gaze into the mirror that shadows death
The metal runs down my shivering cold skin
Tick, tick, tick
Time, there is more time
Thump, thump, thump.

Elizabeth Cyr

Educations Is Where It's At

I am, I am, I said to my Pa
School, I am going, I already talked to Ma.
Study hard, study hard and learn my Son,
Earning a living without Education is not fun.

When you get there talk to everyone.
Associate with the good, not with no puns.
Let them all know Education is where it's at.
They will all help you, and for you go to bat.

Universities are big with lots of people.
More goes here than at a church with a steeple.
Red, yellow, black and white, all Americans:
You must get along with race, be a Good Samaritan

I've told you all I know how to get along.
Respect them and their ways and you won't go wrong.
Treat people like you want to be treated.
This old world will be a better place, not defeated.

Sherrold D. Rogers

Save

The sky turns gray as it fills up with smoke.
The ocean water turns black as it fills with oil.
The land becomes bare as trees are cut down.
The rain forest turns quiet as animals become extinct.
Save us!!

Jennifer Ralston

Happy Birthday Cake

A pain is wrenching the pit been filled
void of feelings kept hidden now jumped and crave and cry
for the one thing that keeps me and set me apart
from a world enclosing a race of people
one for I am not included and cannot be accepted
until I can be considered pretty
What have I done to be damned of such status
What has possessed my will my strength
my inside beauty to leave me wallowing in my sorrow
and self-loathing drowning in what I thought was comfort
now has cursed me
With the eternal fight and battle of what to eat and not to eat
A question that has me chained to a body
I never asked for but continue to feed its need
to expand and explore aspects of a world
that pushed me out before I was born
and has left me with nothing
except Happy Birthday Cake.

Jessica Larrabee

Only You

Burning embers in the fire glow bright,
beyond the flame I hold only you in my sight.

Snow sprinkles the winter trees in an array of white,
angels dance with love this night.

With you in my heart I am never alone—
golden crowns and sticks of stone.

When your arms enclosed my frail frame,
my life was forever changed, never the same.

The strength of a lion and the smile of child,
your eyes full of kindness your voice gentle and mild.

How strong this love for you I hold,
strong as the tales wise men told.

The dawn is breaking as I finish these words,
sweet songs of love- my gift from the birds.

I lie down my pen and I close my eyes,
I think only of you as the wind softly cries.

Brandy Carter

Spring

When you hear the bird's song,
it gives you a clue,
You feel nothing is wrong,
There's so much to do.
And you like to watch the magnificent flowers bloom
Also in the evening you watch the stars shine.
You feel like Cinderella, throwing away her broom
You feel this way because spring is just divine.

Julie Lynn Larson

Flowers of Life

The tension becomes intense
An eruption of hate
Sent for the cause that no one understands
The flowers of conflict rise and bloom
They bloom with the colors of peace
The Cards burn—An act of anarchy?—
No, one of hope
Their seeds spread far from their homeland—East
Forced from a place, to save their life
To stand for the lives of others
The flowers have faded during the Cold winter
Their petals hidden from view
But their spirit moves on,
To live within me and you

Dalton Newsom

The Love That's Within Me

As I sit and wonder why I gaze at
The heavenly blue sky that lies up above me
To ask the same question from time to
Time, again what is the love that within me
My mind racing with even so, much pain and
Sorrow. Tends to lead me straight ahead.
To only find that the question I ask.
Still lies faithful on down the long and
Winding road. The answer I must truly
And surely find for this question still,
Lives deep and ever so buried for into the
Back of my wondering mind, what
Is the love that's within me.
And as I pave, for only a second you, see.
I find that the smell child is playing
Beneath the Oak tree, his laughter,
I hear for and wide shell bring
A smile respond my weary face.
For don't you see he has shone me the answer
Happiness is the love that's within me.

Randal Frank Munday

Love

Sometimes love, isn't all what it seems to be.
It can be filled with happiness, sorrow, or pain
Love can overcome and conquer some of the over
bearing obstacles that people face
Love can bring forth peace in times of war
Love can conquer and beat all odds
Love sometimes can overshadow heartache and pain
Love can be confusing and difficult to understand
Love can weather people through the many storms that they face
Love is in you and love is in me,
But most of all love is what
brings people together.

Tiffany Drain

What Is Love?

A bright orange ray of warmth
that flows thru your body
A fresh crisp breeze that refreshes
your thoughts of that special someone
So what is love?

Hearing the sounds of Mr. Pitter and
Mrs. Patter
As your heart pounds harder when
true love is near
A gentle touch or soft caress as the
tiny hairs on your skin rises from love's conquering

Mesmerized as you look into those enchanting eyes
Picturing the future in your distant thoughts
as they float away with the clouds
And you wonder what is love?
It is everything that can be shared
or felt with someone special

Veronica LaJoyce Bickham

Tears

You're crying tears of sorrow, from your soul's troubled space
Flowing soft as Angels wings, expelling sorrow with grace
Releasing your heart of its agony and pain
While replenishing themselves for when they are needed again

Let the tears flow freely, for there must be a reason.."Why"
your soul felt the need to let go and "cry"
And when the last teardrop falls from your eye
Remember God is there for you
Now was it worth the cry?

Zelda Theresa Partee

Dad

There is no finer person to be had,
than the one we all know as Dad.

How can a hand so firm be so gentle too,
and a voice so stern soothe and comfort you?

He quells the sounds that go bump in the night,
by the touch of his hand yet without a fight.

Parent, teacher, protector and provider too,
there is nothing in this world that Dad can't do.

Dads tend to keep their feelings inside,
but the love for his family Dad just can't hide.

Without hesitation he would lay down his life,
in defense of his beloved children and wife.

So let us thank God for all dads today,
and wish all dads a "Happy Father's Day."

Bernie Conklin

Endings Are Just Beginnings Anyways

I ended a relationship today!
It wasn't going anywhere.
I have too many goals,
to just go drifting.

I opened a new door today!
It is the new door to my future,
Where I go on with my goals
And meet like-minded people.

Endings are just beginnings anyway!
What goes out leaves room for one to enter.
I may begin a new goal today and
Prove that endings are just beginnings anyway.
Endings are just beginnings inside out.

Lauraine T. Feuer-Hutchinson

Lives in Passing: Past and Present

Together a tense calm prevails
As we sit looking at each other
And agony covers the room
As I declare a truce.

Small talk and you and I together
Know our presence compensates all.

Communication we seek despite
All barriers as joy steps hesitantly forth.

The miracle that you and I
Should once more be together
And pain will have to wait until we part.

Nancy Dodge

Our Hearts Will Never Drift Apart

In our lives we do what we can,
For in this world we are only woman and man.
We cannot be perfect as hard as we try,
Yet we are perfect together both you and I.
And in the ocean we call life we are two souls in a boat,
Put together by fate and sent to float.
Where the water carries us is unknown,
But wherever that is will be our home.
And in not knowing what lies ahead,
There are three words that should be said,
To comfort and guide, to give peace and hope,
To help us adjust, and make it easier to cope.
These words can be said when we are happy or blue,
And these three words are "I Love You."

Charles Sanderson

Reverie

I felt the pull of days long past
As I stared into my looking glass.
Nor could I help the tears that came
As easily as the fresh spring rain.
I looked again and as I stood,
Began to go back to my childhood.
I saw again what children see
As they stand before a Christmas tree.
I hung my stocking with love and care
In hopes that St. Nick would visit me there.
I sat before the open heart,
Roasting my toes and being a part
Of each story told, every song that was sung,
Joining in on all the fun.
The sandman came and closed my eyes,
And when I awoke, it was with surprise,
For there upon a throne I sat,
Made of souvenirs from the past,
At my feet, scattered pell mell,
Were many old Jingle Bells.

Mabel R. Yaredick

The Stream and I

Slowly as I watch the ragging running
Stream go by, somehow I wonder where
the end will lie is it like me, with no place
to go no one who cares just moving alone slow.
Hoping someone would come by and say hello
or maybe ask you what do you know. Nothing
that really cares but the wind that blows
above and the sun shining high these
are our only friends don't ask me why.
Maybe one day luck will come our way
and we want have to be alone that day.
Since we are both loners I go down there
twice a day and whisper softly and gently
to a cool soft stream, I know it want answer
back but as water rushes over the rocks it
sounds as though it is speaking to me anyway.
So I sit back and relax and I think will
we ever find someone of our very own
or will we be left all alone as the silence
of a dark and warm summer night.

Shirley E. Daniel

What Do Kids See?

I sit back on my couch and write what's inside me
One question that comes to mind, is what do kids see?
Do they see a good movie, or just people on TV?
Do they see it's a fight or just words with you and me?
Do they see that there is danger, as they run through the house?
Do they see there's a purpose for being "quiet as a mouse"?
Do they see any reason for not doing that?
Do they see that it hurts when they get into a spat?
Do they see why they should be clean and stay neat?
Do they see you get burned if your to close to the heat?
Do they see why not to play in the street?
Do they see why they can't talk to the strangers they meet?
Do they see when they push me, it just makes me mad?
Do they see when I scold them it just makes me sad?
Do they see that this love comes deep from my heart?
Do they see that the bonding was made from the start?
Do we see what it is that they see through their eyes,
It's all the because the I don't knows, and the whys!

Rhonda Clark

Secret Thoughts

Always from a distance, we would usually say Hello
In the door of our building to your lover you would go

I always wanted to talk to you, you seemed to understand
Take a walk in the park, holding each other's hand

On a day like any other I had to say what was on my mind
Would you like to make love and encounter the strange kind

We could read between the lines and then say them
I'd start burning with desire
You'd be getting all my love the kind that would not tire.

But these were just my secret thoughts that I could not say
So I put them down on paper perhaps another day

Kevin O'Brien

Untitled

One dark night two hearts did part,
Alone to begin a brand new start.
Two different roads parting two different lives,
Yet no distance can separate unbreakable ties.
Hearts torn apart yet love lives strong
Forever together no matter what can go wrong.
Years may pass before two reunite,
And so many tears are left to fight.
One heart did break, shattered to pick up,
So many decisions remain, left to confront.
Time passes by, lives live on,
Of a traditional Romeo suddenly gone.
Completely lost accompanied by confusion and fear,
Forced to listen to things you don't want to hear.
Choices to make, forbidden lies,
Living alone because no one complies.
Strength and comfort torn away,
And perfect lives put on delay.
Realize the truth and open your eyes,
Fate can't be changed, No matter how hard you try.

Macy D. Andersen

Point of View (Moon and Sun)

His: As I rose, she laid down.
My blackness took over her beauty.
People sheltered themselves from my sight.
A few of my distant friends could now be seen.
They were my tears,
for I was crying that I could not be seen with her,
could not be as bright as her, could not be as big as her,
could not be her.

Her: He is never consistent,
coming at different times every night,
never appearing clothed in the same way.
The peacefulness he brought, could never be repeated.
Close enough to be touched, but the mystery is not gone.
I am always by myself,
jealous of his company, the magic he plays,
the calmness he brings and the life he lives.

Laura Scagnelli Tellier

Star Gazing

I lie on the wet grass and watch the wind make snow
with the leaves on the ever-changing trees of life.
They were put here to admire and watch.
We live to trip and fall on their branches,
yet we think we are more superior than they.
I am naked with the earth,
though I am caught up in the minds
of thinking in the human race
that I hate with all my heart.
When I die, I would like to become a star
and have the trees to gaze down upon.

Sarabeth Hodge

Situation and Introspect

Drifting in a sea of uncertainty
Within this game which disguises itself as a family,
My anger cripples me.
As I cry in the coming year
Blame is there to provide me with a painful comfort.
Personal demons nip at my ankles,
Only stopping in brief intervals to catch their breath
As I continue running.
Maybe I am one in need of complete correction,
Not just self-improvement when ambition gives way to fear,
Memory and responsibility concede to pressure, and
Individuality and creative thinking are stifled under doubt.
I must be aware of what I need to do
To become more or who I'd like to be;
Because when you lose yourself,
It leaves you even lonelier in your loneliness.

Tina-Marie Hendron

Let It Rain

Though today the rain downs a
steady pour,

Windows are covered by a blanket
of wet, and only to receive more,

I can vision your face enhanced by
a beautiful smile.

I also picture my loving you, as
all is clear, and bright for awhile.

Outside today all is dark accented
by a dreary haze. and wind,

Though through the window of my mind,
You're standing there, and it's summer once again.

Oh that summer, that hot August night.

You and I, with the magic in between,
grew stronger as we held each other tight.

So today let it rain,
let the wind howl with power.

I can escape to a summer's day,
loving you hour after hour.

Fred D. Ritter

Untitled

Sometimes I wonder about this ole world
Sometimes people get mad and slam the door
They don't want to be a man and work it out
They don't want to see what life and love is all about
When they get mad they beat on their wives
All she knows to do is cry
She doesn't want to leave him for someone new
They don't want to face up to reality and realize
They're boys not men
They'll find out true love is where you begin

Ashley Jernigan

Mother Nature's Tools

To see the world through a fly's eyes
is to see a million things,
and to reach your goals you'll have to borrow
some of butterfly's wings.

To speak with words of wisdom
sing a Robin's tune,
and to have the courage of a coyote
howl at the moon.

Amber Rose Pirtle

A Child's Innocence

You take your innocence as a child for granted,
unaware of the troubles that lie ahead of you.
You are anxious to become a teenager;
have friends, relationships and freedoms.

You are shocked that being a teen is a lot different
than you ever imagined.
Your emotions are on a roller coaster,
your heart is content and then broken time and time again.

You are overwhelmed with new responsibilities,
and all you wanted were freedoms.
You are learning some tough lessons about life and now
you long for your childhood days . . .

But you've lost something you will never have again,
the innocence of a child!

Kellie M. Ekiert

Summer

Summer is time off from school . . .
Summer is when we're hot and cool . . .

Summer is time to relax . . .
Summer is time to kick back . . .

Summer is swimming at the pool . . .
To try to stay cool . . .

Summer is getting a tan . . .
Summer is getting buried in the sand . . .

Summer is baby sitting . . .
For brothers and sisters and neighborhood kids . . .

Summer is having fun . . .
In the sun . . .

Summer is staying up late . . .
Summer is sleeping in late . . .

Summer is going to the shore . . .
Summer is fun and lots more . . .

Jennifer Ribecca

Untitled

The night we danced together
it seemed like we should be together forever

The way you held me in your arms
your eyes, your smile you had all the charms.

I could have melted right there
but all I could do was stare

There was many things I wanted to tell you
how my life without you was blue

My dreams were nice that night
wishing you would hold me tight

Wishing my dreams would come true
when you found out I like you

But friends is all you wanted to be.
To my heart you hold the key.

Amanda Belgarde

Untitled

Gaea green blue marble's mystery I have seen
Born of chaos primeval void.
In Tartarus direction some would be
On the other side of the fulcrum Eros in the descending order
Allows Erebus to look down on Him.
And with a cruel smile Nyx is next in the batting order.

John H. LaManque

Cloud Nine

Suffocating so heavily on invisible clouds.
Crying out to be released
To one bold and beautiful.

To encase our desires between us
Kills my very existence.
To see . . . to feel . . . to touch . . .
My physique shakes of lust and sorrow.
Sorrow to whom I shall not seek
For forces greater than I, but not of "us."

Emotions create no boundaries to the forces I imagine.
With great despair I depart,
But shall never leave cloud nine.

Krishna Jenkins

Daffodils

Beautiful golden daffodils, golden as the sun,
I'm sitting here watching you waste away.
All our fun together is all done,
I'll just sit here.

If we never meet again,
I'll see others, but none as sweet as you.
Watching you waste away,
Though I'd hoped we'd never part, it is true.

I shall waste away as well,
Never to see each other again.
In the shadow I see that you're gone,
Good-bye, good-bye, sweet daffodil.

Samantha Rose Zimmerman

Awesome Fire

How many stars uncountable reside
Amidst each blazing galaxy so removed
Their blinding lights are wearied to naught
Before their journey brings them nigh
Where man must peer through glass to see their glow.
How many galaxies seen and unseen
With some so distant that their speeding rays
Have just begun to touch our orbit's path
And some so far they may expire unknown.
What power unimaginable must be
That rules and regulates this awesome fire
Which conquers frigid darkness absolute
Then nurtures blossoms caressed by breeze.

John Niemirovich Jr.

Beautiful Man

I glide into the moon with my yellow teeth in front
I know I can't always get what I want
I watch you fly above the moon
Under the glass eye, I'll see you soon
You hide away from my evil with your arm
Fluffy kittens, we do no harm
I am a well, empty into the sky
Open the clouds, I watch you die
Beautiful man, you read your will
Beautiful man, you drink your last fill
Your dying wish can't fly on home
Next to the wind, you are alone
You're trapped in this world with no soul
Gambling older cow watch it roll!
Guess for the children with their tears
Around the houses, a new atmosphere
I guess who is dying or trying to behave
Trying to move from this heat wave
Beautiful man, you feel my face
Beautiful man, you love, you waste.

Mary Tomaszewski

Consequences

He knew his time was coming and just before he went to a coma
He said he had made awful mistakes and that was his life diploma

Poor mama, had to deal with all the drama
Quiet and with no complaints, she dealt with it
With a smile that anyone would die to know why
She would not cry

But we came to realize that she was teaching us the reality
That we all can change, if we give ourselves a chance

Life simplicity, becomes complex when one starts
Adding inside, things that one does not need to survive

We guessed he was a lover
Of what? We still do not know, and always haunted us
The fact that we seldom saw him sober
We watched him trying, and he told us that he would
But he was too ill to fight

He was a lover and we seldom saw him sober

If you see a stop sign, even if you do not mind
Think twice and do what is right
You might change the course of your life
It goes very fast and there is no coming back!!!

Richard Breglia

My Mother's Hand

Of all the quilts in my mother's chest
I like the crazy quilt the best
I think the reason must be
In the center a tiny hand you can see

It was traced by my grandmother years ago
As mother held her hand on the quilt just so
The hand is much larger now, but just as sweet
As when traced onto the quilt so small and neat.
This hand that rocked my cradle and rolled my curls
For me still knits and purls
And when this hand from age begins to wilt
Will be dearer to me than when traced on the quilt.

Maurine Elkins Arnold

Transcendence

On salty mists of ocean spray, I rise.
Gazing out across the vast gateway of the water world,
the eminence of God's handiwork transcends into my spirit.

Unwinding, my bones give way enervatively as the sizzling,
foaming vapors of the ocean creep into my being.
As I lie limp upon the sand, the water teasingly tickles
my toes and retreats with a hiss.

The morning sunrise bursts through the clouds
and dances upon the water.
The perturbation of a fog horn from the distance
pierces the tranquil ocean—
and I could feel the pulsating rumble within.

Melissa Gibbons

Untitled

They are all a part of what's around us
I am on the outside
Viewing the world from a different point of view
I see people as they are - what they don't see
There are groups of people all of different kinds
The division is there yet they do not see
The world revolves around them
A bubble surrounds their lives
They cannot be harmed and
Are unaware of the world around them
Will they ever wake up from the dream they are living?
Will they ever see what they've done?

Erica Eden

To All Teachers Who Never Believed In Me

Their was a time when I was young and immature.
Though I lived my life too the according of what it was.
I may never have had the 'smarts' of other kids
Nor did I have 'brains' of all your heads.

I remember you laughing at me.
Your tongue declared me 'stupid,' said I would never succeed.
You looked upon me with an incredulous stare.
Doubting me and condemning me of my beliefs.

There are, I am sure, many like myself.
And I cannot lament my sorrow or hatred for life.
But for those of you who saw me as an ignorant gimpy,
I saw yourselves as uncaring and impatient.

I shall not be provoked to curse profanity at you all.
There is simply a lack of intelligence in those words.
And I shall not rip and tear at your hearts!
For I understand how fragile we really are.

To all teachers who never believed in me:
Even if deep inside, you are still just as were.
And find my poem worthless as you would expect of me.
. . . I forgive you . . . with all my recovering heart.

Chris Lakoduk

A Friendship

A friendship is when there's two hearts beat but as one.
A friendship is when her favorite color is yellow and yours
is blue but yet they still match.
A friendship is when your eyes are blue and her eyes are
brown but they see the same thing.
A friendship is when you both can laugh and cry and still be happy.
A friendship is when you both have other friends but you
still have that special relationship.
A friendship is when you have disagreements and you
can push them aside.
A friendship is when two people thousands and thousands of
miles away can still be very close in each others hearts.
I am only eleven years old and I know what having a
best friend is like.
I don't know if I will ever find it again, but I know in my
heart what friendship is.
This is for my best friend Nichole.
I will miss her a lot.

Whitney Horne

High Expectations

I skate out on the ice with the new blades we bought,
remembering the dances and moves, I've been taught.
Yet my hands are clammy; they're cold, and they are numb.
My teeth are chattering - they dance, upon my tongue.
My name is announced over the public address.
I am anxious, I am nervous, I am a mess!
My performance begins and I find that I'm led,
by the sounds of "my" music playing in my head.
My mind puts me through my often practiced routines.
I continue to glide and know what my coach means with:
"keep your mind", on your purpose- don't lose focus"
Or the witches will curse you and hocus pocus.
And just then it happened concentration does break,
the most horrible fall of my life I did take.
The crowd groans then hushes - I lay in a big heap.
But I remembered a promise I have to keep.

I get back up, and smile and continue to skate.
I know I must finish and, I'll finish just great.
I complete my program, I make each turn and twirl
I know in my heart I'm still a wonderful girl.

Nicole Walters

Help

Help I yelp
My brain feels like yellow marshmallow Jell-o
O no my school work
Needs more work
What! I have zits!
Now now this is the pits
But my date
I can't be late
And what about my weight
I hate my weight
And is my hair straight
I need a job
If I want to buy this thing amabob.
I'm not a horse
So of course
I need help

Tina Wittig

Sadness

Sadness is being alone with no place to go
feeling lost and helpless, other people don't know.
Sadness is watching the trees blow in the wind
while you sit alone guzzling gin?
Sadness is watching the sun change the rain
while people with laughter know no pain!
Sadness is watching your best team get beat
while people of the world are born to compete!
Sadness is watching other people have fun
knowing inside that you'll have none.
Sadness is watching her walk away
praying and hoping that she'll come back someday!
Sadness is making a mistake that can't be rectified
no matter what you've done or how hard you've tried.
Sadness is writing this piece and trying to do well,
Sadness is having a blotted mind; Sadness is hell!

Thomas T. Blackwell

Unspoken Thoughts

When the world dies,
Then, and only then, will I be satisfied.
Everyone lives in a fantasy.
Certainly, I wish them to see the reality,
And to see me as I see you.
Then my words shall ring true.
The pictures in your head,
Are not like the ones in mine; but instead,
They give you pleasure in your mind.
Mine gives me pain and a note of unkind.
Wisdom is the only key,
For this knowledge I wish to plea.
There is nothing for me to believe in.
But the words of a dead man.

Melissa Holley

Like It Is

Son, mother knows best
don't worry bout the rest of those so-called friends.
They jus wanna see yo' ends
And don't wanna see 'em met
Bet, they'd love tah see ya regret.
Want ya in the same mess they in
It's a sin,
People like them call themselves friend.
They yo' friend alright but not in the end.
Son, don't get mad
Get glad
I'm jus telling' ya like it is.

Irving Thomas Drake

Indoor or Outdoor Soccer

Indoor is like a box;
With no leaving.
Outdoor is like a bird flying in the open sky;
With no cares.

Indoor is like a cage;
With no escape.
Outdoor is like an open field;
That never stops.

Indoor is like a cave;
That dead ends.
Outdoor is like an ocean;
That never ends.

My eyes go to outdoor;
But my heart goes to indoor.

Michael Harne

Let Them Play

I watch the children at school as they play,
And wonder what each will become some day,
A teacher whose legacy reaches the end of time,
A poet, a writer or even a mime,

A psychiatrist who helps us manage life's strife,
Or a surgeon who could save a little one's life,
A nurse devoting life to that of care giving,
Psychologist, technologist, all make life worth living.

An astronaut who travels in space, dark and fair,
An engineer who designs the craft to get them up there,
A truck driver that keeps the nation's pulse flowing,
A builder of roads that keeps them all going.

Professions galore and one they must choose,
Teach them and guide them, let not one of them lose,
The chance to become what they want to be,
All have a purpose, we must help them see.

A fire fighter, police officer, a husband or wife,
All must choose someday what to do with their life,
I pray our example won't lead them astray,
But while they are children, just let them play

Michael J. Floyd

The Oak By The Gateway

Long by the gateway, o'er shading the farm house,
like titanic guard, in majestic hood,
With arms outstretched, to word off the spear-like
thrusts of the sun, an oak tree stood.

As deep in the earth, in her arms fast entwined,
As stout, hale the hart abeat its big bole,
So deeply in me, for the tree friendship grew,
A rare friend of wood, with rare tender soul.

How else when I'm happy its leaves dance in glee?
And the song in my throat palpitates to the sway
Of the baton - like limbs keeping time, keeping time,
With the forest in chorus and birds gushing gay.

And why when in sorrow, all hearts know the pang,
For joy is ephemeral, and in woe nust atone,
I hear a soft murmur, ah! sympathetic friend
I know by your droop, that I weep not alone!

Oh! long may you stand there, arms spread o'er the farm house.
In sweet benediction, while softly your leaves
Whisper at vespers, their even-song telling
Your world is at peace and only man grieves.

George F. Harwood

Utopia

The flowers in my garden are a potpourri of color
That fills me with everlasting joy and delight
The mingling of the lilac bush
With the enchanting sweetness of the gardenias
The exquisite beauty of the daffodils
Reigning tall and stately
Yet bowing to the roses in their brilliant array
The panorama is an enchanting composite of every hue
Intermingling with its neighbor every size and form
Why, oh why I query, can't the varied people of the universe
Of every different breed and background
Blend and diffuse their own beauty
And encompass the everlasting glory and harmony
of the human race?

Roslyn Kozak

In Remembrance of Life

Life comes, life is, life goes.
Death, from whence we come,
And to which we return,
Is our intrinsic existence in eternity.

Do not ask about the nature of death,
Recall where you were before birth.
As the child asks, "Where did I come from?"
Answer, "You will remember soon enough."

Ask only about the nature of life,
Where the concept of time has meaning.
For every life not yet born will be born in the now,
And every death occurred just a moment ago.

We invented time in order to measure life,
And were comforted, believing we also measured death,
But out sense of comfort is an illusion,
For time passes, just as surely as we do.

Do not measure the time left,
Measure what you do with your portion.
Live! Create, love, work, and play,
Before time again becomes meaningless.

John G. Prinz

No Words Necessary

Wasn't that a beautiful service?
Didn't he look good?
You should really write something—he would like that.
That's what we all want isn't it?
Make it simple, make it pretty.
Make me understand!
Come on, you can write.
Write something to make us feel better.
Write something so he won't be forgotten.
Put our feelings on paper.
Make them less painful!
Then we can just talk about the beauty of the words.
We can stop dealing with the tragedy.
Make it better!
No . . . there are no words to make it better.
My tribute to you is ultimate . . .
blank paper and silence.
You deserve at least that.
I will not forget . . .

Mike Gregory

Because of You

Those words you said made me want to melt
Finally I knew exactly how you felt
No longer did I have to put my feelings aside
No longer my love did I have to hide

That was the sweetest thing anyone had ever told me
And for awhile I thought it would end happily
But like all great things it came to an end
My world came crashing down I knew I couldn't win

My happiness was gone as quick as it came
It seemed as if it was all a simple game
Nothing more than something to do
As if my feelings meant nothing to you

My heart is hurt my feelings cold
I try to let it show my emotions inside I hold
I smile I laugh as if nothing went wrong
I am afraid it won't and can't go on for long

I will continue to search and look
For somewhere out
 is a romance like that in a fairy tale book
Someone who will be my night in shining armor
And I will be his princess

Julie Riggs

Life Is Too Short

Life is too short,
make use of it today.
We will never pass this way again.

For the only thing that lasts is salvation.
Life is too short,
make use of it today.

Lost wealth may be replaced by industries.
Lost knowledge may be replaced by studies.
Lost health may be replaced by temperance or medicine,
but lost life will be gone forever.

Joyce Dawes

Just a Summer Place

A place for just the summer I wish to go
A place where I could do anything
A place for the summer where there is always something to do
A place where the phone doesn't ring

I wish this place for just the summer was here
Even if it's two blocks away
Oh, just where is this place? Oh where?
To see this place for just the summer I would even pay

If this place is a far away place
With lots of flowers and trees to see
To see this place for just the summer through a window of lace
And when I'm there I'll just be me

I found this wonderful place for just the summer to be
I enjoy every alone minute I can gain
I can even see the color blue like the sky in the sea
A place I wish to go for a summer that doesn't have rain

Erin Guinta

Friendship

When you dedicate your heart
to a very special friend,
that special kind of love should never end.
Give me your friendship,
and I'll give you mine
and together we'll stay best friends for a lifetime.
We have took up for each other up till this day
and I'd like it very much for it to stay that way.

Cassie Slott

For Him

I breathe for him.
And how I'm breathing now, I do not know.

He sucked the breath from me when he left,
The breath that once flowed so freely for him . . .

I live for him.
And how I'm living now, I do not know.

He ended the life within me when he left,
The life that once was so griefless
in his presence . . .

I loved him.
And how I still love him now, I do not know.

For he loves me no more, and that's why he left.
But my love for him grows,
And it grows harder for me to breathe . . .

Harder for me to live.

Jaime Goode

Noce/Diaz

As this orb follows its path in space
To complete another circle of flight
Each unerring revolutions trace
Brings a return of the nocturnal blight

His intelligence tinged by fear
His actions spurred by fright
With wire and ore wrestled from the ground
He begins anew his endless fight
The battle to halt its complete surround
This spectre man names night

His brother, a child of the other race
Fears not the waning light
But welcomes its cold embrace
And revels in anticipated delight
Moonrises cold pale glow
Shadows sliced in dark contrast
Quickens the bloods flow
The promise of sensual repast
A ritual founded eons ago.

James Richard Elliott

I Am Anne

I am nothing . . . but I have feelings
I hear voices and gunfire at night
I see only family and the ones who accompany me
I say that gave us a strong feelings, misdirected
I cry tears of sadness
I am nothing . . . lonely with feelings

I am a teenager . . . with feelings
I want to go home, be with my friends, back to school
I need happiness and love
I hope someday things will change for the better
I fear I will someday lose faith and die
I am a teenager . . . with feelings

I am a sensitive, compassionate teenager . . . I feel
I feel deeply at heart that people are still good
I try to imagine I'm going to be free one day
I wonder if I will ever be free again
I dream one day there will be on more hate
I am Anne Frank . . . I am proud to be Jewish

Chris Whitehead

My Children

I am longing for my children and the days
that used to be, for the good times
and the bad times, and the days that used to be.

My heart is breaking as I think of them
lovingly, of the good times and the bad
times and the days that used to be.
I am waiting for them always to come through
the door and my heart will be broken,
not to see them anymore, waiting for
my children patiently.

Adele Rayner

Spring

I love the spring, a time to begin anew
Flowers start to bloom, kissed gently by the dew
Laughter fills the air, as kids go out to play
Birds so sweetly sing, sunshine fills the day
Winter's wounds are healing, summer's coming soon
A perfect time of year, cuddling 'neath the moon
No snow to mar the setting, no leaves to hide the ground
Just colors everywhere, all smiles with ne're a frown

Vince Howard

I Love You

Dedicated to: Jose Rivera III
She's sat and listened to all your crazy lies.
You tell mom "Later," and leave her to cry.

You know you're hurting us, but all you do is laugh
Put on a show, hide in a mask.

You've used us, deceived us, left us behind.
We tell you we love you, but pay us no mind.

I know these words won't reach to your soul.
But our feelings of fear we need you to know.

Mom wonders when the tragic news arrives to our door.
"Sorry, he's gone, we couldn't do anymore."

I hope you understand what I'm trying to say.
"I love you," though I don't say it every day.

We wish we knew you better, that we could understand.
But all you do is turn away when we reach out our hand.

Remember I'll be here, whatever you need.
Bandage your heart whenever it bleeds.

Arcelia Rivera

Beauty So True

Upon my happiness the stars look down
In wonder that my heart can be so free
Without thought they'd give their heavenly crown
In return for the joy I have in thee

All the earth gazes on in jealousy
Desirous that it should be by your side
Ever captivated by your beauty
Which not even the hand of time can hide

Your brilliant smile puts the sun's face to shame
Its radiance cannot compare with you
And roses pale at mention of your name
They can but dream to reach beauty so true

And so I bear creation's endless scorn
For you have cured my heart which once was torn

Nicholas Ryan Bourland

Night Journey

Down into the darkness ride
The shadows of yesterday.
The veil between the worlds parts for me
As I follow,
Hurried by the music of primal fear.

I long to forget those memories past,
Laid like fragments in a cobblestone path,
Which my vagabond spirit
Wishes to tread.

Faint lights blink ahead of me,
As brief and as beautiful
As the glow of flickering candles
In the night.

Watch them burn but a moment,
And then die, only to reawakened.
Into my conscience slither dismal imaginings
and fairy tales. I will not become a slave
to them. My silent vow echoes unheard,
As I close my eyes
To sleep.

Amber Decker

It Came Over The Hill

As I was a watching he came over the hill
A setting backwards upon his horse
As he rode up close, I yelled
"Hey Pilgrim Is something wrong"
Whoa, I heard him yell
And the horse, he did stop
"Why No" he said, "should there be"
I said, "Why are you a sitting backwards on your horse"
He said with a grim, "Well you see
the horse took off so fast
like some thing was a chasing us
And she was going so fast everything was a blur
So I figured she knew where we were a-going.
So I thought I better check and see what was a chasing us
"Well" he said, "Got to be a-going never know it mit be a-gaining"

L. A. Reizenstein

Facing Death (Time, The Great Healer)

I'm in a place where time stands still, yet life keeps going on.
How can I face another day knowing that you're gone?

Death is a heaviness that weighs upon your being.
The eye of the hurricane so eerie and unseeing.

No, this can't be happening, I want to run and scream.
Someone wake me up, let this be just a dream.

The sadness and the pain, how much can I endure?
This helpless, empty feeling - it engulfs my every pore.

I can't step back into the world. I can't even shed a tear.
There are people all around me saying words I cannot hear.

Only my God can help me - now to him I'll pray each day.
I need to try to understand why you had to go away.

You'll always be a part of each new day I start.
You'll not be far away from me, you're always in my heart.

I Love You

Dorothy V. Medlock

On Your Wedding Day

May you know the joy of oneness,
Of love that becomes twice as strong as the years go by.

For, together, you can build a life rich in
understanding, warmth, tenderness, and faith.

In each will be reflected the image of the other
as you travel together thru the wondrous adventure of life.

(And, with God, it can be a wondrous adventure!)

"Make it so"

Ellen Conjour

You and Me

You and me, we would talk all night.
We usually would never fight.
Then one day you found someone new;
So out with the old, in with the new.
I did so much for you,
Didn't you see
That our love came naturally?
I wrote you letters, I did no wrong,
What I am trying to say
Is that everyday you cross my mind
What you really did was left me behind.
I don't know why you did it.
I guess I was not good enough for you our memories
are all I have left of you.
Can't you see all I want is you and me?
But I guess that can't be. I love you respected you,
gave our relationship my all it really did was make it fall
I wonder if I am the problem but that should be unknown
When we fought, I always let you win the thrown
why can't this relationship just be for all eternity? . . .

Jaymie Morales

I Believe

I believe as one we can
Make this dream of peace come true.
I believe, together there's nothing
We can't do.

I've seen miracles before and just the fact
That were still here, proves to me
There's more.
Yes the struggle maybe hard but the
Rewards are great when you know
They come from God.
And if one soul finds peace, before
I'm laid to rest and I believe I've
Done my best . . . I'm blessed.
Amen.

I. Brahim A. Rahman

What Might Have Been

She walks along the moonlit beach
Dreaming things that are out of reach
Sand flows through her fingertips
Her thoughts linger on his lips
She longingly thinks of the way he was
The way he never felt as she still does
The way he would've melted in her arms
The way he'd tease her with his wicked charms
The way his love would give her power
The way he'd hold her, precious as a flower
The steamy passion they'd make one night
The way he'd never give her up without a fight
Regret in her runs deep as does sorrow
God the things she wouldn't give for just one more tomorrow
But her hand is now empty as her heart
Funny how some things finish before they start

Kimberly Morel

What an Irony

That small machine, contrived by man,
With a hallowed piece of metal for a nozzle;
That master author of grief and pains;
That media headline maker - the handgun.
That spreads woes, pains and death;
That separates couple and make wives widows;
That makes mothers childless, and children orphans;
That cuts Presidents down from high office;
That slays in cold blood on duty law officers;
That snaps precious lives out of young and old;
And forever confines fortunate victims to wheelchairs;
That two-step action machine—point and pull;
And many maimed or fall to untimely death.
That gun; the most outrageous outlaw;
That man's most monstrous enemy;
Yet man's most valuable companion,
That Americans wouldn't let go.
What an irony!

Gabriel A. Ekhelar

Gladiators

Gladiators in their chariots of steel roar past
like a swarm of giant insects.
The threat of death is an oppressive storm cloud,
as a gladiator's life ends in a film of black dust.
The crowd buzzes with excitement
as the gladiators pass the scene of disaster with a cruel pleasure;
one less interloper left to destroy their visions of glory.
Gladiators ignore their own fear as they press
toward victory in face of the grim reaper.
A wreath of olive leaves goes to the victor and a
wreath of hemlock to the rest.
The contest will renew on the mourn as the
triumphant gladiator struts again into the eye of the storm
The thrill of winning which dries up the gladiators
fear is dangerous as a cornered lion.

Russell Scales

Tall Pine

Tall Pine, a giant tree,
Made especially for you and me.

If it is in God's plan that I grow old,
I will have to withstand the winter's cold.

The storms that come, the rains that fall,
Or the summer's sun most of all.

Should I manage to survive,
I'll be very happy to be alive

To live out my full life's span,
As tall and straight as I can.

George V. Hatzell

Hate and Love

Hate is the thing that you try to run away,
Hate is the darkness, and hate is the dark shadow
that is in the back of your soul,
hate is the meanest word that the man wrote
when he didn't get love.

Love is everything, Love is every single breath,
Love is a view that heart and this love gives
a seed and has borne a flower that smell the love.
But careful because sometimes the hate and the love
comes together to confuse you, but
don't try to see the hate, just try to see the love
and look for that word that is the most beautiful
word that is living in your heart is the "Love."

Alex Melgoza

There Will Come A Day

There will come a day when our love will
fade away and disappear. There will come
a day when tears will fall like rain and
pain will strike my heart like thunder,
loud and hard but not seen. There will
come a day when words will no longer be
spoken between us and there will be no
more to say, when sadness overlaps our
worlds, and we think of nothing but each other.
Loneliness and pain will be a good friend,
and love will be a word we'll forever
question in our minds. There will come a
day when the light will fade into darkness
and the words we leave unsaid will
tell a thousand tales, alone. There will
come a day when there will no longer
be a you or a me, but there will also
come a day when our broken hearts
will mend and the scars will fade
away and become a distant memory.

Jeny Bellows

Ole Red Brick High School

The beautiful ole red brick high school,
From whence so many of us came,
Taught myself and others some knowledge
In which we all should play the game.

I have many fond and sharing memories
And then some I would as soon forget.
However, most of these many stories
Are cemented solid my mind, even yet.

A lot of that knowledge was of pretty girls,
And guys that seemed to give wonder.
Why them, not me, who were so full of the worlds
Such priceless and gifted candor.

The many years have passed and gone,
And we all are very much the wiser.
I wish then I had only known
Life comes from seeds sown only as an appetizer.

Many things now dwell in this old mind,
As I think of them in jest.
The things linger there are the kind
Which makes memories of the ole red brink high school the best.

Paul E. Summer

Questions—Answers

As I walked the road, and the night grew dreary,
I pondered about life, and a brand new theory.

Will I be courageous, will I be sweet?
What will happen, who will I meet?
Will I be famous, when will I die?
If they come to my funeral, will they cry?

Tomorrow isn't far away,
People come and go each day.
What happens if I die tonight?
Will the road I travel turn out alright?
Will the leaves turn brown, the cardinals blue?
Will they fly away, all too soon?

Questions, there are many, it's true,
But answers, there are all too few!

Katie Barthels

As They Dance On Wishes Bliss

Always,
In random fashion she comes
Spontaneous,
She, a youth spark bathes mother earth below
Holding,
My eyes gaze, she vexingly charms a heavenly scent
Rampaging,
A heart cusp, alive with Fire and Ice
Young bodies,
Foray into a lover's embrace and longingly parade
Seducing, many nubile youth on a rainbow dew
See and Hear,
A stolen momentary kiss of a sirens serenade
Free,
Old loyalties for adorations new
I marvel at their eternal grace
As they dance on Wishes Bliss
Never, to repeat Love
Again

Paul Lepkowski

Indecision

I reached out to touch him,
   but my hands only found the soft whirl of air.
I searched his eyes for the reasons why,
   and saw a battle being fought.
I turned my back to him,
   did not want him to see my thoughts.
Then I felt his breath on my neck,
   it sent shivers down my spine.
I smiled, slowly turned around,
   reached up to stroke the curve of his jaw.
I could feel his muscles quivering,
   momentarily afraid of his decision to trust me.
For a fleeting moment we were one,
   alone in this field of life
   with the grasses dancing at our feet.
Then the clouds covered the sun,
   and the indecision was back.
He tossed his head, mane flowing in the breeze,
   turned and walked away
   only to pause and glance back.
I could feel the power in his gaze,
   this free and wonderful being.
We would come together again,
   maybe for a little longer next time.

Erika L. Walker

Beloved Companion

Beloved companion, I touch the place
Where you once laid your head and
In the dark I seem to hear your gentle breathing.
How long ago and yet how recently
Our breaths entwined as did
Our bodies in the heat of youthful love.

Beloved companion, in my dreams
I take your hand in mine
And clasp it to my breast.
How often has that hand told me of
Your love? How often did your caress
Move me to tears of joy?

Beloved companion, though time has
Divided us, a quiet contentment fills me
As I lie here alone in the dark.
Love immeasurable, memories of your
Gentle breathing, of your tender touch,
Will console until we meet again.

Natalie Joy Woodall

My Unforgotten Friend

There used to be a time
when we were best friends,
We laughed and talked always
never any problems to mend.

But as the years went by,
our friendship slowly faded.
We drifted farther day by day.
Sadly our friendship had not made it.

Still world's apart in these high school years.
I sometimes sit and wonder how she must feel.
Does she miss our friendship, the days we ran and played
and is she just afraid of what I might say?

Or does she really just not care
and rather concentrate on her own new affair?

This is a promise I make today
No matter how much this world may change.
It can wither away, it can even fray.
But I will remember her to the end
and she will always be my unforgotten friend.

Pam Lawson

Love Forever

Since the day you left me
I've never been the same.
The tears just won't stop falling
But I know I'm the one to blame.

The words you said so sweetly
Still ponder in my mind,
The question of if I'll ever get over you
Haunts me all the time.

Now I'm living without you
And, well, life can't get much worse.
Even though you've been gone awhile
My heart still really hurts.

I'm slowly getting better,
But I'll never get over you

Jennifer Mclees

Untitled

We don't know it's there until it slaps
us in the face.
The one thing we've all been looking
for is in this place.
But we can not see it for we are blind.
You don't know it till you take the time.
You've been searching for a love so true.
While it's been waiting just for you.
So take the risk and take the time.
For all I know,
Love is blind.

Kae M. Urling

Savage

I wanted to be the wind
Wild and free, moving, flowing
But you held my hand and wouldn't let go
You wouldn't let me be me.
I wanted to run, so fast
That maybe if I tried I could fly
But you stood in front of me
And I sat patiently as you clipped my wings
My passions, my dreams, they meant nothing to you.
And in the end, I meant nothing too.

Molly R. Vitt

The Little Old Lady With The Blue Hair

The little old lady with the blue hair
Was such a sight to see.
Her husband loved her with such care.
She lived down on one of the Keys.

All skin and bones, she was so thin.
She was only 3 feet, 2 inches.
She could fit herself in a popcorn tin
And boy does she hurt when she pinches.

Her face was so small and round.
Her lips were as thin as pencil lead.
With such a small mouth she barely made a sound
And with her half glasses she read.

Her fingers were only 2 inches long.
Her ring size only a three.
With her hands she directed a song
And sang the songs with glee.

Holly Lawson

Ode To Sarah

My heart is full of loneliness, pain, and
despair
There is a giant empty spot because you're
no longer there.
All I have is memories, I live from
day to day;
My soul has wandered aimlessly, since
you went away.
I miss your little kisses and the sweet
smile on your face.
But I know, my baby angel, that
you're in a better place.
You'll never be forgotten, you death
was not in vain;
Your smile is now the sunshine,
your tears are now the rain.
Dear Sarah you were a precious gift,
from the Lord above;
He sent you for a little while,
to show me how to love.

Melissa Huffman

Escape

Escape the pain
Escape the lies
Escape the hatred that burns inside
Escape the greed and envy that lurks in us all
Escape the truth that which I cannot bare
So why can't I escape this tortured
And senseless soul of mine

Dawn Dorsey

Without You

If I lost you
There'd be nothing more for me to do.
The moon wouldn't glow,
The stars wouldn't shine,
Just because you'd no longer be mine.
To me you're priceless, there is no cost.
If you weren't with me,
Everything would be lost.

Allie Firestone

Mount Love

When I look into the sky at night
I think of the time upon the mountain top
When we sat beneath a willow tree
Holding each other in a firm embrace of love
On the mountain top you told me "I love you"
Under the willow tree we made love
It was there we lost each other
It was there you broke my heart
How can we forget the times we shared
The happiness, the pain, the loneliness
We have forgotten what it means to love
To love forever and unconditionally
Before you left you said you'd love me
How is it that life is fleeting
When my love for you is infinite?
Now I am left holding a memory
When we pass each other on the street
I shall always say, "I love you!"
Look up to the night sky
See what our love has wrought

Marc Andrew Kramer

Locked in the Positive

There is a private Garden where I choose to be,
A serene, special site where one is always free.

Locked into this Garden are energy and will.
Emotions are colorful and full of frill.
Locked out are discouragements and every bitter pill.
Thoughts there are positive—negative ones are still.

Locked into this Garden are appreciation seeds.
Powers are flowing there, where understanding feeds.
Locked out are "No's" and "I Can't Do" deeds.
"Yes" and "I Can" are necessary needs.

Within this Garden one learns inner peace there.
Inspiration is felt to go on every day—anywhere.
Locked out is selfishness and "I Don't Care."
Ideas are creative and judgements fair.

This Glorious Garden is known as the Positive
and I am locked in forever.

I hope all my troubled friends
can join me there together!

Claudette Sternberg

Suffer The Innocent

Yesterday, so happy was I,
roaming my City with a carefree smile,
watching children in the sun,
laughing and playing,
shouting just in fun.

Today, not so carefree am I,
for where is my home,
that used to be,
right on the corner,
now no more can I see,
for only a hole was left for me,
filled with bricks and other peoples debris,
as more homeless people meander like me.

Tomorrow, where will I be
can someone please end this misery?
For my hope cannot last longer,
and when it dies,
so surely will I.

Michelle Murray

High School

School, school is so much fun
Three more years and I'll be done
Going on dates and parties too
Three more years, and still a lot to do
When school is out
I'll probably pout
Everyone will go in opposite directions
To go out and seek their greatest perfections
But right now, I'll take it slow
Because I don't know where I'll go

Courtney Nelson

A Memory

As I look into the majestic sea,
somewhere I know you are watching over me.

And as I walk along on the jet black sand,
I wish I was a little girl and you holding my hand.

As I watch your face in the bright orange light,
I remember your gentle smile, your soft touch,
just a memory, yet it meant so much.

And as I walk I watch the sun fall behind highlands,
I realize one thing, that my love for you will never end.

Jaclyn Morales

I Am Not Alone

Alone I stand and deep in thought,
Alone I greet the day.
Confused and sad, I know you're gone,
But not why you were taken away.

With the coming of dawn, the sun touches me,
And lightens the darkness of night.
Now I tell myself I can stand alone,
Though you are gone from my sight.

But doubt overcomes me once again,
Like a dark and blinding shroud.
I struggle to break away from fear,
As the sun shines from behind a cloud.

Then stronger—higher, the orb of fire,
Shines on the weakness that is me,
Bringing strength as I realize,
"He is as close as memory."

When day is done and the sun's last rays,
Cover the pictures upon the wall.
In the faces of our children, I see you.
And I know—I'm not alone at all.

Rose M. Padilla

What Is Left

A cry goes out,
A whimper as soft as a summer shower,
A mournful tear,
Slowly falling upon the ground,
Only to be snatched up by a delicate rose,
Needing the water to grow tall and strong,
To become all the things you could never be yourself.
A departing bird,
Leaving everything behind,
Only to have a warm place to stay for the winter season.
A lonely song,
Sung by the depressed soul,
That cares nothing of what happiness could be,
And cares nothing about the perfect love,
Because one day, this singer had it all,
They had the type of love that should have never ended,
But the song changed its melody,
And only a sad tune can be heard from this performer,
That says there is no longer anything left to live for.

Denise Briggs

The Nursing Home

Looking around at all the sorrow.
Helplessness . . . so profound.
No hope in view for tomorrow.
The shadow of death all around.

Some are hanging on to memories.
For others, all is forgotten, memories gone.
There are those waiting for loved ones,
And the waiting seems so long.

If only joy could be restored,
And hope seen on each face.
If sadness and pain could be removed,
With love and peace to take their place.

Is a nursing home the place to go,
When it seems life will no longer matter?
Shouldn't this be the time for love and kindness,
Instead of letting all dignity shatter?

As the days turn into years,
And the time comes when we'll depend,
On all our care to come from others
Will the Nursing homes be our end?

Hazel Smith

Combat Zone

The battle of day and night,
Is a never ending fight.

They battle for control of the skies,
And fight on until the other one dies.

But they never die, they keep coming back,
In spite of each other's plan of attack.

The stars we see that shine so bright,
Are simply land mines set by night.

But they fade off by early morning,
And day attacks without warning.

Into the sky, day launches a great ball of fire,
And the clouds keep out night just like barbed wire.

The two meet head to head in a clash called twilight,
Yet day always loses, it just fades out of sight.

Night has control until just around dawn,
That's when day regains strength, packs its gear, and moves on.

It battles with night until the twelfth hour,
Then, in an instant, the day forces lose power.

The cycle is steady, it never ends,
Because there's no allies, no comrades, no friends.

Derek Mitchell

Four Seasons (A Brother For Each Season)

A start of the falls always ready to bear that call, even
when in difference, like in change of temperature from warm
to cool. The flock of feathers ready to spring out of that
lake and head South along with that cool calm breeze and
nevertheless the ever-changing colors of leaves ready for
departure from its branch and never loosing respect from
its tree, as winter sets in with minimal warning of a cold
front and nothing to despair as we must gear up and prepare
for the unpredictable, even when holidays come about bringing
a phony holiday book cover cheer, after that hurdle of
a culprit, we come upon a rewarding spring which brings
nothing but smiles and a fresh welcome to the outdoors, a
delightful chance with mother nature bringing wetness and
cool calm breeze again, for spring flowers to blossom, then only
in the Summer you can see the payoff of the previous season,
nice as it can be, it can also be deceiving with hot
steaming weather, but when it gets ready to blow its top,
it's time to jump into the pool and cool off with an ice cold pop.

Ventura Colon

Woe to the Soul

Woe to the soul contained in this world
Of deceit, dishonor, and greed.
Surrounded by conflicts of color and creed
Surely is something the soul does not need.
What it needs is the love and the kindness of
A generation past;
Overcome by money, greed, and fame,
These qualities did not last.
If someday we hope to find our lost values,
It would take a miracle.
Of course, it would not come from us,
For our minds are too dull.
We only see the bottom line,
Or how much we can earn.
We need to open up our minds,
For it is time to learn.
To learn what love and caring is,
Not how powerful we can become.
In this world, it is a long lost art,
But one which can be found.

Justin Bartz

Loneliness

The chill that runs through my bones
The tears that run down my face.
The fear in my heart that doesn't show.
And the sadness that's in my heart.
It's all because of my loneliness.
With being away from home.
And being away from the love of my family.
Saying goodbye to close friends,
And saying goodbye to love ones.
Never knowing if I'll see them again
never knowing if I'll return.
Not knowing if I stay here long
Not knowing if I'll move away.
Making new friends and having new family,
Should I ever consider them family
Or just a new home that I'll stay in.
The chills, the tears, and the fear
In my heart are all caused by my loneliness.

Crystal Smith

In Celebration of a Friend

I like.
I like the times together spent,
The secrets shared,
The funny talks we always have.
I like the birthday cards you send,
The teasing smiles that know no end
Because were friends.
I smile.
I smile at silly nicknames called,
The private jokes,
The warm advice you always give.
I smile at all the care you've shown,
The way you cheer me upon by phone
When I'm alone.
I know.
I know that people come to change,
That paths diverge, that joys are often left behind.
I know that closeness is a stage.
We'll grow apart. We'll pass with age.
And so our friendship is a phase.

Chistina Trosterod

Congratulating Life and After Life

Mr. And Mrs. T. Doe, is expecting their first child
Congratulations, "It's a boy"
Mr. and Mrs. T. Doe, here's your baby's first toy
Congratulation's "It's a boy"
Mr. and Mrs. T. Doe, time to take him for a walk
Congratulation's, "It's a boy"
Mr. and Mrs. T. Doe, man "Oh" man can he talk
Congratulation's. "It's a boy"
Mr. and Mrs. T. Doe, this is your son's graduation day
Congratulation's "It's a boy"
Mr. and Mrs. T. Doe, your son is getting married by the bay
Congratulation's, "It's a boy"
Mr. and Mrs. T. Doe, grandchildren are on the way
Congratulation's, "It's a boy"
Mr. and Mrs. T. Doe, time to give out birthday presents
Congratulation's, "It's a boy"
Mr. and Mrs. T, Doe, your son's family sends you their blessings
Congratulation's, "It's a boy"
Mr. and Mrs. T. Doe, your days are becoming darker as they lessen
Congratulation's, "It's a boy"
			Angela Miles

Cheater

As I sit in my room and cry,
All I can wonder is why.
Three months of my life you took part,
But in the end you broke my heart.
I realize now that is was all a lie,
You didn't even have enough nerve to tell me good-bye.
I thought you were the one that could be trusted,
But I was wrong when you got busted.
I remember all the things I did for you,
You took me for granted and I didn't even have a clue.
I thought we were the perfect pair,
But now you act like you just don't care.
I wonder if you ever did at all.
And all I can do is bawl.
You used me for what you wanted
And then threw me away like nothing happened.
So I sit in my room and cry all day
And hope that someday I'll be okay.
			Rachel Stevens

Missing and Exploited Children

Dig a grave dig it deep
I know I will stay asleep
You do not have to worry because
I'm in no hurry; in God's hands I rest
I am no longer a pest
Mr. Killer couldn't you see
In my eyes the thriller now
I missed the loved and they miss me too,
Sometimes I sit and cry boo hoo hoo
But I don't worry you will pay I know someday
			Mecca Ali

Southern Spring

The trees put on their overskirt of green
The robins on the lawn announces spring.
The daffodils their golden head nod
The brown grass of winter turns to spring's green sod
The apple and peach blooms are pink and white
While the tree frogs start to talk in the night
The soft spring rain brings out all the blooms
To add their touch to banish winter gloom
It's a bright new beginning that start to unfold
This southern spring that our eyes behold!
			Jewell F. Cristall

The Gift of a Rose

A rose is a rose by no other name
Until it becomes a gift.
A gift from God
That springs from the sod
Who fashioned its petals so fair.
So delicate, so fragile, its fragrance is rare.
Its color that blends
Mid blossoms that flame
So regal its head that bows to the rain;
Shedding petals like snowdrops
'Neath its lofty green stem.
But no rose is sweeter
Than the heart of the Giver
Who plucked the Rose in love of a friend.
			Edith Pearson

Lord

He casts a silver shadow,
and emits a golden glare.
He walks on soft untouched ground.
with lacy flowing hair.
He looks upon his children,
and guides them hand in hand,
helping these, his people, as they follow
his command.
He, their calming light,
He, their ticket back,
He, the one who loves us no matter
what we lack.
			Tammy Curry

Good-Bye

Cold winds blows, as waves brake over the wall.
Mist hides my tears, but it doesn't catch them all.
Peaceful were those nights, walking
hand and hand, melted to your touch.
As we became one in the sand.

Still all alone as you're so far
away, wasting what time we had
going our separate ways.
Didn't know what I wanted
didn't think it was so bad.
Took you for granted, never knew
what I had.

Candles burn bright, find little comfort in there glow.
The heat they provide, does little for my soul.
Watch you lie before me, tears fall like rain,
Resting there so peacefully,
I never felt such pain!
			Gabrielle Saksa

Feelings

I have this feeling
Inside me and
I don't know why it's there,
It comes to me when
I'm alone and fills me with despair.
It brings back the
Pain I once felt and tried to leave behind.
Along with the sudden feeling
That my soul is dying inside,
I do not want to feel this way,
But I can't try to hide.
This feeling can find me anywhere.
It feels my pain inside.
			Melissa Castillo

Fear

Fear is the sound of an oncoming train and your car is stopped on the tracks.
Fear is hearing him call your name while you're frantically trying to hide.
Fear is the sound of a tornado and your knowing it's about to suck up
everything you have and leave all of it scattered about in pieces.
Fear is his footsteps upstairs trying to find you.
Fear is an earthquake. There's no place safe to run.
Fear is his starting to come down the stairs. Your heart is racing.
Fear is a game of Russian Roulette. They're up to the fifth person, and you're number six.
Fear is the waiting as he gets closer and closer. There's nowhere to run.
Fear is the sound of the train much closer and your car still can't move.
Fear is when he finds you and the train smashes into your car.
        Beth Ann King

The Rainforest

Cascading white water plunges to the swift-flowing tributary below,
Swirling and tumbling over massive, sun-bleached stones, forged long ago.
The mighty Amazon River courses through an ancient, fertile land
Of primordial beauty and savage innocence, untouched by the hand of man.

Majestic trees stand silent as sentinels; watching the mystical forest,
Enchanting sounds echo from this primitive world in a spell-binding chorus.
Splendid birds adorned in brilliant plumage flit among tropical greenery,
Creating a blazing union of riotous color that blends with the lush jungle scenery.

Brown-skinned Indians convene around communal huts, sharing tribal folklore;
A timid, speckled-deer pauses to drink, cautiously approaching the river's shore.
Warning of an invader these defenseless inhabitants cannot hope to defeat!

Progress wields a heavy hand, carving jagged roads through the forest's interior.
Man...gratifies his insatiable lust for exploring nature, the need to feel superior!
This haven of refuge...once a sanctuary for native tribes and wild beasts,
Has fallen victim to the outside world; a rainforest under siege!

Awakened to this imminent danger, archaic life-forms are quick to defend!
An unseen virulent presence poses a deadly threat towards arrogant, foolish men.
Surviving the ages, Earth's abundant regions live in harmony with our kind,
That is..................Until now.
        Cyd Charessia Behrensen

On Age and Reunions

Days fly by with unbelievable speed as age claims us as its own.
With eyes grown dim and hair turned gray, we wonder where the years have gone.
We search for that youth, that energy, that has brought us all this way.
We wonder why it gets harder to find with the passing of every day.
But when we get together with dear old friends and reminisce about our youth,
It seems we can conquer the ravages of time and be young again in truth.
If only for a little while, our minds send our mortality away.
We're once again kids with the glow of youth, as we were just yesterday.
        Phyllis K. Rauton

Ideas and Science

All inventions start with an idea or assumption in the mind of man.
It takes science and practical technology to put them into form or plan.
Einstein expounded and proved the validity of his Theory of Relativity.
Other used his ideas to create weapons of destruction and conquers space.
Astronauts can ascend and study earth and stars from another place.

Arthur Clarke, sci-fi writer created "2001 Space Odyssey" and Robot Hal.
In computer-guided space exploration, his ideas now are almost reality.
Artists for many centuries, dreamed of creating intelligence to equal man!
Shelly created Frankenstein, Fritz Lang in "Metropolis" the robot Maria!

Soon artificial Intelligence computers will arrive, which will with man compete.
These ideas, conceived by man, will bring both power and problems complex!
For each invention, like himself, has both negative and positive potential.
The future will reveal how this new power will be utilized—for good or evil!
        Patricia Rosset McQueen

Shadow Lighted Freshman

On the hill of Gauley Bridge,
Stands the High School great and strong,
'Twas here we freshman received the talking,
of things we did that were wrong.

The faculty says we're dumb and ignorant
But these sayings we cannot mind,
We'll try to gain some knowledge.
And leave the ignorance behind.

Let us cross the river of darkness,
And step on the land of light,
We'll soon be in the sophomore year
There's where we'll shine very bright.

When the courses we have completed,
Of our favorite "Gauley Hi,"
The joys of our clubs and ball games,
In our memory will never die.

We'll leave the school for the followers,
Whom we hope will be filled with pep,
So they may carry the spirit,
That we've just taken up.
        Violet R. Ford

Biographies
of
Poets

ABRAHAM, RYAN
[b.] June 15, 1975; Redding, CA; [ed.] Willamette High School (Eugene, OR); [occ.] College Student; [pers.] Poetry is like painting with words. The poet is creating a picture or setting in the mind instead of on canvas. Instead of drawing out and showing what he sees (the painter), the Poet writes down what he sees or feels and the reader imagines for himself the place or conjures up emotions, or sometimes he feels the same way the poet felt while writing the poem. This is why poetry, to me, is the best artistic medium for emotion and imagination.

ACCOMAZZO, ALEX
[pen.] Alexandria; [b.] December 7, 1968; California; [ed.] Gemologist, Musician, singer, songwriter; [hon.] Certified G.I.A Gemologist Degree, Associates in Arts; [oth.writ.] Author of several short stories, including "The Last Breath"; currently working on a historical novel entitled "Another Jewish Wedding"; [pers.] Paraphrased for Beck's song "Loser"—"You can't really write if you can't relate."

ADAM, WINDY
[pen.] Windy Rochelle Adam; [b.] November 20, 1964; Michigan; [p.] Kathryn, Don Henry; [m.] Klaus Adam; July 6, 1991; [ch.] Listel, Natasha, Jason Adam; [ed.] Lake Orion High, Pheonix Academy of Beauty; [occ.] Homemaker; [oth.writ.] A singer, songwriter—I have written several songs for various bands I have been in. I also write lyrics and melodies for others' work. I also write poetry.; [pers.] I write about what moves my heart and soul, life, nature, and spirituality. Occasionally I will write about love or philosophy.; [a.] Roseville, MI

ADELLA JESSEE, ELAINE MARGUERITE
[pen.] Elaine Taylor Jessee; [b.] June 11, 1968; La Mesa, CA; [p.] Carol R. Taylor, CMT Philip L. Taylor, D.D.S.; [m.] Timothy Wayne Jessee; June 14, 1986; [ed.] High School Diploma, Associate in Arts in English; [occ.] Medical Transcriptionist; [oth.writ.] Poem 'Communicate-Understand" The Poets Anthology c. 1994 by CERA, Imperial Valley Press Guest Column Article; [pers.] Mother—my sense of me comes from her, it makes me who I am. Because Mom loves me, nothing can ever take it away. Even if it disappears for a while, remember Mom. She knows I am truly good, and that can never be lost; she knows who I am.; [a.] El Centro, CA

AGBOR-BALYEE, HENRY BATE
[b.] December 20 , 1973; Tiko, Cameroon; [ed.] First School Leaving Certificate, GCE ordinary Levels, GCE Advanced Level, in the process of acquiring BSC—Pol. Science Degree; [occ.] Student; [memb.] Poetsi Corner Creative Writers Club, Ahmadu Bello University Nigeria, Africa, "Young Poet Assembly" Wumba, SW Prounce, the Cameroons West Africa; [hon.] Ray Simpson Poetry Award Jos plateau state Nigeria, 1990, Literary workshop price, Radio BOEA the Cameroon, Best student, literary appreciation, Ahmadu Bello University Zaria Nicerla; [oth.writ.] The great ascention (A play) Poems; "The Rearmost Batallion", "Anguishing Africa", "War Time", "The Most Inglerious Imbecile", "Sink of The Great Ship", "Pandora's Box", "Strive for Letter Power", "My Terrific America" and a lot more; [pers.] "The tendency for growth relies on self-reliance of us; there really can't be any growth without our will for growth. Rewarded goodwill rests in the intenturn of the action not the action itself."; [a.] Urbana, IL

ALBERGO, VITO ROBERT
[b.] July 27, 1973; Park Ridge, IL; [p.] Sebastian Robert and Grace Talarico Albergo; [ed.] B.A. Art History,B.A. Philosophy (Univ. of Illinois) [occ.] Employee of the Art Institute of Chicago; [memb.] National Honor Society of Golden Key, National Honor Society of Phi Kappa Phi; [hon.] Membership in above honor societies, 7 semesters on the Dean's List, Graduating with honors while receiving two degrees concurrently; [oth.writ.] Titles of some of the other poems I have written include: "Aurora's Volcano", "Nurburgring 35", "Phidias's Cup", and "Il Campionissimo"; [pers.] My poetry is humanistic, often pertaining to such themes as the triumph of the human spirit, the heroic individual, and a hand-made artistic tradition; [a.] Chicago, IL

ALEXANDER, ROSHAUNDA
[b.] September 19, 1970; Los Angeles, CA; [p.] Thaddis Alexander, Shirley Alexander; [ch.] Daughter Ameerah Bilal; [ed.] Crenshaw High Los Angeles City College; [occ.] Freelance Writer; [hon.] Professionally awarded for baton twirler, Marshall Arts Award, and awards for creativity; [oth.writ.] I completed a screenplay and many other poems, as well as articles; [pers.] I, Roshauda Alexander, am a born writer who has a gift to inspire people with my words of wisdom and creativity.; [a.] Los Angeles, CA

ALLEN, DAVE MILTON
[b.] February 23, 1963; [p.] Issac Allen (Mother—deceased); [m.] Divorced; October 6, 1991; [ed.] Secondary Culinary Institution; [occ.] Cook; [memb.] American Culinary Federation Inc.; [hon.] Certificates of Participation and Completion; [pers.] I would like to achieve some form of recognition with at least one or two of my talents.; [a.] Fort Myers, FL

ALLEN, HALLET T.
[b.] October 29, 1942; Harrisburg, PA; [p.] C.H. Allen (father), Betty Allen (mother); [ch.] Rebecca E. Allen; [ed.] East Pennsboro High, Enola PA, University of the Philippines, Sam Houston State University; [occ.] Loan Specialist (retired); [memb.] AARP; [hon.] Dean's List, Magna Cum Laude; [oth.writ.] Mainly letters to the editor on a range of subjects; [pers.] I believe in the worth of every person, as seen in the eyes of God throughout creation.; [a.] Waco, TX

ALLINSON, KARA
[b.] June 15, 1984; Natrona Heights, PA; [p.] Amy and Russel Allinson; [ed.] Currently in grade 7 at Huston Middle School in Lower Burrell, PA; [occ.] Student; [memb.] Sylvan Summer Swim League, Burrell Basketball, Huston Middle School Ambassadors, has played piano for 4 years; [hon.] Swim Championships Awards since 1991, 1st Place Reflections Contest 1997 in Photography, National Fitness Award 1991-97, Burrell High Honors Award; [oth.writ.] "Imagine" published in Sparrowgrass Poetry Forum's Poetic Voices of America, Reflections Contest Winner at Huston Middle School; [pers.] I enjoy reading, writing, taking care of my cats and hamster, and I hope to be a teacher someday. My twin sister, Kate, also enjoys writing.; [a.] Lower Burrell, PA

ALONGE, VIVIENNE
[pen.] Vivienne Craig Alonge; [b.] October 29, 1960; Newcastle, TX; [p.] A. W. Craig; [m.] Theo Alonge; May 3, 1980; [ch.] Louise, Mark Anthony, David; [ed.] West Jesmond Primary. Heaton and Kenton Grammar School Hull University; [memb.] National Geographic Soc.; [pers.] My appreciation to my husband Theo and my children; my theory on life: Life is like a roller coaster ride, exciting, scary and you never know when it will end.; [a.] Dallas, TX

ALVARENGA, JENNIFER
[b.] June 13, 1983; Alexandria, VA; [pers.] One reflects their own life off of their writing.; [a.] Springfield, VA

ANYAIBE, OKECHUKWU
[b.] March 21, 1969; Umuaka Imo State, Nigeria; [p.] Mrs. Jessy Anyaibe and Chief-Philip Anyaible; [ed.] (1) Central School Umuaka (elem.). (2) High School-St.Saviours High School Umuaka. (3) Federal Polytechnic Bauchi, Nigeria; [occ.] Laboratory Scientist; [pers.] Great dreams beget great things.

APPLEYARD, GREGORY J.
[b.] February 12, 1961; Jersey City, NJ; [p.] Joan and George Appleyard; [ch.] Gregory Jr. and Amanda; [ed.] Hasbouck Height High, NJ Associate of Police Science US Army; [occ.] Head of Security Poor House, Fort Lauderdale, FL; [oth.writ.] First writing to ever be published; [pers.] Life is like adventure. You have your ups and downs. It is God's way of testing you, and those around you to make you better person. I like to thank my Uncle John, a man who is like a father to me.; [a.] Hollywood, FL

AQEEL, IMAM SULAIMAN R. S.
[pen.] Imam Aqeel; [b.] August 24, 1940; Hot Spring, AR; [p.]William Elrage Bonner Sr., Myrtle Grandy-Bonner; [ch.] Lauren Amanda Aqeel, Stepsons (Charles Lewis Jr., Michael Lewis, etc; [ed.] Goldsten Elementary, Longston High, Arkansas A.M. and N., New University of Arkansas at Pine Bluff 1958-62, Minot State University, Fall 1963, Hot Spring Brian's Business College 1971-74, Henderson State University Spring 1975, Univ. AR at Little Rock summers 1994, 1996, 1997, The School of Paralegal Studies Atlanta, GA 1994-97; [occ.] Notary Public, Bookkeeper, Muslim Minister, Poet, Inventor, Paralegal, USAF (Ret.) 5 June 1967; Disabled American Veteran 100% disabled veteran; [memb.] Omega Psi Phi Fraternity Inc., Elks BPO of W. Disabled Veterans, The American Legion, Ark. Retired Military Assoc. American retired military assoc. Air Force Assoc. Retired Enlisited Association Air Force Sergents Muslim Military Assoc. Amvets, NCOA, AARP, Urban League, The Military Chaplins Assoc., Society of Strategic Air Command, National Assoc. for Military Services AMON/UAPBA/UMNI, Assoc., NAACP, Langston Alumni Assoc. SCLC, Amnesty International, Southern Poverty Law Center, Grand County Inter-faith Council; [hon.] 25 Years award Muslim community, Golden Heart Club 1994 Certificate Award, VFW Certificated Award 1993, Citizens of Year Award 1995 from the Principality of Hutt River Province, Appreciation Award Webb Community Center, Society of the Omega Psi Phi Fraternity, Inc. 1997, Mentoi at the Garland County Juvenile Probation Center; [oth.writ.] Poems published The Sentinel Record Newspaper—Hot Springs, Arkansas; published The Reflection, a poetry quarterly in Arkansas; Of Moonlight and Wishes; [pers.] When one door is not open for you, try the other door—you may not get in the door that you want to enter." The other door that is open you might like even better than the door that was closed.Never Give up a good cause.; [a.] Hot Springs, AR

ARENCIBIA, NELSON
[b.] July 31, 1980; Newark, NJ; [p.] Ofelia Arencibia, Remigio Arencibia; [ed.] Our Lady of Good Counsel Elementary School; [occ.] Student at Our Lady of Good Counsel High School Newark, NJ; [oth.writ.] Other poems published in school newspaper, [pers.] Life is like a set of stairs. When you step up onto different levels and reach the top, don't let anyone push you off.; [a.] Newark, NJ

ARNOLD, AMANDA S.
[pen.] Amanda Arnold; [b.] November 20, 1980; Salem, OR; [ed.] Cascade High School; [hon.] Outstanding Sophomore, Honor Roll, and Drama Award; [pers.] Coming from experience, don't wait too long to tell the ones you love that you love them, because someday it may be too late. I love you, Daddy.; [a.] Aumsville, OR

ASAY, MARY F.
[b.] April 10, 1911; Ala City, AL; [p.] Joseph and Ruth Franklin; [m.] Waters B. Asay; December 19, 1948; [ch.] Mary Ann Whitney, Elizabeth A. Culpepper; [ed.] A.B. University of MD, Graduate Studies 1 year in Doctrinal Program, English, U. of MD A.B. Education, Columbia Teachers' College, New York, MRE Eastern Bapt. Theol. Seminary; [occ.] Retired (teacher); [memb.] Ashton Bapt. Church, American Bible Society of NYC; [oth.writ.] Miscellaneous articles in religious magazines; [pers.] I cherish, learn from, and enjoy children. If I were pursuing a career in writing it would in the field of children and literature.; [a.] Silver Spring, MD

ASH, KRISTIN
[b.] November 28, 1972; Syracuse, NY; [p.] Bonnie Evans, William J. Ash; [m.] Michael A. Eddy; [ed.] BA in Environmental and Forest Biology from SUNY College of Environmental Science and Forestry; [memb.] National Parks and Conservation Assoction; [pers.] I try to reflect nature and fantasy in my works. I have been greatly influenced by the wilderness and by current fantasy novels.; [a.] Batavia, NY

ASIA, JESSE
[b.] May 31, 1983; Twisp, WA; [p.] Debbie Asia and David Asia; [ed.] Student of Liberty Bell High School (8th grade); [occ.] Student; [memb.] Liberty Bell Track team, 4-H Club, and Cross Country Ski team; [hon.] Grand Champion Ribbons at Okangon County Fair, honor roll a school, and Student of the Month at school, [oth.writ.] Stories and poems; [pers.] Everybody has feelings and when you write you put your feelings down on paper with made-up people playing your part in life.; [a.] Twisp, WA

AUKERMAN, ROBERT B.
[b.] April 16, 1939; Cincinnati, OH; [p.] Charles R. and Louise H. Aukerman; [m.] Cecelia; [ch.] Judy, Arlene, Robert; [oth.writ.] Loved one, The Rhyme, Christmas, The Visit, A Child Is Born, School Shoes, Spring, Humble Majesty; [pers.] The Sisters of the Order of the Transfiguration find many ways to help and support. " A Testament to Life" is a "Thank You" to them.; [a.] Littleton, CO

AYERS, JEFFREY G.
[b.] July 19, 1974; Pontiac Mich.; [p.] Lewis and Nancy Ayers; [hon.] Editor's Choice Awards for - Sunshine and Daydreams, Memories of Tomorrow, Whispers at Dusk, The Colors of Thoughts, Into the Unknown, AMoment to Reflect; a Distinguished Member of the International Society of Poets; [oth.writ.] Previously published in: Of Sunshine and Daydreams, Memories of Tomorrow, The Colors of Thought, Into the Unknown, Whispers at Dusk, A Moment to Reflect. Inducted into the International Poetry Hall of Fame, on December 17, 1996; [a.] Toluca Lake, CA

BAKER, CAROL
[b.] January 13, 1948; Rome, GA; [p.] Emmett and Beatrice Earwood; [m.] Grady Baker; June 6, 1979; [ch.] Christina, Melanie and Robin; [ed.] Model High, Rome Beauty School; [occ.] Disabled; [oth.writ.] Several Poems that were inspired by events in my life; [pers.] I love taking notice of the good that people do, and I write about family and nature.; [a.] Cave Spring, GA

BAKER, KATRINA Y.
[b.] May 15, 1978; Flint, MI; [p.] Charles And Easter Baker; [ed.] Graduated from Flint Southwestern Academy 1996, attending Baker College of Flint-Majoring in Accounting; [occ.] Imput Clerk, Indirect Lending Department at NBD Bank; [hon.] National Honor Society, Dean's List, All-American Scholar, Black Scholar; [oth.writ.] I keep a book of personal poems; [pers.] The best poems come from the heart.; [a.] Flint, MI

BAMBINO, ADELE RAYNER
[pen.] Adele Bambino; [b.] October 25, 1929; Union City, NJ; [p.] Alice and William Rayner; [m.] William Caporusso; [ch.] Bill, Bob, Adde, Bruce, Gary, and Paul; [ed.] Emerson High School, Union City, NJ; [occ.] Housewife; [oth.writ.] Purple Heart, Skater; [pers.] I love poetry: it sets my heart on fire, it brings the real me out.; [a.] Edison, NJ

BANKS, DAWN D.
[pen.] Desirre, Dez, Desi; [b.] October 7, 1972; New York; [p.] Janis Lauren Law and Joseph Banks; [ch.] Keeyon Tyriek Banks; [ed.] Associate in Arts Degree—Computer Information Systems; [occ.] Not presently employed; [oth.writ.] Greatest Women Alive, Motherhood, The Gift of Song, Child O' Mine Please Don't Cry, They Followed Me Too, From Here To Nowhere, Carry Me Through The Storm; [pers.] I strive to ensure the reality and religion in my writing. I have been influenced by writers such as the beautiful Maya Angelou.; [a.] Elizabeth, NJ

BARRON, RAMON F.
[b.] October 20, 1960; Chicago, IL: [p.] Manuel Jesus and Armandina Barron; [m.] Susan C. Barron; April 28, 1990; [ch.] Nicole, Christine, Lauren; [ed.] Graduated from W.K. Sullivan Elementary, Graduated James H. Bowen High School, Studied Anthropology and English at Chicago, State University; [occ.] Correctional Officer IDOC Danville Correctional Center; [memb.] Past Member, Treasurer, Comptroller, Vice Chairman and Chairman of the Mexican Community Committee of South Chicago; Past Member, Treasurer and Vice Chair Jesse "Tiny" Chaves Chap. America Q.I. Forum; [hon.] 1997 Quill and Scroll Award; 1993 Officer of the Year for Danville Correctional Center, 1st Runner-Up State Wide; [oth.writ.] Several poems in high school newspaper as well as news articles and editorials. Editorials in local newspaper. Editorial and news articles in Youth Publications; [pers.] One should remain humble in order to learn. One should guard their honor to assure inner peace. One should relish the beauty in our world for it is found everywhere. Peace can be achieved!; [a.] Danville, IL

BATES, SCOTT JAMES
[pen.] S.J. Bates; [b.] April 22, 1964; Noblesville, IN; [p.] Richard Bates, Ginger Brown; [m.] Angela F. Bates; June 8, 1983; [ch.] Marilyn, Amanda, Heather, Scotty and Douglass Bates; [pers.] I created "All I Want to do is Cry" to use as a help/relief to grieving parents who have suffered through still-born children such as our own beloved "Scotty," and my poem is in memory of him.; [a.] Lafayette, IN

BATTLE, MINNIE R.
[pen.] Mommie; [b.] September 17, 1943; Florida; [p.] Annie P. Battle and Johnnie Wallace; [ch.] Marilyn; [ed.] 11th only; [occ.] House person; [memb.] Off Life Living; [hon.] This will be my first one; [oth. writ.] Nothing that I kept, over the years; [pers.] I learned over the years color and different lifestyles are no reason for hate. I use a poem.; [a.] Long Beach, CA

BAUR, MARK
[b.] September 21, 1982; Bad Cannstatt, Germany; [p.] Werner, Baur, Karen Ekman-Baur; [ed.] 9th grade (International School of Stuttgart, Stuttgart, Germany), 10th Grade (Path American High School, Vaihingen, Germany); [occ.] Student— High School; [memb.] Tubingen Hawks Baseball Team, Boy Scouts of America; [hon.] Academic High Honor Roll, ECIS Math Leagues Outstanding Performance Award; [oth.writ.] Various poems have appeared in school-related publications; [pers.] I want my poems to cause the reader to stop and reflect for a moment.; [a.] Ehningen, Germany

BEARD, ANN E.
[b.] October 24, 1964; Houston, TX; [p.] Bill Beard and Nancy Bradshaw; [ed.] Graduated from Westfield High School in Houston, TX in 1984; Received an Associate Degree in Applied Science in 1995 from Blinn College, Brenham TX; [occ.] Clerk # Balance Control for 1st Tennese Bk. in Memphis; [oth.writ.] Have had poems published in my high school newspaper; [pers.] My high school teachers were a big influence in my writing and gave me the support I needed to continue.; [a.] Memphis, TN

BEHNKE, SHERRY
[b.] July 30, 1967; Lindsay, OK; [p.] Mike Jaggars, Carolyn Jaggars; [m.] Mike Behnke; February 14, 1987; [ch.] Kyle Behnke; [occ.] Accountant; [a.] Frisco, TX

BENETEAU, ROSEMARY
[pen.] Rosie; [b.] June 15, 1949; Detroit, MI; [p.] William John-Rose Sardo Maki; [m.] Arthur Beneteau; August 31st, 1985; [ch.] Eric Wayne and Rhonda Jean; [oth.writ.] Done only as a hobby, never published any works until National Library Of Poetry Contest; [pers.] I have my mother and husband to thank, for they are the ones who influenced me to enter my writings, I hope to touch many with my writings.; [a.] Lincoln Park, MI

BIRD, ROBERTA G.
[pen.] Roberta Blair Bird; [b.] September 14, 1912; Lexington, NE; [p.] Benjamin V. and Myrtle Blair [m.] Reinald E. Bird; October 16, 1938; [ch.] Bobbie Jean Bird, Robert Blair Bird; [ed.] A.B. Degree from Phillips Univ. Enid, Oklahoma; [occ.] Retired Teacher; [oth.writ.] My own collection; [pers.] I write for the fun of writing and for my family's enjoyment.; [a.] San Diego, CA

BLACKMON, SHELBY Y.
[pen.] Bet; [b.] May 11, 1959; Memphis, TN; [p.] John, Shirley Blackmon; [ch.] Ashley, Ambee Blackmon; [ed.] High School, Memphis area vo-tech Shelby State, Draughons Jr. College; [occ.] Former Resp. Therapist Tech; [memb.] Frayser Church of Nazarene; [hon.] Editor's Choice Award; [oth.writ.] When I must leave, come to Christ, if it doesn't matter.; [a.] Memphis, TN

BLACKSHEAR, MATT
[pen.] Matt; [b.] February 1, 1975; Irving, TX; [p.] Charles and Sandy Blackhear; [ed.] MacArthur High, Emory-Riddle Aeronautical Univ.; [occ.] Crew Chief on F-16—US Air Force, Luke AFB, AZ; [oth.writ.] Collection of unpublished poems and songs; [pers.] I write about things that are important to me and influence me. Many people have gone through the same things I have and I hope to relate to them through poetry and music.; [a.] Irving, TX

BLACKWELL, THOMAS
[pen.] Dr. Thomas Blackwell; [b.] August 8, 1948; Jackson, MI; [p.] Thomas and Maria J. Blackwell; [ch.] Lesley R. Blackwell; [ed.] Associate in Arts, Bachelor of Arts, Masters—Elem. Ed., Masters—Ed. Leadership, Ph.D—Doctor of Philosophy; [occ.] Educator/Business Owner; [memb.] MEA, Jay-Cees; [hon.] Leadership Development, Outstanding Young Man of America, World Leadershp Award, MEA, Who's Who in American Education, Who's Who in the Midwest, 2000 Notable American Men, Man of the Year Award 1995, Most Admired Men and Women, Who's Who Among America's Teachers, Who's Who in Exec. and Professional; [oth.writ.] Personal Leadership, Hierarchy of Achievement, Quest for Certainty, Junior High Good Grieg, Grow By Thinking Successfully, Restructuring: Methos and Models, Overcoming Harry; [pers.] To achieve a maximum of production which directly affects personal as well as organizational development, through the use of consultation, training and systems of communication networks; [a.[Ypsilanti, MI

BLANCHARD, KIM MARIE
[b.] June 1, 1971; New Bedford, MA; [ed.] B.S.—Psychology, Bridgewater State College; Elementary Education Certification, Bridgewater State College; [hon.] Kappa Delta Pi, Psi Chi, Dean's List; [a.] Lakeville, MA

BLASH, SARAH
[b.] July 28, 1979; [p.] Mary and Gary Blash; [ed.] Mount Clemens High School, Central Michigan University; [occ.] College Student; [memb.] National Honor Society, Business Professionals of America, National Art Honor Society; [hon.] Who's Who Among American High School Students, All-County Tennis Team, Top Ten of Class of 1997, Macomb English Teacher's Association Award, America's Champion Athlete Award; [pers.] Believe in yourself.; [a.] Mt. Clemens, MI

BLAXALL, THELMA
[b.] January 7, 1930; Aberdeen, MD; [p.] Eula Barlow, Russell Fitsburgh Barlow; [m.] John Blaxall; August 12, 1973; [ed.] Haure de Grace High, (R.N.) Wilmington Gen'l. Hosp. School of Nursing; Wilmington College, B.S.; University of Delaware, MA; [occ.] Owner Brick Barn Nursery; writer (in spare time); [memb.] Alumni University Del.; [oth.writ.] None published—continue to write with hope for own book of poetry; influenced by emotions and nature; lover of early history—plans for novel someday; [pers.] I have always written stories, etc. I believe in hard work and have always done my best in anything I have done.; [a.] Georgetown, DE

BOGDANOWICZ, MONIKA
[b.] March 30, 1985; Luban, Poland; [p.] Alex and Lucy Bogdanowicz; [ed.] Graduated Elementary School; [hon.] Intramural Participation, Participation in the School Newspapers, Sixth Grade Promotion, President's Education Awards Program; [oth.writ.] Trapped, Never Again, It Hurts, The Dark Tunnel, Prisoner of Love, Love, Shadow, The Dark Side, Got the Blues, Is It, Where Am I, Does it Matter, The Perfect Man, Could It Be; [a.] Strongville, OH

BOLIN, RENEE E.
[b.] September 15, 1970; Warren, MI; [p.] John and Nancy Bolin; [ch.] Stuart Crayk; [ed.] Life; [occ.] Order and billing supervisor, Crock Shop Inc; [memb.] Wake Board Assc.; [oth.writ.] I've written poems since 1983. My boyfriend Lance, encouraged me to send in "The Journey." I wrote this for my brother Johnny, who died December 15, 1993. Thanks Lance.; [pers.] If you always know, why you've always done, then you'll always get what you've always gotten.; [a.] Ontario, CA

BONONNO, NIAH
[b.] June 27, 1982; Morristown; [p.] Timothy Bononno and Angela Goodrich; [ed.] West Morris Central High School; [occ.] Student; [oth.writ.] First-time publication; [pers.] ". . . And that's why poetry appeals to me so much—because it's so eternal. Nothing else can survive a holocaust but poetry and songs. If my poetry aims to achieve anything, it's to deliver poeple from the limited ways in which they see and feel."—Jim Morrison, Los Angeles; [a.] Long Valley, NJ

BOONE, PAULINE
[pen.] "Boone"; [b.] January 6, 1935; NJ; [p.] Paul Lane, Charlotte Lane (deceased); [m.] Otis Boone (deceased); December 13, 1970 (second); [ch.] Glen Scudder, Lisa Scudder Baccus, Dorian Duren; [ed.] Secretary (Secretarial College); [occ.] Data Entry Machine Operator; [hon.] Merit Award; [oth.writ.] Autobiography, poems, articles in newspapers, editor of a community newspaper; [pers.] I started writing an autobiography about 6 months ago; I hope to finish it in about a year. I would like to also write a book of poems on all ofI nature (different types).; [a.] Paterson, NJ

BOWER, NICOLE
[pen.] Nykole, Bower; [b.] June 14, 1980; Pordennone, Italy; [p.] Stephanie, Bejard Bower; [ed.] High School Senior; [hon.] California speech contest in 1995, printed poem in 1994; [oth.writ.] "Life" only one printed; [a.] Beavercreek, OH

BOYD, BRIAN J.
[pen.] Brian J. Boyd; [b.] January 17, 1983; Ft. Lauderdale, FL; [p.] Mark R. Boyd, Bethany B. Boyd; [ed.] Graduated—St. Mark's School 8th grade, Attending Cardinal Gibbons High School—Ft. Lauderdale FL; [hon.] Headmasters list—ten out of twelve quartes; Athlete of the Year—St. Mark's School; [a.] Lauderhill, FL

BOYLE, DEBRA
[b.] October 14, 1952; Bangor, Maine; [p.] Lyman Clark, Dorothy Clark; [m.] David Boyle; February 14, 1981; [ch.] Kristy Howe, Shawn Ritchardson, Michael Boyle; [ed.] Santa Rosa Jr. College; [occ.] Pest Inspector; [pers.] I write about people and events in my life. Expressing my feelings and emotions in writting helps me in every aspect of my life.; [a.] Petaluma, CA

BRADMAN, FRANCES M.
[pen.] Frani Bee; [b.] May 20, 1938; Belleville; [p.] Deceased; [m.] Daniel A. Bradman Jr; June 20. 1970; [ch.] Danica Joan; [ed.] Belleville High, Kean College in Union; [occ.] County Coordinator for Child Assault Prevention; [memb.] Bethlehem Baptist Church League of Women Voters NAACP; [hon.] National Honor Society, NAACP Family Award Ben Hill Service Award, St. James AMEFCU, Albert P. Vreeland Distinguished Award; [oth.writ.] Primarily used in Church bulletins, for special events or to encourage others in need; [pers.] I was divinely inspired to write four years ago. My writings reflect the goodness, grace, mercy and love of God for all.; [a.] Hillside, NJ

BRADY, DAWN S.
[pen.] Dawn S. Parrish; [b.] June 16, 1949; [ch.] Michael Brant Dial; [ed.] John Marshall High School. I graduated in 1968. I'm going to college to become lawyer—the school is school of paralegal studies; [hon.] Citizenship award; [oth.writ.] I wrote a book called "Helpless Children Needing Help." I'm starting to write a workbook. I wrote another poem. I also wrote a song.; [pers.] The reason why I wrote this poem was because I was abused. I felt that I had to tell other children that they aren't the only ones that have been abused, and you can overcome your fears of abuse.; [a.] Selmer, TN

BRADY, MICHAEL F.
[b.] February 10, 1972; Perth Amboy, NJ; [p.] Linda Schonwald; [ed.] Westfield High, University of San Diego; [occ.] Bartender and Graduate Student Sociology at the New School for Social Research, N.Y.C; [memb.] Public Interest Research Group, Surfrider Foundation; [hon.] Departmental Honors Sociology U.S.D., New School Tuition Scholarship; [oth.writ.] Academic Essays and Short Stories, nothing published; [pers.] Poetry for me has always been a release from the cold, logical drudgery of academic work. I tend to agree with Sartre, who felt that true creativity and meaning are found when searching for a way out.; [a.] Westfield, NJ

BRAINARD, ALICIA
[pen.] Alicia Aileen Brainard; [b.] December 15, 1978; Oklahoma City; [ed.] Preschool-8th Grade, 1 Year High; [occ.] Housekeeping and Laundry at Best Western, Coral Hills; [hon.] Regional Drama Competition; [oth.writ.] (16) Poems, (1) Song; [pers.] If something scares you, don't run away. Face it. If you run every time you get scared, you're going to be running for the rest of your life. This poem is dedicated to Richard Wayne Hendershot II, whom I was thinking of as I wrote.; [a.] St.

George, UT

BRALEY, RUTH
[b.] February 6, 1936; Versailles; [p.] Carl and Myrtle Smith; [m.] Frank Braley; September 9, 1961; [ch.] Carla, Michael, Lena, and Bruce; [ed.] High School; [occ.] Housewife; [memb.] First Southern Baptist Church, American Cancer Society; [hon.] Volunteer of the Year for Cancer Society, Ripley Co. Health Coalition, 30 years teaching Sunday School; [oth.writ.] Funerals, retirements, weddings, own pleasures, and obituaries; published in Through the Looking Glass; [pers.] Putting God and family first, servring others in my church, community and my four children and ten grandchildren; [a.] Versailles, IN

BRANSON, RHONDA
[b.] February 14, 1958; Alexandria, LA; [ch.] James Branson, Jonathan Branson (died May 11, 1995); [ed.] Bolton High School Class of 1976; LSU, Alexandria 1988-89; [occ.] Single mother; [memb.] Northside Baptist Church, Louisiana Organ and Transplant Donation; [hon.] Editor's Choice Award, "A Dedication To My Son" in the anthology "The Colors of Thought"; [pers.] This poem is my gift to my son James for graduation from Louisiana Army National Guard Basic Training and AIT School. I love you.; [a.] Pineville, LA

BRAYTON, AMY C.
[b.] September 24, 1975; Lima, OH; [p.] Richard Brayton, Karen Stitzel; [ed.] Shawnee High; [occ.] Secretary, Microworld, Inc. Lima, Oh/Barmaid, R and D sports Lounge Lima OH; [memb.] American Heart Association; [hon.] Notary Public for the State of Ohio, my commission expires May 16, 2000; [oth.writ.] One poem published in Shawnee H.S.'s 1993 Avatar; [pers.] To let one read my poetry is to allow them to wade through the shallow end of my soul. I enjoy sharing a part of me with strangers and although the form is abstract, it gives me the same satisfaction that a long conversation would.; [a.] Lima, OH

BRENNAN, HELEN T.
[b.] July 15, 1916; Albany, NY; [p.] Anna and Charles Brenna (Deceased); [ed.] Blessed Sacrament Gr 1-8 Albany NY; Hackett Jr. High School; Albany High School; College of St. Rose, Albany; BSS Degree, NY State College, Albany MS degree; [occ.] Retired Elementary Teacher; [memb.] Leisuretimers—Albany; Albany Pub. School Retired Teachers; NY State Ret. Teachers; Silver Streakers; Colmie College of St. Rose Alumni; [oth.writ.] Poems (not published); [pers.] I love poetry and hope that others might enjoy mine.; [a.] Albany, NY

BROOKSHIER, FREDERICK R.
[b.] July 29, 1953; Bellingham, WA; [p.] James and Francis Brookshier; [m.] Deborah R. Brookshier; April 29, 1972; [ch.] Gina Marie, Angela Dawn; [ed.] Lk. Washington High, Misc. Trade Schools; [occ.] Matin Bldg.; [memb.] VFW - Eagles First Bapt. Church; [oth.writ.] Several poems (local pub. only); [pers.] I strive to treat others as I would want others to treat me, to be the best man I can, and to help and support others not so well off.; [a.] Kirkland, WA

BROWN, MIRANDA
[b.] September 8, 1982; Suffolk, VA; [p.] Joyce and Marc Brown; [ed.] Sophomore at present—Isle of Wight Academy; [memb.] Junior Olympic Softball, National Junior Honor Society, Varsity Basketball, Volleyball and Softball and Spanish Club, Student Council Organization and Class Officer; [hon.] 1st place in Veterans of Foreign Wars essay contest. Honor Roll. Presidential Physical Fitness Award (3 yrs. '95, '96, '97); [oth.writ.] My American Hero contest by Veterans of Foreign Wars.(1st place); [pers.] My Granddaddy loved me very much. I wrote the poem for him, even though he'll

never get a chance to read it. I know he would have been very proud of me.; [a.] Carrollton, VA

BROWN, SHENIECE
[b.] August 25, 1978; Seattle, WA; [p.] Ronald Brown and Dorothy Stahl; [ed.] High School graduate; [occ.] College student and sales associate; [memb.] 4-H for six years, Camp Fire Girls for twelve years, Spanish Club for two years, and Environmental Club for two years; [hon.] Art work shown at Maryhill Art Museum and a Community College Art Gallery; [pers.] I am influenced by events in my life, and am related to Robert Louis Stevenson. I was enoucaged by my Grandmother to write poetry. She has taught me a lot about writing.; [a.] Selah, WA

BRUCE III, JOHN BAYLOUS
[b.] February 14, 1967; Beaufort, SC; [p.] Steve Bruce/Patricia Ellis; [m.] Dawn Bruce; August 13, 1988; [ch.] Daughter: Tyler Lea Bruce; [ed.] Raleigh Egypt High School; [occ.] Shipping/Receiving Mgr.; [memb.] Traflagar Village Baptist Church Recreation Ministry Assoc. Director North American Hunting and Fishing Club; [oth.writ.] Several other poems including Father's Day, Baby poems, Birthday poem, and Wedding Day Prayer poem; [pers.] Believe in yourself and write from the heart. Never sugar-coat your writings.; [a.] Memphis, TN

BRUMBAUGH, BRENDA
[pen.] Brenda Gunn; [b.] February 25, 1956; Holden, MO; [p.] Bill and Bonnie Gunn; [occ.] In Process of starting my own Production Co.; [oth.writ.] "Avoid The Tiger," a screenplay currently optioned as a TV movie. "Sweeden Shoes and Breath of Ballet," book of 2 comedy-mystery stage plays.; [pers.] I strive to tell the truth in my writings no matter what price I may end up paying.; [a.] Kingsville, MO

BUBAN, JEFF
[b.] April 28, 1966; Centerville, IA; [p.] Charles W. and Fairie Buban; [m.] Tamara Buban; July 10, 1997; [ch.] Samantha, Lucas, Tim, and Joey; [ed.] Indian Hill's College (G.E.D.); [occ.] Carpenter; [pers.] I would like to thank my Mother, and my wife Tammy, for if there's one thing that can keep a person going it's family.; [a.] Mystic, IA

BUCKLEN, JOHN
[pen.] John Bucklen; [b.] June 5, 1919; Whitewood, VA; [p.] Joseph Bucklen, Watie Bucklen; [m.] May Bucklen; November 10, 1988 (2nd marriage) [ch.] Betty, Marilene, Wanda; [ed.] Elementary School; 1 Year High School; [occ.] Retired Coalminer, Farmer; [memb.] The American Legion, Disabled American Veterans, Amvets, Virginia Sheriffs Institute, Smithsonian Institute, World War II Memorial; [hon.] World War II—Asiatic Pacific Campaign—American Campaign, Occupation Service Silver Star, Bronze Star, 2 Commendations; [oth. writ.] Songs - To tell of His Love, Cobwebs from My Heart, Dreaming of You; [pers.] To see the best in my fellow men and women, to help others to do and be the best that is in them.; [a.] Pounding Mill, VA

BUNCH, ANNIE R.
[pen.] Ruthie; [b.] November 19; Lakeland, FL; [p.] Robert and Catherine Green; [m.] Ralph Bunch; March 11, 1995; [ed.] Masters In Human Relations Counseling (University of Oklahoma) Bachelor of Science: Major Psychology Minor: Sociology (Universtiy of Maryland) Kathleen Senior High School [occ.] Equal opportunity Advisor for the United States Army; [memb.] Person-centered association for studying the approaches of person-centered Therapy. Eventually I will become a member of the American Psychological Association; [hon.] National Defense Medals and Meritorious Service Medals—Military Tour and for my tour in Southwest Asia and the Balkan Region; [pers.] An expressive poem can provide insight to

an issue "Simplistically whereas it may take a book with numerous editions to provide the same insight.; [a.] Glen Burnie, MD

BUNNELL, CHRISTY
[b.] July 4, 1984; Salt Lake City, UT; [p.] Jeannette and Donald Bunnell; [ed.] St. Joseph's Catholic School; [occ.] Student; [memb.] Orchard's Soccer Club, St. Joseph's Parish; [hon.] 20 Academic Excellence Awards: First Honors; [oth.writ.] Other poetry pieces selected for publication; [pers.] Cherish life because you never know when someone will take it from you.; [a.] Vancouver, WA

BURDETTE, DON
[pen.] Joe King; [b.] October 17, 1979; Sharon; [p.] John and Jeanne Burdette; [ed.] I am a senior in high school. (Sharon Senior High School); [occ.] Student; [memb.] National Honor Society; [hon.] National Honor Society; [pers.] Despite popular opinion, power is not ruling people over a thousand mile radius. Real power comes from the ability to make people feel the emotions you wish for them to experience.; [a.] Sharon, PA

BURGES, DANNY
[pen.] Logan; [b.] February 6, 1980; Brooklyn, NY; [p.] Robert and Jeannie Burges; [occ.] Musician; [oth.writ.] Raven's Tears, Therefore I Die, March of the Dead, The Nocturnal Embrace; [a.] Brooklyn, NY

BURNS, EDWARDA LOUISE
[b.] November 15, 1915; Berkeley Springs, WV; [p.] Theresa Atkinson, Irvin Michael; [m.] Paul Emile Burns; November 23, 1946; [ch.] Vincent, Mark, Peter, Elizabeth; [ed.] (1) BS, St. Joseph College, Emmitsburg, MD; (2) BA, Shepherd College, Emeritus Club, Kappa Delta Pi Shepherdstown, WV; (3) Catholic University of America, Junior Engineer, Washington, DC; (4) University of Maryland, 34 hours, Reading Specialist Courses, College Park, MD; [a.] Adelphi, MD

BUTTITTA, CARA LEIGH
[b.] April 1, 1982; Bangor, ME; [p.] James Buttitta and Lydia Buttitta; [ed.] High School Student at Hampden Academy in Hampden, Maine; [pers.] I dedicate this poem to my mother who was a lover of music and poetry until the day she died.; [a.] Newburgh, ME

CAPLAN, JAMIE
[b.] February 27, 1987; Fairfax, VA; [p.] Lori Caplan and Robert Caplan; [ed.] Flint Hill School; (Going into 5th Grade); [occ.] Student; [memb.] USTA Tennis; [a.] Fairfax, VA

CASWELL, CONNIE
[b.] New York State; [ed.] Syracuse University, Syracuse NY; All Nations Christian College, Ware, Herts, England; L'Abril Fellowship, Villars, Switzerland; [memb.] Boston Scottish Fiddle Club; [oth.writ.] 2 Unpublished novels; [a.] Brookline, MA

CASWELL, DARLENE KASI
[b.] March 13, 1957; Daytona Beach, FL; [p.] William and Ollie Boykin; [occ.] Disabled; [oth.writ.] I wrote a song to my mother, and two other poems.; [a.] Woodruff, SC

CASWELL, VIOLET MARIE
[pen.] Crystal Rose Christ; [b.] November 28; Kalamazoo, MI; moved to Miami Beach, FL; [p.] Clarence Le Roy Caswell and Mary Hope Joy Peace; [m.] Gary Dean Shaw; December 22, 1966; (Divorced) January 22, 1988; and Clay Porter Taylor; January 3, 1994; [ed.] Jimtown High, Jimtown Ind. Edwardsburg HI. Edwardsburg, MI, Ext. Brandy-Wine Niles Michigan, South Western Michigan College. "Humman Services." 1988; [occ.] Homemaker; [memb.] "Book Towers," Lake Wales Florida, The Holy Spirit Catholic Church, Lake Wales Florida; [hon.] The Committee to

Promote Cass County I formed, in Edwardsburg, Michigan in Nov. 1979; a group formed a movement for Cass County to secede from the State of Michigan and Become Michiana, Indiana. I got over 3, 000 Signatures. Was in newspapers, news media, Channel 22 News, several TV stations' talk shows—two got Awards and honors for this achievement Cass County, Michigan. I should be remembered in The History Books; [oth.writ.] "The Book of The Soul" 1961 Published went all over the world, "No Never Never Again" 1960; [pers.] I go to The Dundee Baptist Church in Dundee, Florida, where I sing in the Choir. Some realy neat and dear people go there; they provide transportation for me when I am unable to drive. I am writing another book, "With Him, I Am Everything Sacred Love." I dedicate "The Journey of the Soul" to my brother, who is my keeper, Randall Cleave Caswell; to my aunt Mildred Caswell Slevatz; and friend Rev. Jerry R. Wenger: "Thou shalt not, forbidden, take anything forbidden, thou shalt change the face of the earth." [a.] Miami Beach, FL

CHAITOVSKY, CHAVA GILA
[pen.] Chava Chaitovsky; [b.] April 23, 1986; New York City; [p.] Esther and Myron Chaitovsky; [ed.] S.A.R. Academy, Riverdale, NY Yeshiva of North Jersey, Riveredge NJ The Marian School, Engelwood, NJ; [occ.] Student

CHAMBERS, RONNIE
[b.] March 14, 1947; Arab, AL; [p.] Jessica, Thelma Chambers; [m.] Dorothy; December 2, 1966; [ch.] Leticia, Nikki; [ed.] Shipping Receiving; [oth.writ.] Songs; [pers.] I write solely for enjoyment and entertainment for myself and others.; [a.] Lake Wales, FL

CHARETTE, ELLEN
[b.] February 19, 1944; Los Angeles, CA; [m.] Thomas Charette; November 17, 1984; [occ.] Sales Representative Account Manager; [memb.] Alpaca Breeders of Arizona; [pers.] I have been strongly influenced by and have intense feelings about personal and business behaviors of people in the days and times we now live.; [a.] Glendale, AZ

CHURCH, JEFFREY
[b.] September 6, 1970; Great Falls, MT; [p.] Robert Church, JoAnne Church; [m.] Kathleen Church; June 9, 1996; [ed.] University of Montana; [pers.] My writings concern the human experience and how we relate to the natural world.; [a.] Portland, OR

CLARK, JOSEPH
[b.] December 10, 1950; Mullins, SC; [p.] George B. and Myrtle Clark; [m.] Landis C. Clark; July 17, 1983; [ch.] Brian, Joey, and Lance Clark; [ed.] Graduate of Mullins High School—Class of 1969, attended Nashville Auto Diesel College for Automotive Program; [occ.] Shop Instructor for Florence School District; [memb.] Fork Baptist Church; [oth.writ.] Poem published in local newspaper at age 8; [pers.] It is my belief that if one can put into words the ingredients that bring forth a smile or if your thoughts can be shared and you lend to others strength, or just a smile in their heart, then you will leave this world a tiny bit better than you found it!; [a.] Fork, SC

CLARK, MARGOT F.
[pen.] Mfc; [b.] March 7, 1921; Knoxville, TN; [p.] John, Anita Fridge; [m.] David B. Clark; November 26, 1977; [ch.] Elizabeth, Veronica; [ed.] Sulphur High School, McNeese State University; [memb.] Heritage Presbyterian Chruch; [hon.] McNeese Student Union Board, Student Government Association; [oth.writ.] I have a collection of my own poems (not published) called, "Experiences of Life"; [pers.] I would like my poetry to allow those who read it to feel an emotion and to think about experiences in their lives.; [a.] Houston, TX

CLIVER, CAROLYN E.
[b.] October 27, 1935, Indianapolis, IN; [p.] Frederick and Frieda Parker; [m.] Dean O. Cliver, August 13, 1960; [ch.] Blanche (Daughter), Frederick (Son), Carl (Son), Marguerite (Daughter); [ed.] BA and MA from Indiana University; [occ.] Social Worker (Retired); [memb.] AAVW, NOW, Friends of University of California, Davis; [hon.] Unsung Hero 1984 by Madison WI, NAACP; [oth. writ.] The Eagle; [pers.] To calm yourself when you are angry with your children, stop and think how you would feel if something happened to them. This will return your perspective.

CLODFELTER, BRUCE W.
[b.] August 6, 1938; Dayton, OH; [p.] Wendell and Elizabeth Clodfelter; [m.] Divorced; [ch.] Steven William and Scott David; [ed.] University of Dayton Dean's List, Bachelor of Science, Forty (40) Department of Defense courses (misc.), Certifications, Ohio State University; [occ.] Consultant; [memb.] Alumni Club, American Management Association, American Accounting Club, National Contract Management Association, Dayton Masters Track Club; [hon.] 35 Performance Awards (DOD), 3 Professional of Year Award Nominations, 1 Meritorious Service Award, 4 Time South Western Ohio Shotput Champion (93, 94, 95, 96) (Seniors And Masters), 3 Time Medal Winner State of Ohio Shotput Seniors Competition, 93, 94, 95, Over 40 (Seniors/Masters Track and Field Awards; [pers.] Work hard, do good, never quit, trust God, live life fully and believe "The Sky's The Limit."; [a.] Centerville, OH

COGHLAN, RUBY WINIFRED
[b.] July 13, 1909; N. Ireland; [p.] Thomas and Annie McCartney; [m.] John S. Coghlan (Deceased); April 16, 1933; San Francisco; [ch.] Two, a girl and a boy; [occ.] Housewife; [pers.] My husband passed away 25 years ago. I had to sell my home and move into a mobile home park in Santa Rosa.; [a.] Santa Rosa, CA

COLEMAN JR., HOWARD
[b.] September 30, 1980; Fort Pierce, FL; [p.] Barbara and Howard Coleman; [ed.] Currently attending Lincoln Park Academy High School; [memb.] Spanish National Honor Society, National Honor Society, Mt. Olive Missionary Baptist Church, NAACP Youth Group, International Baccalaureate Program, American Heart Association; [hon.] 1st Place in Talent Hunt Competition (recited poem) '97; [pers.] Thank you Jesus Christ for letting my poem be noticed. Thanks Katarsha, my sister.; [a.] Fort Pierce, FL

CONKEY, KELLI
[b.] October 30, 1983; Newport Beach, CA; [p.] Gary and Cheryl Conkey; [ed.] Sierra Vista Middle School; [memb.] City of Irvine Middle School Youth Action Team, Irvine Nova Aquatics; [hon.] Sierra Vista Middle School: Honor Roll, Student of the Month; Youth Action Team Certificate of Appreciation for Community Service, Irvine Unified School District Science Fair—Outstanding Project Award; [a.] Irvine, CA

CONRAD, JAMES
[pen.] Kelly Vick; [b.] March 14, 1968; Boston, MA; [p.] Della Vick, Shermen Berry, [oth.writ.] Many poems and other writtings that are unpublished; [pers.] I dedicate all of my work first to the God of Israel and to His Christ, second to my mother and father, then to the world, and as for me—I ask nothing but to be noticed.; [a.] Central Falls, RI

CONWAY, KRISTY
[b.] September 2, 1969; [m.] Robert Conway; July 5, 1995; [ch.] Megan Kyle Buddy; [pers.] Incest Survivor; [a.] Port Saint Lucie, FL

COOK, VIRGINIA H.
[pen.] Virginia H. D. Cook; [b.] December 12, 1930; Woodburg, NJ; [p.] Henry and Louise Doerrmann; [m.] William T. Cook; May 9, 1953; [ch.] Dwight H. Cook and Michael W. Cook; [ed.] High School Graduate; [occ.] Retired; [oth.writ.] "True Love," another poem I wrote, which is in a book by Sparrowgrass Poetry Forum; [pers.] I enjoy writing poems. We release our inner feelings by writing.; [a.] St. Augustine, FL

COOL, SHANDA
[b.] September 4, 1982; Pikeville; [p.] Leland and Drema Cool; [ed.] Current HS Sophomore at Belfry High School; [occ.] Student; [memb.] National Junior Honor Society; Belfry Academic Team; Belfry High School Yearbook Staff; Principal's Cabinet; [hon.] Woodmen of the World Award; Runyen Elementary Major in Science, History, English, Writing, Mathematics, and spelling, several awards in public speaking; [oth.writ.] Book of poems were published in local library; several short stories published in school newspaper; [pers.] When I write, I reflect my current feelings, whether they be sad or cheerful; that way, my poems always carry a part of me.; [a.] McVeigh, KY

COOPER JR., GARY WAYNE
[pen.] Coop, Coop Dog; [b.] April 7, 1981; High Point; [p.] Susan Cooper and Gary Cooper; [oth.writ.] Several poems yet to be surfaced, but hopefully soon; [pers.] My writings reflect a view of life only the heart recognizes. Life itself is worth no meaning without someone in it to complete it.; [a.] Thomasville, NC

CORBI, CRYSTAL MARIE
[b.] December 23, 1983; New York City, NY; [p.] Leopold and Karen Corbi; [ed.] Freshman year at Howard W. Blake H.S. of Performing Arts, majoring in chorus and creative writing; [hon.] Honor Roll and achievement awards, Middleton Middle School of Technology 1996-1997 graduate; [oth.writ.] "My Teddy Bear", "Nathan", "My Best Friend, Whoever!", "Flower"; [a.] Tampa, FL

CORREA, STEFANIE
[b.] August 14, 1965; Little Rock, AR; [p.] Dick Woodington, Bobbe Kauffman; [ch.] Elijah Porter; [ed.] Brighton High, Front Range Community College; [occ.] Quality Assurance Analyst, Lucent Technologies, Westminster, CO; [memb.] Brighton DECA, Nat'l Wildlife Foundation, Nat'l Arbor Society; [hon.] Wal-Mart Pharmacy: Supportive personnel, certificate of recognition, Confertech Int'l: Certificate of Appreciation, North Elem. School: Outstanding Volunteer Teacher's Aide Award; [oth.writ.] Rainfrost: Buried Treasure of the Pharmacist, Native Americans and Alcohol Abuse (on and off the reservation); [pers.] I tend to write about and photograph things that most people let pass by. My friends say I view life through the eyes of a child. The little things bring the most excitement and pleasure to my life.; [a.] Thornton, CO

CORTEZ, JOYCE
[b.] September 26, 1931; Mesick, MI; [p.] Fred and Mamie Jewell; [m.] Paul Cortez; November 6, 1971; [ch.] Gail, Beverly and Lisa (3 granddaughters); [ed.] High School Diploma from Franklin High School, Los Angeles, have been taking assorted classes ever since but do not have a degree; [occ.] Retired; [oth.writ.] There are dozens of poems and short stories. Two stories are about bank robberies I was involved in as a teller. Once I started on poetry I couldn't seem to stop. If I've lived it, it goes from the pen to the paper in rhyme.; [pers.] I always wanted to write but it may have been an episode of cancer that motivated me to get started. It's like everything I ever wanted to say I am compelled to write now.; [a.] Big Bear City, CA

COVER, CHRISTIANNE
[b.] September 16, 1981; Johnstown, PA; [p.] Tom and Judy Cover; [ed.] Richland High School (sopho-
more); [memb.] Cheerleading; [hon.] Two time PA State Cheerleading Champions (1995 and 1996); [oth.writ.] I have written poetry for five years and this is first time I've shared it to be published.; [pers.] I'm a dreamer but live in reality. I hold on with hope and sometimes let fear have its way.; [a.] Johnstown, PA

CREAL, GREGORY ALLEN
[b.] July 28, 1977; Pascagoula, MS; [p.] Robert Creal, The Late Sarah S. Stevenson; [ed.] John L. Leflore High School; [memb.] Friendship Baptist Church; [pers.] Sex, drugs, and violence, for what they're worth, are killing us.; [a.] Grand Bay, AL

CROCHET, JASON DRU
[b.] January 1, 1975; Port Arthur, TX; [p.] David and Vickie Crochet; [ed.] 12th Grade graduate of Port Nechesgroves High School Sr. 1993; [occ.] Infantry Rifleman in the United States Marine Corps; [memb.] Boy Scouts of America troop 86; [hon.] Southwest Asia with Bronze Star medal, National Defence Medal, Sea Service Deployment Ribon, Sharp Shooter Rifle Badge, Eagle Scout with Bronze Palm, Order of the Arrow (OA); [pers.] Don't let your fears stand in the way of your dreams.; [a.] Groves, TX

CROMWELL, NICK
[b.] September 16, Houston, TX; [p.] Lee S. Cromwell; [m.] Carolyn Cromwell, January 24, 1996; [ch.] Jennifer, Jeanine, Elizabeth, Alexander, Phillip, Kristine, Heather; [ed.] Sophomore in High School; [occ.] Wage Jobs; [memb.] Sons of the Republic of Texas; [hon.] "Who's Who Among American High School Students" nominee; [oth.writ.] None Published; [pers.] Boredom sets into the boring mind.; [a.] Sunrise Beach, TX

CULVER, AMANDA ROSE
[b.] September 12, 1978; [p.] Michael and Cynthia Culver; [ed.] Troy Area High School, attending Lock Haven University of PA; [occ.] Student; [memb.] LHU Marching Band, National Honor Society; [oth.writ.] Several other poems and a few essays but nothing published until this one; [pers.] Writing and music have become a type of therapy for me. It works. I used to be very self-conscious about letting people read my work.; [a.] Gillett, PA

DANIEL, SHIRLEY E.
[pen.] Lane; [b.] December 23, 1950; Atlanta, GA; [p.] Iula Daniel, Solomon Daniel; [ed.] Elementary School, Atl., GA Peter James Bryant High School; C.L. Harpee High; College DEKALB Junior College, Atlanta Junior College Clark College Presents, Clark Atlanta University; [occ.] Asset Protection Agent for Sears, Northlake Mall; [memb.] American Business Women Association (ABWA); [hon.] Business Club-Junior College Courtesy, Award Winner in March 1988. Currently writing as a hobby but I would like to be a poet; [oth.writ.] "Summer Breeze", "Brown Baby's Dad" not published; [pers.] I love all types of poetry and my favorite writer is Mayo Angelou.; [a.] Atlanta, GA

DARCH, SANDRA CHARMAINE
[pen.] Sandy Darch; [b.] August 20, 1945; England; [p.] Eva B. Darch and R.J. Darch; [m.] Harry Celiz; May 11, 1996; [ch.] Shaun James Darch; [ed.] Secondary Modern School, Halesworth, Suffolk, England; [occ.] Homemaker; 3-year stay with Ford Motor Co.; [memb.] Oil Painting and Drawing Schoolcraft College Livonia, MI; [oth.writ.] One poem in local newspaper—Kings Lynn, Norfolk, England; [pers.] I strive to make good in our new land—albeit so different.; [a.] Plymouth, MI

DASKAREV, OGNIAN
[b.] October 28, 1954; Sofia, Bulgaria; [p.] Lubomir, Radka Daskarevi; [m.] Danka Daskareva; November 23, 1973; [ch.] Anna Daskareva; [ed.] Bachelor's Degree in English Language and Literature; [occ.] Recent Immigrant, looking for job;

[oth.writ.] Many unpublished poems; [pers.] Being a pessimist and introvert by nature, I love to depict the dark side of living, loneliness estrangement, despair, alienation, suicide. I love the romantic poets.; [a.] Hasbrouck Heights, NJ

DAVIS, SANDRA
[pen.] Sandra Sue Davis; [b.] February 5, 1953; Oklahoma City, OK; [p.] William Walter and Billie Jean Clary; [m.] James B. Davis; June 20, 1981; [ch.] Two Stepchildren; [ed.] Crooked Oak High School, Oklahoma City, OK; Life iteself; [occ.] Writer, Homemaker, Author and Poet; [memb.] Distinguished Member International Society of Poets; [hon.] Editor's Choice Awards For Outstanding Achievement in Poetry. Presented by The National Library of Poetry, 1996 and 1997. Distinguished Member of The International Society of Poets.; [oth. writ.] "What Is" published by NLP 1996 Anthology "Lyrical Heritage"; "A Voice From Heaven" Pub.NLP 1997 Anthologies "Tracing Shadows" and "Isle Of View"; "Gone Are The Days" Pub.NLP "Best Poems of 1997"; [pers.] I would like to dedicate "Gone Are the Days" to my beloved grandmother Ms. Mamie Marie Carter, a.k.a. "Nan Nan," the most precious angel that ever graced the face of earth; Born October 16, 1908—Died April 10, 1995; [a.] Cypress, CA

DAY, KERRY
[b.] May 30, 1963; Arlington, VA; [p.] Charles H. Day and Betty M. Day; [ed.] Working on my degree in accounting at Nova College; Washington-Lee High School; [occ.] Line Cook at Friday's; [pers.] I always try to write my works from feeling that I have or experienced. I have always been an avid reader of various kinds of writing.; [a.] Alexandria, VA

DE VESTERN, RALPH
[b.] May 8, 1960; Bethesda, MD; [p.] George Alexander Kygoulis, Mary Florence Kygoulis; [m.] Preston Dean Taylor; March 12, 1987; [ch.] Tenequa Malmute, Louie Macaw; [ed.] John P. Stevens High, Middlesex County College, Fairleigh Dickenson University, American Airline School AMR Services, UPS, and Federal Express Courier School; [occ.] Concrete Dispatcher Deputy Weighmaster and Batchman; [hon.] Who's Who 1991, Bravo Zulu Award Federal Express Corporation, Gary R. Alexander's Outastanding Student Award 1978 Karate; [oth.writ.] Saks Fish Avenue's Guide to Salt and Freshwater Fish and How to Housebreak Your New Puppy (Ralph De Vestern AKA/DBA Saks Fish Avenue); [pers.] I dedicate With Equality to the inspiration behind most of my accomplishments and the desire to be worthy of this, Conan King June 12, 1982 to April 24, 1995, a Red White Siberian Husky whom earned the status, "Son." He loved the Piano and Traveled the Country with me.; [a.] West Hills, CA

DEESE, MISTY MICHELLE
[b.] March 19, 1985; Jacksonville, Fl; [p.] Mr. and Mrs. Harbert; [ed.] I am now attending Middle School and plan to finish high school and go to College.; [oth.writ.] I have many other poems and I will continue writing poetry.; [a.] Jacksonville, FL

DEMPS, MARY L.
[b.] January 23, 1955; Albany, GA; [p.] Andrew Demps and Loulla Demps; [ed.] Graduated from Madison High School in Albany, GA; [occ.] Secretary; [a.] Albany, GA

DENNIS, KAREN LEIGH COX
[pen.] Karen Leigh; [b.] January 20, 1967; CA; [p.] James S. Cox, Joyce Lerew; [m.] Carl Dennis; [ch.] Riley Morgan Dennis; [ed.] Bachelor of Arts in English Literature and the Classics from Univ. of California, Santa Barbara; [occ.] Writer; [oth.writ.] Several historical articles published in Local Newspapers. Currently writing children's books; [pers.] One of the greatest gifts we can impart on our children is the love of reading and literature.

Parents, caregivers and teachers have a great responsibility to lead our young ones up the path of limitless imagination, knowledge and wisdom. Reading takes us there.

DENNY, CAROLYN
[pen.] C.J. de L'Isle; [b.] January 16, 1949; Pittsburg, TX; [p.] Bill and Marie De L'Isle; [m.] Weldon Denny; October 28, 1966; [ch.] Tammny, Wynn, Kevin Kirk, Kelly Lynn; [ed.] Mt. Pleasant High, Enrolled in Northeast Texas Community College (NTCC); [occ.] Homemaker; [memb.] High School : Band Booster and Choral Boasters / Church: God Loves Our Women Auxillary, Youth Sponsor, Sanctuary Choir, also Disabled American Veterans Auxilary; [hon.] Iliad Press National Authors Registry: "Words of Love", Summer 1995 Honorable Mention, and 1996 President's Award for Literary Excellence, "Memories" Winter 1997 Honorable Mention; [oth.writ.] Several other poems published in anthologies and hometown newspaper. Several novels and short stodies (to date, unpublished); [pers.] I view life as a gift from God to be spent in eagerness to give Him glory in all I do, say and own, and love as an emotion of action to be measured by what we give of self not by what we get.; [a.] Lone Star, TX

DEREMO, STANLEY K.
[b.] July 2, 1922; Cincinnati, OH; [p.] Deceased; [m.] Rose Mary C. Deremo; September 4, 1948; [ch.] Reda Hutton; [ed.] Xavier University; [occ.] Retired; [hon.] Merchand's Security 1. St Lt. Pinkerton Security 24 yrs. of servive; [a.] Cincinnati, OH

DEVINE, HILTRUD
[b.] October 2, 1937; Germany; [p.] Helene and Walter Jorn; [m.] Gilbert J. Devine; July 13, 1987; [ch.] James A. Steven L. Aultman; [ed.] High School, College in Germany; [occ.] Retired; [memb.] First Christian Church (Disciples of Christ) in Canon City, CO; [hon.] "True Grit" award at Business college honors during my working years at EF Hutton-Shearson Lehman Bros. [oth.writ.] None published; [pers.] "Footprints" (author unknown) gives me a source of strength and comfort—yet I wonder, how much stronger do I need to be?; [a.] Penrose, CO

DEVOID, ADAM
[b.] April 27, 1977; Berlin, NH; [p.] Ronald and Claudette Devoid; [ed.] Berlin High School Class of 1995, Keene State College, Fall 1995 to present; [occ.] Hannaford Superstore in Keene, NH (shiftleader); [memb.] National Honor Society 1992-1995, St. Paul School Advanced Studies Program Alumni (1994), Dean's List Keene State College 1995-1996; [hon.] Keene State College Freshman Challenge Scholarship. Ayling Scholarship. Graduation with high honors; [pers.] I believe that a greater focus should be given to our nation's youth. They are of great importance and I strive to express this in my poems.; [a.] Keene, NH

DILLON, IRIS
[pen.] Iris Dee; [b.] September 20, 1924; New Orleans, LA; [p.] Deceased; [m.] Deceased; May 10, 1939; [ed.] Business College, New Orleans, LA, Tulane University: New Orleans, Denver University, Denver, CO School of Graphology, San Diego, CA; [occ.] Case Manager, SD Home Care; [memb.] In over a dozen service organizations, including Alcoholics Anonymous, Animal Leagues, Christ Church Unity of El Cajon; [hon.] Certified Hospital Chaplaincy Through Christ Church Unity (San Diego), Various Service Awards through work with elderly; [oth.writ.] Tributes and greetings cards for use of friends and businesses; my personal birthday, anniversary, and holidays as well as congratulations. Won a radio poetry contest (2500), comm. flight poetry contest, was published in a local newspaper; [pers.] To do the will of God in my life and express His love in all my endeavors and

relationships.; [a.] San Diego, CA

DISTASIO, JENNA
[b.] September 11, 1981; [p.] Mary Alys and A.J. Distasio; [ed.] Nansemond Suffolk Academy; [occ.] Student, Cheerleader, Student Trainer; [pers.] Poetry is one of the most beautiful and efficient ways to express feeling and experience. Feel it, write it, think it; you will love the clairity and dimension your are words given.; [a.] Chesapeake, VA

DORSEY, DAWN
[b.] November 11, 1981; Steubenville, OH; [p.] Ozell Strawder, Mary Jo Dorsey; [ed.] In High School; [occ.] Going to school and working on my education; [memb.] Simpson United Methodist Church; [oth.writ.] I have other poems but they've never been read by anyone but me and family; [pers.] I basically write about the moods I'm in and how I feel because it's real and a lot of people go through these moods.; [a.] Steubenville, OH

DOSS, KRISTINE
[b.] December 4, 1980; Mountain View, CA; [p.] Todd Doss, Dorothy Henthorn; [ed.] San Benito High School; [occ.] Student; [pers.] You don't know what you can do until you try.; [a.] Hollister, CA

DRINNON, JANIS BOLTON
[b.] July 28, 1922; Pineville, KY; [p.] Clyde Herman and Violet Hendrickson Bolton; [m.] Kenneth C. Drinnon; June 13, 1948; [ch.] Dena Drinnon Foulk, m. David E. Foulk; [ed.] Middlesboro, KY High School: Journalism classes at Lincoln Memorial University, Harrogate, TN, 1947-1948; commercial art certificate from Art Instruction School, 1968; correspondence courses with Newspaper Institute of America; drama instruction and singing lessons with private teachers; [occ.] Homemaker; [memb.] New Hopewell Baptist Church, Knoxville, TN: distinguished member of International Society of Poets; [hon.] Editors choice awards by The National Library of Poetry for eight poems-"When our Purpose Here Is Done" published in The Dark Side of the Moon in 1994, "Blessings" published in The Best Poems of 1995, "My Daily Best" published in Windows of the Soul in 1995, "Going Home" Published in The Best Poems of 1996, "On Call" published in Through the Hourglass in 1996, "He is Real" published in Best Poems of The 90's,"A Better Place" published in In Dappled Sunlight in 1997, "In His Care" published in Through the Looking Glass in 1997. Nominated for Poet of the Year for 1995, 1996, and 1997 by The International Society of Poets. Elected to The International Poetry Hall of Fame. Selected for the Silver 25th Edition of Marquis Who's Who in the South and Southwest and 52nd Edition of Marquis Who's Who in America. Elected to The International Poetry Hall of Fame; [oth.writ.] While attending college, wrote articles for local newspapers. Recently had poems published in anthologies; [pers.] I have always enjoyed the finner things of life and nature, especially those that are spiritually uplifting and bring beauty to the soul. My family has always come first in my life. I have never been much for organizations, preferring to be a doer rather than a participant.; [a.] Knoxville, TX

DUFFY, MICHAEL G.
[pen.] M. G. Duffy; [b.] January 29, 1959; Davenport, IA; [p.] Tom and Virginia Duffy; [ed.] B.S. Child Development, Iowa State Univ. M.A. Therapeutic Recreation, Univ. of Iowa; [occ.] Child Life Coordinator, University Hospital, San Antonio, TX; [memb.] Child ILfe Council, Association for the Care of Children's Health; [hon.] OmicronNu; [oth. writ.] Therapeutic activities for hospitalized children in a professional newsletter; [pers.] My writings reflect the children who have touched my life and my own childhood experiences.; [a.] San Antonio, TX

DUGGER, MELISSA ANN
[pen.] Missy Dugger; [b.] November 29, 1981; Denver, CO; [p.] Mark and Judy Dugger; [ed.] Presently a 10th grader in high school; [occ.] Student; [memb.] Colorado Horse Rescue; [hon.] "A" Honor Roll 7, 8, 9th grades; perfect attendance 9th grade; [oth.writ.] Unpublished personal poems that I have written; [pers.] I want to give all credit for "Friendships and Flowers" to God; [a.] Denver, CO

DURDIN, NANCY HARRISON
[pen.] Nancy Durdin, Nancy Harrison Durdin; [b.] Richard Center, WI; [p.] Carter and Georgia Harrison; [m.] A.C. Durdin IV; April 9, 1988; [ch.] Lori N. and Valerie J., (stepchildren) Gus, Robert, Sarah; [ed.] Bachelor of Science in Nursing, Milton College; Master of Science in Health Administration, California College; [occ.] Director of Nursing Services Valley Manor, Plymouth WI; [memb.] National Association of Dir. of Nursing, Long Term Care Directors of Nursing, Fellow Midwest Geriatic Society, Wisc. Nurses Assoc., American Nurses Assoc., Advisory Council for Assoc. Degree Nurses, YMCA; [hon.] BSN Degree—Magna Cum Laude, Who's Who In American Nursing 1993-1994, ANA Certification in Gerontology; [oth.writ.] Editorial comments in local newspapers; articles in newsletters; I design cards on my computer; [pers.] I try to live a reflective life within a very busy life, to stay aware of the small currents that make up the flow of my life; appreciate each moment.; [a.] Glenbeulah, WI

DUTY, PAT
[b.] October 20, 1954; Baltimore, MD; [m.] Kenneth S. Duty; March 26, 1988; [ch.] Christine Duty and Crystal Duty; [ed.] Essex Community College; [occ.] Systems Analyst; [oth.writ.] Symphony of Life, Heirlooms of Time, Dance to Survival; [pers.] I strive to use my writing to provide healing and encouragement to all who have experienced inner pain and heartache.; [a.] Baltimore, MD

EASTERLY, ANGIE
[b.] April 15, 1982; Dunlap, TN; [p.] Connie, Dale Easterly; [ed.] Sequatchie County School System; [occ.] Student; [hon.] Editor's Choice Award, Published 3 times, school 2nd place poetry award, 7th grade mathematics award; [oth.writ.] She, Lost Love, One Step from Heaven, My Friend, This Sad Day, They Sang, Rookie Deaf ears, The Ride; [pers.] I saw the light through your caring eyes; I felt the world thanks to your caring arms. I love you.; [a.] Whitwell, TN

ECHEVARRIA, GLORYA MIRRA
[b.] April 9, 1975; New Brunswick, NJ; [p.] Charles Mirra and Victoria Roberts; [m.] Gene Echearria; June 4, 1993; [ed.] Level I in computer Technology from Rio Salado, Phx Az; [occ.] Make and design Fashion Jewelry; [hon.] Dean's honor roll 4.0. G.P.A.; [oth.writ.] Poems for my loving husband; [a.] Hackettstown, NJ

EINBINDER, DEANNA
[pen.] Sidney Dean; [b.] October 28, 1941; Chicago, IL; [p.] Kenneth Perkins, Mylle Perkins; [m.] Arnold L. Einbinder; November 5, 1961; [ch.] Stacy, Lisa, Marshall; [ed.] Sullivan High; [occ.] Home Maker, Writer; [memb.] Rare Breed Dog Club, Leonberger Club of America; [hon.] An essay I wrote was used as a teaching tool in a Western Col;. [oth.writ.] Articles published in local newspapers. I am primarily a novelist. I have three historical adventures written, and am currently working on the second book in an historical series.; [pers.] Too many of us are unaware of our relatively brief, wonderful, exciting, often times hard to believe history. I would like to change that.; [a.] Mundelein, IL

EMELUMBA, CHARLES
[b.] February 16, 1958; Ubulu, Imostate Nigeria;

[p.] Nicholas and Geraldine Emelumba; [m.] Edith Emelumba; [ed.] University of Nigeria, NSukka—BA, Philosophy; University of Lagos, Nigeria—MA, Philosophy; [oth.writ.] "Africa, The Drum of Change," "PM . . . My Neighbour," "Songs of the Farmishes" (unpublished), "Man's True Religion" (unpublished); [pers.] "Man's sole duty is to make manifest divinity within." I'm influenced by philosophical essays.; [a.] JC, NJ

ERB, ELISHA
[pen.] Squeaky; [b.] June 29, 1984; [p.] Wendy and Terry Erb; [ed.] Northeastern Middle School; [occ.] Student; [hon.] Honor Roll Awards, Sports Awards (soccer, softball, running, etc.), Art Awards; [oth.writ.] Other poems and stories written on my own, but no publications. Some poems: The Pretty One, He's Gone, Love, Seeing Life, My Lost Love, The Place, The Hood, Heaven, Sunshine, Best Friends, Sorry; [a.] York Haven, PA

ESCOBAR, NATASHA DANIELLE
[b.] December 22, 1988; Brownsville, TX; [p.] Natalie and Danny Escobar; [ed.] Currently (1997-98) at Incarnate Word Academy—4th Grade; [memb.] Tip of Texas Girl Scout B.T. 197, Immaculate Conception Church Choir, Christian dance, art, Palm Grove Sanctuary Summer Program; [hon.] '96-'97 3rd Grade Incarnate Word Academy 2nd place scholastic achievement Iwa Bansa Basketball 2nd place '96-'97 Accelerated reading prog. 2nd place; [pers.] I wish that the world today would be more peaceful. I love my parents with all my heart, soul, and mind.; [a.] Brownsville, TX

FAHRENKAMP, TRACY
[b.] March 12, 1981; Shakopee, MN; [p.] Mark Fahrenkamp and Linda Fahrenkamp; [ed.] New Prague High; [occ.] Student; [hon.] "Excellent" rating for vocal solo, "Excellent" rating to vocal duet, tennis award, 1st year letter in chior; [a.] New Prague, MN

FAIN, ESTHER R.
[p.] Earl, Marie Fuller; [m.] James L. Fain; [ch.] 3: Steven, Leann and Leslie; [ed.] 3 Years grade school Kaaur India El Monte Calif. High School 2 years college 2 years interior decorating; [occ.] Retired GTE Telephone Co.; [pers.] As a small child I lived with my grandmother while my father and mother lived in India. Hearing the trains at night, I longed for my parents, thinking the trains were going all the way to India.; [a.] San Jacinto, CA

FARR, JOHN WESLEY
[b.] November 30, 1988; [p.] Johnny and Mary Kay Farr; [ed.] W.B. Bramlett Elementary School 3rd Grader; [occ.] Student—I will be in 3rd grade 1997-1998.; [memb.] Scouts, Star Wars Fan Club; [hon.] W.B. Bramlett Elementary Young GA Author, Kindergarten (1995) and First Grade (1996); Anthology of Poetry Winner, First Grade (1996), Second Grade (1997); [oth.writ.] The Big Python, The Crocodile Who Needed a Toothbrush; [pers.] I enjoy writing and building. I like to imagine different ideas and question things. I enjoy reading comics.; [a.] Braselton, GA

FEARIN, JESSE LEE
[b.] November 4, 1986; Hancock, IN; [p.] Jeffery and Judith Fearin; [ed.] 4th Grade, Charles A. Beard School, Knightstown, Indiana; [occ.] Student; [memb.] Webelos Scout, Lego Mania; [hon.] Honor Roll, Math, Spelling, Attendance

FERY, JANE
[b.] November 26, 1982; [ed.] Freshman; [oth.writ.] Nothing published; [pers.] Keep your eyes, ears, heart, and mind open, and always have a ready shoulder.; [a.] St. Helens, OR

FIRESTONE, ALLIE
[b.] January 19, 1984; Hayward, CA; [p.] Karen and

Jeff Firestone; [ed.] Niles Elementary School and Pleasanton Middle School; [occ.] Student; [hon.] Various awards in all types of dance and a few in piano; [a.] Pleasanton, CA

FITTS, DIANA
[pen.] De De; [b.] February 24, 1972; Reano; [p.] Lenore and Roger; [ed.] Valle View High School/RC College; [occ.] VRC community workshop for disability; [hon.] High Honor Roll, Principal's List; [oth.writ.] When I Wake Up and See You, seven love poems; [a.] M.V., CA

FITZGERALD, ERIN
[b.] March 17, 1983; [p.] Chuck and Betty Benney; [ed.] 10 years (Pre-K thru 8th) at St. Mary's of the Assumption in Upper Mariboro and entering 9th grade at St. Mary's in Annapolis; [hon.] Physical Education Award, Honor Roll, Service Awards, Dance Competition Awards, Championship Soccer Awards; [oth.writ.] I love to write poems. I have a couple note books of poems that I've written, but this is my 1st poem ever published!; [pers.] I love to write—it soothes my soul and puts me in relaxing moods. I love to write poems for people, especially if it will cheer them up.; [a.] Davidsonville, MD

FITZGERALD, TORITHEA
[pen.] Morning Dancer; [b.] July 5, 1979; Queens Village, NY; [p.] Brinalyn Tuckes, Robert D. Fitzge; [ed.] Attending FIT; [memb.] North Eastern Native American Association; [oth.writ.] "Wind and Leaves" "Love Me He Did Not" "Pain"; [pers.] There are no boundaries when you write what's in your heart.; [a.] Long Beach, NY

FLOYD, RAYMOND L.
[b.] October 26, 1941; Orangeburg, SC; [p.] Jimmie D. and Janie L. Floyd; [m.] Commella L. Floyd; December 31, 1966; [ch.] Dawn Bonique, Heather Lenore, Thomas Hunter; [ed.] Wilkinson High School, CA, Claflin College, M.A.T, University of South Carolina; [occ.] Retired Art Teacher, Owner Novel-Tees/Laser Magic Screen Printing; [memb.] Sickle Cell Anemia Found Board Member, Silver Hill United Methodist Church, Spartanburg Artist Guild; [hon.] Honor Graduate of Claflin College and the University of So.Car.; [oth.writ.] Article Published in School Arts Magazine; [pers.] I pull my ideas from both personal experience as well as my wanting to see and record utopian situations.; [a.] Spartanburg, SC

FORD, VIOLET IVON
[pen.] Vi (Lee) Ford; [b.] April 3, 1925; Arkansas; [p.] Samuel Houston Helms and Lula; [m.] Harley A. Ford; September 19, 1992, second marriage (Lee); [ch.] Four children by former marriage; [ed.] High School.; [occ.] Retired: Senior Citizen; [memb.] I belong at the senior center: Creative writing in Yakima Washington; [hon.] Editor's Award, the Silver Dallas and the Penny One Cent: for outstanding poetry composition: the poetry guild, being published now. In Beyond the Horizon; [oth.writ.] Lots more poems; also novels and children stories and songs. I would love to get my novel published ("The Voice in the Loft"); [pers.] I am 72 years young and love to write. I have loved to write all my life. My latest novel is title "The Voice in the Loft." ; [a.] Yakima, WA

FOX, VIRGINIA E.
[pen.] Jinny/Foxy; [b.] July 25, 1911; New York City; [p.] Jim and Ruby Moore; [m.] William (Bill) Fox; October 3, 1932; [ch.] Wendy and Pat; [ed.] Lyons Township High School, La Grange, IL; Central School of Speech Trainig and Dramatic Art—London England; Just Living and Enjoying Each Day; [occ.] Enjoying life, with family, friends (and excellent health); [memb.] Was a member of "The Fulhma Theater Repertory Co." after graduation in Suburban London long, long ago; [oth.writ.] Primarily personal to close family members, on

special occasions; [pers.] Personally, I have found my Dad's philosophy so true: You can get along with anyone—if it means enough to you; to find his/her interests, likes, dislikes, and finding out a bit to share.; [a.] Templeton, CA

FRECHETTE, ERIK
[b.] June 23, 1977; Tampa, FL; [p.] Lynn and Serge Frechette; [ed.] Graduated East Lake High School June 1995, Presently full-time student at St. Petersburg Junior College; [occ.] Full-time grocery clerk for Publix Supermarkets; Poet; [hon.] Honor Roll, East Lake High School "Pride" Award, Florida Academic Scholars Award of Recognition; [oth.writ.] Many unpublished poems, an incomplete short story in a high school anthology, no other published works to date; [pers.] Read only enough of the past to know what still needs to be done, then run the remainder of the tight rope with me.; [a.] Oldsmar, FL

FREY, DIANA MARIE
[b.] December 26, 1982; Houston, TX; [p.] Joyce and Charles Frey; [occ.] 1997-1998 Ninth grader at Dr. Phillips High School; [hon.] 1997 Disney Dreamer and Doer at Southwest Middle School, Duke University TIP program participant; 1996 Dr. Phillips High School MU Alpha Theta Algebra I 4th place individual, Honor Roll Student; [a.] Orlando, FL

FUNG, VIVIAN H. L.
[pen.] Hoi Ling; [b.] November 24, 1982; Hong Kong; [p.] Sum C. Fung and Pui H. Fung; [ed.] St. Barbara Elementary School, St. Barbara High School; [occ.] Student in H.S. (Freshman); [pers.] I wrote this poem because it shows how I feel toward love. To love someone means to be part of him or her, and I adore romantic poetry.; [a.] Chicago, IL

GABRIELLE, SYLVANA
[b.] San Pedro, CA; [hon.] Editor's Choice; [a.] Los Angeles, CA

GARCIA, KATRINA
[b.] December 24, 1980; Albuquerque, NM; [p.] Diane L. Cochrane; [ed.] Albuquerque Academy; [occ.] Student; [hon.] President's Award for Educational Excellence; [pers.] Without the support of my mother and my grandparents, Art and Dorothy Cochrane, I would never have come this far.; [a.] Albuquerque, NM

GAUFIN, TRESSA
[b.] January 5, 1978; Webster Harris, TX; [p.] Frank and Brenda Gaufin; [ed.] Madera High, Brigham Young University; [occ.] Student at Brigham Young University; [pers.] Sometimes in life we need someone's light to help us back home, to live with our Heavenly Father.; [a.] Madera, CA

GIBBONS, MELISSA
[b.] May 29, 1980; Moore County, NC; [p.] James and Lisa Gibbons; [occ.] Senior at Union Pines High School; [memb.] National Honor Society, V.P Interact Club, Orchestra, UPHS Prayer Meeting; [hon.] Sally Ride, Junior Marshall, NC Close Up, Dean's List, Pembroke State Math Competition, Social Studies Sumposium, NCSAS; [pers.] "Whether therefore ye eat, or drink or whatsoever ye do, do all to the glory of God."; [a.] Whispering Pines, NC

GIGUERE, LINDA
[pen.] Missy; [b.] August 7, 1969; Tewksbury, MA; [ed.] Manatee High; [occ.] Manager—Etsell, Inc., Knoxville, TN; [memb.] Emmett Kelley Society; [oth.writ.] I have several poems. I've been writing since 1986. This is my first entry and my first publication.; [pers.] The miracle of one man's heart comes from his soul, the evil in one man's soul comes from his heart.; [a.] Knoxville, TN

GILES, EVELYN
[pen.] The Gypsy, Evelyn; [b.] March 5, 1918;

Bemidji, MI; [p.] Arthur and Dorothy Thorn; [m.] Divorced; [ch.] 3 sons, 5 grandchildren, 1 great-grandchild; [ed.] Burbank High Graduate, Los Angeles College; [occ.] Retired Bookkeeperk, now complete concentration on writing poetry; [memb.] California Writers; Club (High Desert Chap.), New Poetry Soc., Cactus Wren Garden Club, Cultural Arts Foundation, Hesperia Art Club, Sheriff's Reserve, 4-H Group Leader, Hesperia; [hon.] Tennis Trophy (3), Swimming Awards (5), Best Director (Theatre) Awards (3). Distinguished Member of Int'l Society of Poets, other poetry; [oth.writ.] Closet writing covers many years; Now 2 published, 3 submitted Lyrics for songs, greetings cards; Aventure, Romance, Fantasy. Heartfelt thanks to Blanche, my cousin, who shoved me out of the closet.; [pers.] My wish, my prayer for the people of the world: a togetherness of humanity, the blending of many cultures and colors, creating a beautiful rainbow of peace and good will. Let it be!; [a.] Hesperia, CA

GLENN, YE LANDE
[pen.] Shai Ellis; [b.] January 14, 1982; Union County; [p.] Mr. and Mrs. Glenn; [ed.] Arising Sophomore in High School; [memb.] FBLA, Marching Band, Dance Academy Freshman Class Officer; [hon.] National Honor Society, Smile Award for Dance, Numerous Academic Awards; [pers.] I write my poems so everyone can feel good, to show that this world is for all and we should love and take care of it.; [a.] Buffalo, SC

GOLDBLATT, JENNIEFER L.
[pen.] Jennifer Bupp; [b.] April 6, 1971; Maywood, CA; [m.] Daniel Goldblatt; February 18, 1996; [ed.] Cypress College, CA, A.S. Degree and Radiology Technolist Certificate City of Hope Radiation Therapist; [occ.] Radiation Therapist; [memb.] ASRT—American Society of Radiology Technologists; [hon.] Who's Who in American High School Students 1988, 1989; [oth.writ.] Personal poems that have never been published; [pers.] Growing up I would write poems about friends and boyfriends. My dad would always ask me when I would write a poem about my wonderful parents, I decided to surprise them with a poem at my wedding. It brought tears to there eyes.; [a.] Flagstaff, AZ

GORDON, CORTNEY
[b.] October 28, 1985; Virginia Beach, VA; [p.] Kimberly Gordon, Gerald Gordon; [ed.] Gateway Christian School, Landstown Middle School; [hon.] Honor Roll Student; [oth.writ.] Several unpublished poems nobody has ever heard; [pers.] I wish that all my poems are heard. I want to thank my sixth grade teacher, Mrs. Boyd.; [a.] Virginia Beach, VA

GORIN, PAMELA DOLKART
[b.] June 5, 1941; Chicago, IL; [p.] Ralph E. Dolkart, M. D., Majorie B. Dolkart; [ed.] Yale University, B.A. (1974) Washington University, Ph.D. (1979) University of California, Davis, J.D. (1987); [occ.] Attorney; [hon.] '74 B.A. Cumlaude (Yale University), '86 American Jurisprudence Award (Negotiation and Dispute Resolution), 86-'87 Research Editor University of California, Davis Law Review; [oth.writ.] 19 peer-reviewed scientific publications; [a.] Davis, CA

GRAY II, STANLEY SILAS
[pen.] Silvanus; [b.] February 21, 1980; Greenville, TN; [p.] Stanley Gray, and Mary Gray; [ed.] Light and Life Christian School; [occ.] High School Senior and National Guardsman; [memb.] The Southern League; [oth.writ.] A few poems that I have just written for school and personal expression; [pers.] This has been my first poem of true expression. The relationship with my girlfriend, Chandra Maruhn, has brought our emotions in me that I never knew that I had. Memories of my Papaw, Silas Gray and the reading of the Bible has also added to my poetry.; [a.] Taylor, MI

GREEN, MARGARET CARTER
[pen.] Maggie; [b.] February 15, 1915; Fal, LA; [p.] John Francis Carter, Effie Belle Capshaw Carter; [m.] Lawrence Boone Green; October 18, 1931; [ch.] Jerry Lou, Jefferey Stephen; [ed.] 10th Grade High School; [oc..] Housewife (widow); Past—Real Estate; [memb.] Enon Baptist Church, Franklinton Country Club Garden Club—I have a talent for decorating or have helped many friends; [hon.] Veterans of Foreign Wars, LA Life Magazine for protecting the Pen Creek Natural Area, LA Nature Conservancy of Wild Life and Fishers, March of Dimes; [oth.writ.] I have writtens many poems and ome short stories—I have not tried to have any published until now. I also paint. My time with my grand children is precious to me.; [pers.] I firmly believe that one should always walk a mile in another footsteps before he judges another; put out your hand to help—our Savior did set this example for us.; [a.] Franklinton, LA

GRIEBEL, CARLA ELAINE
[pen.] Mary Anne Devon; [b.] March 16, 1981; Newark, OH; [p.] Glen L. and Nancys Griebel; [ed.] High School; [occ.] Student; [oth.writ.] Have written several short stories; now working on a novel; [pers.] If you have faith in yourself, you will always succeed.

GRIFFITH, GERALDINE
[b.] March 6, 1964; Ft Campbell, KY; [p.] Jeannette Griffith and Albert Griffith; [ed.] BS (Finance)—Penn State University, with Minor in German; working on MBA—DePaul University; [occ.] Benefits Manager Skidmore, Owings and Merrill [a.] Chicago, IL

GUIZZOTTI, JESSALYN B.
[b.] October 29, 1984; Cleve, OH; [p.] Charles and Cheryl Guizzotti; [ed.] Brecksville School System (Current Attendance); [occ.] Student; [memb.] Girl Scouts of America, City of Brecksville Recreational Sports, Brecksville School Choir; [hon.] Silver Award: Girl Scouts of America, Presidential Fitness Award, Pride Patrol Organization: Brecksville School System; [oth.writ.] "Spring" published in River of Dreams (poem); "Halfway Perfect" submitted for publication (Book); [pers.] I strive to show that sullen and sad predicaments may culminate in happiness and tranquility. I am influenced by the poetry of Shel Silverstein and the writings of Judy Blume.; [a.] Brecksville, OH

GUNTER, TWYLA
[pen.] SAA; [b.] October 1, 1964; Wayne Co., GA; [p.] Keith and Nell Anderson; [m.] Brad Lee Wade; July 18, 1997; [ch.] Holly, Rebecca, Jeffrey, Kyle; [ed.] High School Graduate, one year of college; [occ.] Sales at Gainesville Jewelry; [oth.writ.] Many Spiritual Poems; [pers.] To God be the glory for all things. The talents we have are from Him and to be used to glory Him. To Him be praise and glory and honor forever.; [a.] Alto, GA

HALL, LACIE BETH
[b.] March 29, 1980; Smithfield, VA; [p.] Phyllis Cornett and Thomas Hall; [ed.] Senior at Smithfield High School (plan to go to college to become a doctor); [memb.] National Beta Club; [hon.] National Beta Club, named who's Who Among America High School Students; [oth.writ.] Write poems and short stories in small hardbound blank books for myself; [pers.] I believe a person's emotions are one the most personal things one can share. By writing your feelings in a poem and sharing that work with others, you show them a small piece of your soul.; [a.] Smithfield, VA

HALLINAN, CANDICE
[b.] January 12, 1980; Spoke, WA; [p.] Tammy Hallinan, Chris Hallinan, Dan Hoffman; [ed.] David Prouty High School; [oth.writ.] Several poems and short stories published in the school newspaper "The Prowler"; [pers.] Poetry is a way of express-

ing the viewpoint of the author. In poetry, one poem's never better than the other, if they are written honestly. I have nothing to offer but the chaos in my own mind.; [a.] Spencer, MA

HANDY, MICHAEL J.
[b.] September 9, 1982; Niskayuna; [p.] Cindy and Gerald R. Handy; [ed.] Cableskill-Richmondville High School; [occ.] Freshman; [memb.] Young American Bowling Alliance, Long Path North Hiking Club; [hon.] Outstanding author award for poetry from Cableskill-Richmondville Middle School; [oth.writ.] "The Cabin"; [a.] Cableskill, NY

HARBERTS, VICTORIA
[pen.] Victoria Seabring; [b.] April 4, 1958; Akron, OH; [p.] Donna and James Smallwood; [m.] Brian L. Harberts; September 3, 1988; [ch.] Christina and April Harberts; [ed.] East Bay High School—11th Grade Completed; [occ.] S.C. School for the Deaf and Blind, Security Officer; [hon.] (World of Poetry) Award of Merit Certificates, A Lonely Little Boy, My Brother And I—Golden Poet 1991; [oth.writ.] Looking Through The Eyes Of A Child. Without A Home, Why Don't You Marry Your TV, My Brother And I, Nature, My Man, A Mother's Job, A Lonely Little Boy; [pers.] I strive to reflect what was, what is, and what may be.; [a.] Grambling, SC

HARDIN, DENISE M.
[b.] November 3; Chicago, IL; [p.] James and Dorothy Turner; [ch.] Khiry J. Shepherd; [ed.] Wendell Phillips High School, Chicago, IL, Northeasthern University, Chicago State University Chicago, IL; [occ.] Child Protective Investigator Chicago, IL; [a.] Dolton, IL

HARDING, EBONY
[b.] March 6, 1981; Baltimore, MD; [p.] Tyrone and Betty Harding; [ed.] Western Senior High School; [memb.] Sometimes Literary Magazine, Native American Society; [hon.] Environmental Award; [oth.writ.] Novel: Rajanee; Except published in school newspaper; MI Vida (My life); Race Relations; [pers.] I hope that my writing will encourage young people to read more.; [a.] Baltimore, MD

HARGROVE SR., RANDY
[pen.] Randy Raging; [b.] March 12, 1960; Evansville, IN; [p.] Thomas and Lavada Hargrove; [m.] Debbie Hargrove; February 14, 1997; [ch.] Randy II, Leslie, Lucas, Jayme, Sage; [ed.] High School Graduate; [occ.] Extrusion Operator (18 years) Crescent Plastics; [oth.writ.] Michael, Ray, Jesse's Last Prayer, Jayme, Lucus, The Final Salute, Tiffany, Rachael, In God We Trust, Young Love, Crazy Kind Of Love, From Grandpa To Grandma, Time With Tim, Donna My Love; [pers.] A wise man once said, "Don't worry, be happy." God has given us all the power to heal. It's called laughter and laughter is love. I live my life by these words.; [a.] Evansville, IN

HARRELL, WAYNE A.
[b.] November 15, 1949; Eastman Dodge, GA; [p.] Augustin O. Harrell Bobie E. Dowty; [ed.] Associates Degree—Electronic Engineer; [occ.] Security Officer; [hon.] Retired 55G US Army 1968-1987; [pers.] I dream of walking and talking with life under a distant star.; [a.] Augusta, GA

HARRINGTON, TYLER B.
[b.] October 22, 1969; Lincoln, NE; [p.] Richard and Judith Harrington; [ed.] Lincoln High School, Cuyamaca Community College; [occ.] Transportation Worker, Casa De Las Campanas, Rancho Bernardo, CA; [pers.] I tend to explore the element of pain and loneliness in my writing yet, at the same time, giving the reader hope in spite of suffering. The works of Edgar Allan Poe and the lyrical styling of the British rock group Pink Floyd have a great deal of influence on my writing.; [a.] San

Diego, CA

HARRIS, HALLEY R.
[b.] August 5, 1976; Everett, WA; [p.] Melody Patrick, Michael Patrick; [ed.] Marysville Pilchuck High School, Everett Community College; [occ.] Attack Helicopter Mechanic, US Army; [pers.] "I still talk in my sleep. I still dream. How can there be perfect stillness when my brain's so noisy?"—365 TAO, Edgar Allan Poe, Emily Dickinson, Brian Edwards—Thank you.; [a.] Arlington, WA

HARTWAY, DARLENE D.
[b.] October 25, 1957; San Francisco; [ed.] Ms. Hartwa,y a native San Franciscan, attended San Francisco State Univ. and was English Major.; [occ.] Ms. Hartway works for Progress Foundation as a Mental Health Specialist.; [oth.writ.] Ms. Hartway is currently working on her first book, which will be titled "A Braid and a Weave," due to the interelated nature of each piece of work contained in the book.; [pers.] For me "The greatest deliverance" is my personal statement regarding what matters most in life—telling the truth about who we really are and how powerful that is.; [a.] Berkeley, CA

HARVATIN, ILA FAYE
[pen.] Kitten; [b.] July 6, 1937; Johnston Co, NC; David and Grace Vinson; [m.] Richard Theodore Harvatin Sr; March 22, 1959; [ch.] Robert, Judy, Angela, Richard Jr; [ed.] High School, and Life; [occ.] Housewife; [memb.] ACBL Bridge Club; [oth.writ.] I have written many poems in the past this will be the first one published; thank you.; [pers.] Many of my poems were written while my husband served in Vietnam with the 5th Spaniard Forces Sp. When he came it was wonderful and has been ever since.; [a.] Fayetteville, NC

HARWOOD, GEORGE F.
[pen.] George F. Harwood; [b.] September 28, 1907; New York, NY; [p.] John Harwood and Margaret Reardon; [m.] Mildred Brazis; May 5, 1931; [ed.] High School, finished at night courses, had to work to help my mother, days. Father died when I was 10 years old; [occ.] Retired; [memb.] American Legion, Past Commander Fairfield post #741950; [hon.] Purple Heart; At age 18 I took up violin. After studying for 3 years, I was accepted in Bridgeport Symphony, second violin section under director Fuduk Foti.; [oth.writ.] Loved poetry, never took too seriously. Just wrote for my own pleasure. I saved very few.; [pers.] World War II, drafted 1944 served with 28th Division; wounded in Germany, in the Huertgen Forest, small town called Germeter; [a.] Fairfield, CT

HATZELL, GEORGE VERNON
[b.] February 22, 1922; Penalosa, KS; [p.] Clarence Irma Hatzell; [ed.] Grade - High School Plains, Liberal, KS; have two diplomas: Motel Mgr. School L.A. Cal Lewis Hotel - Motel School Wash. DC; [hon.] I have been emp. as waiter / dining room supervisor Old Faithful Inn, Yellowstone ND; [pers.] The law of abundance manifests in my life, and that which is needed for my sustenance will come unto my through this operation of divine love and law.; [a.] Tulsa, OK

HAWKINS, LYDIA C. COPPOLA
[pen.] Lydia Coppola; [b.] July 5, 1944; Brooklyn, NY; [p.] Joe Coppola, Dorothy Coppola; [m.] James Hawkins; December 23, 1989; [ch.] Christina, Lisa Anne; [ed.] Newton High Rio Salado Community College; [occ.] Administrative Assistant, Board of Equalization (BOE) Phx, AZ; [memb.] IAAO National and Local Chapters; [oth.writ.] Several poems written over the years for personal enjoyment; [pers.] I wrote this poem as a special remembrance to my beloved daughter, Lisa Anne, who was married on May 10, 1997.; [a.] Scottsdale, AZ

HAYS, RYAN RICHARD
[pen.] Ryan Richard Hays; [b.] August 9, 1982; Boynton Beach, FL; [p.] Pat and Mike Hays; [ed.] Freshman at Apex High School, Apex, North Carolina; [memb.] Ducks Unlimited; Honor Roll Society; [hon.] Honor Roll; [oth.writ.] The Giver of Life; [pers.] I dedicate this poem to Lottie Stiles, who passed away June of 1996.; [a.] Cary, NC

HENDRON, TINA-MARIE
[b.] February 2, 1972; Chicago, IL; [p.] Christine and Ronald J. Hendron; [ed.] George Washington High, College Credit in Psychology; [occ.] Teacher's Aide—Eight Grade English, Gallistel Language Academy, Chicago, IL.; [hon.] National Honor Society, Senior Year English Award; [pers.] I believe everyone should look deeply into themselves and communicate the truth and goodness that comes from within. I try to express honest emotion in my writing.; [a.] Chigaco, IL

HENRY, MATTHEW
[b.] October 14, 1954; Toledo, OH; [p.] John and Joanne Henry; [m.] Amy Pearson; June 20, 1981; [ed.] A.S. Cabrulo Couge, Santa Cruz, CA 1985 B.A.-University of Oregon, Eugene, OR 1995 M.Div.-American Baptist Seminary of the West, Berkeley, CA, M.A.-Graduate Theological Union, Berkeley, CA; [occ.] Seminarian and Asst. Pastor of a Chinese Methodist Church in Chinatown, S.F.; [memb.] Phi Alpha Theta Ministers Council-ABC/USA; [hon.] Graduated: "Honorable Mention," Cabrillo College, "Magna Cumlaude", University of Oregon, Scholarships: Odd fellows Scholarship (1985), G.T.U. Presidential scholarship (1995); [oth.writ.] In progress; [pers.] As a Cleric and Historian, I am inevitably drawn to our common human story and where individual lives intersect it at various points, both backward and forward in time. "Up Front at His Funeral" grows out of this.; [a.] Berkeley, CA

HENSON, TARA
[b.] November 18, 1981; Carroll; [p.] Richard and Karen Henson; [ed.] I'm attending Guthrie Center High School—I'll be Sophomore in Fall of 1997 (15 years old); [occ.] Student; [memb.] 4-H Art Club; [pers.] I like to look at what the future may hold for us. I include that in my poems. I also got a great deal of ideas from art pieces.; [a.] Bayard, IA

HENTHORNE, NANCIE
[b.] September 17, 1941; Santa Rosa, CA; [p.] Violet and Leroy Henthorne; [ch.] Anastacio De Leon Gallardo, Edward Scott Gallardo, Phillip Todd Gallardo and five grandchildren; [occ.] Home Health Care Provider; [pers.] This poem was written for and dedicated to my son, Edward Scott Gallardo, with love and tender feelings.; [a.] Covelo, CA

HEWITT, BRENT
[pen.] B. L. Hewit; [b.] April 12, 1959; Lansing, MI; [p.] Bill and Jo Ann Hewitt; [m.] Kelly; June 15, 1985; [ch.] Megan and Shawn; [ed.] Petuskey High School, Central Michigan University; [occ.] High School Special Education Work Co-ordinator; [hon.] Have recited at The Northern Michigan Bliss Fest, and at The Stone Circle; [oth.writ.] Not So Long A Walk, Summer Daze, The Brook, Nature's World, Grandma, A Child Inside, many more; [pers.] I have been greatly influenced by: Max Ellison, Frost, Benet, Edna St. Vincent Millay.; [a.] Petoskey, MI

HIGGINBOTHAM, MELISSA
[b.] September 14, 1979; Indianpolis, IN; [p.] Jean and Keith Higginbotham; [ed.] Ben Davis High School; [hon.] Eight First Place Awards in Solo and Ensemble Competitions, for the Flute and Piccolo; [pers.] By writing poetry and playing music, I've found and I can release my frustrations and emotions in a clear and more positive way.; [a.] Indianapolis, IN

HILL, TISHA LYNN
[b.] June 11, 1976; Los Angeles, CA; [p.] Lorraine Windsor, Robert Hill; [m.] Lamond Nicholson; [ed.] Manhattan Center for Science and Mathematics, Coppin State College; [occ.] (Student trainee) Customs Inspector; [hon.] Honors scholarship Maryland Law Enforcement Scholarship; Scholar Athlete of the Year (1996-97), President's Athlete award (tennis); [oth.writ.] "Thought" published in Through Sun and Shower"; [pers.] I must first thank God for blessing me with the inspiration I've found through true love. I have been creatly blessed with a true angel, Lamond.; [a.] Baltimore, MD

HINCKLEY, DELMAR LEROY
[pen.] Del Hinckley; [b.] October 11, 1964; Rexburg, ID; [p.] Marlene and LeRoy Hinckley; [ch.] Melinda, Seth, Danielle, Ashley, Hali and Sara; [ed.] Salt Lake Community College Automotive Tech, High School Skyline High; [occ.] Public Relations with Sandstar Family Entertainment; [memb.] Hobbies: I enjoy working with computers and on cars. In my spare time, I enjoy writing poems for friends and when I feel something inspirational comes to mind; [hon.] Selected as a semi-finalist in the National Library of Poetry Contest "Beneath a Rainbow" of and also selected for The Sound of Poetry; [oth.writ.] Personal poems written for friends and family; [pers.] In loving memory for my grandmother, Verman May Quinton Pack, who passed away 13 October 1994. I have found it easier to write my feelings out in words of love and caring—a great talent and enjoy sharing it with others.; [a.] Idaho Falls, ID

HOANG, PHUONG
[b.] February 5, 1986; Vietnam; [p.] Hoang Hoanh; [ed.] 5th Grade; [a.] San Francisco, CA

HOSKINS, MANDY
[b.] May 18, 1979; Roswell, NM; [p.] James and Regena Hoskins; [ed.] Roswell High School, currently enrolled in a writing course with the Institute of Children's Literature; [hon.] Outstanding Journalism—High School Newspaper (Coyote Howler); [oth.writ.] Poems and stories in high school newspaper; [pers.] I enjoy writing because you can decide what happens, whether it ends happy or not.; [a.] Roswell, NM

HOWARD, LUCINDA
[pen.] Lucinda Tanner Howard; [b.] February 12, 1949; Lamar, MO; [p.] Curtis Tanner, Marianna Tanner; [ch.] Shaun Howard, Joel Howard; [occ.] Owner of Automobile Interior Design and Repair Business; [pers.] My sensitivity and emotions that go into my poems stem from the life I have been dealt. I want the reader to experience my sadness.; [a.] Richardson, TX

HULSE, CAROL LYNN
[pen.] Carol L. Hulse; [b.] September 26, 1944; Redmond, OR; [p.] Norman Gore and Shirley Smith; [m.] Richard Hulse; August 16, 1979; [ch.] Coleen, Cathi, Chris, Cari and Craig; [ed.] Cubberly H.S., Palo Alto, CA; [occ.] Legal Assistant, Oregon Health Sciences University, Portland, OR; [memb.] National Assoc. of Legal Secretaries (NALS); Portland Assoc. of Legal Secys; Marion-Polk Counties Legal Secys. Assoc.; [oth.writ.] My first publication. Have several poems and (original) puns I would love to publish!; [pers.] My perception of God's love, nature's beauty, man's character and animals' antics are expressed in my writings.; [a.] Salem, OR

HUMMEL, THOMAS P.
[b.] May 14, 1954; Midwest; [p.] Thomas Joseph Hummel, Rita Hummel; [m.] Mary E. Hummel; October20, 1995; [ed.] Bachelor of Science in Commerce, Finance Major, from a Major Catholic Universtiy; [occ.] Mortgage Broker; [oth.writ.] "They Hung Love Upon A Tree", a poem; Come

Closer to God, a book of Christian Poetry, published in November 1997 by Watermark Press. I have also written a second book of poetry called Be "Friends With God"; [pers.] I am humble servant of Jesus Christ. I try to do His will in this life, to be happy with Him forever in the next life in Heaven.

HUTCHINGS, JENNIFER
[b.] April 29, 1982; Austell, GA; [p.] Linda Jackson, Steve Hutchings; [ed.] 10th Grade, attending Pine Ridge Elementary, Snellville Middle School, South Gwinnett High School; [occ.] High School Student; [hon.] Young Author Awards 3 times; [oth.writ.] None published; [pers.] I love writing poems, a way to express my feelings and relaxation.; [a.] Loganville, GA

HUTCHINSON, LAURINE FEUER
[pen.] Paris Kelly; [b.] January 7, 1953; West Palm Beach, FL; [p.] Marilyn and William Feuer; [m.] Ronald Mark Hutchinson; February 9, 1995; [ed.] Pacific Palisades High School; U.C.L.A. 2 years, transferred to (1972-1974) University of Mass., Amherst ELE, BA 1977; Mass. College of Art—Teaching Extension 1979, Mass. College of Pharmacy MS 1984; [occ.] Fundraiser in WGBH Channel 2 (PBS); [memb.] Sigma Delta Tau; HSUS member; PETA; Conducts Computerized Program Survey, Renews Memberships, Generates Goodwill among members; [oth.writ.] Two Short Stories, Copywrited but unpublished—female private investigator, Three Books of poems written by myself and friends through the 60's, 70's, and 80's; [pers.] I believe in living a moral decent life, doing no harm to others, animals, and people, and living my life towards those goals. I also believe in magic.; [a.] Salem, NH

HYATT, HILDA
[b.] February 26, 1909; Switzerland, Co. IN; [p.] Jesse M. and Minda Elaine (Ford) Lewis; [m.] Charles Edmond Hyatt; February 28, 1935; [ch.] Dale M.; [ed.] New Marion High School, New Marion In. Two years at Ball State University Muncie, In; [occ.] Retired Farmer's Widow; [oth.writ.] Poems: "Mother", "A Dropped Dog", "Memories", the poems "Mother", "A Dropped Dog" and "1995 Apple Crop" were published in our Country Paper, "Osgood Journal"; [pers.] I love people, nature, animals and birds. I was greatly influenced by other poems about dogs and cats. The poem about the "1995 Apple Crop" really happened the way the poem says.; [a.] Osgood, IN

INIQUEZ, ADELA G.
[b.] September 19, 1977; Downey, CA; [p.] Lupita Salcido, Ben Iniquez; [ed.] Signmaker—L.A. Signs and Banners; [memb.] KCET membership; [hon.] High School Drama Award; [oth.writ.] Several unpublished collections of original poems and essays; [pers.] My best way to express myself is my writing. It keeps me healthy. Writing is a very positive thing for me, no matter what I write about.; [a.] Downey, CA

INMAN, TERESA A.
[b.] March 22, 1957; Seattle, WA; [p.] Frederick and Lola Bishop; [m.] Steven R. Inman; September 1, 1984; [ch.] Steven Ray Jr, Darrick Christopher and Nichole Mary Ann; [ed.] Fort Vancouver High Clark Community College; [occ.] Accounting Supervisor, America the Beautiful Dreamer; [oth.writ.] Several poems used as poster, decor at local parties; [pers.] My poems are written in a hope that I can reflect life as 'Shades of Grey' and not as life seems, 'Black and White.'; [a.] Vancouver, WA

ISDELL, MARGARET
[pen.] Margaret; [b.] December 23, 1929; [p.] Mr and Mrs Frank Lee Doughty; [m.] Lillian Sarah Sturgis; January 22, 1961; [ch.] 1 child—Terry Lynne Williams; [ed.] Graduate of Central High

School 13 years trained by John H. Dulany and 26 years and 7 months with C&P Telephone Co. of Virginia; [occ.] Retiree of C&P Telephone Co. (no Bell Atlantic); [memb.] Cosmetique, right now member of God Holy Church, lifetime wit C&P and Bell Atlantic.l; [hon.] Memorabilia from C&P Telephone and a lot of Perfect Attendance awards from John H. Dulany Foods—I was Food Inspector for about 3 years or more; an award for a Preferred Customer Global and also achieved 100 for 26 years and 7 months, loyalty tests when I retired at C&P and Bell Atlantic also; [oth.writ.] My life has no closed closests I have nothing to hide. I do work for the Lord, Holy Bible etc. I am Chef of my kitchen at home called Margaret's Kitchen. I am especially good at baking and cook it all, and am also a Housekeeper. I really enjoy life.; [pers.] I don't drink any alcohol. I don't smoke. I have self-discipline with people. I walk in God's good world of Light I grow gardens and Flowers.; [a.] Qwuinby, VA

ISLA, TYENA A.
[b.] May 4, 1979; San Jose, CA; [p.] Debra A. Wood and Richard Isla; [ch.] Joslin Aloha Isla; [occ.] Fulltime mother; [pers.] I love you Joslin Aloha, my little angel.; [a.] Patterson, CA

IVEY, ROBERT PERRY
[b.] May 28, 1978; Forsyth, Ga; [p.] Robyn McDonald, Barry Ivey; [ed.] First Presbyterian Day School, Macon, GA; Mercer University, Macon, GA; [occ.] Fulltime Student; [memb.] Kappa Alpha Order; [pers.] My thoughts pound my head, spinning around like two howling dogs writing for reasons, reasons to be, reasons to live, reasons to breathe in one poetic kiss.; [a.] Macon, GA

JACKSON, JR., CLARENCE
[b.] June 21, 1980; Southwest, MS; [p.] Linda and Clarence Jackson; [ed.] South Pine High; [memb.] Future Farmers of America; [hon.] Math Award; [oth.writ.] I have several unpublished poems: Love and Affection, Childhood, and Never Alone; [pers.] Unlike some of today's poets, my poetry comes from the heart. When it comes form the heart it's real, it's real enough to feel.; [a.] McComb, MS

JAMES, CHERYL D.
[b.] March 24, 1960; Brooklyn; [p.] Carol and Frank James; [ch.] Expecting my first child; [occ.] Dispatcher for the N.Y.P.A.; [pers.] I am a sensitive person who writes about my deep feelings and life. I hope people can relate.; [a.] Brooklyn, NY

JOECKEL, CAROLE J.
[b.] December 18, 1937; Fairmont, MN; [m.] Rollin H.; January 19, 1957; [ch.] Kevin R., Kris R; [ed.] High School Graduate; [occ.] Retired; [oth.writ.] Poetry set to music, for special occasions, at Immanuel Lutheran Church in Fairmont; [pers.] I see poetry in every living form, and 8n each new day, as God inspires my talent.; [a.] Fairmont, MN

JOHNSON, GARROLD
[b.] November 2, 1953; Edmonson; [p.] Everett and Mable Johnson; [m.] Janice Johnson; April 27, 1973; [ch.] Shannon Chirty; [ed.] 8th Grade; [occ.] Disable; [memb.] Member of God's Family; [oth.writ.] Stand Firm, I've Got News for You, A Dear Friend, My Homeland, I Know I'm Saved, The Old Gospel Way, My Guiding Light, My Lord is Great, and more; [pers.] Jesus Christ Lord! He and I wrote 11 poems, and I am so thankful.; [a.] Brownville, KY

JOHNSON DUNN, KATIE LYNNE
[pen.] Kat; [b.] June 2, 1986; Maryland; [p.] Lori and Bob Dunn; [ed.] Crofton Middle School; [occ.] 6th Grader; [memb.] Anne Arundel County Division 1 Soccer; Viola Player (4th Year); [hon.] Honor Roll; [pers.] One might be surprised to find out I am only 11 years old but I can only write about my life and how it relates to me.; [a.] Crofton, MD

JOHNSON II, BERNARDINE M.
[b.] February 19, 1969; Washington, DC; [p.] Bernardine M. Johnson and Francis W. Johnson Sr; [occ.] Clerk, Counter; [a.] Mechanicsville, MD

JOHNSTON, PHILLIP
[pen.] P.J.; [b.] March 23, 1979; Columbus, IN; [p.] Maggie Kibler, Tom Kibler; [ed.] Santa Fe High; [hon.] Wendy's Heisman Scholar, National Young Leader, Boys State Delegate, Who's Who Among American High School Students; [pers.] The tricked mind only surrenders to perceptions as the mere deception can blind you to truth.; [a.] Lakeland, FL

JONES, COMMIE ELL
[pen.] L (Commie Ell Jones); [b.] January 6, 1955; Tarboro, NC; [p.] Martha Elaine Carroll and Elbert Rudd; [ch.] Jediah, Seriah, JonPaul; [ed.] Johh F. Kennedy H.S., J. Sargeant Reynolds CC, VCU, University of Richmond (continuing studies); [occ.] Adminisrative Assistant at Virginia Union University; [memb.] Genesis Gospel Group, BW Robertson Choir, Federal Employee Women's Group, Sigma Tau Upsilon of JFKHS, 1973 Class Reaunion Committee Member, Radio Announcer of Cedar Street Memorial Church, Treasury Committee, Nurse Committee; [hon.] Queen of JFKHS, certificate of achievement CSX corporation, Stock award for employee achievement CSX Corp., Asst for GRE Test Administrative VUU, US Dept. of Educ. Rep. for title III-VUU; [oth.writ.] Have a collection of over 42 poems to be copywritten and published; [pers.] Life to me is an open book of journeys, passages, secrets, adventures, and challenges to be lived in its entirely to the utmost in peace, harmony, and love with hope that we will pass over.; [a.] Richmond, VA

JONES, VICTOR
[b.] January 25, 1918; Washington; DC; [p.] Florence and Robert Jones; [m.] Deceased; May 28, 1970; [ch.] 3; [ed.] High School, Cornish School (Radio Announcing), National Radio Institute (Servicing), YMCA—Communication Course, Photography Class—University of Washington; [occ.] Retired—Seattle City Light Co; [hon.] Newspaper National Snapshot Award, (1) First Place Award B-W Week of June 3, 1963 (same picture) (2) Honorable Mention Grand Finals—1963; [pers.] The inspiration for the poem was a high school girl friend who I was really fond of.; [a.] Bonney Lake, WA

JUSTUS, JILL NICOLE
[b.] March 17, 1985; Columbus, OH; [p.] Richard and Kimberly Justus; [ed.] I will be a 7th grade student at Hamilton Middle Schoo.l; [hon.] I've made Honor Roll every grading period, every year. I have an grade point average of 3.8; [oth.writ.] I like writing poems for my family and friends. I write all types of poems. I keep a journal of all my poems.; [pers.] I like writing poetry because it lets me express my feelings.; [a.] Columbus, OH

KASELNAK, JOHN
[pen.] Jack Kasenak; [b.] March 2, 1928; Minneapolis, MN; [p.] Andrew Kaselnak, Lillians Burgess; [m.] Joann Kaselnak (deceased); August 27, 1952; [ch.] Patrick John, Michael Patrick, Robert Anthony, Michele Marie; [ed.] GED/Edison High School, Naval Justice School, CPO Academy; [occ.] Retired Navy (30 years) Permanently Retired, Volunteer; [memb.] American Red Cross, American Legion, Fleet Reserve Assn., National Association Uniformed Services, Eucharistic Ministry, Mary Mother Catholic Church; [oth.writ.] "The Skater" and "The Skater—A Sequel"—not published; [pers.] I try to reflect either humor or true events in my writings.; [a.] Eagan, MN

KECK, NELDA WARD
[pen.] Nelda Ward Keck; [b.] July 17, 1930; Okla, (Fox); [p.] Hays B. and Nora Elliott Ward; [m.] Bob G. Keck; August 24, 1951; [ch.] Bob Nelson Keck, Karee Keck Hopkins; [ed.] BRE (Bachelors in Religious Education) Degree; [occ.] Retired-University Administrative Associate, Dept. of Germanic Languages; [memb.] University of Texas and Austin; [hon.] Validectorian—High School Graduating Class, President's Excellence Award and The University of Texas at Austin in 1980; [oth.writ.] Other poetry: "Autumn Reflections" "Our Danny Boy"; [pers.] Be beautiful inside, in your hearts, with the lasting charm of a gentle and quiet spirit which is so precious to God.; [a.] Springer, OK

KEMPFF, MELANIE A.
[b.] June 20, 1957; Guate Mala; [p.] Betty and Gerhard Kempff; [ch.] Jeffrey; [ed.] Diploma of Nursing, Certified in Pediatrics; [occ.] Pediatric Nurse; [memb.] Redeemer Lutheran Church, Sierra Club; [hon.] Published poem in "Amidst the Splendor"; [oth.writ.] Poetry; [pers.] Children are our most precious commodity and we must do all we can to protect our children.; [a.] Greenacres, WA

KESSINGER III, RAYMOND
[pen.] Bulldog Vampyr; [b.] December 14, 1972; Portland, OR; [p.] Raymond Kessinger Jr., Patricia G. Kessinger; [ed.] General Studies G.E.D; [occ.] (T.V.B.S) Tualaitin Valley Builders Supply, St. Helens Oregon; [memb.] Gladiator's Paintball Team Capt. at Enchanted Acres Paintball Park; [hon.] Editor's Choice Award for "Alone" in Isle of View; [oth.writ.] Some scripts and poems—unpublished; [pers.] Eat your cereal with a fork, and do your homework in the dark.; [a.] St. Helens, OR

KILLING, LINDA A.
[b.] August 31, 1958; Boston, MA; [p.] Margaret A. Blum; [ch.] Michael Anthony, Christopher Charles; [ed.] Malden High; [occ.] Facility Specialist, Nynex, Sangus MA; [memb.] First Baptist Church Education Committe - Board of Christian Education; [oth.writ.] Several poems published in work papers, school papers; [pers.] A dedication to my beloved brother "Tony" who I've always looked up to; [a.] Malden, MA

KINDER, MELISSA
[b.] October 18, 1977; Colorado; [p.] Mark and Merrie Kinder; [ed.] Alameda High School, Concorde Cancer Institute; [occ.] Medical Assistant; [oth.writ.] "Leaving My Imprcssion", "To Say Goodbye"; [pers.] "Live for now."; [a.] Lakewood, CO

KIRKPATRICK, MARGIE LUNSFORD
[pen.] Margie Kirkpatrick; [b.] November 14, 1941; Brashear, TX; [p.] Leroy and Manah Lunsford; [m.] Ralph Dewey Kirkpatrick; June 13, 1960; [ch.] 4 Sons; [ed.] Graduated Orangefield HS Attended Lamar Univ.; [occ.] Writer; [memb.] Church of Christ, GOP; [hon.] Diamond Homer Award for Poem "Oklahoma City," 1996, from Famous Poets Society; [oth.writ.] Religious Articles in The Preceptor mag; poem "Oklahoma City" in Famous Poems of the Twentieth Century; [pers.] Poetry is part of the soul of man. Poetry expresses my heart. Poetry can laugh and cry at the same moment.; [a.] Inez, T

KITTS, VALERIE O'ROURKE
[pen.] H.L., [b.] February 16, 1964; Bronxville, NY; [p.] Frank and Sue O'Rourte; [m.] Howard Kitts; November 28, 1993; [ed.] B.A. (Communications Studies) University of MD, University College, Spr. '95; [occ.] Freelance Writer, Copy and Print Shop Technician; [memb.] ISP; [oth.writ.] "The Flaw" Published in Through Sun and Shower (1997); [a.] Washington Grove, MD

KLAASSEN, BARBARA E.
[m.] Frans M. Klaassen; [ch.] Donnette, Jamie, Desiree, Nicole; [ed.] Mt. Vernon, Univ. of Houston and Martan, TX A and M; [occ.] Business Owner, Writer, Sculptor, Painter; [oth.writ.] Poems and short stories for periodicals—none lately; [pers.] Traveled extensively, lived abroad and studied art, several showings in Europe—portraits and still lifes. Certified Hypnotherapist. Currently writing on alternate creation theory; [a.] Hawkinsville, GA

KRAMER, MARC ANDREW
[b.] August 23, 1975; Levistown, NY; [p.] David Kramer, Gail Kramer; [ed.] Mac Arthur H.S., Long Island University C.W. Post Campus; [occ.] Student; [hon.] Dean's List, Magna Cum Laude, Pi Gamma Mu, Phi Eta Sigma, Phi Sigma Tau, Pi Sigma Alpha; [oth.writ.] Articles for The Pioner, articles for Perspectives, articles for the Hillel Times; [per.] It is enough that I exist. I believe that one sould always try to share a smile with everyone. I also believe that we must accept that this is how life is, but then realize we can change the present for our future.; [a.] Levitown, NY

LA LENA, GRETCHEN
[b.] April 14, 1983; Marlton; [p.] Frank and Chris La Lena; [pers.] Through my writing I express the way I feel. This was one of my dreams to see one of my poems in a book.; [a.] Blue Anchor, NJ

LAM, KAILY
[b.] December 14, 1983; Honolulu, HI; [p.] Leighton and Lani Lam; [occ.] Student 8th grade; [hon.] Punahou School Bishop Memory Book; [oth.writ.] Horses of Hawaii, now they lay me down to sleep; [pers.] I write because it expresses the way I feel about life. It is a way to let out my fantasies and dreams. To me, writing is a link to my inner self.; [a.] Honolulu, HI

LANGHORN, AZITA
[b.] March 30, 1962; Tehran, Iran; [p.] Mr. and Mrs. Ansari; [m.] Peter Langhorn; January 7, 1984; [ch.] Faith Langhorn; [ed.] Bachelor of Business of Administraton, Clear Lake High, Houston, Texas, University of Houston, Houston, Texas; [occ.] Business Owner; [memb.] Unity Church, Laguna Hills, CA; [oth.writ.] not published; [pers.] I am interested in the process of life in all its glory—beginnings and endings and everything in between.; [a.] Lake Forest, CA

LAWRENCE, STEVEN
[b.] February 4, 1980; New York, NY; [p.] Jessica Currie; [ed.] Attended Brooklyn Technical High School; [occ.] Writer; [memb.] Ice Hockey in Harlem; [hon.] Dave Wilk Community Service Award; [oth.writ.] Several unpublished poems; [pers.] In my poems I try to let people take a look into my everyday life and struggles so that they can have a better understanding of my people.; [a.] Brooklyn, NY

LEACH, RACHELL
[b.] September 28, 1981; Salem, OH; [p.] Dianne Leach; [ed.] Entering 10th Grade at Heartland Christian School; [occ.] Student; [memb.] Believers Christian Fellowship Church, Salem, OH; [hon.] Recieved a Blue Ribbon for Drama Competition; [oth.writ.] I write short stories and other poetry.; [a.] Salem, OH

LENHART, NORMA
[pers.] I dedicate this poem to all mischievous young boys, especially my two sons Jim and Brian, and my beautiful daughter Jennifer.; [a.] Warren, OH

LEPKOWSKI, PAUL
[pen.] Michael Anthony; [b.] November 16, 1952; Milwaukee, WI; [p.] Francis and Anthony Lepkowski; [m.] Divorced; [ch.] Joseph, Paul, Andrew; [ed.] Graduate University of Wisconsin. Milwaukee, Attending Florida Atlantic University, Boca Raton, Florida; [occ.] Secondary Teacher Sunrise Middle, Ft. Lauderdale Fl; [memb.] Museum of Art Fort Lauderdale, Museum of Discovery and Science Fort Lauderdale, young professionals, Fort

Lauderdale Broward Council for the Social Studies Phi Delta Kappa Broward Dade; [hon.] Dean's list, Cum Laude, Teacher of the Year 1992, numerous Education Awards; [oth.writ.] Published essays on educational issues and editor, publisher for professional newsletter; [pers.] Writing is the personal expression of thoughts, feelings, and emotions reflecting the human condition. It is a never ending journey of self-discovery.; [a.] Coral Springs, FL

LEWIS, BOBBIE J.
[b.] August 16, 1936; Tyler, TX; [ed.] Attended Lincoln High, Dallas TX, Attended Velma B's Cosmotology Academy Of Dallas; [occ.] Retired; [hon.] Have been a gospel singer since the age of 5 yrs.; Have written more songs and poems than I can number; [oth.writ.] Have written a copy righted message to women titled "Dynamic Women"; [a.] Dallas, TX

LIDDELL, KELLY P.
[b.] March 17, 1969; Orlando, FL; [p.] Howard R. and Fran E. Smith; [m.] Kevin D. Liddell; April 15, 1995; [ch.] Kirstin Brianna Liddell; [ed.] Evans High, Westside Tech.; [occ.] Full-Time Mom; [pers.] My inspirations are Kevin and Kirstin. Love Mommy.; [a.] Clermont, FL

LINWOOD, CONSUELLO
[pen.] Connie; [b.] March 6, 1981; Chicago, IL; [p.] Otto and Rebecca; [ed.] Juniorr in High School—Lincoln Way Community High; [pers.] Putting my thoughts on paper helps me stay light-hearted and free.; [a.] Frankport, IL

LOCKSON, CURTRICE
[pen.] Renee, CFRL, Renee Bleu'air; [b.] February 24, 1975; Oakland, CA; [p.] Deborah Lockson; [ed.] James Logan High; [oth.writ.] Several poems, short stories, erotica, and songs; [pers.] I hope to one day complete a full-fledged screen play, and publish my erotica.; [a.] Fremont, CA

LOCKWOOD, NATALIE
[pen.] Madeline Lowe; [b.] August 9, 1977; Rochester, NY; [p.] Albert and Beverly Lockwood; [ed.] School of the Ants High School S.U.N.Y Oswego; [hon.] Poetry Merit Award from the National Library of Poetry; [oth.writ.] Poem titled "Rebirth" which was published in another anthology titled Through the Looking Glass; [pers.] As a poet and a writer, the only thing that matters is that everything matters. Everything is important.; [a.] Rochester, NY

LONGENBERGER, DANIEL E.
[b.] July 17, 1971; Berwick, PA; [p.] Bonnie L. Golla, Lowell Longenberger; [m.] Heidi Longenberger; April 11, 1992; [ch.] Travis Aaron; [ed.] Berwick Senior High US Army Tactical Transport Helicopter Repairman Course; [occ.] Military Helicopter Repair Technical Inspector; [memb.] National Rifle Association, Paralyzed Veterans of America (Hon.1997); [oth.writ.] Several Poems yet to be Published; [pers.] I mainly write from the heart, or both personal feelings and life experiences I find writing as a great outlet for emotions that are otherwise hard to express.; [a.] Berwick, PA

LOUDEN, JENNA BOND
[pen.] Andre Carson, Gaudia Spirare; [b.] December 17, 1982; Baltimore, MD; [p.] Karen Bond and Eric Louden; [ed.] Current High School Sophomore (Class of 2000) at Friends School of Baltimore, Graduate of Grace and Saint Peter's School (Elementary); [memb.] The Baltimore Museum of Art; [hon.] Ninth Grade Honor Roll; [oth.writ.] "The One I first loved", "Doing Nothing at All"; [pers.] "If you asked me what I came into this world to do, I will tell you: I came to live out loud."—Emile Zola. I'd like to thank my guardian angels, especially my angels on Earth.; [a.] Baltimore, MD

LOVELAND, TABATHA LYNN
[pen.] Tabby Loveland; [b.] December 04, 1981; Bend, OR; [p.] Robin Jones, Darrell S. Loveland; [ed.] Yelm High School; [memb.] Yelm High School, Cheerleader; [a.] Yelm, WA

LOVELESS, CALANA D.
[pen.] C. D. Love; [b.] July 29, 1972; St. Louis, MO; [p.] Rev. C. D. and Mrs. T. E. Loveless; [m.] John M; June, 1998; [ed.] Nova Southeastern University, currently pusuing MBA; Florida A and M University; [occ.] Excutive Assistant; [memb.] Association of Black Sociologists; [oth.writ.] Stories, essays, poems—non-published currently; [pers.] It is true that as we age we lose our memory. I have met entirely too many adults who have forgotten all they should have learned in kindergarten.; [a.] Tamarac, Fort Lauderdale, FL

LUKE, GOLDIE MAE
[pen.] Tommy or Goldieloch; [b.] June 24, 1926; Apollo, PA; [p.] Carrie and James Ahens; [m.] Edward Luke (deceased January 8, 19960; May 15, 1964; [ed.] 10th Grade; [occ.] Retired, worked at Cartle Medical Hospital; [hon.] Got a trophy from Castle Hospital for a best tray line workers and also for a certification for not missing a day work; [a.] Niles, OH

MACGILLIVRAY, ROBIN
[b.] June 23, 1981; St. Paul; [p.] Lorrie and David Macgillivray; [hon.] Regional History Day and Young Conference; [pers.] I enjoy writing stories and poems. I have always hoped that I could get published. My philosophy of life is center life on the well-being of others and not on your own.; [a.] White Bear, MN

MACKEY, ANGELA MAY
[pen.] Angela Mackey; [b.] May 10, 1957; Washington, DC; [p.] Robert Mackey and Mary Ellen Mackey; [ch.] Adrienne, Stephanie, Rachael, Christien; [edu.] Clear Creek High, LaVonne's Academy; [occ.] Hairstylist and Housekeeper; [memb.] Our Saviour's Church; [hon.] Semi-finalist in the National Library of Poetry contest; [oth.writ.] Lots of writings, just never sent off for someone else to read; [pers.] I have learned one very important lesson through my journey in life so far: never give up.; [a.] Lakewood, CO

MALERBA, RACHEL
[b.] August 22, 1984; Long Island, NY; [p.] Janet and Peter Malerba; [ed.] 7 years; [occ.] Student; [hon.] Accepted to a poetry reading where I read my poem; [oth.writ.] Several writings I've written in my journal; [pers.] I think all poems relate to something that is going on in your life or someone else's; they really express feelings.; [a.] Ridge, NY

MANDERS, ELIZABETH
[b.] January 19, 1979; Monterey Park, CA; [p.] Ernest and Robin Heim; [m.] November 7, 1987; [ed.] Rancho Cucamonga High; [occ.] Student; [hon.] Writer of the Year 1996-1997, Rancho Cucamonga HS Writers Club; [pers.] "Love immensely, Laugh a lot."; [a.] Rancho Cucamonga, CA

MANET, SALLIEHOOD CYNTHIA
[b.] August 18, 1936; Newport News, VA; [p.] Col. and Mrs. Walter D. Buie; [ed.] BA Queens College Charlotte NC., MA 1975 Fla State University, Ph. D. 1978 Fla. St. University (High School St. Genevieve's of the Pines Asheville, NC. Catholic Convent School Academy; [occ.] Retired Art Teacher Elementary Sch. Teacher; [hon.] First Prize three act play contest Bainbridge Arts Festival 1993, Exhibit in Juried Art Shows; [oth.writ.] Poems short stories ever since I could write, often printed in local papers; [pers.] Since a child I have felt close empathy with naturally revelled in its wonder, beauty, sadness. Acutely sensitive, I share what I feel through my art, painting and poetry and short stories, with appreciation of the masters.; [a.] Thomasville, GA

MANLEY, DOROTHY M.
[b.] August 19, 1954; Meridian, MS; [p.] John H. Bishop, Roxie M. Bishop; [ch.] Johnny Lee Neal; [ed.] Pelahatchie Attendance Center Meridian Jr. College; [oth.writ.] One poem published in the Fan Club Newsletter of a County Music Star.; [pers.] I have been writing stories and poems since I was a child, with the hope that someday I could share them with the world.; [a.] Meridian, MS

MARINCE, RICHARD J.
[pen.] R. J.; [b.] August 27, 1933; Philipsburg, PA; [p.] Walter and Anna Marince; [ed.] B.A. MA. Penn State University, PA; English Instructor DuBois Campus of P.S.U.; [occ.] Artist; [memb.] Presque Isle Artist Assoc., Red Cross Volunteer; [hon.] National Honorary Society, 3rd Place PA Art Senior Citizen '95 Show; [oth.writ.] Unpublished book on 1.) Flagship Niagara, 2.) Ship The Wolverine 3.) Presque Isle 4.) Erie Tours 5.) Chautaugua Inst. Tute, NY Pub. Poetry in College English Textbook; [pers.] Love and Happiness Makes The World Go Round. God Bless!; [a.] Erie, PA

MARSH, BERTHA
[b.] November 26, 1907; Dragoon, AZ; [p.] Jesse and Maggie Wien; [m.] W.R. Marsh, (deceased); 1924; [ch.] 5 Daisy May, Willie Marie, Beryl Ellen, Contance Joan, Bedford Jackson (Jack); [ed.] High School graduate; [occ.] Retired; [oth.writ.] Several poems published in local newspapers family history, stories of pioneer days, [pers.] My Grandfather, Amas H. Wein, came to AZ with the 6th Calvary in 1876 and later establised to protect the settlers from Indians the Wein family in the vicinity of the Cochise stronghold, in Cochise country. Our whole family interested in mining and ranching. Many of the heirs still live in the general area. I am now residing in AZ pioneers originally home, which was established miners, and at present houses. We pioneers have lived in AZ for 30 years or more.; [a.] Prescott, AZ

MARTINEZ, MILAGROS FRAU
[pen.] Margeline Del Mar; [b.] January 20, 1947; Santurce, Puerto Rico; [p.] Victor Frau, Dolores Frau; [m.] Francisco Martinez; [ch.] Hector Gabriel Guerrero; [ed.] Caribbean University College (basic); [occ.] Translator; [memb.] Seventh-Day Adventist Church, Puerto Rico Society of Georgia, Amnesty International; [hon.] Dean's List. Published in Gallery of Artistry Anthology by the Poetry Guild (August 97), also will be published by the Sparrowgrass Poetry Forum in their Anthology titled, "Poetic Voices of America"; [oth.writ.] Fifty Children's Fiction Stories (In Spanish); Thousands of poems (thirty three years worth of them, both in Spanish and English); a couple of novels; several poems published in local newspapers both in PR and GA; [pers.] A true successful life is measured by its loving usefulness to humanity. I'd like to dedicate this poem to my beloved, heroic husband, Francisco.; [a.] Hapeville, GA

MASON, JOSHUA ELI
0[b.] February 9, 1982; Huntsville, AL; [p.] Donna Mason, Kymmie Mason; [oth.writ.] Several poems that have never been published.; [pers.] In my writings, I try to bring out the beauty and romance in a dark and dismal life.; [a.] New Market, AL

MATTHEWS, JEROME
[pen.] Billy Pac'soo; [b.] December 1, 1949; Shaw, MS; [p.] Katie Mae and Josiah Matthews (Deceased); [ed.] Chicago Art Institute 1970 Chicago, IL Advertising/Design Michigan State University Lansing, MI Human Behaviors; [oth.writ.] Jerome Matthews (Deceased) is the writer of "What A Beauty" also of other poems, artist and children's books he has completed two according to the Lakeshore Times; [pers.] Jerome Matthews is my brother. He sent me this poem, along with many

other poems he had written. I choose the poem in particular, for this poem is one of the most beautiful to me.; [a.] Joliet, IL

MAYE, CHARLES
[pen.] Charles Kenneth Maye; [b.] January 18, 1970; Los Angeles, CA; [p.] Vern Maye, Nina Maye; [ed.] Fairfax High, California State University, Northridge; [occ.] Screenwriter; [hon.] Poet of the Night, Mahogany Cafe, Hov., Tex; [oth.writ.] Screenplays, once upon a passion, Summa'Time, and S.O.V.L. poems and song lyrics; [pers.] It has been said that I have a way with words. I disagree—words have a way with me.; [a.] Los Angeles, CA

MCCLEARY, DONECE M.
[b.] February 8, 1952; Los Angeles, CA; [p.] Donald and Lauchette McCleary; [ed.] Venice High School, ICS (International Correspondance School); [occ.] Secretary and Catechist, St. John Baptist de la Salle Catholic Church, School of Religious Education, Granada Hills, California; [a.] Granada Hills, CA

MCCLURE, RANDY L.
[pen.] Randy Lee; [b.] July 19; Bloomfield, IA; [p.] Wayne McClure, Betty McClure; [occ.] Self-Employed, Contractor; [memb.] International Poets Society; [hon.] 1984 Monster Arm Wrestling National Champion; [oth.writ.] Many Poems; [pers.] Chase a dream—it might be your salvation; [a.] Eldon, IA

MCCULLOUGH, DEBORAH
[pen.] Darlene M; [b.] October 10, 1952; Memphis, TN; [p.] Deborah Gardner Minister; [ch.] Dedric and Sheilonda McCullough; [ed.] Finished High Schoo,l Some College; [occ.] Business Manager/owner; [oth.writ.] Poems, Book-unpublished titled "Letting Go". Short essays; [pers.] My writings are inspired by what I feel in my heart and by my surroundings, and most of all by the memories of my dear mother. Writing, for me is a deeply moving experience.; [a.] Matteson, IL

MCDONALD, TROY
[b.] September 27, 1979; Indio, CA; [p.] Jeanettia McDonald; [ed.] High School; [pers.] I grew up in a very small retirement desert community. My single mother, an older sister and myself made a life for ourselves in this remote location. I had Independent School Study for my four years of High School; I graduated June 1997. I have always had a lot of time to reflect on life—I'm sure this is where my poetry comes from.; [a.] North Shore, CA

MCKISSICK, AMY
[b.] November 28, 1974; Athens, GA; [p.] Barry and Robyn McKissick; [ed.] AS Science, AS Respiratory Therapy; [occ.] Clerk, Walton Country Magistrate Vourt Criminal Division; [memb.] Debutantes of Monroe Alumni, Gainesville College Alumni, Enimett Kelly Jr. Society; [hon.] Editors Choice Award for poem "He's the Only One"; [oth.writ.] Windows on the World 1990 "He's the Only One"; American Poetry Anthology 1989 Six additional poems; [pers.] Love that which you believe and believe in that which you love unconditionally, completely. All else will come to you.; [a.] Monroe, GA

MCKNIGHT, CHRISTEL BELLE
[b.] December 11, 1973; Chicago; [p.] Lydia Mae Smith and Arthur Mcknight; [occ.] Social Service Work; [oth.writ.] Day Ol' Cornbread; [pers.] In my writings I always want to project innocence and pride, that in some way has been stripped from the world. Also I strive to be a cultural Optimist.; [a.] Richfield, MN

MCMAHAN, JOHN T.
[pen.] Johnny Trey; [b.] March 31, 1963; Geneva, OH; [p.] John T. McMahan Jr. and Kay S; [m.] Pamela K. MacMahan; October 18, 1986; [ch.] 1,

John T. McMahan IV; [ed.] Wimington College; University of Vienna, Austria; Lakeland College; Bowling Green State University; Kent State; Cleveland State; [occ.] Manager of Family-Owned McMahan-Spafford Inc; [oth.writ.] Book of 100 poems called "Animus" which includes 2 short stories "Oddybie's Babylon" and "Habsburgergasse FUNP"; 5 Record Albums 1988 - Where is the right road? 1992 - Guilty of Love, 1993 - Child of the Wildwood, 1994 - Rescue Me, 1996 - Yesterday; Currently working on Album - "Den of Desire" with Steve Hayes of Cleveland, OH and City Blue with Mark Luthandt of Mentor, OH; 6 Children's books about Bobby "The Blue Bull"; [pers.] "A story is not complete without a catharsis, when a lyric's flame and music's muscle meet."; [a.] Rock Park, OH

MCMILLAN, RACHEL C.
[b.] July 8, 1919; Chicago, IL; [p.] Alonzo J. D. Cobb, Adlean Cobb; [m.] Divorced; June 25, 1949; [ch.] Adjora Faith McMillan Stevens; [ed.] Speleman College, GA. Governors State University, IL. International Graduate School, MO; [occ.] Retired teacher, educator; [memb.] BD of Directors Green Leaf U. MO Harris YMCA Advisory Bd Phi Delta Kappa Sorority, Am Can Society, Deacon of Good Shepherd United Church of Christ, Remys Dtrs; [hon.] 40 years Silver Service pin PDK sorority, Gld watch 50 years Alumnae Speleman College, 1995 Outsanding Christian Woman, Special Recognition 1979 Award International Black Writers, Incorporation Community Service '93; [oth.writ.] Doctoral Dissertation 1985, Krinon Magazine 1987, Chryso poets 1997; [pers.] I continue to be committed to and involved in life, as I age gracefully while striving toward fulfillment of my potential and keep on a-keeping on.; [a.] Chicago, IL

MEDINA, CORY A.
[pen.] Cory Medina; [b.] November 4, 1981; Elyria, OH; [p.] Eugene and Patricia Medina; [ed.] Sophomore at Brookside High School; [occ.] Student at Brookside High School—Sheffield, Ohio; [oth.writ.] A few other poems, none that have been published; [pers.] I write poetry for myself and to express my thoughts and/or feelings. I want to thank my friends and family for their support on entering this contest; [a.] Sheffield Lake, OH

MEISENHOLDER, ROB
[b.] October 1, 1979; Plainview, LI; [p.] Al and Arlene Meisenholder; [ed.] Graduated From Bay Shore High School, Attending Suffolk Community College in the fall; [hon.] Student of the month award foreign Language May 1997, Lynn Clark Award for excellence in Latin; [oth.writ.] I have a series of unpublished works that I feel are noteworthy and hope to have them published in the near future; [pers.] The best way to escape reality is to make your dreams become a reality. I will stop at nothing to live my dreams, both literally and figuratively.; [a.] Bay Shore, NY

MELENDEZ, ELYSIA INENA
[b.] December 28, 1980; Branford, CT; [p.] Pedro J. Melendez and Bohdanna Bonias; [ed.] Brandford High School, grade 11; [occ.] Student; [memb.] Blue Coffee (writing club) S.A.D.D.; [hon.] R.J. Julia Award for participation, honors 1st, 2nd, and 4th quarters both grades 9 and 10; [oth.writ.] This book of ours (school book); [pers.] "The world is a book; those who do not travel read only one page."—St. Augustine; [a.] Middletown, CT

MERKULOV, OLEG A.
[b.] June 21, 1969; Voronegh, Russia; [p.] Lubov Stephanovna and Alexie Fedotovitch Merkulov; [m.] Beth Lynn Merkulova; July 23, 1994; [ed.] Latvia State University - Bachelor's Degree in Philology; [occ.] Bellman at the Madison Hotel, Washington, DC; [oth.writ.] Several articles published in "SM-Segodnya" - Riga, Several poems in Russian.; [pers.] Under the most extreme circum-

stances they will not betray you. They will not let you forget the human values. They will sacrifice their lives for you. People around you - the real angels. Be one of them yourself.; [a.] Alexandria, VA

MERREL, JASON
[b.] June 16, 1978; San Jose, CA; [p.] Fuerrett Merrel, Sharon King; [ed.] Gustine High School, Modesto Junior College; [occ.] Handicap Camp Counselor for Christian Berets, student; [memb.] First Baptist Church of Nowman, First Baptist Church of Modesto; [pers.] In Christ I can do all things according to His will. I also believe that to bring a smile to a face is the greatest accomplishment.; [a.] Gustine, CA

MERRITT, RUBY M.
[b.] January 2, 1928; Holden, W. Va; [p.] Charlie and Mary Bumgarner; [ch.] 4; [ed.] High School, Logan County; [occ.] Retired; [memb.] Songwritters Guild Of America (1995) Nashville, Tennesee; [hon.] Certificate of Associate Membership 1995, Joined the guilds ranks of composers and lyricists George David Weiss, President; [oth.writ.] "What A Dream" and "Not Waiting For You" being recorded by Heart Land Records, Kansas City, MI "Jesus Is The One" and "Heavenly Store" being recorded by Amerecord Record Company, Hollywood, California; [pers.] For the insight to feel and be thankful know what I write. I have studied, and bought many books to learn the art of songwriting. I also love poems.; [a.] Chapmanville, WVA

MESSINGER, JR., GARTH REED
[pen.] G.R; [b.] January 8, 1979; Salisbury, MD; [p.] June and Garth Messinger; [ed.] Junior in High School; [occ.] Learning to be a electrician; [hon.] Made Honor Roll 6 out of 8 terms. Made all-star in Varsity Soccer at a Lancaster, PA, tournament in the 8th grade and lettered in Varsity Soccer when a Freshman. Got an award from the Saint Jude's Children Hospital for a Marathon for school; [pers.] "Even though life has its ups and downs, you should come back with more pride and confidence."; [a.] Salisbury, MD

MEYERS, ROBERT
[b.] December 3, 1951; Lincoln, NE; [p.] Robert and La Yera Meyers; [ed.] Graduated Lincoln High School in 1970; [occ.] Disabled; [oth.writ.] My Mother, My Brother Died in Vietnam, Why Me, My Best Friend, Eldergarden, I Must be getting Older; [pers.] My family has been after me for years to send in one of my poems; now I'm glad I finally did.; [a.] Greeley, CO

MHLANGA, ERASMUS
[b.] August 2, 1969; Zimbabwe, Africa; [p.] Amos and Rose Mhlanga; [ch.] Jasmine Tsitsidzashe Mhlanga; [ed.] Business Administration Degree; [occ.] Writer for Dorrance Publishing House. Pittsburgh, PA; [hon.] Perfect attendant student and 4.0 student; [oth.writ.] Author of the book, "The Wit and Wisdom of Nelson Mandela," published in 1996 by Dorrance Publishing Co., Inc. I'm also an author of the upcoming book, "Life In Africa", and many more children and adult books to come; [pers.] To all my poem and book fans, "May God find in your past the strength to shape your future."; [a.] Nashville, TN

MICHEL, GEORGE L.
[pen.] George Leo Michel; [b.] May 21, 1921; Akron, OH; [p.] William and Elda Shipman Michel; [m.] Deceased; November 20, 1944; [ch.] Timothy Wayne, Stephen Lawrence; [ed.] High School Kenmore, Akron O,; Johnson Bible College, Knoxville, TN. Christian Theological Seminar, Indianapolis, TN; [occ.] Chaplain (Part-time) Wayne County Care Center, Wooster, OH; [memb.] Central Christian Church, Wooster, Disciples of Christ Minister; [hon.] Poems is local newspaper world of poetry recipient (Golden Award) (Silver Award); [oth.writ.] Nothing of note; Except poems, unpub-

lished, used for Retirement recognition, volunteer worker's appreciation poems; [pers.] Serving as Chaplain in Retirement years, my poems bring to light the needs of the Elderly.; [a.] Wooster, OH

MILENBERG, JASMIN
[pen.] Jasmin Milenberg; [b.] October 15, 1981; Ft. Rodge, IA; [p.] Em and Dorothy Milenberg; [occ.] Attending high school in Fort Dodge, IA; [memb.] Band, Chair and 4-H; [oth. writ.] Many poems and stories; [a.] Fort Dodge, IA

MILLER, JANE
[b.] December 13, 1981; Salt Lake City, UT; [p.] Del Miller and Radon Hackworth; [occ.] High School Student—Full Time; [hon.] Poetry Contest in the 7th grade; [oth.writ.] Poems published in a school newspaper and magazines; [a.] West Valley, UT

MILLER, WILLARD
[b.] November 16, 1945; Fairmont, WV; [p.] Marion W. and Sarah R. Miller; [m.] Judith Joan Miller; January 21, 1978; [ch.] (5) Duane, Connie, Diane, Gary, and Rob; [ed.] Elementary Hagon S WV. Jr. High River Side Morgantown, WV. Completed High School G.E.D. Ft. Sill Oklahoma— 1968; [oc.] Material Handler- High lift OPTR, Swing in Slide Janesville, WI; [memb.] Bethel Baptist Church Janesville, WI; [hon.] Army- December 29, 1965- December 17, 1968- Vietnam Tour 1966-67; [oth.writ.] Dedication to My Father, a Tribute to Hank Williams Sr. and Of Wisconsin, None have been published; [pers.] Humility! The best teacher of man. To speak and write from the heart, of unique people, places and things I meet and see. My inspiration comes from the music of Hank Williams.; [a.] Janesville, WI

MITCHELL, DEREK
[b.] March 13, 1979; Manchester, NH; [p.] Tom Mitchell, Mary Mitchell; [ed.] Hooksett Memorial Jr. High, Manchester Central High School; [occ.] Department Head of Sanitational Maintenance, Hooksett Space Center; [memb.] UNH Upward Bound Program, DECA International, Multiple Video Stores; [hon.] The Upward Bound Strider Award, Two ECLIPSE Awards, Two Academic Honors Awards, Three Summer Achievement Awards, A DECA Trophy, A DECA Silver Medal and many DECA Certificates; [oth.writ.] Several poems and many stories for "The Pipeline", a UNH newsletter; [pers.] My poetry is the end result of my brain and my heart getting together and trying to communicate.; [a.] Hooksett, NH

MITCHELL, JERRY M.
[pen.] Teddy Bear; [b.] October 17, 1979; Danville; [p.] Kimberly Bryant; [m.] Jerry Davis; [ed.] Senior at Geoge Washington High School; [occ.] Helping Children at Church; [hon.] Choir Award, Selected by schools to read my poems in different churches and other schools; [oth.writ.] I have written short stories such as The Fallen Night Tears that I cry, and other poems such as Outstanding Boy, Alone, Longing for Love; [pers.] I thank God for the gift of writting. I thank my grandmothers, Lula Mitchell and my auntie Tonya Diggs they are very special to me—love ya.; [a.] Danville, VA

MOORE, JAMES
[pen.] Quiet Storm; [b.] April 6, 1970; Douglas, GA; [p.] Henry and Jessie Moore; [m.] Deena Moore; January 16, 1994; [ch.] Kassendra D. Moore; [ed.] Coffee High School, American River College; [occ.] Full-time student; [memb.] Boys and Girls Club Santa Ana, NAACP, African American Unity Club; [hon.] Who's Who Among Junior High School Students, Military Awards 2 Meritorious Mast, numerous letters of appreciation, sea service deployment, Good Conduct Nedal, Kuwait Liberation Medal, National Defense Medal; [pers.] I can die for my country; will I ever be treated as an equal?; [a.] Carmichael, CA

MORALES, JAYMIE
[b.] December 18, 1984; Los Angeles, CA; [p.] Ellen Sklover and Dr. Ray Morales; [ed.] Birch Elementary School, Now attending Merrick Avenue Middle School; [oth.writ.] The first one I ever published.; [pers.] Life is my nspiration. Do well, and doubt not.; [a.] Merrick, NY

MORRIS, PAT R.
[b.] February 23, 1972; Phoenixville, PA; [p.] Grace and Edward, Fink Beiner; [ed.] Upper Perkiomen High School Western Montco Vo-Tech School; [occ.] Data Entry, RX Returns, Palm, PA; [pers.] I write mostly, To Help People Around Me, Get Through Rough Times. It Makes Them Feel There's Always Someone There, When They Need Them The Most; [a.] Barto, PA

MORRIS, SHIRLEY
[pen.] Shirley (Reichard) Morris; [b.] September 2, 1942; Arkoma, OK; [p.] Ernest and Clara Reichard; [m.] Widow and Charles H. Morris; September 27, 1967; [ch.] 1 son, Andy Greenwood; 1 daughter, Donna Kinne; [ed.] Graduate of Spiro High School, Graduate of Melli's Beauty College; [occ.] Stockroom Attendant with James Rivers/Ft. Smit, Ar. Division for 30 yrs; [memb.] Member of Calvary Miss. Bap. Church in Van Buren Ar./Member of Delightful Doll Society; [oth.writ.] Published in newspapers, Published in "Windows of the Soul" Nat'L Lib. of Poetry 1996/Also Sparrowgras "Poetic Voices of America" Spring 1997; [pers.] In my writings I strive to express feelings in my heart,; [a.] Van Buren, AR

MOYES, ALMA
[b.] July 19, 1929; Alma, MI; [p.] James and Ethel Taylor; [m.] Elton Moyes; February 19, 1994; [ch.] Five children; [occ.] Retired Housewife— took care of children; [memb.] AARP, church, Bowling; [hon.] For volunteer at nursing home and at senior center; [oth.writ.] Just poems to friends and 8children and grandchildren; [pers.] I love music (gospel). I sing solos at church. I love camping, my church family, volunteer work.; [a.] Mt Pleasant, MI

MUNDAY, RANDALL FRANK
[b.] September 23, 1959; Taxlorsville, NC; [p.] Audrey Munday, Frank Munday; [m.] Jody Munday; June 1, 1991; [ed.] 12 years, Whittenburg Elem. (8), Alexander Cential High (4); [occ.] Owner of small trucking Co. in Claremont NC, Randall Munday Trucking; [memb.] Walnut Grove Baptist Church; [hon.] Driver of the Year/and Driver of the Month; A and A+ in essay, in high school; [oth.writ.] None, at the moment but I have, an idea, for one right now, on more poetry; [pers.] I would love too win grand prize, so I could buy a new typewriter (mine is broken) to make my work easier. I'm thinking about writing a novel; ifHillary Clinton can do it, so can I.; [a.] Claremount, NC

MURRAY, ROBYN L.
[b.] July 27, 1961; Teaneck, NJ; [p.] Melva, Cortland; [ed.] Bachelor Science Nursing from William Paterson College, Wayne NJ; [occ.] Critical Care Cardiac Nurse; [memb.] National League for Nurses, International Society of Poets, Distinguished Member; [hon.] Dean's List W.P.C. School of Health and Science. Phi Theta Kappa National Honor Society; [oth.writ.] I enjoy writing poems, lyrics for songs, and short stories; [pers.] Follow the rules of wisdom and fate, never ignore mistakes that you make. Learn to accept what you have been dealt...open your eyes so pain can be felt.; [a.] Paterson, NJ

NAGGAR, ROGER
[pen.] Naggz; [b.] January 5, 1980; East Meadow, NY; [p.] Karam Naggar and Marianne Naggar; [ed.] East Meadow High School; [occ.] Sound Technician for 28 Orange Street; [memb.] 28 Orange Street; [oth.writ.] Several unpublished poems wait-

ing to be released; [pers.] The "Beat" writers have been my greatest influence. "I'm going to try speaking some reckless words, and I want you to try to listen recklessly."—Allen Ginsberg; [a.] East Meadow, NY

NASHTAR, SYEDA NAHEED
[pen.] Naheed Nashtar; [b.] M.P., India; [p.] Nashtar Khairabadi and Sarfaraz Fatima; [ed.] M.A.M. Phil., Linguistics and Hindi; [occ.] Associate; [memb.] Member of Aligarh Association, Atlanta; [oth.writ.] Poems published in Indian magazines; [pers.] Poetry is the expression of powerful feelings a mirror of life. I have been greatly influenced by Shelley and Keats.; [a.] Lawrenceville, GA

NAVARRO, ANTONIO TONY
[b.] September 26, 1922; Havana, Cuba; [p.] Antero Navarro, Aurora Perez-Zuazo; [m.] Avis Hedges; December 28, 1954; [ch.] Antonio Jr., Avis, Alex; [ed.] Belen Jesuit School, Havana-Georgia Tech., Atlanta, GA, B.S. In Chem. Engineering (CH.E.); [occ.] Retired, P.R. Consultant, Director, Author, Columnist (In the Miami Herald); [oth. writ.] "Tocayo," a Cuban Resistance Leader's True Story; [a.] Key Biscayne, FL

NAVARRO, JUDITH (REITZ)
[b.] November 29, 1940; Nebraska; [p.] Henry and Katherine Reitz; [m.] Lou Navarro; August 18, 1962; [a.] El Sobrante, CA

NELSON, AMBER LUCETTA
[b.] February 19, 1983; Williston, ND; [p.] Peggy and Vern Nelson; [ed.] Crenora Public School; [pers.] This is dedicated to my Aunt Donna Ring. For those that dream there is no such place as far away.; [a.] Zahl, ND

NELSON, DAVE
[b.] December 19, 1982; Norwalk CT; [p.] David Nelson, Joanne Nelson; [ed.] High School Student, Norwalk High School (Sophmore); [occ.] Student, Drummer in Garage Band; [memb.] Model United Nations Club, Lacross Team; [oth.writ.] Composes own music lyrics for band; [pers.] My poetry is my best way of expressing my feelings with words.; [a.] Norwalk, CT

NEWMAN, ELIZABETH
[b.] January 3, 1980; Alexandria, VA; [p.] Jeff Newman and Kathy Newman; [ed.] Fairfax High School; [memb.] National Honor Society, Senator of 1998 Student Government, Student Advisory Council member, Keyette, Spanish Honor Society, Future Business Leaders of America; [hon.] Scholar Athlete Award; [a.] Fairfax, VA

NOLET, AMBER B.
[b.] February 28, 1983; Groton, CT; [p.] Gary C. Nolet, Kathryn M. Nolet; [ed.] I just graduated from eighth grade, and am now entering my high school years.; [occ.] Student; [memb.] Art Club, Swim Team, Dancing—Gotta Dance Studios, Freshman Band (Saxophone), on my 8th grade Volleyball team; [hon.] I won medals for playing the Saxophone, Ribbons for Swimming, I was honored as The Most Outstanding Art Student; [oth.writ.] Never been published before, but I write others poems, and stories. "First Love", "Christmas Wish" and "Losing the One You Loved" are just a few of my poems; [pers.] I would like to say that my poem "Drug Addict" was inspired by my cousin Kristen. Now she's straightened up, and I'd like to wish new luck in staying straight.; [a.] Villa Park, IL

NORIEGA, JOSEPH ANTHONY ORTIZ
[oth.writ.] "The Child" published in the National Library of Poetry anthology "A Moment In Time" and "Christie" to be published in "Montage of Life" by the National Library of Poetry; [pers.] Dedicated to a dear friend Caryn Clark. Might all of us come to know our gargoyles only to be rid of them in sanctuary.

NOTTINGHAM, KERRI
[b.] March 8, 1988; Greensboro, NC; [p.] Joe and Vicky Nottingham; [ed.] Entering 4th grade—Varner Elementary Powder Springs, GA; [occ.] Student; [memb.] Target - Gifted Student (Program) Class at Varner, Powder Springs 1st United Methodist Church; [hon.] Bowling, Honor Roll Student, Star Reader, Social Studies, Star Reader, Social Studies Achievement Award, Language Arts Achievement Award; [oth.writ.] Various Poems; [a.] Powder Springs, GA

NOWICKI, CHERI LYNN
[b.] October 1, 1984; Warren, MI; [p.] John and Nancy Nowicki; [ed.] Eastland Junior High—8th Grade; [occ.] Student; [memb.] National Junior Honor Society, Bethel Lutheran Church Youth Group, E.J.H.S. Band; [hon.] "Gold" Presidential Academic Award; [pers.] I enjoy writing—usually on the spur of the moment. Thank you, Mrs. Hill, for your support in my early years.; [a.] Roseville, MI

ODOM, BRANDY
[b.] July 1, 1982; Levelland, TX; [p.] Randy and Kathy Odom; [ed.] Pampa Middle School now Lakin High School; [memb.] Wesleyan Church; [hon.] State Softball Runner-Up team, 1st Place in Soccer Tournament, 2nd Place in Volleyball Tournament, 4 First Place finishes in track, 7 second Place finishes in track, Team Captain in Volleyball, Ranked 14 in class out of 297 kids, 3 Third finisher in track, straight A student, won 1st Division in solo and ensemble for band; [a.] Lakin, KS

OGBRU, IRENE
[ch.] Three; [ed.] Univ. Education; [occ.] Dietitian/Nutritionist and novelist; [oth.writ.] Novels: "I'm Born a Woman, Not Daddy's Son"; "Power of Women"; [pers.] Writing novels and poems is my best personal intuition and visions for the human race's special reconciliation towards God's love of creation, and woman is the mirror and love of His creation.; [a.] Eagon, MN

OSVATICS, DEBORAH MARIE
[b.] October 1, 1959; Manhattan, NY; [p.] Philip and Rachel Militano; [m.] Steven C. Osvatics Sr.; [m.] December 31, 1992; [ch.] Desiree' Angel, Steven Charles Jr., Cassandra-Marie, Taylor William; [ed.] Sewanaka High School, Briarcliffe Business School, attended UMBC; [occ.] Housewife and "Mom"; [memb.] St. Paul's Lutheran Church, Spina Bifada Association; [hon.] Honor Vocal Award; [oth.writ.] I enjoy writing poems, write for songs and greeting cards; [pers.] No matter what the day's challenges may be, there's always a greater sense of life with my husband and children.; [a.] Mechanicsville, MD

OVERSTREET, VIVIAN
[b.] May 22, 1960; Mobile, AL; [p.] John and Edwina Clearman; [m.] Franklin M. Overstreet; December 6, 1969; [ch.] Julie Elizabeth (20), Amanda Jill (3), Franklin William (deceased); [ed.] Graduated from Vigor H.S. in 1968, Graduated from Mobile Infirmay School of Radiologic Technology in 1970, Received Registered Technologist Degree; [occ.] Bookeeper—Overstreet Trucking; [memb.] ARRT; [a.] Creola, AL

PADILLA, ROSE M.
[b.] July 20, 1928; Dearborn, MI; [p.] Joseph and Marie Kreskoff; [m.] John Padilla; August 7, 1947; [ch.] 9 Children; [ed.] Olathe High, Colorado State University; [occ.] Retired Computer Operator; [hon.] Phi Theta Kappa; [oth.writ.] As an Air Force Family we moved often. Occasionally I had poetry published in local newspapers at several tour of duty locations.; [pers.] I wrote this poem after watching the sunrise shortly after the death of my husband. I tend to write poetry when I have been moved deeply by some occurence that is compelling to me.; [a.] Tonopah, AZ

PAGEL, JESSICA
[pen.] Krishna Jenkins; [b.] January 3, 1983; Green Bay, WI; [p.] Christine and Glenn Pagel; [ed.] Currently in Bay Port High School; [occ.] Child Care; [hon.] To me a person's awards and achievements are their friends and family 'cause everything else is just material things.; [pers.] Writing is only way to look head-on into the soul, so enlighten and enjoy.; [a.] Green Bay, WI

PAISSON, ANTHONY DALE
[pen.] Paisano; [b.] October 26, 1959; Anchorage, AK; [ch.] Shane Anthony Paisson; [ed.] High School Graduate; [hon.] I won the 1984 Los Angeles Golden Glove Award as a Junior Middle Weight; [oth.writ.] I would like to dedicate this work to my son Shane Anthony Paisson and to Benjamin Klee Mann, who I love as a son, in hopes that they will forever follow their hearts and dreams and dare to be free!; [a.] La Mirada, CA

PALMER, VICTOR M.
[pen.] Remlop - Remlap; [b.] April 10, 1924; Morenci, MI; [p.] Arthur C. and Florence Palmer; [m.] Dema E. Palmer; January 18, 1946; [ch.] Four Children (Daughters); [ed.] Twelve Years; [occ.] Retired; [memb.] Stages Youth and Family Council, The American Legion, The Vets, The Writers Mill; [hon.] Won 2nd Place in tall tales story contest; [oth.writ.] 12 other published poems; [pers.] I have limited abilities in my writings...But I still keep trying. "Let him be kept from paper, pen, and ink...so may he cease to write and learn to think."

PALMERIO, COLETTE J.
[pen.] Colette; [b.] April 5, 1977; Freehold; [p.] John and Donna Palmerio; [ed.] Holy Family School (Elem.) Lake Wood High School, Ocean County College; [occ.] New Talent Management; [memb.] Saint Mary of the Lake Church, Math Tutor, Ocean County College 1996-1997; [hon.] National Honor Society 94-95, President's Academic Award (94-95) High School Year Book Award (94-95) Honor role (91-95), National Dean's List (95-97); Who's Who Among High School Students (94-95); [oth.writ.] "I Love Him" poem published 1997 in previous anthology; [pers.] I hope my writing will touch and inspire the youth. Influenced by: Nancy Abrams (Former Teacher); [a.] Lake Wood, NJ

PANZARINO, CAREY
[b.] May 31, 1974; Delhi, NY; [p.] Colleen Panzarino and Rocco Panzarino; [ed.] Continuing education; [occ.] Gourmet Cook; [a.] Santa Barbara, CA

PARMAN, CAROL
[b.] February 1, 1938; Rockwell City, IA; [p.] Bernard and Maxine Moriarty; [m.] Doyle Parman; March 12, 1988; [ed.] Some College Secretarial Degree Dean's List, IA Western Community Coll 1985; [occ.] Farm Wife; [memb.] DCCW (Diocesan Council of Catholic Women), Iowa Genealogical Society, Kansas City Christian Writers Network; [hon.] Won 1st Place for State of Missouri in the 1994 Great American Think Off Sponsored by the New York Mills Regional Cultural Center in MN; [oth.writ.] Published in various local newspapers In IA and MO, our Sunday Visitor, Rural Missouri, The Catholic Mirror; Write speical poetry for birthdays and anniversaries (Story of life poems); write for 12-step publications; [pers.] Have been writing stories or poems since 5th grade. My mother writes poems and influenced me in writing letters, she always encouraged our talents. I want to help others through my own 12-step experience; writing is healing; [a.] Grant City, MO

PARTEE, ZELDA T.
[b.] November 18, 1952; [ed.] Graduate of: Douglas High, Johnston School of Nursing - Union Memorial Hospital; [occ.] Nursing; [hon.] Elected

as a member of The International Poetry Hall of Fame; [pers.] My talent is a gift from the Lord. Being a Romantic at heart I feel that "Poems are expressions of emotions that are never torn apart, when written through each beat of the heart."; [a.] Randallstown, MD

PARTLOW, MARGARET E.
[b.] January 1, 1935; Barke, VT; [p.] William and Evelyn Farnhain; [m.] Clarence I. Partlow; October 25, 1952; [ed.] H.S. Some College, Lots of Courses and training; [occ.] Retired Professional Librarian; [pers.] I wrote this poem standing at my kitchen shelf. I feel it's never too late to try things. It just "popped" out. I think the poem is quite good.; [a.] Grand Isle, VT

PATEL, POONAM
[b.] November 3, 1983; Lusaka, Zambia; [p.] Arvindkumar and Gitaben Patel; [ed.] Beginning Eighth Grade; [occ.] Student; [hon.] Teachers Honor Roll, Good Citizenship, Good Student, Perfect Attendance, and other school awards, Beta Club, Art awards; [oth.writ.] Journey, Winter Love, Colors of Fall, Cool Winter, Spring, Summer (all of the above are unpublished poems); [a.] Memphs, TN

PATNODE, SANDY
[b.] January 1, 1951; Morristown, NJ; [p.] John Buskey, Eileen Buskey; [m.] John Patnode; February 26, 1993; [ch.] Andrew Carl, Frank Michael; [ed.] Windham High School, Tampa College; [occ.] Specialty Producst Manager, Bessette Printers, Springfield, MA; [memb.] POPAI, American Marketing Assoc., National Advertising Assoc.; [a.] Marlborough, CT

PEARCE, BARBARA BURKE
[b.] January 11, 1955; New York, NY; [p.] James Burke, Frances Burke; [m.] Robert Pearce; April 26, 1980; [ed.] Notre Dame Academy—Miami, FL; [occ.] Clerical Work in Family Construction Business; [hon.] 1996 Overall Champion Adult Tonopah, NV Cowboy Poetry Gathering; [pers.] I strive to touch the hearts of the people who read my poems. If I make you smile or shed a tear, I've reached my goal.; [a.] Las Vegas, NV

PEMBERTON, IRENE C. HANSEN
[b.] July 11, 1906; Omaha, NE; [p.] Hans and Lula Hansen; [m.] Lewis N. Pemberton, deceased 1968; January 1, 1958; [ed.] 1921-1924 Gr. Omaha Technical High Business Administration 1925-33, 1 year Chicago Bible Institute, Teacher Missionary Zion Center Omaha, Boys degree Omaha University '41 Sociology, Grad. Social Wk., 3 years USC California; [occ.] Recently completed 2 years art course art intruction school Minn., received Blue Ribbon, writer to date; Poems distributed widely uplifting—many toward the better life; [memb.] Kountze Choir member 14 yrs, Danish Brotherhood, fellowship, ELC Evangelical Lutherm Church; [hon.] Several poems have been written for special occasions, the crowd's response is my reward—many publications have shown; "Editors Choice," an award, was granted to me by John Campbell, Editor published of "Selected Works of our Worlds' Best Poets"; my 3 poems appear in this publication—it was the first anthology of over 15 to date; [oth.writ.] A special message and a poem given at a class reunion in behalf of the classmates no longer with us. Play writings. "Patty Sue's Birthday Party" was among many dramatic speeches written in for children; [pers.] So many people seem to have lost hope today. When I look to my Savior and Lord for guidance in setting up the poem, there is always a clear sense of direction to feed His sheep. So my poems teach a lesson of hope; often comedy breaks through so the lessons depicted leave a firm imprint, long to be remembered.; [a.] Omaha, NE

PETERS, BARBARA J.
[b.] January 12, 1943; Washington, DC; [p.] Valerie V. and Andrew E. Peters; [ch.] Valerie Antoinette

and Kenneth Allen; [ed.] D.C. Public Schools Eastern HE School, Wash, DC, Attended University of the District Of Columbia, Southeastern Univ.; [occ.] Retired from Federal Government

PETERSON, GREG A.
[b.] February 3, 1951; Aue Claire, WI; [p.] Alvin and Barbara Peterson [m.] Sandra K. Peterson; September 4, 1971; [ch.] Andrew John and Amber Marie; [ed.] BS, Southern Illinois University at Carbondale; [occ.] US Navy Master Chief Petty Officer; [pers.] The river of life can be turbulent, swift, or stagnant. You can float along and not be involved or you can swim and live life instead of life living you.; [a.] Honolulu, HI

PIERCE, KATIE
[b.] July 25; Athens, OH; [p.] Lily and Late Luster, Pierce Josephe Willison (current Dad); [ed.] Briggs High

POPELY, HELEN I.
[b.] April 8, 1918; Traveskyn, PA; [p.] Vincent and Barbara Egry; [m.] Julius Popley (Deceased); August 14, 1943; [ch.] William (dec.), Ronald, Richard; [ed.] Ligonier High, PA; Lakeland College, WI (B.A., Eng.), French Studies - France, Quebec, USA; [occ.] (Ret.) School Teacher, 27 years Calumet Park, IL (Jr. High); [memb.] Enr. Program for Gifted Children; Jr. High Natl. Hon. Soc. Comm., PTA Board, Elected to Local School Board (8 yrs.), Amer. Assoc. Teachers of French, Chicago Chapter; [hon.] Scholarship to University of Deb Recen, Hungary (1939), exc. publicity work local PTA Chicago; [oth.writ.] Press releases to local news papers for home church, original articles for monthly church publication, numerous poems and a few children's plays never submitted anywhere, feature writer for college newspaper; [pers.] We owe it to ourselves and to society to do the best we can with what we have been given, be it talents or material wealth, etc., and share what we have or know with others.; [a.] Calumet Park, IL

POSSESSKY, KAREN
[b.] Edward and MaryLou Possessky; [ed.] BA in English and Sociology from Clemson University; [occ.] Social Work, Graduate Student at University of Pittsburgh (full-time); [memb.] Delta Delta Delta; [a.] Pittsburgh, PA

POUND, CHEYRL KAY
[b.] July 24, 1944; Prague, OK; [p.] Ernest and Kathleen Ogburn; [m.] Virgil Pound; February 24, 1963; [ch.] Schelley, Renee and Marty; [ed.] Northwest Nazarene College; [occ.] Homemaker; [memb.] Church of the Nazarene; [a.] Issaquatt, WA

PRASHAD, TIFFANY M.
[b.] December 17, 1983; New York; [p.] Gopall (father), Rookmin (mother); [ed.] George Gershwin Jr. High, Franklin K. Lane H.S.; [occ.] Student; [oth.writ.] Several poem put in Jr. High Year book; [pers.] I am inspired by what I see and how I interpret it.; [a.] Brooklyn, NY

PROEHL, VICKI
[b.] March 16, 1983; Waseca, MN; [p.] John and Denise Proehl; [ed.] 8th Grade; [occ.] Student; [memb.] Waseca Christian Assembly Youth Group. School Band; [pers.] A friend of mine commited suicide back in May 27, 1997. It just goes to show how fragile our lives are.; [a.] Waseca, MN

PUTMAN, JERRY D.
[b.] December 22, 1952; Monroe, LA; [p.] Lifford and Louise Putman; [ch.] Jared Michael Putman; [ed.] Graduated Oak Grove High School - 1971; [occ.] Office Manager Cox Funeral Home; [memb.] VFW Post 3977- Oakgrove, LA; [oth.writ.] Have written 14 other poems, none submitted or published; [pers.] Oakgrove, LA

QUAST, ELIZABETH
[b.] January 23, 1984; Le Sueur, MN; [p.] John and Cynthia Quast; [ed.] Currently attending Sibley

East Jr. High School (7th grade, 1996-1997) [occ.] Student; [memb.] An Alumna of the People to People Student Ambassador Program (1997), Trumpet Player for School Band, Youth League of Zion Lutheran Church; [hon.] (1996) President Clinton's Outstanding Academic Achievement Award, Peer Tutor at Sibley East Jr. High, Certificate of Commendation from Governor Arne Carlson for the D.A.R.E. Program, Letterman pin for being on the "A" Honor Roll three times in 1996-1997 1997 MN Academic for Excellence Foundation Award; [a.] Henderson, MN

QUICK, JOHN H.
[b.] October 18, 1951; Sault Ste Marie, MI; [p.] John and Evelyn Quick; [m.] Joni Quick; April 6, 1974; [ch.] Sara Quick; [ed.] BS Computer Science, College of Engineering, Arizona State University MS Systems Management, Institute of Systems and Safety Management, University of Southern California; [occ.] Programmer / Analyst and University of Maryland Graduate / Undergraduate Computer Science Instructor; [memb.] IEEE Computer Society American Computing Machinery American Mathematical Association; [hon.] Outstanding Loving Man of America 1986; [pers.] "Sometimes a person has to go a very long distance out of his way to come back a short distance correctly."—The Zoo Story, by Edward Albee; [a.] APO, AE

QUIGGINS, LARRY P.
[pen.] Bug; [b.] January 6, 1962; St Louis, MO; [pers.] The world is a complex place, filled with complex creatures. It's too bad that they can't all get along and work together. Life happens only once.; [a.] St. Charles, MO

RAHMAN, MUKLESUR
[b.] March 1, 1960; Sylhet, Bangladesh; [p.] Haji Abdus Salam and Kulsuma Begum; [m.] Rehana Yeasmin Choudhury; February 5, 1988; [ch.] Syeed Ahmed Nabil and Jerin Tasnim; [ed.] B.A. (honors), M.A. (Philosophy) from Dhaka University, Dhaka, Bangladesh; [occ.] Espresso Bar Manager, New York City, NY, former Lecturer, Moinuddin Women's College, Sylhet, B'desh; [memb.] Jatiyo Party, a national political party of Bangladesh and Bangladesh College Association; [oth.writ.] Several poems were published, one book of poems "Calls in Conscience are Heard" and a book of articles "Progressive Awareness Expressed in Intimate Moments" were published in Bangladesh; [pers.] Indulgence in soul searching stimulates me to write for my "self". So to say, my literary pursuits are devoted to my self-satisfaction. Satisfaction consists in creation. I search for my soul in plurality that embodies society and life. The dream of a beautiful world and pious wish for the wellbeing of the mankind make me a creator in imagination.; [a.] New York, NY

RANDOLPH, CHEILON
[b.] January 28, 1978; Detroit, MI; [p.] Timothy Randolph, Gay Randolph; [ed.] Oak Park High, Wayne State University; [memb.] was Member of Health Occupation Students of America (HOSA); [pers.] My poems are a reflection of me and everything around me. They come from within my soul.; [a.] Oak Park, MI

RAUTON, PHYLLIS K.
[b.] September 6, 1944; Charleston, SC; [p.] Joe and Edna Prather; [m.] Mel Rauton, Sr.; February 25, 1964; [ch.] Mel, Jr., Melinda, Jay; [ed.] Grad. Gordon H. Garrett High School 1962, attended Univ. of Georgia '62-'64 Grad. College of Charleston 1975; [occ.] Sec-Treas. Melcer Tile Co., Inc; [memb.] Dorchester Waylyn Baptist Church, Member of "The Charleston Flappers" (Dance group to preserve the "Charleston"), Member Lowcousty Model "A" and AACA Clubs; [hon.] Performed on Today Show with Charleston Flap-

pers, was Salutations of High School Class; [oth.writ.] Many more, most are personal-Love never tried to let anyone but friends and family read. Two poems were read at funerals (one at Dad's, one at a dear friends); [pers.] My poetry allows me to release what's in my heart. Usually when I write I am inspired or deeply moved by something or someone. For me "Things of the heart" are expressed better on paper.; [a.] Charleston, SC

RAY, HILLOL
[pen.] Hillol Ray, Hee Ray (means Diamond); [b.] Calcutta, India; [p.] Nibaran Chandra and Angur Lata Ray; [m.] Manjusree Ray; December 7, 1981; [ch.] Brian, Ryan; [ed.] MS Environmental Engg, North Dakota State Univ., BS Civil Engg, Univ of Calcutta, India; [occ.] Environmental Engineer, US EPA, Dallas TX; [memb.] American Assn. for the Advancement of Science, etc.; [hon.] Who's Who in APAC (Asian Pacific American Community), Personal recognition from Francine Cousteau of The Cousteau Society, Inc. in France, etc.; [oth.writ.] poems published in NLP anthologies; [pers.] Often we ignore the long term effects of our inner peace to cherish the material possessions for a short term on earth.; [a.] Garland, TX

REED, HELEN
[pen.] Minnie Harvery

RENFRO, KHRYSTAN PAGE
[pen.] Panther Moon, The Stream; [b.] April 14, 1967; Springfield, IL; [m.] Michael Stella; October 18, 1997; [ed.] Graduate of Sacred Heart Academy; [occ.] Medical Records Coordinator Professional Natural Bodybuilder; [memb.] WNBF, World Natural Bodybuilding Federation, Professional Bodybuilder; [hon.] 1989 IL Body building champion, 1995 Pro-World Natural Top Ten Finisher, 1997 Pro MS. International Natural Championships. Placed in the top ten; [oth.writ.] Sunday's Pain—published summer of 1994 in Poetic Voices of America, Sparrowgrass anthology, Feature writer, For Midwest Muscle Bodybuilding magazine, out of Baraboo WI; [pers.] A job is done when a poet can touch the spirit of a stranger, by leaving their words inside that person's soul. It is then I know... that I have left my truest reflections, somewhere etched deep within the soul I wished to tap.; [a.] Framingham, MA

RHODES, RYAN W.
[b.] January 19, 1976; Salt Lake City, UT; [p.] Alick Rhodes, Renee Rhodes; [ed.] West Jordan High, Life; [occ.] U.S. Army Infantryman; [oth.writ.] Passion Hidden, How to Bring a Heart About, Light Shadows, Softly Sleeping (not yet published); [pers.] May water never flow thicker than blood.; [a.] West Jordan, UT

RICHARDSON II, PAUL JOSEPH
[pen.] Malacca; [b.] February 4, 1970; Houston, TX; [p.] Bonnie Lockwood; [ch.] Alan and Austin; [ed.] UNC, UNF, Naval NFAS, NNPS, ANO NPTU; [occ.] Student, Network Specialist PGA Nat'l Hdqtrs; [memb.] Ren and Stimpy Fan Club, Premed Society, UNF; [hon.] NC Chancellors Scholar, UNC, Gulf War and other service medals; [oth.writ.] Essays on Epistemology, Sexual Psychology, Anthropology, and lots of Poetry; [pers.] I want to know who the real 'Me' is.; [a.] Jacksonville, FL

RICKARD, KENNETH K.
[pen.] Ken and Kenny; [d.] June 21, 1922; Schoharie; [p.] Silas and Edith Rickard; [m.] Virginia M. Rickard (died April 14, 1997); September 5, 1942; [ch.] 2; [ed.] High School—graduated in 1941 from Schoharie Central School; [occ.] Retired; [memb.] B.M.I; [hon.] Member of International Poetry Hall of Fame October 1, 1996; Brenda Lee gave me award in '82 Kentucky Fried Chicken contest; [oth.writ.] I write 6 kinds of music. I love country and gospel.

RIGGS, JULIE
[b.] February 27, 1981; Elizabethtown, Kentucky; [p.] Martha and Cotton Riggs; [ed.] Larue County High School; [occ.] Student; [pers.] God has given me the gift of being able to turn my personal experiences into writing that come not only from my mind, but my heart as well; [a.] Hodgenville, KY

RILEY, RACHAEL
[b.] May 24, 1979; Mariemont, OH; [p.] James and Barbara Riley; [ed.] High School Diploma Bethel Tate, Kathleen Wellman Modeling Diploma; [hon.] Varsity Cheerleader—3 years cheered in Macy's Day Parade; Cheerleading Scholarship to Tiffin University; [oth.writ.] I write all the time yet never took the steps to publish any pieces, besides this one. I plan to start though. My love is with writing; I plan to try and go all the way with it.; [pers.] I am greatly moved by passionate writings; Shakespeare is a personal favorite. "In all writing my mind, my emotion, must move my pen. . . .", [a.] Hamersville, ON

RITTER, FRED D.
[b.] January 26, 1972; Flint, MI; [p.] William Ritter/Shirley Collins; [ed.] Clio High; [occ.] Warehouse Opperative; [pers.] I want my writings to reflect love and emotion not noticed merely on the surface, but felt deep from within, where the truest beauty lies.; [a.] Folsom, CA

RIVERA, JULIE
[b.] September 23, 1978; Brooklyn, NY; [p.] Elba Iris Figueroa (Mother); [ed.] City-As-School in Manhattan, Freshman At Brooklyn College; [hon.] Two Leadership Awards, An all-credit Award. Master of Ceremonies in H.S. Graduation; [oth.writ.] Poem Written and read at Graduation, an autobiographical excerpt of my life written for a scholarship, (Didn't get it, but it didn't hurt to try!), wrote a children's play for J.H.S.; [pers.] All my writing is based on what I observe of myself, other people and my personal experiences growing up: the good, the bad and the totally insane. It helps me discover my fears, faults, battles and my accomplishments as a Hispanic, a female and a teenager. Writing is my therapy.; [a.] Brooklyn, NY

ROBINSON, LILY
[b.] November 23, 1984; Atlanta, GA; [p.] Sue and Lewis Robinson; [ed.] Wesleyan School; [hon.] Honor Roll; [oth.writ.] I have written quite a few poems and stories, which have been published in our school magazine.; [a.] Atlanta, GA

RODRIGUEZ, ADRIAN
[pen.] Mr. Sisco; [b.] May 18, 1974; El Paso, TX; [p.] Maria and Jesus Rodriguez; [m.] Maria Luisa Lopez; March 18, 1995; [ch.] Matthew Angel, Mark Anthony; [ed.] Riverside High; [occ.] Shuttle Driver Hampton Intercontinental; [oth.writ.] "Aztec Valentine Dream", "A Chicano Rhyme", "I Do Love You", "Guess Who", "Am I Dreaming", "Two The Point", "I Sing", "Tupac R.I.P.", "Baby I'm For Real"; [pers.] "I'm just a soul who's intensions are good, Oh Lord please don't let me be misunderstood."; [a.] Houston, TX

ROSALES, ROSE
[pen.] Marie; [b.] April 18, 1971; Corpus Christi, TX; [p.] Yolanda Plancarte; [m.] Jesse Gonzales; [ch.] Mark, Daniel, Johnny; [a.] Corpus Christi, TX

ROSE, CAROL
[b.] June 7, 1940; Oakland, CA; [m.] William R. Rose; February 6, 1965; [ch.] None; [ed.] B.A.-University of Oregon Graduate Work-Univ. of Oregon, S. OR. Unive. and Univ. of Colorado; [occ.] Former High School Teacher; presently: Artist, Writer, Poet; [oth.writ.] Autobiography, other poetry; [pers.] The cultural arts are one of the leading avenues for enlightenment and understanding. Art, in all its wide-ranging aspects, is the province of every human being. It is simply a matter of beginning and doing. When the artist, inside of us, nurtured and alive, whatever the effort or work may be, that special person becomes an inventive, searching, caring, self-expressive creature.; [a.] Medford, OR

ROSE, PHILIP
[ed.] Boston College (BA) Syracuse University (MS); [occ.] Counselor and Teacher; [oth.writ.] I write a regular column on men's issues for our local newspaper and I've written a number of workbooks and educational pieces for adult new readers; [pers.] I'm a musician, a parent and a husband. I was raised Irish Catholic and now on a deep spiritual and emotional journey. All these things inform and shape my poetry.; [a.] Syracuse, NY

ROSS JR., WILLIAM J.
[b.] February 23, 1967; Manayunk; [p.] William and Anne Ross; [ed.] I have attended "The Walnut Street Threatre School" and study acting under Actors Studio Veteran Sidney Kaye currently; [occ.] Struggling Actor Returning to School in fall; [memb.] "Walnut Street Theatre" "The Neighborhood Playhouse School of the Theatre - phila"; [hon.] Journalism Award from Royborough High School, was published in school paper, also once in Phila. Daily News; [oth.writ.] I've written many poems and songs off and on since age 15 "Mind Healer", "Born Blind", and "What I Expected" are among my proudest efforts; [pers.] I am influenced by my surroundings and relationships, from which I draw my greatest inspiration. I am told Elisabeth Barrett Browing was a cousin of my great, great grandmother Loise Barrett Maxwell.; [a.] Philadelphia, PA

ROWLAND, JESSICA
[pen.] Junior Chatman; [b.] July 14, 1982; Petersburg, VA; [p.] Vicki and Wade Rowland; [ed.] Greensville County High School; [occ.] Student at Greenville County High School; [memb.] High Hills Baptist Church, Greensville/Emporia 4-H Livestock Program; [hon.] 1st place in a high school poetry contest, a poem published in the Anthology of Poetry by Young Americans; [oth.writ.] Poems in school and local newspaper; [pers.] If you believe in yourself and work hard, anything is possible.; [a.] Jarratt, VA

ROY, CANDICE LYNN
[pen.] Candice L. Roy; [b.] May 24, 1983; Cincinnati, OH; [p.] Jeff Roy, Teresa Roy; [ed.] Carthage Elementary, Central Baptist School, and Mason Middle School; [hon.] Different academic awards from school; [oth.writ.] A small story book that was published in my school library, Central Baptist. Other writings that were done in and for school; [pers.] My favorite writings are those which the topics move me deeply. I find it easier to write about things that bother me.; [a.] Mason, OH

ROZELL, SONYA
[b.] March 25, 1974; Lexington, MS; [p.] Calvin Ramsy; [m.] Daniel Bailey; February 14, 1997; [ch.] Schantia Bailey; [ed.] McClain High School Tougaloo College; [occ.] Telecommunications and Data Entry; [memb.] Eastern Star, American Heart Assoc.; [hon.] Salutatorian of High School Class; [pers.] I never thought in a million years that a poem of mine would actually go this far. Thanks to my husband I got that chance to see.; [a.] Baton Rouge, LA

RUHL, MARTHA W.
[b.] February 22, 1929; Rexmont, PA; [p.] Isabella and Michael Keath; [m.] Allen H. Ruhl; June 30, 1951; [ch.] 1 daughter and 2 sons; [ed.] 12 year Graduate Cornwall High School; [occ.] Housewife; [memb.] Harmony United Methodist Church—Lay Leader, in Pastor's Absence I present the sermons; [pers.] I just love to write poetry that rhymes, mostly. I like to write special day poetry: Mother's Day, Father's Day, Easter and Christmas, etc.; [a.] Elverson, PA

SANTULLANO, MICK LAN
[pen.] Michael; [b.] May 21, 1957; [p.] Dr. Michael and Phyllis; [ch.] Matthew; [ed.] Northern Illinois University. Shimer College Waukegan. IL; Bachelor of Science in Political science and Psychology; [occ.] Qualified Mental Returdation Professional; [oth.writ.] Whole Science Value Theory (Shimer College Express) Trailblzer (Hilltop Records Hollywood CA.); [pers.] I've many different length stories...to songs, sociological essays...to poems, aimed towards advancement inspiration, excitement, healing and delight. With the right exposure I will.; [a.] Wauconda, IL

SAPORITO, JOANN M.
[pen.] Joann Morgan; [b.] November 28, 1930; Sikeston, MO; [p.] Walter and Stella White; [m.] William Morgan; July 31, 1949; [ch.] Jane Morgan DiBiasio, M.A., Capt. Deborah S. Morgan, USAF; [ed.] B.E. plus graduate study; [occ.] Retired from GTE; [memb.] Bible Study Teacher, American Arthritis Fnd., Pinellas County Poets Council; [hon.] Community Leaders and Noteworthy Americans 1976-1977, Honorary acknowledgement for teaching classes for GED testing in inner-city deprived areas; [oth.writ.] Poems published in newspapers magazines and religious-affiliated papers; [pers.] I try to reflect that perseverence in a goodly and worthwhile endeavor will be beneficial to self and others, and when we are gone others will know we passed this way.; [a.] Clearwater, FL

SARGEANT, ANGELA M.
[pen.] Angie Sargeant; [b.] October 6, 1968; Columbus, OH; [p.] Charlese Teresa Satterfield; [m.] William David Sargeant; May 15, 1992; [ch.] Kesha, Kolte Hannah; [ed.] South Hopkins, High School, Madisonville Health Technology Center, Madisoville Vocational Technical School; [occ.] X-Ray Technologist; [memb.] ASRT; [oth.writ.] "Hidden Memories; [pers.] Thank God for this blessing, Treasure each moment as if it where your last. Take time to notice the little things about the one you love, Be patient when things don't go your way. Don't take for granted the love God gave you. Most important, be aware of the moments that are becoming. Memories right before your eyes!; [a.] Murray, KY

SCALES, RUSSELL
[b.] June 25, 1973; Middletown, NY; [p.] Thomas and Julie Scales; [ed.] Marywood University Wallen Paupack High School; [occ.] Freelance Writer; [hon.] Dean's List 1st Honors; [oth.writ.] Film Treatment, televesion, script, radio, and TV commercials; [a.] Tafton, PA

SCHLUNDT, GORDON DEAN
[pen.] Dean Gordon; [b.] May 19, 1934; Indiana; [ch.] Cindi, Dau; [occ.] Retired; [memb.] I.S.P, T.I.P, Hall of Fame; [hon.] Eleven Consecutive Ed. Choice Awards, NLP, Grand Prize Winner - Through Sun And Shower Anthology 1997; [oth.writ.] Songs, Magazine, Articles, Various Newspapers, (Local); [pers.] Who can say what Science and Technology will achieve in the next 100 years? Cryogenics may indeed become perfected enough to be a viable reality for mankind.; [a.] Mattoon, IL

SCHMIDT, VICTORIA
[b.] July 19, 1908; St. Louis, MO; [p.] Gottfried Schmidt and Anna Christine (Juenger) Schmidt; [ed.] AB Harris Teachers College, St. Louis 1929, MA Columbia U., NY, NY 1930, Ed. U. Colorado, Boulder, Colorado 1952; [occ.] Teacher St. Louis Public Schools 1929-1948, Professor Harris Teachers College 1949-1978, Professor Emeritus Harris-Stowe College, Primary Candidate US Congress from St. Louis 1974, 76, 78, Primary candidate MO State Representative 1980, Traveling and Writing, Retired School Employees of St. Louis,

Parliamentarian; [memb.] Library of Congress Associates, International Society of Poets, American Museum of Natural History, Explorers Club, Smithsonian Institute; [oth.writ.] Victoria's Story - Reincarnation - God's Love Returned, Vantage Press 1992, Bible Stories from Heaven, MS 1979, More Victoria's Story, MS, Poem - Matrix of Our Lives 1995, Poem- Life-Death 1996, Peom- Time 1996, Poem- Lament 1995; [pers.] Have traveled all over the world including all five continents and both polar regions. Survived plane crash and two train wrecks. Each day is a special gift to be lived fully. My writings carry a message to the world.; [a.] St. Louis, MO

SELPH, WILLIAM
[b.] November 30, 1958; Miami, FL; [p.] John Selp and Jane Selph; [m.] Jane Watson; August 14, 1989; [ch.] Carlton A. III, Angela Mann; [ed.] Morris Knolls High New Jersey; [occ.] Iron Worker, Mogensen Steel Erectors Inc. Cedar Rapids NE; [hon.] Purple Heart, Silver Star, 3 Presidential Clusters; [pers.] If was looking through the eyes of an angel, those eyes would belong to Hazel Paul.; [a.] Rowan, IA

SFAKIANOS, MICHELE
[b.] July 9, 1962; Homestead, FL; [p.] Pat Banister and Mary M. Banister; [m.] John Sfakianos; July 27, 1996; [ch.] Jenna Moore, Jason Moore [ed.] In Computer Programming and in Nursing; [occ.] Registered Nurse; [oth.writ.] "Returning to Work" 1997 Nursing Spectrum Magzine; [pers.] I love to write from the heart, to express suppressed feelings.; [a.] Homestead, FL

SHANK, DAVID
[b.] December 18, 1982; Hagerstown, MD; [p.] Reverend David and Cindy Shank; [ed.] Orems Elementary, Baltimore, MD. Stemmers Run Middle School, Balt. MD. Baker Middle School, Damascus High School, Damascus, MD; [occ.] Student; [memb.] National Jr. Honor Society Member, Youth Council, Montgomery United Methodist Church; [hon.] Inducted into National Jr. Honor Society, 1995, Writer of the Year, Baker Middle School, 1996, Honors Classes, Honor Roll, Elementary, Middle and High School; [pers.] I strive to better myself every day in every way. My writings reflect my personal feelings and emotions, most of which are centered upon the American Experience 1860 to the present.; [a.] Damascus, MD

SHELTON, NICOLE
[b.] September 20, 1982; Fort Worth, TX; [p.] Rhonda Baker; [ed.] 8th grade, going to 9th; [hon.] A honor roll, perfect attendance, solo/ensemble; [oth.writ.] "Hello" also published, and many more unpublished.; [pers.] I love to read Edgar Allen Poe, and began writing poetry in 6th grade.; [a.] Springtown, TX

SIMON, PATRICIA A.
[pen.] Patricia A. Simon; [b.] May 11, 1943; Harford Co., MD; [p.] William L. and Hilda M. Wilson; [m.] Roger Simon; June 24, 1961; [ch.] Jeffrey Scott; [ed.] North Harford High School, Ruth's School of Beauty Culture; [occ.] Bookeeper for Roger Simon and Sons Paving Co.; [memb.] Upper Crossroads Baptist Church, Arthritis Foundation; [oth.writ.] Church and school newsletters have published several of my poems.; [pers.] I believe there to be much beauty in this lifetime. We only need to take time to find it. Many of my writings are of things I see or think I see.; [a.] Jarrettsville, MD

SMALL, ELDOREEN E.
[pen.] Eldoreen Small; [b.] August 23, 1952; Barbados, WI; [p.] Eustace Small, Clarice Small; [ch.] O'Neale Small, died March 22, 1993, Laura May Small; [ed.] Trent's Secondary High, Metropolitan High School, Medgar Evers College (CUNY); [occ.]

Home Health Aide, Substitute Paraprofessional; [memb.] Member of Mount Zion Tabernacle Choir, Treasurer for the Sunday School Dept. and a Sunday School Teacher; [oth.writ.] None that was published; [pers.] I express my feelings by putting my thoughts on paper in words. I am a romantic at heart and I sometimes feel what others are feelings and I put actions into words.; [a.] Brooklyn, NY

SMART, PHYLLIS
[b.] November 7; Brockton, MA; [pers.] Days of darkness may seem endless, but it is a fact that the sun eventually will shine.; [a.] Brockton, MA

SMITH, AMY J.
[b.] October 31, 1983; Houston, TX; [p.] Tim and Le Ann Smith; [ed.] 8th Grade, Monroe Middle School; [occ.] Student; [memb.] Mount Olive Lutheran Church, Show Choir at Monroe Middle School; [hon.] Monroe Middle School Honor Roll, Presidential Physician Fitness Award; [oth.writ.] Other poems written for family and friends; [pers.] I write from my heart and put my feelings into my poetry.; [a.] Green River, WY

SMITH, BEVERLY A.
[pers.] That God loves us no matter how the world proceeds us, because it's God, not the world, that has made us, so when you see yourself, see God and truly enough will be enough.; [a.] Lauderdale Lakes, FL

SMITH, JOHN E.
[b.] November 16, 1969; Coaterville, PA; [p.] William and Valiree Smith; [m.] Lisa Smith; September 15, 1995; [ed.] Coatesville Area Senior High (Cash) Medix/Rets Medical Asst. U.S. Army 1993-1996 U. of Chicago German; [oth.writ.] I have a lot of poems which are my secrets to my strength, courage and the beautiful places, people and things I experimented in my life and a closeness with my greatest listeners my wife (Lisa) and God.; [pers.] When through human eyes all that is beautiful is even more beautiful through Jesus's eyes.

SMITH, PAULA MARIE
[b.] March 1, 1962; St. Louis, MO; [p.] Paul and Barbara Robinson; [m.] Russell Keith Smith; June 3, 1989; [ch.] Shanon Marie LaBrot and Jason Keith Smith; [ed.] Grammar: Lafayette - St. Louis MO; High School - Melville Sr. High MO; [occ.] Work for Eagles Club; [memb.] Fraternal Order of Eagles #4231; [oth.writ.] My writings are pure and heartfelt. God and my family give me my words for us little people. Thank you Lord.; [a.] Mammoth Spring, AR

SNELL, KATHY
[b.] October 3, 1982; Memphis, TN; [p.] Larry and Sharon Snell; [ed.] Went to elementary school at Immanuel Lutheran, going to high school at Cordova; [pers.] I don't usually write. But when I do its usually about one of my dreams of becoming an actress.; [a.] Atoka, TN

SNYDER, BONITA L.
[b.] July 18, 1961; Camp Springs, MD; [p.] William and Edith Hocker; [m.] Milton M. Snyder; June 16, 1984; [ch.] Cody Robert, Cheryl Lynn; [ed.] Thomas Stone High School, Charles County Community College; [occ.] Artist/Sculptor; [memb.] Victorious Tabernacle; [a.] Union Bridge, MD

SPARKS, CARMEN
[b.] May 12, 1981; Fort Smith, AR; [p.] Paul Sparks and Rita Hogan; [pers.] This is written for a very special person, whom I will always love and admire, the one who inspired me.; [a.] Fort Smith, AR

SPOHN, DENA M.
[b.] June 30, 1958; Stanbaugh, MI; [p.] Russell and Kathleen Hepler; [m.] (former) George E. Spohn III; June 29, 1977; [ch.] Shaun, George, Jennifer, and Michael; [ed.] Pardeeville, WI, Portage Turner HS Portage, WI, Clovis Community College, Clovis, NM (Assoc. Arts May '96); [occ.] Homemaker/

student; [oth.writ.] "The Tower" a short story published in the fall 1995 anthology, New Mexico English Journal; a few poems, published in my hometown newspaper, as an adolescent; [pers.] I greatly appreciate those, poets who are not afraid to be unconventional and who can express a wide range of emotions. My favorite poet is Sylvia Plath.; [a.] Clovis, NM

SPRAGUE, BETTIE
[b.] July 13, 1946; Elkin, NC; [p.] William and Mary Todd; [ch.] Marie, Chris, Debbie, Rene, Sion, Deborah; [ed.] Sparta High, Bee Country Col., Dobson College, Duke, Baylor, I hold a degree in applied science; [occ.] Environmentalist; [memb.] National Beta Society forward by Faith Missons; [hon.] NBS for Outstanding Character and achievement; [oth.writ.] "Our Disposable Society"; [pers.] I strive to help others see and appreciate the beauty and wonder of themselves and the world around them. I have been influenced by living close to nature.; [a.] Souderton, PA

SPRAQUE, ROXANNA JEAN
[pen.] Roxanna J. Spraque; [b.] September 18, 1942; Klameth Falls, OR; [p.] Dr. Boyd F. Spraque, Georgiana Spraque; [ed.] BA, MA, Phd; [occ.] Special Education, High School; [memb.] Phi Kappa Phi and Association for Supervision and Curriculum Development (ASCD); [hon.] "Thanks to Teachers Excellence Award" Designing Curriculum for State, WA and National Level; [oth.writ.] Letters to the President about Educational Concerns; [pers.] As my loving mother always told me, "Never lose sight of your Jack Rabbit." We must keep your eyes focused on our goals if we are able to obtain them.; [a.] Sacramento, CA

SPROAT, JAMES C.
[pen.] Jim Sproat; [b.] June 27, 1982; Richmond, IN; [p.] Saundra Huelsman, Jim Sproat; [ed.] Irm O High; [occ.] Student; [oth.writ.] No others published; [pers.] Love lasts forever; if you find true love, never let it go.; [a.] Columbia, SC

STAFFORD, DARLENE P.
[pen.] Pennie Nichels; [b.] April 23, 1931; Alexandria, MN; [p.] Ronald J. and Ethel Pennie; [m.] Col. H. Carlisle Stafford, Jr; September 2, 1982; [ch.] David and Zonia Nichelson; [ed.] MBC Professional College, Emory University, Candler School of Theology; [occ.] Hospice Executive Director; [memb.] National Assoc. of Female Executives, Business and Professional Women, Contact International, Peale Center for Living Hospice of Northeast Georgia; [hon.] Teacher of Year, Certified Counselor Service Resolution Services Award; [oth.writ.] Pigeon - Holes Vagabond Mind; [pers.] Christ is the beginning, center and completion of my life. Family and friends are the bonus.; [a.] Clarkesville, GA

STAFFORD, STACIE M.
[b.] July 23, 1974; Piqua, OH; [p.] Onie L. Stafford; [ed.] Grad JHS; [occ.] Wendy's (fast food); [oth.writ.] A song "If My Heart Could Talk It Would Be Arrested"; [pers.] I come from a single parent home. I go to Zion Baptist Church. Music is my first love—it has been a dream of mine to write professionally, and to be a songwriter and musician professionally as well. I also graduated from Troy High School.; [a.] Troy, OH

STAFMAN, ED
[b.] January 9, 1954; Key West, FL; [p.] George and Marilyn Stafman; [m.] Beth Lee; July 14, 1984; [ch.] Laura, Logan; [ed.] H.S. - Brooklyn Technical H.S. (1971), S.U.N.Y. at Stony Brook, B.S. 1975, Florida State Univ. College of Law, T.D., 1977; [occ.] Criminal Defense Attorney

STASEVICH, LESA S.
[pen.] Elles; [b.] November 2, 1941; Troy, NY; [p.] Agnes and Lee Simonds; [m.] Michael Stasevich;

May 14, 1982; [ch.] Daughter, Tracy Brower; [ed.] Saratoga Springs, High School 1958, Saratoga Springs, NY, State University of NY, Plattsburg, BS Ed 1962; [occ.] Retired November 96 Early El. and Spec. Ed. teacher; title 1 reading Veterinarian Assistant and Breed and Raise own Arabian Horses; [memb.] NEA (National Ed. Assoc.), MEA; [hon.] Kappa Delta Pi (honors) Graduate 1962 Cum Laude; [oth.writ.] Many unpolished, unpublished; [pers.] My writings are inspired by the beauty and wonders of the natural world, animals, children and personal experiences.; [a.] Fennville, MI

STEIN, ERICA LYNN
[p.] Erica Jasmine; [b.] January 29, 1970; Long Island, NY; [p.] Arlene and Alvin Stein; [m.] Involved with Steven Eriksen; April 4, 1997; [ed.] New School For Social Research; [occ.] Web Site Designer/Creator Http: Home, earthlink, net/ 2ric3is my page; [oth.writ.] Published by C/Net the computer company - web-site reviews. First place winner for fictional short story on America Online, pursuing a carrer as a writer. Also fiction for humorous web-pages; [pers.] I believe to try because if you don't, you'll never know. I dislike car accidents, but I love new experiences. I love my two cats dearly, and Steve, my boyfriend.; [a.] Massapequa Park, NY

STEPHEN, FLORA
[b.] May 22, 1907; Manila, P.I; [p.] Alton and Grace Hall (deceased) [m.] Lawrence R. Stephen (deceased); August 10, 1929 (married 54 yrs); [ch.] (3) Flora Homan, Joan Clements, Lawrence A. Stephen, 7 Grandchildren, 5 Great Grandchildren; [ed.] Elementary School-Bishop CA Linfield Col. Prep-McMinville OR Graduated from San Jose State Teacher's Col. San Jose, CA (now SJ state University) (Went on to each all 8 grades in a one room schoolhouse); [occ.] At age 90, a homemaker; [memb.] First United Methodist Church-SJ CA. United Methodist Women, Women's Group of Montevalle, WILPF (Women's Int'nl League for Peace and Freedom), San Jose State University Alumni (I support many other groups); [hon.] None that stand out except that perhaps it was an "honor" to be the first white baby born on the Island of Manila in the P.I. as my father was a Missionary teacher there. Awards: Well, one that I remember (but that that I worked hard to achieve) was my Private Pilots License-at age 63; [oth.writ.] Many poems and verses written for family and friends and for my "memory" book. This-my 2nd to be published my 1st was in a book of poems and short stories "Lady of the Lake" by Jackie Hall; [pers.] I have a deep and abiding love for my God, and my family. I cherish my family, my friends, and all of God's creations. I enjoy my flower garden with the squirrels and the many kinds of birds that visit me there.; [a.] Scotts Valley, CA

STERNBERG, CLAUDETTE F.
[pen.] Claudette Sternburg; [b.] March 16, 1937; Louisville, KY; [p.] Mr. and Mrs. Joseph Fante; [m.] Robert A. Sternberg; November 24, 1960; [ch.] Scott J. and Joseph A.; [ed.] B.A. Degree, Cum Laude Ursuline College, Louisville, KY; Majors: Elem. Ed. and Social Science; Minor: Philosophy; [occ.] Housewife; [memb.] Corpus Christi Church, Newman Center, Tampa Palms Ladies Club, Original New Tampan Grads, Hospice Auxilliary, Friends of the New Tampan Regional Library; [hon.] Who's Who in American Colleges 1954 and 1955, Kappa Gamma Pi Honorary Society, AAUW; [oth.writ.] Recently 30 original poems and many meditations; [pers.] I write poetry to express my inner feelings and others seem to relate to those same reactions. "Locked in the Positive" was inspired by my husband's 5 year fight against Leukemia.; [a.] Lutz, FL

STEWART JR., JAMES G.
[pen.] Jim Stewart Jr.; [b.] December 9, 1956; Camp LeJuene; [p.] Jim Sr, Mary C. Stewart; [ch.]

James G Stewart III, Jennifer Remee; [ed.] GED DeVry and 126 credits towards B.S; [occ.] Disabled (broke back in 1986); [memb.] NRA, St. Michael and All Angels Episcopal Church; [hon.] National Defense Medal (USN 1974) and Dean's List at DeVry; [oth.writ.] A couple in small-town papers, inclusions in a half dozen books with The National Library of Poetry as well as in 2 books through Sparrowgrass Poetry Forum; [pers.] My poetic endevors are generally inspired by portions of my life, both negative and positive.; [a.] Phoenix, AZ

STRICKLAND, JENNIFER
[pen.] Jenny Lynn; April 17, 1983; St. Mary's, OH; [p.] Ken Strickland, Kim Strickland; [ed.] St. Mary's Memorial High School; [occ.] High School Student; [memb.] St. Paul's United Church of Christ, 4-H Club, Naylor Dancers Competition Team, MHS Majorettes; [hon.] Honor Roll Student, Midwest Talent Search Participant, Outstanding Scolastic Achievement Award; [oth.writ.] First place winner in district and regional power of the pen writing competitions, poems published in magazines and bulletins; [pers.] Writing is not only a past time, but therapy for me. My pen and paper provide an outlet for every feeling. "Shoot for the moon, and if you don't make it, you'll still be a star."; [a.] St. Mary's, OH

STRINGFELLOW, AARON J.
[b.] May 12, 1982; Washington, DC; [p.] Vera Jackson-Stringfellow; [ed.] 10th grade, St. Alban's [occ.] Student; [memb.] Nat'l Mathematics Assoc.; [hon.] Science Fair first place/ 8th grade - School Univ. District of Columbia - Yes Program; [a.] Cheverly, MD

SUDERS, JOSEPH S.
[pen.] Josef Anthony; [b.] February 2, 1959; Altoona, PA; [p.] Richard E. and Clementine T. Suders; [m.] Young S. (Lee) Suders; July 2, 1987; [ch.] Crystal J.J., Michael, Aaron, Hanali; [ed.] H.S. Graduate; [occ.] Building Materials Sales Associate, also U.S. Army Retired; [oth.writ.] Several poems over the past 20 years; [pers.] My goal is to publish a book of my poems and other stories so that others may enjoy, live and learn from them. "The best is yet to come to be, from thee."; [a.] York Haven, PA

SULLIVAN, DEBORAH D.
[pen.] Debbie; [b.] March 4, 1964; Nashville, TN; [p.] William McGaw and Gwendolyn Sartain; [m.] Patrick N. Suliva, Jr; January 15, 1983; [ch.] Nakeeah G. Sullivan, Wendy J. Sullivan; [ed.] Bellevue High School - G.E.D.; [occ.] Co-Owner and Laborer of Concrete Design Systems; [memb.] Songwriter's Club of America and Midwestern Songwriter's Association; [oth.writ.] Many poems, some of which are published. Also, many country music songs; [pers.] If it were not for my very dear husband Patrick making me feel special and somewhat talented, I would not have continued to write. Thanks with all my heart.; [a.] Antioch, TN

SULMAN, LAURIE A.
[b.] New York; [p.] Lois M. Sulman, Michael Sulman, brother Robert M. Sulman; [hon.] Dean's list; "The Eyrie Award for Distinctive Service," specifying the free verse "Foreward" (i.e. preface) and "Afterword" to "The Eyrie," annually published humanities magazine of Tallahassee Community College; award for a poetic contribution to another issue of "The Eyrie," appointed to editorial staff of said magazine. Other honors include (partial listing) early recognition in a Canadian-based youth competition, at eleven years of age: awarded first prize in poetry, and first prize in art.; [a.] Lynbrook, NY

SUMMERFORD, JANICE K.
[pen.]J K Summerford; [b.] July 3, 1951; Warren, AR; [p.] Lewis (Tip) and Dorothy Thompson; [m.] Donnie J. Summerford; February 5, 1988; [ch.]

Michael Douglas, Christina Lyma; [ed.] I have an Associate Degree in Data Processing from UAM in 1992. I have a BS in Business Administration from UAM in 1994, I graduated as Salutatorian of New Edinburg High in 1969; [occ.] I am currently writing poems and am about to open my own business. I am self-employed—own JK's Appraisal Service. I'm also a notary public for Drew County.; [memb.] I am a member of Pentecostal Church of God of Warren, AR.; [hon.] I was salutatorian of New Edinburg High School in 1969. I received honorable mention of graduation ceremony of UAM in 1994. I am a member of Certified Appraisers Guild of America as a Certified Personal Property Appraiser.; [oth.writ.] I have a lot of poems written but none are in publication yet; [pers.] I was inspired to write poems years ago but am recently widowed and am really getting a good grip onwriting poems for the glory of God.; [a.] Monticello, AR

SUSI, LOU
[b.] July 3, 1969; Malden, MA; [oth.writ.] Home-made scrapbooks of poetry and other writings, published in the Lowell Pearl and Bijaxous; [pers.] I want to submerge myself further into the dream and the dreaming world and weave a myth from the fibres this life offers unto me.; [a.] Watertown, MA

TATE, ANGELA D.
[pen.] Angie Tate; [b.] July 13, 1969; Kansas City, KS; [p.] Frank and Linda Nelson; [m.] William J. Tate, Jr.; August 18, 1990; [ch.] Kristin Nicole and Nickolas Edward; [ed.] Piper High School, Kansas City Kansas Community College; [occ.] Construction Loan Processor/Loan Closer; [memb.] Maywood Community Church-Member Since 1979; [hon.] Music Scholarship to Kansas City Community College; [oth.writ.] I've written other poems, but I've never tried to enter them in a contest or have them published; [pers.] I like to write about matters that have to do with my life experiences. Poems are the way I express my feelings.; [a.] Kansas City, KS

TAYLOR, LISA YOLANDA
[b.] October 9, 1973; Ripley, TN; [p.] Larry and Lillie Taylor; [ed.] Ripley High School, and Alabama A and M University; [occ.] Student; [memb.] Holly Grove Baptist Church, Ripley, TN. Union Chapel Baptist Church, Huntsville, AL. Alpha Kappa Alpha Sorority, Inc, Church Young Women's Auxillary, Co-ARM Youth Counselor; [hon.] Alabama A and M University's Dean's List and Honor Roll, Alpha Kappa Mu Honor Society, Poetry voted "Best Work" and "Most Outstanding Work" Winner in Alabama A and M University Poetry Contest, Magna Cum Laude Graduate; [oth.writ.] A poem published in school newspaper. Wrote several news stories for channel 48 (Huntsville, AL) newscasts; [pers.] My personal philosophy on life is "If my mind conceives it and in my heart I believe it, then I can achieve it."; [a.] Ripley, TN

TAYLOR, TANISHA
[b.] April 8, 1976; St. Andrew, JA; [p.] Mavis Powell, Clarence Taylor; [ed.] Bachelor of Science, Biology Mercy College; First year Medical student, New York Medical College; [occ.] Student, formerly a product support specialist, Wyeth Ayerst; [memb.] Who's Who Among Students in American Universities and Colleges; [hon.] Alpha Chi, Beta Beta Beta Biological Honors Society; National College Honors Society, Dean's List, Valedictorian for Class of '97 Mercy College, Gold Medal in Biology President's Medal for Academic Excellence; [oth.writ.] Other personal unpublished poems in my Reflection Series; [a.] Yonkers, NY

TAYLOR, VICKY ANN
[pen.] Miss Vicky, Vicky Ann; [b.] July 31, 1958; Fairfield, AL; [p.] Eddie Richardson Jr., (deceased) Ruth Hans Johnson; [ed.] Jackson Solomon Abrams High, Bessemer, AL, Miles College (Bachelor of

Science), Fairfield, AL; [occ.] Maintenance Administrate, Bell Atlantic, Greenbelt, MD; [memb.] Glendale Baptist Church; [hon.] Dean's List [Awards] play(s) Dare To Dream - Best Female Drama 2/21/90, Faith Freedom and Dem Dreams (Participants 2/15/89, Miss United Negro College Fund (UNCF 1978) Perf. Award(s) FBI (9/30/86-11/30/87); [pers.] I strive in my writings of inspiration to encourage the soul, and daily to express the importance of God's love through sharing a kind word or deed to mankind.; [a.] Washington, DC

TEBOW, MATT
[b.] February 9, 1975; Spokane, WA; [p.] Michael and Jacqueline Tebow; [ed.] Kent Meridian High School, Green River Community College (AA), University of Washington (Junior standing); [occ.] Part time at United Parcel Service; [memb.] The Mountaineers, National Eagle Scout Association (NESA); [hon.] Eagle Scout; [oth.writ.] Poem published in Puget Soundings Magazine June/July 1986; [pers.] My goal in writing poetry is to reflect observations made about myself and in nature.; [a.] Kent, WA

TEMPLIN, SHANNON
[b.] May 31, 1973; New Mexico; [p.] Shelby Jean Cornett; [m.] Tony A. Templin; July 4, 1993; [ch.] Shaun and Sara; [occ.] Furniture Delivery; [a.] Batesville, AR

THARPE, LAKISHEA
[b.] March 16, 1984; [p.] Sharon and Billy Tharpe; [ed.] Weaver Elementary School, Weaver High School; [hon.] I have received many awards at school for different achievements, honor roll, etc.; [oth.writ.] I have a few poems that my friends and family have read; none of them were ever published before.; [pers.] My writings represent the mood that I am in, the way that I feel. I mostly write just for the fun of it. It makes me happy to express feelings that way.; [a.] Anniston, AL

THECKSTON, KRISTIN
[pen.] Cecket Theckston; [b.] May 22, 1973; Woodburg, NJ; [p.] Peter and Barbara Buchert; [m.] Separated; [ch.] Daniel and Nicholas Theckson; [ed.] West Deptford High, Star Technical Institute, Bayada Nurses; [occ.] Certified Nurse's Aide at Pitman Manor; [oth.writ.] Obsessions, Wanted, 24 hours (short stories) numerous poems but I have never been published; [pers.] I can't help but wonder sometimes, am I in love or obsessed? The symptoms are the same.; [a.] Thorofare, NJ

THOMPSON, MARTA
[b.] January 9, 1933; Oklahoma; [p.] Cecil Fox - Virginia Fox; [m.] Lelon Thompson; April 5, 1970; [ch.] Three; [ed.] High School; [occ.] Housewife; [memb.] Church of Christ; [pers.] I was inspired to write this poem after the death of my mother. I wrote it for my sister Mary Sue after our experience on the day before she died.; [a.] Visalia, CA

THOMPSON, PHIL
[pen.] Mr. E., P6, Cornball Helius; [m.] Mirna Del Carmen; Sept. 21, 1991; [ch.] Austin Cooper; [oth.writ.] Albums include Clay, Totem Pole, No Recoil (with brother, Dan), Cable Crossing, and Bad Vibes; [pers.] Les Claypool and Neil Peart are two major heroes, though Zappa put out the best combination of thought-provoking lyrics and mind-tickling sound. I crave for the world to appreciate the importance of Raymond Scott's genius to the past 50 years of Western music.; [a.] Pensacola, FL

THORNTON, JAMIE LEE
[b.] September 14, 1983; Good Sam; [p.] Norma and James Thornton; [ed.] Currently in school and middle school; [occ.] Student; [hon.] Honor roll, outstanding achievement, music, art (many times), safety, student of the month (3 times) scholarship awards, stock market game, reading, and writing etc.; [oth.writ.] Many poem and stories that have

not yet been published; [pers.] Always write what you feel. No matter what other people think of your writings, it will always be a work of art in your eyes.; [a.] Loxhatchee, FL

TIBBS, BARBARA J.
[pen.] B.J. Tibbs; [b.] October 13, 1963; Warrensville, OH; [p.] John and Ruth McDevitt; [m.] David Allen Tibbs; September 6, 1986; [ch.] David, Jason, Andrew, Keith, and Kevin; [ed.] Nordonia High School; [occ.] Homemaker; [pers.] My writing is my way of expressing my feelings.; [a.] Maple Heights, OH

TILDON, JAMES M
[b.] June 24, 1948; Havre de Grace, MD; [p.] Morgan E. Lucinda E. Tildon; [m.] Kim Fllinger Tildon; September 30, 1991; [ch.] (son) Adam James, (dau.) Morgan; [ed.] Aberdeen Senior High School; [occ.] Peach Bottom Nuclear Security; [memb.] The Church of Jesus Christ of Latter Day Saints; [oth.writ.] The Gift Emotions; [pers.] Envy is a costume worn by those who wish momentarily to be someone else.; [a.] Aberdeen, MD

TIPTON, VIOLA ELIZABETH
[pen.] Viola E. Tipton; [b.] September 28, 1913; Near Hagerville, AR; [p.] Solen Andarmenda Williams; [m.] Rex. M. Tipton; March 3, 1934; [ch.] 2 Daughters and one son; [ed.] Took GED; One year art in college when I was 53 years old; [occ.] Artist and collector of dolls and all kinds of collectables; [memb.] 50 year member of First Baptist Church member of AR., River Valley Art Center in Russellville AR; [hon.] An art store here in town borrowed my peach painting, sent it to Ohio, got poster made, and sold them during our peach festival. The Lyons Club borrowed my painting, the new peach festival got it reduced in size, put it on envelopes, and sold them at the post office for charity.; [a.] Clarksville, AR

TOMASZEWSKI, MARY
[b.] May 25, 1984; Trenton, NJ; [p.] Elizabeth Smith, Edward Tomaszewski; [occ.] Student; [oth.writ.] Other poetry; [pers.] I write what's in my mind, and there is a lot in my mind. I write whatever my mind tells me to write and most of the time it makes sense.; [a.] Trenton, NJ

TREMBLAY, JUDY
[b.] April 26, 1978; Montgomery, AL; [p.] William George & Bonny Lee Tremblay; [ed.] Grace King High School, Belhaven College; [memb.] Caledonian Society of MS, Machenzie Society on the Americas; [hon.] Who' Who Among Am. High School Students, National Dean's List; [oth.writ.] Several non-published poems, poems published in college literary magazine and church newsletter; [pers.] I believe that my talents come from God, and I wish to use the gift of poetry to help others know that they are not alone in their struggles.; [a.] Metairie, LA

TROSTEROD, CHRISTINA
[b.] January 21, 1984; Portchester, NY; [p.] Jackie Trosterod Vincent Trosterod; [ed.] Louis M. Klein Middle School—8th Grader; [occ.] Student and Babysitter; [hon.] I got a scholarship to Manhattanville College for a writing program; [oth.writ.] Poems and stories published in school newspaper; [pers.] Writing is an exploration. Hopefully one day everyone will explore the great world of poetry writing.; [a.] W. Harrison, NY

TYSON, BLAZE A.
[pen.] Blaze; [b.] December 28, 1967; Indiana; [p.] Mary Tyson; [ch.] Anthy R. and Tore L. Tyson; [ed.] High School Graduate; [occ.] Clerk, Pro Wrestler; [oth.writ.] Lots of writings, none published yet, all of life experiences; [pers.] Thanks to Ranell for the inspiration she's and beautiful friend. Love ya, Rae.; [a.] Kissimmee, FL

ULLO, GWENDOLYN K.
[pen.] Gwen Ullo; [b.] June 16, 1955; Anadarko, OK; [p.] Ernie Thomason and Louise Jaques; [m.] Larry E. Ullo; August 17, 1973; [ch.] Larry Michael, Amanda Kaye; [ed.] Farmington High School Graduate, Farmington, NM; San Juan College, Farmington, NM; [occ.] Homemaker; [oth.writ.] Several poems published in local newspapers and college publications. Wrote and published family history titled Long Road Back; [pers.] I strive to reflect, through my poetry, short stories and other writing, the beauty and reality of life as seen through the eyes of a conservative, Christian homemaker.; [a.] Farmington, NM

VAN BALEN, CAROL G.
[b.] January 24, 1942; San Francisco, CA; [p.] Willard J. Mulherin, Thelma G. Ferguson; [m.] Robert Van Balen; February 8, 1964; [ch.] Shane Robert, Sherri Renee, Terrie Lynn; [ed.] San Lorenzo High School; [occ.] Retired; [memb.] Sacramento Valley Shetland Sheepdog Club, Sacramento Valley Caledonian Club; [oth.writ.] This was my first writing and I hope to be writing more.; [pers.] I was inspired by seeing my first grandchild at my daughter's ultrasound.; [a.] Citrus Heights, CA

VANMYERS, DORI
[pen.] Dr. Dori; [b.] March 11, 1983; Brooklyn, NY; [p.] Diane and Joseph VanMyers; [ed.] Currently Attending Churchill Jr. High; [pers.] I wish to study medicine after high school, but write on my free time. I would like to thank Ms. O'Mara, my eight grade teacher, who helped and encouraged me in writing during our lunch.; [a.] East Brunswick, NJ

VILLALOVAS, MARY ANN
[b.] June 16, 1961; Denver, CO; [p.] Florentino Villalovas and Mary Candy Maynes; [ch.] Javier and Christina Gomez; [ed.] Sweetwater High, Our Lady of the Lake University, Institute of Army Education; [occ.] Equipment Sales Representative in San Antonio, Texas; [oth.writ.] Poems published by the Poetry Guild; [pers.] Inspiration and imagination have freed the limitation of my work; I have been blessed.; [a.] Schertz, TX

VILLEGAS, LYVIA M.
[b.] October 22, 1946; Manila, Philippines; [p.] Lutgardo (deceased) and Virginia Mendoza; [m.] Rudy G. Villegas; November 21, 1990; [ed.] University of the Philippines School and College of Nursing; Columbia University Teachers College, NY, NY; UCLA School of Nursing Post-Masters Family Nurse Practitioner Certification Program, Los Angeles CA; [occ.] Family Nurse Practitioner, Orange County Health Care Agency, Santa Ana, CA; [memb.] University of the Philippines Nursing Alumni Association International (UPNAAI), PNA of Southern California, California Coalition of Nurse Practitioners, Sigma Theta Tau International; [hon.] Clinical Practitioner of the Year 1997 awarded by the Philippines Nurses Association of Southern California, Academic Internship Program Award to develop and promote a mentor program, Azusa Pacific University, Azusa, CA; [oth.writ.] Writer for the Poetry Corner, a section of the MCAH Chatter (work newsletter), co-author of two publications on the report of the high-risk home health nursing clinical specialty program, Azusa Pacific University School of Nursing, Article in the Mentor Connection in Nursing (1998); [pers.] Faith in God is an absolute empowerment in living life and love. I celebrate all the challenges bestowed in me. Struggles are sweet and akin to victory.; [a.] Irvine, CA

VITELLO, JESSICA
[b.] May 25, 1982; Butte, MT; [p.] Patricia and Christopher Vitello; [ed.] Marshfield High School; [memb.] Marshfield Schools Softball Team, Pen and Exit Club, Medical Explorers; [hon.] Marshfield High School Honor Rolls; Marshfield Schools Gifted Education Program; Student Council President;

Marshfield Schools Honor Choir; MHS Renaissance Program; [a.] Marshfield, MO

VOGL, MARIA
[b.] September 14, 1966; Spencer, IA; [p.] Robert and Bonnie Wuebker; [m.] Randy Vogl; November 3, 1989; [ch.] Hadley Maria, Joseph Randall; [ed.] Emmetsburg High, Briar Cliff College Emmetsburg, IA, Sioux City, IA; [occ.] (Former) Weekly Reporter, Copy Editor for Daily News; [memb.] Good Shepherd Catholic Church, Early Childhood Family Education Board; [oth.writ.] News, feature stories published as a daily and weekly reporter; [pers.] As a reporter, I would have liked to have interviewed Ernest Hemingway, my all-time favorite writer.; [a.] Jackson, MN

VOLOVELSKY, MICHELLE
[b.] December 2, 1986; Miami Beach, FL; [p.] Paul and Irma Volovelsky; [ed.] Going into 5th grade in Treasure Island Elementary, North Bay Village, FL; [occ.] Student; [hon.] Two Principal's Award trophies, One 3rd place Science Fair Award (trophy), and many honor certificates; [oth.writ.] Only writings for school assignments; [pers.] I was born on December 2nd of 1986 in Miami Fl. My parents and my older brother are from Russia and arrived to the U.S. in the early 70's.; [a.] Miami Beach, FL

WALKER, DANIEL P.
[pen.] The Rabbi of the Railroad; [b.] September 28, 1949; Portland, OR; [p.] Robert E. Walker, Dorothy Parker; [m.] Deceased; [ch.] David, John, Fister; [ed.] General Education Development Medical Care Treatment, Ford Automotive Transition, Draughon Norton Business College; [occ.] Disabled Vietnam Veteran; [memb.] Crestview Chamber of Commerce; [oth.writ.] Hobos Christmas Phony Lies, Unity, Forever to You True, The Final Day, Memorial day, Mid-Summer Morning Dream, The Bank of Dreams, You've Got the Power, The Patriot; [pers.] I finally arrived at a place in my life, to reflect and find rhyme and reason in my life so late in season, no more rails or box cars for me, for now I am free.; [a.] Crestview, FL

WATERMAN, JANET LEE
[pen.] Janet McCollough Waterman; [b.] March 25, 1958; Hood River, OR; [p.] Leonard and Frances McCullough Sr.; [m.] Noble Waterman, Jr., September 27, 1974; [ch.] Steven Noble and Michael Joe Waterman; [ed.] Van Horn High School, Longview College Blue Springs, MO; [occ.] Marketing, ITI marketing services Inc. St. Joseph MO; [memb.] MO P.T.A; American Heart Assoc. American Cancer Assoc; Toys for Tots; United Way; Special Olympics; MO Police Chief Fund; [hon.] Numerous awards for volunteer work from Mt. Washington on Elementary and Kansas City School district, and a number of awards for marketing; [oth.writ.] Several poems, songs and a children's story book, unpublished. Also I portrait characters from the past annually during the Trails West festival in St. Joseph MO, the home of the Pony Express; [pers.] I believe in three things in life: God, You can't return what you don't receive and respect's one of those things. In order to receive a positive outcome you must start with a positive outlook.; [a.] St. Joseph, MO

WEBSTER, KRYSTA
[b.] November 9, 1980; Sain Eugene Hospital; [p.] DR. and Peggy Webster; [ed.] High School Junior, I plan to attend a university and study to become a physician someday; [occ.] Attending Dillon High School in Dillon, SC; 8[memb.] SADD, Fellowship of Christian Athletes (FCA), Yearbook/Editorial Staff, Poem Writer for the Wildcat News, Gifted and Talented 8Classes, Foreign Language Club, Anchor Club, Beta Club; [hon.] Honors and 8AP Classes in School, Gifted and Talented Student; 1994 National Awards 8Academy Scholar, Hoby

Ambassador for DHS, 1997 Miss Tenn Latta, 1997 Miss 8Wildcat, straight A student; [oth.writ.] Various county and regional essay 8winners, poem writer for the Wildcat News, poem published in McGregor Itill 8Publishing, Inc. Annual High School Poetry Anthology for 1996-1997; [pers.] 8Poetry is the best representation of the heart, mind, soul, and entire 8being. Therefore, never underestimate the beauty that lies within the 8delicacy of the poem.; [a.] Dillon, SC

WERNER, SARAH
[b.] March 7, 1983; Dallas, TX; [p.] Joanne Werner, Keith Werner; [ed.] Junior High School; [occ.] Student; [hon.] "A" Honor Roll at Lake High Lands Junior High School, Judges Choice for Prose in Cultural Arts Fair; [pers.] Always look toward the sun and towards love and goodness.; [a.] Dallas, TX

WESTCOTT, JAY
[b.] December 29, 1975; St. Joseph Hospital; [p.] Rick and Linda Westcott; [m.] Theresa Royce-Westcott; August 29, 1996; [ch.] Jonathan Westcott; [d.] Attending Schoolcrafts College of Culinary Arts in Michigan; [occ.] Pantry Cook in Executive Cheif Craig Common's Common Grill in Chelsea, MI; [memb.] Schoolcrafts Gourmet Club; [pers.] Press on. Nothing in the world can take the place of persistence. Talent will not; nothing is more common than unsuccessful men with talent. Genius will not; unrewarded genius is almost a proverb. Education will not; the world is full of educated derilects, persistence and determination alone are omnipotent.

WHITE, MELODY
[pen.] M.W. Spencer; [b.] August 16, 1970; New York, NY; [p.] Annie W. White (Mother); [ch.] Jade A. S. Fortune; [ed.] Walton High School, Westchester Business Institute, Bronx Community College; [occ.] Unit Secretary Montefiore Medical Ctr., Bronx, NY; [memb.] Formerly a member of St. Edmunds Episcopal Church and formerly a member and supporter of the Smithsonian Institute; [hon.] Dean's List; [oth.writ.] Solstice published in the Nautilus Magazine and in one of the previous volumes volumes of the National Library of Poetry; [pers.] I write what I feel and believe in.; [a.] Bronx, NY

WHITTEN, MARK
[b.] March 25, 1977; Daytona, FL; [p.] Tom and Pat Whitten; [ed.] Franklin Road Academy, the University of Tennessee; [occ.] Student; [memb.] Christ Church, Young Life, Kappa Sigma Fraternity; [hon.] FL Christian Athelete of the Year, '95 Capt. of Football Team, a Franklin Road Academy Linemar of the Year 1995; [oth.writ.] "Our Voices" Williamson County Literary Review, Franklin Road Academy Newspaper and Library Magazine; [pers.] God Blesses everyone with different talents and I have been fortunate to have received the gift of writing poetry. I enjoy writing about the blessings of the Lord and the trying times of teen-aged love.; [a.] Brentwood, TN

WIECKHORST, KATHRYN
[pen.] Luke Van Reenen; [b.] January 1, 1984; Wantagh, NY; [p.] Kathleen Wieckhorst, James Wieckhorst; [ed.] Abbey Lane and Summit Lane Elementary, Wisdom Lane Middle School; [memb.] National Junior Honor Society, school sports teams, Levittown Athletic club softball teams; [hon.] National Junior Honor Society, MADD article winner; [oth.writ.] County winning article published in the Levittown Tribune for MADD in 1994; [pers.] I try to answer everyday questions in my poems. I love poetry. It is an important part of my life.; [a.] Levittown, NY

WIGGINS, LAURA
[pen.] Laura Wiggins; [b.] October 3, 1962; Allegan MI; [p.] Clarence and Rose Wiggins; [ed.] Graduated Western KY University-Emphasis Social and

Behavioral Sciences; [occ.] Assistant manager for group home for special needs adolescents; [memb.] Radcliff 1st Assembly of God; [oth.writ.] "The Dark and Bloody Land-III" was part of a series of ten poems written about Kentucky; [pers.] Most of my poetry reflects an emotional voice coming from either history or personal experience.; [a.] Radcliff, KY

WILLIAMS, KIMBERLY ANN
[b.] January 11, 1967; Chicago, IL; [p.] Rosie and Fred Williams; [ch.] Tharlon Jones, David Bray; [ed.] Academy of Our Lady; Iowa State University; [oth.writ.] I have numerous poems, all collected in a book I am compiling called "Thoughts On Life"; [pers.] My poetry is my own creation it comes from my soul. Since 15, I have been doing my first love. I hope enlightens many people.; [a.] Chicago, IL

WILLOUGHBY, KAREN C.
[b.] January 7, 1967; Baltimore MD; [p.] Cecelia Ghee, Edward Ghee; [m.] Sean Willoughby; November 17, 1990; [ch.] Phylicia Ghee, Christian Willoughby; [ed.] Randallstown High School, Catonsville Community College; [occ.] Pharmacy Technician; [memb.] Sought Out Reedemed Church and United Way; [hon.] First Contest entered. American Literary Press wanted to publish my poems in the; [oth.writ.] I have been writing poems for years. I have several other poems I would like published.; [pers.] My poems are based on my emotions and personal experiences. My poems are from my heart. My parents are my inspiration.; [a.] Baltimore, MD

WILSON, JAMES
[b.] August 3, 1955; Atmore, AL; [p.] Willis and Lorie Wilson; [oth.writ.] I have several unpublished poems: Dark Ingenuities, Divine Disgust, Imagine Sime, the list goes on; [pers.] I have always had a passion for the world of science fiction and fantasy, because they both can transport you to many-faceted horizons.; [a.] Atmore, AL

WILSON, JOHN CHARLES
[b.] October 13, 1983; Asheboro, NC; [p.] Thomas and Louise Wilson; [ed.] Guy B. Teachey Elmentary, Asheboro NC; South Asheboro Middle Asheboro, NC; Asheboro High School, Asheboro, NC; [memb.] Calvary Baptist Church Asheboro, NC; All-American Scholar; National Honor Society; Woodmen of the World; United States Achievement Academy; [hon.] Highest English Average SAMS 94-95; Highest Social Studies Average SAMS 96-97; Spelling Bee Winner Teachey School 93-94; Peer Connector SAMs 95-96; Young Scholar SAMS 95-96; Quiz Bowl Winner SAMS 94-95; Beta Club SAMS 94-97; President Education Award SAMS 97; [oth.writ.] The Bandit: The Kidnapping of Kitty Catterus; The Bandit: The Lost Handkerchief; "Decisions and Choices" (poem), "Love" (poem); [pers.] It is my goal for people to realize that even though there is destruction in the world there are still good things to write about and enjoy. I have been influenced greatly by my 7th and 8th grade English teachers, Mrs. Nancy Cranford and Mrs. Cookie Sprouse.; [a.] Asheboro, NC

WILSON, JUSTIN
[b.] December 20, 1981; [p.] Jim Wilson, Mary Wilson; [ed.] Clyde Boyd Junior High and Charles Page High School; [occ.] Student; [memb.] Charles Page High School Band, Hyechka Music Club, C.H.A.O.S.; [hon.] School Academic Awards including the American Legion Award and the Masonic Lodge Award; [oth.writ.] Many other unpublished poems and a few short stories; [pers.] I am very glad to have my first poem published. I also love music and play the Oboe and Piano and I enjoy all the arts.; [a.] Sand Springs, OK

WINTER, JAMES E.
[pen.] Jym Zyne; [b.] July 22, 1978; Las Cruces, New Mexico; [p.] James Patrick Winter, Trinna

Sue Riddle; [ed.] Received High School Diploma May 17, 1996 from Hot Springs High School, Truth or Consequences NM/presently attending Albuquerque Job Corps Center; [occ.] Learning Framing Carpentry at AJCC, October 1996-present; [memb.] Republican Party; [hon.] Student of the Month (Terrific Tiger) February 1996/Office positions at AJCC trashman January-March 1997, Cleaning Officer April-May 1997; [oth.writ.] All At Ease (1994), The Campfire Story (1997); [pers.] I live only for the emotional stimuli I give myself by thoroughly correcting my own writing. No one has paid attention to my absolute negative view of reality. I enjoy spite in its purest and most educated form, as I know others do.; [a.] Albuquerque, NM

WOODALL, NATALIE JOY
[b.] January 5, 1946; Adams, NY; [p.] Fay C. Woodall, Margaret Dudley Woodall; [ed.] Independent Scholar and part time Newspaper reporter for Oswego Palladium -Times; [memb.] American Philological Ass'n; Modern Language Ass'n; Women's Classical Laucus; Order of the Eastern Star; Grace Evangelical Lutheran Church; American Ass'n of University Women; [hon.] Woodrow Wilson Dissertation Fellowship; Newspaper Fund Fellowship; Outstanding Young Women of America; [oth.writ.] Contributor to four biographical encyclopedias; Articles in classical studies; Articles on Latin American studies; John Milton and Nineteenth-Century Women Writers; [a.] Oswego, NY

WOODING JR., PERRY D.
[pen.] Da'I.Z.M, Mr. Theatrical; [b.] August 16, 1966; Jersey City, NJ; [p.] Corretta P. Wooding and Perry D. Wooding Sr.; [ch.] Natasha, Tiffany, Shakira, Monet; [ed.] Jersey City State College; [occ.] Supervisor, Port Liberte' Homeowners Assoc.; [memb.] Playaz Club, and Uniminds Writers Organ.; [oth.writ.] A book entitled "The 5 Senses and the 4 Elements of Human Nature through Poetry." (Uniminds) also a multitude of lyrical compositions, (Vital Signz Unlimited); [pers.] A notation of inspiration to all our loved ones that are deceased, at least they rest in peace, we are driven from that which God has given to the living, which beith the memories of them that we keep within. "A better place"; [a.] Jersey City, NJ

WOODS, SANDRA J.
[pen.] S. Smith; [b.] November 20, 1963; Bernice, LA; [p.] Bobby and Ellen Wiltcher; [m.] Todd Smith; [ch.] David, Jereme, April Woods; [ed.] High School Diploma from Ruston High School, Ruston LA.; [occ.] Homemaker; [hon.] All state softball, Jr. High School Volleyball team, Jr. High School gymnastics team, 2 first place awards for poetry; [oth.writ.] 1st place poems in poetry contest greeting cards; [pers.] I have always been amazed with the world of poetry to be able to express my thoughts with such beauty and grace.; [a.] Springfield, MO

WORTH, ASHLEY
[b.] September 19, 1983; Livermore; [p.] Mark Worth and Laura Worth; [ed.] Junction Ave Middle School; [memb.] 4-H, Color Guard, and the United Spirit Association; [hon.] 3 year winner of good medal for Oral Interpretation in the Academic Olympics 6th - 8th grade, Award for Academic Excellence in Science; [oth.writ.] A Biography of My Grandmother's Daily Life, "When My Grandmother Was A Girl" published in the local newspaper; [pers.] I write, hoping to fill my work with spirit so it is enjoyable to read and it makes people happy.; [a.] Livermore, CA

YANG, YANG
[pen.] Kelly; Kelly Yang; [b.] August 29, 1984; Tianjin, China; [p.] Meiying Wang and Yinong Yang; [ed.] Previously Finished 7th grade, scheduled for 8th grade fall '97; [hon.] All my life I have picked up uncountable amounts of recognitions—

all very influencing towards my success. However, probably the most encouraging award would have to be the unsuspected metal for my first English essay.; [oth.writ.] I have written poems published in several books—including my own—and have also written many many short stories worldwide.; [pers.] The one philosophy I have to is to dream. To achieve, one must dream, and to succeed, one has to believe in their hearts that those dreams are fully theirs to obtain. Strive hard to grasp those fantasies and no longer will they be nonsense but reality and life.; [a.] Chula Vista, CA

YANULAVICH, ANN
[b.] August 1, 1958; Pittston, PA; [p.] Al and Edna Yanulavich; [ed.] Immaculate Conception Wyoming Area High School, LCCC (Luzerne County Community College); [occ.] Laborer; [memb.] Distinguished Member in the International Society of Poets, 1977; [hon.] Editor's Choice Award 1977 (National Library of Poetry); [oth.writ.] "Fight Until The End" published in a "A View From Afar"; Several dozen poems I'm starting to publish in near future; [pers.] I like to thank 3 special people who influenced me to share my poetry with others. I've been writing since I was 8 years old.; [a.] W. Pittston, PA

YAREDICH, MABEL RUTH REDFERN MAZE
[pen.] Mabel R. Maze; [b.] November 13, 1911; Farmersville, IL; [p.] Isaac Milton and Lucinda (Ballard) Redfern; [m.] Archie Paul Maze, Aleksa Yaredich (deceased); [ch.] Beverly J. (Maze) Smelser, Linda L. (Maze) Callies; [ed.] Springfield, Illinois Public High School, Betty Stuart School for Girls and various public relations in-service training seminars in Home Ec Business/Retail Sales; [occ.] Retired; [memb.] Daughters of America, retired; [hon.] Popularity Queen (DOA), Flag Bearer (DOA), Arthur Murray Dance Contest, 2nd place for fox-trot and tango. Valedictorian of physical therapy class at Charlevoix Health Care and Rehabilitation Center; [oth.writ.] Various poems, not published but used at different events/ competitions at Charlevoix. Also short stories of daily life; [pers.] I'm grateful and proud that my poem has been selected for publication. Thank you so much. I like to write about little happenings in my daily life, especially things I recall of years past, amusing things.; [a.] St. Charles, MO

YEARWOOD, STEPHEN A.
[pen.] Iyawo; [b.] May 6, 1948; Trinidad; [p.] Alnoresy Vanory Casey; [ed.] St. Johns High Guyana, South America; [occ.] Refrigeration Technician; [memb.] Member of the International Society of Poets; [hon.] Editor's Choice Award; [oth.writ.] Poems published: (some) Come See My Ways, Give Respect, Or So It Seems, One for the Road; [pers.] The world's tallest building is built on the shoulders of reinforced belief. The elements of life intrigue me.; [a.] Brooklyn, NY

YHONQUEA, LARCENIA
[pen.] Lar; [b.] May 3; [m.] September 1969; [ch.] Eight; [ed.] H.S.G./College Col. Library Educational Media Associate, International Trade Degree; [occ.] School Librarian, Substitute Teacher; [memb.] Library Associations, First Presbyterian Church of Clev., National Council for Black Children; [hon.] North East Adoption Agency, National Dean's List, 1983-1984 1985-86, National Veterans Assoc., Iowa Maple School Cleve., Cuyahoga Comm. College; [oth.writ.] Hair, Nap Time, Grandmother, Flight of a Wounded, Dove, Caught and others; [pers.] When angels whisper I listen.; [a.] West Point, MS

YOST, JAMES E.
[b.] April 23, 1923; Pennsauken, NJ; [p.] Herman Yost and Sarah Yost; [m.] Helen Kozloski; October 26, 1946; [ch.] James Richard, Roger Gordon, Stephen Philip; [ed.] Woodrow Wilson Senior High, Art instruction, Inc; Philadelphia Technical

Institute and Central Bible College (Corp. Course); [occ.] Retired Engineering, Design Draftsman; [memb.] Somerdale Republican Club, Fountain of Life Center A/G (Assembles of God); [oth.writ.] I have compiled a variety of manuscripts (Biblically oriented), but not submitted as yet for possible publication. I endeavor to arouse more interest in mankind to his relationship with God, his creator.; [a.] Somerdale, NJ

ZALOUM, BASILE H.
[b.] 1949; Lebanon; [p.] Homer Zaloum, Rose Zaloum; [m.] Sharon A. Zaloum; [ch.] Alex; [ed.] Central Michigan University-MBA E Cole Des Lettres De Legon- Psychology; [occ.] Principal, Market Entry USA; [memb.] American Society For Training Association For Psychological; [hon.] Sigma Iota Epsilon; [oth.writ.] Corporate and Marketing Communication; [a.] Arlington, VA

ZEPEDA, MARIO A.
[b.] June 13, 1957; El Salvador; [p.] Angelica Zepeda; [ed.] Dispanoamerica, College; Lookdale Vocational Institute (Canada); [occ.] Food preparation, Liovauni Restorante; [oth.writ.] Some plays (not published), and a short story in progress; [pers.] I try to find out solutions through communication in my writings. The new screen players one my inspirations.; [a.] Cliffside Park, NJ

ZIVKOVITCH, JESSICA
[pen.] Joy Zee; [b.] October 20, 1982; Wayne, NJ; [p.] Joanne and Jovica Zivkovitch; [ed.] Attending high school, currently beginning 10th grade; [occ.] High school student; [memb.] National Junior Honor Society; [hon.] Excellence in Scholarship by the Administration and faculty of Southern Regional School District; [pers.] The glass is always half-full.; [a.] Barnegat, NJ

ZOOK, CHRISTOPHER RYAN
[pen.] Ryan Zook; [b.] April 13, 1980; Fairfax, VA; [p.] Michael and Cindy Zook; [ed.] Student— Fairfax High School; [hon.] Spanish Honor Society, National Honor Society, Math Honor Society, Honor Roll, V. Golf Team, Letter with 3.5 Award, Golf Captain, Best of the Best, Varsity Math Team Letter, Varsity Tennis Letter; [a.] Fairfax, VA

*Index
of
Poets*

Index